MANAGEMENT SCIENCE IN BANKING

EDITED BY

KALMAN J. COHEN
Distinguished Bank Research Professor
Duke University

and

STEPHEN E. GIBSON
International Operations Group
Chemical Bank

WARREN, GORHAM & LAMONT
Boston and New York

CONTRIBUTORS

PARVIS AGHILI, *Development and Investment Bank of Iran*
DAVID M. AHLERS, *Cornell University*
R. Y. AWH, *Mississippi State University*
RAYMOND V. BALZANO, *Baxter Travenol Laboratories*
H. PRESCOTT BEIGHLEY, *Federal Home Loan Bank of Chicago*
JOHN H. BOYD, *Northwestern University*
STEPHEN P. BRADLEY, *Harvard University*
E. EUGENE CARTER, *University of Illinois at Chicago Circle*
KALMAN J. COHEN, *Duke University*
ROBERT H. CRAMER, *University of Wisconsin—Madison*
DWIGHT B. CRANE, *Harvard University*
JOHN DAVIS, *Bank of Oklahoma, N.A.*
LEON DERWA, *Societe Generale de Banque and Liege University*
JAMES F. DINGLE, *Bank of Canada*
MICHAEL E. ECHOLS, *University of Wisconsin—Milwaukee*
PETER C. EISEMANN, *Georgia State University*
J. WALTER ELLIOTT, *University of Wisconsin—Milwaukee*
FRANK J. FABOZZI, *Hofstra University*
FREDERICK S. HAMMER, *The Chase Manhattan Bank, N.A.*
THOMAS R. HARTER, *Federal Home Loan Bank of San Francisco*
WOLFGANG P. HOEHENWARTER, *The World Bank*
JOSEPH J. HORTON, JR., *Slippery Rock State College*
MICHAEL J. HOSEMANN, *Louisiana National Bank of Baton Rouge*
G. DAVID HUGHES, *University of North Carolina at Chapel Hill*
DONALD P. JACOBS, *Northwestern University*
R. C. JONES, *Schering-Plough Corporation (USA)*
ROBERT L. KRAMER, *A. J. Wood Research Corporation*
MORTON LANE, *J. F. Eckstein and Company*
SHIMON D. MAGEN, *University of the District of Columbia*
STEVEN F. MAIER, *Duke University*
ROBERT B. MILLER, *University of Wisconsin—Madison*
SHYAM L. MOONDRA, *The Chase Manhattan Bank, N.A.*
S. R. MORRISON, *National Westminster Bank Ltd.*
YAIR E. ORGLER, *Tel-Aviv University*
ALBERT A. POOL, *First American National Bank of St. Cloud, Minnesota*
S. R. QUAY, *Wells Fargo Bank, N.A.*
ROBERT REBACK, *Donaldson, Lufkin & Jenrette*
RANDALL S. ROBINSON, *The Babcock & Wilcox Company*
MARC H. ROYER, *Banque Bruxelles Lambert*

DAVID P. RUTENBERG, *Queen's University*
RICHARD A. SHICK, *St. Bonaventure University*
MARK G. SIMKIN, *University of Hawaii*
RALPH H. SPRAGUE, JR., *University of Hawaii*
BERNELL K. STONE, *Georgia Institute of Technology*
HOWARD E. THOMPSON, *University of Wisconsin—Madison*
MICHAEL R. THOMSON, *Mellon Bank, N.A.*
SAL TROVATO, *Estee Lauder, Inc.*
JAMES H. VANDER WEIDE, *Duke University*
JAMES A. VERBRUGGE, *University of Georgia*
W. H. WAGNER, *Wells Fargo Bank, N.A.*
DON R. WATERS, *Northeast National Bank (Fort Worth, Texas)*
DANIEL L. WHITE, *Georgia State University*
KENNETH J. WHITE, *Rice University*
R. P. WHITEMAN, *National Westminster Bank Ltd.*

TABLE OF CONTENTS

Part VI   THE LOAN PORTFOLIO

Part VII   OPERATIONS AND CORPORATE SERVICES

Part VIII   THE TRUST PORTFOLIO

PREFACE

Despite the rapidly increasing complexity of problems facing the management of financial institutions in today's competitive environment, too little attention has been given to using management science techniques to structure and simplify bank management problems. The reasons generally expressed for not utilizing management science tools are not cost, inapplicability, or lack of regard for their usefulness. Instead, management generally reports a lack of knowledge of such techniques as linear programming and computer simulation as the primary reason that commercial banks do not apply management science techniques on a broader scale. A second, related reason is the inability of traditional bankers to use quantitative techniques due to their lack of knowledge of organizing and implementing management science.

Although management science techniques have been successfully applied in banks, there is a greater potential for future applications. If this potential is to be realized, a new breed of bankers who understand the capabilities of management science tools must evolve. Of equal importance to future bank managers is an appreciation for the organization and planning that are needed for successful implementation of new management techniques such as optimization models or computer-based simulations.

Many financial institutions have attempted to generate more innovative management through the hiring of MBAs. MBAs quite often have been exposed to the use of management science techniques and other innovative approaches to management. Because the reluctance of some banks to implement management science is based largely on a lack of knowledge, employing MBAs is one way to remove obstacles to the use of scientific management techniques. The potential of this approach will likely depend on the nature of MBA education in bank management science.

This book is intended for use in graduate level courses in commercial bank management (or, more broadly, management of financial institutions). The emphasis is on increasing the reader's knowledge of current attempts by management science researchers to apply scientific techniques to banking problems. The discussions include applications from a wide variety of bank management areas. While some of the techniques discussed have direct application to specific banking problems, others could be applied in many different problem situations to structure and analyze complex interacting decision variables.

We frequently emphasize that the aim of management science is to help executives solve complex problems. While several techniques discussed do provide solutions to specific problems, the more general goal is to enable management to devote more time to broad policy planning and objective setting. These are often neglected as management becomes involved in dealing with routine but pressing problems. Management science is not meant to replace careful analysis by experienced managers; instead, it is intended to focus that analysis on key decision issues. The behavioral problems which can arise from a misunderstanding of this point are significant, and should be understood in attempting to implement management science.

The editors have not attempted to critique the technical aspects of the research presented in this book. We decided to forego critical comments, because we felt that such analysis would prove worthwhile for readers to undertake in evaluating the potential of these techniques in actual use. Further, including such critical analysis would have made the book excessively long. Our goal of exposing readers to a wide range of management science applications is best met by leaving critical analysis to them. In contemplating implementation of any of the models presented, a thorough critical analysis would, of course, be an essential first step.

Many of the research articles included in this book contain significant levels of quantitative analysis. Because the text is aimed at graduate level students, we have assumed that readers have some knowledge of calculus, linear programming, and statistics. Every effort has been made to avoid including unnecessary quantitative analysis. Readers will find that in many chapters a careful examination of the verbal material (with only limited attention to the mathematics) will provide an adequate understanding of the analytical approaches being used and the banking areas to which they may be applied. Readers who have an adequate quantitative background, on the other hand, will generally benefit from a careful reading of the mathematical portions of the chapters.

Successful implementation of management science techniques involves more than simple recognition of a potential application. The use of these techniques involves careful consideration of behavioral implications, cost effectiveness, and viable alternatives. Some discussion of these essential considerations is provided in the introductory material to Part I. The ability of bankers to effectively implement management science should improve as more applications are attempted and knowledge gained from the experience.

Most of this book is devoted to discussions of management science models that have been or potentially might be successfully implemented in banks. These models are intended to help executives deal with planning, decision making, and control problems in a variety of banking areas. The topics covered range from day-to-day problem solving in the operations management area (Part VII) and considerations of retail marketing management (Part II), through rather complex models for bank balance sheet management (Part IV) and bond portfolio management (Part V), to long-term capital structure and planning considerations for banks and bank holding companies (Part X). Other banking areas considered are the loan portfolio (Part VI), the trust portfolio (Part VIII), and electronic funds transfer systems (Part IX). Applications of forecasting and simulation techniques to a variety of bank planning problems are discussed in Part III.

This book includes a wide assortment of management science techniques varying from the applications of forecasting and simulation techniques discussed in Part III to the innovative techniques made possible by electronic funds transfer systems. Because balance sheet management models based on linear programming formulations have been used successfully, linear programming techniques are examined in some detail in Part IV. Additionally, the reader is provided with several statistical models, particularly in the discussions of retail marketing (Part II) and operations management (Part VII). The exposure provided to a diversity of management science techniques applied to a variety of banking areas should enhance the reader's appreciation for the usefulness of these analytical approaches in banking.

Every effort has been made to illustrate not only the great potential for applying innovative management techniques in banking, but also the drawbacks of using more sophisticated management techniques. While the editors feel that management science techniques have a valuable potential for commercial bank management, this book has carefully avoided overselling that potential. Many of the techniques have been successfully applied to "real world" situations, and others have been tested on a trial basis in actual situations. The promising results of such applications point to the potential of management science as an aid to executives in dealing with the growing complexity of the commercial banking environment.

To the authors and copyright holders of the articles which have been reprinted in this book, we as editors express our thanks. We recognize that their contributions are important landmarks in the growing literature of the field. The Bank Administration Institute has been especially generous in allowing us to reprint many articles which have appeared in their journals—*Journal of Bank Research* and *The Magazine of Bank Administration*. Specific acknowledgments to the copyright holders of each reprinted article appear on the first page of each chapter.

KALMAN J. COHEN
STEPHEN E. GIBSON

Part I

IMPLEMENTING MANAGEMENT SCIENCE

BEFORE examining potential applications of management science techniques in banking, attention should be given to the complex task of implementing these techniques. The failure of many attempted applications of management science techniques has resulted from poor implementation procedures. These poor procedures are in turn the result of inadequate planning and organization which are critical aspects of implementation.

Kalman J. Cohen provides a framework for approaching implementation decisions in Chapter 1, "A Realistic Approach to Implementing Management Science." The article sets forth a realistic management philosophy aimed at insuring that management science models are used once they have been designed and placed on line. The article examines the role of the executive in the problem-solving process and the implications of this role for designing management science models.

Chapter 2 focuses on the relevant question: "How widely used are management science techniques in the actual management of American commercial banks?" Frank J. Fabozzi and Sal Trovato report the results of their survey on this question in the article, "The Use of Quantitative Techniques in Commercial Banks." Fabozzi and Trovato also focus on the factors that influence the use of quantitative and management science techniques in banking.

It is unfortunate that many potentially valuable applications of these techniques in banking fail because of poor planning for implementation or even a total disregard for the importance of implementation problems. Experience has shown that neglect of this key aspect of utilizing management science will prove disastrous.

Chapter 1

A REALISTIC APPROACH TO IMPLEMENTING MANAGEMENT SCIENCE*

By Kalman J. Cohen

*This article is reprinted, with permission, from *The Magazine of Bank Administration,* Vol. 45, No. 9 (September, 1969), pp. 28-31 and 64.

Recent advances in the development of quantitative models for finance and banking, along with the increasing utilization of electronic computers, have made it feasible to adopt a management science framework in approaching many types of financial problems. A realistic philosophy concerning the manner in which management science models should be utilized in order to improve financial planning and decision making is set forth in this article. As indicated below, this is the approach which has been successfully followed in two major American corporations with which I am familiar (and which undoubtedly is the pattern employed in many other companies as well). The so-called "implementation problem," which is concerned with how to get executives actually to utilize either existing or newly developed management science models, also is considered. The article concludes by examining the relative roles that traditionally trained executives and management scientists should play in the problem-solving process.

The term "management science" refers to the application of quantitative techniques and scientific concepts to help executives solve the planning, decision making and control problems of large, complex organizations. Any management science approach to problem solving utilizes formal models. Since a model is an abstraction of reality, it must necessarily be "incomplete" or "inaccurate" in some respects.[1] The real world is itself far too complex to manipulate and understand without the aid of the intellectual simplifications that models represent. The real basis for judging the usefulness of a model is not whether it is entirely accurate (which it never is) but, rather, whether it contains enough relevant features of the world so that it can be effectively used by executives to improve their performance.

Utilizing Mathematical Programming Models

Since the focus of this paper is on the use of management science models for financial planning and

[1] Many people who do not understand the process by which management science models can in fact be implemented often falsely criticize the management science approach. They look at the management science models, and they indicate that these models are unrealistic because this particular factor or that specific aspect of the world are not taken into consideration. It can be obvious that many features have been left out of the model because of the explicitness with which any good management science model is formulated. Thus, one can see not only exactly what is in such a model, but one can also readily note what has been left out. Since every "model" is necessarily an abstraction of reality, it is clear that any formal management science model can never portray the world as it really is, in every detail.

Conventionally trained businessmen who criticize the quantitative approach fail to recognize a most important point: a person who applies thirty years of experience and who uses judgment and wisdom in making business decisions in effect is using some models that are implicit in his head. These subjective models are not the same as the real world which objectively exists. These subjective models are never well formulated; rather they are generally implicit, subconscious, and ill-understood. Hence, it is often not easy to know exactly what is wrong with these subjective models, i.e., to identify the aspects of the real world that are left out of them. You can be sure, however, that a great deal is left out.

decision making, let me specifically consider the type of management science model which is most commonly suggested for this purpose, i.e., mathematical programming models. In particular, mathematical programming models have been applied with notable success in the investment planning process at Standard Oil Co. of New Jersey (and its various subsidiary and affiliated companies) and in the dynamic balance sheet management processes at Bankers Trust Co. Neither of these corporations is utilizing mathematical programming models in an automatic, routine fashion. Instead, some creative dialogues and interchanges take place that involve conventionally trained executives, "management-oriented" management scientists, the models that are programmed in the computer and a data base. It is important to realize that in practice management science models (especially those involving mathematical programming) are utilized in a far more flexible manner than their bare-bones mathematical formulations might indicate.

Even though authors (myself included) discussing a linear programming model for bank dynamic balance sheet management may talk about an "optimal" solution in some mathematical sense, one must recognize that the model of the world being utilized is not necessarily correct. Given that the real business situation is only approximated by the model, that some of the inputs are not always accurately known, that the model contains many expressions of policies that management may not be absolutely convinced are correct and that many forecasts (which might be wrong) are used to generate some inputs, then it is clear that the "solutions" produced by the model to real world problems are not going to be truly optimal. All that we can hope for is that the solutions obtained with the aid of the model are better than the solutions that we otherwise would have arrived at using the same degree of effort.[2]

Let us consider more specifically how a mathematical programming model is utilized in practice. Long before anything even approaching an "optimal" solution is acted upon, a great deal of conversation and an exchange of ideas takes place that involves executives, management scientists and the model itself. In this process, the mathematical programming model in the computer serves as an extension of the peoples'

[2] There is one important reason why it often is the case that the use of a mathematical programming model will produce better decisions than conventional procedures. The model can simultaneously consider all aspects of a particular problem, whereas traditional methods frequently focus on what is only a subset of the crucial issues. The more comprehensive viewpoint permitted by the mathematical programming model in effect transforms all of the assumptions that are made concerning the nature of the business and the values of input data into specific implications concerning the courses of action that might be taken. There is, however, a price that must be paid in order to obtain such an overall understanding of the situation. Because of its greater complexity, a relevant mathematical programming model requires a great deal more effort to develop and implement than the traditional procedures which it is designed to supplant.

brains. In effect, the computer model serves as another member of the committee that "sits" around the table "discussing" what should be done. In this process, the resulting plans and decisions are very much influenced by the human components, and not just by the mathematical programming model in the computer.

One example of a creative, flexible use of a mathematical programming model would be to explore relationships among various possible goals. Goal programming techniques have been specifically developed for this purpose. The more common linear programming models can also be used in a similar manner, however. For example, a linear programming model is typically formulated in terms of one goal; nonetheless in practice it can be used to explore the consequences of alternative goal formulations. In this way, LP models are not necessarily used to optimize only a single goal, but to establish trade-off relationships that exist among many goals. Other common but imaginative uses of mathematical programming models would be sensitivity analyses to determine how important is an accurate knowledge of inputs, to what extent some ill-understood constraints need to be specified more accurately, etc.

The Implementation Problem

One reason why management science efforts in banks and business firms often fail to improve the planning and decision making proc-

ess is that from the outset the projects are organized in the wrong way. If the executives of a company are so busy "on the firing line" making day-to-day and week-to-week decisions that they can seldom spare half-an-hour to talk to their management scientists, then the management science analysts become "the boys in the back room." It is then difficult for them to learn enough about the real business world so that they can build relevant models. If the "back room" management scientists are successful in formulating a model that they feel could be relevant, this is usually communicated to the executives in a written memorandum. These decision makers all too often merely put the memorandum into a desk drawer or a waste basket, usually without understanding it and certainly without acting upon its recommendations. In this manner the so-called "implementation problem" arises, which is the problem of how to induce executives to utilize management science models to improve their planning and decision making activities.

My own pessimistic viewpoint is that the implementation problem is almost impossible to solve, once it has arisen. In an optimistic vein, however, I feel that it is possible to organize the management science activities in a business firm so that the implementation problem will not arise. To illustrate how this can be done, let me describe the realistic approach to the implementation of management science which has been successfully utilized in Bankers Trust Co., where I have been a consultant for the past decade. At Bankers Trust, we have found it possible to eliminate the distance between the executives "on the firing line" and the management science analysts "in the back room." In practice we bring these two groups together in frequent meetings and discussions, and they effectively collaborate in developing and implementing truly relevant management science models. Since our management scientists do not generally know very much about banking when they start, it is necessary for them to learn what are the crucial problems of banking, what are the new opportunities that might be exploited, what types of information are available, how good are the data, etc. Our management science analysts in practice learn this through the eyes, ears and mouths of the experienced bankers. Effective learning can occur only when these two different types of people can work together and communicate in ordinary banking language. In effect, the bank executives are teaching the management scientists a great deal about the banking business. At the same time, the management science analysts are gradually winning the confidence of the senior officers. Then both groups can jointly determine the types of considerations that will be embodied in the models, and together they can decide how the models will be utilized.

Most of the bank's executives themselves never learn any mathematics or computer programming,

because it is unnecessary. But the executives understand the economic and banking substance of the models, have an intuitive (i.e., a "big picture") understanding of the solution techniques, realize how the models could be used, appreciate when it is dangerous to use them, are aware of the qualitative considerations that have been left out of the models, know what extensions may be feasible, etc.

For effective, two-way communication to occur between executives and analysts, we found it essential to recruit "management-oriented" management science analysts, i.e., people who have the ability (and perhaps also the motivation) to become senior corporate officers someday. They must have the types of personalities and human relations skills that permit them to interact effectively with older, conventionally trained bankers. The resulting communication, of course, takes place in the ordinary language of the executives, rather than in terms of technical jargon or mathematical symbols.

When management-oriented scientists work jointly with senior executives to develop the economic substance and banking meaning of the management science models, the results are usually very relevant to the executives' problems. The models are to some extent unrealistic in that many aspects of reality are not incorporated in them. They are utilized, however, in a way which involves a great deal of interaction, many reruns and insightful interpretations of the results. This realistic approach produces far better results in practice than would be obtained either by "conventional" (people only) decision making techniques or by "straw man" (computer only) management science models that are run only once to generate allegedly "optimal" solutions.

The Respective Roles

Let me now consider more explicitly the role of the traditionally trained executive in the management science efforts. If management science is going to be profitable for a business firm, it has to change the way in which planning and decision making take place. If all the executives think that they are doing a great job and that there is no need for any change, management science is not going to help that corporation. On the other hand, if some executives realize that, no matter how good a job they might have done in the past, the environment is becoming more competitive (perhaps in part because competitors are effectively utilizing new management science tools), there are new kinds of markets emerging, the problems are growing more difficult and that they themselves may not in fact have been doing the best possible job in the past, then there is a good possibility of profitably using management science in that firm. It is important, however, to realize that the conventional executive cannot alone and unaided develop and implement useful management science models. Some knowledge of the mathematical tools and the computer systems (which need not

be overwhelming in terms of academic research standards) is necessary. Most executives do not have this type of technical knowledge.

On the other hand, it is also essential to realize that the young management scientist who might have had a sound academic training, and perhaps even some experience in another industry before coming to work in his present corporation, is not going to develop and implement these tools by himself. Traditional executives and management scientists must work together in order to develop and implement relevant management science models. There must be a team approach to the management science efforts.

The most effective way to accomplish this, in my opinion, is to have the management scientists who work in a given area invited to attend every management meeting that has anything to do with that particular area of the firm.[3] Initially the management science analysts will be silent observers, but gradually they will be asked questions by the traditional officers present, and eventually the analysts will be brought into the decision making process. I feel that this type of development should be encouraged. It will lead to mutual understanding and effective communication between more conventionally trained and older bank executives and the younger management scientists. Hence, when the development of a management science model is finished, there should not be great difficulty in implementing it.

In the process of building the model, the managers are involved in numerous discussions of goals, constraints and alternative courses of action. These discussions will change the manner in which the executives think. Also, the management scientists in this process are themselves becoming effective managers. Because of the comprehensive understanding they obtain of the company's problems from their management science work and because of their frequent exposure to senior officials, the management science analysts are well along the road to becoming corporate executives. There will, of course, always be some management-oriented management science analysts who will prefer not to become general managers but instead to remain staff specialists (or even some who will leave the business world and

³The extent to which the management scientists actually attend these meetings will vary over time. In the early stages of the project, the management science analysts will find it useful to attend almost all of these meetings, since they will be learning what the problems are, observing the process by which decisions are made, and becoming acquainted with the executives involved. During the intermediate stages of the project, the analysts should probably curtail the time that they spend in general management meetings in order to have enough time for building and analyzing the management science models. Once the models have been developed to the point where they should be utilized in the management process, the analysts will find themselves participating in increasing numbers of meetings to help executives formulate plans and make decisions. At some stage the management science analysts must decide whether to become managers in this particular area of the firm (in which case they will continue to attend and participate in all relevant meetings), or else to continue on their careers as management scientists (in which case they will start working on other projects).

return to an academic career). In the future, however, there will be an increasing number of senior corporate officers who have been management scientists earlier in their careers. This does not mean that management scientists will "take over" banks and other corporations in the future any more than it would now be proper to say that engineers have "taken over" oil companies and that actuaries have "taken over" life insurance companies.

Let me again stress that management science efforts require the enthusiasm of and cooperation from senior management before they can be successfully implemented. Traditional executives should realize that the growing use of management science need not necessarily cause them to be insecure in their jobs, and they certainly will not be replaced by computers. Unfortunately, however, some particular subset of present-day executives, those who refuse to learn and adapt to new ways of doing things, will be replaced by other executives who are willing and able to keep up with the times.

An analogy that illustrates this point is to consider what happened to the drivers of horses and wagons around the turn of the century when the internal combustion engine was introduced. It undoubtedly is true that there were a few horse-and-wagon drivers who never learned to drive automobiles and trucks, and who consequently may have eventually lost their jobs. Most of the horse-and-wagon drivers, of course, did learn to become chauffeurs, and they found gainful employment (probably at higher wages) driving trucks and automobiles. The blame for the loss of work of those few horse-and-wagon drivers who refused to learn new and more efficient ways of transporting passengers and hauling freight should lie with them, and not with the internal combustion engine.

In order for today's executives to learn to utilize management science techniques to improve their planning and decision making processes, they do not have to become management scientists themselves. Instead, as I have already indicated, they need only hire management-oriented management scientists, organize the management science effort in the proper manner and learn to interact effectively with their management scientists. Neither management scientists nor computers will truly "run" any corporation in the future, any more than it is fair to say that corporations today are "run" by telephones, jet airplanes and dictating machines. Today's corporations are, in the last analysis, "run" by people. The fact that today's executives have learned to utilize telephones, jet airplanes and dictating machines means, however, that their corporations are "run" today in a far different and more efficient manner than would be the case if these particular tools were not being used. In much the same manner, people will "run" the corporations of the future. In the future, however, executives will make in-creasing use of such tools as management science models, computer-based information systems and the like.

As the business world becomes more complex and more competitive, it is increasingly important for executives to learn to utilize new and more powerful tools to improve their planning, decision making and control activities. For this to happen, organizational doors must be opened to permit management scientists to attend meetings that heretofore had been considered to be "in bounds" only for members of senior management. Otherwise, the management science analysts will not be able to gather information and to build effective management science models that will help the top-level executives improve the planning and decision making process. It takes a special type of management scientist to be effective in this particular role. He must not only be a good mathematician and econometrician, but he must also possess a great deal of tact and diplomacy, the ability to communicate freely and easily both orally and in writing, and perhaps even the personal desire to become a senior corporate executive some day. This type of management-oriented management scientist can successfully make the transition from "analyst" to "manager" to "executive." As he does so, the corporation for which he works will be more profitable as the effective implementation of management science techniques improves the quality of the plans and decisions that are made.

Chapter 2

THE USE OF QUANTITATIVE TECHNIQUES IN COMMERCIAL BANKS*

By Frank J. Fabozzi and Sal Trovato

*This article is reprinted, with permission, from *Journal of Bank Research*, Vol. 7, No. 2 (Summer, 1976), pp. 173-178.

The objective of this paper is to summarize the principal findings of a survey on the use of quantitative techniques by 92 commercial banks. Mail questionnaires were employed to obtain an overview of the applications of quantitative techniques by commercial banks. Of the 400 questionnaires sent, 92, or 23%, were returned.

There were two constraints imposed upon us in conducting this investigation. First, because this project was not funded, cost was a primary factor in our decision to mail out only 400 questionnaires. Secondly, in constructing the questionnaire, we requested only limited information in order to encourage the return of questionnaires. Although there were numerous potential questions that could have been included, we decided to

concentrate on determining partial answers to the following questions: What quantitative techniques were currently being used and in what areas of a commercial banking operation? Why are some techniques not being used? What do bankers feel is the future for such techniques?

Applications of Quantitative Techniques to Commercial Bank Operations

Each commercial bank was asked if they currently utilize any of the following quantitative techniques: Linear programming, queuing theory, simulation, Monte Carlo process, PERT, game theory or statistical sampling. Thirteen of the banks did not use any of the techniques mentioned. Of the non-users, 12

Figure 1. Use of Quantitative Techniques by Deposit Size

Technique	Total Users	Less than $99.9 No.	(%)*	$100-499.9 No.	(%)*	$500-999.9 No.	(%)*	$100-1500 No.	(%)*	Over $1500 No.	(%)*
Linear Programming	29	2	(11)	3	(16)	7	(26)	7	(44)	10	(83)
Queuing Theory	9	—	(—)	—	(—)	2	(7)	2	(13)	5	(42)
Simulation	33	4	(22)	6	(32)	4	(15)	7	(44)	12	(100)
Monte Carlo Process	7	—	(—)	—	(—)	—	(—)	2	(13)	5	(42)
PERT	25	2	(11)	3	(16)	4	(15)	7	(44)	9	(75)
Game Theory	—	—	(—)	—	(—)	—	(—)	—	(—)	—	(—)
Statistical Sampling	43	1	(6)	6	(32)	10	(37)	14	(88)	12	(100)

Deposit size (in millions)

*Percentage of users within the respective deposit size class.

have deposits of less than $500 million. All of the banks in the sample with deposits of $1 billion or more used at least one of the quantitative techniques mentioned.

The distribution of users by deposit size for each technique are presented in Figure 1. Game theory was not reported as being used by any bank. This result may be partially due to the manner in which the authors constructed the questionnaire. Banks were asked if they employed a technique but were not given a description of the technique. Perhaps some banks classify game theory as simulation. In determining the number of different techniques employed by deposit size, not unexpectedly, the number of techniques employed by banks increases with deposit size.

Bankers were asked to give specific applications for the techniques they employed. Figure 2 reports the specific applications cited.

Linear programming models for asset and liability management are well documented in the literature.[1] The increasing number of services offered by commercial banks necessitated a systematic method for determining the profitability of a service or service department. Because of the interdependence of service departments in many industrial firms, linear programming models have been suggested for profitability accounting in such instances.[2] These models apparently now have been adopted to commercial banking. Two surprising omissions of linear programming's applicability are in the area of bond portfolio selection

[1]See, for example, Cohen and Hammer [1967], Cohen [1972] and Chambers and Charnes [1961].
[2]See, for example, Demski [1967], Kaplan and Thompson [1971] and Samuels [1965].
[3]The applicability of programming models to bank portfolio selection is demonstrated by Cohen and Thore [1970], Crane [1971] and Fried [1970]. Cohen and Hammer [1965] and Percus and Quinto [1956] have illustrated how linear programming can be applied to competitive bond bidding.

and competitive bond bidding.[3]

All applications of queuing theory and the Monte Carlo process were for teller staffing.[4] None of the 11 banks reporting the use of simulation for teller staffing reported using queuing theory and the Monte Carlo process. It is possible that the respondents classified the combined use of these techniques that are necessary for the teller staffing model as simulation. It has been suggested that the EDP and proof departments of a bank can employ simulation models in the same manner.[5] Banks in the survey reported such uses.

Commercial banks are currently under pressure to improve their investment performance in order to compete with other financial institutions for pension funds. Simulation can be used to provide the bank's portfolio manager with the return on alternative portfolios under various economic conditions. Surprisingly, only seven banks cited this as an application.

The dynamics and uncertainty involved in asset and liability management can be handled within the mathematical programming context by using chance constraints and dynamic programming. Alternatively, the problem can be dealt with by using simulation.[6]

Simulation was also cited as being applied to analyze the impact on the acquiring bank of an acquisition of another bank. Simulation was also employed to examine the consequences of a change in the service charge on demand deposits. However, this technique was not reported as being used for training employees.[7]

[4]Byerly [1960] illustrates how queuing theory and the Monte Carlo process can be applied to teller staffing.
[5]Cohen and Hammer [1966, p. 543].
[6]Cohen and Hammer [1966, p. 65].
[7]The Stonier Graduate School of Banking and the Pacific School of Banking currently employ simulation in training students. Bankers Trust Company first adopted a simulation program for training bank personnel in late 1960.

Figure 2. Specific Applications by Deposit Size

Techniques and Applications	All Banks		Deposit size (in millions)									
			Less than $99.9		$100-499.9		$500-999.9		$1000-1499.9		Over $1500	
	No.	(%)*	No.	(%)*	No.	(%)*	No.	(%)*	No.	(%)*	No.	(%)*
Linear Programming:												
1. Profitability accounting	15	(16)	1	(6)	2	(11)	3	(11)	3	(19)	6	(50)
2. Asset and liability mgmt.	12	(13)	1	(6)	—	(—)	1	(4)	4	(25)	6	(50)
3. Teller staffing	10	(11)	1	(6)	2	(11)	—	(—)	2	(13)	5	(42)
4. Proof and transit	17	(18)	—	(—)	1	(5)	5	(19)	4	(25)	7	(58)
Queuing Theory:												
1. Teller staffing	9	(10)	—	(—)	—	(—)	2	(7)	3	(19)	4	(33)
Simulation:												
1. Teller staffing	11	(12)	1	(6)	2	(11)	1	(4)	2	(13)	5	(42)
2. Proof and transit	8	(9)	1	(6)	2	(11)	1	(4)	1	(6)	3	(25)
3. Investment models	7	(8)	1	(6)	—	(—)	—	(—)	2	(13)	4	(33)
4. Financial planning	8	(9)	1	(6)	—	(—)	1	(4)	2	(13)	4	(33)
5. Computer timing	6	(7)	—	(—)	—	(—)	1	(4)	2	(13)	3	(25)
6. Acquisition studies	2	(2)	—	(—)	—	(—)	—	(—)	—	(—)	2	(17)
7. Service charge analysis on demand deposit accounts	5	(5)	—	(—)	2	(11)	—	(—)	1	(6)	2	(17)
Monte Carlo Process:												
1. Teller staffing	7	(8)	—	(—)	—	(—)	—	(—)	2	(13)	5	(42)

Techniques and Applications	All Banks		Deposit size (in millions)									
			Less than $99.9		$100-499.9		$500-999.9		$1000-1499.9		Over $1500	
	No.	(%)*	No.	(%)*	No.	(%)*	No.	(%)*	No.	(%)*	No.	(%)*
PERT:												
1. Project scheduling	10	(11)	2	(11)	1	(5)	2	(7)	2	(13)	3	(25)
2. Programming projects	3	(3)	—	(—)	1	(5)	—	(—)	—	(—)	2	(17)
3. Data processing planning	11	(12)	—	(—)	1	(5)	2	(7)	2	(13)	6	(50)
4. General planning	2	(2)	—	(—)	—	(—)	—	(—)	—	(—)	2	(17)
5. Trust	1	(1)	—	(—)	—	(—)	—	(—)	1	(6)	—	(—)
6. Term loans	3	(3)	—	(—)	—	(—)	—	(—)	1	(6)	2	(17)
7. Certificates of deposit	1	(1)	—	(—)	—	(—)	—	(—)	1	(6)	—	(—)
Statistical Sampling:												
1. Marketing-research, studies	7	(8)	—	(—)	—	(—)	1	(4)	—	(—)	6	(50)
2. Market penetration and planning	9	(10)	—	(—)	1	(5)	1	(4)	1	(6)	6	(50)
3. Marketing bank services	16	(17)	2	(11)	—	(—)	2	(7)	4	(25)	8	(67)
4. Proof and transit	12	(13)	1	(6)	—	(—)	—	(—)	3	(19)	8	(67)
5. Credit work	15	(16)	—	(—)	1	(11)	2	(7)	3	(19)	9	(75)
6. Auditing	37	(40)	1	(6)	3	(16)	5	(19)	16	(100)	12	(100)
7. EDP systems design	1	(2)	—	(—)	1	(5)	—	(—)	—	(—)	—	(—)
8. Branch site studies	12	(13)	2	(11)	1	(5)	1	(4)	3	(19)	5	(42)
9. Transit end-point analysis	3	(3)	—	(—)	2	(11)	—	(—)	1	(6)	—	(—)
10. Commercial loans	11	(12)	—	(—)	—	(—)	—	(—)	3	(19)	8	(67)
11. Student loans	3	(3)	—	(—)	—	(—)	1	(4)	—	(—)	2	(17)
12. Welfare processing	2	(2)	—	(—)	1	(5)	—	(—)	1	(6)	—	(—)

* Percentage of users within the respective deposit size class.

PERT was cited as being used in the trust department for term loans and for certificates of deposit. Nothing more specific was said, but it is likely that the timing and planning of cash flows in these three areas was why PERT networks were being used.[8]

Statistical sampling had the greatest number of decision-making applications. The most common was in the marketing area where marketing research, market penetration and marketing of all bank services were mentioned. Like linear programming and simulation, statistical sampling was also used by some banks for proof and transit. The application of statistical sampling to credit work, commercial loans and student loans most likely involves credit scoring models and/or loan portfolio evaluation models.[9]

It is interesting that applications have not been concentrated wholly in the larger banks. Of the 32 applications cited in Figure 2, 12 are being used by banks with less than $100 million in total deposits. Since this is the least representative group in terms of its universe, it is an encouraging sign.

Reasons for Not Using Quantitative Techniques

It is important to understand why banks did not use specific quantitative methods. For those techniques the banks did not use, bankers were asked the reasons why there was no usage. Interestingly, cost apparently had little to do with a bank not using quantitative techniques to aid in decision making. The main reason was lack of understanding of the techniques and their applicability to banking problems for all except game

theory and statistical sampling. The main reason game theory is not applied is because bankers felt there is no need for it at the present time. Those banks which did not use statistical sampling gave the main reason for non-usage as lack of qualified personnel to adapt the techniques to the computer.

Future Use of Quantitative Techniques

The banks that did not use a given technique were asked if they felt the technique would receive wider use in the next 10 to 15 years. The responses shed some encouragement on the possibility of greater use of quantitative methods in the future. It appears that linear programming, queuing theory, simulation, PERT and statistical sampling could all be on the threshold of gaining wider acceptance by the banking community as decision-making tools.

Some larger banks have already assembled their own management science staff. Also, there are several factors that should serve to foster the introduction of more applications. First, most graduates of business colleges now hired by banks are generally acquainted with the basics of operations research. As these individuals move into a position where they can exert strong direct influence on decision making, they might give these techniques greater consideration. Secondly, as the individuals involved in the adoption of some quantitative technique at their bank or at least present in its formative stages move into top management positions, they might encourage the use of more quantitative techniques. Finally, top management will encourage further use of quantitative techniques once they realize that such models do not replace decision makers but rather permit them to make better decisions. □

[8]Thore [1970] developed a model for programming credit networks under uncertainty.

[9]Such models were developed by Orgler [1966] and [1969].

REFERENCES

Byerly, Richard A., "The Use of Mathematical Models in the Analysis and Improvement of Bank Operations," *NABAC Research Bulletin*, Vol. 1, No. 5 (May 1960), pp. 12-19.

Chambers, D. and A. Charnes, "Intertemporal Analysis and Optimization of Bank Portfolios," *Management Science*, Vol. 7, No. 4 (July 1961), pp. 393-410.

Cohen, Kalman J., "Dynamic Balance Sheet Management: A Management Science Approach," *Journal of Bank Research*, Vol. 2 (Winter 1972), pp. 9-19.

Cohen, Kalman J. and Frederick S. Hammer, "Optimal Coupon Schedules for Municipal Bonds," *Management Science*, Vol. 12, No. 1 (September 1965), pp. 68-82.

————— (editors), *Analytical Methods in Banking*, Homewood, Illinois: Richard D. Irwin, Inc., 1966.

—————, "Linear Programming and Optimal Bank Asset Management Decisions." *Journal of Finance*, Vol. 22, No. 2 (May 1967), pp. 147-165.

Cohen, Kalman J. and Sten Thore, "Programming Bank Portfolios under Uncertainty," *Journal of Bank Research*, Vol. 1, No. 1 (Spring 1970), pp. 42-61.

Crane, Dwight B., "A Stochastic Programming Model for Commercial Bank Bond Portfolio Management," *Journal of Financial and Quantitative Analysis*, Vol. 6 (June 1971), pp. 955-975.

Demski, Joel S., "An Accounting System Structured on a Linear Programming Model," *The Accounting Review*, Vol. XLII, No. 4 (October 1967), pp. 701-712.

Fried, J. "Bank Portfolio Selection," *Journal of Financial and Quantitative Analysis*, Vol. 5 (June 1970), pp. 203-227.

Kaplan, Robert S. and Gerald L. Thompson, "Overhead Allocation Via Mathematical Programming Models," *The Accounting Review*, Vol. XLVI, No. 2 (April 1971), pp. 352-364.

Orgler, Yair E., "Evaluation of Consumer Loan Portfolios with Credit Scoring Models," Washington, D.C.: Federal Deposit Insurance Corporation, 1966.

—————, "Selection of Bank Loans for Evaluation: An Analytical Approach," *Journal of Finance*, Vol. 24, No. 1 (March 1969), pp. 75-80.

Percus, Jerome and Leon Quinto, "The Application of Linear Programming to Competitive Bond Bidding," *Econometrica*, Vol. 24, No. 4 (October 1956), pp. 413-428.

Samuels, J., "Opportunity Costing: An Application of Mathematical Programming," *Journal of Accounting Research*, Vol. 3, No. 2 (Autumn 1965), pp. 182-191.

Thore, Sten, "Programming a Credit Network under Uncertainty," *Journal of Money, Credit, and Banking*, Vol. 2, No. 2 (May 1970), pp. 219-246.

Part II

RETAIL MARKETING

IN an effort to enhance profitability, commercial banks have become increasingly competitive at the retail level. This emphasis on improving retail profitability has generally taken two forms. One approach has been to increase the volume of retail activity through expanded services, price competition, and innovative technology such as the cash dispensing machine. The second has been to focus on the cost factors involved in providing retail services. Obviously, most banks utilize a combination of both approaches, and one goal of strategic planning is to determine the maximum amount of services that can be provided at an acceptable cost level.

An important area of competition for most banks is attracting retail deposits. Deposits are the primary source of bank funds and make up nearly 90% of total commercial bank liabilities. The trade-off between maximum service and minimum cost forms the basis for strategies concerning retail demand deposits. Some banks feel that deposits are extremely valuable and as a result provide free checking services to customers who maintain a specified minimum balance. There are banks that go even further and provide free checking to all customers regardless of their balances in an effort to establish the highest possible volume of total retail services. On the other hand, many banks carefully scrutinize the cost of providing checking services and attempt to determine the exact benefit derived from various levels of deposits.

Chapter 3 examines the profitability of checking account arrangements. John H. Boyd focuses on the minimum balance arrangement in his article, "Bank Strategies in the Retail Demand Deposit Markets." Boyd's analysis reveals the extent to which short-term profitability suffers when banks lower service charges, increase advertising, and lower minimum balance requirements. Most strategic planners who choose the highly aggressive approach to attracting customers are aware that short-term profitability can suffer. Boyd's article provides a more exact analytical approach, however, which could provide much greater accuracy in balancing this key trade-off between profits and growth potential.

Aside from varying service charges or minimum balances, banks also advertise heavily to increase deposits and use of bank services. Determination of an optimal advertising expenditure consistent with the potential market is an important element of strategic planning and yearly budgeting. G. David Hughes provides in Chapter 4 an analytical framework that relates advertising expenditures to sales (increased retail business volume and loans). His article, "Predicting Bank Deposits and Loans," takes into account other marketing efforts and the environment within which the bank competes. Hughes illustrates the need for a predictive model that isolates controllable variables, which can then be incorporated into the bank's strategic plan in the form of performance goals. Using three savings banks as an example, Hughes points out that predictive marketing models must reflect the firm's goals, planning horizons, and general marketing strategy. Goals and strategies would then be expressed in specific terms, such as dollar share.

One of the greatest challenges to bank marketing abilities may arise as part of the movement toward an electronic funds transfer system (EFTS) (discussed in more detail in Part IX). EFTS is based on consumer use of bank cards and automatic tellers. One area of great concern is the acceptance level among consumers of depersonalized electronics and their willingness to utilize the system if it is made available. EFTS in general entails a large initial capital outlay for the electronics and facilities. Therefore, banks have been confronted with key investment decisions that rest in part on their ability to make effective and accurate market analyses. The result has been a reluctance on the part of bank management to commit themselves to full scale EFTS.

R. Y. Awh and Don R. Waters suggest an approach to this type of market analysis in Chapter 5, "A Discriminant Analysis of Economic, Demographic, and Attitudinal Characteristics of Bank Charge-Card Holders: A Case Study." The article provides a methodology that addresses key variables in analyzing the market potential of an electronic system. Socio-economic data and attitudinal characteristics are evaluated, and the conclusion reached is that attitude toward the use of credit cards is a key factor in determining the activity level of a card holder. This work by Awh and Waters is extremely valuable in providing guidelines for performing market research and analysis.

Discriminant analysis can also be utilized in the determination of promotional strategy issues, such as market segmentation. Analysis based on demographic and life-style variables can reveal the most effective use of media and the most receptive target audience. This approach to developing promotional strategy is described by Albert A. Pool in Chapter 6, "Application of Discriminant Analysis in Formulation of Promotional Strategy for Cash-Dispensing Machines." The article focuses specifically on promotional efforts for cash dispensing machines. The cash dispensing machine is, of course, a key element in the total electronic funds transfer system discussed in Part IX.

Management science techniques such as discriminant analysis are aimed at providing a bank manager with tools that will enable him to view all aspects of a decision clearly. The use of techniques such as those described in this part does not insure that decisions will become automatic. Rather, the use of careful market analysis will provide a better understanding of the relationships among key variables in the decision process. The actual decision still remains in the hands of the executive who must interpret the meaning of these relationships in light of the goals, planning horizon, and environment of the bank.

Chapter 3

BANK STRATEGIES IN THE RETAIL DEMAND DEPOSIT MARKETS*

By John H. Boyd

*This article is reprinted, with permission, from *Journal of Bank Research,* Vol. 4, No. 2 (Summer, 1973), pp. 111-121.

This study investigates the pricing of retail (households' and individuals') checking accounts, and attempts to define an optimal strategy for a bank. The subject has received little attention in the literature. However it is a topic of great current interest to many bank managers who are presently utilizing a variety of complex pricing schemes for such accounts. A few banks in various parts of the country now offer truly free checking plans, under which the depositor pays no service charge regardless of his account balance or activity; and a number of others are seriously considering this policy.

This analysis concentrates on the widely used "minimum balance" type plan in which the depositor may avoid any service charge if his account balance is continuously maintained above some minimum level specified by the bank. A micro model of the bank is constructed and solved, assuming that its objective is to maximize the total profit contribution of retail checking accounts. It is further assumed that the bank controls three critical variables which influence the demand for such accounts: The service charge, the balance requirement and advertising. A general solution of the model shows the relationship between these three decision variables and other "exogenous" variables, such as market interest rates and reserve requirements, which are not subject to control by bank management.

The model is applied to a real-world situation in which operating costs, interest rates, reserve requirements and deposit demand can be quantified. For this purpose estimates of operating costs are taken from the Federal Reserve's *Functional Cost Analysis*. Estimates of deposit demand are taken from an earlier empirical study which fitted regression equations over a 1970-1971 sample of Chicago area banks. Utilizing these data an optimal strategy is developed to maximize profits. The optimal (theoretical) strategy is then compared to the typical strategy employed by the sample of Chicago banks.

Finally, several different policies are simulated to demonstrate their effect on deposit growth,

profits, etc. The simulations indicate that the optimal strategy does better than the typical strategy, in the sense that it increases the profit contribution of demand deposit operations by about 14%. A free checking (zero service charge) policy is also simulated for purposes of comparison. Use of this strategy is shown to result in a substantial increase in deposit growth and a substantial reduction in profits. The simulations indicate the inherent trade-off between short-run profitability and long-run growth. Free checking is the extreme case in which growth is at a maximum, current profits at a minimum. Thus the choice of an optimal strategy must depend on a bank's discount rate, its planning horizon and on its willingness to sacrifice profits in order to achieve other objectives such as increased market share, accelerated growth, etc.

The Demand for Minimum-Balance Checking Accounts

A previous study by the author analyzed theoretically and empirically the determinants of demand for checking accounts. As here, the analysis focused on retail accounts of the minimum balance type [Boyd, 1973]. With such accounts the depositor may avoid any service charge if his account balance is continuously maintained above some prespecified minimum, B. If at any time his balance drops below B, a service charge, S, will be billed to the account.

The earlier study assumed that the number of accounts held by a bank would depend on its service charge, its balance requirement, its expenditure on advertising, p, and on a vector of exogenous variables, L, which were beyond its control. If N = number of accounts,

$$(1) \quad N = N(S,B,p,L), \frac{\partial N}{\partial S} \leq 0, \frac{\partial N}{\partial B} \leq 0, \frac{\partial N}{\partial p} \geq 0.$$

As indicated by the partial derivatives, it was hypothesized that advertising can be effective for attracting depositors, and that number of accounts is negatively related to the service charge and balance requirement, both of which represent costs to the account holder.

It was further assumed that changes in B or S would have systematic effects on the average size of account, A, held at the bank. This average size relationship was derived from a micro theoretical model of the individual depositor, in which his assumed objective was to maximize investment income, net of bank service charges and transactions costs. Upon solution the model indicated that as S was raised, those depositors who did not leave the bank would respond by holding larger account balances than they did previously, i.e. $\partial A/\partial S \geq 0$. It further indicated that as B was increased, those depositors who chose to remain with the bank would similarly increase their cash balances in an attempt to meet the balance requirement. However, this effect would not continue indefinitely. If B was raised high enough, a point would be reached at which the depositor's opportunity cost in holding cash balances exceeded the rate of return which he could achieve by investing his funds elsewhere. And increases in B beyond that point would actually diminish his optimal demand deposit balance. Summarizing these relationships:

$$(2) \quad A = A(S,B,L'), \frac{\partial A}{\partial S} \geq 0, \frac{\partial A}{\partial B} \lessgtr 0,$$

where L' is a vector of variables exogenous to the bank, which affect account size.

The hypothesized relationships, (1) and (2) were tested empirically using regression equations over a 1970-1971 sample of Chicago area banks. Almost without exception, the empirical results were in accord with the theory. Average size of account was positively and significantly related to the service charge, and significantly related to the minimum balance requirement. The relationship with B was non-linear and concave to the origin as suggested by the theoretical model. Growth in number of accounts was negatively and significantly related to the service charge, and positively and significantly related to advertising. The minimum balance requirement never entered as a significant factor explaining growth however. This last finding is difficult to justify and, as discussed in the earlier study, may be explained by problems in statistical estimation.

The Micro Model

The purpose of this section is to present a micro-theoretical model of a bank, integrating the earlier results concerning individuals' and households' demand for checking accounts. The model will explicitly recognize the distinction between number of accounts and average size of account,

and will assume the functional (demand) relationships (1) and (2) to hold. In that regard, its structure is importantly dependent on the previous empirical work.

The objective function is defined as the profit contribution of retail demand deposits, π, where,

$$(3) \quad \pi = NAr(1-R) - NC + NSE - NP$$
$$= N[Ar(1-R) - C + SE - P] = N\alpha.$$

r = the average rate of return on loans and investments held by the bank, R = the reserve requirement for demand deposits, C = bank operating costs per checking account, S = the service charge, E = the percentage of accounts which pay the service charge in any period $(0 \leq E \leq 1)$, P = advertising/number of accounts and α = average profits per account. R is constant and it is therefore assumed that the bank will always stay fully loaned up. It is further assumed that the bank invests its funds in a perfect market so that r is exogenously determined. C is assumed constant so that operating costs are a linear function of number of accounts; increasing or decreasing returns to scale are ot allowed.[1]

Since the empirical tests ii licated that bank policy can affect the growth rate of demand deposits, the model must take account of more than a single period. It is assumed therefore that the bank attempts to maximize the present value of all profits, present and future, generated by its retail demand deposit operations or ϕ,

$$(4) \quad \phi = \sum_{i=0}^{m} \pi_i/(1+k)^i,$$

where i represents time period and k is the bank's discount rate. Number of accounts is assumed to grow at a rate g so that in period i, $N_i = N_{i-1}(1+g)$. Assuming that $g < k$, and that the bank has an infinitely long planning horizon so that $m \to \infty$, equation (4) can be simplified,[2]

$$(5) \quad \phi = \frac{N_o(1+k)[Ar(1-R) - C + SE - P]}{k-g}.$$

In accordance with the empirical findings it is assumed that depositors behave according to equations (1) and (2), and that these equations summarize the market (demand) constraints confronting the bank. Finally, it is assumed that the proportion of depositors paying the service charge in any period, E, is a function of the balance

---

[1] Only advertising directed toward retail checking account customers is included in P.

[2] This type of infinite horizon model has become commonplace in the financial theory of the firm. For a discussion of its derivation and implications see, for example, [Dobrovolsky, 1971, Chapter 4].

requirement and the average size of account such that,

(6) $\quad E = E(B, A), \dfrac{\partial E}{\partial B} \geq 0, \dfrac{\partial E}{\partial A} \leq 0.$

As the model is constructed, the bank sets three decision variables, P, S and B. For simplicity it is assumed that these variables are fixed during the first period and then maintained through time at their initial values.[3] Differentiating the objective function, (5), with respect to the decision variables, S, B and P, subject to the market demand constraints, (1) and (2) and subject to constraint (6) defines the first-order conditions for an optimum when these partial derivatives are set equal to zero.

(7) $\quad N_i \left[\dfrac{\partial A}{\partial B} r(1-R) + S\left(\dfrac{\partial E}{\partial B} + \dfrac{\partial E}{\partial A}\dfrac{\partial A}{\partial B} \right) \right]$

$\quad + N_i \dfrac{\left[Ar(1-R) - C + SE - P \right] \dfrac{\partial g}{\partial B}}{k-g} = 0.$

(8) $\quad - N_i + \dfrac{N_i \left[Ar(1-R) - C + SE - P \right] \dfrac{\partial g}{\partial P}}{k-g}$

$\quad = 0.$

(9) $\quad N_i \left[\dfrac{\partial A}{\partial S} r(1-R) + E + S\dfrac{\partial E}{\partial A}\dfrac{\partial A}{\partial S} \right]$

$\quad + \dfrac{N_i \left[Ar(1-R) - C + SE - P \right] \dfrac{\partial g}{\partial S}}{k-g} = 0.$

Conditions (7), (8) and (9) have the usual marginal cost-equals-marginal revenue interpretation, except in this case cost and revenue are spread over a number of periods. Each condition has the interesting property that it relates profitability to growth, and reflects a trade-off between the two. We first examine the effect of changes in the decision variables on single-period profitability. In any arbitrary period i,

(10) $\quad \dfrac{\partial \pi_i}{\partial B_i} = N_i \left[\dfrac{\partial A}{\partial B} r(1-R) + S\left(\dfrac{\partial E}{\partial B} + \dfrac{\partial E}{\partial A}\dfrac{\partial A}{\partial B} \right) \right],$

(11) $\quad \dfrac{\partial \pi_i}{\partial P_i} = -N_i,$

(12) $\quad \dfrac{\partial \pi_i}{\partial S_i} = N_i \left[\dfrac{\partial A}{\partial S} r(1-R) + E + S\dfrac{\partial E}{\partial A}\dfrac{\partial A}{\partial S} \right].$

It is clear that the left-hand expressions in marginal conditions (7), (8) and (9) represent

[3] This assumption greatly simplifies the structure and solution of the model. However, it ignores the possibility that the true optimal solution may be one in which S, B and P are changing through time.

$\dfrac{\partial \pi_i}{\partial B_i}, \dfrac{\partial \pi_i}{\partial P_i}$ and $\dfrac{\partial \pi_i}{\partial S_i}$ respectively. Since by assumption advertising affects the growth rate in number of accounts, a change in period i advertising has no effect on the number of accounts until period $i+1$ so that in (11) $\dfrac{\partial \pi_i}{\partial P_i} = -N_i =$ the marginal cost of advertising. And since $\dfrac{\partial \pi_i}{\partial P_i} < 0$ the bank can always raise current profits by cutting back on advertising.

Changing the service charge has several same-period effects as shown in equation (12). $N_i \dfrac{\partial A}{\partial S} r(1-R)$ measures the change in portfolio income, as depositors adjust their average account size in response to a change in S_i. Since $\dfrac{\partial A}{\partial S} \geq 0$, $N_i \dfrac{\partial A}{\partial S} r(1-R)$ will be non-negative. $N_i \left[E + S\dfrac{\partial E}{\partial A}\dfrac{\partial A}{\partial S} \right]$ is the change in total service charge revenue, resulting from a marginal change in the service fee S_i. This expression is complex and could in principle be either positive or negative. As the service fee is raised, any increase in revenue is offset to some extent by the fact that depositors will increase their average balances.

As demonstrated in equation (10) changing the minimum balance requirement also has several same-period effects. $N_i \dfrac{\partial A}{\partial B} r(1-R)$ is the change in portfolio income which results as depositors alter their average account balances in response to a change in B. Since $\dfrac{\partial A}{\partial B} \gtreqless 0$, it is impossible to state *a priori* whether an increase in B will raise or lower portfolio income. $S\left(\dfrac{\partial E}{\partial B} + \dfrac{\partial E}{\partial A}\dfrac{\partial A}{\partial B} \right)$ is the marginal change in service charge revenue resulting from a change in the balance requirement B. Since $\dfrac{\partial E}{\partial B} \geq 0$, *ceteris paribus*, increasing B will raise service charge revenue. However, depositors will respond to a change in the balance requirement by adjusting their average account balance, A, and this secondary effect may either increase or decrease total service charge revenue collected by the bank.

Growth Effects

If the objective were to maximize single period income the bank would set $\dfrac{\partial \pi_i}{\partial P_i} = \dfrac{\partial \pi_i}{\partial S_i} = \dfrac{\partial \pi_i}{\partial B_i} = 0$. However, each of the decision variables, S, B and P influences the rate of growth over time in addition to its effect on profitability within each single period. Let $d =$ an artificially defined decision variable which affects only growth in number of accounts. If d is changed for a single period, period i, the entire effect will be reflected in g_{i+1} so that,

$$(13) \quad \frac{\partial \phi_i}{\partial d_i} = \frac{N_i \alpha \frac{\partial g_{i+1}}{\partial d_i}}{1+k} + \frac{N_i \alpha \frac{\partial g_{i+1}}{\partial d_i}(1+g)}{(1+k)^2} + \frac{N_i \alpha \frac{\partial g_{i+1}}{\partial d_i}(1+g)^2}{(1+k)^3} \cdots$$

Assuming an infinite horizon and $g < k$,

$$(14) \quad \frac{\partial \phi_i}{\partial d_i} = \frac{N_i \alpha \frac{\partial g_{i+1}}{\partial d_i}}{k-g}.$$

The right-hand expressions in marginal conditions (7), (8) and (9) are analogous to $\frac{\partial \phi_i}{\partial d_i}$, and measure the change in discounted future profits resulting from a single period change in one of the decision variables. Thus, conditions (7), (8) and (9) may be interpreted in the following manner. During any period i, P, S and B must be set so that $\frac{\partial \phi_i}{\partial P_i} = \frac{\partial \phi_i}{\partial S_i}$ $= \frac{\partial \phi_i}{\partial B_i} = 0$. Changing a control variable will affect current profits, as shown in (10), (11) and (12), and also future profits, as shown in (14). At the margin the sum of these present and future effects, discounted for futurity, must equal zero. Since the choice of period i is arbitrary, these conditions will be fulfilled in all future periods as well as in the initial period.

The Trade-Off Between Profits and Growth

The optimal values of P, B and S are not independent. Combining equations (7), (8) and (9) with the definition of α and rearranging:

$$(15) \quad \frac{\frac{\partial \alpha}{\partial P}}{\frac{\partial g}{\partial P}} = \frac{\frac{\partial \alpha}{\partial B}}{\frac{\partial g}{\partial B}} = \frac{\frac{\partial \alpha}{\partial S}}{\frac{\partial g}{\partial S}} = -\frac{\alpha}{k-g}.$$

The control variables will be set so that the ratio, marginal change in profitability per account/ marginal change in the growth rate, is the same for each. Since it is assumed that $k > g$, and since $\alpha > 0$ is a requirement for positive profits, these ratios will be negative. By assumption $\frac{\partial g}{\partial B} \leq 0$ and $\frac{\partial g}{\partial S} \leq 0$. Therefore according to (15) at the optimum

solution, $\frac{\partial \alpha}{\partial B} \geq 0$ and $\frac{\partial \alpha}{\partial S} \geq 0$. In other words, B and S are not set at the values, $\frac{\partial \alpha}{\partial B} = \frac{\partial \alpha}{\partial S} = 0$, which would maximize profitability per account. In fact if α is strictly concave then B and S are lower than they would be in a single period model. By increasing either the balance requirement or the service charge, the bank could raise current profits; however to do so it would sacrifice some future growth. Similarly, current earnings could be increased (subject to some decline in future growth) if advertising expenditures were set at a lower level than that defined by (15). There is an inherent trade-off between growth rate and current profitability, and it is clear that the optimal strategy need not maximize either.

Solving the Model for Specific Values of the Exogenous Variables: Implications for Optimal Bank Strategy

The next step is to apply the model to the real world, in which operating costs, interest rates, reserve requirements, etc. can be quantified. By assuming specific values for the exogenous variables it is possible to solve the first-order conditions, (7), (8) and (9), for P, S and B. If the model is correctly structured and if the estimates of the exogenous terms (presented in Figure 1) are accurate, the solution values, P^*, S^* and B^* should approximate optimal policy for a real-world bank. For this purpose cost estimates are taken from the Federal Reserve's *Functional Cost Analysis*, and demand parameters are taken from the author's earlier empirical study. A discount rate of 10% per annum is arbitrarily assumed. The actual equations for growth, service charge revenue, average size of account, etc., are presented in an Appendix. The model is solved for a finite horizon of 20 quarters. This modification is necessary because the tractability of the infinite-horizon model depends on the assumption $g < k$, and the empirical growth equation is not constrained to insure this inequality.[4]

Advertising

Initial attempts at solving the model gave unreasonably large values for P^* and, in fact, suggested that a bank could increase profits almost indefinitely by raising advertising expenditures. This result is largely due to the fact that the empirical growth equation assumes $\partial g/\partial P$ is constant.[5] That assumption may be acceptable for

---

[4] Optimal values of the decision variables are calculated using an iterative search method and therefore the solutions are approximate.
[5] See Appendix.

Figure 1. Exogenous Variables: Values Assumed and Sources

	Variable	Definition	Value	Source
1)	$r(1-R)$	Average Rate of Return (annual) on Investment of Demand Deposit Funds, Net of Reserves	.0511	Federal Reserve, *Functional Cost Data*, 1971.
2)	C	Average Bank Cost (Fixed and Variable) Per Minimum-Balance Checking Account (Quarterly)	$5.73	Federal Reserve, *Functional Cost Data*, 1971.
3)	N_O	Beginning Number of Minimum-Balance Checking Accounts	5337	1970-71 Sample of Chicago Area Banks. (5337 = sample average).
4)*	P^*N	Advertising Expenditure (Quarterly) Includes Only Advertising for Demand Deposit Accounts	$4485	1970-71 Sample of Chicago Area Banks ($4485 = sample average).
5)	k	Discount Rate (Annual)	.10	Assumed.
6)	A_O	Beginning Average Account Balance	$1021	1970-71 Sample of Chicago Area Banks ($1021 = sample average).

*Advertising is not truly an exogenous variable, although in this section it is treated as one.

values of advertising close to the sample mean; but it seems clear that a bank cannot continue to increase its advertising budget without experiencing decreasing returns. These results are still of some interest, for they suggest that the typical sample bank could raise its profits through increased advertising for demand deposits. But due to the obvious problem with the growth equation, final solutions for B and S are calculated assuming that P is exogenous and fixed at the sample mean. This procedure may introduce some error, but the solution values of B and S do not seem to be greatly affected by moderate changes in advertising.[6]

The Minimum Balance Requirement

Upon solution the optimum value for the minimum balance requirement is approximately $349. This is about 30% higher than the mean balance requirement for the sample of Chicago area banks, which is $269. B^* is very stable and changes little in response to changes in the exogenous variables. This stability is in large part due to the assumption that growth in number of accounts is independent of the balance requirement, or that $\partial g/\partial B = 0$. As mentioned earlier, we were unable to establish such a relationship empirically even though it seems likely that one exists. When $\partial g/\partial B = 0$, B^* is the value of B which maximizes single-period profits; and $349 is very close to the value of B which,

according to the empirical estimates, maximizes the average size of account.[7]

The Service Charge

The solution values of S^* is $1.70. This is about 30% lower than the mean service charge for the sample of Chicago area banks, which is $2.44. Unlike the balance requirement, S^* is sensitive to changes in the exogenous variables. Figure 2 shows S^* plotted against C, the cost of servicing a minimum-balance checking account. The two are positively related so that holding all the other variables constant, the lower the bank's cost, the lower its optimal service charge.

The bottom quadrant in Figure 2 shows the present discounted value of total profits, assuming that the service charge is set at S^* and, alternatively, assuming that it is set at zero. For all reasonable values of C profits with $S = 0$ are less than the profits which can be achieved with a positive service fee. And if C is more than about $6.50, a zero service charge will result in losses and, therefore, in a negative discounted value of total profits.[8]

[6] For example, a doubling of P has almost no perceptible effect on B^* and S^*.

[7] If, as we suspect, there actually exists a relationship between growth and the balance requirement such that $\partial g/\partial B < 0$, then the true optimal solution for B will be something less than $349. That conclusion is implied by equation (7) assuming that α is strictly concave in B.

[8] In this section of the paper, a number of results are derived with $S = 0$, e.g. assuming that the bank offers free checking. This special case is included for purposes of comparison, in terms of its impact on profits, growth, etc. However, it must be pointed out that the results regarding free checking should be interpreted very cautiously. None of the sample banks used in estimating the deposit demand equations offered this plan. Therefore, in examining this case we are extrapolating beyond the range of the underlying data, and at $S = 0$ the demand elasticities may be considerably different than they are at the sample means.

Figure 2.

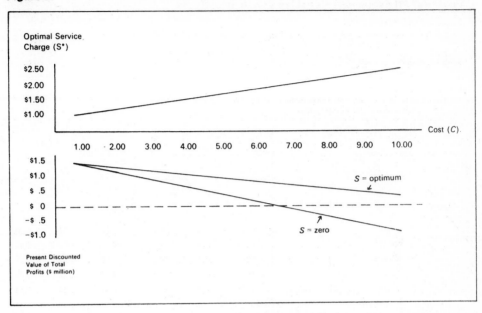

Figure 3.

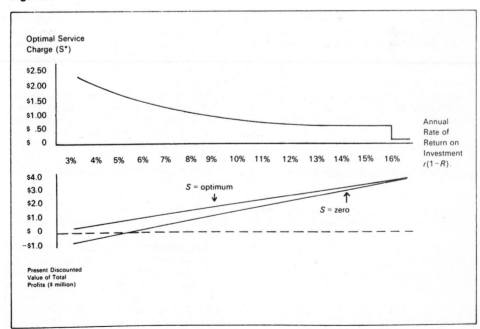

Figure 4. Simulating Three Pricing Strategies for Retail Checking Accounts; All Exogenous Variables Constant*

Strategy (1): $S = \$2.44, B = \$269.$
These are the *average* values for service charges and balance requirements, calculated from the sample of Chicago area banks.

Strategy (2): $S = \$0, B = \$349.$
"Free Checking".**

Strategy (3): $S = \$1.70, B = \$349.$
The Optimal Strategy. These solution values of B and S maximize the present discounted value of total profits.

Strategy:	Number of Accounts			Average Size of Account ($)			Total Deposit Balances ($ Million)		
	(1)	(2)	(3)	(1)	(2)	(3)	(1)	(2)	(3)
End of Quarter									
4	4962	7821	5638	1023	612	958	5.08	4.79	5.40
8	4661	12261	5989	1024	514	943	4.77	6.30	5.65
12	4495	17295	6248	1024	491	940	4.60	8.48	5.87
16	4403	22567	6425	1024	485	939	4.51	10.94	6.03
20	4352	27962	6545	1024	484	939	4.45	13.52	6.14

*All exogenous variables are set at the values listed in Figure 1. Advertising is held constant at the sample mean of $4485.
**If the service charge is zero, depositors have no reason to meet the balance requirement and variations in B should have no effect on deposit demand. However, the statistical demand equation does not account for this fact and to run the simulations it is necessary to specify a value for B even when $S = 0$. $349 is the optimal solution value for B, e.g. the value which maximizes present discounted profits. As a result, the simulation of strategy (2) gives the highest level of profits which could be expected with zero service charges. If there is any bias therefore, it is in favor of free checking.

In Figure 2, S^* is plotted against $r(1 - R)$, the rate of return on investment after provision for reserve requirements. The slope is negative, indicating that the higher the interest rate, the lower S^*. For any reasonable interest rate $S^* > 0$, and by setting the service charge at the optimum the bank can achieve positive profits. This is not true if $S = 0$, however, for in this case whenever $r(1 - R)$ is less than about 5% the bank will sustain losses.[9]

The Break-even Point

Figures 2 and 3 show that as demand deposit operations become increasingly profitable, (i.e. as costs fall or as interest rates rise), the optimal service charge S^* decreases. Since $\partial g/\partial S < 0$, the bank will increase its rate of growth by lowering the service fee. At the same time, however, as S is lowered, average profitability per account, α, will fall. This occurs because the average size of account is diminished, and so in general is the expected service charge revenue per account.

[9] Figure 2 shows that at one point S^* is discontinuous, falling abruptly from $.70 to $.20. This discontinuity occurs because there are two local maximums for S. At $r(1 - R) \approx 16\%$ the "optimum optimorum" shifts from one local maximum to the other.

For any given values of P, S and B, there exists a break-even point at which average revenue per account just equals average cost. This break-even point depends on operating costs, interest rates and the reserve requirement, but as noted above it also depends on the service charge set by the bank. In general, the higher S, the higher the level of costs which can be tolerated without resulting in losses. And similarly, the higher S, the further interest rates must fall to push the bank below its break-even level. A zero service charge requires the most favorable conditions for the bank to operate profitably. As shown in Figures 2 and 3, when $S = 0$ the break-even point occurs at $C \approx \$6.50$ and at $r(1 - R) \approx 5\%$. Although we have little confidence in the exact figures, it is interesting to observe that these break-even levels are not far from the average values of C and $r(1 - R)$ listed in Figure 1.

Since future interest rates and operating costs cannot be predicted with perfect accuracy, these results have interesting implications for the risk associated with demand deposit operations. By setting a low service charge the bank may be able to grow rapidly, increase its market share, and still maintain a positive profit margin. However, its

Figure 4 (Continued)

	Quarterly Service Charge Revenue ($1000)			Quarterly Income from Investment of Deposits ($1000)			Quarterly Costs Attributable to Demand Deposit Operations ($1000)*		
Strategy:	(1)	(2)	(3)	(1)	(2)	(3)	(1)	(2)	(3)
Quarter									
4	11.7	0	12.0	64.9	61.2	69.1	32.9	49.3	36.8
8	11.0	0	12.7	61.0	80.5	72.2	31.2	74.8	38.8
12	10.6	0	13.3	58.8	108.4	75.0	30.3	103.6	40.3
16	10.4	0	13.6	57.6	139.8	77.1	29.7	133.8	41.3
20	10.2	0	13.9	56.9	172.8	78.5	29.5	164.7	42.0

*Includes advertising expense

	Average Profitability Per Account, Per Quarter ($)			Quarterly Profits ($1000)					
Strategy:	(1)	(2)	(3)	(1)	(2)	(3)			
Quarter									
4	8.79	1.52	7.85	43.6	11.9	44.2			
8	8.75	.47	7.70	40.7	5.8	46.1			
12	8.71	.28	7.68	39.1	4.8	48.0			
16	8.69	.27	7.69	38.2	6.0	49.4			
20	8.67	.29	7.70	37.7	8.1	50.4			

Present Discounted Value of
Total Profits ($1000)

Strategy (1):	655.2
Strategy (2):	143.4
Strategy (3):	748.5

average account size will be relatively small and it will collect little in service charge revenue. In combination, these two factors will result in a low value of α—e.g. the average profitability per account will be small. As a result, the bank will have little margin to absorb an unforeseen rise in operating costs or decline in interest rates without suffering losses. In achieving a high rate of growth, it has necessarily sacrificed some current income; but in addition, the bank has magnified its exposure to the risk of imperfect forecasting.[10]

The analysis has assumed that the cost of servicing retail demand deposits is a simple linear function in number of accounts. To the extent that cost is systematically lower for small accounts than it is for large accounts, this assumption may have biased the results against low service charge policies. It seems clear however that for a given level of total deposits, bank operating costs will fall as the average size of account increases. Or in other words, it is cheaper to service a small number of large accounts than it is to service a large number of small accounts.[11] Therefore α may still be expected to fall with the average size of account, even if costs are not strictly a linear function of the number of depositors.

[10] Although it is not done here, a more complete model would explicitly account for the risk preferences of management, which would influence the choice of an optimal strategy.

[11] This conclusion is supported by some results presented in [Daniel, Longbrake, and Murphy, forthcoming].

Simulating Different Strategies

To clarify the relationships discussed in the preceding section, three different bank strategies have been simulated, assuming that all exogenous variables are held constant at the values listed in Figure 1. The simulations are presented in Figure 4. They are intended to show the general relationship between growth, profitability, average size of account, etc., and the specific values in the table must be interpreted cautiously. The underlying equations are presented in the Appendix.

In accord with the preceding discussion, free checking (Strategy 2) yields the fastest growth in number of accounts and the smallest average account balance. It also results in the highest level of costs and that fact, in conjunction with zero service charge revenue, yields the lowest profitability among the three strategies. The optimal strategy (Strategy 3) results in a moderate rate of growth in number of accounts, service charge revenue, investment income and profits.

The "typical" strategy (Strategy 1) results in the highest average account size and the highest profitability per account. However it produces a modest decline in number of accounts, deposit balances and total profits. This is not an unreasonable conclusion, for the definition of a typical strategy guarantees that about half of the banks competing in the market offer service charges and balance requirements which are less than "typical." One would expect that in an imperfectly competitive market these low-pricers will gradually expand their market share, at the expense of banks with higher values of B and S.[12]

Summary and Conclusions

In devising a strategy for retail checking account operations a bank should be aware that its policies will affect the size composition of deposits, as well as the number of accounts that it holds. Changes in average size and/or number of accounts will in turn affect its investment income, its service charge revenue and its operating costs. The bank may increase its growth rate by raising advertising expenditures, lowering service charges and, probably, by lowering its minimum balance requirement. However a policy which maximizes growth is not likely to maximize current profits and vice versa. Therefore it is important that bank management recognize this trade-off in its decision making.

An increase in growth obtained by lowering service charges will be partially offset by a decline in average account size. This decline in average account size tends to diminish profitability per account, and move the bank toward the break-even point at which average cost equals average revenue. In other words, a low service charge, high growth policy will result in some reduction in current profits. Moreover it will reduce the profit margin available to absorb any future rise in operating costs or decline in interest rates, thus magnifying the risks associated with imperfect forecasting. In general, the choice of an optimal policy must depend on a bank's discount rate, its planning horizon, and on its willingness to sacrifice some profits in order to achieve other objectives such as increased market share, accelerated growth, etc.[13]

□

---

[12] Since the earlier results indicated that the typical sample bank could raise its profits by increased advertising, the simulations were rerun assuming advertising at twice the sample mean. Profits did increase as expected, but the relative ranking of strategies 1, 2 and 3 was unaffected. Additional simulations were run assuming a longer 40 quarter horizon, and again the rankings remained unchanged.

[13] This study suffers from two deficiencies which should be mentioned as possible areas for future research. First, it has ignored the fact that in many cases a bank provides more than a single service to the same individual. Therefore it may be perfectly rational for it to accept unprofitable demand deposit accounts if the resulting losses are offset by other, more profitable relationships with the same customer. This full customer-bank relationship is undoubtedly important, but unfortunately it is difficult to quantify given the present accounting systems at most banks.

We have ignored another important problem by assuming that a bank can devise an optimal strategy without specifically accounting for the probable reaction of its competitors. Many banks must be concerned with this problem particularly if they are large or have a substantial share of their deposit market.

REFERENCES

Boyd, John H., "Consumers' Demand for Checking Account Balances." Unpublished Working Paper, Northwestern University, 1973.

Cohen, Bruce C., "Deposit Demand and the Pricing of Demand Deposits." *Quarterly Journal of Economics*, LXXXIV (August, 1970).

Daniel, D., W. Longbrake and N. Murphy, "The Effect of Technology on Bank Economies of Scale for Demand Deposits." *Journal of Finance*, forthcoming.

Dobrovolsky, Sergei, *The Economics of Corporation Finance*. New York: McGraw-Hill, 1971.

Functional Cost Analysis: 1971 Average Banks. Federal Reserve System.

Klein, Michael and Neil Murphy, "The Pricing of Bank Deposits: A Theoretical and Empirical Analysis." *Journal of Financial and Quantitative Analysis*, VI (March, 1971).

Status of Bank Marketing. The American Bankers Association, 1970.

Weiss, Steven, "Commercial Bank Price Competition: The Case of 'Free' Checking." *New England Bank Review*, September/October, 1969.

APPENDIX

1) $q = .00425 - .058S + 134. P/A$

2) $SE = -.0096B + .0000145B^2 + 3.54S - .794 S^2$

3) $A^* = -1701. + 12.54B - .018B^2 + 268.S$

4) $A_i = A_{i-1} + .3(A^* - A_{i-1})$

5) $N_i = (1+g) N_{i-1}$

6) $\pi_i = N_i [A_i r(1-R) - C + SE - P]$.

Note: Equations (1), (2) and (3) are regression estimates from a 1970-1971 sample of Chicago area banks. The simulations were run assuming a partial adjustment mechanism in which A_i = average size of account in period i, and A^* = long-run equilibrium average account size. This equation assumes that average account size responds to changes in B and S with some lag. The speed-of-adjustment coefficient, .3, is arbitrarily assumed. It results in a fairly rapid adjustment to equilibrium, which is 76% complete at the end of one year, and 95% complete at the end of two years. Equation (5) gives the number of accounts in period i, and equation (6) defines the profit contribution of retail checking accounts. For the simulations, E (equation 2) is constrained to be non-negative.

Chapter 4

PREDICTING
BANK DEPOSITS
AND LOANS*

By G. David Hughes

*This article is reprinted, with permission, from *Journal of Marketing Research* published by the American Marketing Association, Vol. 7 (February, 1970), pp. 95-100.

Because banks spend over one-quarter billion dollars for advertising [13], their concern for optimal levels of advertising expenditures is natural. The familiar question, "How much should we spend for advertising?" may be answered with operations research techniques if an objective function can be described. But this function requires a prediction of deposits and loans. This study attempted to identify the variables that should be included in prediction models for three savings banks in Boston. For details, see [3].

METHOD

A detailed case study revealed that quite different goals were used by one bank when developing its strategy: the dollar volume of deposits, the market share of deposits, the number of depositors, and the share of depositors [2]. Equations reflecting each of these goals were used to see if goals differed among the banks examined.

Banks can aggressively alter controllable variables such as dividend rates, loan rates, and advertising, or identify a market segment and adapt to the needs of this segment. The strategy actually used will determine which variables should be included in a prediction model. Since the case study did not reveal a clear strategy, the most likely variables were included in the equations in an attempt to identify strategy or lack of strategy.

A bank with a short planning horizon will react quickly to competitive advertising and dividend rates while a bank with a long-range horizon will rely more on its own plan than the short-run behavior of competitors. Thus, the planning horizon will determine the importance of variables in models of prediction. Three planning horizons—intermediate, annual, and long-range—were examined.

Models to predict deposits included two variables that could be controlled by the banks (dividend rate and advertising expenditures) and three which could not (effective buying income per household, common stock dividend rates, and earnings rates). Similarly, models to predict loans used two controllable variables (interest rates on loans and advertising expenditures) and three uncontrollable ones (government bond rates, consumer expenditures for durables, and effective buying income per household).[1]

Variables took three forms—absolute, first difference, and lagged. The first model used absolute variables in a hyperbolic form to examine the relationship between the earnings-price ratio of common stocks, savings banks' dividend rates, and dollar volume of deposits (Figure). The second model used the first differences of variables to examine the relationships between the independent variables of advertising expenditures, common stock dividend-price ratios, common stock earnings-price ratio, bank dividend rates, and effective buying income, and the dependent variables of savings deposits, expressed as dollar volume, number of accounts, and the market share of each (Table 1). The market for share calculations was defined as all Boston savings banks. Each of these dependent variables represented a possible savings bank promotional goal. The third model (Table 2) used the same variables as the second, but in the lagged form [4]. The fourth model used the lagged variables to identify the determinants of demand for loans by savings banks (Table 3).

FINDINGS

Hyperbolic (Absolute) Model

It was hypothesized that there would be two types of savings bank depositors. One would be insensitive to the activities of the stock market and the second would be sensitive, depositing in his savings account according to the spread between the bank dividend rate (Div_i) and the earnings-price ratio of common stocks (E/P). In the model,

$$\text{Deposits} = a + b \, [1/(E/P - Div_i)],$$

the volume of despoits insensitive to the stock market is represented by the constant a, which is the horizontal asymptote in the Figure. The influence of the stock market is represented by the coefficient b, the slope of

---

[1] Sources of data are as follows: advertising price index, *Boston Globe* (combined morning-evening daily flat rate) as reported in the *Editor and Publisher International Yearbook*, 1947–1961; bank variables including dollar deposits, number of depositors, dollar loans, number of loans, value of premises, advertising expenditures, dividend and loan rates were taken from The Commonwealth of Massachusetts, Division of Banks and Loan Agencies, *Annual Reports of the Commissioners of Banks, Section C* for the years 1946 to 1962; "Consumer Price Index, Boston, Massachusetts, All Items, 1947 Forward," Series A-11, U. S. Department of Labor, Bureau of Labor Statistics, Washington, D. C.; Earnings-Price Percentage (E/P) was computed from Moody's price per share of industrial stocks. Their earnings per share at the annual rate and government bond yields (U.S. taxable, 3–5 years), were from U. S. Office of Business Economics, *Business Statistics, A Supplement to the Survey of Current Business, 1965*, Washington: U. S. Government Printing Office, 1965, 107–8, 91; expenditures for durables per capita, U. S. Department of Commerce, Office of Business Economics, *The National Income and Product Accounts of the United States, 1929–1965*, Washington: U. S. Government Printing Office, 1966, 48–9; population, households, and effective buying income were taken from the annual "Survey of Buying Power," *Sales Management* (1947–1961).

OBSERVED DEPOSITS, ALL BOSTON SAVINGS BANKS

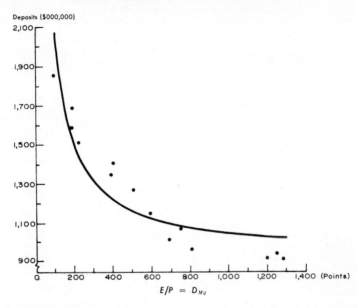

$$E/P = D_{Mg}$$

the curve. This slope performs an important role in determining if savings bank dividend rates should be altered. If the spread $(E/P - Div_i)$ is less than 300 points (Figure), a slight increase in savings bank dividend rates will increase dollar deposits substantially. If the spread is 700 points or more, even a large increase in dividend rates will have little effect on deposits in savings banks.

Coefficients of elasticity were computed for each of the savings banks using the hyperbolic model. There was little difference among banks—.27, .37, and .32.

To determine if these coefficients were unique to Boston they were computed for all savings banks in New York State, including a large savings bank in New York City and a medium-sized and a small bank in upstate New York. The results were .39, .30, .35, and .40 respectively. Thus, the model seems to be applicable to more than the Boston banks.

The hyperbolic model fits the data well ($r^2_{adj.} = .83$) but the Durbin-Watson statistic (d) revealed positive serial correlation in the residuals, which was to be expected in time-series data. One technique for reducing

Table 1
FIRST DIFFERENCE MODEL: DEPOSITS ($n = 14$)

	Constant	Δ Advertising Expenditures[a] ($000)	Dividends (D), Price (P), Earnings (E) on NYSE (points)		Δ Effective Buying Income/ Household $	R^2 [b]	Positive Serial Correlation in Residuals (Durbin-Watson)
			$\Delta \dfrac{1}{D/P - Div_i}$	$\Delta \dfrac{1}{E/P - Div_i}$			
All Boston Savings Banks							
Δ Deposits ($000)	5.31×10^4			2.58×10^7 [c]		.525	Yes
Δ Deposits (No.)	$-1.54. \times 10^3$			1.43×10^7 [d]		.346	No
Bank A							
Δ Deposits ($000)	8.95×10^3			6.12×10^6 [c]		.568	Yes
Δ Share Deposits (No.)	$-.002$			-1.57 [c]		.336	?
Bank B							
Δ Deposits ($000)	4.85×10^3			2.82×10^6 [c]		.633	Yes
Δ Deposits (No.)	1.80×10^3		2.36×10^4 [d]			.371	No
Δ Share Deposits ($000)	5.80×10^{-4}	5.72×10^{-5} [d]				.311	?
Bank C							
Δ Deposits ($000)	1.10×10^4			5.89×10^6 [c]		.460	No
Δ Deposits (No.)	1.09×10^3			1.32×10^6 [d]		.208	?
Δ Share Deposits ($000)	8.11×10^{-5}		1.24×10^{-3} [d]		8.55×10^{-6} [e]	.577	?
Δ Share Deposits (No.)	-9.17×10^{-5}		1.07×10^{-3} [d]	-1.30 [d]	1.16×10^{-5} [e]	.648	No

[a] Constant dollars. [b] Adjusted. [c] Significant at .01 level. [d] Significant at .05 level.

Table 2

KOYCK MODEL OF LAGGED VARIABLES: DEPOSITS ($n = 14$)

	Constant	Deposits $(t-1)$	log Advertising[a] (log $000)	Dividends (D), Price (P), Earnings (E) on NYSE (points)		Effective Buying Income/ Household $	R^2 [b]	Positive Serial Correlation in Residuals (Durbin-Watson)
				$\dfrac{I}{D/P - Div_i}$	$\dfrac{I}{E/P - Div_i}$			
Ali Boston Savings Banks								
Deposits ($000)	-4.15×10^5	.90[e]	1.02×10^5 [d]		1.34×10^7 [d]		.996	No
Deposits (No.)	2.39×10^5	.65[e]			1.07×10^7 [e]		.820	No
Bank A								
Deposits ($000)	-4.10×10^4	1.22[e]		9.94×10^4 [d]			.991	?
Deposits (No.)	3.91×10^4	.72[e]					.649	No
Share Deposits ($000)	.03	.86[e]					.929	Yes
Share Deposits (No.)	.04	.79[e]			-1.05[d]		.938	?
Bank B								
Deposits ($000)	-1.38×10^4	.97[e]	5.67×10^3 [d]	3.32×10^4 [d]	1.27×10^6 [e]		.997	?
Deposits (No.)	-2.07×10^4	.76[e]		3.27×10^4 [d]		5.33[e]	.955	No
Share Deposits ($000)	.02	.61[e]	4.06×10^{-3} [e]				.958	?
Share Deposits (No.)	.01	.86[e]					.904	No
Bank C								
Deposits ($000)	-1.95×10^4	1.16[e]					.987	No
Deposits (No.)	-1.69×10^4	1.13[e]	1.49×10^3 [e]				.969	No
Share Deposits ($000)	.12		$-.002$[e]	.002[e]		1.08×10^{-5} [e]	.963	No
Share Deposits (No.)	.10					6.87×10^{-6} [e]	.914	No

[a] Constant dollars.   [b] Adjusted.   [c] Significant at .01 level.   [d] Significant at .05 level.   [e] Significant at .07 level.

serial correlation is the transformation of data into first differences before fitting regressions. This transformation was consistent with savings bank marketing goals, defined frequently in terms of annual changes in deposits [2].

First-Difference Model

Equations which were significant using the first-difference model are summarized in Table 1. The findings suggest that when the promotional goals of these banks are defined in terms of annual changes in dollar volume of deposits, number of accounts, or share of each, the determinants of deposits (the influence of the stock market and effective buying income per household) are beyond the control of the bank. The one exception is the case of Bank B, where advertising expenditures were associated with the *share* of dollar deposits. This is the role that advertising is expected to play when products or services are homogeneous, which is the case with savings banks. The fact that only Bank C's market share was sensitive to annual changes in income suggests that this bank may be using a strategy of market segmentation by directing its promotional effort to those segments with increasing income.

Defining the goal of marketing efforts in terms of first differences ignores the many economic stimuli that do not produce an effect until the following period and may continue to produce decreasing effects through subsequent periods. The Koyck [4] model for lagged variables was used to reflect the cumulative effect of bank promotional effort.

Koyck Model of Lagged Variables

Several researchers have applied the Koyck model to the relationship between advertising and sales. Nerlove [6] explored the relationship for agricultural commodities, Palda [7] for a proprietary drug, and Lambin [5] for a consumer nondurable. The present study seems to be unique in its application of the model to a consumer service.

Original plans called for converting all dollar deposits to real dollars with the aid of the Consumer Price Index. It was doubtful, however, that this would represent the decision process of the saver who, with inflated dollars, was choosing between a savings bank and the stock market. The structural relationship between dividend rates and dollar deposits might be damaged by deflation. The final choice was detemined pragmatically: the relevant equations were fitted with and without deflating deposits. In every case, more variance was explained without the CPI than with it. Therefore, deposits were not deflated when fitting the regressions reported in the tables, nor was effective buying income per household. Other dollar values, advertising expenditures and durable goods expenditures per capita were deflated by appropriate indices so that deposits were related to *units* of advertising or durable goods.

Another transfomation was use of the logarithm of advertising expenditures in the Koyck model. This form reflects the diminishing returns of advertising, an effect noted by many researchers. There is no general agreement that advertising is subject to diminishing returns. See, for example, Simon [9].

Table 3

KOYCK MODEL OF LAGGED VARIABLES: REAL ESTATE LOANS (n = 7)

	Constant	Loan (t − 1)	log Adv.[a] (log $000)	$r_i - r_1$ (points)	$r_i - GBY$ (points)	Expenditures for Durables per Capita[a] ($)	Effective Buying Income/ Household ($)	R^2[b]	Positive Serial Correlation in Residuals (Durbin-Watson)
Bank A									
Loans ($000)	1.47×10^5			-1.02×10^4[c]		86.56[c]	4.15[d]	.949	No
Loans (No.)	-2.42×10^4			-556.11[d]				.980	No
Share Loans (No.)	$-.14$					.002		.762	?
Bank B									
Loans ($000)	-2.91×10^4	.730[c]	6059.29[c]			127.91[c]		.999	No
Loans (No.)	-2.86×10^3	.793[c]				22.49[c]		.985	No
Share Loans ($000)	.004	.51[c]			1.49×10^{-4}[d]			.924	No
Share Loans (No.)	.03	.65[c]						.912	No
Bank C									
Loans ($000)	-1.09×10^5	.99[c]					22.30[d]	.983	No
Loans (No.)	179.64	1.29[c]						.963	No
Share Loans ($000)	.007	1.09[c]						.856	No
Share Loans (No.)	$-.002$	1.22[c]						.920	No

[a] Constant dollars. [b] Adjusted. [c] Significant at .01 level. [d] Significant at .05 level.

The Koyck model for deposits, summarized in Table 2, was superior to the first difference model. There were significant coefficients for each of the four promotional goals, R^2 increased, and the number of coefficients with positive serial correlation declined. But most of this improvement was because of the lagged variable (Deposits$_{t-1}$). Ten of the 12 lagged variables accounted for 90% or more of the variance.

This variable has been interpreted by Palda as the cumulative effect of previous promotional effort.

Since the coefficient of the lagged variables reflects the annual cumulative effect of past promotional effort and environment, the annual rate of decay will be one minus this coefficient.   For example, all Boston savings banks had a decay rate of .10 per year (1.00 − .90) for volume of dollar deposits. Banks A and C, in contrast, were fortunate to have growth rates of .22 and .16, respectively.

Five of the 14 equations had significant coefficients for the advertising variable, but only two of these coefficients were in equations of market share, as oligopoly theory would predict. Futhermore, the advertising coefficient for the share of dollar deposits for Bank C was minus instead of plus. It would appear that, in the long run, advertising is not conforming to the role of determining only market share. The fact that three coefficients were associated with the dollar volume or number of deposits suggests that advertising does expand the demand for savings.

Koyck Model for Loans

The yield on government bonds was introduced because the savings banker may invest in bonds instead of mortgages. To reflect the competition among savings bankers for mortgage loans, a variable was introduced that measured the spread between a bank's loan rate and the lowest loan rate among Boston savings banks. Ex-penditures for durable goods were used as a proxy variable for the need for a loan because loans are frequently made for such purchases. Because of a change in the Commissioner's Annual Report for Savings Banks, the annual loan rate was available for only seven years.

The findings for the loan model are summarized in Table 3. From 83 to 97% of the variance was explained by the lagged variable, loan (t − 1), for Banks B and C. The demand for loans from Bank A was influenced most strongly by the spread between its rate and the lowest rate in Boston ($r_i - r_1$). Advertising performed an important role in determining the dollar volume of loans for Bank B. Bank C, with a loan rate equal to the lowest in Boston, was relatively uninfluenced by these variables, with the exception of the influence of income when the goal is defined in terms of dollar volume of loans.

DISCUSSION

Goals and Planning Horizons

The influence of the several variables examined depended on the marketing goals (absolute or share of dollar deposits or number of accounts), the marketing strategies, and the planning horizon (annual changes or cumulative effects). When the planning horizon included only annual changes (Table 1), the uncontrollable variables were the most influential. If we assume that the equation with the best fit for each bank (highest R^2) represents its goal, it appears that the three banks did not have the same short-range marketing goals. Banks A and B attempted to maximize dollar deposits ($R^2 = $ .568 and .633 respectively) while Bank C focused on share of the number of deposits (.648). Perhaps Bank C adapted its marketing strategy to that market segment with increasing income.

If the planning horizon is longer than one year, so that the cumulative effect of previous effort is considered, most of the variance is associated with the lagged variable, but the number of cases where advertising is an important variable increases. Thus, the effect of advertising seems to emerge only when the cumulative determinants of demand have been removed. If we use the best fitting equation to identify the long-range strategy of each bank it appears that each bank is concerned with maximizing its dollar deposits in the long run. The short-run strategy of Bank C may just be a means toward this long-range end.

Negative advertising coefficients that are highly significant are most perplexing. The negative sign associated with the share of deposits of Bank C is an example. Since the advertising of Bank C was not objectionable, it is unlikely that people avoided the bank because of its advertising. Several other hypotheses are worth noting.

A negative advertising coefficient could result if expenditures did not keep pace with increased advertising costs so that real units of advertising declined. This effect did occur with Bank C for two of the 14 observations.

Advertising has a dual role. It is used to increase or to stop a decline in deposits. In the second role, advertising expenditures might have been increased after Bank C's share of the dollar deposits declined. This relationship would yield a negative sign. In six of the 14 years, Bank C lost market share. Thus, the negative sign suggests that Bank C's advertising strategy was both offensive and defensive. In the latter case, deposits determine advertising rather than vice versa.

None of the absolute loan activity (Table 3) was associated with the yield on U. S. government bonds. Perhaps the lack of a relationship is explained by the fact that these bonds carried rates that were 148 to 245 points lower than the lowest loan rate, which was too much to pay for security and liquidity. In 1967, quality corporate bonds were purchased by many savings banks because of their high yields, liquidity, and ease of administration. According to one banker, the yield of a mortgage must be 75 points higher than a corporate bond to justify the servicing expense of the former [1].

The long-range goal of the three banks with regard to loans seems to be maximizing the dollar volume of loans. The strategies for reaching this goal vary among banks. Bank A loans were identified with the short-run spread in loan rates, while loans for Banks B and C seemed to be determined by long-run cumulative effects.

Strategies

The most prevalent short-run strategy for attracting deposits was adapting dividend rates to the earnings-price ratio of common stocks on the market, for which the hyperbolic model could be useful. When the short-run goal was maximizing the share of the number of depositors, the strategy seemed to be two-fold—adaption of the bank's dividend rate to the dividend-price ratio of common stocks and identification with that market segment that had increasing income.

The long-run strategies were more complicated despite the fact that the three banks seemed to share the long-range goal of maximizing dollar deposits. The most complicated strategy was that of Bank B. Advertising performed the dual role of increasing the absolute volume of deposits and the market share of deposits. The setting of deposit dividend rates would seem to require adaption to the dividend and earnings rates of common stocks.

Limitations of the Findings

Several limitations of these findings should be made explicit, especially the assumption that high correlation means causation. While the independent variables used here seem to be the appropriate ones, there is always the possibility that the relationship existed because of a correlation with a third, unidentified variable. Rather than accept these results as definitive, they should be viewed as hypotheses to be tested by experimentation. Second, motives for saving are not fully known, and the variables explored here were limited to available time series data. Savings in the Boston area were known to vary by income class, family size, age of family head, and occupation of family head [12]. While the number of people employed in Greater Boston increased by only 6% between 1950 and 1960, the composition changed considerably. For example, the high-saving group of professionals increased by 42% [11]. The lack of annual data for these variables precluded their use. A third limitation is the assumption that advertising expenditures represent advertising effectiveness, which is not necessarily the case. A small, well-written ad can be more effective than an expensive, poorly-designed one. Some media are more effective than others. But the lack of data required this simplifying assumption.

CONCLUSION

Models for the optimization of advertising expenditures require a prediction model that will relate controllable and uncontrollable variables to that variable which reflects the marketing goal of the firm. Using three savings banks as an example, it was demonstrated that models for the prediction of demand must reflect the firm's goals, planning horizon, and marketing strategy. When these are unknown, which is probably the general case, regression techniques such as those described here may help to identify the implicit goals, horizons, and strategies of the firm in question as well as those of its competitors.

REFERENCES

1. "Bond Men Sweep Out the Shop," *Business Week,* (July 1, 1967), 93–4.
2. G. David Hughes, "The Boston Five Cent Savings Bank: Evaluating Advertising Strategy," Boston: Graduate School of Business, Harvard University, Inter-collegiate Case Clearing House 9M54, 1964.
3. ———, "The Marketing Systems of Three Savings Banks," *Research Program in Marketing, No. 32.,* Institute of Business and Economic Research, University of California, Berkeley, California, October, 1967. (Mimeographed.)
4. L. M. Koyck, *Distributed Lags and Investment Analysis,* Amsterdam: North-Holland Publishing Co., 1954.
5. Jean-Jacques Lambin, *Investissements Publicitaire et Étude de Rentabilité,* Louvain, Belgium: Centre de Perfectionnement dans la Direction des Entreprises, Université Catholique de Louvain, 1967.
6. M. Nerlove, *Distributed Lags and Demand Analysis for Agricultural and Other Commodities,* Washington: U. S. Dept of Agriculture, 1958.
7. Kristian S. Palda, *The Measurement of Cumulative Advertising Effects,* Englewood Cliffs, N. J.: Prentice-Hall, Inc., 1964.
8. *Sales Management,* (June 10, 1963), 20–2.
9. J. L. Simon, "New Evidence for No Effect of Scale in Advertising," *Journal of Advertising Research,* 9 (March 1969), 38–41.
10. Lester G. Telser, "Advertising and Cigarettes," *Journal of Political Economy,* 70 (October 1962), 471–99, 480.
11. U. S. Bureau of the Census, *U. S. Census of Population: 1960, Vol. I, Characteristics of the Population, Part 23, Massachusetts,* Washington: U. S. Government Printing Office, 1963, 16.
12. U. S. Bureau of Labor Statistics, *Consumer Expenditures and Income, Boston, Mass., 1960,* BLS Report No. 237-7, November, 1962.
13. Lawrence N. Van Doren, "Bank Ad Dollars in '66: Over a Quarter Billion," *Banking,* (March 1966), 67–74.

Chapter 5

A DISCRIMINANT ANALYSIS OF ECONOMIC, DEMOGRAPHIC, AND ATTITUDINAL CHARACTERISTICS OF BANK CHARGE-CARD HOLDERS: A CASE STUDY*

By R. Y. Awh and Don R. Waters

*This article is reprinted, with permission, from *The Journal of Finance*, Vol. 29, No. 3 (June, 1974), pp. 973-980.

BANK charge-cards are fast emerging as one of the newest media of exchange and credit in the American economy: the use of bank charge-cards allows the consumer to obtain his merchandise and borrow up to thirty days without interest, and longer with interest. However, there is an important obstacle that hinders a widespread use of bank charge-cards that may bring us closer to the so-called "cashless, checkless society": while a large number of card-holders are active users of their charge-cards, a significant portion of the card-holders have never activated their accounts. What are the factors that make a cardholder an active or inactive user? The economic and financial literature does not provide us with an answer, since it is conspicuously lacking studies dealing with inactive cardholders. The objectives of this study, therefore, are (1) to establish the extent to which differences exist between active and inactive bank charge-cardholders in terms of selected economic, demographic, and attitudinal characteristics, and (2) to ascertain the relative importance of various characteristics in differentiating between active and inactive cardholders.

I. DIFFERENTIATING CHARACTERISTICS

In order to identify the factors that make a cardholder an active or inactive user, the authors examine two broad groups of characteristics or variables. The first group of variables are *economic and demographic*. This group of characteristics includes the quantitative variables traditionally employed in describing various markets: (a) income, (b) age, (c) education, and (d) socio-economic standing.[1]

The second group of characteristics includes three *attitudinal* variables: (a) use or non-use of other credit cards, (b) attitude toward credit, and (c) attitude toward bank charge-cards. The number of credit cards (other than bank credit cards) used by a cardholder, e.g., oil company credit cards, department store credit cards, and travel and entertainment credit cards, is used as an indicator of his "inclination to use credit cards." A card-holder is characterized as "inclined" to use credit cards if he uses two or more of these other credit cards; otherwise, as "less inclined" to use credit cards.

---

1. The socio-economic index of the cardholders is assigned on the basis of their particular occupations. The ratings are obtained from the "Socio-economic Index for Occupations in the Detailed Classification." See Albert J. Reiss, Jr., *Occupations and Social Status* (New York: The Free Press, 1961), p. 114-138.

The difference in attitudes for credit in general and for bank charge-cards in particular may help to explain why some cardholders use their bank charge-cards and others do not. Thus, two Likert-type scales were developed: one to measure the cardholders' attitudes toward bank charge-cards, and another to measure the cardholders' attitudes toward credit.[2] On the basis of the scores on these scales, the attitude of each cardholder is quantified in a trichotomous fashion. For instance, if a cardholder's attitude is favorable, his attitude score is +1; if his attitude is neutral, his score is 0; and, if his attitude is unfavorable, his score is −1. Thus the mean value of the attitude for the active or inactive group will be either positive (favorable), zero (neutral), or negative (unfavorable). The closer the group mean is to +1, the more favorable is the attitude of the group.

II. Sampling Design

The active and inactive cardholders used in this study were randomly selected from the active and the inactive files of an interchange commercial bank.[3] A sample of 600 cardholders each was drawn from the active and inactive master files. Each member of the samples was mailed a questionnaire designed to acquire their economic, demographic, and attitudinal characteristics. Of the 600 active cardholders to whom questionnaires were sent, 312 responded with usable returns; of the 600 inactive cardholders, 257 responded with usable returns. In order to determine whether the characteristics of the respondents differ from those of "non-respondents," a sample of 50 cardholders each was taken from the active and inactive non-respondents. The sample elements were personally contacted and/or mailed a personal letter. The procedure generated 25 active responses and 27 inactive responses. The analysis of this data showed that, at 10 per cent significance level, the characteristics of non-respondents did not differ significantly from those of the respondents.

III. Linear Discriminant Analysis

Our task is to establish, from the responses of active and inactive bank-card users, the relative importances of various characteristics (or variables) in differentiating between active and inactive cardholders. A statistical tech-

2. This portion of the questionnaire lists various statements which indicate an individual's attitude toward credit and bank charge-cards, and asks the respondent to indicate whether he strongly agrees, agrees, is undecided, disagrees, or strongly disagrees. A few examples of the attitude statements that were listed in the questionnaire are: Debt is bad. Credit buying is good because it makes savings possible. Credit should be used only in case of an emergency. A person should not buy unless he has the cash. Credit buying is good because it allows for present enjoyment rather than future enjoyment.

3. An interchange bank is a licensee bank that has the right to issue bank charge-cards to agent banks, or Class B banks, within a given area. The interchange bank is responsible for all services related to the charge-card program (i.e., issuing, billing, advertising, etc.). The interchange bank is the recipient of the profits and is subject to the losses of the charge-card program, which it directs.

nique well adapted for this purpose is the linear discriminant analysis developed by R. A. Fisher. Consider a set of variables, $x_1, x_2, \ldots, x_n$, by means of which it is desired to discriminate between two groups of cardholders. Let

$$Z = w_1x_1 + w_2x_2 + \ldots + w_nx_n$$

represent a linear combination of these variables. What is needed is to determine w's in such a way that this linear discriminant function's ability to differentiate between the members of the two groups is maximized. Fisher's technique does this by assigning w's (referred to as weights or linear discriminant function coefficients) in such a manner that the ratio of the variance between the two groups to the variance within the two groups is maximized.

Utilizing the weights (w's) of the discriminant function, the importance and relative importance values of each characteristic can be obtained. Such importance values make it possible to evaluate each characteristic in terms of its contribution to the difference between the two groups. The *importance value* of the ith characteristic (I_i) is obtained as follows:

$$I_i = w_i(\bar{x}_{ia} - \bar{x}_{ii}),$$

where w_i is the discriminant function coefficient for the ith characteristic, and $(\bar{x}_{ia} - \bar{x}_{ii})$ shows the difference in the group means of the ith characteristic for the active and inactive cardholders.[4] A *relative* importance value shows the importance value of a particular characteristic relative to the sum of the importance values of all characteristics. That is, the relative importance value of the ith characteristic (R_i) is given by

$$R_i = \frac{w_i(\bar{x}_{ia} - \bar{x}_{ii})}{\Sigma w_i(\bar{x}_{ia} - \ddot{x}_{ii})}, \qquad i = 1, n.$$

Once the discriminant function is known, it is possible to compute the Z value for each cardholder by substituting the values of the cardholder's characteristics into the discriminant function. Performing this operation for each active and each inactive cardholder yields a frequency distribution of Z values, for each group, from which mean values ($\bar{Z}_a$ and $\bar{Z}_i$) are computed. The average of these means, $(\bar{Z}_a + \bar{Z}_i)/2$, is then used as the critical value in classifying the cardholders. For example, if the mean Z for the active cardholders is 20 and the mean Z for the inactive cardholders is -10, the midpoint between the two Z values is 5. Thus, if an individual cardholder has a Z value of above 5 he is assigned to the active rating classification; if the cardholder has a Z

4. Frederick Mosteller and David L. Wallace, "Inferences in an Authorship Problem," *Journal of the American Statistical Association,* Vol. 58 (June, 1963), pp. 282-283.

value of less than 5 he is assigned to the inactive classification.[5]

The assignment of cardholders to either the active or the inactive classification in accordance with the above procedure will, in all likelihood, result in some of the cardholders being misclassified. That is, some of the cardholders that are members of one group may, on the basis of their Z values, be classified as members of the other group. The extent to which cardholders are properly classified by the discriminant function indicates the efficiency or discriminating ability of the function.

IV. EMPIRICAL RESULTS

Utilizing a computer program titled "Discriminant Analysis for Two Groups,"[6] the following information was secured from the questionnaire data: (1) the mean value for each characteristic for each group, (2) the discriminant function coefficients for each characteristic, and (3) the Mahalanobis D^2 statistic which is converted into a variance ratio (F) for the purpose of testing the significance of the discriminant function.

A. Difference in the Mean Values

Table 1 shows the mean values of the seven characteristics studied for the active and inactive cardholder groups. The last column in the table presents

TABLE 1

GROUP MEANS OF THE CHARACTERISTICS OF THE ACTIVE AND INACTIVE CARDHOLDERS

| | Activity Rating | | |
Characteristics	Active $(\bar{X}_{ia})$	Inactive $(\bar{X}_{ii})$	Difference $(\bar{X}_{ia} - \bar{X}_{ii})$
x_1: Income, in thousands of dollars	14.14	11.59	2.55[a]
x_2: Age, in years	44.14	53.44	9.31[a]
x_3: Education, in years	14.35	12.19	2.16[a]
x_4: Socio-economic standing	61.30	46.31	14.99[a]
x_5: Other cards in use, in percentages	80.82	37.70	43.12[a]
x_6: Attitude toward credit, in percentages	48.97	13.49	62.47[a]
x_7: Attitude toward bank charge-cards, in percentages	69.52	29.37	98.89[a]

[a] Significant at .01 per cent level.

5. See M. G. Kendall and A. Stuart, *The Advanced Theory of Statistics*, Vol. 3, 2nd Ed., p. 319.
In many cases, it is wise to allow for reserved judgement on borderline cases, and not to insist on an allocation to one of two classes. This means in geometrical terms, that we wish to divide the sample space into three regions R_1, R_2, and D_{12}. If a member falls into R_1 we allocate it to population 1; if it falls into R_2, to population 2. If it falls into D_{12}, we admit that the data are insufficient to make a satisfactory judgement.
In order to set up the region D_{12}, we merely have to decide on what misclassification probabilities are tolerable, define R_1 and R_2 in terms of them, and assign D_{12} to the remainder of the sample space (Kendall and Stuart, p. 327).

6. "Discriminant Analysis for Two Groups," *Biomedical Computer Programs* (Los Angeles: Health Science Computing Facility, University of California, 1956).

the differences in the mean values of the active and inactive groups for each of the seven characteristics. The difference in group means for each of the seven characteristics was statistically significant at the one per cent level. Specifically, the active cardholders possess a significantly higher educational attainment, a higher level of income, a higher socio-economic standing, and a lower age as compared with the inactive cardholders. "Other cards in use" shows the proportion of the active and the inactive cardholders who use two or more other charge-cards. Clearly, the active cardholders are more inclined to use credit than are the inactive cardholders: 80.8 per cent of the active cardholders use 2 or more other credit cards as compared with only 37.6 per cent of the inactive cardholders who do so.

The active cardholders have more favorable attitudes toward both credit in general and bank charge-cards in particular than do the inactive cardholders. This is evidenced by the relatively high, positive group mean attitude values for the active cardholders as compared with the negative group mean values for the inactive cardholders.[7] It is interesting to note that as a group the active cardholders favor charge-cards more than they favor credit and that the inactive cardholders disfavor charge-cards more than they disfavor credit. Thus the sentiments of the active and inactive groups differ most with respect to bank charge-cards.

B. *The Discriminant Function*

While the test of significance of the differences between the mean values of the characteristics provide an initial insight into the differences between the active and inactive groups, it fails to recognize the interrelationships that may exist among variables. The linear discriminant analysis takes into consideration such interrelationships among variables, and determines the weights (w's) of each variable in such a way that the linear combination of all variables will best discriminate between the active and the inactive cardholders.

We experimented with discriminant functions based on different sets of variables: four discriminant functions based on the first four, first five, first six, and all seven variables of Table 1 were obtained. The discriminant function with the greatest discriminating ability was the one that incorporated all seven variables. This seven-variable discriminant function is as follows:[8]

$$z = .00000x_1 - .00010x_2 + .00008x_3 + .00004x_4$$

$$+ .00128x_5 + .00037x_6 + .00184x_7.$$

Associated with this discriminant function is a Mahalanobis D^2 statistic of 1.36, which gives the variance ratio (F) of 36.64. With 5 and 538 degrees of freedom, the discriminant function is significant at .01 level. This discriminant

---

7. For the ease of tabular presentation, the trichotomous attitude scores are converted into percentages. Thus the closer the group mean is to +100 per cent, the more favorable is the attitude toward credit or bank charge-cards.

8. See Table 1 for the descriptions of x_i variables.

function correctly classified 78 per cent of the cardholders into their proper groups.

C. *The Relative Importance Values*

While the discriminant function based on *all* of the characteristics is relatively successful in discriminating between the two groups, some of the characteristics are more important as discriminators than are others. The data contained in Table 2 reveals the "discriminative importance" of each of the characteristics in distinguishing between the two groups.

The relative importance values reveal that, of the seven characteristics, *"attitude toward bank charge-cards"* is by far the most important in differentiating the active from the inactive cardholders. With an importance value of .00181, attitude toward bank charge-cards has a relative importance value of 42.3 per cent. The relative importance value of a variable indicates the relative contribution this variable makes to the overall difference between the two groups of cardholders.

Age is the second most important characteristic in differentiating between the cardholders. With an importance value of .00093, age has a relative importance

TABLE 2

DISCRIMINANT FUNCTION COEFFICIENTS, DIFFERENCES IN GROUP MEANS, IMPORTANCE VALUES, AND RELATIVE IMPORTANCE VALUES OF THE SELECTED CHARACTERISTICS OF THE ACTIVE AND THE INACTIVE CHARGE-CARDHOLDERS

Characteristics	Discriminant Function Coefficient (w_i)	Differences in Group Means $(\overline{X}_{ia} - \overline{X}_{ii})$	Importance Values (I_i)	Relative Importance Values (R_i)
x_1: Income	.00000	2.55	.00000	00.0
x_2: Age	−.00010	−9.31	.00093	21.7
x_3: Education	.00008	2.16	.00017	4.0
x_4: Socio-economic standing	.00004	14.99	.00059	13.8
x_5: Other cards in use	.00128	43.12	.00055	12.8
x_6: Attitude toward credit	.00037	62.47	.00023	5.3
x_7: Attitude toward bank charge-cards	.00184	98.89	.00181	42.3

value of 21.7 per cent. Of the cardholders surveyed, it was found that the 42.2 per cent of the inactive cardholders are above 60 years of age whereas only 11.3 per cent of the actives are above 60 years of age. It appears that a high age reduces the likelihood of an individual being an active cardholder: older people's spending patterns probably do not call for a significant amount of credit and charge-card utilization. The negative discriminant function coefficient associated with age further evidences the nature of the relationship between age and bank charge-card utilization.

The characteristic of tertiary importance in differentiating between the active and the inactive cardholders is *socio-economic standing*. With an importance value of .00059, socio-economic standing accounts for 13.8 per cent of the difference between the two groups of cardholders. The positive weighing of this characteristic indicates that an individual with a relatively high social standing is more likely to be a user of the bank charge-card than is a person of relatively lower social standing. This finding is contrary to the contention that lower social classes utilize the card as a means of engaging in "free spending" (buy now, pay later).[9]

TABLE 3

PROPORTION OF BANK CHARGE-CARDHOLDERS AGREEING WITH SELECTED ATTITUDE
STATEMENTS PERTAINING TO BANK CHARGE CARDS, BY ACTIVITY RATING

Attitude Statement	Activity Rating		Proportion Test Statistic	Null Hypothesis
	Active Per Cent	Inactive Per Cent		
1. I fear the consequences of overspending with a bank charge card	36.0	64.6	6.8	Reject
2. The cost of using the bank charge card is too much	38.0	42.8	1.1	Accept
3. Bank charge cards cause excessive use of credit	54.6	78.2	5.8	Reject
4. It is unwise to use any charge card, including a bank charge card	6.2	21.0	5.2	Reject
5. Bank charge cards are a desirable contribution to the community by the banking system	72.3	35.8	8.73	Reject
6. Bank charge cards should be used only in case of an emergency	26.1	59.0	7.94	Reject
7. I dislike all charge cards	4.8	30.9	8.23	Reject
8. Bank charge cards provide a needed service	81.3	37.9	3.6	Reject
9. Bank charge cards are safe and risk free	31.9	18.5	7.24	Reject
10. It is too easy to overspend with a bank charge card because of their wide acceptability	37.6	67.3	7.24	Reject

9. Instead, it may indicate the presence of another situation wherein is found an active cardholder of a rather high social standing being forced to use credit (bank charge-cards) to engage in conspicuous consumption in order to cling to his status. This is somewhat of an allusion to the findings of Matthews and Slocum. They contend that within the higher social classes are found not only the "status seekers" but also the "status clingers" who must keep their performance on a high level.

See H. Lee Matthews and John W. Slocum, Jr., "Marketing Strategies in the Commercial Bank Credit Card Field" (Chicago, Illinois: Bank Public Relations and Marketing Association, 1968), pp. 33.

Following socio-economic standing in importance is the *"other cards in use."* With an importance value of .00055, this characteristic accounts for 12.8 per cent of the difference between the two groups of cardholders. The positive weighing of this characteristic indicates that an individual is more likely to be a user of the bank charge-card if he is also a user of other types of credit cards. This may be interpreted to mean that credit card use is somewhat of a habit; one who is accustomed to using other types of credit cards may also, as a matter of habit, use the bank charge-card.

The remaining three characteristics—*attitude toward credit, education,* and *income*—have relative importance values of 5.3, 4.0, and 0.0 respectively. Obviously, these characteristics account for a minimal amount of the overall difference between the active and the inactive cardholders, for together they contribute less than 10 per cent to the overall difference between the cardholders. It is quite interesting to note that our discriminant function assigns no discriminating power to the income variable. Essentially, this indicates that income is of no importance in determining whether or not an individual will use or not use the bank charge-card.

The fact that the discriminant function is able to classify correctly nearly 8 out of the 10 cardholders clearly shows that the characteristics of the active and inactive cardholders are different. Thus a strategy appropriate for intensifying card utilization by the active cardholders may not be appropriate in "activating" the inactive accounts. The bank charge-card promoters may have to consider the two groups of cardholders as two different "markets," in which two distinct strategies must be pursued.

IV. ATTITUDES TOWARD BANK CHARGE-CARDS

Since the attitude toward bank charge-cards is found to be the most important factor in differentiating the active from the inactive cardholders, the ten attitude statements included in the questionnaire are reproduced in Table 3. For each statement we tested the null hypothesis, at the one per cent level of significance, that there is no difference between the proportions of the active and inactive cardholders. All such hypotheses (except statement No. 2) were rejected.

It is clear from the table that the inactive cardholders' unfavorable attitudes toward bank charge-cards stem primarily from (a) their fear that charge-cards may induce them to rely on credit excessively and (b) their belief that bank charge-card utilization should be confined to emergency needs. This finding has an important implication for activation strategies, for a big selling point of bank charge-card advertisements is "convenience"—which a majority of the inactive cardholders may preclude as an acceptable reason for activating their accounts.

Chapter 6

APPLICATION OF DISCRIMINANT ANALYSIS IN FORMULATION OF PROMOTIONAL STRATEGY FOR CASH-DISPENSING MACHINES*

By Albert A. Pool

*This article is reprinted, with permission, from *Journal of Bank Research*, Vol. 5, No. 1 (Spring, 1974), pp. 13-19.

In the past 20 years, competition in banking has been increasing at rates surpassed by few industries. In a rapid movement toward a less-check environment, banks have begun to realize the importance of carefully segmented markets for their increased product lines. Most banks have doubled their product lines in the past decade. The industry has increased its spending for advertising from $38 million in 1950 to $192 million in 1960 and to more than $400 million in 1972 ["Now Banks Are . . . , 1972].

A number of new products have been introduced during this period. Many banks have doubled the number of services offered during the past decade. One unique product that several banks have adapted to keep pace with this movement toward automation as well as appeal to specific market segments is the cash dispensing machine (CDM).

Market studies were conducted prior to the introduction of the CDM;[1] however, most of the results were held in confidence. This pattern of introduction with a certain lack of precision and marketing refinement has typified these current new banking products.

In August of 1972, the first bank introduced four cash dispensing machines into the Salt Lake City market. Less than 90 days later, a competitor entered the market with three identical machines. Finally, a third bank entered the market with CDMs during the Spring of 1973. In the year since its introduction, the number of users of this service has increased enough to draw profiles of the innovative users and nonusers to aid in promoting this product.

The Pretest

A pilot study was conducted using discriminant analysis to separate users from nonusers to allow for a more accurate application of this competitive tool. It was expected there would be significant differences between users and nonusers based

[1] See ["1971 National Bank . . . , 1971] and ["A Consumer Banking . . . , 1971].

totally upon secondary data gathered from CDM and instalment loan (nonuser) applications. The purpose of this pretest was to determine if there was any difference based upon consumer profiles between the users and nonusers using only these secondary data. It was fully recognized that some spurious correlations would enter into the explanation at the onset of the pretest (as will be explained later).

The hypotheses were:

H_o: "There is no significant difference between the user and the nonuser of the CDM."

H_1: "There is a difference between the nonuser and the user of the CDM."

Secondary data about the CDM users were available from the approved CDM applications. Instalment loan applications (of verified nonusers of CDM) were selected to examine the difference between the users of one service and another as well as users and nonusers of CDM. All 18 variables that were common to both applications were used in the analysis. In all, 142 users and 103 nonusers were randomly sampled. Figure 1 shows the mean values for the users and nonusers for these self-selected pretest variables.

A stepwise discriminant analysis was conducted upon the 142 users and the 103 nonusers using the variables listed in Figure 1. Of the significant self-selected variables presented in Figure 2, it should be recognized that a CDM user is required to maintain a checking account and therefore could not maintain only a savings account at this bank. Based upon mean values, the dwelling value for users of CDM was less than that of the nonusers, as were ages and total family monthly income (see Figure 1). Initially, it appeared that users were younger, with a relatively high monthly income and dwelling unit value for this market, and did not maintain additional checking accounts at other banks as much as did the nonusers.

The coefficients were normalized for these significant variables to observe their relative impor-

Figure 1. Variable Values for Users and Nonusers

Variable	User	Nonuser
Dwelling Value	$18,613*	$19,955*
Age	27.5 years*	43.6 years*
Marital Status		
Married	78%	85%
Separated/Widowed	6%	7%
Single	16%	8%
Number of Dependents	1.7*	2.5*
Spouse Employed	Yes	Yes
Total Family Monthly Income	$1,508*	$1,882*
Total Value of Automobiles	$3,666*	$3,268*
Home or Rent Monthly Payment	$ 98*	$ 83*
Auto Monthly Payment	$ 41*	$ 34*
Checking Account (only at this bank)	51%	25%
Savings Account (only at this bank)	None	18%
Checking and Savings (only at this bank)	49%	23%
Checking Account (only at other bank)	5%	14%
Savings Account (only at other bank)	10%	8%
Checking and Savings (only at other bank)	5%	12%
Use Savings and Loan Services	9%	15%

* Mean values for each group.

tance within the user and nonuser groups [Morrison, 1971]. Using these betas (Figure 2), the relative importance within the nonusers of bank references over age, income and dwelling unit value is clearly highlighted. Based upon betas gathered from these secondary data, the importance of bank references overshadowed the three demographic values both for the users and the nonusers.

A V_1-type validation sample of 42 cases of users and 30 cases of nonusers (30% in each case) was used to avoid both the model building bias and the sampling error bias [Frank, Massy and Morrison, 1965]. The probability of an individual being correctly classified was computed to be 87% both for the sample building the discriminant function and for the validation sample [Morrison, 1971] as is shown in Figure 3.

This successful classification of self-selected variables gathered from secondary data indicated the potential applicability of a stepwise discriminant function in building predictive profiles of CDM users and nonusers to develop segmentation criteria for the market. The spurious relationships of checking to CDM user was recognized fully, as instalment loan users were required in most cases

Figure 2. Significant Variables in Segmenting CDM Users From Nonusers

	Discriminant Coefficient		Standardized Discriminant Coefficient**	
	User	Nonuser	User	Nonuser
Dwelling Value Home or Rent	.20596†	.10891†	.02306	.01037
Age	.04402†	.20250†	.00337	.01396
Total Family Monthly Income	−.01457*	.17201*	−.00999	.03659
Check Only at This Bank	20.97681†	13.40502†	41.75320	33.51255
Check and Save at This Bank	21.30902†	13.47889†	42.41445	38.51111
Save Only at This Bank	16.63940†	13.05952†	16.63940	39.57430
Check at Other Bank	11.94437†	9.52773†	50.29208	24.43076

† Significant at 1% level (2-tailed test)
* Significant at 10% level (2-tailed test)
  Trivial Variables
** Discriminant Coefficient divided by its standard deviation

Figure 3. Normalized Confusion Matrix for CDM Users and Nonusers

Actual Membership	Predicted Group Membership	
	Users	Nonusers
Users	.96	.04
Nonusers	.25	.75
Validation Sample		
Users	.87	.13
Nonusers	.09	.91

to maintain a checking account during the time of their loan. This pretest was a relatively inexpensive (less than $400) method of systematic "fishing" to see if any difference existed. Using these results, management decided to proceed with the survey in the market.

The Survey

A questionnaire was designed using accepted demographic measures, opinions of bank services, and activities, interests and opinions [Wells and Tigert, 1972]. A five-point Likert scale was used in grading the responses. Typical questions were:

"Attending a symphony, play, or ballet is much more enjoyable than taking a weekend trip."

"The CDM is much too risky because I could lose all of my money that I had in the bank if my card were lost or stolen."

The hypotheses were:

H_0: "There is no significant difference between users and nonusers."

H_1: "There is a difference between the user and the nonuser of CDM."

The questions were based both on life-style concepts as well as demographic factors. In a study conducted in 1971, 21 life-style factors

Figure 4. Customer Response Card

were found to be significant from several hundred originally considered [Granzin, 1971]. These 21 significant factors were the basis of the questionnaire design.

The respondents were handed a card[2] (see Figure 4) by the interviewer and asked to answer each of the 40 questions with a response ranging from strong agreement to strong disagreement. Questions requiring the card for a response were grouped together in the first part of the questionnaire. The reaction of the respondents to the card was very positive and extremely favorable, according to the interviewer.

The sample of users and nonusers was selected randomly from bank records. Fifty-five nonusers were interviewed as were 44 users. The interviews were conducted between the hours of 5:00 p.m. and 8:30 p.m., Monday through Saturday in the homes of the respondents.

A stepwise discriminant analysis of this ordinal data was used in building the profiles of users and

[2] Card designed by author and Donald Young, Salt Lake City artist.

nonusers. A V_I validation sample of 40% of total observations in each class was employed. The normalized confusion matrix for the six significant ($p > .05$) variables (Figure 5) indicates successful classification of users both in the function building and in the validation samples.

The entry level was set into the program at the F level necessary for inclusion at a $p > .05$ [Blalock, 1972]. The significant variables (Figure 6) included two opinions of bank services, one activity and three demographic questions.

The resulting profiles using these significant variables indicated that the CDM user is seven years younger, lives in typical dwelling unit (home, apartment or condominium), understandably plans to use the CDM service in the future more than the nonuser, views the CDM as an insurance against running out of cash and prefers symphonies, plays and ballets to weekend trips. Additionally, there were more female card holders than male.

This information, combined with the listening and viewing patterns obtained in this survey, was

Figure 6. Significant ($p > .05$) Variables in Discriminant Analysis of CDM Users and Nonusers

Step Number		Mean Responses	
(Entry into Function)	Variable	User	Nonuser
1	"Plan to Use CDM in Future"	4.1*	2.5*
2	"Live in Dwelling Other than Apartment, home, or condominium"	None	16%
3	Sex	M = .4 F = .6	M = .6 F = .4
4	"CDM is a way to keep from Running out of Cash"	3.9*	2.5*
5	Deletion of variable #1		
6	"Prefer symphony, ballet, play to a weekend trip"	2.4*	2.0*
7	Age	40.9 (years)	47.5 (years)

* (1 = disagreement to 5-agreement)

Figure 5. Normalized Confusion Matrix for CDM Users and Nonusers

Actual Membership	Predicted Membership	
	User	Nonuser
User	.88	.12
Nonuser	.22	.78
	Validated Sample	
User	.83	.17
Nonuser	.40	.60

Figure 7. Evaluation of Past Promotional Methods

	Percentage Hearing of CDM	
Medium	Users	Nonusers
Word of mouth	11	7
Radio-TV	23	36
Newspaper	0	6
Billboard	0	0
Bank (Contact or direct mail)	64	36
Never heard of it	2	15

applied in the formulation both of promotional strategy and the execution of advertising tactics.

Noting the effects of past promotional efforts, 64% of the users stated they had heard about the CDM from the bank through direct mail or personal contact, significantly different from the 36%

of nonusers ($p > .05$) who heard of the service in the same manner (Figure 7).

Additionally, the reported ineffectiveness of print and outdoor in both groups as well as the effectiveness of electronic should be noted. Their implications toward media scheduling is obvious as are the indicated preferences in radio stations and television programs (Figure 8) as classified by program content.

One additional analysis was conducted using the same technique. The level for inclusion was not specified; rather, the iterative steps were limited to 10. Three additional variables entered as significant ($p > .05$). The mean values for these additional variables, included in Figure 9, provided additional guidance in the establishment of

Figure 8. Listening and Viewing Preferences for CDM Users and Nonusers

Favorite Program (TV)	(Percentages)	
	User	Nonuser
Documentary	27	18
Mystery	7	6
Sports	12	18
Drama	27	15
Comedy	11	14
Variety	14	18
Western	2	6
Quiz Shows	0	5
Favorite Station Type (Radio)		
Folk/Western	9	13
Jazz	0	0
Popular Contemporary	55	58
Rock	9	13
Classical	18	16
Talk Station	9	0

Figure 9. Additional Significant Variables

Variable	Mean User	Mean Nonuser
"Seeks Financial Help in Planning"	3.11	3.73
"CDM is Too Complicated for me"	1.55	2.33
"Checking Services are generally good"	4.43	4.76

(1.00 = disagreement and 5.00 = agreement)

Figure 10. Profile of CDM User and CDM Nonuser

CDM User	CDM Nonuser
Slightly prefer symphonies, plays and ballets to weekend trips.	Prefer weekend trips to symphonies, plays and ballets.
Want some degree of financial advice in planning.	Desire greater amount of financial advice than Users.
See CDM as insurance against running out of cash.	Insurance aspect not as powerful; almost neutral response.
CDM definitely not too complicated to operate.	CDM somewhat complicated to operate.
Will use CDM in future.	Neutral response; indifferent to future use of CDM.
Very good service on checking account.	Excellent service on checking account.
Print and outdoor had no effect at all in knowledge (initial) of service.	Outdoor had no effect while 5% heard of CDM initially in print medium.
Electronic accounted for 23% of initial knowledge.	Electronic accounted for 36% of initial knowledge.
Bank contact and DM accounted for 64% of initial knowledge.	Bank contact and DM accounted for 36% of initial knowledge.
Favorite TV was documentary for 27%.	Favorite program was documentary for 18%.
11% preferred sports	18% preferred sports
27% preferred drama	15% preferred drama
9% listen to western radio	13% listed to western radio
55% listen to contemporary pop radio	58% listen to contemporary pop radio
9% listen to talk stations	None listen to talk stations
None live in mobile homes	16% live in mobile homes

guidelines for advertising strategy in marketing the CDM.

The user does not seek as much help in planning his financial services as does the nonuser. Also, the user definitely does not feel that the CDM is too complicated for him to operate. Additionally, the nonuser feels more strongly that he is getting rather good checking services than does the user.

Based upon the findings above, the following profile (Figure 10) is presented. This profile is developed using only those significant variables from the discriminant analysis. It should be noted that mean values are available for each question introduced in the questionnaire.

Summary

The combination of a profile based upon significant demographic and life-style variables, combined with media preferences and indications of past promotional effectiveness served both as an evaluation of advertising effectiveness as well as a foundation for future promotional strategy. Application of techniques similar to this one could provide an additional tool to the promotional manager to assist him in the segmentation of his markets. □

REFERENCES

"A Consumer Banking Study," National Family Opinion, Inc., (unpublished), Toledo, Ohio, 1971.

Aaker, David A., *Multivariate Analysis in Marketing: Theory and Application*, Wadsworth, Inc., Belmont, California, 1971.

Blalock, Hubert M. Jr., *Social Statistics*, McGraw-Hill, New York, 1972.

Cooley, William W. and Paul R. Lhones, *Multivariate Data Analysis*, John Wiley and Sons, Inc., New York, 1971.

Frank, Ronald E., William F. Massy, Donald G. Morrison, "Bias in Multiple Discriminant Analysis," *Journal of Marketing Research*, August, 1965.

Granzin, Kent L., "A Study of Life-Style Concepts," unpublished, 1971.

Kerlinger, Fred N., *Foundations of Behavioral Research*, Holt, Rinehart, and Winston, Inc., New York, 1968.

Massy, William F., "Discriminant Analysis of Audience Characteristics," *Multivariate Analysis in Marketing: Theory and Application*, David A. Aaker, Wadsworth, Inc., Belmont, Calif., 1971, pp. 117-126.

Morrison, Donald G., "On the Interpretation of Discriminant Analysis," *Multivariate Analysis in Marketing*, David A. Aaker, Wadsworth, Belmont, California, 1971, pp. 135-136.

"1971 National Bank of Detroit Cash Dispenser Study: A Marketing-Oriented Exploration of Consumer Response to the Service and of the Size and Character of Its Potential Market." (Confidential, unpublished) Market Planning and Research Department, National Bank of Detroit, Detroit, Michigan, 1971.

"Now Banks are Turning to Hard Sell," *Business Week*, June 24, 1972.

Robertson, Thomas S. and James N. Kennedy, "Prediction of Consumer Innovators: Application of Multiple Discriminant Analysis," *Multivariate Analysis in Marketing; Theory and Application*, David A. Aaker, Wadsworth, Inc., Belmont, Calif., 1971, pp. 142-152.

Veldman, Donald J., *Fortran Programming for the Behavioral Sciences*, Holt, Rinehart and Winston, Inc., New York, 1967.

Wells, William D., and Douglas J. Tigert, "Activities, Interests and Opinions," *Market Segmentation, Concepts and Applications*, James F. Engel, Henry F. Fiorillo and Murray A. Cayley; Holt, Rinehart and Winston, New York, 1972.

Part III

FORECASTING AND SIMULATION

AMONG the most difficult problems facing bank management is the need for effective planning. The difficulty arises from the uncertainty of the future environment within which the bank will operate. While management cannot predict the exact nature of future events, it is not limited to random guesses. Generally, management plans on the basis of experience with past events that are expected to recur. The use of management science techniques can improve on this heuristic approach by providing a predictive framework based on management's knowledge of key relationships among variables. Simulation, for example, is one systematic approach to using current data to make the best possible estimate of future events. By varying key elements in their estimates, planners can see the impact of different strategies on future performance. This technique has been used with substantial success as a planning tool; its biggest contribution has been in organizing relevant data and defining key relationships.

In developing a useful predictive model, analysis of past experience is the basic building block. Utilizing time series analysis or other econometric tools, the model builder can determine relationships involving key decision variables. A mathematical model based on these relationships can then be tested to see how well it would have predicted past events. If an appropriate statistical methodology is utilized, a "good fit" with past events is a reasonably reliable indicator of a forecasting model's validity. Robert H. Cramer and Robert B. Miller discuss the essentials of forecasting model building in Chapter 7, "Development of a Deposit Forecasting Procedure for Use in Bank Financial Management." The article focuses on a time series model and its implications for bank financial management. The basic stages of model building are examined, and the important issue of updating the model is also explored.

Banks are most concerned with forecasting external market conditions such as loan demand, interest rates, return on investments, and deposit flow. Michael R. Thomson illustrates in Chapter 8 that models aimed at forecasting these variables need not be overly complex. Thomson's article, "Forecasting for Financial Planning," provides a useful framework for identifying key decision variables and developing a useful planning methodology. Thomson also addresses the question of forecast reliability and the availability of necessary input variables. The article provides a good overview of the link between forecasting models and the planning process.

The longer the planning horizon involved in forecasting, the greater the uncertainty. Accordingly, updating model inputs is necessary to maintain the accuracy of forecasts. Unfortunately, long-run planning models have up to now received the bulk of attention. The greater reliability of short-run forecasts, however, makes them suitable for applications that involve short-run decisions. Raymond V. Balzano explores a valuable short-run application in Chapter 9, "A Model to Forecast a Bank's Daily Net Clearing House Liability." If a bank is able to forecast its clearing house obligations accurately, then it can free excess funds for other uses that yield a net return. Balzano outlines a methodology based on time series analysis, but short-run forecasting is clearly not limited to this application. The methodology described in the article might have numerous other applications in the management of commercial banks. In many cases, a short-run model can become part of a long-term overall planning model.

The increased capabilities of the computer have led to greater use of forecasting and planning tools. Simulation, the most widely used of these tools, lends itself to computerized analysis. Programming a simulation model is often relatively straightforward, and, once developed, simulation models are reasonably simple to use. The limitations of these models stem from their dependence on management's estimates of key parameters. Nevertheless, simulation can offer a significant advantage over heuristic approaches to strategy formulation in a commercial bank.

In Part III we examine three representative simulation models. While the models are extensive and detailed, in practice these simulation planning tools are relatively easy to use, especially once the model has been programmed. Leon Derwa provides a good introduction to the development of a computer-based planning model in Chapter 10, "Computer Models: Aids to Management at Societe Generale de Banque." The model described has been implemented at a major bank in Belgium with good results. The model is actually several submodels combined in one computer package. One of the submodels is a deposit forecasting component similar to that discussed by Balzano in Chapter 9. The relationships among key variables are diagrammed by Derwa to illustrate the extent of detail in the model. Derwa's article concludes with the accurate observation that psychological problems usually outweigh technical obstacles in applying a management science model to management problems.

In Chapter 11, "Simulation at Banque de Bruxelles," Marc H. Royer focuses on policy decisions of the bank and forecasting net profit under various policy options. Like Derwa in Chapter 10, Royer has included an examination of input data and provided a diagram of the interrelationships among key simulation variables. Royer emphasizes that this model is intended as an aid to management and not as a replacement for sound judgment. The model provides a scientific approach to evaluation of the consequences of policy decisions in a commercial bank.

One of the most extensive computerized simulation models developed for bank planning purposes is BANKMOD. In Chapter 12, "BANKMOD: An Interactive Simulation Aid for Bank Financial Planning," Randall S. Robinson examines this management aid, developed at the Bank Administration Institute. Thus far, BANKMOD has experienced limited use. The reason for the lack of wide acceptance is probably behavioral and not related to the technical aspects of the model. BANKMOD is unique in that it addresses total bank planning. Its application could be relatively simple, since it has been made available to banks on a time-sharing basis by the Bank Administration Institute. Acceptance of broad-based total planning tools such as BANKMOD may increase as more executives become aware of their applications and value in the difficult task of bank planning.

In today's competitive banking environment, a major activity of bank planners and market researchers is the evaluation of potential branch bank expansion. The use of forecasting techniques in this planning area is receiving greater attention as the cost of initial investment in branch sites rises. Chapter 13, "Forecasting Branch Bank Growth Patterns," by Robert L. Kramer, evaluates the potential for using growth models in this key planning and forecasting area. Basically, the aim of the model is to forecast branch growth potential over time. Kramer details the procedure for developing a growth curve and suggests further work which is needed in this area.

The critical planning issue involving expansion through branch banking is also discussed in Chapter 14, "The Use of Simulation in Selecting Branch Banks," by E. Eugene Carter and Kalman J. Cohen. They suggest an approach to the problem of branch bank selection which deals directly with the uncertainty inherent in committing resources to a capital investment with risky returns. The uncertainty arises from such variables as market share, deposit growth rates, revenues, and costs.

71

Typically, the banker would determine these factors based on past experience and make his "best estimate" of returns. Carter and Cohen suggest that "risk analysis" can provide a more systematic view of the impact of key variables and market factors. Their approach combines a model for discounted cash flow analysis with a methodology for varying key parameters. An example is discussed. The article emphasizes that investment decisions should hinge not only on expected outcomes but also on the uncertainty inherent in these expectations.

The articles in this part examine various simulation and forecasting models which can aid bank management in dealing with the problems of an uncertain future. These aids to management are intended to support, not replace, careful planning. In applying them, behavioral resistance to unfamiliar management techniques must be anticipated and dealt with. Several of the techniques and models presented have been successfully applied in banks, particularly to planning problems. In many cases, forecasting and simulation can offer a significant improvement over traditional approaches to planning, but only if management fully understands their potential uses and inherent problems.

Chapter 7

DEVELOPMENT OF A DEPOSIT FORECASTING PROCEDURE FOR USE IN BANK FINANCIAL MANAGEMENT*

By Robert H. Cramer and Robert B. Miller

*This article is reprinted, with permission, from *Journal of Bank Research,* Vol. 4, No. 2 (Summer, 1973), pp. 122-138.

In a recent article Cohen [1972] discusses a management science approach to dynamic balance sheet management for a bank. Under the management science approach bank executives use an optimization technique (e.g., linear programming) as a "guide to their thinking" and thereby improve the effectiveness of their planning and decision making.

An important consideration in the practical application of an optimization technique is the extent to which the uncertainties associated with input data requirements can be analyzed. Forecasts are needed for interest rates, loan demand, and deposit levels for most banking oriented optimization techniques to function. Decisions should be based on accurate forecasts that properly portray the nature of a bank's environment.

The purpose of our research is to identify and estimate the parameters of a time series model for bank deposits and to determine the implications of the modeling procedure for bank financial management. The modeling procedure for interest rates and loan demand is felt to be similar to the one developed for deposit levels and this topic is left for future research.[1]

To show the role of time series modeling in the management science approach, Figure 1 presents a flow chart of the dynamic financial management process. The first section of the flow chart illustrates the role of statistical analysis. The past data series is fed into a modeling technique and a forecast is generated based on the time series model. The second section of the flow chart indicates that the forecast serves as a basis for applying an optimization technique (e.g. linear programming, chance constrained programming). The final step is the decision making by bank executives where information from the optimization technique as well as other factors enter into the decision making process.

An essential part of the dynamic management process according to Cohen [1972] is the interaction between management scientists and bank executives. This interaction is shown by feedback loops and a monitoring function in Figure 1. The implementation of the financial management process will cause trial and error adjustment where bank executives will re-examine their thinking and management scientists will restructure their statistical analysis and optimization techniques. The result of this adjustment will be an improved framework for decision making.[2]

Section I of this paper reviews previous research on bank financial management. It is a conclusion of this section that the improved statistical analysis of input data series would lead to better specified optimization techniques. To date, the results of optimizing techniques have not corresponded well with actual operating results. Section II presents the time series model building and forecasting procedure as shown in Figure 1. Section III applies this procedure to three types of data sources: Deposit levels of all banks (U.S. money supply), a group of large New York banks and a small midwestern bank. Section IV summarizes our research and discusses implications for the financial management process for banks.

I. PREVIOUS RESEARCH ON BANK FINANCIAL MANAGEMENT

In discussing previous research on bank financial management, one's first inclination is to categorize the research by the type of optimization technique employed. Categorizing research in this manner, however, suggests that the financial management process shown in Figure 1 begins with the selection of an optimization technique. In such a case, the researcher would first select an

---

[1]Ultimately uncertainty should be expressed by specifying a joint probability distribution of all random elements. However at present it is practical only to deal with one or two elements, as suggested by Cohen and Thore [1970, p. 48, 57]. There is undoubtedly interaction between loan demand and deposit levels and future work should consider these factors jointly.

[2]The goal here is similar to the one set forth by Holt, Modigliani, Muth and Simon [1963] in relating the decision making of a manufacturing company to sales fluctuations. They relate patterns of forecasted and unforecasted sales to adjustments in inventory, work force and plant size. The dynamic financial management process ultimately must relate forecasted and unforecasted deposit levels (as well as loan demands and interest rates) to adjustments in different categories of assets and liabilities.

Figure 1. Dynamic Financial Management Process

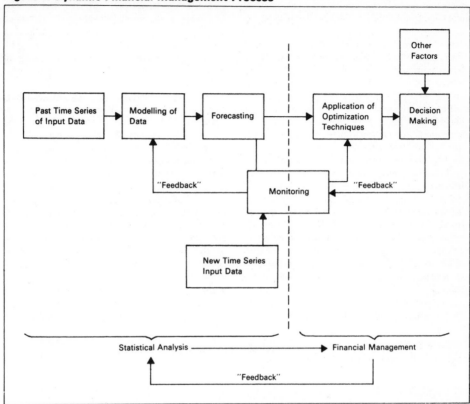

optimization technique (e.g. unconstrained maximization, the method of Lagrange multipliers, stock adjustment, linear or non-linear programming, chance constrained programming, dynamic programming) and then make assumptions about key environmental parameters in order to use the technique. Much of the previous research in bank management has proceeded in this manner.

Because sound *a priori* reasoning usually precedes the choice of a technique, the above procedure of first choosing an optimization method often produces interesting normative conclusions. However, the correspondence of actual data with optimum solution values from these techniques has been poor. For example, Fried [1970] compared the solution values from a chance-constrained programming model with data for 10 large banks in the Seventh Federal Reserve District. He finds that the results are inconsistent with the hypothesis "that banks act as if they conformed to the model as specified." More recently Aigner and Bryan [1971] used the La-

grangian multiplier technique in formulating the constrained maximization of the utility of a bank's liquidity position. The model was empirically tested by using the Wednesday position of a single bank. The authors conclude that "while the empirical results were generally consistent with the theory, they were sufficiently bad for us to be dissatisfied with [the model] as specified."

Perhaps the reason we are left with the above results is that research has been too technique oriented. The development of a dynamic method for balance sheet management involves not only the interaction between management scientists and bank executives as Cohen [1972] suggests, but the interaction between *a priori* reasoning (by both of these groups) and empirical findings. Thus we need to follow the feedback loop shown at the bottom of Figure 1 where a round of statistical analysis precedes further development of optimization techniques. The work of Dewald and Dreese [1970], Hester and Pierce [1968] and Melnik [1970] has shown that bank asset structure is related to deposit changes. Hence, it is useful to review the literature on bank financial planning by classifying planning techniques according to the assumptions made about the bank's deposit level. The classification is presented in Figure 2 with the type of deposit generating function listed in the left column. Next the author-article reference is given and then the type of optimization technique for bank planning is listed.

Figure 2 shows that the range of assumptions made about the deposit generating function is quite vast. Assumptions range from the rather naive notion that deposit levels are given at a set level to the rather vague notion that deposit levels be based on some (unspecified) probability distribution.

Figure 2 also shows that as the form of the deposit function becomes more complex, the optimization technique tends to become more sophisticated. The techniques range from linear programming associated with a given deposit level to chance constrained and dynamic programming associated with a probability distribution for the deposit level.

Only one author (to our knowledge) has explicitly stated a probability distribution for deposit levels and that was Edgeworth who in 1888 specified that deposit levels would follow the law of error (i.e. the normal distribution). He stated that: ". . . the law of error may be predicated of the variables with which the banker is concerned, so far as their quantity depends upon a variety of agencies, the fortunes and actions of a heterogeneous public." [Edgeworth, 1888, p. 114.]

Given the assumption of a deposit generating function, Edgeworth went on to describe an optimization technique for maximizing the expected return on an asset portfolio. A formal model or set of solutions, however, was not presented.

Although Edgeworth did not formally deal with time series models, he did recognize the problem of time series components:

". . . But it may be objected that some fluctuations in banking business are known to depend, not upon a fortuitous aggregation of small causes, but upon regular and unique events, such as the quarterly payment of dividends . . . And of course, if this change in conditions were considerable, the series so mutilated might not fluctuate according to the normal law of error. We must distinguish the undulations . . . from the tides . . . The normal law of fluctuation applies not so

Figure 2. Research on Bank Financial Management Classified by Deposit Generating Function

Deposit Generating Function (D = Deposit Level)	Article (Author, Title)	Optimization Technique
D, Given	Chambers and Charnes [1961]	Linear Programming
	Cohen and Hammer [1967]	Linear Programming
$D_{t+1} - D_t$, Given where t designates time period	Bryan and Carleton [1967]	Stock Adjustment Model
$f(Z)$ = probability distribution Z = deposit decline	Orr and Mellon [1961]	Maximum Expected Profit
	Porter [1961]	Maximum Expected Return
$D_t + A(t)$ where $A(t)$ = deposit anticipation	Aigner and Bryan [1971]	Maximum Expected Utility (of net revenue)
	Kane and Malkiel [1965]	Maximum Expected Utility (of return and variance of return)
$f(D)$ = probability distribution	Poole [1968]	Minimum Expected Cost
	Cohen and Thore [1970]	Two Stage Linear Programming Under Uncertainty
	Fried [1970]	Chance Constrained Programming
	Gray [1970]	Dynamic Programming
$$f(D) = \frac{1}{\sigma\sqrt{2\pi}} e^{-\frac{1}{2}\left(\frac{D-\mu}{\sigma}\right)^2}$$ where μ = mean deposit level σ = standard deviation of deposit distribution	Edgeworth [1888]	Maximum Expected Return

much to the ebb and flow of tides, as the undulatory motion which is relative to, superadded on, those periodic movements." [Edgeworth, 1888, p. 114-115.]

Our emphasis in this paper is on the regular events in a time series. It is our goal to model the "tides" that affect deposit levels and thereby reduce the "undulatory motions" to a minimum. This modeling process is the subject of the next section.

II. FORECASTING PROCEDURE AND DECISION MAKING

The purpose of this section is to provide a detailed discussion of the time series modeling and forecasting procedure shown in Figure 1, and also to relate this procedure to bank decision making.

A. Past Time Series

The primary statistical input in Figure 1 is a fairly lengthy series of past observations of deposit levels (daily, weekly or possibly monthly). Some judgement must be exercised in choosing the amount of data. If not enough data points are used the modeling and forecasting stages will be too easily influenced by chance variations, while if data from too far into the past are used, archaic patterns are likely to be introduced into the model and hence the forecasts.

B. Modeling

Our basic modeling technique is the one thoroughly discussed by Box and Jenkins [1970]. The basic idea of the Box and Jenkins approach is to develop, by empirical means, a parametric model which well describes the time series of interest. Once a model has been decided upon, forecasts of future observations may be obtained. It is important to keep the number of parameters

as small as possible while obtaining an adequate representation of the series. This is called the principle of parsimony by Box and Jenkins [1970, pp. 17-18]. A brief summary of the proposed modeling technique is presented below under the headings "models" and "model building." Application of the technique to some interesting series is presented in Section III.

B-1. Models. The basic building block of the parametric approach to the time series modeling is the expression

$$(1) \quad w_t - \eta_1 w_{t-1} - \ldots - \eta_{p'} w_{t-p'} = \tau_0 + a_t$$
$$- \tau_1 a_{t-1} - \ldots - \tau_{q'} a_{t-q'},$$

where $\{w_t\}$ is an observable series and $\{a_t\}$ is a sequence of unobservable random "shocks" into the system such that the a's are mutually statistically independent and each has a normal distribution with mean zero and variance σ^2. The parameters $\eta_1, \eta_2, \ldots, \eta_{p'}, \tau_0, \tau_1, \ldots, \tau_{q'},$ and σ^2 are assumed to be unknown but estimable from the data and to satisfy certain regularity conditions which guarantee the stationarity of the series $\{w_t\}$. Stationarity insures that $E(w_t)$ and $Var(w_t)$ are the same for all values of the index t, and $Cov(w_t, w_{t'})$ is some function of the difference $|t - t'|$ alone.

It is convenient to introduce a backshift operator denoted by B. B is an operator such that $Bf(t) = f(t-1)$, $B^2 f(t) = f(t-2), \ldots, B^s f(t) = f(t-s)$, etc. where f is some function of t. Using this notation, equation (1) may be written as

$$(2) \quad (1 - \eta_1 B - \ldots - \eta_{p'} B^{p'}) w_t = \tau_0$$
$$+ (1 - \tau_1 B - \ldots - \tau_{q'} B^{q'}) a_t.$$

Models written in terms of the backshift operator are especially useful when one is trying to interpret the models because seasonal and other time related factors stand out very clearly. This point will be illustrated in the data analysis presented below.

It is well known that many important economic time series have definite trends and are therefore

Figure 3

Verbal Description of the Model	Model Expressed in Terms of Equation (2)
1. Autoregressive	$(1 - \eta_1 B - \ldots - \eta_{p'} B^{p'}) w_t = a_t$
2. Purely Moving Average	$w_t = (1 - \tau_1 B - \ldots - \tau_{q'} B^{q'}) a_t$
3. Simple Random Walk	$(1 - B) Z_t = a_t$
4. Simple Exponential Smoothing	$(1 - B) Z_t = (1 - \theta B) a_t$
5. Simple Exponential Smoothing of a Seasonally Adjusted Series	$(1 - B)(1 - \Phi_1 B^s - \ldots - \Phi B^{P_s}) Z_t$ $= (1 - \theta B)(1 - \Theta_1 B^s - \ldots - \Theta_Q B^{Q_s}) a_t$
6. General Seasonal Model	$(1 - \phi_1 B - \ldots - \phi_P B^P)(1 - \Phi_1 B^s - \ldots - \Phi_P B^{P_s}) w_t$ $= \tau_0 + (1 - \theta_1 B - \ldots - \theta_q B^q)(1 - \Theta_1 B^s - \ldots - \Theta_Q B^{Q_s}) a_t$

not stationary. Hence if the model discussed above is to be useful, it must be extended to include non-stationary series. This can be done in many ways. One of the more useful ways is by means of differencing. For example, if the observations Z_1, Z_2, ..., Z_T come from a non-stationary series, it can often be shown that the first difference series $w_1, ..., w_{T-1}$, where $w_t = Z_{t+1} - Z_t = (1 - B)Z_{t+1}$, is well described by a form of the stationary model in (2). In this case the series $\{Z_t\}$ is said to be non-stationary in level (see [Box and Jenkins, 1970, pp. 85-94]). This idea can be extended to more complicated differences to account for seasonal effects. For example, suppose the seasonal effect is non-stationary in level with period 12. Then the series $w_t = Z_{t+13} - Z_t = (1 - B^{12})Z_{t+13}$ would have a stationary component of period 12 (although it may have non-stationary effects of other periods). (See [Box and Jenkins, 1970, pp. 300-305].)

In order to point out the relationship between model (2) and other models appearing in the literature we have prepared Figure 3. The following remarks refer to Figure 3:

> If $\tau_0, \tau_1, ..., \tau_q$ are all zero, then (2) is the defining equation of an autoregressive model. On the other hand, if $\tau_0, \eta_1, \eta_2, ..., \eta_p$ are all zero, then (2) defines a purely moving average model. Because (2) combines these two well-known models, it is said to define a mixed autoregressive-moving average model.

> The parameter τ_0 is a linear trend term. The model could be generalized to include more complicated deterministic trends, but for purposes of expository simplicity this has not been done.

> The simple random walk model in entry 3 may be put into its more familiar form by noting that $(1-B)Z_t = Z_t - Z_{t-1}$, so that the model is $Z_t = Z_{t-1} + a_t$, i.e., the current observation is the previous observation plus a random "shock." The important random walk model with a deterministic drift may be obtained by simply adding the τ_0 term to the model in 3.

> It is pointed out by Muth [1960] and by Box and Jenkins [1970, pp. 107-108] that the model in item 4 is nothing more than the familiar exponential smoothing model. In particular, letting $\lambda = 1 - \theta$ and $\bar{Z}_t = E(Z_t|Z_{t-1}, \lambda)$, i.e., the conditional expectation of Z_t, given the value of Z_{t-1} and the "smoothing constant" λ, produces the expression,

(3) $\bar{Z}_t = \lambda Z_t + (1 - \lambda)\bar{Z}_{t-1}$.

Expression (3) can be compared to equation (1) of Winters [1960] and equation (2) of Crane and Crotty [1967]. The simple exponential smoothing

model is easily generalized to the case where the original series is seasonally adjusted and then smoothed exponentially. The result is the simple exponential smoothing model with seasonal adjustment. (See item 5 in Figure 3). This model can in turn be generalized to the case where some other operation besides exponential smoothing is carried out after seasonal adjustment. (See item 6 in Figure 3). The general seasonal model in item 6 is discussed in [Box and Jenkins, 1970, pp. 300-305]. By multiplying the operators together in item 6, one obtains the form (2). For example, suppose the model were

$$(1 - \phi B)(1 - \Phi B^{12})w_t = (1 - \theta B)(1 - \Theta B^3)a_t.$$

The left-hand side of this model is

$$(1 - \phi B)(1 - \Phi B^{12})w_t$$
$$= (1 - \phi B - \Phi B^{12} + \phi \Phi B^{13})w_t,$$

so that $\eta_1 = \phi, \eta_2 = ... = \eta_{11} = 0, \eta_{12} = \Phi, \eta_{13} = -\phi\Phi, \eta_k = 0, k \geq 14$. Similarly one obtains $\tau_0 = 0, \tau_1 = \theta, \tau_2 = 0; \tau_3 = \Theta; \tau_4 = -\theta\Theta, \tau_k = 0, k \geq 5$.

B-2 Model Building. Given a set of time series data $Z_1, ..., Z_T$, one follows an iterative procedure in obtaining an appropriate model for the data. This procedure includes three stages: Identification, estimation and diagnostic checking.

a. *Identification.* The first step in identification is to calculate the sample autocorrelation function (sacf) defined by

$$r_k = \frac{\sum\limits_{t=1}^{n-k}(w_t - \bar{w})(w_{t+k} - \bar{w})}{\sum\limits_{t=1}^{n}(w_t - \bar{w})^2},$$

where n is the number of observations and $\bar{w}$ is the average of the w's, which are functions of the Z's. The sacf is calculated for a number of lags k and compared to known shapes of theoretical autocorrelations associated with various models that can be represented by (2). The theoretical autocorrelation function of a stationary series $\{w_t\}$ is defined by $\rho_k = E(w_t - \mu)(w_{t+k} - \mu)/E(w_t - \mu)^2$, where $\mu = E(w_t)$. For example, a purely moving average model of order 1 is a special case of (2) with all η's and $\tau_0, \tau_2, ..., \tau_q$ equal to zero. The theoretical autocorrelation function of this process is $\rho_0 = 1, \rho_1 = -\tau_1/(1 + \tau_1^2), \rho_k = 0, k \geq 2$. If the sacf had approximately this shape (except for sampling error), then one would tentatively identify the data generating model as purely moving average.

The most important characteristic of the sacf of most stationary series is that its values tend to become small after a relatively small number of lags (damped behavior). On the other hand, if observations $Z_1, \ldots, Z_T$ come from a non-stationary series, and if the sacf is calculated for these data, it will tend to exhibit the opposite behavior. If such a pattern is encountered, one differences the data and calculates the sacf of the differenced series to see if it follows a stationary pattern. Once a stationary series has been produced by appropriate differencing, one can begin searching for a model to describe this stationary series.

b. *Estimation.* Once the form of the model has been chosen the unknown parameters are estimated from the data. It is very important that the estimation be done efficiently, so that the adequacy of the fitted model may be examined. Box and Jenkins [1970, pp. 231-238] discuss a general least squares algorithm for obtaining efficient parameter estimates, and this is the algorithm we have employed.[3]

c. *Diagnostic Checking.* Once the parameters of the model have been estimated, one can obtain a series from this model which should imitate the behavior of the observed data. To check this, one calculates residuals by subtracting the modeled values from the actual values of the series. If the model fits the data adequately, these residuals should behave approximately like random deviates. The behavior of the residuals can be checked by calculating their sacf. If the model is adequate, this function should be close to zero for all lags except the zeroeth lag, since the theoretical autocorrelation function of random deviates is $\rho_0 = 1$, $\rho_k = 0$ for $k \geq 1$.

If, on the other hand, the autocorrelation function of the residuals exhibits a pattern, the model may be modified to account for this pattern. For example, suppose a first order moving average model is fit to the data, and the sacf of the residuals seems to follow the pattern $r_0 = 1$, $r_1 \neq 0$, $r_k = 0$ for $k \geq 2$. Then one may entertain the possibility that the data follow a second order moving average model, i.e.,

$$w_t = (1 - \tau_1 B - \tau_2 B^2) a_t.$$

The stages of estimation and diagnostic checking are repeated for this model. If the residuals then behave approximately randomly, the model is accepted. If not, further modification may be made.

The process of choosing a model, obtaining a least squares fit of the data to the model, examining the residuals of the least squares fit, and modifying the model if necessary, sets our approach apart from approaches which choose a model *a priori* and judge the model strictly on the basis of the forecasts it generates. We would argue that if we can model all (or almost all) of the significant trends and autocorrelations in the data, then our model should produce the best forecasts one can hope for using time series methods.

C. Forecasting

Once a suitable model for the past data has been found, it is relatively easy to generate forecasts of future observations. Suppose $Z_1, \ldots, Z_T$ are the observed values of a time series. Two questions naturally arise: 1) What is the best guess at some future value of the series Z_{T+r}, say, and 2) is there a measure of the potential error in this guess? It turns out that an efficient forecasting function is the conditional expectation of Z_{T+r}, given the information obtained up to and including time T. If this forecasting function is employed, it is easy to obtain an estimate of the standard error of the forecast and hence error bounds for the forecast. A detailed derivation of the necessary formulae is given in [Box and Jenkins, 1970, pp. 126-132, 135-137, 306-310].

D. New Input Data

Even after a model has been adopted, new observations will be collected as time passes. We will discuss two ways in which these data may be used—the updating of forecasts and the monitoring of the model.

While it would be bad practice to ignore the new data, it would probably be too tedious to remodel and reforecast each time a new observation was obtained. An alternative technique is simply to update existing forecasts in light of the new observation. Again this is rather simple, given a suitable parametric model. (See [Box and Jenkins, 1970, pp. 132-135] for details.) Updating has the effect of making the forecasts adaptive in nature, i.e., trend components are modified in the light of new observations. This feature is especially important when dealing with economic time series exhibiting quite erratic behavior. Updating will be illustrated in the data analysis portion of the paper.

E. Monitoring

It often happens in economic time series that the parameters of the model, and sometimes even the form of the model, will change over time. A quality control technique for detecting changes is discussed in [Miller, Wichern and Hsu, 1971].

---

[3]A listing of a FORTRAN program (written for a UNIVAC 1108 computer) which carries out the estimation and the forecasting discussed in the next two sections may be obtained from the Program Librarian, Madison Academic Computing Center, 1210 W. Dayton St., Madison, Wisc. 53706.

Figure 4. Sacf of Money Supply, Z_t

1–12	.99	.98	.98	.97	.96	.95	.95	.94	.94	.93	.92	.92
ST.E.	.04	.08	.10	.12	.13	.15	.16	.17	.18	.19	.20	.21
13–24	.91	.90	.90	.89	.88	.88	.87	.86	.86	.85	.85	.84
ST.E.	.21	.22	.23	.24	.24	.25	.26	.26	.27	.27	.28	.28
25–36	.83	.83	.82	.81	.80	.80	.79	.78	.78	.77	.77	.76
ST.E.	.29	.29	.30	.30	.31	.31	.32	.32	.32	.33	.33	.33
37–48	.76	.75	.75	.74	.74	.73	.73	.72	.72	.71	.71	.70
ST.E.	.34	.34	.34	.35	.35	.35	.36	.36	.36	.37	.37	.37
49–52	.70	.70	.69	.69								
ST.E.	.37	.38	.38	.38								

Figure 5. Sacf of First Difference of Money Supply, $(1-B)Z_t$

1–12	−.01	.01	−.29	.20	.02	−.21	−.20	.03	.24	−.29	−.10	−.16
ST.E.	.04	.04	.04	.05	.05	.05	.05	.05	.05	.06	.06	.06
13–24	.63	−.05	−.01	−.20	.18	.04	−.26	−.21	.05	.29	−.25	−.06
ST.E.	.06	.07	.07	.07	.07	.07	.07	.08	.08	.08	.08	.08
25–36	−.13	.56	−.06	−.10	−.21	.17	.13	−.23	−.22	−.05	.26	−.22
ST.E.	.08	.08	.09	.09	.09	.09	.09	.09	.09	.09	.09	.10
37–48	.01	−.10	.55	−.04	−.14	−.23	.10	.12	−.21	−.13	−.06	.26
ST.E.	.10	.10	.10	.10	.10	.10	.10	.10	.10	.11	.11	.11
49–52	−.27	.02	−.05	.75								
ST.E.	.11	.11	.11	.11								

Figure 6. Sacf of $(1-B)$ $(1-B^{13})Z_t$; Z_t is Money Supply

1–12	.27	.19	−.10	−.03	−.01	.08	.05	−.01	−.02	−.06	−.19	−.26
ST.E.	.04	.05	.05	.05	.05	.05	.05	.05	.05	.05	.05	.05
13–24	−.43	−.06	.07	.17	−.02	−.11	−.13	.01	.14	.10	−.02	−.07
ST.E.	.05	.06	.06	.06	.06	.06	.06	.06	.06	.06	.06	.06
25–36	.02	−.07	.00	−.04	.01	.07	.13	.01	−.16	−.11	−.05	.15
ST.E.	.06	.06	.06	.06	.06	.06	.06	.07	.07	.07	.07	.07
37–48	.12	−.03	−.30	−.28	−.19	−.11	−.04	−.02	.07	.08	.02	−.04
ST.E.	.07	.07	.07	.07	.07	.07	.07	.07	.07	.07	.07	.07
49–52	−.08	.11	.22	.69								
ST.E.	.07	.07	.07	.08								

Figure 7. Results from Fitting Model (4) to U.S. Money Supply

Parameter	Estimate	Approximate 95% Confidence Interval
ϕ_{52}	.98	[.92, 1.03]
θ_1	.35	[.26, .44]
θ_{13}	.56	[.47, .64]
θ_{52}	.34	[.21, .46]
σ^2	.5748	[.51, .67]

Autocorrelations
Data—The estimated residuals—Model (4)
Mean of the series = .035
St. error of mean = .036
Number of observations = 429

1–12	-.02	.07	-.11	.02	-.04	.01	-.06	.13	.05	.04	-.02	-.03
ST.E.	.05	.05	.05	.05	.05	.05	.05	.05	.05	.05	.05	.05
13–24	.05	-.06	-.00	.10	-.02	-.02	.03	-.01	.03	.04	-.03	.03
ST.E.	.05	.05	.05	.05	.05	.05	.05	.05	.05	.05	.05	.05
25–36	.03	-.05	-.05	.02	.08	-.09	-.03	-.03	-.06	-.01	-.05	-.06
ST.E.	.05	.05	.05	.05	.05	.05	.05	.05	.05	.05	.05	.05
37–48	.04	-.07	-.07	-.06	-.01	-.07	-.08	-.02	.06	-.04	.01	-.01
ST.E.	.05	.05	.05	.05	.05	.05	.05	.05	.05	.05	.05	.05
49–52	-.04	.01	-.07	.00								
ST.E.	.05	.05	.05	.05								

Mean divided by St. error = .96518

To test whether this series is white noise, that value 59.926 should be compared with a Chi-square variable with 47 degrees of freedom.

This technique, or modifications of it, could be used to compare the behavior of the past data with that of the new data. If the behaviors appear drastically different, then remodelling would be necessary.

F. Decision Making

Ideally, a bank management decision takes into account all relevant factors. We feel that among these factors may be not only the actual values of time series forecasts and their standard errors but the form of the model which led to the forecasts. For example, if the model of a series differed radically from that of exponential smoothing this may be significant information to a manager whose forecasting department routinely uses exponential smoothing. It may also be useful to know the nature of seasonal components of the series. Such components usually stand out clearly in the parametric model. The final section of this paper discusses some implications of time series modeling for the financial planning process.

III. DATA ANALYSIS

The time series modeling aspects of Section II will now be illustrated using three interesting series.

A. Data Series

a) The series of weekly average U.S. money supply (demand deposits plus currency) figures reported in the *Federal Reserve Bulletin* from January 4, 1961 through June 24, 1970.

b) The series of weekly average demand deposits for a group of large New York City banks as reported in the *Federal Reserve Bulletin* from May 3, 1960 through April 29, 1970.

c) The series of demand deposits at the end of each Wednesday of a small midwestern bank from January, 1965 through July, 1970.

In section III-B the modeling of the money supply series is discussed in some detail. Then the models for the two bank deposit series are briefly presented and some comparisons made. In section III-C forecasts based on the models are displayed and discussed. In section III-D the nature of the forecast functions is discussed in more detail.

B. Modeling

Figures 4, 5 and 6 display the sacf's of the money supply series, its first difference $(1 - B)Z_t = Z_t - Z_{t-1}$, and the function

$$(1 - B)(1 - B^{13})Z_t = Z_t - Z_{t-1} - Z_{t-13} + Z_{t-14}.$$

Standard errors are shown to help pick out significantly large autocorrelations. The sacf in Figure 4, since it does not die out, confirms the fact that the money supply series is non-stationary in level. The sacf in Figure 5 is quite ragged, but its most salient feature is the collection of large values at lags 13, 26, 39 and 52. These "spikes" suggest non-stationarity of period 13 and indicate inspec-

Figure 8. Results from Fitting Model (5) to U.S. Money Supply

Parameter	Estimate	Approximate 95% Confidence Interval
θ_1	.36	[.26, .46]
θ_{13}	.55	[.47, .63]
θ_{52}	.36	[.26, .46]
σ^2	.5745	[.51, .66]

Autocorrelations
Data—The estimated residuals - Model (5)
Mean of the series = .034
St. error of mean = .036
Number of observations = 429

1–12	-.01	.07	- 11	.02	-.03	.01	-.05	.13	.06	.05	-.02	-.03
ST.E.	.05	.05	05	.05	.05	.05	.05	.05	.05	.05	.05	.05
13–24	.05	-.06	00	.10	-.01	-.02	.03	-.02	.03	.03	-.03	.03
ST.E.	.05	.05	05	.05	.05	.05	.05	.05	.05	.05	.05	.05
25–36	.03	-.05	-.05	.02	.08	-.09	-.04	-.03	-.06	-.01	-.06	-.06
ST.E.	.05	.05	05	.05	.05	.05	.05	.05	.05	.05	.05	.05
37–48	.04	-.07	- 07	-.06	-.01	-.07	-.08	-.01	.05	-.04	.00	-.01
ST.E.	.05	.05	05	.05	.05	.05	.05	.05	.05	.05	.05	.05
49–52	-.05	-.00	- 08	.01								
ST.E.	.05	.05	05	.05								

Mean divided by St. error = .93656

To test whether this series is white noise, the value 38.09 should be compared with a Chi-square variable with 26 degrees of freedom.

tion of the function $(1 - B)(1 - B^{13})Z_t$, whose sacf is shown in Figure 6. The most interesting of the significant autocorrelations in Figure 6 are at lags 1, 13 and 52, since they can be interpreted as indications of weekly, quarterly and annual fluctuations in the data. While not shown in Figure 6, the 104th lag autocorrelation is also significant, suggesting that either the series is non-stationary in lag 52 or that it exhibits autoregressive-moving average behavior in that lag. The sacf in Figure 6 also suggests moving average behavior in the first and thirteenth lags. These remarks may be summarized in the model

$$(4) \quad (1 - \phi_{52}B^{52})(1 - B^{13})(1 - B)Z_t = (1 - \theta_1 B)(1 - \theta_{13}B^{13})(1 - \theta_{52}B^{52})a_t.$$

Some results from fitting this model appear in Figure 7.

Note in Figure 7 that the 95% confidence interval for ϕ_{52} contains 1, suggesting that we might set $\phi_{52} = 1$ and use the 52nd seasonal difference instead of a seasonal 52nd order autoregressive term in the model. The model then would be

$$(5) \quad (1 - B^{52})(1 - B^{13})(1 - B)Z_t = (1 - \theta_1 B)(1 - \theta_{13}B^{13})(1 - \theta_{52}B^{52})a_t.$$

Some results from fitting this model appear in Figure 8. We note that the estimate of σ is .76

billion dollars and contains 425 degrees of freedom. The model in (5) may be interpreted as exponential smoothing in weeks, quarters, and years. Alternatively it may be thought of as simple exponential smoothing of an appropriately seasonally adjusted series.

By going through a similar analysis procedure as the one just outlined, models were developed for the collection of large New York banks and the small local bank. The model for the New York banks is

$$(6) \quad (1 - \phi_{13}B^{13} - \phi_{26}B^{26} - \phi_{52}B^{52})(1 - B)Z_t = (1 - \theta_1 B)a_t,$$

where $\hat{\phi}_{13} = .13$, $\hat{\phi}_{26} = .29$, $\hat{\phi}_{52} = .42$, $\hat{\theta}_1 = .82$, and $\hat{\sigma} = 1.057$ billion dollars (413 degrees of freedom). Note that the model is exponential smoothing of a seasonally adjusted series. The model for the local bank is

$$(7) \quad (1 - B^{52})(1 - B)Z_t = (1 - \theta_1 B)(1 - \theta_{52}B^{52})a_t,$$

where $\hat{\theta}_1 = .49$, $\hat{\theta}_{52} = .69$, and $\hat{\sigma} = 967$ thousand dollars (236 degrees of freedom). Again an exponentially smoothed, seasonally adjusted model is obtained.[4]

[4]It should be noted that although all of the above models involved exponential smoothing of a seasonally adjusted series, there is no guarantee that this is the appropriate model type for all banks. Also the parameter structure of any model type will differ substantially from case to case as the above results indicate.

Figure 9. Forecasts, Forecast Limits, and Actual Values of Money Supply. Forecast Origin is July 24, 1968

Legend: Actual Values
    Forecasted Values — — — — — —
    Lower 95% Forecast Limits ——————
    Upper 95% Forecast Limits _____

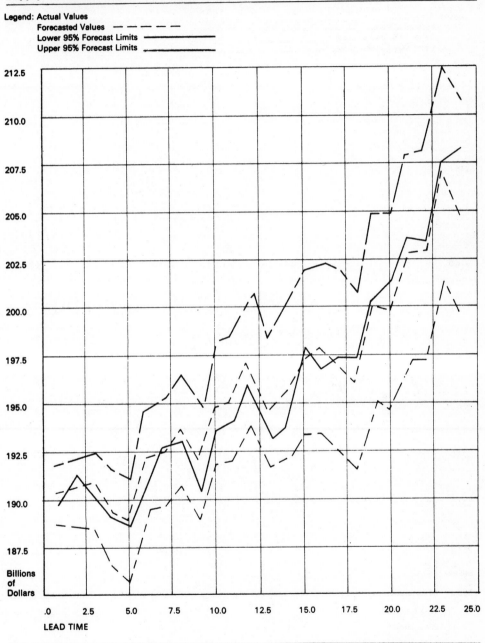

**Figure 10. Forecasts, Forecast Limits, and Actual Values of Money
Supply. Forecast Origin is June 24, 1970**

Legend: Actual Values
Forecasted Values   — — — — — —
Lower 95% Forecast Limits _____
Upper 95% Forecast Limits — — _____ — — _____

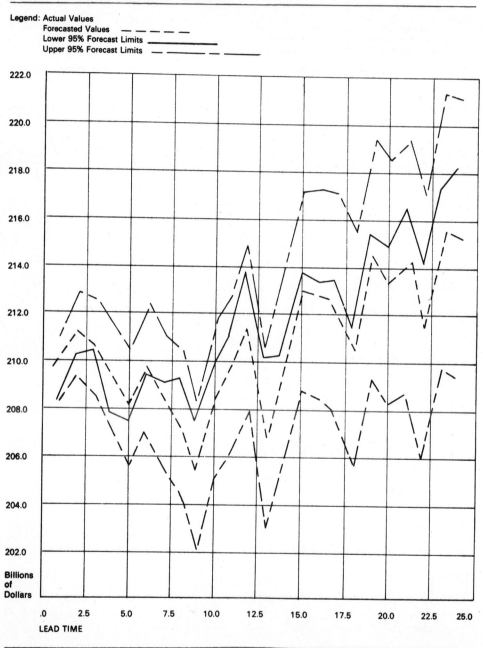

Figure 11. Updated Forecasts of Money Supply from Lead Times 1, 6 and 12

Lead Time	Forecasts Updated From			
Date	July 1, 1970	August 5, 1970	Septembe: 16, 1970	Actual Value of Money Supply
July 1, 1970				208.3
July 8, 1970	209.3			210.3
July 15, 1970	213.7			210.5
July 22, 1970	208.3			207.7
July 29, 1970	206.9			207.3
August 5, 1970	208.9			209.4
August 12, 1970	207.4	207.7		209.0
August 19, 1970	206.6	206.9		209.2
August 26, 1970	207.1	204.5		207.2
September 2, 1970	207.5	207.9		209.9
September 9, 1970	208.5	208.9		211.1
September 16, 1970	210.5	210.9		213.9
September 23, 1970	205.8	206.1	208.8	210.1
September 30, 1970	208.3	208.6	211.3	210.2
October 7, 1970	211.6	212.0	211.6	213.7
October 14, 1970	211.5	212.3	214.9	213.2
October 21, 1970	211.1	211.3	214.0	213.3
October 28, 1970	209.2	219.7	212.4	211.3
November 4, 1970	213.2	213.8	216.5	215.3
November 11, 1970	212.2	212.7	215.9	214.9
November 18, 1970	212.8	213.3	217.0	216.3
November 25, 1970	210.1	210.6	214.5	214.1
December 2, 1970	214.2	214.7	213.3	217.4
December 9, 1970	214.0	214.5	213.2	218.3

All Figures are in Billions of Dollars

The New York banks series exhibits strong weekly, quarterly, semi-annual and annual effects, while the local bank exhibits only weekly and annual effects. The total money supply, of which the two other series are components, exhibits weekly, quarterly and annual effects. The strong quarterly effect in money supply and New York banks presumably reflects, at least in part, action by the Federal Reserve.[5] Apparently the small local bank is immune to such action, as the quarterly effect does not appear.

C. Forecasting

Figures 9 and 10 display forecasts for the money supply series for the 24 weeks following July 24,

1968 and the 24 weeks following June 24, 1970, which is the end of the modelled series. Also shown are 95% forecast limits and the series values actually observed in these periods. Note that the forecast limits widen as forecasts are made further away from the forecast origins. This happens because the series is non-stationary and illustrates the nature of the uncertainty involved in attempting to make long-term forecasts.

To illustrate the process of updating we have provided updated forecasts from lead times 1, 6 and 12 in Figure 11. See [Box and Jenkins, 1970, pp. 132-138] for a discussion of updating.

Figure 12 shows long-term and continually updated forecasts for the New York City banks for the 24 weeks following April 29, 1970. Continually updated forecasts are simply forecasts made one period ahead every time a new observation becomes available. It can be seen from Figure 12 that the continually updated forecasts track the actual

[5]Federal Reserve policy is a basic source of uncertainty because of the difficulties the Fed has in implementing its own policies. Recent articles in the *Monthly Review* of the Federal Reserve Bank of New York *Monthly Review*, July 1970, Oct. 1970, Apr. 1972 discuss the difficulties the New York Fed has in controlling monetary aggregates according to a prescribed policy.

Figure 12. Forecasted, Continually Updated and Actual Values of Demand Deposits of Large New York City Banks. Forecast Origin is April 29, 1970

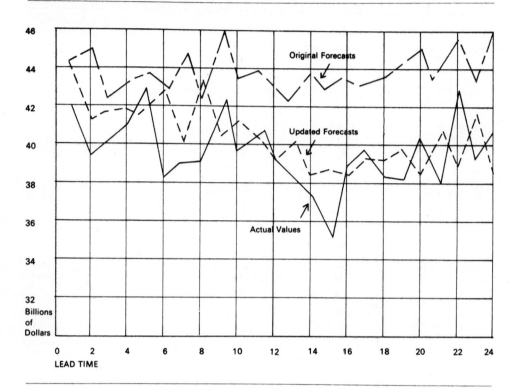

values of the series more closely than do the long-term forecasts, as would certainly be expected.

While graphical comparisons are very useful, it is advisable to have a quantitative measure of the effectiveness of a forecast. One measure which appears to be useful is Theil's index of forecast efficiency presented in [Theil, 1966]. The index is defined by

$$T = \sqrt{\frac{\sum\limits_{k=1}^{24} (Z_{T+k} - \hat{Z}_T(k))^2}{\sum\limits_{k=1}^{24} (Z_{T+k} - Z_{T-1+k})^2}},$$

and is clearly a comparison of sums of squared forecast errors from two forecasting methods: Our own and the method which consists of continually

Figure 13. Theil Coefficients

Money Supply		New York Bank		
Origin	Long-term forecast	Origin	Long-term forecast	Continually updated forecast
July 24, 1968	.610	April 29, 1970	1.9088	.9463
June 24, 1970	.797			

updating forecasts by using the current observation to forecast the next observation. Theil's index is presented in Figure 13 for all the cases considered above.

D. Forecast Models

In this section the money supply is used to explain the nature of the forecasts generated by

86

our modeling procedures. Recall that the money supply model is

$$(5') \quad \begin{aligned} &(1-B^{52})(1-B^{13})(1-B)Z_t \\ &= (1-\theta_1 B)(1-\theta_{13}B^{13})(1-\theta_{52}B^{52})a_t. \end{aligned}$$

The product of operators on the left-hand side of (5') can be expanded to yield

$$1 - B - B^{13} + B^{14} - B^{52} + B^{53} + B^{65} - B^{66},$$

while the product of operators on the right-hand side of (5') can be expanded

$$\begin{aligned} &1-\theta_1 B - \theta_{13}B^{13}+\theta_1\theta_{13}B^{14}-\theta_{52}B^{52} \\ &+\theta_1\theta_{52}5^{53}+\theta_{13}\theta_{52}B^{65}-\theta_1\theta_{13}\theta_{52}B^{66}. \end{aligned}$$

Thus (5') can be written as

$$(8) \quad \begin{aligned} Z_t =\ & Z_{t-1}+Z_{t-13}-Z_{t-14}+Z_{t-52}-Z_{t-53} \\ & -Z_{t-65}+Z_{t-66}-\theta_1\theta_{13}\theta_{52}a_{t-66} \\ & +\theta_{13}\theta_{52}a_{t-65}+\theta_1\theta_{52}a_{t-53}-\theta_{52}a_{t-52} \\ & +\theta_1\theta_{13}a_{t-14}-\theta_{13}a_{t-13}-\theta_1 a_{t-1}+a_t. \end{aligned}$$

The forecast of Z_{T+1} standing at forecast origin T is given by $\underset{T}{E}(Z_{T+1})$, where E stands for conditional expectation at time T, given all past information. Thus

$$(9) \quad \begin{aligned} \hat{Z}_T(1) =\ & \underset{T}{E}(Z_{T+1}) \\ =\ & Z_T+Z_{T-12}-Z_{T-13}+Z_{T-51}-Z_{T-52} \\ & -Z_{T-64}+Z_{T-65}-\theta_1\theta_{13}\theta_{52}a_{T-65} \\ & +\theta_{13}\theta_{52}a_{t-64}+\theta_1\theta_{52}a_{T-52} \\ & -\theta_{52}a_{T-51}+\theta_1\theta_{13}a_{T-13}-\theta_{13}a_{T-12} \\ & -\theta_1 a_T, \end{aligned}$$

since $\underset{T}{E}(a_{T+1}) = 0$ and all the other quantities in (9) are known. (The Z's are observed data, and estimates of the a's are generated by the model fitting procedure. In actual forecasting the θ parameters would be replaced by point estimates. There is some evidence to indicate that this procedure introduces only slight errors into the forecast limits when the number of data points is large. See [Box and Jenkins, 1970, pp. 267-269].) The forecast of Z_{T+2} is $\hat{Z}_T(2) = \underset{T}{E}(Z_{T+2})$ and is given by

$$(10) \quad \begin{aligned} \hat{Z}_T(2) =\ & \underset{T}{E}(Z_{T+1})+Z_{T-11}-Z_{T-12}+Z_{T-50} \\ & -Z_{T-51}-Z_{T-63}+Z_{T-64} \\ & -\theta_1\theta_{13}\theta_{52}a_{T-64}+\theta_{13}\theta_{52}a_{T-63} \\ & +\theta_1\theta_{52}a_{T-51}-\theta_{52}a_{T-50} \\ & +\theta_1\theta_{13}a_{T-12}-\theta_{13}a_{T-11}, \end{aligned}$$

since $\underset{T}{E}(a_{T+1}) = \underset{T}{E}(a_{T+2}) = 0$. The value of $\underset{T}{E}(Z_{T+1})$

in (10) is simply $\hat{Z}(1)$ which is obtained in (9). Continuing in this manner forecasts may be obtained recursively. It is clear that when the lead time l is greater than 64, the a's will no longer contribute to the forecasts. Thus when $l > 64$, the forecasts are

$$(11) \quad \begin{aligned} \hat{Z}_T(l) =\ & \hat{Z}_T(l-1)+\hat{Z}_T(l-13)-\hat{Z}_T(l-14) \\ & +\hat{Z}_T(l-52)-\hat{Z}_T(l-53)-\hat{Z}_T(l-65) \\ & +\hat{Z}_T(l-66), \end{aligned}$$

where

$$(12) \quad \hat{Z}_T(l) = \begin{cases} Z_{T+l} & \text{if } l \le 0 \\ \hat{Z}_T(l) & \text{if } l > 0 \end{cases}.$$

The function in (11) satisfies the difference equation

$$(13) \quad (1-B^{52})(1-B^{13})(1-B)\hat{Z}_T(l) = 0,$$

where B operates on l. Note that this is the homogeneous difference equation associated with the model in (5').

Multiplying (13) by $(1+B+...+B^{51})(1+B^{13}+B^{26}+B^{39})$, the following expression is obtained:

$$(14) \quad (1-B^{52})^3 \hat{Z}_T(l) = 0.$$

In expression (14) the index l may be thought of as having the form $l = 52n + m, n = 0, 1, 2, ..., m = 1, 2, ..., 52$, so that n represents years, and m represents weeks within a given year. Then for a fixed week, m, B^{52} operates on n according to the relation $B^{52}(n) = n-1$. Thus for a fixed week, the difference equation in (14) has solution

$$(15) \quad \hat{Z}_T(52n+m) = A_0^{(m)} + A_1^{(m)}n + A_2^{(n)}n^2,$$

where $A_0^{(m)}$, $A_1^{(m)}$, and $A_2^{(m)}$ are constants which must be determined from the series. As an example consider $m = 1$, that is, first weeks. The forecast function for first weeks of the years is simply a quadratic function of n, the number of years: $A_0^{(1)} + A_1^{(1)}n + A_2^{(1)}n^2$. A similar remark holds for the other weeks of the year, but note that there is a different set of coefficients $A_0^{(m)}$, $A_1^{(m)}$, $A_2^{(m)}$ for each week. Figure 14 displays these weekly coefficients.

IV. Summary and Conclusions

It has been our purpose in this paper to present a model building approach to deposit forecasting and to discuss its role in the dynamic financial management process of a bank. The model building approach is seen to have a number of features which make it particularly useful in financial management.

The time series modeling enables the researcher to discover the type of model that "best" fits the past data rather than beginning with a predetermined form of a model.

The model building procedure involves three stages: Identification, estimation and diagnostic checking. The latter stage represents an iterative process where further identification and estimation of the model is carried out until the residual error in fitting the model is reduced to an appropriate level. The iterative procedure is used in the initial modeling of data as is demonstrated for the money supply series and can also be used for subsequent revisions. These revisions could result from new data or other modifications deemed necessary by the monitoring function.

Once the time series model is constructed, it can be readily used in forecasting. Two types of forecasts can be generated, the "long range" forecast and periodically updated forecast. Theil's index of forecasting efficiency indicates that for the New York banks data, the continually updated forecasts perform more efficiently than the long range forecasts, as would be expected.

We chose to update every week and forecast only one week ahead, but this was not necessary. Updates do not have to be made every period. The frequency of updating is determined by the decision maker. In addition updated forecasts for many periods into the future can be obtained.

The time series modeling and forecasting procedure fits in well as a component of the dynamic financial management process. The procedure generates forecasts needed by optimization techniques, and its iterative nature is well adapted to the "feedback" and monitoring relationship in the management process.

This last feature is the most important because it facilitates communication between the management scientist and the bank executives. In model building, care is taken to include only those parameters which have a time series interpretation (weekly, monthly, quarterly, annually, etc.) and hence can be easily recognized by bank executives. The forecasting results fit into the bank executive's present framework. It gives him a long range forecast which is useful in the long range planning function that many banks have established. Also it gives him updated forecasts which could be generated monthly for budget reviews.

The results of applying the time series modeling and forecasting procedure suggest a number of issues for the management scientist to consider in developing optimization techniques. First, the time series models for the various deposit series are quite complex. Second, the forecast limits widen in a nonlinear fashion as estimates are extended farther in the future. Third, the updated forecasts prove to be more efficient than the "long range" forecasts.

Figure 14. Weekly Coefficients of the Forecasting Function of Money Supply

m	$A_0^{(m)}$	$A_1^{(m)}$	$A_2^{(m)}$
1	206.50000	1.40001	−2.60000
2	214.10001	−2.00000	−2.10000
3	208.10001	2.45000	−3.05000
4	212.90000	−4.49999	−1.30000
5	204.00000	2.55000	−3.05000
6	207.00001	.85000	−2.85000
7	208.09999	.20000	−2.60000
8	212.90000	−4.05000	−1.65000
9	206.70000	2.85001	−3.25000
10	211.70000	1.45000	−3.15000
11	210.99999	5.00001	−3.80000
12	207.70000	3.00001	−3.50000
13	201.40000	5.55000	−3.85000
14	202.30000	6.85001	−4.25000
15	202.20000	6.15001	−4.05000
16	201.00001	7.40000	−4.40000
17	193.49999	11.60001	−5.30000
18	197.20000	10.70000	−5.20000
19	200.40000	7.70000	−4.40000
20	203.90000	6.25001	−4.05000
21	206.60000	2.90001	−3.30000
22	211.80000	3.65000	−3.95000
23	214.80000	2.75000	−3.55000
24	215.90001	5.00000	−4.40000
25	209.99999	7.60001	−4.40000
26	205.89999	7.75000	−4.45000
27	208.50000	5.60001	−4.00000
28	204.60000	6.85001	−4.25000
29	206.20000	4.50000	−3.70000
30	202.60000	5.00001	−3.80000
31	208.60000	.00001	−2.80000
32	210.80000	−3.70000	−1.70000
33	206.89999	1.85001	−3.15000
34	206.70000	−2.80000	−1.70000
35	210.90000	−6.74999	−1.05000
36	207.70000	−1.20000	−2.40000
37	209.59999	−4.99999	−1.40000
38	204.10000	− .64999	−2.35000
39	205.90000	−5.34999	−1.25000
40	212.70000	−8.50000	− .70000
41	207.90001	−4.39999	−1.60000
42	206.39999	−4.69999	−1.50000
43	204.00000	−4.74999	−1.45000
44	207.00000	−6.49999	−1.30000
45	208.90000	−7.60000	− .90000
46	208.50000	−5.50000	−1.60000
47	209.70000	−8.84999	− .55000
48	210.89999	−10.39999	− .40000
49	209.89999	−5.39999	−1.90000
50	214.80000	−12.34999	− .05000
51	210.10000	−6.65000	−1.45000

Although present models are not available to deal with all the issues raised above, the two stage linear programming under uncertainty technique described by Cohen and Thore [1970] appears to be workable. The technique has two "stages." In the first stage, control variables are set and in the second stage, stochastic movements in deposits (or other parameters) occur. The time series model could serve in two capacities in this technique. First, forecasts could be examined to determine the point in time where forecast errors are too high in the bank executive's judgement. This time period could serve as the planning horizon for the optimization technique. Second, the time series model could be used to predict the stochastic movements in deposits for the second stage of the model.

Dynamic financial management is a complex problem with many facets. This paper has explored one of these facets in the hope that the problem can be handled in a more realistic context. □

REFERENCES

Aigner, D. J., and W. R. Bryan, "A model of short-run bank behavior" *Quarterly Journal of Economics*, 1971.

Box, G. E. P., and G. M. Jenkins, *Time Series Analysis, Forecasting, and Control*, San Francisco, Holden-Day, 1970.

Box, G. E. P., and D. A. Pierce, "Distribution of residual autocorrelations in autoregressive-integrated moving average time series", *Journal of the American Statistical Assoc.* 65, 1970.

Bryan, W. R., and W. T. Carleton, "Short-Run adjustments of an individual bank," *Econometrica*, April, 1967.

Chambers, D. and A. Charnes, "Intertemporal analysis and optimization of bank portfolios," *Management Science*, July, 1961.

Cohen, K. J., "Dynamic balance sheet management: A management science approach," *Journal of Bank Research*, Winter, 1972.

Cohen, K. J., and F. S. Hammer, "Linear programming and optimal bank asset management decisions," *The Journal of Finance*, May, 1967.

Cohen, Kalman J., and Sten Thore, "Programming bank portfolios under uncertainty," *Journal of Bank Research*, Spring, 1970.

Crane, D. B., and J. R. Crotty, "A two-stage forecasting model: exponential smoothing and multiple regression," *Management Science* 13. 1967.

Dewald, W. G., and G. Richard Dreese, "Bank behavior with respect to deposit variability," *The Journal of Finance*, September, 1970.

Edgeworth, F. Y., "The mathematical theory of banking," *Journal of the Royal Statistical Society*, 1888.

Fried, Joel, "Bank portfolio selection," *Journal of Financial and Quantitative Analysis*, June, 1970.

Gray, Kenneth B., Jr., "Managing the balance sheet: A mathematical approach to decision making," *Journal of Bank Research*, Spring, 1970.

Hester, D., and J. L. Pierce, "Cross-Section analysis and bank dynamics," *Journal of Political Economy*, 1968.

Holt, C. C., F. Modigliani, J. F. Muth, and H. A. Simon, *Planning Production, Inventories and Work Force*, Prentice-Hall, New Jersey, 1963.

Kane, E. J., and B. G. Malkiel, "Bank portfolio allocation, deposit variability, and the availability doctrine," *Quarterly Journal of Economics*, February, 1965.

Melnik, Arie, "Short run determinants of commercial bank investment, portfolios: An empirical analysis," *The Journal of Finance*, June 1970.

Miller, R. B., D. W. Wichern, and D. A. Hsu, "Detecting variance changes in time series models", Technical Report #284, The University of Wisconsin, Statistics Department, 1971.

Monthly Review, "A day at the trading desk: An address by Alan R. Holmes," Federal Reserve Bank of New York, October, 1970.

Monthly Review, "Interpreting the monetary indicators," Federal Reserve Bank of New York, July, 1970.

Monthly Review, "Open market operations and the monetary and credit aggregates—1971," Federal Reserve Bank of New York, April, 1972.

Muth, J. F., "Optimal properties of exponentially weighted forecasts of time series with permanent and transitory components," *Journal of the American Statistical Association* 55, 1960.

Orr, Daniel, and W. G. Mellon, "Stochastic reserve losses, and expansion of bank credit," *The American Economic Review*, September, 1961.

Pegels, C. C., "Exponential forecasting: some new variations," *Management Science* 15, 1969.

Poole, William, "Commercial bank reserve management in a stochastic model: implications for monetary policy," *The Journal of Finance*, December, 1968.

Porter, Richard C., "A model of bank portfolio selection," *Yale Economic Essays*, Fall, 1961.

Theil, H., *Applied Economic Forecasting*, Amsterdam: North-Holland Publishing Co., 1966.

Winters, P. R., "Forecasting sales by exponentially weighted moving averages," *Management Science* 6, 1960.

This research was partially supported by funds from the Wisconsin Alumni Research Foundation.

Chapter 8

FORECASTING FOR
FINANCIAL PLANNING*

By Michael R. Thomson

*This article is reprinted, with permission, from *Journal of Bank Research*,
Vol. 4, No. 3 (Autumn, 1973), pp. 225-231.

Financial planning for asset and liability management is increasingly important to banks seeking profits and competitive position. Increased reliance on purchased funds, narrowing of rate differentials and growing competition from non-bank institutions all contribute to this position. Since these financial plans are so vital to the bank, simple prudence requires that they be understood and developed in as systematic a way as possible.

A minimum of five steps can be identified in the asset and liability planning process. Briefly stated, these are: 1) Definition of the environment, 2) identification of major alternative strategies, 3) evaluation of the strategies, 4) selection of the strategy and 5) implementation. All of these steps are necessary to the smooth functioning and efficient use of the planning process and all major elements in the bank become involved in one or more of them. While removal, or the serious weakening, of any one of these elements would prevent the whole system from functioning properly, my remarks here will focus on the first of these steps. In particular, systems for developing and maintaining forecasts of the external environment will be examined. Specific comments will be directed to loan, deposit and interest rate forecasts.

The Forecasting Framework

In order to establish a reasonable forecasting system to support the planning process, the requirements of that system must be made known by the planner. At a minimum these specifications must include descriptions of the variables to be forecast and definitions of the time horizons relevant to the planning system. In the context of bank planning, the variables might include volume and cost/price information associated with major balance categories and operating processes. Forecasts of loan demand, deposit availability, interest rates and operating costs are examples of these variables that come easily to mind. The level of detail in the forecast will depend upon the purpose of the financial planning system and the time horizon(s) involved. The forecasting system described below is designed for a macro-planning process and, as such, deals with highly aggregated variables.

The problem of defining a relevant time horizon is not an easy one. If the horizon is too short, too many variables are fixed or beyond managerial control. As the horizon lengthens, not only are forecasting problems compounded, but interaction among available decision variables becomes quite complex and difficult, if not impossible, to understand and model. As with all human situations, compromise seems the best solution. In the task of bank resource allocation, the best compromise appears to involve multiple time horizons. In the short run—out to one quarter— the bank may make significant alterations in its securities and borrowed funds portfolios. At least one set of forecasts must be available to exploit opportunities and respond to shifting conditions in this time interval.

Two-year time horizons are usually sufficient to cover the next turning point in the business cycle. Cyclical variations in volumes and rates should be forecast in order to manage the bank's response in the most advantageous way. Decisions made over this time interval will reflect these cyclical conditions and may shift the allocation of resources between loans and securities as well as alter the bank's basic loan supply position.

Finally, true strategic planning, reflecting permanent shifts in asset and liability allocations, requires forecast horizons out five to ten years. Here deep-seated fundamental shifts in the economy, industry and competitive environment must be discussed and projected.

Three additional general remarks can be made about the forecasts. First, the level of detail diminishes with the length of the time horizon. At the short end, weekly or monthly forecasts are called for. For the cyclical, intermediate range horizon, quarterly forecasts are adequate. And finally, long-term forecasts can generally be made annually. The forecasting system should update each forecast at the frequency of its shortest contained time unit. Second, care should be taken

Figure 1. Commercial and Industrial Loans[1]

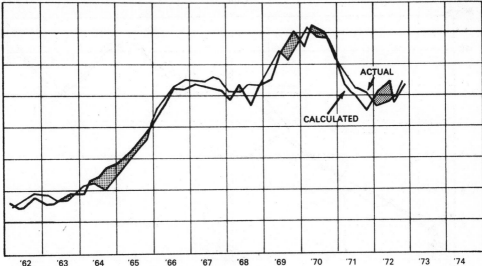

Estimating Equation:

$$C \& I \text{ Loans} = A_1 + A_2 \text{ Inventory Investment} + A_3 \text{ AAA Bond Yield}$$
$$+ A_4 \text{ Plant and Equipment Expenditures-Durable Goods}_{-1}$$
$$- A_5 \text{ Cash Flow} - A_6 \text{ Cash Flow}_{-1} - A_7 \text{ Cash Flow}_{-2}$$

[1] Seasonally adjusted average of weekly figures excluding acceptances.

to ensure that where forecasts overlap they are consistent. They will usually require that the longer forecast change to conform to the shorter one which will be based on more current information. Finally, the forecasting system must contain review procedures to ensure internal consistency among the elements of the forecast. While this may seem obvious, it is frequently neglected and impairs the integrity of the overall forecast.

In summary, the forecasting framework defines a set of variables and time horizons relevant to the planning process. Typically the variables will reflect aggregate asset and liability items, interest rates and costs associated with them. The time horizon definitions are tabulated below:

Financial Planning

Forecasting Horizons

Horizon	Period Measure	Number of Periods	Frequency of Update
Short	Month	3-12	Monthly
Intermediate	Quarter	4-8	Quarterly
Long	Year	5-10	Annually

The Forecasting Process

Bank business is highly responsive to the economic conditions prevailing in the markets they serve. Shifts in income, consumption expenditures, investment decisions, inflation expectations and government policies are quickly reflected in the balance sheet and income statement. For this reason the logical first step in the forecasting process is to begin with a projection of basic economic conditions, both nationally and regionally. Once these macro forecasts have been made, their impact upon the bank can be measured and projected. Since interest rates, with perhaps the exception of bank-administered rates (e.g., prime and savings rates), are determined in national economic markets, the determination of these forecasts should be made at this stage. Because of this, our subsequent remarks on interest rates will be limited to a few techniques which are useful in assessing the internal consistency of these forecasts.

Once the general economic forecast has been made, this information must be systematically combined with internal bank data to determine new forecasts of variables of immediate interest to the planning process. The responsiveness of bank loans, for example, to changing external condi-

Figure 2. Plant and Equipment Expenditures Durable Goods Manufacturers

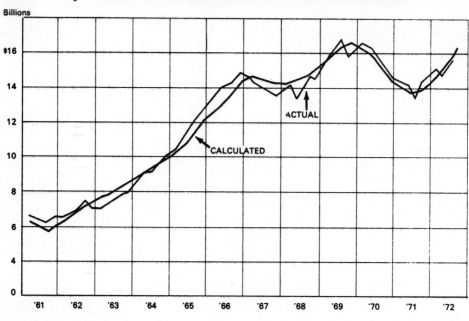

Figure 3. Change In Total Loan Volume

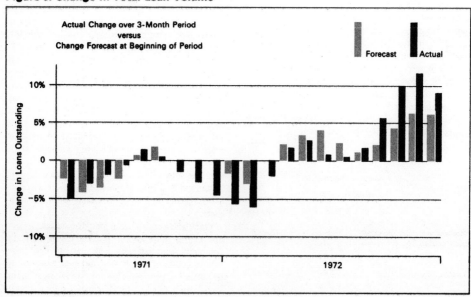

tions and internal policies must be investigated and determined. Given this determination, a consistent set of loan forecasts is relatively easy to generate and update. More fundamentally, the linking of all major variables back to the economic forecasts helps to ensure the overall integrity of the forecasting system.

In order to keep the forecasting system under control, some ongoing, routine forecast review process should be established. This effort of monitoring the discrepancies between forecasts and actual events will focus research attention on those parts of the system which appear to be in trouble. In truth, this is simply the manufacturer measuring and maintaining the quality of the product.

The forecasting process then, in theory at least, is relatively simple. For the bank three major steps are involved: 1) General economic forecasts, 2) specific bank variable forecasts and 3) quality controls. While in one sense these steps are taken sequentially, due to the dynamic nature of the problem, they are all really continuous.

Even though the link between the economy and the bank will be unique for each bank, some insights might be gained from an examination of a particular set of forecasting techniques.

Loan Demand

Loan demand is perhaps most clearly defined at the short end of the forecasting spectrum. Over the next one to three months loan volumes will respond primarily to customer desires and not bank policy shifts. Opportunities to control volumes, however, increase rapidly as the horizon stretches out to two years and major changes in market position are possible in the long run. Fortunately for the forecaster, banks rarely change policy direction in major ways; hence, loans granted can serve as an adequate proxy for loan demand. With this caveat that past supply is serving as a proxy for past demand, a forecasting system for commercial or business loans will now be described.

In general economic terms, business loans arise from the financial requirements of corporations. These requirements are basically determined by the corporate spending plans and cash flow positions. Whether or not the requirements are fulfilled by banks as opposed to other sources will depend, to some extent, upon relative prices. A model developed on this basis allows an intermediate loan forecast to be directly developed from the basic GNP forecasts. For example, the highly volatile commercial loan demand shown in

Figure 4. Money Supply¹ as Percent of Gross National Product

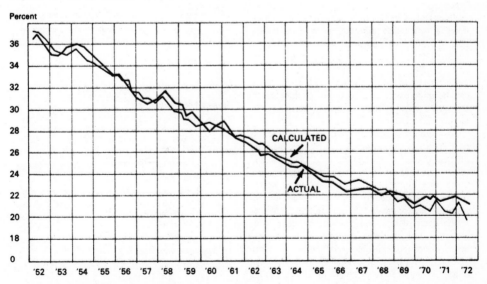

¹ Currency plus demand deposits.
Money Supply/GNP = 5.195 + .583 Percent Change, GNP Deflator
 + 38.607 Exp (–.00875 Time) – .321 Three-Month Treasury Bill Rate

Figure 1 can be "successfully" forecast in this way.[1]

Success as used here is defined by a standard error of forecast small enough to make the forecast useful to the planning process. For this particular equation, the standard error is about 2%-3% of next quarter's loan demand. Forecasts farther into the future are obviously less exact as they must contend not only with the errors of the model, but also with the errors associated with forecasts of the independent variables. Nevertheless, the model tracks cyclical swings in demand fairly well and serves as the basis for eight quarter forward forecasts of loan demand.

Because of the importance of loans and swings in loan demand, this forecast is checked for reasonableness in a couple of ways. First, independent equations forecast total commercial and industrial (C & I) loan volume at all large commercial banks. Then market-share statistics are computed to ensure that there are no unusual or abrupt changes in this measure. Second, the basic economic forecast itself is partially validated, by models of plant and equipment expenditures, the most important variable in the loan equation. Leading indicators of these expenditures include net new orders of durable goods manufacturers and capacity utilization rates in the manufacturing sector. Polynomial lag equations using these independent variables provide good results and forecast lead times of almost three quarters (see Figure 2).

Short-run estimates of loan demand are developed in somewhat different ways. Due to the normal lead time associated with loan requests, lending officers are in a unique position to forecast borrowings and repayments of their major customers up to three months out. Such forecasts can be quite acceptable in terms of their errors and given suitable operating procedures can be made on a regular weekly basis.

An alternative, quantitative procedure for short-term forecasts can be developed by utilizing data on the volume of outstanding lines of credit and other company-managed borrowing agreements. Since lines of credit and revolving credit agreements are the predominate institutional mechanism for developing and dispensing loans, changes in the levels of these agreements are useful leading indicators of loan demand. The standard errors associated with these relationships compare favorably with those generated by the direct loan officer polling process. A record of 21 consecutive

forecasts made using this technique is shown in Figure 3 based upon the equations shown in Figure 5.

All three of these independent forecasting procedures provide forecasts for one quarter out. Since the standard errors are all roughly comparable, judgment must be used in arriving at the final forecast. In exercising this judgment, care must be taken to ensure consistency with forecasts for other variables for the same quarter and with forecasts for future time periods.

With some care the cyclical (intermediate) loan forecasting equation may be used to forecast longer-term trends. Caution must be exercised here, however, since much of the loan growth of the past 10-15 years has arisen from the general decline in debt-equity ratios of corporations. If this trend slows, then so will corporate demand for borrowed money. Under these conditions estimating equations based on historical data are apt to systematically overestimate the corporate demand for loans in the coming years.

Deposit Flows

As with loan demand, different forecasting techniques are relevant to different time horizons

Figure 5. Three-Month Loan Equations

These forecasting equations are based on the following variable definitions:

L = Total domestic loans.

TCL = Total lines of credit and firm commitments.

CL = Change in loans last month to current month.

$P\text{-}CP$ = Spread between prime and commercial paper rates.

$L+1$ = Loans one month into future.

$L+2$ = Loans two months into future.

$L+3$ = Loans three months into future.

30-Day Loan Equation

$$L+1 = 38.9 + .96\,L + .02\,TCL + .60\,CL - 21.3\,(P\text{-}CP)$$
$$\quad\ (4.2)\quad(103.0)\ (3.2)\qquad(9.3)\qquad(-4.1)$$

Coefficient of Variation: 1.1%
R^2: .999
Degrees of Freedom: 125

60-Day Loan Equation

$$L+2 = 99.3 + .89\,L + .06\,TCL + .86\,CL - 52.7\,(P\text{-}CP)$$
$$\quad\ (5.1)\quad(46.9)\ (4.0)\qquad(6.4)\qquad(-4.9)$$

Coefficient of Variation: 2.2%
R^2: .994
Degrees of Freedom: 124

90-Day Loan Equation

$$L+3 = 150.5 + .83\,L + .10\,TCL + 1.09\,CL - 75.0\,(P\text{-}CP)$$
$$\quad\ (5.2)\quad(29.2)\ (4.5)\qquad(5.3)\qquad(-4.7)$$

Coefficient of Variation: 3.2%
R^2: .987
Degrees of Freedom: 123

[1] Standard regression techniques are used in developing the specific relationships between the variables. Because of the confidential nature of the data, the regression equation statistics are not reported here.

in forecasting deposit trends. In the short run, exponential smoothing provides a relatively effective technique. Relying on the high inertia associated with deposit levels and the relative stability of seasonal factors, these forecasts are quite accurate in the short run. Errors of about 1% of actual values are typical.

The intermediate forecasting of deposit levels is considerably more difficult, particularly if the impact of changes in demand deposits on profits is considered. For savings deposits, economic models relating deposits to personal income flows and the interest rates on competing instruments offer some hope of producing acceptable results. Demand deposits, on the other hand, will respond primarily to shifts in monetary policy and differences between regional and national economic growth rates. Anticipating and understanding shifts in Fed policy is not easy. Measuring the responsiveness of the bank's deposits to shifts in that policy is somewhat easier. Such relationships allow the forecaster to produce a variety of projections based upon alternative Fed actions. The final monetary policy used in the deposit forecasting process here must be consistent with the general economic forecasts and interest rate projections made earlier.

In the long run, it is more convenient to view monetary policy as endogenous to the economic system rather than exogenous. The money supply will grow at that rate dictated by changes in GNP and payment system technology. The secular trend of velocity which has been up for the past 20 years should continue. Money (M1), currently about 20% of GNP, should decline to 15% over the next ten years, if past trends continue. This trend is starkly visible in the data shown in Figure 4. In absolute terms, of course, the money supply will increase due to the strong anticipated growth in GNP. If GNP rises at an average annual rate of 7% over the decade, money supply will increase by 50% over the current level. Since currency maintains a fairly stable relationship to GNP, this forecast allows for long-run demand deposit growth of only 3%-4% per year on a national basis, a rather bleak outlook when compared to the forecasts of loan demand.

Interest Rates

As stated earlier, comments in this section will be limited to techniques which can be used to ensure consistency among rate forecasts. This consistency is extremely important when many later decisions will depend upon relative cost or profitability calculations. The desired end effect can perhaps most easily be achieved by reducing

the number of interest rates actually forecast to a minimum. The forecaster can then rely on historical relationships between rates on alternative instruments and differing maturities to produce the rest of the desired forecasts. The approach here is a fairly obvious one and the actual form used is somewhat a matter of taste. The equation shown in Figure 6 can be used, for example, to establish bounds on municipal bond yield term structures. Equations with similar characteristics will also work for U.S. Treasury securities.

As most money market instruments are close substitutes on both the demand and supply side, their rates should, and do, move in harmony. If this were not the case, then the concept of the "floating" prime rate would never have been possible. Admittedly, the rates in this market at the present time bear no resemblance to their former selves.[2] However, political intervention has always, in the short run, been able to distort markets and frustrate their economic function. Since the current rate relationships cannot persist in a meaningful way without creating serious problems for

Figure 6. Municipal Bond Interest Yields Term Structure Relationships

$$R(M) = -.36 + 1.1\,R(1) + .39\log M - 3.1\,D_2$$
$$ (-8.81)^* \quad (89.5) \quad\;\; (40.3) \qquad (-6.5)$$
$$ -6.5\,D_5 - 10.0\,D_{10}$$
$$ (-13.5) \quad\; (-20.6)$$

$R^2 = .965$ Degrees of Freedom = 404
Standard Error = 0.17

Variable Definitions

$R(M)$	AAA Municipal Bond yield of maturity M.
M	Years to maturity of bond. Has values 2, 5, 10.
D_i	Smoothing variable related to changes in the one-year rate, $R(1)$. It is a dummy variable with the subscript indicating the appropriate coefficient for each maturity.

Equation was estimated using monthly observations from June 1964 through December 1972.

*Numbers in parentheses are *t*-statistics associated with the parameter.

the banking industry and the general economy, one must expect to see a gradual return to normal conditions over the next few quarters. In the interim, unfortunately, forecasting these rates will be very difficult indeed.

It might well be appropriate to interject a word of caution at this point about the use of the quantitative techniques in general. As the prime rate problem amply illustrates, there will always

[2] Spring 1972. Subsequent events have tended to validate the assertions made here.

be short-run events of a nonquantifiable or non-repetitive nature. Since these cannot be incorporated into studies of past rate or volume relationships, they will not be a part of any purely quantitative forecast. It becomes the responsibility of the forecaster then to understand these conditions and to make the necessary modifications to the forecasts. Pure equations in other words will almost always produce forecasts inferior to those produced by a competent individual using the equations as one of the many inputs.

Summary

The forecasting system and techniques which have been discussed here are not in any way unique. Nor are they in most instances highly sophisticated. Their chief value is that they establish a set of routine operating procedures which work. The system produces timely, consistent, appropriate, and controllable forecasts. With this base of information, the rest of the planning process may proceed to completion.   □

Chapter 9

A MODEL TO FORECAST A BANK'S DAILY NET CLEARING HOUSE LIABILITY*

By Raymond V. Balzano

*This article is reprinted, with permission, from *Journal of Bank Research*, Vol. 6, No. 3 (Autumn, 1975), pp. 228-231.

As the federal funds rate remains at high levels, it is even more imperative that banks strive to maintain a zero surplus in their Federal Reserve account. The degree to which this account is closely maintained depends on the bank's size and the activity of the account. Small banks with low account activity will only keep a rough estimate of their exact reserve position. While being certain to maintain the legally required minimum, the cost of carefully minimizing surpluses will outweigh the benefits gained. Large banks with high activity can ill-afford a high surplus cash position, especially with the recent high federal funds rate. For example, an average daily surplus of only $1 million would have added over $100,000 to a bank's interest expense in 1974.

To help solve this problem, larger banks have set up cash desks that are responsible for maintaining the bank's Federal Reserve account at the minimum required level. This is accomplished by either buying or selling federal funds during the day as transactions draw money from or deposit money into the bank's Federal Reserve account. While it is true that the required reserve position only has to balance on settlement day, the cash desk does not want to take the chance of getting caught on settlement day with a large surplus or deficit because of the wide variation in rates on that day. The market is very unpredictable on settlement day and the rates have varied from less than 1% to more than 20%. Therefore, the cash desk will attempt to hold the surplus cash position down to zero each day. This assumes that the cash desk's responsibility is only to maintain the minimum required level and does not attempt to play the market. The situation where the cash desk also plays the market will be addressed at the end of this article.

The Problem

One problem area for the cash desk is the bank's daily net clearing house liability, which will be referred to as net clearings. Net clearings is the difference between the checks Bank A receives that are drawn on other banks and the checks that the other banks receive that are drawn on Bank A. Each day the bank sends the checks it has received that are drawn on other banks to the clearing house. The clearing house then determines each bank's net position and either draws that amount from the bank's Federal Reserve account if the net position is negative, or deposits that amount in the bank's account if the net position is positive. The daily net clearings figure for many banks is a very large percentage of its Federal Reserve account. The problem arises because the banks do not receive the daily net clearings figure until the early afternoon. Due to both the size of the figure and its late arrival, it is difficult to accurately project the bank's final cash position until late in the day, unless one uses some method of forecasting the net clearings.

The Benefits

The benefits that any forecasting model can provide depend on its accuracy and the previous system used. The ability of any forecasting to produce reliable, accurate results is essential. The most unsophisticated forecasting model is blind guessing, which anyone is capable of doing. Blind guessing assumes no knowledge and anyone that relies on it probably will not be in business for long. The next step up the forecasting ladder is educated guessing, which claims a great number of practitioners, some of whom are very successful. Educated guessing can provide an acceptable degree of accuracy, but to do so often involves an extended period of "education" which can be very costly. More sophisticated modelling techniques attempt to provide quick and accurate forecasts while eliminating most of the "education" process. The test of any forecasting method is the ability to predict more accurately than any other devised method.

The benefit that arises from a model to forecast the daily net clearings is in its ability to reduce the uncertainty by providing the bank's cash desk with the best information available as early in the day as possible. Armed with a projection of what this substantial figure will be, the cash desk is better able to plan its position throughout the day, with a reduced danger of having to drastically alter its plan late in the day. It is especially beneficial on settlement day because it reduces the risk of getting caught late in the day with a large surplus or deficit when the cash desk must accept any market rate it can get.

The Model

A multiseasonal model[1] was developed to forecast net clearings. Two very pronounced seasonal patterns are present in the data. The primary pattern is the day of the week. The weekend creates a backlog of clearings and the Monday figure is always very high. Tuesday falls

[1]The model utilized exponential smoothing

Figure 1

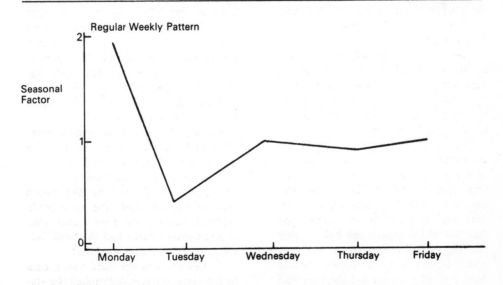

101

off substantially from Monday and is the lowest day of the week. The final three days vary only slightly and are average days. Figure 1 illustrates this weekly pattern.

The daily pattern is complicated by the numerous Monday holidays, which in effect create a three day weekend. The three day weekend intensifies the normal pattern and shifts it back one day. Thus Tuesdays are extremely high, Wednesdays are very low and Thursdays and Fridays average. Figure 2 illustrates the Monday holiday weekly pattern. This Monday holiday pattern causes two problems in developing this type of model. When calculating the day of the week averages to get the initial seasonal factors, the Tuesday and Wednesday averages will reflect both patterns together, and neither pattern separately. This can be overcome by calculating a regular week Tuesday and Wednesday average. The second problem arises when trying to recalculate the seasonal factors during a Monday holiday week. First it was treated as two seasonal patterns. This proved to be inaccurate because regardless of the order the calculations are made, the first will bias the second. The solution to this problem is to view the two patterns not as two different seasonal patterns, but as two variations of the same pattern. Therefore, the smoothing model developed has two loops, one for the regular weekly pattern and one for the Monday holiday weekly pattern.

The secondary pattern is the day of the month (see Figure 3). After the day of the week pattern is removed, a pattern exists throughout the month. The day of the month pattern peaks on the 16th and are generally above unity the last half of the month and below unity the first half of the month. It was generally felt that the monthly pattern would have a small peak around the 10th due to the amount of billing which permits discounts for bills paid on or before that date. To arrive at the initial factors, the seasonal patterns were removed in several different orders. At no time did this peak around the 10th occur.

One word of caution must be given. The patterns in net clearings data have two components. One is the institution of the clearing house and how it operates. This can be considered constant and causing similar patterns for all banks. The second component is the individual bank. Such characteristics as its size, market sphere and percentage of local market could cause changes in the basic pattern. The patterns presented here should not be considered industry norms in any sense; they are only the patterns observed in one set of data. Each set of data must be carefully studied to discover its own patterns.

Three years of daily data were available when the model was developed. The first two years of data were used to calculate the initial patterns. The next step was to choose an objective function and to find the set of parameters that would optimize the function. The objective function must be one that the user agrees is a fair representation of what is expected from the system. In this case the objective function was to minimize the mean absolute deviation (MAD). A secondary statistic used was the algebraic sum of the errors, which gave the forecasts bias.

Finding the best parameters is complicated by the size of the model. The normal procedure is as follows:

1) Pick a set of parameters.

2) Go through the first two year's data and update daily the appropriate seasonal factors, the base factor (the average daily figure) and the trend factor (the average daily increase).

3) Go through the third year's data in the same manner and collect the sta-

Figure 2

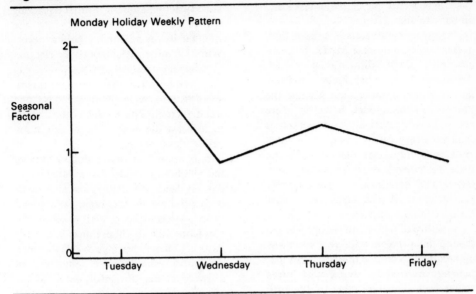

Monday Holiday Weekly Pattern

Figure 3

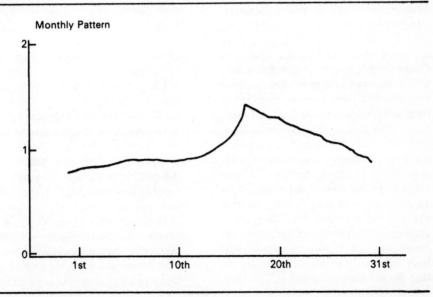

Monthly Pattern

tistics necessary to judge the system.

4) Pick a new set of parameters and go back to step 2.

The set of parameters is chosen that, in this model, minimize MAD. In a single loop, single dimensional model, there are only three parameters, and one large simulation run can quickly find the best set. In this model, however, there are five parameters and the computer time necessary can become prohibitive, even on a very large machine. Testing three parameters over ten values each takes 1,000 iterations, while testing five parameters over the same ten values takes 100,000 iterations.

An approximation can be used to get around this problem with very little loss of accuracy. Varying the first four parameters over wide ranges with three values each, find the value of the fifth parameter that minimizes MAD. By running a number of simulations, with three values of the fifth parameter in each, over a narrowing range, the best value of the fifth parameter can be found rapidly. Then fix the value of the fifth parameter and repeat the process for the other four. After values have been fixed for each of the five parameters, pick two of them and vary these again over 20 values each, centered around the value determined of the first pass. Continue this process until the values of the parameters that minimize MAD are fairly stable on successive runs. While there is a danger of finding a local minimum rather than a global minimum, each time this method was compared with a brute force massive simulation, the results were remarkably similar.

Once the parameters are chosen, it is an easy matter to build a program that the user can run each day. The parameters are built into the program and the initial seasonal factors along with the base and trend factors are in a data file that the program accesses.

The user first enters the last prediction and the actual amount for that day along with the day of the week, date and whether it was a Monday holiday week. With this information about the last prediction and its accuracy, the model can then update all of the appropriate seasonal factors as well as the base and trend factors. The model is then ready to forecast the next day's, or any number of days' net clearings.

It is important that a daily exponential smoothing model be updated every day. It feeds on daily data and needs it to preserve its accuracy. Occasionally an odd occurrence, such as some mishap at the clearing house, may cause one day's actual net clearings to be abnormal. The model should have some way of communicating this information to the program so the misleading information does not affect future forecasts. This can be accomplished by entering a special code number instead of that day's actual net clearings.

The Results

The model has been used daily for over nine months. One statistic that has been kept to judge the forecast's accuracy is the mean absolute deviation as a percent of the average net clearings. Figure 4 lists these results.

Unfortunately no comparable data was available against which the accuracy of the model could be judged. The previous system used in this instance was one of educated guessing. The person in charge of the cash desk had performed this job for a number of years and no records had been kept of the daily net clearings estimate.

However, after a couple of months of running the model, the person that had previously been estimating the net clearings figure had built up enough confidence in its accuracy to begin relying on

Figure 4

Month	Mad/Average Net Clearings %
February	13.98%
March	13.41%
April	8.78%
May	13.93%
June	10.33%
July	10.51%
August	13.48%
September	9.41%
October	10.72%

the model. It was felt that the model provided more consistently reliable information than was previously available. While many different statistics can be used to show accuracy, user acceptance determines whether a model will be employed, and this model has been successfully implemented.

Playing the Market

Throughout the development of this model it was assumed that the cash desk's responsibility was only to maintain the minimum required level of reserves and not to play the market. Since only the banks' average amount in its Federal Reserve account over a one week period must meet the required reserve level, the cash desk can play the market by buying excess funds on days when it feels the rates are low and by carrying less than the required amount of reserves on days when it feels the rates are high.

To be successful at such an operation requires two pieces of information—a rate forecast and a volume forecast. While daily rate forecasts are beyond the scope of this paper, the model does provide daily volume forecasts of one of the major components of total volume. On the first day of the reserve calculation week, the cash desk can obtain an estimate of each day's net clearings. This gives the cash desk a better idea of the total flow of funds into or out of the reserve account for the week. The total required reserve amount for the week is already known. Based on the rate forecast, the cash desk can then formulate a federal funds investment policy for the week. As each day's actual net clearings figure comes in, the model can be updated, a new forecast made for the remainder of the week and any necessary adjustments in the investment policy made.

Conclusion

Even though the daily actual net clearings figure's late arrival and wide variations cause problems for the cash desk, its patterned nature makes it amenable to time series forecasting. Such a time series forecasting model that utilizes these patterns has been developed and has provided results that were acceptable to the user group. This model can also be used if the function of the cash desk is expanded to include playing the market. □

Chapter 10

COMPUTER MODELS: AIDS TO MANAGEMENT AT SOCIETE GENERALE DE BANQUE*

By Leon Derwa

*This article is reprinted, with permission, from *Journal of Bank Research,* Vol. 3, No. 2 (Summer, 1972), pp. 84-94.

The use of computer models to improve management decision making in banks has proceeded with somewhat mixed results in many institutions. This paper will present the experience of Societe Generale de Banque in developing models that contribute to the decision making process. It should be noted that the discussion will be limited to those models that have given good results and are currently operating at Societe Generale de Banque.

First, a brief distinction between two mathematical management methods: Econometrics and operations research. Econometrics is a collection of mathematical techniques which make it possible to state the forms and values of relationships between economic variables. So far as possible, economic theory has to provide a working hypothesis, suggesting the variables to be considered and the form the functions should take. There is, however, the danger that the calculated relationships may be chance phenomena, so that a model that appears significant today and passes the statistical tests, provides no more than a distorted image of reality when it is applied tomorrow. It is therefore necessary to produce econometric models that can be easily modified. Models 1 and 2, described later in this paper, are econometric models.

Operations research, as opposed to econometrics, is normative in the sense that it seeks to obtain an optimum with respect to a given criterion. It has to be remembered that we are thinking entirely in terms of an optimum related to the description of the problem and to the criterion chosen. This is illustrated by models 3, 4, 5 and 6 which discuss certain operations research models constructed by SGB.

Frequently the first venture in mathematical economics in a firm is an attempt to develop an overall model for the entire company. The effort is usually unsuccessful because of the complexity of the task, which leads to much discouragement, and because it takes too long to obtain positive results. The approach at SGB was somewhat different. The first steps were directed toward models of limited application that can be made operational within a reasonable time period, but each is considered with an eye to the eventual overall model. The different models thus are considered as pieces of a jig-saw puzzle which, when ultimately joined together, will create the general model. Models 7 and 8 show how SGB is progressing on the road to the general model.

Finally, there is a summary of our experience and a statement of the philosophy of SGB regarding the general management model for a firm.

Deposit and Credit Forecasting Model

In banking, deposits constitute the raw material of the industry. Thus, it is especially important to forecast the manner and extent of deposit expansion so that any *anomaly* in their growth can be identified at the earliest possible moment. The principle followed is to distinguish between the permanent component of the time series—also known as the "cycle + trend"—and the seasonal and accidental variations.

First, the seasonal variations are removed from the time series by the Winters formula. Next, the values of the variables are estimated by the stochastic method of Theil and Wage. This is a form of exponential smoothing, in which the smoothing coefficients are such as to give a minimum value to the sum of the squares of the forecasting errors. Using the smoothing coefficients, it is possible to estimate the values of the series for a given number of periods by reference to the last available observation. This method applied to deposits makes it possible to forecast the figure for several months in advance, with an error factor of less than 1% (see Figure 1). Knowledge of the seasonal coefficients makes it possible to calculate the most probable course for the target deposit figure. A calculated confidence interval above and below the course figure, indicates the probability of reaching the target by reference to the volume of deposits already brought in (see Figure 2).

In processing the data, the model is handled on the 8K IBM 1130. The computer is assisted by a Benson Plotter. The system is fully integrated.

Past observations are retained on the disk, comprising the amount of each of the different types of deposit at different branches. The information given each month consists only of the last observation available for each series, thus limiting the risk of error and the need for additional checking. The program calculates the forecasts and automatically draws the graph embodying the results. It is also possible, on request, to draw the graph representing any specific series.

The credit forecasting model has just started operating in the bank. At present, it is working only for the bank as a whole and not for each branch as is the case with the deposit model. The credit forecasting model is based on techniques similar to those utilized for the deposit forecasting model.

Rates of Interest[1]

Another important element in the management of a bank is an understanding of the mechanism by which interest rates are determined and, if possible, the ability to forecast these rates. The explanatory variables used in this model are of two types: Conjunctural (i.e. estimated volume of order books; steel production; and similar series) and monetary (velocity of circulation of sight deposits; increases in the supply of money; difference in rates for the dollar in the free and official markets; etc.).

The conjunctural variables are strongly correlated, and cannot be introduced as they presently exist into a multiple regression model. In order to avoid the multicollinear effect, they are dealt with by factor analysis, and the first principal component is used as the general conjuncture index. The next item calculated is the time lag between the rate of interest and the explanatory variable (i.e. the conjunctural index and the monetary variables) which gives the best correlation. For variables for which there is no time lag, the future values are calculated by the model shown in Figure 1.

A step-wise regression, taking into account the optimum time lags and the smoothed values, makes it possible to estimate future values of interest rates. The wisdom of the choice of variables is confirmed by the fact that the step-wise procedure brings in all the series used in the explanatory model.

1 This factor analysis, step-wise regression model has been developed in a publication by the Study Department of Societe Generale de Banque, *Interest Rates in Belgium: Contribution to an Econometric Study*.

Figure 1.

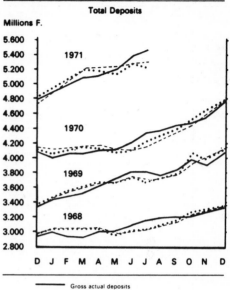

Total Deposits

Millions F.

- Gross actual deposits
- Deseasonalized actual deposits
- Deseasonalized and smoothened actual deposits

Financial Engineering[2]

Sigma is a linear programming financial engineering model. The model is designed to solve the following problem: A firm has decided upon an investment plan, and the question is how to finance the investment most advantageously for the company, taking into consideration the various legal and financial constraints involved. The solution is of interest to the financial management of firms, whether they be industrial firms or banks. It is also useful for the lending officer, who is better able to appraise the health of a company when it applies for credit.

The few financial engineering models that are operational are simulation models. Sigma, on the other hand, is also an optimization model that checks in advance the compatibility of the assumptions regarding the firm's growth.

From the mathematical standpoint, Sigma is based on linear programming. From the financial standpoint, Sigma uses the theory of opportunity costs. The objective function to be minimized is the sum of the finance sources weighted in terms of the opportunity costs. A unique feature of the system is that the equations of the linear model are introduced as data. This makes it possible for

2 The Sigma model has been developed in a publication by Societe Generale de Banque, *Sigma has been designed for you.*

Figure 2.

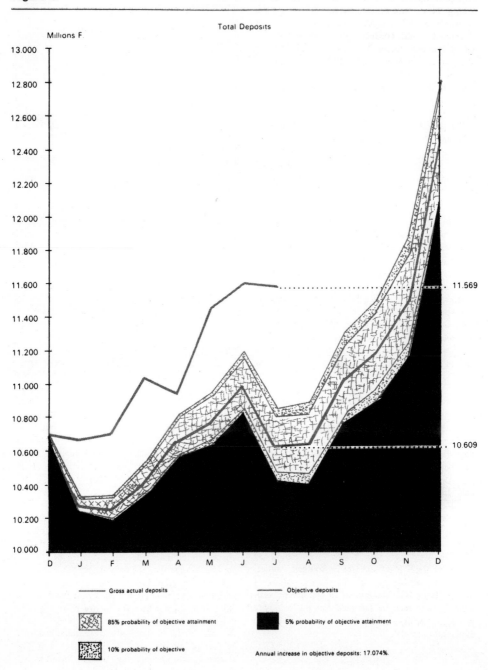

Total Deposits

Millions F.

- Gross actual deposits
- Objective deposits
- 85% probability of objective attainment
- 5% probability of objective attainment
- 10% probability of objective
- Annual increase in objective deposits: 17.074%.

Figure 3.

July 1971

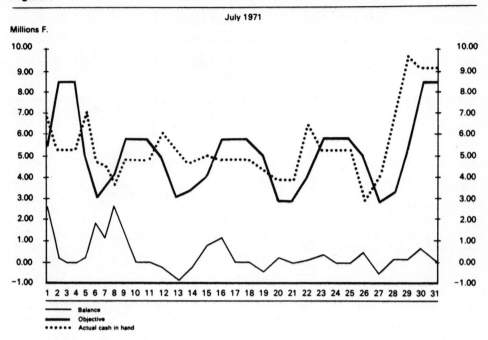

Millions F.

- Balance
- Objective
- • • • • • Actual cash in hand

the analysts to describe, in detail, the financial structure and policy of the firms to be studied.

Sigma is a pluri-annual model. Beginning with the equations for the first year, through the constants brought in for ensuing years, the complete model input is generated in MPS form. Various MPS programs make it possible to modify and process this collection of data. Using the MPS Report Generator, it is possible to print the results in the familiar form of balance sheets, profit and loss statements and financial tables.

Sigma also makes it possible to test the coherence of the component items of the firm's finance policy and, if there is any incompatibility, to indicate the causes. Provided the policy is practicable, Sigma gives a projection of the future balance sheet and profit and loss accounts of the firm, assuming it carries out the optimum financing policy. The model also facilitates a study of the degree to which the recommended solution may be affected by variations in the constants of the system, such as the cost of resources, the amounts to be invested and similar items. The analysts thus have the necessary elements for a detailed exposition of the consequences ensuing from any modification in the financial policy or in the initial assumptions.

Cash Balances

Cash balances held in branches of the bank represent a sizable amount of unproductive capital. It is in the interest of the bank to reduce such amounts to as low a level as is practical and possible. The problem is part of the general class of stock problem. The question is one of determining the amounts to be delivered and the delivery dates that will minimize the total cost, which is the weighted sum of the costs of storage, supply and shortage.

There is no way of knowing with any high degree of certainty how much in cash balances a bank branch will need. The following facts have, however, been ascertained:

The cash requirements follow a symmetrical distribution. In conformity with statistical tests, fitting the normal curve is acceptable.

The parameters of this distribution vary from one branch to another, and, for any individual branch, between one day of the week and another.

Under the normal assumptions, if a branch holds at the beginning of a period a sum which covers the average plus twice the standard difference for the period, the probability of shortage is extremely small. This makes it possible to calculate the amount to be delivered; the difference

Figure 4. Simulation Plan for Societe Generale de Banque

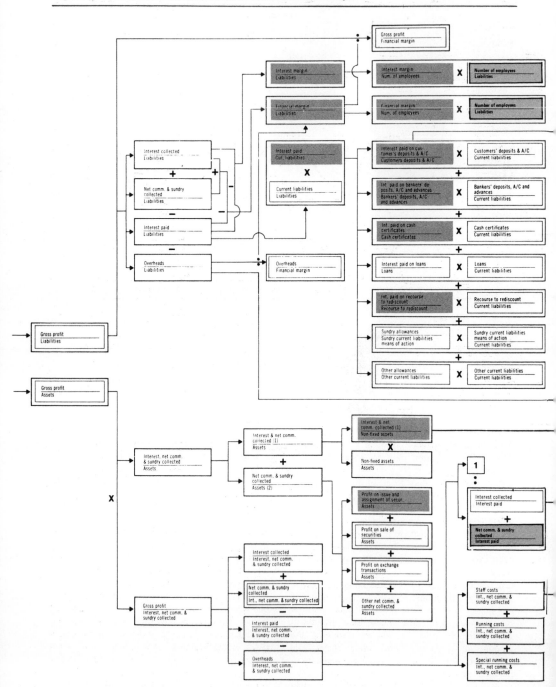

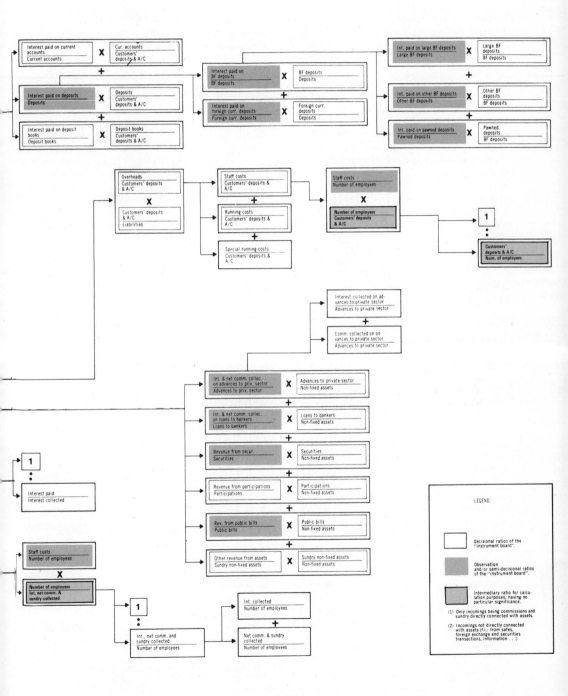

between the above theoretical amount and the funds still available. The resulting figure may be positive or negative, indicating whether funds should ·be supplied or withdrawn. The model is required to calculate not only the amounts to be delivered but also the frequency of supply. After calculating all possible transport policies for the week, the one chosen is that showing the smallest total cost.

In order to make the model more realistic, a number of other factors are taken into account. Among these are the denominations of notes and the shorting for bundling, the number of counter positions per branch and such factors as end-of-month or quarterly settlements. The validity of the method was tested by simulation. It was found that through use of the model it was possible to reduce the cash holdings by more than 40% without increasing risk of shortage. There are various calculated ratios produced by which performance is measured and the various branch offices compared.

The system was tested on the 1130, and when the experience was considered satisfactory, application was transferred to the 360. The 1130 is still used each month to draw the control graphs (Figure 3).

Portfolio Management Model

The object of security portfolio management is to obtain a sufficient return without undue risk. In order to maintain the total return from a portfolio, its composition must be limited to those securities on which the return is highest. In most cases, however, the movements in the prices of these securities are strongly correlated, so that the risk in such a portfolio is high. Other things being equal, a higher degree of diversification tends to decrease the risk.

This portfolio management model is a Markowitz quadratic programming model. The Markowitz model determines the mix of issues comprising the so-called "efficient" portfolios. Efficient portfolios, of course, refer to those portfolios which, for a given return, comprise the smallest degree of risk. The components of the return are the changes in prices and in the dividend or interest income received. The components of the risk are the uncertainty of forecasting relating to each security (measured by the variance) and the high or low degree of co-variation of the securities among themselves.

From a mathematical standpoint, minimizing the risk and therefore the total variance of the portfolio is a problem of quadratic programming.

Since the aim of the model is to calculate the whole boundary line of efficient portfolios, the Markowitz algorithm is a parametric quadratic program. The input of a Markowitz program is extremely heavy. The variance-co-variance matrix between all the shares used in its composition is time consuming to set up.

The program input is of the "Sharpe" variety. The future values of the shares are estimated in the form of a linear relationship with one or more financial indices that may be linked with one another. The correlation matrix is estimated from these relationships, but the possibility exists to feed into the program correlations that have been explicitly calculated elsewhere. The program makes it possible for securities to be classed in groups with an indication of the maximum amount per group and per security. In addition, many types of constraints or limitations are accepted, provided they are linear.

The program output is of a two-fold nature. First, it provides a list of efficient portfolios for each return specified in the program, indicating the risk and the percentage composition. Secondly, for each iteration, a series of technical data can be obtained, making it possible to follow the development of the algorithm. A particular result of these data is the possibility of calculating the dual cost of each constraint, so that the manager in charge can see how much it costs him to depart from the optimum by adding to the problem the task of satisfying any specific condition. In our view, these data are the most useful. They supply indications, expressed in terms of budgetary cost, of the relationship to the policy followed in the management of the portfolio.

Using the Sharpe method requires forecasting the evolution of the general indices of the stock exchanges. At present, Societe Generale de Banque possesses a model for the Brussels Stock Exchange[3]. Thus, the model can already calculate optimum Belgian portfolios. At present, data are being gathered on the Paris, Frankfurt, Amsterdam, London and New York Stock Exchanges. These data will make it possible to construct forecasting models for those exchanges. These models, in turn, will enable the bank to utilize the portfolio optimization method for the French, German, Dutch, British and American securities.

Arbitrage Model

The arbitrage service in a bank is involved in trading of foreign currencies. If foreign exchange

---

[3] The model will be described in a forthcoming publication by Societe Generale de Banque.

Figure 5. First Essay at Constructing an All-Over Model at Societe Generale de Banque

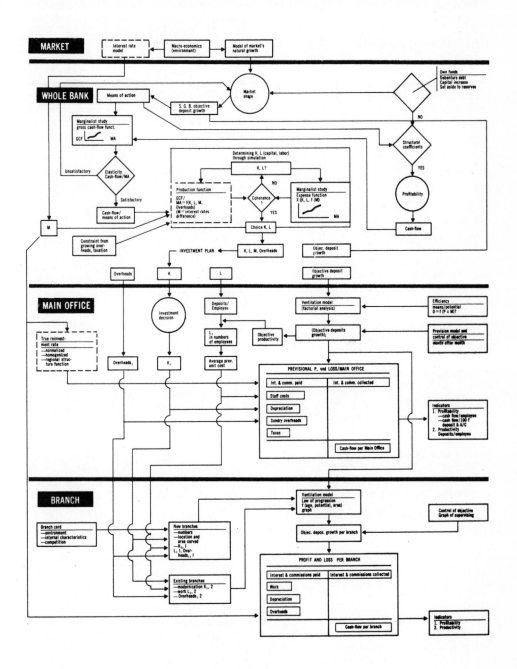

markets were perfect, the price of a given currency would be identical in all countries. In practice, however, information is not available instantaneously, and there are a number of distorting factors which create price differences. The purpose of arbitrage is to take advantage of the small differences in price that exist, while at the same time, contributing to the levelling of markets. The great number of data items and their combinations, and the frequent price variations, indicate the advantage of using a computer.

The purpose of this dynamic programming model is to take account of the data available and indicate in each case the best way of carrying out an arbitrage operation—by sale or purchase, or by borrowing or lending foreign currencies. The model also deals with indirect ways of carrying out a given operation. For example, a sale of Sterling against Deutsche Marks may, under certain circumstances, be carried out most advantageously through the French Franc.

The model also makes it possible to identify cycles, i.e. to exchange one currency for another, convert it into a third currency, and so on, so that the trader eventually returns with a profit in the currency from which the activity started. The imperfections of the market are such that cycles of this type are often available.

The repeated calculation of all the combinations is avoided by using a dynamic programming algorithm. It thus makes it possible to calculate only the simplest optimal paths and to combine them in a complex cycle procedure. Each of the 16 arbitrage operators at the bank has a display unit, which is useful for interrogating the model.

Profit & Loss Simulation

The profit and loss account simulation model is the closest analytical representation of the bank in its economic and commercial environment. It is based on existing accounting diagrams which it sets out in the form of ratios, comparing in pairs the various items in the balance sheet and profit and loss accounts.

The system facilitates a quick determination of the results that may flow from a policy decision by management, or from external changes, such as business conditions, monetary policy or wage settlements. It provides a projection of the balance sheet, profit and loss accounts and cash flow, resulting from each set of assumptions, or from a change in any of the established data. The system can be used for short-term purposes in management and budgetary forecasting. It also helps in the periodic appraisal of target attainment, and in

the diagnosis of the causes of discrepancies between target and achievement. On the longer term the model makes it possible to study the consequences of various policies and medium-term strategies in the light of possible changes in external conditions.

From the technical point of view, the model is conceived as a form of decision tree (see Figure 4) which makes it possible to proceed step by step and examine the chief factors converging on the essential objectives of the bank. It is thus possible to trace the chain reaction to a change in one of the ratios for a district head office of the bank, whether the change is deliberate (as a voluntary act of management) or involuntary (resulting from economic or commercial conditions). The consequences of such a decision influence the achievement of the targets of the district office concerned, and ultimately the situation of the bank itself.

Management Information System

In running any firm, two different levels of activity can be identified: The conduct of current operations, and medium- and long-term administration. It is the second level—establishing objectives, resource allocation and control—that constitutes management.

At the operational level, decisions can usually be programmed and the necessary data are easier to determine. This is why computers are primarily used at the operational level. The management information system, or MIS, is involved with attempts to use the computer to facilitate and systemize the work of the senior management in business firms. The further we move away from the operational level, the more difficult it is to draw up systematic rules for decision-making. The questions that must be taken into account are always more numerous and the direct or indirect consequences of decisions are more difficult to forecast.

Establishing an MIS therefore presupposes: 1) Setting up a basis of important data that faithfully represents the firm in its economic, competitive and commercial backgrounds, and 2) establishing a model for the firm, facilitating decision-making at each level and showing the consequences of possible policy decisions of management or changes in the environment.

Societe Generale is undertaking this two-fold effort in building its MIS. At the model level, profit and loss account simulation seems to be a promising approach. The application of a model of the Sigma type, or better yet, a more general model of convex programming, will normally be the next stage. The constitution of the basic data is already at an advanced stage. It will include file information describing the economic environment (chronological series, input-output matrices); competition (a series of bank balance sheets); companies (customers or non-customers); marketing data; the structure of the bank (personnel and building files), and the essential data contained in the operational files.

As was noted, Figure 5 shows the philosophy of the bank regarding the general management model through a chart of the main elements of a simulation plan for Societe Generale de Banque as a whole.

One final word in conclusion: The psychological problems raised by introducing models into management are much more difficult to solve than the technical ones connected with mathematics or data processing.   □

Chapter 11

SIMULATION AT BANQUE DE BRUXELLES*

By Marc H. Royer

*This article is reprinted, with permission, from *Journal of Bank Research*, Vol. 5, No. 4 (Winter, 1975), pp. 237-245.

The computer has become an indispensable tool for banks, and can be particularly useful in the planning process of an enterprise. It is the aim of this paper to show how the Banque de Bruxelles,[1] through simulation and with the aid of a computer, has been able to assess the impact of external economic circumstances and bank policy decisions on its net profit.

The objective of simulation is to determine one or several values for a variable named "dependent" given several values of "independent" variables. Simulation enables one to answer the question "what if . . ." and to see the impact of the assumptions on the dependent variable. The design of a simulation plan has a twofold advantage —it gathers together all the elements of a problem, and it requires a close analysis of the problem [Charlent, 1965, pp. 657-664]. In fact, the plan often clears up a subconscious intellectual approach. Simulation normally involves large amounts of computations; hence it would generally be impractical were it not for the availability of high-speed computers.

Simulation of Net Profit at Banque de Bruxelles

The elements affecting a bank's profit are numerous. It would be impossible (and certainly irrelevant) to inventory all accounts and sub-accounts which can exert an influence on that profit. Thus, when devising a simulation plan, one is obliged to "stop" somewhere. The stopping point often is determined by the degree of significance of the data as far as control (drawing a distinction between data that can be "manipulated" and that which cannot[2]) and availability are concerned.

Technically, the simulation plan appears as a decision tree which recalls the classical Dupont ROI Chart [Derwa, 1972, p. 94]. Figure 1 shows that the plan is essentially composed of ratios— rates of interest and proportions. In fact, the simulation plan, as it appears, is a breakdown—in form of ratios—of the profit and loss statement of the bank; it details, up to the point mentioned above, all operating revenues and expenses. The plan has to be read from right to left. The arrows indicate the flow of the computations and such flows allow for the assessment of the cumulative effects of changing any ratio in the simulation plan. (This can be seen more specifically on Figure 2 where the account "interests collected" has been isolated.) By means of simple mathematical relations, the dependent variable (net profit) has been linked with the independent variables. There are no unusual or intriguing aspects about the computational procedures and equations. The plan is, in effect, a mathematical translation of an accounting structure.

The input factors (which will be discussed later) are considered to be known or at least estimated in advance. Ideally, it would be interesting to have those inputs with their probability distribution, and build a probabilistic model. Practically, this last approach has to be abandoned because these distributions are not known. What we can determine, however, are the inputs with their error percentages (one could determine, for instance, the interest rate on time deposits with an error of, say, 5%). The simulation plan offers this possibility. The inputs can be introduced with their estimated error percentage and the model automatically computes the effects of those errors on the output, according to known rules of error propagation.

As far as computer programming is concerned, the plan has been split into several modules, easier to write and to check.[3] Then they are merged into a global simulation plan. (This does not mean that it is impossible to "work" on an individual module. The program has enough flexibility to sort out each of these modules). The program has been

---

[1] Banque de Bruxelles is Belgian's second largest bank with over $5.0 billion in deposits and 1,000 branches.

[2] Those which cannot be manipulated are called "exogeneous" variables. They are generally imposed by the market (interest rates, loans etc) or by the Authorities (devaluations, regulations, etc.)

[3] The modules are: Interest collected, interest paid, miscellaneous profits, overhead expenses and depreciation.

Figure 1. Simulation Plan

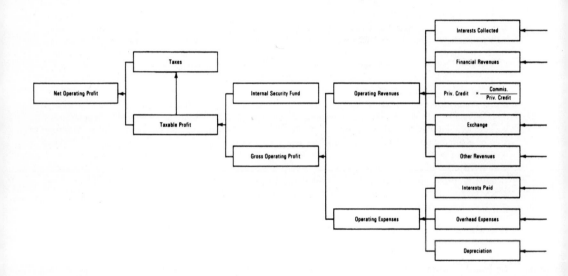

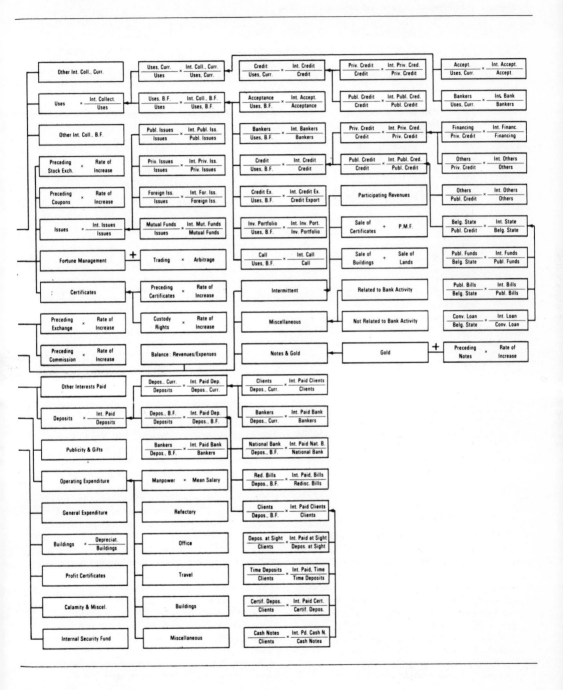

Figure 2. Interests Collected Module

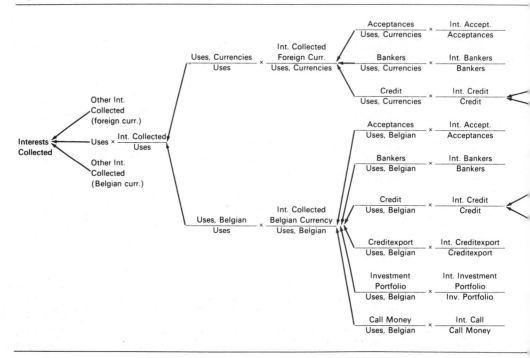

written in BASIC, a language that allows for the use of time-sharing. It is completely conversational; the computer asks questions about input and output mode, error calculations, etc. and the user has only to answer those questions. The simulation model can thus be utilized by persons not familiar with computers and computer programming.

Example of Utilization

The first task in order to use the simulation plan is to determine the parameters to be fed into the program. This can be done in two ways. First, we may evaluate directly those different inputs. They can be introduced in two forms—a percentage (ratio) and/or raw data; the program then computes the corresponding percentages. It would be redundant to give a complete list of all the inputs used. Let us simply show those needed, say, for the "interest collected" module. This is done in Figure 3 which should be viewed with Figure 2 in mind. The whole simulation plan needs a total of 88 input data.

A second way to determine the parameters is to use a specially designed program that determines

those inputs according to various hypotheses the user can make. Three types of informations are entered into this program: 1) Historical information, such as the latest balance sheet and income statement, 2) management plans and assumptions on future evolution and 3) management constraints such as regulations, ratios to be maintained, etc. The input program also can take account of the dependence of any variable on another (for instance, we may consider that acceptances represent a certain percentage of the total clients' deposits, and so on).

As far as the assumptions are concerned, they can cover a period up to five years and five typical assumptions are possible for each item of the balance sheet and the income statement from which we start. They are listed in Figure 4.

Figure 5 shows a typical example of output. It represents the simulation of the "interests collected" account.[4] The other output reports are more or less the same.

Simulation can allow the user to consider many more alternatives than could be done on a manual basis [Johnson, 1973, pp. 43-49]. Figure 6 illus-

[4] If there is a translation problem, please see Figure 2.

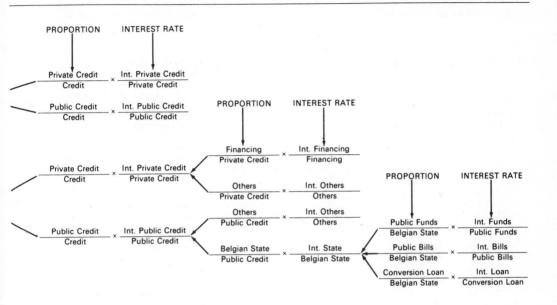

trates the kind of question that can be directed toward a simulation model. The problem to analyze was as follows: When making loans in Belgian franks, the bank has two possibilities—making loans to the state or to private customers. Starting from a 50-50 situation, what could be the percentage variation of interests collected when moving away from that point? In other words, how do interests collected vary when we have, say, 60% credit made to the state and 40% to private customers, or a 25-75 proportion? Figure 6 gives an answer to this question.

Two additional remarks should be made at this point: 1) The relationship happens to be linear because all other things have been considered equal;[5] and 2) the slope of the line is positive due to the fact that the rate of interest associated[6] with private credit is higher than that associated with public credit.

[5] The sentence, "all other things being equal," appears often in econometric literature. It often shows the inability of the econometrist to consider simultaneous variations of other variables. This is not the case here. "All other things being equal" is used for the simplicity of the example.

[6] The reader will have seen that the computer calculates intermediary interest rates—weighted averages of the rates of the corresponding subaccounts. For instance, Figure 5 shows that the rate of private credit, in Belgian franks is 7.112%, weighted average of 10.0 and 6.5%.

Results Achieved

The time horizon considered in this simulation plan is not limited; so, simulations covering very long periods of time are possible. However, the farther one goes, the more difficult it becomes to evaluate the different parameters of the plan. This last remark should be a warning for those who try to use a simulation plan as a forecasting device. It is, of course, possible to utilize this simulation plan to forecast the net profit of the bank. (This has been done on a one-year basis and the results obtained are good; for instance, for the period 1972-1973, gross profit was forecasted with an error of 0.2%, net profit with an error of 5% and profits on interest collected with an error of 4.1%.) However, for longer periods of time, other techniques—such as econometric models and exponential smoothing—should be considered.

The simulation plan has been devised and is being used in the corporate planning department of the bank. Perhaps at this point, some words of explanation on the bank's structure are needed. At the top, the powers are delegated by the following bodies: The general assembly of shareholders, the Board, the Management Committee and the vari-

Figure 3. Input Data for the Interests Collected Module

Inputs,[1] if given in the form of a ratio	Inputs,[1] if given in the form of raw data.
Foreign Currencies	
1. Rate private credit	Interests collected on private credit
2. Rate public credit	Interests collected on public credit
3. Rate acceptances	Interests collected on acceptances
4. Rate bankers	Interests collected on bankers
5. Proportion private credit/credit	Volume private credit
6. Proportion Uses, currencies/Uses	Volume public credit
7. Proportion acceptances/Uses, currencies	Volume acceptances
8. Proportion bankers/Uses, currencies	Volume bankers
9. Other interests collected[2]	Other interests collected[2]
Belgian Francs	
10. Rate public funds	Interests collected on public funds
11. Rate public bills	Interests collected on public bills
12. Rate conversion loan	Interests collected on conversion loan
13. Proportion public funds/State	Volume public funds
14. Proportion public bills/State	Volume public bills
15. Total uses[3]	Volume conversion loan
16. Rate financing	Interests collected on financing
17. Rate other private	Interests collected on other private
18. Rate other public	Interests collected on other public
19. Proportion financing/priv. credit	Volume financing
20. Proportion priv. credit/credit	Volume other private
21. Proportion other public/publ. credit	Volume other public
22. Rate acceptances	Interests collected on acceptances
23. Rate bankers	Interests collected on bankers
24. Rate creditexport	Interests collected on creditexport
25. Rate investment portfolio	Interests collected on inv. portfolio
26. Rate call money	Interests collected on call money
27. Proportion accept./Uses, Belgian	Volume acceptances
28. Proportion bankers/Uses, Belgian	Volume bankers
29. Proportion creditex./Uses, Belgian	Volume creditexport
30. Proportion Inv. portfolio/Uses, Belgian	Volume Investment portfolio
31. Proportion call/Uses, Belgian	Volume call money
32. Other interests collected[2]	Other interests collected[2]

[1] Volume in millions, interests in thousands, rates and proportions in %.
[2] Exception—these are commissions (interests not generated by funds).
[3] Exception—this is raw data.

ous directors of departments. The structure is functional and geographical: Central Administration centralizes the usual departments of a bank —financial operations, credit, accounting, etc. Five groups (to which 18 offices and more than 1,000 branches report) divide the national market. Among the departments of Central Administration there is one called Studies and Commercial whose tasks are threefold: Studies, planning and marketing.

In 1967, a management by objectives system was introduced in the bank. The function of plan-

Figure 4. Possible Assumptions for Input Data

Code	Possibility
1	1 rate of increase, constant over 5 years.
2	5 different rates, one for each year.
3	5 different values, one for each year.
4	1 percentage constant over 5 years, and the corresponding item on the B.S. or I.S.
5	5 different percentages, one for each year.

Figure 5. Example of Output: Interests Collected

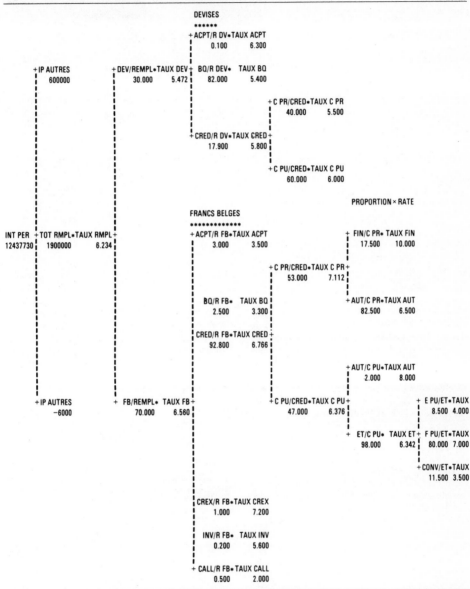

ning, essential in setting objectives, is the part of MBO where simulation comes in. The main task of the simulation plan devised at Banque de Bruxelles is to test the coherence of the objectives for future years. Indeed, it is not enough that a decision be logical because it corresponds to proposed objectives with available means and satisfactory profitability; it is also necessary that it be compatible with all other actions decided upon (for example, equilibrium between deposits and credits, balance between internal and external constraints, etc.). This coherence of the agreed objectives is done by means of the simulation plan.

Figure 6. Impact of Credit Allocation on Interests Collected

Proportion	Private credit / Total credit	Percentage variation of interests collected
	75	+1.83
	70	+1.47
	65	+1.10
	60	+0.73
	55	+0.37
	50 — Starting point	
	45	−0.37
	40	−0.73
	35	−1.10
	30	−1.47
	25	−1.83

Thus far, and because the simulation plan is relatively new, this is accomplished on a one-year basis. It has been estimated that it would be dangerous, if not doomed to failure, to consider immediately a longer span of time; people must first be educated into a simulation perspective, and resistance to change, particularly in a bank with deeply-rooted traditions, is great. But the goal is to incorporate the simulation model into a pluri-annual plan which would combine short- and long-term objectives.

Conclusion

The plan, hereabove described is not, nor can it be, a substitute for sound judgment and careful planning, but it can facilitate management decision-making and evaluate more scientifically the consequences of general policy decisions. Moreover, it enables those decision-makers to dispose of the useful and necessary information which is required for sound judgment. If we consider that strategic planning involves the study and appraisal of different alternatives, simulation represents a formidable tool for such planning. □

REFERENCES

Charlent, J., "La gestion scientifique en banque," *Revue de la banque,* 1965, No. 7.
Derwa, L., "Computer Models: Aids to Management at Société Générale de Banque," *Journal of Bank Research, Summer* 1972.
Johnson, H. G., "Financial Modelling for the Smaller Bank," *The Bankers Magazine,* Winter 1973.

Chapter 12

BANKMOD: AN INTERACTIVE SIMULATION AID FOR BANK FINANCIAL PLANNING*

By Randall S. Robinson

*This article is reprinted, with permission, from *Journal of Bank Research*, Vol. 4, No. 3 (Autumn, 1973), pp. 212-224.

Bank Administration Institute recently released a computer-based aid, called BANKMOD, to facilitate financial planning in a bank. BANKMOD's primary purpose is to help the bank executive arrive at superior planning decisions in connection with financial assets and liabilities—or, phrasing it differently, in connection with financial sources and uses of funds—over a planning interval that may range from one month to two years. The user has access to reports that cover projected balance sheets, income statements (including income both before and after security gains or losses), unrealized security gains or losses, liquidity, capital adequacy, surplus or deficit of funds, and various other aspects of overall bank status and performance. BANKMOD can be tailored to suit banks of different sizes and different circumstances. The software is "interactive" in that it provides for extensive give and take, through a terminal, between the user and the planning system. The software is being made available on a national time-sharing utility.

The goal of this paper is to present a brief, essentially nontechnical, description of the new planning aid and of methods for utilizing it. Topics discussed include basic facts about BANKMOD, features of particular interest to users, operating procedures and applications. An annotated BANKMOD reference list is given at the conclusion of the paper.

What Is BANKMOD?

BANKMOD is a computer program designed mainly to assist a banker who is doing comprehensive medium-term financial planning, which encompasses planning for such activities as investment in municipal bonds and issuance of large certificates of deposit. From the user's point of view, the program offers help along two broad lines: Carrying out computations and expediting, the planner's job.

BANKMOD's computations parallel, in principle, the steps taken in a conventional hand-prepared plan: The user specifies a course of action under consideration, together with assumed starting conditions and future conditions, and then a projection is made of the anticipated results. One of the aid's functions is to vastly increase the speed with which the voluminous calculations for a detailed plan of this type may be completed. In addition, BANKMOD incorporates certain provisions for reducing the amount of data needed; this is so especially in the realm of forecasted yields and interest rates.

In common with its typical hand-prepared counterpart, a BANKMOD medium-term plan does not subdivide time into periods as short as days or weeks. It subdivides, instead, into either months or quarters. If the user elects to produce a plan that looks ahead month by month, he may extend his projection over a total time interval of anywhere from one to 12 months. Should he choose a quarterly plan, the total time viewed in his study may cover from one to eight quarters.[1]

Beyond performing computations entailed in projections, BANKMOD helps in a number of ways to make the process of planning faster and easier. For example, a user may request forms, adapted to the planning framework he has established, that guide him in the compilation of necessary data. After data has been assembled, he can undertake, at one sitting at a terminal, as much or as little of the task of plan construction as he wishes. The program responds quickly to his instructions. He enjoys a great deal of freedom of choice as he interacts with the aid to enter data, try out possible planned actions and call for various reports. Data, once entered, may be stored so that it need not be entered again. Many checks are executed by the program to assist in preventing errors.

Financial Decisions. A BANKMOD plan is built up from individual balance sheet categories and, in cases where balance sheet categories are subdivided, from individual category subdivisions.

[1] The gist of the foregoing two paragraphs is that BANKMOD implements a discrete, deterministic, dynamic simulation model. By way of further technical classification, it is also a multiloop nonlinear feedback model. There is very little modeling of policy; a loop is closed, in most cases, by having the user observe the status of the simulation and then stipulate appropriate decision-variable values.

Figure 1. Financial Decisions Defined in BANKMOD

Associated BANKMOD Balance Sheet Category	Possible Decisions

Assets

Daily Funds Sold: Federal funds sold and securities purchased under agreements to resell.
→ Specify level, for entire category.

Money Market Loans: Loans to security dealers and brokers to carry security inventories.
→ Specify level, for entire category.

Asset CDs: CDs, issued by other banks, which are held as short-term investments.
→ Specify amounts purchased and amounts sold, for selected groups based on maturity.

Acceptances and Commercial Paper: Acceptances and commercial paper held as short-term investments.
→ Specify amounts purchased and amounts sold, for selected groups based on maturity.

Treasury Bills: U.S. Treasury bills held as an investment.
→ Specify amounts purchased and amounts sold, for selected groups based on maturity.

Governments: U.S. Treasury securities held as an investment—notes, certificates and bonds.
→ Specify amounts purchased and amounts sold, for selected groups based on maturity and coupon rate.

Agencies: Investment securities issued by various U.S. federal agencies.
→ Specify amounts purchased and amounts sold, for selected groups based on maturity and coupon rate.

Municipals—Prime: Tax-exempt municipal securities rated Aaa or Aa.
→ Specify amounts purchased and amounts sold, for selected groups based on maturity and coupon rate.

Municipals—Good: Tax-exempt municipals not classified prime.
→ Specify amounts purchased and amounts sold, for selected groups based on maturity and coupon rate.

Liabilities, Reserves and Capital Accounts

Daily Funds Purchased: Federal funds purchased and securities sold under agreements to repurchase.
→ Specify level, for entire category.

FRB Borrowing: Borrowings from the Federal Reserve.
→ Specify level, for entire category.

CDs—Money Market: Large negotiable CDs issued by the bank.
→ Specify amounts issued, for selected groups based on maturity.

Holding Company Paper: Because of the reserve requirement imposed upon the issuance of holding company paper to obtain funds to support loans, BANKMOD treats holding company paper (if any) as a source of funds for the bank and retains the associated loans on the books of the bank.
→ Specify amounts issued, for selected groups based on maturity.

Capital Notes: Debt securities issued by the bank to expand its capital base.
→ Specify amounts issued, for selected groups based on maturity.

Equity: Capital stock issued.
→ Specify number of shares issued or number of shares repurchased.

To illustrate, the asset category *Buildings and Equipment* is treated as a single unit for planning purposes while the category *Prime Municipal Bonds* is subdivided into security groups based upon time to maturity, yield, and coupon rate.

The finished plan, recorded in such forms as projected balance sheets and income statements, shows expected bank-wide progress which comes about in part from factors the bank will control, more or less, and in part from uncontrollable factors. How is planned progress likely to vary in the event there are changes in the approach taken to factors under the bank's control? This question may be investigated by means of working out several alternative plans—each incorporating a different approach.

The primary task for which BANKMOD was created is to assist in the investigation of different managerial approaches to those particular controllable factors associated with financial investment (i.e., bank investment, not trust investment) and financial fund-acquisition. Planned actions regarding such factors are called financial decisions in this paper. More specifically, the financial decisions upon which BANKMOD focuses attention are those enumerated in Figure 1. Decisions to buy a given quantity of Government bonds, with selected maturity and coupon rate, or to issue a given quantity of capital notes, with selected maturity, are examples.

Besides stating contemplated financial decisions, a BANKMOD user sets forth all of the other information needed to fill in a plan. This additional information combines, in effect, data on nonfinancial factors assumed to be under the bank's control, or nonfinancial decisions, with data related to uncontrollable factors; it pertains to such topics as: Loan levels, deposit levels and levels of other nonfinancial balance sheet categories; interest rates and yields; regulatory rates and requirements; depreciation; dividends and other income and expense; taxes; loan loss rates; measures of liquidity and capital adequacy; and security pledging.

It would be logical at this point to ask: Since a BANKMOD plan applies to the entire bank, and since the information that must be supplied incorporates (directly or indirectly) nonfinancial decisions, why can't BANKMOD be employed to explore changes not only in financial decisions but also in nonfinancial decisions, such as those influencing loans and deposits? The answer is: It can. Nothing about BANKMOD precludes utilization for the study of nonfinancial decisions.

Because BANKMOD was designed especially to facilitate financial planning, it possesses features which make experimentation with financial decisions more convenient than experimentation with nonfinancial decisions. For instance, when a user stipulates a feasible financial decision, BANKMOD totally traces out the decision's consequences; when a user wants to put forward a nonfinancial decision, in addition to specifying it he must check to be sure that its ramifications have been reflected properly in all prerequisite information furnished to the program. Another illustration is that the user has the option of entering data on financial decisions, based upon his on-the-spot evaluation of where the plan stands and where it is headed, during the time a projection is being generated by the computer, but he does not have a similar opportunity to enter data on nonfinancial decisions while the computer-aided computational development of a plan is in progress.

Features of BANKMOD

Seen from the user's perspective, certain features of BANKMOD play a major part in shaping its practical value and, at the same time, constitute distinguishing characteristics when comparing BANKMOD with other planning aids. Some of the main features of this type will now be reviewed.

Furnishes Statement Projections. Turning attention first to computational aspects, BANKMOD is a simulation aid; that is, it simulates (or projects) the bank's progress resulting from a stipulated managerial course of action together with assumed initial and future conditions. A simulation aid may be contrasted with an optimization aid in which many alternative courses of action are automatically screened and those that give rise to the best anticipated outcomes, as judged by some very definite way of evaluating outcomes, are identified, all in a single computational run.

Generally speaking, but not necessarily true in every case, an optimization aid of given scope embodies a less realistic portrayal of complex activities than does a simulation aid of the same scope. This occurs because procedures for automatically locating superior courses of action can be incorporated, in most instances, only when more stringent restrictions on methods of description are observed. With the foregoing point in mind, one can say that BANKMOD, at its level of detail, places emphasis on attempting to describe the bank with a relatively high degree of accuracy or realism.[2]

A related consideration is that most planners are accustomed to selecting courses of action for study and then appraising them through projections. So BANKMOD enhances a process that is familiar to most users and for which they already have an intuitive feeling.

Determines Yield Curves and Security Market Values. A significant ingredient of the BANKMOD simulation is its taking into account security market values as well as security book values, thereby permitting coverage of such measures as net income (after security gains or losses and associated tax) and unrealized security gains or losses. In connection with security market values, the program includes features to ease the burden of supplying relevant data. Two basic ideas are involved. First, when entering the fundamental data of yields and corresponding times to maturity, a user is not called upon to list every maturity that may come up. Instead he enters yields applicable to only a designated few maturities and then BANKMOD fits a curve to fill in the rest. Second, it is not necessary to provide a curve of yield versus maturity for each security category, only for the four categories *Daily Funds Purchased* (maturity is not varied in this case), *Governments, Agencies and Prime Municipals.* Other curves are worked out by BANKMOD based upon a user-specified spread (difference), which may vary with maturity, between the contemplated curve and one of the initially-entered four.

To illustrate, consider securities in the BANKMOD category *Prime Municipals* and consider a particular planning period: Second quarter 1974, for example. To enter data on the relationship he anticipates will prevail then between purchase yield and time to maturity, the user specifies yields corresponding to only three maturities—1 year, 5 years and 30 years, respectively; BANKMOD subsequently fits a curve so that it may calculate yields for all maturities which come under scrutiny. Now, should the user contemplate purchasing *Prime Municipals* in that future planning period, he states the amount, maturity and coupon rate. BANKMOD then extracts, from the previously-entered curve, the yield accompanying the stated maturity, and combines it with the other purchase data to compute a purchase or market price.

Continuing this example, suppose the user is thinking about selling *Prime Municipals*. The purchase price is determined by BANKMOD, along lines just reviewed, and then the sale price is calculated by introducing an assumed spread between the two prices; the user has previously furnished a curve that expresses his judgment about how that spread will vary with maturity. In a similar manner, stipulated relationships, varying with maturity, between purchase yields on *Prime Municipals* and purchase yields on *Good Municipals* and between purchase prices and sale prices of *Good Municipals,* are utilized in BANKMOD to find the purchase or sale price for *Good Municipals.*

Program is Interactive with Provision for Efficient Entry of Information. The other features to be discussed in this section concern the software aspects of BANKMOD. First of all, the program is installed on a national time-sharing utility and the planner utilizes it through a terminal. BANKMOD is interactive in the sense that the user and the computer move together, step by step, in the process of entering data and building projections, without any need for the computer to interrupt with a long delay in carrying out its part of the joint task.

In addition to its capability for giving a fast response, BANKMOD incorporates a number of characteristics directed toward making the interaction between user and program efficient. One of these is that a user is able to follow straightforward groundrules, standardized throughout BANKMOD, when entering information.

For instance, many interactions are started by a specific question from BANKMOD that asks for a verbal reply. To illustrate, when BANKMOD prints the question BALANCE SHEET (Y, N)?, the user answers either Y, for yes, to obtain a listing of the balance sheet or N, for no, if he doesn't want the listing. The program also provides several questions that call for numerical data. For example, at the point where balance sheet amounts applicable at the very beginning of the plan are to be supplied, BANKMOD prints ENTER BOOK VALUES and then prints each balance sheet category followed by a question mark. The user reads B&E?, for example, and replies with the number 20, which would mean he has specified the initial value 20 (million dollars) for the category *Buildings and Equipment.*

Another type of information entry revolves around the command, or instruction, which a user selects from several authorized commands. An example is the command *BAL: it may be entered, at various times, to obtain a balance sheet

² It is noted parenthetically that BANKMOD will delineate the implications of a suitably stated course of action whatever its source—be it the planner himself or a comparable optimization aid. Two recent references on the optimization approach to bank financial planning are: Cohen, Kalman J. and David P. Rutenberg, "Toward a Comprehensive Framework for Bank Financial Planning," *Journal of Bank Research,* Vol. 1, No. 4 (Winter, 1971), pp. 41-57; and Cohen, Kalman J. and Frederick S. Hammer, "Linear Programming and Optimal Bank Asset Management Decisions," *The Journal of Finance,* Vol. 22, No. 2 (May, 1967), pp. 147-165.

listing.

By means of giving commands and answering questions, a planner has much flexibility in shifting from one BANKMOD function to another and in controlling things done within a function. Should the user, while sitting at a terminal, temporarily forget a command or other groundrule regarding information input, he can look it up quickly in a small folder called *BANKMOD Reference Card.*

Safeguards Against Errors and Breakdowns Are Built In. BANKMOD contains many checks to help prevent an element of erroneous information, accidentally entered by the user or created when initially-accurate information is garbled during transmission to the computer, from going undetected. The program conducts tests on a data item for correctness and consistency with other data. If an error has been uncovered, depending upon the circumstances either the last BANKMOD question is repeated or else an appropriate message is printed.

In addition, BANKMOD applies a number of safeguards against the possibility of a breakdown in program operation resulting from a user's mistake or from poor data transmission. In the rare event a difficult situation does arise, the user can look in the *BANKMOD Reference Card* to refresh his memory about what emergency procedures to follow.

Violation of a data-entry groundrule or restriction constitutes an error, so it might be said that BANKMOD's limitation of such restrictions represents a means of reducing error as well as promoting ease of use. One important restriction-limiting feature, not previously mentioned, is that a user does not have to place the information he is entering in a very narrowly-defined position, on a line of terminal printing. As long as the information is applicable at its point of entry, is in the proper form and, in the case where several items of data are given, is in the proper sequence, it may be positioned in any empty space on the line.

Forms to Aid in Compilation of Data Are Available. A user may employ BANKMOD to request customized forms that will help him compile his planning data and organize it in a manner convenient for subsequent entry. These forms are generated by BANKMOD itself; they incorporate all relevant details of the user's own plan, such as dates and selected balance sheet categories. Data forms are produced on an offline printer at the computer facility, in quantities chosen by the user and then mailed wherever the user has stipulated.

Some Data May be Stored and Some Entered on Cards. Two other noteworthy features are concerned with the job of supplying data to BANKMOD. First, much data can be stored in computer files so that it need not be re-entered each time the planner sits down at a terminal. Some is stored automatically upon entry; this includes data on the overall planning framework, the position of the bank at the outset of the plan, assumed future conditions in those aspects not likely to be varied during experimentation with a given plan (e.g. tax rates and pledging information) and assumed future conditions in those aspects likely to be varied during experimentation (e.g. basic yields and levels of loans and deposits). Other data may be stored at the user's option; in this classification are one or more additional sets of data on assumed future conditions, of the variable type, and one or more sets that describe complete courses of action for financial decisions. Every stored data file regarding either decisions or variable future conditions is assigned a name so that it can readily be applied, by name, when desired. The planner is free, through one means or another, to delete any automatically-stored or optionally-stored data and replace it with something else.

Second, whereas in most instances the user must arrange to have data grouped, without BANKMOD's assistance, into planning categories or category subdivisions and then must enter the grouped data through a terminal, in the case of the initial portfolio of *municipal bonds* (prime and good) he can elect to utilize BANKMOD for those functions. If he chooses that option, the user prepares a computer punched card for each bond in the initial municipal portfolios, mails all cards to the computer utility and finally, working with BANKMOD at a terminal, gives instructions which result in execution of the required grouping and entry.

A BANKMOD Plan is Tailored to Suit the Planner and His Bank. The general specifications of a BANKMOD plan may be adapted in many respects to conform to different planning preferences and to the needs of banks of different sizes and circumstances. The user decides to produce either a monthly or quarterly plan and he chooses a total planning interval of from one to 12 months or from one to 8 quarters. He selects monetary units of either thousands or millions of dollars. He may or may not include those BANKMOD balance sheet categories designated optional: There are seven optional asset categories and four optional categories under liabilities, reserves and capital accounts. A user defines and names various categories for loans and for demand deposits not backed by pledged securities. And he specifies, for each security portfolio in which holdings may be grouped by yield, the number of different yield groups and the numerical yield values associated with each group.

Many Different Reports May Be Requested. Throughout BANKMOD a user may pick and choose among many different kinds of reports, and different reporting time spans, in response to his judgment of what best meets his needs at the moment. Available reports encompass virtually all matters of potential interest including the structure of the plan, the initial bank status, assumed future conditions such as yields and interest rates, any planned financial decisions that are stored in computer files and, of course, the intermediate or final result of each planning projection or simulation.

Reports of the type last mentioned, upon which a user concentrates when he undertakes the actual development of a projection, are listed in Figure 2. The status and progress reports of Figure 2 offer choices that provide important flexibility for the planner. He can select reports on different topics, such as balance-sheet position or earnings. He can ask for a concise summary, such as a Flash Report, or a more fully detailed presentation, such as an Earnings Report. And he may focus on either a single period, by means of Data Display and Snapshot Reports, or on the entire multi-period plan, by means of Horizon Reports. A related helpful feature, where no choice is entailed, is that several of the Snapshot Reports show results before recently-entered decisions, results after recently-entered decisions and the associated amount of change in results; this before-and-after format assists a user with analysis of the short-run impact of the financial decisions he has in mind.

Operating Procedures

To further clarify how BANKMOD can aid a planner, some of the procedures involved in the operation of BANKMOD now will be reviewed, briefly (see Figure 3). BANKMOD's program is made up of subprograms called *modes,* each of which does a specific job. Figure 3 names all modes and summarizes their respective functions.

A user must finish several preliminary tasks before he may launch into the actual development of projections. The first of these is to define desired structural characteristics of the plan, such as period length and optional aspects of the balance sheet. That is accomplished in the For-

mulate Mode. He also will specify, in the Mailing Label Mode, a name and address under which items are mailed to him from the computer utility. Then, through the Input Forms Mode, the planner requests data forms that incorporate his previously-designated structural features; the forms come to him by mail.

After forms have been received, required elements of information covering assumed future conditions and the bank's initial position are recorded in appropriate form blanks. The initial position data thus prepared is entered at the terminal in the Real State Mode; that portion concerning initial municipal bond holdings may be handled by the alternative method of being recorded on punched cards and entered at the computer utility under BANKMOD control (Real State Mode). Data on future conditions is entered through the Assumption Mode. In connection with this data, the segment related to assumptions the user might vary from period to period or simulation to simulation will consist of one or more complete sets, with each set being given a name. For example, the planner could enter three different possible views of the future reflecting, say, optimistic, best-guess and pessimistic outlooks.

At this stage the user may obtain well-labeled listings of some or all data so far entered as well as of market yields calculated from yield data. He places his order through the Query Mode and elects to receive the listings either at his terminal or by mail from the computer utility. Listings thereby acquired can be employed to check data accuracy, supplementing the verification of accuracy performed along the way and to consult for reference during plan development. Should any information revealed by a listing not coincide with what was intended, appropriate steps in the data-entry process may be repeated until everything is satisfactory.

Now, if at the outset the planner has in mind certain financial decisions, he could store them in a file, or files, through the Decision Mode. Such a file is assigned a name that can be cited during the course of plan construction. Alternatively, he could enter those decisions period-by-period while the projection is being generated, in the Simulate Mode, and then store them for future use or not as he sees fit. Once decisions have been stored, whether entered in the Decision Mode or Simulate Mode, a terminal listing of that file may be obtained for reference—through the Decision Mode.

Of course a user need not handle all of the foregoing prerequisite activities personally. He

Figure 2. BANKMOD Managerial Reports on Planned Bank Progress

Reports on projected bank results, available in the Simulate Mode (see Figure 3).

Data Display Reports

Time. Shows current status of bank at point in plan where report is requested.

Information. User designates selected balance sheet category. If category has no associated portfolio, report gives book value; otherwise gives book value, overview of portfolio, and details of portfolio holdings (part of portfolio description is standard and part optional).

Snapshot Reports

Time. Shows current status or progress during current period (month or quarter).

Information. Five different reports available:

  Funds Report—Summarizes net funds (cash) surplus or deficit and, at user's option, related cash flows.

  Flash Report—Presents synopsis of status and performance in terms of six primary measures. For each measure includes value before recently-entered (or new) decisions, value after new decisions, value of resulting change and graph of percentage change.

  Analysis Report—Gives eight additional status and performance measures that supplement the basic measures of the Flash Report. Same before-and-after format as Flash Report.

  Earnings Report—A detailed, thirty one line-item, report on earnings in three sections: interest income and expense; net operating income and net income; and unrealized gains or losses on securities. Before-and-after format comparable, but not identical, to that of Flash and Analysis Reports.

  Balance Sheet Report—Complete balance sheet.

Horizon Reports

Time. Shows status or progress period by period over all planning periods.

Information. Five reports:

  Horizon Funds Report—Funds surplus or deficit: cumulative and single-period value given for each period.

  Horizon Flash Report—Same measures as Flash Report. Value of measure in each period presented.

  Horizon Analysis Report—Same measures as Analysis Report. Displays value of measure in each period.

  Horizon Earnings Report—Conveys information similar to that contained in an Earnings Report. Value of each information element given for each period.

  Horizon Balance Sheet Report—A summary of the balance sheet rather than a detailed balance sheet. Values presented period by period.

---

might, for instance, arrange for clerical personnel to enter data which he would subsequently check by inspecting listings.

Having arrived at this point, a planner is ready to undertake the main business of building plans, in the Simulate Mode. He starts by designating the particular set of Named Assumptions, that describe future conditions, to be applied. In addition, should there be stored decisions and he wants to apply a group of them, he may specify a set of decisions. Then he constructs his projection, proceeding from the beginning of the plan to the end, period by period. In each period he can enter decisions, or enter additional decisions if stored decisions are already applied, call for vari-

ous Data Display and Snapshot Reports to disclose the short-term results, then enter other decisions, and so on, repeating this process until he is satisfied with results at the present stage. After a full projection is completed, he may request Horizon Reports that show final results across all periods and serve as a record to which he can refer when comparing the newly-created projection with others. Any number of different projections may be developed in this manner, each based upon a different future outlook, or a different pattern of decisions or a different combination of outlook and decisions.

In the event the user wishes to rest but a projection is in progress, he may interrupt with

Figure 3. BANKMOD Subprograms, Called Modes, and Activities Carried Out By the User with Each

Formulate Mode—User tailors the plan structure to suit his bank and his planning preferences.

Mailing Label Mode—User specifies a name and address to be employed when material is mailed to him from the computer utility.

Input Forms Mode—User orders customized forms which help him assemble data for entry in the Real State and Assumption Modes. Forms are produced on an offline printer at the computer utility and then mailed.

Real State Mode—User enters or modifies information that describes the bank's position at the beginning of the plan. This information includes balance sheet amounts and holdings in security portfolios.

Assumption Mode—User enters or modifies data regarding assumed future conditions. One group of such data, called Unnamed Assumptions, consists of factors the user is not likely to vary from period to period or from simulation to simulation; another group, called Named Assumptions, consists of factors he may wish to vary. A single set of Unnamed Assumptions and one or more sets of Named Assumptions are entered.

Query Mode—User may obtain printed listings, for convenient reference while working in the Simulate Mode, of input data supplied in the Formulate, Real State, and Assumption Modes and of yields calculated by BANKMOD from assumption data. These listings may be produced at the user's terminal or on an offline printer at the computer utility. A terminal listing of data on stored decisions may be requested in the Decision Mode.

Decision Mode—User has an opportunity to enter one or more sets of financial decisions into stored files. He also may modify, delete, or list decisions currently stored.

Simulate Mode—User develops and revises his plans, period by period. Decisions may be entered directly or may be taken from stored files—created either during previous simulations or during previous interactions with the Decision Mode. Reports shown in Figure 2 are available.

the command *PAUSE and leave the terminal. When he returns later, signs on and asks for the Simulate Mode, the program will resume just where it stopped.

A planner at all times enjoys the freedom to transfer readily from one mode to another. He might, for example, carry out some projections in the Simulate Mode, then go to the Assumption Mode or the Decision Mode in order to add more data, or change existing data, and finally go back to the Simulate Mode and construct projections incorporating the new data.

When there is a continuing program of planning, periodically the time interval viewed in a plan must be altered—by shifting dates ahead one period, say. After such an alteration, it is not necessary to start totally from scratch with BANKMOD. The original plan structure and original Unnamed Assumptions may be retained, if desired. Revised data will be needed for the initial bank position, Named Assumptions and stored decisions (if any).

Applications

What are the different ways BANKMOD could be applied productively? In this section four possible types of application will be noted: Financial planning, profit planning, training and providing ideas to bankers who are developing other aids.

One might say that BANKMOD addresses itself to the task of total-bank planning with particular emphasis on planning financial decisions. We have seen that a BANKMOD plan does *not* exclude or overlook the effect of nonfinancial decisions—as a trust department plan might exclude the results of decisions in commercial banking, for example. What BANKMOD does is handle nonfinancial and financial decisions differently, for the purpose of making the trying out of various financial decisions especially convenient.

BANKMOD's contribution to a planning effort consists in part of helping the user identify, organize and store relevant data. Another phase of its contribution is that it performs the extensive computational job of converting data into projections. A third aspect, tied to the second, is that it encourages the planner to search for courses of planned action which give rise to improved bank performance in his plan.

The quest for improved performance could involve just experimentation with financial decisions (BANKMOD's natural role), just experimentation with nonfinancial decisions or experimentation with both types. Regardless of which of these possibilities characterizes the planner's experimentation, two basic ideas about BANKMOD hold true, and deserve comment.

The first point is that BANKMOD, because it generates projections, permits the user to strive for, and measure progress toward, virtually any kind of improvement he might contemplate. In other words, by and large the aid has no philosophical approach to performance embedded in it; instead, it indicates progress in very many dimensions so that the planner is free to be guided by whichever dimensions he believes are important.[3] Thus, widely different points of view may be brought to bear by different planners, even though all probably will have in mind the same general goal of determining how the bank may obtain superior performance (indicated by values and trends in such measures as net operating income per share and net income per share) while meeting actual or assumed requirements (such as having funds available when needed and operating within regulatory restrictions).

The second basic idea is that BANKMOD can help a planner adjust his plan in light of the inevitable, often great, uncertainties about the future pattern of factors wholly or partly outside the bank's control. By working with several different future outlooks, described in different Named Assumption data files, the user may investigate how unexpected future circumstances could alter bank performance. And he may seek a course of action that seems superior taking into account the various possible future situations and their associated chances of occurrence; planned actions selected from this perspective very likely will not be the same as those selected when only one future outlook is considered.

There is no standard procedure for bringing uncertainty into the picture with BANKMOD. Generally speaking, however, the user will draw upon two types of studies. One entails developing contingency plans. That is, take a given description of the future and search for a corresponding superior course of action; take a second description and search for its corresponding superior action (probably different from the first); and so on. In this way a planner may explore how much of an impact changes in future circumstances have on the choice of action. The second kind of study might be termed "sensitivity analysis."[4] The notion is to take a particular course of action and generate projections from it under several different assumed future climates. Resulting projections indicate how greatly bank performance might vary from what is anticipated in the event the single course of action under consideration is adopted. Sensitivity analysis can be carried out, of course, for a second course of action, a third and others.[5]

Financial Planning. Financial planning is the terminology adopted herein for BANKMOD's normal role of facilitating experimentation with financial decisions when nonfinancial decisions are given or fixed.

It is possible that nonfinancial decisions will present little chance for management discretion during the future time interval viewed by the planner. In that case, financial planning will be the primary method of improving the bank's planned performance. On the other hand, management may have significant latitude with nonfinancial actions through the planning interval. If so, the planner could identify several alternative nonfinancial courses of action, take the first one and find a corresponding superior set of financial decisions, then take the second and find a corresponding set of financial decisions for that, and so forth. This process should culminate in finding a plan which represents a particularly favorable combination of financial and nonfinancial decisions.

Profit Planning. The name profit plan often is given to the bank's periodically-produced plan which is summed up at the level of the balance sheet and income statement. Within this usage, financial planning, previously defined, is a special aspect or phase of profit planning and not a separate activity—even though it might turn out to be worked on separately in the bank.

BANKMOD could support creation of the profit plan, or similar overall plan, in the following ways. Simply stated, they include aiding with experimentation (under various assumed future conditions) in financial decisions, nonfinancial decisions or both types. A final possibility is no experimentation—using BANKMOD just to project the anticipated consequences of one specified financial and nonfinancial course of action. All of these are feasible, but they don't take advantage of BANKMOD's facilities in equal measure. The most advantageous, from the stand-

---

[3] BANKMOD does embody a viewpoint about performance to a limited extent. The views of its designers are conveyed in the information displayed in reports and in other design features.

[4] This refers to examining the sensitivity of the plan to variations in assumptions about the future, with a fixed set of decisions. Contingency planning is also sensitivity analysis, but of a different variety; it shows the plan's sensitivity to variations in future assumptions when decisions are adapted to the assumptions.

[5] To take full advantage of tools available for analyzing uncertainty, a planning aid would incorporate random variables and associated probability distributions. Random variables are commonplace in theory but not in planning practice. BANKMOD encourages the user to investigate the possible impact of future surprises and to hedge his plan accordingly. When implemented, such investigation and hedging ought to lead to substantially better results compared with the familiar procedure of developing a single, best-guess plan. Their implementation, moreover, should help prepare a planner to appreciate the potential practical value of probabilistic methods, which provide greater insight at the cost of greater complexity.

point of utilizing BANKMOD features, are in connection with trying out financial decisions or trying out financial and nonfinancial decisions.

Training. BANKMOD's ability to reveal, either concisely or in detail, how a bank's progress is determined by the complex interplay of decisions, the economy and other factors makes it potentially valuable for training prospective bank officers. It could provide, for example, an experimental laboratory in which trainees try out decisions and vary assumed future conditions interactively. Or it could help an instructor to prepare hypothetical bank histories that would be discussed during a training session.

Insights Applied to Other Aids. Bank management science specialists and computer programmers who are developing decision aids for their own banks may find BANKMOD to be a useful source of ideas.

Conclusions

BANKMOD is the property of the Bank Administration Institute. The program is installed on a national time-sharing utility to which banks in the United States and Canada may gain access. Arrangements to do so must be made *with the Institute.* Inquiries regarding the terms of access, or regarding other subjects having to do with BANKMOD, should be sent to the Director of Research, Bank Administration Institute, Post Office Box 500, Park Ridge, Illinois 60068.   ☐

Views presented in this paper are the author's; they are not official views of the Bank Administration Institute, which developed BANKMOD and holds all rights to it. The experience of the author with BANKMOD consisted first of having participated in originating and staffing the BANKMOD project, while serving as the Institute's Research Division Director, and later having prepared material for a BANKMOD user's course, in the capacity of a consultant. Appreciation is expressed to BAI officials for their invitation to give this report.

REFERENCES

BANKMOD Annotated Demonstration Run. Park Ridge, Illinois: Bank Administration Institute, 1972. A reproduction of the input and output from an illustrative run with BANKMOD.

BANKMOD Reference Card. Park Ridge, Illinois: Bank Administration Institute, 1972. Small folder to which the user may refer when he is working at a terminal. Furnishes a compact summary of facts about BANKMOD operation.

Clowes, George A., Kenneth E. Reich, and Wolfgang P. Hoehenwarter. *Introduction to BANKMOD.* Park Ridge, Illinois: Bank Administration Institute, 1972. Nontechnical overview of BANKMOD and its application. Covers basic ideas.

Gray, Kenneth B., Jr., "Asset Management Planning by Way of the Computer," *The Weekly Bond Buyer for the Capital Market Investor,* Vol. 186, No. 4101 (November 15, 1972), pp. 10+. An interim report on BANKMOD. Emphasizes the need for and methods of financial planning.

Gray, Kenneth B., Jr., and Wolfgang P. Hoehenwarter. *BANKMOD Computer System Reference Manual.* Park Ridge, Illinois: Bank Administration Institute, 1972. Gives technical information about the simulation model and program design in BANKMOD. Of interest to management science specialists and computer programmers.

Hoehenwarter, Wolfgang P. and Kenneth E. Reich, "BANKMOD—An Interactive Decision Aid for Banks," American Federation of Information Processing, *Conference Proceedings,* Vol. 39 (1971 Fall Joint Computer Conference), pp. 639-649. Summary written while BANKMOD was under development. Highlights simulation modeling and software features.

Reich, Kenneth E. with introduction by Kenneth B. Gray, Jr. *BANKMOD System Guide.* Park Ridge, Illinois: Bank Administration Institute, 1972. This is the primary reference for users of BANKMOD. It contains a complete, detailed explanation, accompanied by numerous illustrations, of how to operate and apply the planning aid.

Reich, Kenneth E., Kenneth B. Gray, Jr., and Wolfgang P. Hoehenwarter, "Balance Sheet Management: A Simulation Approach," *Journal of Bank Research,* Vol. 1, No. 3 (Autumn 1970), pp. 59-62. Early progress report that briefly describes BANKMOD.

Chapter 13

FORECASTING BRANCH BANK GROWTH PATTERNS*

By Robert L. Kramer

*This article is reprinted, with permission, from *Journal of Bank Research,* Vol. 1, No. 4 (Winter, 1971), pp. 17-24.

One of the most common functions performed by bank marketing research groups is estimating branch business potential. A number of reasonable methods for performing this task have been described in trade publications and at bank marketing conferences (see, for example [1], [3], [4], [9] and [15]). These procedures are generally concerned with estimating the total ultimate potential of banking business of the area, and at times, the share of this total that will be achieved by a new branch. These are difficult tasks. Anticipating the time pattern of growth toward these potentials is harder still. Few, if any, procedures have been discussed publicly for predicting the pattern of branch growth from the initial state of zero accounts to the anticipated potential—three, four or five years hence.

This paper describes a model designed specifically to confront this latter problem: Forecasting the time pattern of branch growth. Although a number of alternative formulations were explored, it employs a simple power function, based only on the length of time since the branch appeared.

Use of Growth Models

Predicting growth patterns is important for three reasons. First, growth patterns affect branch budgets and forecasted profit levels, staffing requirements, physical facilities and marketing strategies. Thus, a good model of growth patterns directed toward achieving the potential predicted for the branch would be a valuable planning tool.

Secondly, it is generally recognized by those responsible for branch location that even though their overall record may be very good, some branches will do substantially better than anticipated while others will fall far short of expectations. If these deviations could be predicted early in the life of a branch, appropriate action could be taken sooner.

A third potential benefit of a growth model is to measure the effects of special promotions (not the normal branch opening promotion) or the opening of competitive institutions. The results of such events are frequently obscured by other factors. For example, Bank A's two year old branch may continue to grow even after Bank B opens a nearby office. It would be difficult, it not impossible, without some idea of the normal growth pattern, to assess the impact of the additional competition. A growth model, if proven reliable, could provide a standard of comparison for those and many other situations.

At this point, an important distinction should be made between the *level* to which a process grows and the *pattern* it follows in achieving that level. We are concerned only with the latter. The level of business that a branch bank attains depends on a tremendous variety of factors, most of which are relatively slow to change (e.g., size and characteristics of the relevant population; the number, location and appearance of competitive institutions within and near its trading area; the marketing strategies employed by the bank and its competitors; the personality and marketing efforts of the branch manager and his staff; etc.). All these factors bear on what might be termed the branch's "mature" size and, therefore, on the decision to open a branch in that location. Once the branch is opened, however, the effects of these variables are already present.

A new branch is obviously not expected to achieve its full deposit potential immediately. Rather, some form of time-dependent growth pattern is likely to exist. People do not open bank accounts very frequently. New relationships are usually established when a person moves (either his residence or his place of work), recognizes a need (perhaps as a result of bank marketing efforts) or experiences some major dissatisfaction with his present bank.

A new branch, located more conveniently than existing banking offices, may be sufficient reason to switch banks. Much of the branch's clientele can be expected to arrive early in its life, as people and businesses for whom the new branch is more convenient than any other, or those attracted by the initial promotion, open accounts there. However, there may be considerable inertia: People may not be aware of the new branch right away, may not respond to the stimulus immediately or may wait until a convenient time, such as the end of a quarter, to transfer accounts.

Thus, after the initial spurt, there may still be a reasonably large influx of customers—less than the early growth, but greater than that normally experienced by established branches. Eventually, the growth rate might be expected to settle down to merely reflect the growth of the area's population and use of bank services in general. Thus, the curve would be expected to rise rapidly at first, then continue to increase, but at a decreasing rate, as the branch approaches maturity.

Growth Models in Other Industries

Growth curves have been applied to numerous other marketing problems. Several mathematical formulations have been developed, corresponding to variations in the underlying behavioral processes assumed. "The market characteristics have an important bearing on the outcome of any market penetration process. In order to carry out the share computations, it is necessary to predict the share as a function of time. There are many forms of market growth curves, depending on the product, economic, political and social environment, and state-of-the-art." [6] Several of these models are described briefly below.

Crawford (1966) compares the sales growth of a new product to the trajectory of a missile. Given the intended target and knowledge of the relevant physical laws, it is possible to calculate a series of points through which the rocket must pass if it is to reach its destination. The model used is of the form: $Y_t = a + bt + ct^2 + dt^3 + et^4$, where Y_t is the cumulative sales as of period t.

Other researchers have employed "penetration" or "saturation" curves to describe new product growth. These models assume that there is some ceiling, L, toward which the cumulative sales curve grows; that the sales increment in each time period is proportional to the remaining distance between present penetration and the ceiling, and that the ratio between successive sales increments is constant. The sales increment in the tth period is $\triangle Y_t = rL(1-r)^{t-1}$, where r is the "growth constant." [7] This model has been applied successfully to a number of new grocery products.

Another school treats new product adoption as a learning process (see, for example, [8] and [11]). This approach assumes the probability of purchasing a brand in period t is a function of the previous purchase probability and of whether the

brand was actually purchased in the preceding period. Numerous modifications of this basic model have appeared in the marketing literature. One example is $\triangle Y_t = (1-a) Y_t (L-Y_t)$, where Y_t, $\triangle Y_t$ and L are defined as above, and a is the "learning" rate.

Still others have modeled new product adoption as a "diffusion process." (see, for example, [5], [12], [13] and [14]). This approach, based on social interaction among potential purchasers, is of the form $dY/dt = k(1-Y)t$; where Y is the cumulative proportion of customers adopting the new product and k is a constant indicating individual receptivity. [5]

Although these models may have validity in other applications, none seems to fit the branch growth problem particularly well. Virtually all of the numerous surveys designed to discover bank selection factors have concluded that convenience is of overwhelming importance and that recommendations or other social interaction plays a secondary role at best. Another weakness of the diffusion process model is purely empirical: It produces an S-shaped cumulative sales curve, whereas every bank branch studied exhibited the expected "decelerating growth" shape. The theoretical basis of the learning model is inappropriate to the bank selection decision, since the latter is a one-time choice, whereas that model is based on the effects of repeat purchases and experience, characteristic of consumer packaged goods. The penetration model is concerned with the cumulative numbers of new triers, whereas the branch growth pattern refers to accounts net of closings. The theoretical foundation of the trajectory model seems somewhat weak for marketing applications in general. Thus, it was considered desirable to explore still other model formulations.

The Data Developed

The model presented here was developed using data from Bankers Trust Co. which has approximately 90 branches in the New York metropolitan area. Nineteen of these were opened between 1958 and 1966. The bank's Branch Administration Division maintains monthly records of account openings and closings at each branch, for three major consumer services: Regular checking, special checking and savings accounts. This information is kept for a period extending back ten years. Thus, monthly data on the number of active accounts at most of these newer branches were available for the first several years of their operation. This study was concerned only with checking accounts. Not all of the branches were used in determining the model parameters. Monthly data for the first four years life of each of the 13 branches opened between 1958 and 1963 (all of those for which the data were available) were used to estimate parameters. (The selection of a four-year period was based on several factors: Availability of sufficient data, visual examinations of typical growth patterns and capacities of the computer programs to be employed.) These were then tested on data from the six branches opened between 1964 and 1966.

The use of numbers of accounts rather than balances as the primary dependent variable is consistent with the bank's normal practices. It has been found more accurate to forecast this variable, then multiply it by an average balance figure (appropriately adjusted for area socio-economic characteristics) than to estimate total balances directly. (Number of accounts is considered important by regulatory authorities because it seems to be a better measure of "service to the community"—a major factor in approving applications—than does total balances.)

Model Development

Since this model is concerned with the *pattern* of account growth rather than the actual number of accounts that the branch eventually acquires, the dependent variable was standardized to facilitate comparison across branches by dividing each monthly observation by the number of accounts at the end of the first year of operation of that branch: $Y_t = N_t / N_{12}$. This procedure was also helpful in applying the model for forecasting purposes. All forecasts could be expressed in terms of a per cent of first year total number of accounts.

All data were recorded on paper tape for input to a computer through a time-sharing terminal. Figures for each service (regular and special checking) were recorded separately. Thus, there were 26 different series (2 services, 13 branches) of 48 monthly observations each. In later phases of the analysis, the data were pooled in various ways and re-analyzed.

Each of the original data series was run through a regression curve-fitting program. Although the program used includes six different functional forms, only three of these were of *a priori* interest (because the others involve the inverse of the independent variable):

1) $Y_t = a + bt$ (linear model)
2) $Y_t = at^b$ (power function)[1]
3) $Y_t = ae^{bt}$ (exponential model)[2]

[1] Equivalent to: log Y_t = log a + b log t = a' + b log t
[2] Equivalent to: log Y_t = log a + bt = a' + bt

The only measure of goodness-of-fit provided by the program was the index of determination (r^2). Based on this measure, the model that fit best for nearly every series was number 2 (see Table 1). This model was subjected to further analysis.

Since the goal of the study was to develop a model that could be applicable to all branches, tests were made to determine the effect (if any) of various branch characteristics and to decide whether data from different branches in the sample could legitimately be pooled to develop bank-wide parameters. Three branch characteristics were considered: Type of neighborhood served (4 residential branches versus 9 commercial branches), age (6 branches opened between 1958 and 1962 versus 7 opened in 1963) and size (6 larger branches, with an average of about 1,700 total checking accounts at the end of the first year versus 7 smaller ones, with an average of about 900 accounts).

The first test was to examine the coefficients of the best-fitting regression model ($Y_t = at^b$) for each service for each branch. The average and standard deviation of each coefficient was computed for each subgroup, and t-tests performed to uncover any significant differences. The only pair of coefficients that differed significantly was the b coefficient between the two size groups. Similar tests were used to examine possible differences between growth patterns of the two types of checking accounts. No differences were found (see Table 2).

TABLE 1. Index of Determination (r^2) for Individual Branch Regressions

Model:	1		2		3	
Branch	$Y_t = a + bt$		$Y_t = at^b$		$Y_t = ae^{bt}$	
	Reg.	Spec.	Reg.	Spec.	Reg.	Spec.
A	.92	.92	.99	.99	.76	.79
B	.86	.89	.97	.96	.71	.69
C	.98	.89	.98	.97	.91	.84
D	.96	.95	.97	.96	.90	.90
E	.96	.93	.98	.98	.87	.75
F	.92	.85	.98	.86	.79	.58
G	.64	.71	.89	.94	.52	.63
H	.94	.79	.99	.96	.82	.69
I	.95	.80	.99	.82	.82	.49
J	.95	.86	.99	.97	.86	.77
K	.88	.90	.99	.98	.75	.75
L	.94	.94	.97	.96	.88	.67
M	.98	.97	.97	.93	.81	.96

TABLE 2. Tests for Differences Between Groups at Branches

Model: $Y_t = at^b$

	a	b
Residential (n=4)	39.83	.378
Commercial (n=9)	37.27	.400
t-score of difference	.83	.73
Old (n=6)	40.4	.371
New (n=7)	36.1	.409
t-score of difference	1.89	1.06
Large (n=6)	40.4	.371
Small (n=7)	36.1	.423
t-score of difference	1.95	2.44
Regular Checking (n=13)	35.2	.429
Special Checking (n=13)	36.1	.429
t-score of difference	.25	.01

TABLE 3. Test of Regression Model With Dummy Variables for Branch Characteristics

641 Observations

Model:	$Y_t = at^b$	$Y_t = at^b X_1{}^c X_2{}^d X_3{}^e$
r^2	.915	.922
S.E.E. (%)	.106	.101
F-Stat. for Regr. Eqn.	6864	1898
regr. coeff. (std. err.)		
a	3.632 (.004)*	3.595 (.004)*
b	.3932 (.005)*	.3932 (.005)*
c	—	.0666 (.008)*
d	—	.0010 (.008)
e	—	.0018 (.008)

* coeff. signif. diff. from zero at 1% level
X_1 = branch size (log X_1 = 0 if large (≥1250 accts); = 1 if small (≤1250 accts))
X_2 = branch age (log X_2 = 0 if old ('58-'62); = 1 if new ('63))
X_3 = branch area (log X_3 = 0 if commercial; = 1 if residential)

TABLE 4. Pooled Regression Statistics for Growth Pattern Models

$Y = at^b$

Service	Regression Coefficients and (standard errors) a	b	Standard Error of the Estimate	R^2
Regular	32.33 (1.005)	.4291 (.0053)	1.126	.91
Special	34.80 (1.007)	.4193 (.0084)	1.206	.80
Total	34.58 (1.004)	.4241 (.0050)	1.170	.92

A second, more rigorous, test involved multiple regression analysis with dummy variables used to represent the branch characteristics. The coefficients of year of opening and area type were not significantly different from zero. The coefficient for size was significant (see Table 3). However, considering the very small improvement in the standard error of the estimate resulting from the additions of this variable against the simplicity of the time-only model, it was decided to omit the size variable.

Runs were made for the final model ($Y_t = at^b$) with data from all branches pooled, one each for special checking, regular checking and total checking. The total checking model was selected as most appropriate (see Table 4).

The model equation, along with the 90% confidence intervals was then plotted and compared with the actual data for the sample branches. Not surprisingly, about 93% of the sample observations fell within the limits. More importantly, about 93% of the observations for the six holdout branches fell within the confidence interval (see Table 5).

TABLE 5. Observations Outside of 90% Confidence Intervals For Growth Pattern Model

	Original 13 Branches	7 Holdout Branches
Too high	28	13
Too low	15	3
Within limits	601	226
Total	644	242
% Outside Interval	6.6%	6.6%

Testing the Model

As part of the process of deciding to apply for a new branch (and as part of the application itself), the bank's branch locations group makes projections of the number of accounts expected at the end of each of the first several years of the branch's life. In addition, once a branch has opened, the manager makes annual forecasts of volume for planning and budgeting purposes. Thus, two alternative sets for forecasts were available for the holdout sample branches. If the model, even in this highly simplified version, could compare favorably with these present methods, a more complete version should be well worth developing.

Unfortunately, the three forecasts are not made on the same basis. The branch locations projections are made six months to two years before the branch actually opens. The branch manager makes his projections late in each calendar year for the end of the next calendar year. The model's forecasts are assumed to be made at the end of the first year's operation for all future years. Thus, the three sets of forecasts are made at different points in time and cover different periods. Nevertheless, this is the relevant group of forecasts among which comparisons must be made.

One might expect the branch manager's projections to be most accurate and branch location's to be least precise. The latter group, however, has more experience in making such forecasts and uses a larger number of factors in making them. The model uses only one variable at a single point in time (number of accounts after one year). Thus, we might expect the model to perform poorly.

Second year and third year observations for the six holdout branches were compared with the projections made by each of the three methods. (Fourth year figures were not yet available.) For eight of the 12 figures, the model provided far better forecasts than either of the other two. In the other four cases, the branch manager's predictions were best. (However, in one of these instances, the model differed from the manager by only six accounts and in another by 14 accounts, out of a third year total of about 1,000 at each branch.) All four of these cases were third year forecasts, for which the manager had more recent information than the model (see Table 6).

The average error in the 11 forecasts by the model was −3.5%, compared to +21% for the managers and +119% for Branch Locations. Since some of the forecasts erred in each direction, the average of the absolute values of the errors is a better measure of overall accuracy. The ranking, however, is unchanged: Model, 7%; managers, 22%; Branch Locations, 128%. Because the averages are also strongly affected by outlying values, median absolute errors were computed. Although the relative performance of the three methods were slightly closer by this measure, the rankings were still unaffected (see Table 7).

It seems fair to conclude that the model offers a substantial enough improvement over present methods to warrant further study.

Directions for Further Study

First, we might consider the inclusion of additional variables to explain the remaining deviations between the model and actual results. Among these might be population growth rate, opening of additional nearby branches, special promotions, etc.

Secondly, we have been dealing only with numbers of accounts. In order to translate this into profits, it is necessary to make assumptions about balances. This would be difficult enough if balances were static, but they are not; the average balance of a new account follows a growth pattern too. Like the number of accounts, the level to which the average balance grows is likely to vary

TABLE 6. Comparison of Forecasts

Branch	Year	Locations	Manager	Model	Actual
N	1	605	650	—	698
	2	765	1220	929*	999
	3	900	1400*	1103	1289
O	1	1800	980	—	898
	2	2500	1459	1195*	1149
	3	3200	1414*	1420	1280
P	1	850	460	—	557
	2	1060	936	741*	811
	3	1200	1158*	881	1119
Q	1	1840	640	—	450
	2	2600	720	599*	578
	3	3090	725*	711	722
R	1	1080	1390	—	544
	2	1400	974	724*	746
	3	1690	1040	860*	933
S	1	2142	1525	—	674
	2	2416	1855	897*	905
	3	2663	970	1066*	1037

* Forecast closest to actual

TABLE 7. Forecast Errors

Branch	Year	Locations	Manager	Model
N	2	− 23%	+ 22%	− 7%
	3	− 30	+ 9	−14
O	2	+118	+ 27	+ 4
	3	+150	+ 10	+11
P	2	+ 31	+ 15	− 9
	3	+ 7	+ 3	−21
Q	2	+350	+ 25	+ 4
	3	+328	0	− 1
R	2	+ 88	+ 31	− 3
	3	+ 81	+ 11	− 7
S	2	+167	+105	− 1
	3	+157	− 6	+ 3
Average Error [a]		+116%	+ 28%	− 4%
Avg. Absolute Error [b]		+124	+ 28	+ 7
Median Absol. Error [c]		+103	+ 13	+ 5.5

[a] Computed by dividing algebraic sum of % errors by 12
[b] Computed by dividing sum of absolute values of % errors by 12
[c] Median of absolute values of % errors

from branch to branch, but the pattern may be similar across branches. Thus, another extension of this work would be to develop a growth model for account balances. The two models could then be combined to produce forecasts of total branch balances.

A related phenomenon is that of multiple account usage. Usually, a new customer opens only one account at the branch. As times passes, however, he may either find the need for additional services or find that the services he had been using at a competing institution can be obtained more conveniently at the new branch. Over a period of time, it would be reasonable to expect the average number of accounts per customer to increase, at least during the first several years of the branch's life. This process too could be modelled.

Finally, all of the models concerned with growth patterns should be integrated into a model of business potential in order to estimate the specific volume of deposits, loans and numbers of accounts that can be anticipated at any point in time. This, of course, is a major undertaking which will probably require substantial effort and a considerable period of time for completion. ☐

REFERENCES

1. Aaronson, Howard S., Jr., "Trading Area Analysis," *Talks on Bank Marketing*, American Bankers Association, New York, 1965.
2. Allen, Ralph W., "Factors Influencing Market Penetration," *Management Science*, Sept., 1966.
3. American Bankers Association, *A Guide to Selecting Bank Locations*, New York, 1965.
4. Brown, Thomas G., Jr., "Trading Area Analysis," *Talks on Bank Marketing*, American Bankers Association, New York, 1965.
5. Coleman, James, Elihu Katz, and Herbert Menzel, "The Diffusion of an Innovation among Physicians," *Sociometry*, Dec., 1967.
6. Crawford, C. Merle, "The Trajectory Theory of Goal Setting for New Products," *Journal of Marketing Research*, May, 1966.
7. Fourt, Louis A., and Joseph W. Woodlock, "Early Prediction of Market Success for New Grocery Products," *Journal of Marketing*, Oct. 1960.
8. Haines, George H., Jr., "A Theory of Market Behavior after Innovation," *Management Science*, July, 1964.
9. Herman, Raymond O., "Determining Your Bank's Penetration of its Area Potential," *Proceedings—March Marketing Meeting*, American Bankers Association, New York, 1967.
10. Kelly, Robert F., "Estimating Ultimate Performance Levels of New Retail Outlets," *Journal of Marketing Research*, Feb., 1967.
11. Kuehn, Alfred A., "Consumer Brand Choice—A Learning Process?" in Frank, Kuehn, and Massy (eds.) *Quantitative Techniques in Marketing Analysis*, (Homewood, Ill., Richard D. Irwin, Inc. 1962).
12. Lionberger, H. F., *Adoption of New Ideas and Practices*, (Ames, Iowa: The Iowa State University Press, 1960).
13. Rogers, Everett M., *Diffusion of Innovation* (New York: Free Press of Glencoe, 1962).
14. Shaw, Steven J., "Behavioral Science Offers Fresh Insights on New Product Acceptance," *Journal of Marketing*, Jan., 1965.
15. Taylor, Barney C., "Locating Profitable Office Sites," *Banking Magazine*, March, 1965.

Chapter 14

THE USE OF SIMULATION
IN SELECTING
BRANCH BANKS*

By E. Eugene Carter and Kalman J. Cohen

*This article is reprinted, with permission, from *Industrial Management Review*, Vol. 8, No. 2 (Spring, 1967), pp. 55-69.

Abstract

This paper applies risk analysis simulation to branch bank selection, with suggestions for non-banking applications. Investment in a particular branch is usually done after comparing anticipated returns of proposed branches. These anticipated returns are computed on the basis of the most likely single values expected for deposits, costs, and other variables. Risk analysis adds another dimension to the decision. By constructing a model of a branch's investment performance, one can study how the return is affected by the *uncertainty* inherent in forecasts of variables. Depending on management's risk preference, the choice of one investment over others depends not only on the *most likely* anticipated return, but also on the *variability* in that return.

Introduction

In many areas state legislation permits banks to establish branch operations. These branches, in effect, are small community banks, with the parent bank's name, coordination, and control. In deciding where to establish a branch, the bank faces problems similar to a grocery chain locating stores, a petroleum company placing stations, and the like. In this paper, the decision to invest in one branch rather than another is treated as a capital budgeting problem, and computer simulation is used to provide information about the degree of uncertainty inherent in expectations about the profitability of a proposed branch.

The profitability of a future branch bank depends upon such factors as the market potential of the area it serves, the share of this potential market actually tapped by the bank, the total amounts of the bank's deposits and its mix between demand and time deposits, the earnings yield realized and the expense ratios incurred by these deposits, the deposit growth rates that will materialize, and the size of the initially required investment. The most sophisticated approach

currently used by bankers would be to use their experience and judgment in making the "best possible estimate" of each of these critical factors, and then apply the resulting numbers to compute the rate of return to be anticipated if the branch were actually opened. This procedure ignores the fact that each "best possible estimate" of any critical factor is itself only one point in a range of possible values that this factor may assume, and it thus may lead to an erroneous viewpoint about the degree of reliance which should be placed on the computed rate of return. In particular, the fact that proposed branch A has an anticipated rate of return of 15 per cent per year while proposed branch B has an anticipated rate of return of 20 per cent per year does not necessarily imply that B is a better investment than A, since the uncertainties surrounding the "best possible estimates" of the critical factors associated with B may be much greater than the corresponding uncertainties for A's critical factors. Thus, uncertainty inherent in a branch's return is an important element to be considered in evaluating alternative investment opportunities.

Risk analysis simulation is an approach to capital budgeting which has been operational for several years in a number of major industrial firms.[1] While it is a technique which is readily transferable to many problem areas in banking (i.e., situations in which a decision is required about a major commitment of funds, the returns on which are uncertain), this paper specifically discusses its applicability to selecting the locations for new branch banks. In this context, risk analysis simulation can be considered to be a procedure for quantifying the extent to which uncertainty is present in the rate of return anticipated from a proposed branch bank.

[1] An excellent expository discussion, and one general example of an industrial application of risk analysis simulation, is given in Hertz [6].

A model is developed which incorporates the interrelationships between such critical factors as demand deposits, time deposits, revenues, expenses, and other variables. Given potential branches with various characteristics, the rate of return concept is used to show why one branch might be favored over the others. Then, adding risk analysis simulation, the effect of uncertainty on the expected rate of return is shown. Finally, this paper demonstrates that the desirability of an investment pivots not only on the *estimated* rate of return, but also upon the *variability* of this estimated rate of return.

Computing the Rate of Return for a Proposed Branch

The upper left-hand corner of Figure 1 shows that the average level of time and demand deposits in the branch during the first year of its operation depends on the "market" demand and time deposit potentials, and on the share of these potentials captured by the bank in the first year. A representative interest rate (the prime rate) is used as an element in determining both operating costs and revenues for the bank, because interest rates affect costs as well as represent revenues. Then, by suitably combining the yearly rental charges, the prime rate, and the demand and time deposits for the first year, revenue and operating cost for the branch in the first year are computed.

Part of the initial investment in the branch (upper right of Figure 1) is expensed as a current operating expense; e.g., advertising expenses would be treated in this manner. The remaining investment is depreciated over the life of the branch; e.g., capital equipment would be so treated. Combining the expensed portion of the investment, the depreciation for the first year, and the revenue and operating cost for the first year, before-tax profits are calculated. The marginal corporate income tax rate, applied to the before-tax profits, gives the branch's profit after taxes for the first year. All non-cash charges (depreciation each year, and the fraction of the initial investment outlay that was expensed) must be added back to the profits after taxes to generate the net after-tax cash flow of the branch for the year. Since the total investment outlay is considered to be a cash outflow at the time the branch is established (i.e., at the time 0), the portion of the initial outlay that is tax deductible as a first-year expense should not be treated as a first-year cash outflow.

The second year carries over three particular items from the first year. The first is the prime rate, and in this model the prime rate in any given year is related to the prime rate in the preceding year. Likewise, depreciation will carry over to successive years. Finally, after the first year of the branch's life, its deposits in the next year are computed by applying some particular growth rate to the preceding year's deposits. The initial growth rate is generally the highest that will be experienced during the entire lifetime of the branch. After the branch reaches maturity, its deposits will grow at the average rate experienced by the bank as a whole. Between the initial year and the time when the branch matures, its deposits will grow at successively decreasing rates.

Figure 1 shows the general flow of important variables for the proposed branch in the second and following years. From the demand and time deposits of the current year, a demand and time deposit figure for the following year is computed, using the growth rates just described. Again, the prime rate and yearly rental join with the demand and time deposits to give current operating cost and revenue. Bringing in depreciation, before-tax profit for that year for the branch is computed, and the marginal tax rate gives after-tax profits. Adding back the non-cash expense of depreciation (note that the actual capital outlay being depreciated has already been taken into account as an initial cash outflow), the branch's cash flow for this year is computed.

For this branch bank problem, projections of revenues and expenses are made for a number of years. Y_0 (a negative number) is the cash outflow for the initial investment. In later years, Y_i represents the cash inflow from the investment, which is the revenue for year i minus the expenses, minus the taxes on the profits, plus the non-cash expenses. Thus, the cash inflow is the after-tax profit plus the non-cash expenses for the period. Then the rate of return is the r for which

$$\sum_{i=0}^{n} \frac{Y_i}{(1+r)^i} = 0$$

where n is the number of years in the hori-

Figure 1   Flow Chart of Yearly Branch Operations

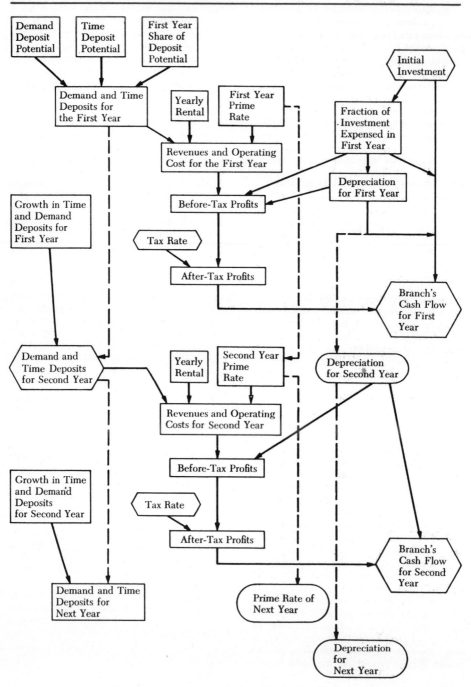

152

zon.[2]

It is clear that the assumptions of perfect forecasts of a single value represent a gross simplification. There are inevitably many critical uncertainties involved in attempts to predict the relevant aspects of the future. The risk analysis simulation technique has been designed to start from the premise that most forecasts can be made meaningfully only in the form of probability distributions. In risk analysis simulation, a computer is used to generate a realized value from each of the probability distributions of the major factors shown in the flow charts.[3] Once these specific numbers have been generated, the rate of return is computed. The process is then repeated; the computer generates another set of realized values from each of the probability distributions, and once more a rate of return is computed. This is done a large number of times; in the illustrative results presented below, it has been done 250 times for each of the proposed branch locations. As a result, a whole distribution of rates of return for any branch is obtained. In effect, this distribution of rates of return shows the probability that any specified rate of return will actually be achieved if the branch is established.

The Model

There are four principal steps in building a model:

First, the relationships among the major variables must be postulated. In the branch bank case, costs depend on investment, depreciation, the prime rate, the level of deposits, and so on. Revenues from deposits were based on the prime rate and the level and mix of demand and time deposits.

Second, the relationships decided upon must then be quantified. The equations defining the relationships may be complex or relatively simple, depending on the accuracy desired in the model, the comparative importance of the particular variable being estimated, and the mathematical sophistication of the model builder.

Third, the equations have to be assembled into a computer program. This model required a total of 700 statements in the IBM programming language, Fortran IV.[4]

Finally, following trial runs in which all programming errors are discovered and eliminated, the resulting program is run for the actual simulation. The time and expense will vary depending on the desired accuracy/cost trade-off as well as the number of alternative branches being considered.[5]

The flow charts and commentary presented indicate the approach taken in this paper to analyzing prospective branch banks. Although the paper will focus on the distribution under uncertainty of rates of return of proposed branches, it is also possible to compute the risk distributions for present value of branches, for the growth in deposits, and for other relevant outcome criteria. The present model is for illustrative

---

[2] Another criterion for judging capital expenditures, the present value, alters the calculations to find the net present value, *given* the cost of capital rate, r. Partially because the rate of return method assumes that cash throw-offs are reinvested at the same rate earned on the original project whereas the present value reinvests the cash throw-offs at the cost of capital, these two concepts do not always rank projects in the same way. Terborgh [13] shows an interesting example of four projects in which the present value ranking is exactly opposite the rate of return evaluation. In general, whenever they lead to different results the present value method is superior to the rate of return approach. Lorie and Savage [8] have shown that the rate of return may not be unique; one investment may have more than one rate of return. Hirsheifer [7] points out that the rate of return and present value both ignore borrowing and lending opportunities open to the firm. In addition, Weingartner [14] and Näslund [11] present mathematical programming approaches to the capital budgeting problem.

This paper uses the rate of return calculation because the differences in the rate of return and present value measures would be minimal in the examples used, and the rate of return simplifies the presentation and makes it more familiar to bankers who are used to thinking of it in terms of bond yields.

[3] It may be useful to indicate briefly how a computer generates random variables in the simulation. Random drawings from most probability distributions are based upon any one of the many library subroutines which generate numbers that appear to be randomly distributed in the interval 0,1. Various transformations are employed to convert these uniformly distributed random numbers to a sequence of random numbers possessing any specified probability distribution.

[4] However, 250 statements were in subprograms from the IBM SHARE library which are available to all users, and 150 of the remaining statements were in programs which, while developed especially for this model, could be used by a firm in many other areas. One example of the last is the internal rate of return calculation.

[5] A larger number of trials for each branch will produce a more accurate probability distribution of the rate of return. This advantage is offset, however, by the disadvantage of greater costs in computer time. The following procedure might be useful in arriving at a reasonable accuracy/cost trade-off.

For a particular branch, some very large trial size (e.g., 5,000 trials) could arbitrarily be accepted as a standard. The cumulative distribution of the rate of return for that branch for the 5,000-trial case would then be used as a reference point for computing a "squared-error" measure of the cumulative distributions produced by other trial sizes. This squared-error measure is found by squaring the deviation of each observation from the standard at 5 per cent intervals, summing for all the intervals and finally taking a square root of this sum. For this purpose, the 5,000-trial run can itself be regarded as consisting of 50 independent observations of 100 trials each, 20 independent observations of 250 trials each, 10 independent observations of 500 trials each, etc. The squared-error measurement for each trial size should then be averaged over the number of independent observations, in order to generate the desired cost/accuracy trade-off relationship. (The costs of computer time for the various trial sizes can easily be measured, of course.)

Table 1   Definitions of Variables

t = the year of branch operation, $t = 1, \ldots,$ L ($t = 0$ is the time the branch is established.)	$\bar{g}_M$ = mean mature growth rate in the branch's deposits
L = lifetime of the branch (number of years)	σ_M = standard deviation of mature growth rate in the branch's deposits
C_o = initial outlay required to establish branch	$\bar{g}_t$ = mean growth rate in the branch's deposits in year t, $t = 1, \ldots, L - 1$
C_t = current costs (excluding depreciation) of operating branch in year t, $t = 1, \ldots, L$	σ_t = standard deviation of growth rate in the branch's deposits in year t, $t = 1, \ldots,$ $L - 1$
D_t = average level of demand deposits in the branch in year t, $t = 1, \ldots, L$	
T_t = average level of time deposits in the branch in year t, $t = 1, \ldots, L$	p_t = prime rate of interest in year t, $t = 1,$ $\ldots, L - 1$
D^P = demand deposit potential for the branch	r = rate of return of the branch over an L-year lifetime
T^P = time deposit potential for the branch	
A = annual rental cost for the branch	F_t = after-tax cash inflow from branch in year t, $t = 1, \ldots, L$
s^T = share of time deposit potential initially realized by the branch	θ = marginal tax rate on corporate profits
s^D = share of demand deposit potential initially realized by the branch	R_t = annual revenues for branch, $t = 1, \ldots, L$
g_t^D = actual growth rate in the branch's demand deposits in year t, $t = 1, \ldots,$ $L - 1$	π_t^B = before-tax profits of the branch in year t, $t = 1, \ldots, L$
g_t^T = actual growth rate in the branch's time deposits in year t, $t = 1, \ldots, L - 1$	π_t^A = after-tax profits of the branch in year t, $t = 1, \ldots, L$
M = number of years required for the branch to reach maturity	h = fraction of the initial outlay required to establish the branch that is depreciable, the remainder of the initial outlay being expensed in the first year
$\bar{g}_I$ = mean initial growth rate in the branch's deposits	H_t = depreciation charges for the branch in the year t, $t = 1, \ldots, L$
σ_I = standard deviation of initial growth rate in the branch's deposits	N = number of histories simulated for the branch

purposes only and is not intended to be totally realistic or to furnish all the risk distributions of proposed branches along all of the dimensions which management may consider relevant.

Before a computer can be used for the simulation trials, it is necessary to define explicitly the relationships postulated. Table 1 defines the variables used in the model.

Figure 2 indicates the probability distributions for many of the major relationships in this model. Although the growth rates in time and demand deposits are related to a normal distribution with a mean growth rate ($\bar{g}_t$) and a standard deviation (σ_t), this mean and standard deviation are allowed to change over time.

From time $t = 2$ until time $t = M$, the maturity date, the mean growth for each year ($\bar{g}_t$) and the standard deviation (σ_t) is

$$\bar{g}_t = \bar{g}_I - \frac{t-1}{M-2} (\bar{g}_I - \bar{g}_M)$$

$$t = 2, \ldots, M,$$
$$(M > 2)$$

$$\sigma_t = \sigma_I - \frac{t-1}{M-2} (\sigma_I - \sigma_M)$$

This process provides a linear interpolation between the initial growth rate and the mature growth rate.[6] For $t = M + 1$ through the rest of the life, L,

$$\left.\begin{array}{l} \bar{g}_t = \bar{g}_M \\[2mm] \sigma_t = \sigma_M \end{array}\right\} \quad t = M + 1, \ldots, L-1$$

From these growth rates, the demand and time deposits in subsequent years are

$$D_t = (1 + g^D_{t-1}) \, D_{t-1}$$
$$t = 2, \ldots, L$$
$$T_t = (1 + g^T_{t-1}) \, T_{t-1}$$

---

[6] As an example, take $\bar{g}_I = 20$, $\bar{g}_M = 8$, $M = 5$. The linear interpolation makes each year decrease by 4, and
$\bar{g}_1 = 20$
$\bar{g}_2 = 16$
$\bar{g}_3 = 12$
$\bar{g}_4 = 8$

The revenues of the branch are

$$R_t = B_t^1 D_t + B_t^2 T_t, \qquad t = 1, \ldots, L$$

In general, B_t^2 will be larger than B_t^1. The higher revenues associated with time as compared to demand deposits reflect both differences in the Federal Reserve's legal reserve requirements and also portfolio composition effects that stem from differences in the capital backing requirements of the Federal Reserve examiner's criteria.[7]

In estimating current operating costs (C_t), economies of scale[8] enter into the cost of demand deposits. The current costs from time deposits are proportional to the level of time deposits, and are directly linked to the prime interest rate (p_t). Current costs (C_t) are, then, related to the annual rental (A) and the deposit levels $(D_t$ and $T_t)$.

When demand deposits are less than 2.7183 million,

$$C_t = A + A_t^1 D_t + A_t^2 T_t$$

and when demand deposits are equal to or more than 2.7183 million,[9]

$$C_t = A + A_t^3 D_t + A_t^4 \ln D_t + A_t^2 T_t$$

where the parameters are distributed as shown in Figure 2.

Of the initial investment (C_o), a fraction (h) is depreciated over the life of the branch (L).

$$H_t = \frac{hC_o}{L}, \, t = 1, \ldots, L$$

---

[7] For a general discussion of the relevant asset management considerations, see [2], Part II.

[8] See [9], pp. 30-33, 40ff.

[9] At the pivot point under conditions of certainty, the linear and curvilinear equations will be equal. In addition, their slopes will be equal. Then
$$sD = .02D + .015 \ln D$$
$$s = .02 + \frac{.015}{D}$$
where s is the expected value of the slope coefficient (A_t^1) in the linear equation, and as shown in Figure 3, .02 and .015 are the expected values of A_t^3 and A_t^4, respectively. Solving the two simultaneous equations,
$$D = e = 2.718282$$
$$s = .0255182$$
When demand deposits are below 2.7183 million dollars, the current costs arising from the handling of these deposits are assumed to be proportional to the level of deposits. When demand deposits are equal to or greater than 2.7183 million dollars, the current costs from the demand deposits are related to the level of demand deposits and the natural logarithm of the demand deposits.

and a fraction $(1-h)$ is expensed the first year,

Investment expensed first year $= (1-h) C_o$

Pre-tax profits (π_t^B) for the branch are then calculated from current revenue (R_t), current costs (C_t), and the investment depreciated (H_t) and expensed $(1-h)C_o$ that year.

$$\pi_t^B = R_t - C_t - H_t - (1-h) C_o, \qquad t = 1$$

$$\pi_t^B = R_t - C_t - H_t, \, t = 2, \ldots, L$$

Allowing for a marginal tax rate on corporate profits of θ, after-tax profits (π_t^A) are

$$\pi_t^A = (1 - \theta) \, \pi_t^B, \, t = 1, \ldots, L$$

The paper previously explained the necessity of adding back the noncash expenses for the year to avoid double counting. Then, the yearly net after-tax cash inflow (F_t) for the proposed branch is

$$F_t = \pi_t^A + H_t + (1-h) \, C_o \qquad t = 1$$

$$F_t = \pi_t^A + H_t \qquad t = 2, \ldots, L$$

The rate of return (r) is the rate for which

$$-C_o + \sum_{t=1}^{L} \frac{F_t}{(1 + r)^t} = 0$$

The prime interest rate (p_t) begins at 4 per cent, for $t = 1$, in each simulation. For each subsequent year $(t = 2, \ldots, L)$, the prime rate depends on the prime rate of the previous period, p_{t-1}, with the probabilities of change previously shown in Figure 2. The prime rate is limited to the interval 2½ per cent to 5½ per cent. This in effect defines a one-period Markov process.[10]

Inputs

For the illustrative results presented here, many of the variables in the model were con-

---

[10] In a more realistic model, the deposit growth rates and the prime interest rate both may be related to some general index of economic activity. Hence, during any year these variables in fact may not be independent, as assumed in this model. To the extent that they are considered important, modifications of this type can readily be introduced into the model before it is actually applied.

Figure 2°   Probability Distributions Used

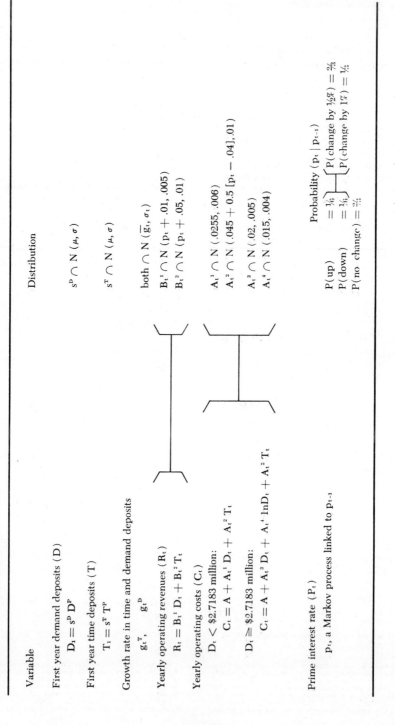

Variable	Distribution
First year demand deposits (D)	
$D_1 = s^D D^P$	$s^D \cap N(\mu, \sigma)$
First year time deposits (T)	
$T_1 = s^T T^P$	$s^T \cap N(\mu, \sigma)$
Growth rate in time and demand deposits	
$g_t^T, \quad g_t^D$	both $\cap N(\bar{g}_t, \sigma_t)$
Yearly operating revenues (R_t)	
$R_t = B_t^1 D_t + B_t^2 T_t$	$B_t^1 \cap N(p_t + .01, .005)$ $B_t^2 \cap N(p_t + .05, .01)$
Yearly operating costs (C_t)	
$D_t < \$2.7183$ million:	
$C_t = A + A_t^1 D_t + A_t^2 T_t$	$A_t^1 \cap N(.0255, .006)$ $A_t^2 \cap N(.045 + 0.5[p_t - .04], .01)$
$D_t \geq \$2.7183$ million:	
$C_t = A + A_t^3 D_t + A_t^4 \ln D_t + A_t^2 T_t$	$A_t^3 \cap N(.02, .005)$ $A_t^4 \cap N(.015, .004)$
Prime interest rate (P_t)	
p_t, a Markov process linked to p_{t-1}	Probability ($p_t \mid p_{t-1}$)

P(up)   = 1/6 ⎱ P(change by 1/2%) = 2/3
P(down)   = 1/6 ⎰ P(change by 1%) = 1/3
P(no change) = 2/3

°Throughout the paper, "∩ N (X, Y)" means the variable is distributed as a normal distribution with *mean*, X, and *standard deviation*, Y.

Table 2   Characteristics Of Proposed Branches

Variable	Normal Distribution Parameters°	Potential Branches				
		A	B	C	D	E
Initial Investment	μ	75,000	100,000	300,000	100,000	300,000
	σ	7,500	10,000	30,000	10,000	10,000
Demand Deposit	μ	7,500,000	7,500,000	7,500,000	Skewed	7,500,000
Potential	σ	1,500,000	1,500,000	1,500,000		500,000
Time Deposit	μ	2,500,000	2,500,000	2,500,000	Skewed	2,500,000
Potential	σ	500,000	500,000	500,000		140,000
Annual Rental	μ	100,000	100,000	· 100,000	100,000	100,000
	σ	0	0	0	0	0
Initial Growth Rate	μ	20%	20%	20%	20%	20%
	σ	5%	5%	5%	5%	2.5%
Mature Growth Rate	μ	10%	10%	10%	10%	10%
	σ	2%	2%	2%	2%	1%
Fraction of Investment	μ	75%	75%	75%	75%	75%
Depreciated	σ	5%	5%	5%	5%	5%
First Year Share of Deposit Potential (Skewed)	mode	12%	20%	25%	20%	25%
Expected Return Under Certainty		4.1%	16.6%	14.1%	16.6%	14.1%

° μ = Mean
  σ = Standard Deviation

sidered as deterministic and the same for all prospective branches. These were:

L (the branch's life)   = 20 years
θ (marginal tax rate)   = 48 per cent
N (simulation runs per branch) = 250

For each of the proposed branches many of the particular variables were generated from the normal distributions with the means and standard deviations shown in Table 2.

Although many of the distributions fit the normal curve, particular ones do not. Figure 3 shows the shape of the distributions used for the share of potential market (s^T and s^D) for all the different branches, and the distribution used for the time and demand deposit potentials (T^P and D^P) for Branch D. Both these distributions are skewed so as to allow values higher than the "most likely" value with greater frequency than values lower than the "most likely" value. This skewness can be explained by noting that a given market share

may not be realized, but there is a small chance that the proposed branch will be unusually successful in capturing the deposit potentials. In a like manner, Branch D's time and demand deposit potentials allow for a potential market which is unusually large.

In brief, the essential differences in the branches may be summarized as follows:

Branch A has the lowest investment and lowest first-year share of deposit potential. Table 2 also shows that Branch A has the lowest expected return under certainty.

Branch B has a moderate investment and a moderate first-year share of deposits. It has the highest return under certainty.

Branch C has the highest investment and the highest first-year share of deposits. Note, however, that Branch C's return under certainty is less than Branch B's, indicating that the higher market share captured in the first year is more than offset by the higher initial investment.

Branch D has the same investment and first-year share of deposits as B, but the dis-

Figure 3   Skewed Distribution

Frequency

.6

.5   Share of Potential Market

.4

.3

.2

.1

Branch

A	4.0	8.0	12.0	16.0	20.0	24.0	28.0	32.0
B	6.6	13.3	20.0	26.6	33.3	40.0	46.6	53.3
C	8.3	16.7	25.0	33.3	41.6	50.0	58.3	66.3
D	6.6	13.3	20.0	26.6	33.3	40.0	46.6	53.3
E	20.0	22.5	25.0	27.5	30.0	32.5	35.0	37.5

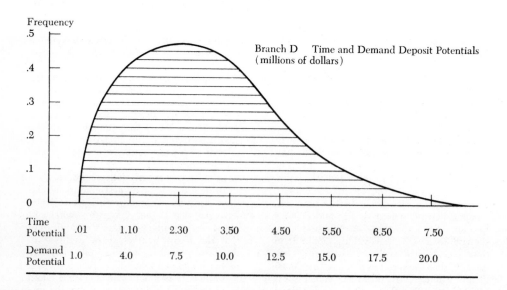

Frequency
.5

.4   Branch D   Time and Demand Deposit Potentials
                                (millions of dollars)
.3

.2

.1

0

Time Potential	.01	1.10	2.30	3.50	4.50	5.50	6.50	7.50
Demand Potential	1.0	4.0	7.5	10.0	12.5	15.0	17.5	20.0

tributions for its demand and time deposit potentials are skewed, and reflect much greater uncertainty. Under certainty, it shares the highest return with Branch B.

Branch E has the same high investment and first-year share of deposits as Branch C, and likewise has the same return under certainty. However, the uncertainty present in Branch E is substantially less than any of the other proposed branches.

Results

Figure 4 shows a bar chart, or histogram, for each of the proposed branches, indicating the probability of a given rate of return in 5 per cent intervals. Compared to Branches A and C, Branches B and D have substantially greater uncertainty in the rate of return which can be realized. Conversely, Branch E shows a tight clustering of the returns under uncertainty. A 15 per cent range contains substantially all of the returns from the computer simulation of Branch E, indicating that the bank can be relatively certain that Branch E's actual return will be within the 15 to 30 per cent interval.

Figure 5 illustrates one useful way of understanding the risk simulation results. Here, and in subsequent figures, the horizontal axis indicates the rate of return, and the vertical axis shows the probability of a return *at least as good* as that point. For example, if one-tenth of the simulation trials had a return of 15 per cent or less, then the probability of a return of *at least* 15 per cent would be .90.

Consider Branches D and E as two mutually exclusive alternatives available to the bank. Although D has a higher rate of return under certainty than E (16.6 per cent compared to 14.1 per cent), the probability of a non-negative return is much higher with Branch E (1.00 versus .92). More striking than this fact, Branch E has an even greater likelihood of a return of 5 per cent or more compared to Branch D (.97 compared to .79). But Branch D has one

chance out of three of a return of 30 per cent or more, whereas Branch E has virtually no chance of a return of 30 per cent or more.[11] None of these factors stems from the fact that Branch E has a lower return under certainty than Branch D. The important point is that simulation and risk analysis present useful data which the "expected return under certainty" does not give management. Clearly, the final decision depends on the risk preference function of management, other things constant.

Now consider Branches A, B, and C as being mutually exclusive possibilities for the establishment of a single real branch. They differ only in that each has a different distribution of initial investment outlays, to which there corresponds a different distribution of first-year market share initially realized. The certainty rates of return for the Branches are 4.1 per cent for A, 16.6 per cent for B, and 14.1 per cent for C. The frequency distributions for all these branches show a great deal of variability in rates of return, with the rates of return for Branch B being the most variable. Comparison of the distributions shown in Figure 6 show that Branch A is dominated by both B and C. This means that there is a greater probability that any given rate of return will be achieved by B and C than by Branch A. Hence, Branch A is not as good an investment as either Branch B or Branch C, regardless of management's degree of risk aversion. Note, however, that neither Branch B nor Branch C dominates the other. Branch C is a somewhat more conservative investment than Branch B; i.e., Branch C is considerably less likely to generate a high rate of return, but it is also less likely to generate a loss or a low rate of return.

Comparisons based on risk show that A is the worst possible choice, while the choice between B and C depends on management's risk preferences. Even though Branch C requires a much greater initial investment outlay than Branch B, a conservative management should prefer Branch C, while a venturesome management would be inclined to prefer Branch B.

All these comparisons assume that management is basing its branching decision on the rate of return as an investment criterion, rather than using the rate of deposit growth as the criterion. Although banks *should* base their investment decisions on a profitability concept such as the rate of return or net

[11] There are other useful ways of expressing the results of the simulation. For example, lower and upper 5 per cent confidence levels can be estimated. The lower 5 per cent confidence level (−5.6 per cent for Branch D and 11.2 per cent for Branch E) means that there is one chance in 20 of a return less than the indicated rate; the upper 5 per cent confidence level (70.0 per cent for Branch D and 24.5 per cent for Branch E) implies one chance in 20 of a return greater than the indicated rate. These confidence levels can be valuable indicators of the uncertainty present in the rate of return of a proposed branch.

Figure 4   Rate of Return Histograms

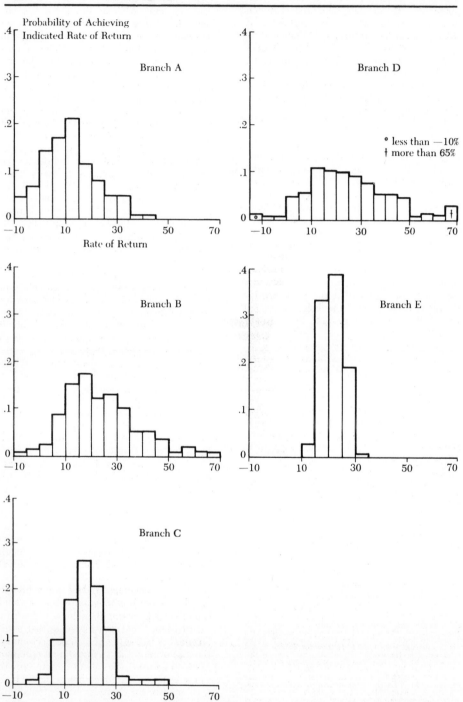

Figure 5   Cumulative Rate of Return Distributions

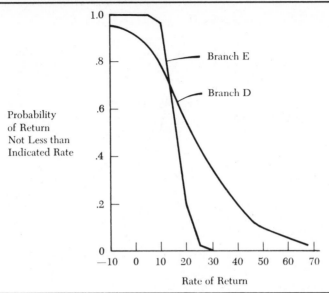

present value, some recent research[12] raises doubts about whether bank management does behave in this manner.

Conclusion

The examples presented here indicate the extra information about branch location and investment decisions which is available to bank management using risk analysis simulation. The paper has shown the weakness of relying solely on an expected rate of return computed from the "best guess" of many input variables.

There are limitations to this present paper, some of which were intentional oversimplifications for the sake of illustrating the risk analysis simulation technique. In addition to the simple assumptions about current revenues and operating costs depending solely on deposit levels and the prime rate, there is the more important oversimplification present in the potential demand and time deposit figures. Particular distributions of market potentials for each branch are accepted as given. Very little work has actually been done in developing a rigorous procedure for a bank to use in arriving at this sort of market estimate. This is one of the most important variables, and

[12] See [3] and [4].

the simulation outlined would not be at all realistic without a far more accurate, explanatory model of this "market," which is simply used here as a gross concept. Although work needs to be done in this area, it is beyond the scope of this paper.[13]

Another question must be how the bank can develop the required probability distributions. The relation of costs and revenues to the prime rate, number of employees, number of accounts, nature of business, and so forth can generally be found through appropriate regression analyses. The first-year share of market and the growth rates can

[13] Perhaps a starting approach can be suggested. First, what are the significant variables that affect deposit levels? Some plausible variables would seem to be:
1. The number and nature of business firms in the proposed branch's immediate and outlying areas, their average sales volume, and their average number of employees.
2. The number of residences in the area, the average income of the residents and the range of income, the age distributions of residents, etc.
3. The existence of bank branches. This problem relates to the "market share" problem, noted in Hartung and Fisher [5].
4. The amount of money to be spent in launching the branch through advertising, etc.
Second, certain variables in the above list (plus others) may be found to be more significant than others through regression analysis with data from existing branches. The significant variables can then be studied in depth.
Third, from the study of existing branches and the significant variables, the bank can make reasonable estimates of the potential market for proposed branches. Whatever the technique, the bank needs to be especially careful in estimating this potential deposit figure, for obviously it is a key variable in the profitability of the proposed branch.

Figure 6   Cumulative Rate of Return Distributions

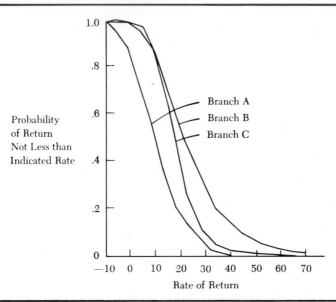

also be found by careful study of existing branches. However, in lieu of the suggested regression analyses, the familiar "subjective survey" of key officials can be made. This survey often takes the form of asking the person to estimate the most likely value of X, then to indicate X' and X" on either side of X, so that he is two-thirds confident the final value will fall in this interval. There are more sophisticated variants of this theme, but basically it does rely on subjective estimates by personnel expected to be aware of the main factors. Although this approach may be the only one practical in some situations, generally a more objective technique such as regression analysis would be better.

One of the major gaps in the model is the lack of interdependency among the proposed branch banks. For example, the profitability of proposed branches A and B may depend on various common elements, such as the prime rate. Adjacent branches may have common deposit potential "markets," and a higher growth in one's deposit levels may result in a lower growth in the other deposits. Similarly, there are interdependencies between the success of one branch and what happens to branches which are already established.

One approach to interdependencies of proposed investments is given in Cohen and Elton.[14] To summarize, first the model would specify for each current or anticipated branch and for the bank as a whole what the cash flow for each project depends upon. This model would necessarily include the various interrelationships among the branch banks. Next, the returns for each project and for the bank as a whole would be simulated, period by period. The present value for each of the branches would be computed and retained trial by trial. When the simulation is complete, the variances, covariances, and means for the present values of all the branches would be computed. A quadratic programming approach would then be used to calculate an efficient frontier of portfolios of branch banks.

The quadratic programming technique combines various investments in branch banks to generate the efficient frontier which indicates the *maximum return* possible for a *given variation* (standard deviation) of returns, or alternatively, the *minimum variation* possible for a *given* return. The efficient frontier is really a boundary. Points to the left of it are undesirable, since they

[14] See [1].

have a lower return and as much variation as a boundary point. Points to the right of the boundary are unattainable, since these points have the same variation but a higher return, and the quadratic programing solution already has given the highest return possible for a given variation.

The point to pick on the efficient frontier (which determines the set of new branch banks to open) is that point that maximizes the market value of the bank's stock. This point depends upon the market's trade-off between risk and return. For a particular bank, selecting the point would require estimating the trade-off for various combinations of branches it is considering. In practice, it would mean comparing the bank to other banks that react to similar underlying variables and have the same risk-return combination. Once the point of the efficient frontier curve is found, then the quadratic programming solution which generated the curve would indicate the optimum combination of proposed branches to be built.

There are, of course, other areas of business in which the techniques of risk analysis simulation could be useful. Many capital budgeting decisions occur in which a decision is required about a major expenditure of funds the returns on which are highly uncertain. A few examples are illustrations of representative problems to which the risk analysis technique can be applied. First, the costs, savings, and service benefits from a large installation of data-processing equipment typically can be estimated only with great uncertainty. Second, the effects of alternative promotional expenditures on profitability can be described at best in terms of subjective probability distributions. Third, the prospects inherent in potential merger possibilities depend on a number of highly uncertain political and economic forces.

In all these situations the risk analysis simulation procedure can be employed. Usual analyses ignore the problem of uncertainty and assume that all relevant variables can be accurately forecast. In contrast, the risk analysis technique, by providing an understanding of the entire probability distribution of returns, is conducive to decision making on a more rational basis.

In addition to the benefits derived from a simulation analysis, the steps required for simulation have several indirect benefits.

First, the "forced quantification" requires the assessment of the many variables in a critical way. Second, the distributions required for effective simulation force the management to think about the possible ranges and likelihood of several variables. No longer is an official able to indicate merely that he thinks the branch will have an average of $5,000,000 in deposits. When will this level of deposits be realized? How will the deposits grow? How likely is the deposit figure to lie outside $5,000,000 ± 10 per cent? Thus, the slipshod casual answer is automatically rejected in favor of one requiring more thoughtful consideration. Finally, simulation requires rigorous analysis of the interdependencies of the various factors, coupled with a complete study of how costs and revenues are affected by changes in various factors. The resulting analysis may reveal that familiar ideas about earnings being tied directly to deposit levels or the prime rate being the main determinant of profits are grossly oversimplified. Not only may familiar variables be found to be less important than was previously thought, but other variables may be found that turn out to be very important. Thus, benefits from the mathematical rigor forced by simulation accrue to management from areas other than mere risk analysis.

References

1. Cohen, Kalman J. and Elton, Edwin J. "Inter-Temporal Portfolio Analysis Based on Simulation of Joint Returns," *Management Science,* forthcoming.

2. Cohen, Kalman J. and Hammer, Frederick S. (eds.). *Analytical Methods in Banking.* Homewood, Ill.: Richard D. Irwin, Inc., 1966.

3. Cohen, Kalman J. and Reid, Samuel Richardson. "The Benefits and Costs of Bank Mergers," *Journal of Financial and Quantitative Analysis,* December, 1966, pp. 15-57.

4. Cohen, Kalman J. and Reid, Samuel Richardson. "Effects of Regulation, Branching, and Mergers on Banking Structure and Performance," *Southern Economic Journal,* forthcoming.

5. Hartung, Philip H. and Fisher, James L. "Branch Switching and Mathematical Programming in Market Expansion," *Management Science,* August, 1955, pp. B231-B243.

6. Hertz, David B. "Risk Analysis in Capital Investment," *Harvard Business Review,* January-February, 1964, pp. 95-106; reprinted as Chapter 23 in [2].

7. Hirscheifer, J. "On the Theory of Optimal Investment Decision," *Journal of Political Economy*, August, 1958, pp. 329-352; reprinted as Part IV, Section 1 in [12].

8. Lorie, James H., and Savage, Leonard. "Three Problems in Capital Rationing," *Journal of Business*, October, 1955, pp. 229-239; reprinted as Part II, Section 4 in [12].

9. Luftig, Paul. "Evaluating Capital Expenditures in Branch Banking," unpublished dissertation submitted to the Stonier Graduate School of Banking at Rutgers — The State University, 1962.

10. McMillan, Calude and Gonzalez, Richard F. *Systems Analysis: A Computer Approach to Decision Models.* Homewood, Illinois: Richard D. Irwin, Inc., 1965, Chapters 2, 5 and 6.

11. Näslund, Bertil. "A Model of Capital Budgeting Under Risk," *Journal of Business*, April, 1966, pp. 257-271.

12. Soloman, Ezra. *The Management of Corporate Capital.* Glencoe, Ill.: The Free Press of Glencoe, 1959.

13. Terborgh, George. "Some Comments on the Dean-Smith Article on the MAPI Formula," *Journal of Business*, April, 1956; reprinted as Part V, Section 6 in [12].

14. Weingartner, H. M. *Mathematical Programming and the Analysis of Capital Budgeting Problems.* Englewood Cliffs, N.J.: Prentice-Hall, Inc., 1963.

Part IV

BALANCE SHEET MANAGEMENT

In Part III we examined various forecasting and simulation models which help bank management assess the consequences of policy decisions. As suggested in Robinson's discussion of BANKMOD (Chapter 12), the emphasis of simulation models has been on organizing and translating data into projections of future performance. Although simulation is widely used in bank profit planning with good results, its value is limited in some respects by the quality of inputs that must be provided by management. Some of these inputs involve simple accounting relationships, but others require an understanding of sophisticated interrelationships among management decision variables.

Linear programming (LP) models, by comparison, relate more directly to the actual decision process and are less dependent on managements' understanding of key relationships. For bank balance sheet management, LP models provide the optimal size and composition of assets, liabilities, and capital accounts over a multiperiod planning horizon. Because the LP model often involves liability and capital management as well as asset management, the title of Part IV is "balance sheet management" rather than "asset management." Linear programming provides management with a dynamic planning tool that actually develops values for key decision variables. Management inputs are in the form of constraints on and policies concerning such variables as funds available for investment, acceptable risk levels, volume of portfolio trading, loan limits, and regulatory requirements. Models such as those examined in Part IV have been implemented successfully in some commercial banks.

Despite successful applications of the linear programming balance sheet management model, use of this technique has not spread as rapidly as might be expected. In general, behavioral aspects of utilizing the LP model are responsible for the slow growth in its use. The basic behavioral problem stems from managements' lack of familiarity with the capabilities and applications of linear programming. Compounding this is a general uneasiness resulting from not understanding the mathematics by which an LP model arrives at an optimal solution. The mathematical nature of this technique can intimidate bank executives, even though successful use of the linear program does not require knowledge of the underlying mathematics. Most LP models can be packaged so that management inputs information in a familiar form.

Experience with linear programming applications has shown clearly that management's total involvement and commitment is a key to successful implementation. A "hands off" attitude on the part of those who must utilize and provide input for the model is usually disastrous. Communication between the management scientist-designer and the manager-user is the key factor for success. While such communication is usually important in the application of any management science technique, it is even more essential in utilizing a linear programming model.

It should be emphasized again that linear programming is a technique for providing management with a better understanding of critical aspects of their decisions. The use of an LP model for bank balance sheet management cannot in any sense replace management's careful establishment of key policy constraints and guidelines, which actually determine the solution provided by the model. The value of linear programming is its ability to translate management policy into optimal short-run decisions and long-term planning guideposts. Understanding of the nature of LP models and their applications will probably continue to evolve, alleviating many traditional managers' uneasiness with the technique. The result could be much greater use of the LP approach in bank management.

Part IV focuses on bank financial planning models using linear programming and some of its extensions. The preponderance of LP-based models reflects the editors' opinion that the full potential of this approach to balance sheet management has not yet been realized. This potential includes structuring an investment portfolio, setting transfer prices, capital budgeting, lease management, determining optimal asset mix, and suggesting capital structure. In Chapter 15, "Linear Programming Models for Optimal Bank Dynamic Balance Sheet Management," Kalman J. Cohen and Frederick S. Hammer provide a thorough description of LP models for determining the optimal size and composition of the asset, liability, and capital accounts of a commercial bank. The nature of input variables, constraints, and the model's basic equations are discussed.

The approach described by Cohen and Hammer has been successfully applied at Bankers Trust Company. Kalman J. Cohen discusses this application, which he helped formulate and implement, in Chapter 16, "Dynamic Balance Sheet Management: A Management Science Approach." The article focuses on the interaction between management scientists and traditional managers, and underscores our earlier emphasis on the importance of behavioral elements in the application of linear programming models. Behavioral problems can be overcome, and if management determines policies toward risk, regulatory compliance, and constraints on certain actions, an LP model can provide the optimal allocation of the bank's resources to meet those policies.

The allocation decision involved in balance sheet management is continuous and changes with shifts in the environment. Financial planning is aimed at determining an optimal allocation of the bank's resources over future periods as well as the present. Because of the uncertainty inherent in forecasting the future environment, a problem arises in developing a multiperiod model. The attempts to deal with multiperiod decision making under uncertainty are varied. Three articles are presented here which focus in part on future uncertainties.

In Chapter 17, "Forecasting vs. Allocational Efficiency in Bank Asset Planning: An Integrated Evaluation," Michael E. Echols and J. Walter Elliott explore the importance of forecasting in an allocational model. Echols and Elliott compare the results of an allocational model under conditions of certainty with those of an allocational model combined with a forecasting model. The comparison points out the return that can be realized through improved forecasting of allocational model inputs. Improvement in a bank's ability to forecast interest rates, for example, would greatly improve the results of the bank's LP planning model. In general, forecasting is among the most difficult aspects of allocational model building. Nevertheless, the results of multiperiod models are superior to those of single-period allocational models.

Theoretically, it might be desirable to statistically analyze frequency distributions of key input parameters to help determine their expected values. This approach, however, is not practically feasible. The complexity of intertemporal joint probability distributions limits their use and information value. Parvis Aghili, Robert H. Cramer, and Howard E. Thompson have analyzed one alternative to the complexity of such an approach in Chapter 18, "Small Bank Balance Sheet Management: Applying Two-Stage Programming Models." The two-stage programming model (or "programming with recourse") which they describe may offer a practical method for incorporating uncertainty into an allocational planning model. Aghili, Cramer, and Thompson found that the model produced results very similar to those of a "real world" small Midwestern bank.

In Chapter 19, "Short Term Money Management for Bank Port-folios," Morton Lane focuses on the short-term aspects of balance sheet management. Lane's emphasis is on development of short-term financial policies incorporating projections of such variables as deposits and interest rates. A numerical example is provided which illustrates the nature of variables, inputs, output, and limitations of the LP balance sheet formulation.

Following several applications of linear programming in bank financial management, the final article in Part IV examines a comprehensive use of an intertemporal linear programming model for financial planning. In Chapter 20, "Toward a Comprehensive Framework for Bank Financial Planning," by Kalman J. Cohen and David P. Rutenberg, numerous bank activities are incorporated into the LP formulation to develop an overall long-range planning model. However, a "total" planning model of this type may not prove feasible for all types of bank financial decision making, as Cohen and Rutenberg point out in their summary. The reason for the model's limited applicability is its level of aggregation and implicit centralization. Some detailed decisions need to be made on a less aggregate level and a more decentralized basis. The Cohen and Rutenberg article does provide the framework for the development of a total planning model incorporating numerous bank activities.

The integration of the model with a bank's decision structure points to the need for consideration of decision structure in applying a planning model. A model that involves various levels of decision making must be applied with caution, since running an LP repeatedly to solve small problems may prove infeasible. The Cohen and Rutenberg article provides insight into the potential for applying linear programming in bank balance sheet management. It also illustrates that this application can be broadened to encompass nearly all of a bank's financial activities in a financial planning model. Cohen and Rutenberg conclude with a discussion of risk and uncertainty.

Despite its limitations, linear programming offers a practical aid in the complex tasks of bank financial planning and balance sheet management. Behavioral problems in implementing the LP model are largely based on misunderstanding, lack of information, and poor communication. As more bankers become acquainted with this approach to financial management and planning, bank applications of linear programming will increase. This approach can be extremely useful in developing a consistent strategic plan for a bank, given management's attitude toward risk and its forecast of economic conditions. An added benefit of the model is its ability to generate fresh examinations of critical planning issues by bank management.

Chapter 15

LINEAR PROGRAMMING MODELS FOR OPTIMAL BANK DYNAMIC BALANCE SHEET MANAGEMENT*

By Kalman J. Cohen and Frederick S. Hammer

*This article is reprinted, with permission, from *Mathematical Methods in Investment and Finance,* edited by Giorgio P. Szego and Karl Shell, North-Holland Publishing Company, Amsterdam and American Elsevier Publishing Company, Inc., New York, 1972, pp. 387-413.

1. Introduction

Dynamic balance sheet management, an area on which senior bank management focuses major attention, is concerned with determining the size and composition of the bank's assets, liabilities and capital accounts over a multiperiod planning horizon. Because of its importance, it is not surprising that many different approaches to this problem have appeared in both the banking and the academic literature. These approaches that have been suggested range from self-reliance on 'wisdom', inflexible heuristics expressing the perceived relationships between assets and liabilities, simulation, static and intertemporal linear programming formulations and a variety of other analytical approaches. Unfortunately, much of the sophisticated literature which has appeared has been presented at a level of abstraction that precludes practical application.

Several years ago the authors reported on an alternative approach that extended well beyond existing literature in developing a rigorous and practical method for obtaining an 'optimal' solution to the bank dynamic balance sheet management problem (which we then called the "asset management problem")[1]. In that earlier article, an intertemporal linear programming model was discussed whose decision variables included stocks and flows associated with various types of assets, deposits and capital, as well as promotional efforts. The model incorporated constraints relating to funds availability, risk, management policy, market restrictions and portfolio trading; the effects of forecast errors and of feed-back relationships between loans and deposits were also discussed. Alternative criterion functions and the possibility of introducing time periods of varying length into the model were also considered.

The earlier article did not employ any mathematical symbolism, in order to make its approach more accessible to non-mathematically oriented readers. The present paper fulfills a promise made in the previous article: 'A more detailed and mathematical explanation will be contained in a forthcoming publi-

---

[1] Kalman J. Cohen and Frederick S. Hammer, 'Linear programming and optimal bank asset management decisions', *Journal of Finance* 22, No. 2 (May, 1967), pp. 147–165.

cation'. [2] This paper, then, presents the component equations and explicit structure of the model discussed earlier. [3]

It should be noted that the approach taken herein to the dynamic balance sheet management problem involves presentation of a rather wide array of alternative intertemporal LP models. Thus, different criterion functions are considered along with a general approach to incorporating a time horizon made up of periods of various lengths. Many different types of constraints are discussed, but not all of them need necessarily be present in each version of the model that is implemented. The variables are presented in complete generality with respect to 'types' and 'maturity classes' of various accounting categories; the actual set of variables that will appear in a particular version of the model depends upon how these 'types' and 'maturity classes' are specified. Some variables might be treated as being either endogenous or exogenous (or even omitted entirely from the model), depending upon some choices made by the model formulator. The authors have purposely developed a large class of models in order to provide the user in a practical situation with a relatively complete kit of alternative approaches to various parts of the problem which can be melded together to fit the actual requirements of a given situation.

2. Some conventions

2.1. *Balance sheet variables*

The following variables, each of which is expressed in terms of the average balance in the corresponding account during time period t, will be used to represent a bank's balance sheet during any period:

Assets (Y_t = total assets):
$$C_t \quad = \text{cash}$$
$$A_{jt} \quad = \text{daily assets}$$
$$I_{jmt} \quad = \text{investments}$$
$$L_{jmt} \quad = \text{loans}$$
$$F_t \quad = \text{fixed assets}$$

---

[2] *Ibid.*, footnote 5, p. 149.

[3] The authors have freely utilized some of the material that was contained in their earlier article, in order to make this paper understandable in its own right. Those readers who wish additional explanation of the reasons for various relations appearing in the model and/or who contemplate implementation of the model should also carefully read the earlier article.

Liabilities and capital (Z_t = total liabilities and capital):
$\quad B_{jt}$ = daily liabilities (i.e., borrowed funds)
$\quad D_{jt}$ = demand deposits
$\quad S_t$ = savings deposits
$\quad E_{jmt}$ = time deposits
$\quad H_t$ = other liabilities
$\quad K_{jmt}$ = capital

In the above variables, the subscript j refers to the type and the subscript m to the maturity class of the corresponding asset or liability account; the subscript t refers to the time period.

For convenience in expressing the constraints of the model, some of these accounts are classified into the following particular type and maturity categories (note that this classification is not necessarily mutually exclusive or collectively exhaustive):

A_{jt} = daily assets:
$\qquad$ $j = 1$ refers to 'Federal funds sold'
I_{jmt} = investments:
$\qquad$ $j \in G$ refers to 'government securities'
$\qquad$ $j, m \in M$ refers to 'readily marketable investments'
$\qquad$ $j, m \in P_{j*}$ refers to 'investments which are pledgable
$\qquad\qquad$ against demand deposits of type $j*$'
$\qquad$ $j, m \in R$ refers to 'investments which are usable for re-
$\qquad\qquad$ purchase agreements'
B_{jt} = daily liabilities:
$\qquad$ $j = 1$ refers to 'borrowings from the Fed'
$\qquad$ $j = 2$ refers to 'borrowings under repurchase agreements'
D_{jt} = demand deposits:
$\qquad$ $j* \in P$ refers to 'demand deposits which require pledged
$\qquad\qquad$ assets'
E_{jmt} = time deposits
$\qquad$ $j \in C$ refers to 'certificates of deposit'
K_{jmt} = capital
$\qquad$ $j, m \in B$ refers to 'borrowed capital funds'
$\qquad$ K_{tt} refers to 'total capital funds during period t'
$\qquad$ K_{et} refers to 'equity capital funds during period t'

2.2. *Average and spot balances*

As indicated, the variables specified above all refer to average balances during time period t. In an earlier model developed by Chambers and Charnes [4], it was assumed that all flows occur instantaneously at the start of a time period. In this situation, spot balances and average balances would be equal at each instant during the time period. In the present models, on the contrary, flows are assumed to occur at constant rates during a time period, and spot balances equal average balances only in the middle of the time period.

In this model the spot balance at the end of a period is denoted by a prime (′) after the upper-case symbol representing the corresponding average balance. E.g., since I_{jmt} refers to the average balance during period t of investments of type j and maturity class m, then I'_{jmt} refers to the spot balance at the end of period t of investments of type j and maturity class m. With this notational convention, the relationship between average and spot balances for any account, e.g., investments, may be expressed as follows:

$$I_{jmt} = \frac{1}{2}(I'_{jm,\,t-1} + I'_{jmt}). \tag{1}$$

Analogous expressions hold for the other accounts.

These linear flow assumptions within a period are, of course, made only for those stocks which cannot in fact be adjusted instantaneously in banking, i.e., most loan accounts and certain categories of investments and deposits. However, for certain instantaneously adjustable items like daily assets (loans to government dealers, Federal funds sold, etc.), the Chambers-Charnes assumptions remain relevant. In addition, the realities of the marketplace will restrict the maximum rates at which the levels of various balance sheet categories can be altered.

Because of these assumptions concerning flows, it is clear that although *on average* the balance sheet will balance within each period, it is not necessary that this relationship hold for every instant of each period. Thus, in moving from one balance sheet position to another, if changes in *sources* are preponderantly in instantaneously adjustable categories (e.g., Federal funds bought) and changes in *uses* are in assets which take longer to adjust (e.g., commercial loans), the implied *spot* balance sheets at the beginning and end of the planning period will not necessarily balance.

2.3. Notational conventions

To accomodate the wide variety of considerations needed to portray the banker's problem in some detail, the following conventions are also utilized as

---

[4] D. Chambers and A. Charnes, 'Inter-temporal analysis and optimization of bank portfolios', *Management Science* 7, No. 4 (July, 1961), pp. 393–410; reprinted in Kalman J. Cohen and Frederick S. Hammer (editors), *Analytical methods in banking* (Homewood, Illinois, Richard D. Irwin, Inc., 1966), chapter 4.

modifications of the basic balance sheet variables defined in section 2.1 above.

For each 'stock' variable denoted by an upper-case Roman letter, there is a corresponding 'flow' variable which is denoted by the corresponding lower-case Roman letter. (E.g., i_{jmt} refers to the rate – stated in terms of dollars per year – at which investments of type j and maturity class m are purchased during period t.) Where applicable, a superscript q is added to a flow variable to indicate that the flow is a *sale* rather than a purchase. (E.g., i_{jmt}^q refers to the rate – stated in terms of dollars per year – at which investments of type j and maturity class m are sold during period t.)

Coefficients and parameters are frequently (although not exclusively) denoted by Greek letters.

R_{jmt}^x denotes the after-tax interest rate net of marginal processing costs, marginal default losses, etc. applicable to the related stock or flow variable (as $x = i, I, A, l, L, E$, etc.) of type j, maturity class m, in period t.

g_{jmt}^i and g_{jmt}^l denotes the after-tax capital gain (loss, if negative) factor on selling investments (i) or loans (l), where applicable, of type j, maturity m, in period t.

2.4. *Intertemporal links*

While relationships involving a variable in different time periods can be easily portrayed by simply varying the subscript t, different symbolism is needed to accomodate the various flow rates which can characterize the different variables in the models. Thus, let Γ_{jmt}^i denote the fraction of investments (i) of type j and maturity class m in period t which flow into maturity class $m - 1$ in period $t + 1$. Γ_{jmt}^l, Γ_{jmt}^e and Γ_{jmt}^k are defined similarly pertaining to loans (l), time deposits (e) and capital (k).

V_t denotes the length of period t within the planning horizon. It is not necessary, of course, to divide the planning horizon into time periods of equal length. It becomes increasingly difficult to forecast the economic climate the further into the future one looks. In addition, management is more interested in greater detail concerning near-term activity than it is about actions which will occur only in the longer-term future. Thus, it may be useful to utilize relatively short time periods in the early stages of the planning horizon, and longer stretches of time in the later periods. For example, if five planning periods are to be employed stretching over a four-year horizon, one might usefully regard the first two periods as each being three months long, the third period as six months long, the fourth period as one year long, and the fifth period as two years long. For this example, one would have $V_1 = V_2 = 0.25$ years, $V_3 = 0.5$ years, $V_4 = 1$ year and $V_5 = 2$ years.

The flow variables are all expressed in terms of annual rates. The lengths of the planning periods will appear as parameters in the intertemporal links defining spot balances, as the following example indicates for investments:

$$I'_{jmt} = (1 - \Gamma^i_{jm, t-1}) I'_{jm, t-1} + \Gamma^i_{j, m+1, t-1} I'_{j, m+1, t-1} + V_t (i_{jmt} - i^q_{jmt}). \qquad (2)$$

The spot balances for loans, L'_{jtm}, and for time deposits, E'_{jtm}, are defined in an exactly analogous manner. The spot balances for capital, K'_{jtm}, are more complex and are discussed in the following section.

The intertemporal links that have been defined for the model imply that within any time period, the spot balance of an account will change in a linear manner, but that between any adjoining time periods, the spot balance will change in an exponential manner.

2.5. The definition of capital

Since capital plays a pivotal role in determing the risk posture of any alternative bank portfolio, more detailed consideration must be given to the definition of this variable. We have previously indicated that K_{jmt} refers to the average balance of capital of type j and maturity m during period t. If the analog of eq. (2) were utilized to define the spot balance of capital of type j and maturity m at the end of period t, one would have:

$$K'_{jmt} = (1 - \Gamma^k_{jm, t-1}) K'_{jm, t-1} + \Gamma^k_{j, m+1, t-1} K'_{j, m+1, t-1} + V_t (k_{jmt} - k^q_{jmt}). \quad (3)$$

Eq. (3) correctly expresses the manner in which the amount of a particular type and maturity of capital (e.g., capital notes which have a remaining life to maturity of 15 years) will vary as a function of merely the passage of time and the issuing and repurchase of this categorie of capital. For borrowed capital funds, nothing more is needed. For equity capital, however, some other considerations must be introduced in order to develop a complete portrayal of the factors which cause equity capital to vary over time. It is useful to define some auxilliary variables to denote various additional types of intra-period endogenous capital changes.

Let k_{1t} denote the components of after-tax net operating earnings directly associated with the endogenous balance sheet accounts during period t. k_{1t} is defined in eq. (4) below. Note that this is not only net of taxes, but it is also net of marginal processing costs, marginal default losses, etc., in view of the definition of R^x_{jmt} given in section 2.3 above.

$$k_{1t} = V_t \left(\sum_j R^A_{jt} A_{jt} + \sum_{j, m} R^I_{jmt} I_{jmt} + \sum_{j, m} R^L_{jmt} L_{jmt} \right)$$

$$- \sum_j R_{jt}^B B_t - \sum_j R_{jt}^D D_{jt} - R_t^S S_t$$

$$- \sum_{j,\,m} R_{jmt}^E E_{jmt} - \sum_{j,\,m} R_{jmt}^K K_{jmt} \Bigg) \, . \tag{4}$$

Let k_{2t} denote the after-tax capital gains (or losses, if negative) during period t resulting from the sale of investments and loans. This is defined as:

$$k_{2t} = V_t \Bigg(\sum_{j,\,m} g_{jmt}^i \, i_{jmt}^q + \sum_{j,\,m} g_{jmt}^l \, l_{jmt}^q \Bigg) \, . \tag{5}$$

Define k_{3t} as the after-tax promotional expenditures of the bank during period t. This is determined by the marginal income tax rate of the bank, τ, and by the pre-tax promotional expenditures during period t, p_t, as follows:

$$k_{3t} = (1 - \tau) p_t \, . \tag{6}$$

To the extent that promotional expenses (e.g., advertising, give-aways, etc.) affect the bank's loan and deposit market shares, the determination of desired levels of these expenses falls within the purview of dynamic balance sheet management. If the way in which these expenses affect the relevant market shares is both understood and can be expressed linearly, these relationships can be added to the model and the optimal level of these expenditures determined endogenously. In the formulation of the model presented in section 3 below, we have not included such relationships; without them, p_t should be regarded as an exogenous variable.

Let ni_t denote the after-tax net income of the bank during period t. This will largely be determined by k_{1t}, k_{2t} and k_{3t}. In addition, however, there will be some exogenous components affecting net income which are not directly related to decision variables of the LP model. Such exogenous components would include fixed operating expenses of the bank, net earnings from trust operations, etc. We shall let k_t^e represent the net after-tax exogenous components of net income during period t. We then have

$$ni_t = k_{1t} + k_{2t} - k_{3t} + k_t^e \, . \tag{7}$$

Let div_t denote the aggregate volume of dividends paid by the bank during period t. Capital funds are reduced when dividends are paid. If the value of dividends to stockholders is known, the imputed yield can be assigned to the dividend variable in the criterion function. In this case, the model can be used to determine the optimal dividend level. This approach is overambitious at present, given the current state of financial theory. Thus, for now a more pedestrian approach will be employed. This requires adding constraints (see section 3.2.3 below) describing the bank's dividend payout policy. Such an approach allows the model to reflect the impact of dividends paid on future available capital funds.

It is now possible to define the bank's total capital funds at the end of period t, which is denoted by K'_{tt}. Utilizing eqs. (3) through (7) and the accompanying discussion, it follows that

$$K'_{tt} = \sum_{j, m} K'_{jmt} + ni_t - \text{div}_t .$$

(8)

The equity capital of the bank at the end of period t, denoted by K'_{et}, is then simply

$$K'_{et} = K'_{tt} - \sum_{j, m \in B} K'_{jmt} .$$

(9)

Note that the summation on the right-hand side of (9) is over the non-equity classes of capital.

It should be realized that these endogenous changes in capital specified above are not incorporated merely in homage to the fetish of precise forecasts. The amounts of capital actually available to the bank at future times will depend heavily upon exogenous factors which cannot be predicted perfectly. In evaluating the yield-risk trade-offs of a given decision, however, it is essential that its impact on future capital funds be made explicit. Thus, endogenous changes in capital are included in the model in order to extend the comprehensiveness of the interactions considered in making present dynamic balance sheet management decisions.

3. The model

Utilizing the conventions defined in section 2, the model can be described in three stages: intra-period constraints, intertemporal constraints and the criterion function.

3.1. *Intra-period constraints*

In each period within the planning horizon, a variety of constraints might be imposed. These may be grouped into five major categories.

3.1.1. Risk constraints

One of the key factors in this model is the set of risk constraints imposed upon each balance sheet within the planning horizon. The capital adequacy formula developed by the examiners of the Board of Governors of the Federal Reserve System is used for this purpose in both the present model and the earlier Chambers and Charnes model [5]. The intended function of the capital adequacy constraints in such programming models is to insure that plans formulated with the aid of the model do not subject the bank to an excessive degree of risk.

The underlying concept of the Federal Reserve Board of Governors (which we shall henceforth abbreviate as FRBG) examiners' capital adequacy formula is that the function of bank capital is to protect the depositor against possible loss. In other words, capital is a buffer that protects the depositor against the risks and uncertainties inherent in banking. If, because of undue vicissitudes, the bank comes upon hard times and somebody has to lose out, it is intended that the losers be the stockholders who supply the bank's capital funds rather than the depositors.

We can thus view the capital adequacy formula as providing the bank with a score which is the ratio of actual capital funds to 'required' capital funds. The amount of capital funds 'required' to protect the bank's depositors against possible losses is determined in a manner which will soon be discussed. For now, let us note that the higher the score of a bank on this formula, the less is the degree of risk to which it is exposed (according to the FRBG). In principle, one might suppose that a bank should score 100% or higher on the FRBG formula.

It is important to note, however, that a score of 100% or more on the FRBG capital adequacy formula is not a rigid legal restriction which must be met by a bank at all times at any cost. As originally specified by the FRBG, the capital adequacy formula incorporates a severe degree of conservatism — a degree that would not be tolerated by the management of any aggressive commercial bank. Thus, even though the *form* of the constraints may be sensible, the specific *numbers* employed by the examiners should be modified to fit both the economic circumstances and management policies of a particular bank [6].

The rationale underlying the FRBG formula is a complicated leverage restriction that combines a capital adequacy test with a liquidity test. This measure-

---

[5] *Ibid.*

[6] For a discussion of various ways in which the FRBG capital adequacy formula could usefully be improved as a basis for the risk constraints in a deterministic LP model, see Kalman J. Cohen, 'Improving the capital adequacy formula', *Journal of Bank Research* 1, No. 1 (Spring, 1970), pp. 13–16.

ment becomes more restrictive as the need for potential liquidity becomes greater — i.e., as assets become less current, liabilities become more current or trust operations become relatively larger. In this respect, the FRBG capital adequacy formula provides a measurement of bank risk which is more comprehensive than the ratios and rules of thumb usually employed by bankers to gauge safety and liquidity.

In section 2.1 above, we have defined a set of balance sheet variables which conveniently serves as a means of expressing most of the relationships in the LP model. In order to express the risk constraints in mathematical notation, however, it is useful to introduce another set of variables which partition the bank's balance sheet in a different manner. It should be recognized, of course, that any particular balance sheet account will correspond both to one of the balance sheet variables defined in section 2.1 above as well as to one of the balance sheet variables to be defined below. Thus, e.g., the average balance of Treasury bills held by the bank during period t can be designated both as I_{jmt} (for appropriate values of j and m) and as U_{2t}.

The following variables (all denoting average balances during period t) are used to represent the bank's balance sheet for the purposes of expressing the risk constraints:

Assets:

U_{1t} = cash (e.g., vault cash, float, deposits at the Fed)
U_{2t} = primary reserves (e.g., Treasury bills, dealers day loans)
U_{3t} = secondary reserves (e.g., 2-year governments, 1-year municipals)
U_{4t} = minimum risk assets (e.g., 3-year governments, 2-year municipals)
U_{5t} = intermediate risk assets (e.g., 5-year governments)
U_{6t} = portfolio assets (e.g., C and I loans)
U_{7t} = fixed, special and other assets (e.g., premises)

Liabilities and capital:

W_{1t} = demand deposits
W_{2t} = time deposit excluding CDs and a few other types
W_{3t} = other deposits (e.g., CDs) and borrowing from the Fed and from other banks

K_{tt} = capital

It is now possible to describe in some detail the manner in which the FRBG capital adequacy formula determines the amount of capital funds 'required' to protect the bank's depositors against possible losses. This is determined in three states.

179

First, the direct capital requirement against assets during period t, denoted by DCR_t, is a linear function of the various types of assets held by the bank:

$$DCR_t = \sum_{n=1}^{7} \alpha_n U_{nt} . \tag{10}$$

The rationale for imposing direct capital requirements against assets is that in the normal course of banking business, there will be some shrinkage in value, i.e., capital losses, as a result of holding assets. Some assets, e.g., low-grade bonds and particular loans, may default. Other assets which have no default loss are frequently turned over at a capital loss during the normal course of business, e.g., tax switching of bonds. In either case, some amount of capital is required to support these potential losses, as specified in (10). In general the longer the maturity or the greater the default risk of an asset, the greater will be the amount of capital required as direct backing against it [7].

Second, the provision for liquidity required against liabilities during period t, denoted by PLR_t, is a linear function of the bank's liabilities:

$$PLR_t = \sum_{n=1}^{3} \beta_n W_{nt} . \tag{11}$$

PLR_t will determine a second source of required capital on the basis of con-siderations related to possible shrinkage in the bank's deposits and other sour-ces of funds. For any given structure of liabilities, a potential need for liquidity is determined. In general, the more likely it is that a type of liability will shrink in total volume, the greater is the potential liquidity that is required to meet this deposit withdrawal or liability shrinkage. Hence, the potential liquidity needs of the bank will increase, according to the capital adequacy formula, as the bank's liabilities become more current [8].

The main sources of liquidity for meeting shrinkages in the bank's liabilities are its assets: $U_{1t}, U_{2t}, ..., U_{7t}$. Note that these asset accounts have been de-fined in order of decreasing liquidity, so that U_{1t} is the most liquid group of assets, U_{2t} the next most liquid group of assets, ..., and U_{7t} is the least liquid group of assets. To the extent that funds for meeting potential contractions in deposits and other liabilities must be obtained by liquidating longer-term and less liquid assets, for which there is likely to be greater shrinkage in value in the

---

[7] The values of the parameters in eq. (10) suggested by the FRBG are: $\alpha_1 = 0.0; \alpha_2 = 0.005; \alpha_3 = 0.04; \alpha_4 = 0.04; \alpha_5 = 0.06; \alpha_6 = 0.10; \alpha_7 = 1.0$.

[8] The values of the parameters in eq. (11) suggested by the FRBG are: $\beta_1 = 0.47; \beta_2 = 0.36; \beta_3 = 1.00$.

event of their forced liquidation, additional capital requirements are imposed on the bank. The specific nature of these additional capital requirements is defined in (12)–(16) below.

For this purpose, three auxiliary variables are introduced:

X_{1t} = liquidity to be provided by assets in categories U_{4t}, U_{5t}, U_{6t} and U_{7t};
X_{2t} = liquidity to be provided by assets in categories U_{5t}, U_{6t} and U_{7t};
X_{3t} = liquidity to be provided by assets in categories U_{6t} and U_{7t}.

The values of these three auxiliary liquidity variables are defined in the following expressions [9]:

$$X_{1t} = \max \begin{cases} PLR_t - \sum_{n=1}^{3} \gamma_n U_{nt} \\ 0 \end{cases} \tag{12}$$

$$X_{2t} = \max \begin{cases} X_{1t} - \gamma_4 U_{4t} \\ 0 \end{cases} \tag{13}$$

$$X_{3t} = \max \begin{cases} X_{2t} - \gamma_5 U_{5t} \\ 0 \end{cases} \tag{14}$$

Note that X_{1t} will be different from zero only if the potential liquidity requirements to meet contractions in liabilities cannot entirely be met from liquidating such assets as cash, primary reserves and secondary reserves. Analogous remarks apply to X_{2t} and X_{3t}. With the parameter values suggested by the FRBG (see footnote 9), the less liquid are the assets which provide funds to cover contractions in liabilities, the lower the percentage of book value that it is assumed will be realized from the liquidation of the assets.

The amount of required capital to meet potential contractions in liabilities during period t, denoted by KCL_t, is determined in eq. (15) [10]:

$$KCL_t = \sum_{n=1}^{3} \delta_n X_{nt} . \tag{15}$$

Although the parameters in (15) need not be monotonic, there will be a monotonic non-decreasing relationship between the provision for liquidity required against liabilities, PLR_t, and the required capital to meet potential contractions in liabilities, KCL_t. In particular, KCL_t is a piecewise linear non-decreasing

---

[9] The set of the γ's suggested by the FRBG is: $\gamma_1 = 1.0$; $\gamma_2 = 0.995$; $\gamma_3 = 0.96$; $\gamma_4 = 0.9$; $\gamma_5 = 0.85$.

[10] The values of the parameters in eq. (15) suggested by the FRBG are: $\delta_1 = 0.065$; $\delta_2 = 0.040$; $\delta_3 = 0.095$.

function of PLR_t. Together, (12)–(15) imply that:

$$KCL_t = 0 \quad \text{if} \quad PLR_t \leqslant \sum_{n=1}^{3} \gamma_n U_{nt} \tag{16a}$$

$$KCL_t = \delta_1 (PLR_t - \sum_{n=1}^{3} \gamma_n U_{nt}) \quad \text{if}$$

$$\left. \sum_{n=1}^{3} \gamma_n U_{nt} < PLR_t \leqslant \sum_{n=1}^{4} \gamma_n U_{nt} \right\} \tag{16b}$$

$$KCL_t = \delta_1 (\gamma_4 U_{4t}) + (\delta_1 + \delta_2)(PLR_t - \sum_{n=1}^{4} \gamma_n U_{nt}) \quad \text{if}$$

$$\left. \sum_{n=1}^{4} \gamma_n U_{nt} < PLR_t \leqslant \sum_{n=1}^{5} \gamma_n U_{nt} \right\} \tag{16c}$$

$$KCL_t = \delta_1 (\gamma_4 U_{4t}) + (\delta_1 + \delta_2)(\gamma_5 U_{5t})$$

$$\left. + (\delta_1 + \delta_2 + \delta_3)(PLR_t - \sum_{n=1}^{5} \gamma_n U_{nt}) \quad \text{if} \right\} \tag{16d}$$

$$\left. \sum_{n=1}^{5} \gamma_n U_{nt} < PLR_t . \right\}$$

The third and final source of required capital in the FRBG examiners' ca-pital adequacy formula can be regarded as being exogenously determined, since these needs for capital relate to decisions that are not being planned en-dogenously within the linear programming model. The only exogenous source of capital presently considered in the capital adequacy formula relates to trust operations. Substantial capital losses can be incurred if the bank is proven negligent in the management of its fiduciary activities. Hence, the greater the volume of the bank's trust operations, the more capital is required. In particu-lar, KAT_t will denote the amount of required capital against trust operations during period t. This is an exogenous item that is to be provided as input to the LP model [11].

In summary, the bank's 'required' capital during period t, denoted by RC_t, is defined as the sum of the capital requirements determined by three different sources: (a) direct capital requirements against assets, DCR_t; (b) required capital to meet potential contractions in liabilities, KCL_t; and (c) required capital against trust operations, KAT_t. Thus,

$$RC_t = DCR_t + KCL_t + KAT_t. \tag{17}$$

The FRBG examiners' capital adequacy formula assigns a capital adequacy score to the bank which is the ratio of the bank's actual total book capital, K_{tt}, to its required capital, RC_t; i.e., the bank's capital adequacy ratio during period t is K_{tt}/RC_t. The higher the capital adequacy ratio of the bank, the less risk the bank is assuming. Let η_0 be defined as the minimum value of the capital adequacy ratio which the management of the bank is willing to achieve. As we have already indicated, η_0 could be less than 1.0, since the minimum acceptable value of the capital adequacy ratio is more an expression of management policy than a rigid legal requirement. Thus the final form of the risk constraint in the LP model is:

$$K_{tt} \geqslant \eta_0 (RC_t). \tag{18}$$

All of the expressions (10) through (18) inclusive together constitute the risk constraints for period t. Not all of these expressions would, however, actually become row constraints in the initial tableau for the LP model. (16) is clearly redundant when (12)–(15) are present. Furthermore, the identities contained in (10), (11), (15) and (17) are definitional in nature, and can be eliminated from the tableau (along with the corresponding variables). There will remain four inequality constraints, stemming from (12), (13), (14) and (18), that essentially enter the tableau to express the risk constraints for period t. The auxiliary variables X_{1t}, X_{2t} and X_{3t} must be included in the set of endogenous variables to be determined by the LP model's solution.

Finally, it should be noted that the risk constraints are piecewise linear, rather than strictly linear, in nature. Nonetheless, ordinary LP computer codes adequate for solving the LP model. In particular, an optimal solution will force

---

[11] The FRBG suggests that KAT_t should be three times the amount of gross annual income generated by all trust activities in the bank.

each of the X_{it} ($i = 1, 2, 3$) as close to zero as possible. Furthermore, a positive value for X_{3t} is less desirable than a positive value for X_{2t}, which in turn is less desirable than a positive value for X_{1t}. Therefore, the non-linearities can be safely ignored, and the resulting LP solution will in fact satisfy the piecewise linear risk constraints.

3.1.2. Funds availability constraint

On an average balance basis, the total uses of funds must equal the total sources of funds during any time period. This is equivalent to stating that on an average balance basis during period t, the balance sheet must balance, i.e., the sum of the bank's assets, Y_t, must equal the sum of the bank's liabilities and capital, Z_t. The appropriate definitions are provided in (19) and (20), and the funds availability constraint is expressed in (21).

$$Y_t = C_t + \sum_j A_{jt} + \sum_{j, m} I_{jmt} + \sum_{j, m} L_{jmt} + F_t \tag{19}$$

$$Z_t = \sum_j B_{jt} + \sum_j D_{jt} + S_t + \sum_{j, m} E_{jmt} + H_t + \sum_{j, m} K_{jmt} \tag{20}$$

$$Y_t = Z_t. \tag{21}$$

3.1.3. Liquidity buffer

The LP model assumes that deposits are expressed as average balances over a planning period. It is clear, of course, that actual deposits will fluctuate from day to day within a planning period. These fluctuations are consistent with the model's implicit assumption that the average levels of deposits are accurately known. For planning purposes, some minimal liquidity buffer of cash and near-cash items must be provided. This buffer will be utilized in making the daily adjustments required by these fluctuations in deposits. Such considerations are incorporated by a constraint, (22), which requires that on average some minimal amount of cash, daily assets and readily marketable investments be held throughout the planning period. This minimal amount, of course, depends upon the magnitude of the day-to-day swings expected in deposits, and hence the parameters ϵ_1 and ϵ_2 are to be estimated on the basis of the bank's own historical experience.

$$\epsilon_1 C_t + \sum_j A_{jt} + \sum_{j, m \in M} I_{jmt} \geq \epsilon_2 \sum_j D_{jt}. \tag{22}$$

3.1.4. Policy considerations

There are many time-honored and well-established heuristics used to gauge bank safety and liquidity, e.g., the ratios of governments to assets, capital to risk assets, loans to deposits, etc. Sophisticated observers have long realized that each of these heuristics involves only a limited, narrow view of the overall portfolio balance problem. These rules of thumb are superseded by the more comprehensive measure of the Federal Reserve Board of Governors examiners. Nonetheless, so long as such heuristics remain in vogue, bank management must be sensitive to possible adverse reaction by stockholders, depositors and others to balance sheet positions which imply ratios which greatly deviate from 'accepted' ranges.

Policy constraints can easily be added to express these conventional measures. Thus, for example, (23) imposes a lower bound on the bank's ratio of governments to assets; (24) imposes a lower bound on the bank's ratio of capital to risk assets; and (25) imposes an upper bound on the bank's ratio of loans to deposits. The parameter values in these policy constraints would normally be set at the outside perimeters of what is deemed by management as acceptable. The dual variables obtained in solution to the linear programming problem are especially pertinent in evaluating the impact of limited constraints of this type. If the duals indicate that the opportunity costs of these restrictions are unduly high, management may well wish to reevaluate the necessity of adhering closely to policy restrictions of this type

$$\sum_{j,\, m \in G} I_{jmt} \geqslant \eta_1 Y_t \tag{23}$$

$$K_t \geqslant \eta_2 \left(Y_t - C_t - \sum_{m,\, j \in G} I_{jmt} \right) \tag{24}$$

$$\sum_{j,\, m} L_{jmt} \leqslant \eta_3 \left(\sum_j D_{jt} + S_t + \sum_{j,\, m} E_{jmt} \right). \tag{25}$$

Since the market for certificates of deposits is of relatively recent origin, bankers may not yet be confident of the extent to which this money market instrument can be relied upon as a source of funds in all economic climates. Thus it is not clear *ex ante* whether under particular economic conditions it will be possible to increase the stock of these funds, or even to roll them over as outstanding certificates mature. Hence, as a policy matter, management may wish to avoid placing undue reliance upon this particular source of funds.

Policy constraints of this type can be expressed in either of two ways: as a maximum percentage of total deposits, as in (26); or as an absolute upper limit, as in (27). Obviously the force of such constraints can be modified from period to period within the planning horizon to reflect management's expectations concerning changes in the state of monetary conditions over the planning horizon.

$$\sum_{m,\,j\in C} E_{jmt} \leqslant \eta_4 \left(\sum_{j} D_{jt} + S_t + \sum_{j,\,m} E_{jmt} \right) \qquad (26)$$

$$\sum_{m,\,j\in C} E_{jmt} \leqslant \theta_{1t}. \qquad (27)$$

3.1.5. Market restrictions
The policy constraints outlined in section 3.1.4 above are internally generated. In addition, a set of restrictions must be imposed to reflect the limitations on a bank's freedom of action which arise from the economic and institutional realities of the marketplace.

Under normal economic conditions, there is a limit on a bank's ability to make at prevailing market terms loans of a particular type and quality. Thus, (28) constrains the rate at which the bank can make new loans of various types to be no greater than the forecasted demand for them. In a tight monetary environment, of course, it may appear that the bank can make all the new loans for which resources can be mustered, i.e., that loan demand for the bank is far higher than funds available. In these circumstances, these demand constraints become redundant, and the rate at which the bank makes new loans is determined through interaction with other parts of the model.

$$l_{jmt} \leqslant \lambda_{jmt}. \qquad (28)$$

There are many types of daily liabilities, each of which can be used only to a limited extent as a source of funds. Constraints must be added to the model to represent these limitations. For example, through its experience and contacts in the marketplace, a bank may believe that there is an absolute maximum dollar amount of Federal funds that it can buy at any one time, as reflected in (29). Similarly, it is possible to borrow either from the Federal Reserve System or under repurchase agreements only to the extent that suitable securities are available as collateral, as constraint (30) indicates.

$$B_{1t} \leqslant \theta_{2t} \tag{29}$$

$$B_{2t} \leqslant \eta_{5t} \sum_{j,\, m \in R} I_{jmt} . \tag{30}$$

Some types of daily assets and daily liabilities are dealt with in the same market. For example, a bank may feel that in order to maintain its market position as a net purchaser of Federal funds, it must also sometimes be active as a seller. Under these conditions, the minimal amount of Federal funds sold can be expressed as a linear function of Federal funds bought, as shown in constraint (31).

$$A_{1t} \geqslant \eta_{6t} B_{1t} . \tag{31}$$

Many depositors (especially public authorities) require a bank to maintain collateral against their deposits in the form of specific types of assets. Thus, the minimal amounts held of appropriate assets must be related to the volume of relevant deposits, in the manner indicated by constraint (32).

$$\sum_{j,\, m \in P_{j*}} I_{jmt} \geqslant \eta_{7t} D_{j*t} \qquad j* \in P* . \tag{32}$$

Because of legal reserve requirements, float considerations and correspondent bank relations, the bank must maintain a minimal level of cash. This minimal level, of course, is related both to the size and composition of its deposits, as constraint (33) specifies.

$$C_t \geqslant \sum_{j} \rho_{1j} D_{jt} + \rho_2 S_t + \sum_{j,\, m} \rho_{3j} E_{jmt} . \tag{33}$$

The maximum rate during a period at which a bank can sell any type of security of marketable loan must be related to the amount available for sale at the beginning of that period. Hence, a series of upper-bound constraints is added to the model, as shown in (34) and (35). Such constraints would be formulated, of course, only for those types of securities and loans which in fact are marketable.

$$i_{jmt}^{q} V_t \leqslant I'_{jm,\, t-1} \tag{34}$$

$$l_{jmt}^{q} V_t \leqslant L'_{jm,\, t-1} . \tag{35}$$

3.2. *Intertemporal constraints*

Each of the constraints specified in section 3.1 above have been couched in terms of variables pertaining to a *single* planning period. A similar set of intra-period constraints would be formulated for *each* period within the planning horizon. In order to link the variables pertaining to *different* time periods, one must explicitly indicate how balance sheets depend upon both initial stocks and decisions made in earlier periods within the planning horizon. To do so, there are at least three major considerations: intertemporal links, endogenous changes in capital, and loan-related feedback mechanisms.

3.2.1. Intertemporal links

It is necessary to be able to express the manner in which, for any given balance sheet category, its average balance during a period, its spot balances at the beginning and end of the period, and its rates of purchase and sale within the period are interrelated. Appropriate definitional identities, which we call intertemporal links, are incorporated in the model for this purpose [12]. These intertemporal links were already discussed in sections 2.2 and 2.4 above. In particular, constraints of the form (1), formulated in terms of each relevant balance sheet account, and constraints of the form (2), formulated for each type of investment, loan and time deposit, would be included in the model.

3.2.2. Endogenous changes in capital

It should be clear that the amount of available capital funds during any period depends in part upon decisions made in both the same and preceding periods within the planning horizon. Changes in capital occur as (a) interest is paid and received, (b) securities are traded at capital gains or losses, (c) expenses are incurred for promotional efforts aimed at changing the bank's loan and deposit market shares, (d) dividends are declared, etc.

Since considerations such as these are an integral part of the bank's dynamic balance sheet management problem, decisions concerning the relevant variables must consider the trade-offs involved between induced changes in the volume of capital funds (i.e., in the constraint matrix) and present and future yields (i.e., in the criterion function) generated by these variables. Thus,

---

[12] When formulating an LP model, it is often convenient for the model builder to incorporate definitional identities as constraints. This permits him to write various relationships in the model in the form which seems most natural to him. Prior to running an LP computer program to obtain the solution to the model, however, it is wise to use appropriate algebraic manipulations (which themselves can easily be programmed) to eliminate all definitional identities. This will reduce the numbers of rows and columns in the LP tableau, and hence save running time and computational costs.

changes in capital which occur for reasons such as those enumerated above should be explicitly included in the model. Each of these factors can be easily accommodated, thereby allowing their effects to be included when determining optimal dynamic balance sheet management decisions [13].

In section 2.5 above, we discussed most of the considerations relevant to incorporating the effects of endogenous changes in capital into the model. In particular, eqs. (3)–(9) indicate the types of definitional identities which are to be included. The one remaining consideration which must be elaborated upon in regard to endogenous changes in capital relates to constraints which describe the bank's dividend policy.

There are various possible dividend policies which a bank may have. Most (if not all) reasonable dividend policies can be formulated as suitable linear inequality constraints. For example, suppose that the bank never wishes to reduce its dividend rate, and that it wishes its dividends to be at least some specified percentage of its net income. These considerations are reflected in constraints (36) and (37).

$$(\text{div}_t) / V_t \geqslant (\text{div}_{t-1}) / V_{t-1} \tag{36}$$

$$\text{div}_t \geqslant \eta_8 (ni_t). \tag{37}$$

The reasons why the lengths of the time periods, V_t and V_{t-1}, appear in (36) is that the model may have time periods of different length; as (36) is formulated, the time rate of dividend payments will be monotonically non-decreasing. Obvious changes can be made in (36) and (37) to reflect more sophisticated types of dividend policies. For example, (37) might be modified by summing both sides over several time periods, reflecting a policy that the minimum payout ratio may be achieved on an average basis over several time periods, rather than necessarily in each period. When time periods shorter than quarters are used in the model, then (36) and (37) must be modified to reflect the fact that dividends are typically paid on a quarterly basis. Finally, if new stock may be issued during the planning horizon, then (36) should be reformulated on a per share basis, rather than on an aggregate basis.

---

[13] It should not be assumed, of course, that these considerations imply that future levels of capital funds can be precisely forecasted. On the contrary, changes in capital will occur for various reasons exogenous to the model. For example, changes in fees and commissions received from trust operations and bond trading activities can at best be forecasted imperfectly. Since these other functions are basically independent of dynamic balance sheet management, their effect on capital funds can be included in forecasts made externally and supplied as input to the model. Thus, the overall estimates of capital funds used in each of the model's periods are only forecasts based upon the bank's best expectations.

3.2.3. Loan-related feedback mechanisms

Bankers often make loans at contract rates which are less than the market rates of interest obtainable on alternative investment instruments (e.g., tax-exempt municipal securities). Clearly this is not necessarily an irrational action on the part of the banker. To the extent that a present loan makes available both present and future deposits, it generates resources which sustain additional earning assets. Thus the present value of the stream of future income earned on these assets should be considered as an increment to the present value of the contract interest earned on the loan. Evidently, in the banker's judgment, the implied 'imputed rate' is more than enough to overcome the stated differential in the contract rates. This phenomenon must clearly be considered by the model in determining optimal dynamic balance sheet management decisions.

One approach to doing so would be to suppose that demand deposits are affected by the volume of loans made in that period and in previous periods within the planning horizon. In particular, (38) is one possible way of expressing this loan-deposit feedback relation.

$$D_{jt} = D_{jt}^e + \sum_{h=1}^{t} \sum_{k,\,m} z_{kh}^{jt} l_{kmh} . \tag{38}$$

In (38), D_{jt}^e is the exogenously forecasted level of demand deposits of type j during period t that would result if there were a neutral effect of loans made on demand deposits; z_{kh}^{jt} reflects the impact of loans of type k and maturity m made during period h on demand deposits of type j during period t.

If it were believed that there are similar feedback relations between the demand for loans during a period and the amount of loans made during previous periods, then this loan-loan feedback relation could be formulated as in (39).

$$\lambda_{jmt} = \lambda_{jmt}^e + \sum_{h=1}^{t-1} y_{jmh}^t l_{jmh} . \tag{39}$$

In (39), λ_{jmt}^e is the exogenously forecasted level of loan demand of type j and maturity m during period t that would result if there were a neutral effect of loans previously made on current loan demand; y_{jmh}^t reflects the impact of loans of type j and maturity m made during period h on loan demand of type j and maturity m during period t [14].

---

[14] Note the implicit assumption as (39) is formulated that the loan-loan feedbacks do not extend across loan types and maturities. This assumption could, of course, be eliminated by suitably reformulating (39).

As indicated in section 2.5 above, one might in principle wish to incorporate promotional expenditures, p_t, as an endogenous variable in the LP model. In order to do so, it would be necessary to understand the manner in which the bank's demand deposits and loan demand are affected by current and past promotional expenditures. If this were understood, and if the effects were linear, then they could be incorporated into the right-hand sides of (38) and (39). In the absence of such knowledge, however, it would be beyond the scope of this LP model to determine the optimal level of promotional expenditures.

Unfortunately, although bankers continually refer to the importance of loan-related feedback mechanisms, very little is known concerning either the structure or magnitude of these relationships. In practice, it may prove necessary to assume that endogenously induced changes in demand deposits and loan demand are relatively small compared to the general levels of demand deposits and loan demand which might be forecasted at the beginning of the planning horizon. To the extent this is true, the loan-related feedback mechanisms might be eliminated from the model [15]. At the very least, the model provides a structural vehicle which allows the practitioner to experiment with alternative forms of inter-period relationships which may, in fact, improve demand deposit and loan demand forecasts.

3.3. *Criterion function*

The various types of intra-period and intertemporal constraints which comprise the model have been discussed in sections 3.1 and 3.2 above. It is left to specify the criterion function that will be used, i.e., to define the goals that the bank is striving to maximize by its dynamic balance sheet management decisions during the planning horizon.

Rather than delineating a single criterion function that must be used, three possible choices will be discussed [16]:

---

[15] Two alternative approaches which might be adopted when loan-related feedback mechanisms are not explicitly incorporated in the model are discussed in Cohen and Hammer, 'Linear programming and optimal bank asset management decisions', *op. cit.*, p. 158.

[16] With respect to each of these criterion functions, there are two points to be noted. First, the question of possible dilution effects on stockholders' equity from new stock issues can be handled by selective reruns of the model. Dean W.W. Cooper, of Carnegie-Mellon University, has suggested that the solution on a per share basis may be directly obtained by formulating the criterion function in linear fractional form, i.e., as a ratio of two linear functions of the decision variables. (See A. Charnes and W.W. Cooper, 'Programming with linear fractional functionals', *Naval Research Logistics Quarterly,* 9, Nos. 3 and 4 (Sept.–Dec., 1962), pp. 181–186). Second, it is assumed throughout this section that endogenous changes in capital are incorporated into the constraints of the model.

(1) maximize the value of the stockholders' equity at the end of the final period of the planning horizon, as expressed in (40);

(2) maximize the present value of the net income stream during the planning horizon, as expressed in (41);

(3) maximize the present values of the net income stream during the planning horizon plus the present value of the stockholders' equity at the end of the final period of the planning horizon, as expressed in (42).

It will be seen that while arguments can be advanced for each of these criterion functions, the authors generally favor the third alternative.

$$\text{Max } K'_{eT} \tag{40}$$

$$\text{Max } \sum_{t=1}^{T} \prod_{\tau=1}^{t} \left(\frac{1}{1+\rho_\tau} \right) ni_\tau \tag{41}$$

$$\text{Max} \left[\sum_{t=1}^{T} \prod_{\tau=1}^{t} \left(\frac{1}{1+\rho_\tau} \right) ni_t + \prod_{\tau=1}^{T} \left(\frac{1}{1+\rho_\tau} \right) K'_{eT} \right]. \tag{42}$$

In (41) and (42), ρ_τ is the rate used to discount flows of net income during period τ; these discount rates may differ from period to period during the planning horizon.

3.3.1. Maximize horizon value

There are two major reasons for considering this criterion function, as expressed in (40). First, it avoids the necessity for determining a rate at which to discount monetary receipts and disbursements which occur during various time periods. The difficulties associated with choosing the proper discount rate are well known and need not be belabored. Second, this criterion implies a willingness to sacrifice current income if doing so will lead to a higher value of stockholders' equity at some future (but not too far distant) date.

3.3.2. Maximize present value of net income

There are three general reasons why the maximization of the present value of net income, as specified in (41), might be preferred to the maximization of the horizon value of equity, as specified in (40), for the criterion function of the LP model:

(a) not all earnings opportunities are explicitly incorporated as decision variables in the linear programming model;

192

(b) increasing degrees of uncertainty are implicitly attached to more distant forecasts; and

(c) it is felt that shifts in the time pattern of the net income stream will affect the market's valuation of the bank's stock.

For any of these reasons, most bankers would prefer the form of criterion function expressed in (41) to that expressed in (40). This choice, however, immediately leads to a problem: what discount rate should be employed in computing present values?

Conceptually, the most plausible candidates for determining the proper discount rate are: (a) the bank's cost of capital; (b) the rate at which the stock market implicitly capitalizes net income in determining the market value of the bank's stock; or (c) management's subjective time rate of preference for net income.

Most modern economists would agree that on a theoretical basis, the bank's cost of capital should be used. There is a practical drawback in so doing, however, since few economists agree on an operational procedure for determining this rate.

In lieu of this, it may be somewhat easier operationally to estimate the implicit rate at which the stock market capitalizes the bank's net income. It may be possible to determine this rate using econometric techniques when a suitable bank equity valuation model becomes available. It should be noted, however, that employing any such rate implicitly assumes an acceptance of the 'traditional viewpoint' that, within conventionally accepted limits of leverage, raising additional debt capital does not change the cost of equity.

Finally, if no more objective basis for determining the proper discount rate can be agreed upon, one can always fall back upon management's subjective time rate of preference for net income. Some clever interviewing is clearly required in order to obtain consistent agreement concerning this rate. In the absence of consensus, the model can be rerun to determine the sensitivity of the implied optimal decisions to the choice of discount rate [17].

3.3.3. Maximize present value of net income plus terminal valuation

The third possible criterion function, expressed in (42), is essentially a combination of the preceding two, and hence much of the foregoing discussion remains applicable. In order to understand the reason for adding terminal valua-

---

[17] Some additional considerations favoring the use of present value of net income as the criterion function, with the discount rate representing management's subjective time rate of preference for 'net income now' rather than 'net income later', are presented in Kalman J. Cohen and David P. Rutenberg, 'Toward a comprehensive framework for bank financial planning', *Journal of Bank Research,* 1, No. 4 (Winter, 1971), pp. 41–57; see esp. section A.

tion to the second criterion function, (41), note that it is really only the optimal decisions for the first period that must be known. These are the only decisions that can be immediately implemented.

The phrase, 'optimal first period decisions', must be interpreted, however, as the first step in a plan that is optimal in a long-run sense. Later time periods are included in the planning horizon only because we do not know how to modify the criterion function to reflect the consequences of present decisions on future opportunities. If these consequences were understood, they could be explicitly incorporated within the criterion function. This would enable us to deal with a sequence of single-period models to generate a path of decisions which is optimal in the long run.

The value of T in a T-period model should be chosen where the set of first-period decisions becomes insensitive to further increases in T. By adding the terminal valuation of the stockholders' equity to the second criterion function, it is possible to obtain with only T periods the same first-period decisions that would be made if net income were discounted over a longer time horizon. By not including terminal valuation, one implicitly assumes that stocks held at the end of the planning period are worthless.

4. Summary

This paper provides a detailed mathematical description of a linear programming approach to bank dynamic balance sheet management decisions which the authors first described in verbal terms over five years ago. Section I of this paper briefly discusses the nature of the dynamic balance sheet management problem, and it indicates that this paper should be regarded as presenting a general class of intertemporal LP models. In practice, the user would typically include only a subset of the features herein described in formulating a specific LP model to meet the requirements of a particular bank. Section 2 introduces much of the mathematical notation utilized, and it also discusses the nature of the intertemporal links (which interrelate average balances, spot balances and flows) and the definition of bank capital. The general intertemporal LP models are described in section 3, where separate subsections are devoted to discussions of intra-period constraints, intertemporal constraints and the criterion function. The LP models include comprehensive risk constraints, various policy considerations, economic and institutional realities of the marketplace, and a variety of different dynamic effects which must be considered in order to make optimal dynamic balance sheet management decisions.

Specific versions of the general class of intertemporal LP models described in this paper have been usefully implemented in at least one major American commercial bank (Bankers Trust Company) for at least a five-year period

(1962–67). It is beyond the scope of this paper to discuss the improvements in the dynamic balance sheet management process which resulted from the judicious use of these LP models. Readers interested in learning about the experiences that the authors have had in the successful implementation of these models should consult some of their other publications [18].

[18] For discussions of the practical advantages which can result when these intertemporal LP models are incorporated in the dynamic balance sheet management process, see:

(a) Kalman J. Cohen, 'Dynamic balance sheet management: A management science approach', *Journal of Bank Research,* 2, No. 4 (Winter, 1972), pp. 9–19.

(b) Kalman J. Cohen, Frederick S. Hammer and Howard M. Schneider, 'Harnessing computers for bank asset management', *The Bankers Magazine,* 150, No. 3 (Summer, 1967), pp. 72–80;

(c) Cohen and Hammer, 'Linear programming and optimal bank asset management decisions', *op. cit.*

Some examples of additional modelling considerations which go beyond the LP models actually implemented at Bankers Trust Company but which should prove useful in practice are provided in:

(a) Cohen and Rutenberg, 'Toward a comprehensive framework for bank financial planning', *op. cit.*;

(b) Cohen, 'Improving the capital adequacy formula', *op. cit.*;

(c) Kalman J. Cohen and Sten Thore, 'Programming bank portfolios under uncertainty', *Journal of Bank Research,* 1, No. 1 (Spring, 1970), pp. 42–61.

Chapter 16

DYNAMIC BALANCE SHEET MANAGEMENT: A MANAGEMENT SCIENCE APPROACH*

By Kalman J. Cohen

*This article is reprinted, with permission, from *Journal of Bank Research*, Vol. 2, No. 4 (Winter, 1972), pp. 9-19.

The theme of this paper is that traditionally trained bank executives (with the aid of a new breed of people, management scientists) can utilize some new and sharp tools of analysis in order to make more effective plans and decisions for their banks. These new tools are embodied in management science models. In order to utilize them effectively, traditional executives must understand the banking and economic assumptions inherent in the models, although they need not be familiar with the underlying technical details.

This paper discusses one particular management science model that was successfully used for several years to improve the dynamic balance sheet management process at Bankers Trust Co. in New York. The model is briefly described and some examples of how it has been usefully applied are provided. The paper concludes by discussing the roles of traditional executives in the formulation and implementation of this type of management science model.

Introduction

The phrase *asset management* is commonly used by many bankers to mean *portfolio management*. Some bankers think of their bank's portfolio in narrow terms, focusing only on the investment securities held by the bank. Indeed, some useful tools are available to improve the management of the narrowly defined investment portfolio; but such a narrow viewpoint can be unnecessarily costly to a bank. Maximum advantage can be obtained for the bank from its investment portfolio only if it is managed within the much broader context of bankwide financial planning over a time horizon stretching several years into the future.

In particular, decisions concerning the composition of the investment portfolio (e.g., how it should be split between governments and municipals, what its maturity structure should be, etc.) cannot be made optimally if the investment portfolio is viewed as an entity in itself. It is misleading to view the portfolio management problem as

one of trying to maximize the current yield of the funds now allocated to the investment portfolio. Because banks expect to make loans in the future, management must consider the interactions that exist between the various segments of the investment portfolio and the lending policy of the bank. In effect, the entire asset side of the bank's balance sheet should be simultaneously planned.

Active management of the bank's liabilities and capital accounts has become an increasingly important part of portfolio management during the past decade. This reflects the ability that banks now have to borrow capital by issuing debentures and the emergence of important discretionary sources of funds for banks, such as certificates of deposits (CDs) and Eurodollars. Hence, the interdependencies which exist among all the various balance sheet accounts of the bank must be recognized if maximum benefits are to be obtained for the bank. This is why *balance sheet management* is a more appropriate phrase to use than either *portfolio management* (which focuses too narrowly on the investment securities) or *asset management* (which looks only at the left-hand side of the balance sheet). The entire balance sheet of the bank should be regarded as the portfolio for which financial planning is to be undertaken.

The word *dynamic* is used to precede the phrase *balance sheet management* to convey the idea that optimal decisions regarding the investment securities that the bank should buy or sell today, how aggressively the bank should bid for CDs, etc., cannot be made in a static or a short-run context. Such decisions should recognize the dynamic character of the banking marketplace and the economy. Bankers need to assess the implications of their outlook for the future on the decisions to be made today. Intelligent current decisions are virtually impossible to make solely by examining the present state of the bank and the economic outlook for only the next few months. A proper financial plan for the bank must encompass a time horizon spanning several future years.

In planning over a meaningful future time

period, e.g., five years ahead, care must be exercised so as not to misinterpret what these plans actually mean. Such plans do not necessarily provide accurate predictions of what the bank will do over the next five years. Management should not look ahead for the sake of deciding now what the bank will do four or five years hence. Rather, management should look ahead in order to determine the implications of its currently held predictions about the future for those decisions that must soon be implemented. Any predictions of the future might well prove to be wrong. If the predictions made now turn out to be wrong, new predictions should be made on the basis of what will then be current information. Using the latest available information and predictions, management should then make new plans for the future. This process of planning and replanning is the essence of sound bank financial management. Hence, the phrase *dynamic balance sheet management* is more appropriate than any of the more narrow phrases commonly used by bankers to denote the central financial planning problems of a bank.

I am discussing in this paper how a management science model can help bank executives improve their process of dynamic balance sheet management. This is certainly not to suggest that bank executives should be replaced by mathematical models or that computers should run the investment portfolio (or make other financial plans) for a bank. Instead, I am suggesting that traditionally trained bank executives can increase their effectiveness in financial planning and decision making by properly utilizing management science models.

A Model For Dynamic Balance Sheet Management

For approximately a decade during the 1960s, I was a consultant to Bankers Trust Co. in New York. During that period I was deeply involved in the formulation and implementation of the linear programming model for dynamic balance sheet management which will now be briefly described.[1]

The linear programming model helps bank executives determine an optimal sequence of balance sheet positions for the bank over a multiperiod planning horizon which stretches several years into the future. This sequence of balance sheets is said to be "optimal" in that it results

---

[1] A more complete description of this model has been published in [3].

[2] For some examples of additional considerations which go beyond the model that was actually utilized at Bankers Trust Company, see [2], [4] and [5].

in the largest possible present value of the bank's net income, subject to a variety of constraints on the bank's safety, liquidity and other relevant considerations, and given the bank's initial balance sheet position and its economic forecasts over the planning horizon.

Although it is not necessary here to provide a detailed description of this model, it is helpful to indicate the types of banking and economic considerations which are incorporated in it. The model itself is capable of extension, so that many types of additional considerations which some bankers may feel are essential to include in bank financial planning can be incorporated in this general type of model.[2]

Risk Constraints. One of the most important considerations in this model is the set of risk constraints that are imposed upon each balance sheet within the planning horizon. A modified version of the capital adequacy formula developed by the examiners of the Board of Governors of the Federal Reserve System is used for this purpose. The function of these capital adequacy constraints is to insure that plans formulated with the aid of the model do not subject the bank to an excessive degree of risk.

The capital adequacy formula is a leverage restriction which combines a capital adequacy test with a liquidity test. This formula takes a comprehensive view of the bank's mix of assets and liabilities. It seeks to determine whether the bank has enough capital to protect its depositors against the vicissitudes of banking that might reasonably be expected to occur. In part, the capital adequacy formula can be regarded as an institutional constraint. The reason is that if a bank is undercapitalized, then regulatory agencies will instruct the bank to obtain more capital.

In the model, however, the main function of the capital adequacy formula is to serve as a way of expressing management's attitudes concerning the proper balance among risk, liquidity and yield considerations. In a financial planning model that is used within a bank, it is important for management to understand the underlying reasons for the various constraints. Management has recognized that the modified capital adequacy formula provides an operationally useful definition of risk. Hence, they can use the model to explore the tradeoffs that exist between risk and return.

Other Constraints on Each Planned Balance Sheet. In addition to the risk constraints, there are many other types of constraints that must be satisfied by each future planned balance sheet within the horizon. Restrictions are imposed to prevent the bank from planning to lend or invest more funds than it has available for these purposes, after considering all of its sources of liabilities, reserve requirements, etc. Sets of constraints are added to reflect some policy considerations that bank management may feel are appropriate. Examples of these would be lower bounds on the acceptable ratios of governments to assets and of capital to risk assets, upper bounds on the ratios of loans to deposits and of CDs to total deposits, etc.

Additional types of constraints are imposed to reflect the limitations on a bank's freedom of action that arise from the economic and institutional realities of the marketplace. Some minimal liquidity buffers of cash and near-cash items must be provided to permit the bank to make short term adjustments required by day-to-day fluctuations in its deposits. The predicted demand for new loans by customers is reflected in upper limits on the amounts of new loans that the bank can make. There are many types of short term liabilities, each of which can be used only to a limited extent as a source of funds; constraints are imposed to represent these limitations. In order to have continued access to some sources of short term liabilities (e.g., Federal funds purchased), the bank may need to be active on both sides of the market (e.g., sometimes to sell Federal funds, even though on balance it wishes to be a net purchaser); these considerations are reflected in suitable constraints. Some depositors (e.g., public authorities) require the bank to maintain collateral against their deposits by the pledging of appropriate assets; these pledging requirements are reflected in the constraints. The bank is constrained to maintain at least the level of cash and cash items required by legal reserve requirements, float considerations and correspondent bank relations. Finally, the bank is permitted to generate additional funds by selling investment securities that it holds prior to their maturity.

Dynamic Mechanisms. The constraints that have been mentioned in the two preceding subsections apply to each planned balance sheet position of the bank during the planning horizon. Several additional types of constraints are present in the linear programming model to represent the dynamic mechanisms that link successive planned balance sheet positions of the bank. These dynamic mechanisms in effect specify the manner in which future planned balance sheets depend upon the bank's initial balance sheet and decisions to be made in earlier periods within the planning horizon.

Some of these dynamic mechanisms are entirely straightforward, reflecting inventory-type relation-

ships and the passage of time. Thus, for example, if the bank now purchases government bonds maturing in nine years and holds them until maturity, then one year from now the remaining time to maturity of these bonds will be eight years, one year after that it will be seven years, etc. Additional constraints reflect the dynamic manner in which the bank's capital funds at the end of any period depend in part upon decisions made in that and earlier periods within the planning horizon. Thus, the bank's capital funds will change as interest is paid and received, securities are traded at capital gains or losses, expenses are incurred, dividends are declared, etc. The final set of dynamic mechanisms that can be incorporated in the model reflect the manner in which the bank's current lending policy will affect its future loan demand and its current and future levels of deposits.

Objective Function. The three preceding subsections have indicated the type of balance sheet constraints and dynamic mechanisms that can be incorporated in the linear programming model. In order to complete the model's formulation, it is necessary to specify the nature of the objective function which the bank is trying to maximize. From a mathematical viewpoint, a great deal of flexibility exists concerning this objective function. In practice, it is important that the bank's senior executives participate in determining the most appropriate way to measure the bank's profit performance over the planning horizon. In many instances, bankers will agree that the present value of the bank's net income during the planning horizon is an appropriate manner in which to specify the objective function in the model.

Decision Variables. In using the linear programming model for planning a sequence of future balance sheets for the bank, it is important to understand what items are considered as decision variables, i.e., what factors are viewed as being at least partially subject to control by the bank. Depending upon the exact form of model that is being utilized, any or all of the following items can be regarded as decision variables that are at least partially under the bank's control: Cash and cash items, short term earning assets, investment securities purchased and sold, new loans made, demand deposits (to the extent that they reflect "compensating balances" for new loans made), CDs, Eurodollars used to support domestic loans, short term borrowed funds and capital notes issued.

Input Data Requirements. Several different categories of input data are required before an optimal solution to the linear programming model can be obtained. Information must be provided concerning the bank's initial balance sheet at the beginning of the planning horizon. Forecasts must be made of future interest rates, loan demand and deposit levels over the planning horizon. Some other miscellaneous factors that have an impact upon funds availability, capital requirements, etc., must also be predicted. Finally, numerical values need to be specified for various parameters of the model which reflect management policies and marketplace realities.

Practical Applications Of The Model

The preceding section has described the banking and economic content of a linear programming model for dynamic balance sheet management. I shall now discuss some of its practical applications at Bankers Trust Co. between 1962 and 1967, the period of time during which I was most extensively involved as a consultant in the formulation and implementation of this model. In considering practical applications, emphasis will be placed on the insights and understanding that executives can derive from interacting with this type of model and with the management scientists who have been involved in its development.

Many people without technical training have an erroneous view of the manner in which linear programming models are used in practice. They regard the process as one in which the management scientists provide the single best set of input data for the model, run the computer to obtain an optimal solution and then instruct the executives to implement this solution. Any attempt to utilize a model in this way would either lead to its complete rejection by the executives involved or else to a system of "pushbutton decision making" in which executives would be replaced by computers. Hence, this erroneous view does not describe the process by which the model is used in practice.

The actual process by which this type of linear programming model affects dynamic balance sheet management in a bank is considerably more subtle. There will develop over time a series of dialogues or conversations involving conventionally trained bank executives, management scientists, the mathematical model that is programmed in the computer and a data base (that may also be resident in the computer). In practice, instead of running the model only one time during any planning cycle in order to determine what management ought to do, the model is run many times.

Analyzing Uncertainties. One reason for running this model many times during any planning cycle is that neither the executives nor the

management scientists believe that they can accurately forecast the future over a several-year planning horizon. As indicated in the preceding section, among the data inputs required by this model are forecasts of future interest rates, loan demand and deposit levels over the planning horizon. Since forecasts are required, but we do not believe that these forecasts can be entirely accurate, the obvious way of proceeding is to make several alternative forecasts, each of which stems from a plausible economic scenario describing future events.

The model is then solved repeatedly, each time using one of the plausible future economic scenarios as the basis for generating the required input data. The various solutions of the model are then compared. Determinations are also made as to what will happen if any solution is implemented and each of the alternative future economic scenarios were to develop. Any particular solution may be "optimal" for only one of these scenarios, and we need to compute how the bank will be affected when that solution is implemented and the future develops in some other manner.

It sometimes will turn out that the range of uncertainties regarding future economic developments is not critical for the decisions that need to be implemented currently. In other words, regardless of which of the plausible alternative future economic scenarios develops, the optimal actions to be taken during the first period of the planning horizon are substantially similar. When this turns out to be the case, then bank executives and management scientists are able quickly to agree on a course of action. There is no need for them to spend much time discussing the relative likelihoods of the alternative future economic scenarios, since such discussions will not alter the present actions that should be taken. Before the linear programming model was utilized, however, such irrelevant debates concerning future economic developments were relatively commonplace.

Often, however, the choice of current actions for the bank is much more difficult because these actions critically depend upon which of the alternative plausible future economic scenarios is assumed. In such circumstances, the first-period components of the optimal solution of the model will change substantially when the model is rerun with different forecasts. When this occurs, there is no easy, automatic way of reaching decisions. Bank executives are called upon to exercise judgment and to make difficult choices.

Any situation in which executives must reach decisions in the face of uncertainties that can critically affect the outcomes of these decisions requires some risks to be taken. When such decisions are made in an entirely intuitive manner, the nature of the risks is implicit and unquantified. The key new element which the use of the linear programming model introduces is the ability to determine explicitly and quantitatively the magnitudes of the risks involved. In other words, the executives are placed in a position in which they can take "calculated risks" rather than "blind risks." In this situation it is clear that the management scientists, the model and the computer do not replace the judgment, wisdom and experience of the executives. Instead, they provide sharper tools that enable the executives to explore and understand the logical implications of their policies and outlooks for the future. In the end, however, it is the executives who ultimately make the final decisions.

One additional aspect of the use of the model to analyze uncertainties should be mentioned. While it is naive to expect that perfect forecasts can ever be made, within limits it is possible to improve the relative accuracy of forecasts by devoting more scarce resources (e.g., money, people, computer time, etc.) to making them. The linear programming model can be used as a tool to help determine the magnitude of the benefits that the bank might expect from various degrees of improvement in forecast accuracy. These estimates of benefit can then be used by the executives to help determine the extent to which additional scarce resources should be devoted to improving the forecasting process within the bank.

Relaxing Constraints and Testing Interactions. Many of the internal policy considerations that have been incorporated in the constraints of the model reflect the somewhat vague feelings of executives rather than precise guidelines to which the bank must necessarily conform. When this is the case, then many comparative runs of the model can usefully be made in order to help the executives better understand the nature and impact of their policies. An outstanding example of this type of analysis is provided by the manner in which the constraints imposing a minimum value on the ratio of governments to assets have been treated at Bankers Trust Co.

Initially, the model did not include any constraints on the governments-to-assets ratio. When some early runs of the model were discussed with management, they expressed considerable uneasiness about the results. The model was indicating that the bank should switch large amounts of its investment securities out of governments and into municipals. While this type of switch seemed to be very profitable, it implied balance sheets for the bank with far lower ratios of governments to assets than other large commercial banks had at that time. At first, the management scientists did not understand why this should make the bank executives feel uncomfortable.

A series of dialogues concerning the governments-to-assets ratio involving the bank executives and the management scientists then developed. We found that management did adequately understand the nature of the risk constraints and the liquidity buffer constraints that had been incorporated in the model. We found that management was willing to assume that the various alternative economic forecasts (which they themselves had provided) that were used as inputs to the various model runs satisfactorily represented their future outlook. We found that management understood sufficiently well the other relevant aspects of the model. Nonetheless, management was unhappy about the resulting ratios of governments to assets that were implied by the various solutions to the model. At that time, we management scientists felt that risk and liquidity considerations were already adequately provided for by the model and that any attempt to impose governments-to-assets ratio constraints in the model could only lead to poorer performance for the bank.

After further conversations, however, we began to realize that the executives indeed had good cause to be worried. Their concern was not based on the types of risk and liquidity considerations that were already reflected in the model. Rather, they were rightly concerned with some more subtle factors which had not been explicitly quantified and indeed which had been omitted from the model.

In particular, the possible reactions of corporate treasurers and of investors in the market for bank stocks were the basis for management's worries. If the bank were to publish a balance sheet in which the ratio of governments to assets was far lower than in other major commercial banks, it was felt that corporate treasurers and investors might begin to view the bank as being unsound. Once that would happen, then corporate treasurers might begin to withdraw millions of dollars of deposits from the bank and investors might begin to sell their holdings of the bank's stock (precipitating a drop in its price). After the management scientists understood that these were the reasons for management's discomfort with balance sheets showing an extremely low governments-to-assets ratio, we agreed that the model should be appropriately modified.

In principle, the most desirable way of modifying the model would have been to build into it relationships indicating the manner in which the bank's demand deposits and its stock price are affected by its governments-to-assets ratio. Unfortunately, we did not feel that we understood these phenomena well enough to do so. Hence, the alternative that we adopted was to impose direct constraints that required each planned balance sheet for the bank to have at least some minimum specified value for the governments-to-assets ratio. When this minimum ratio is specified at a conventionally acceptable level, then we can be sure that the bank will not suffer losses of deposits or declines in its stock price as a result. Furthermore, we can use the model to determine the opportunity costs, in terms of the tangible quantitative factors incorporated in the model, of such constraints.

When we first reformulated the model in this manner, we used 16% as the minimum acceptable ratio for governments to assets. The resulting solutions to the model were then acceptable to management. Next, however, we showed management the results of a similar series of model runs in which the minimum acceptable governments-to-assets ratio was stipulated as 15%. Management was surprised at how much more profitable the bank would be over the planning horizon if the governments-to-assets ratio would be permitted to decline to 15% rather than remain at 16%. In management's judgment, this projected increase in tangible profitability over the planning horizon was more than enough to compensate for the increased intangible risks from less favorable attitudes towards the bank that the lower governments-to-assets ratio might lead corporate treasurers and stockholders to develop. Management then went on to ask us to produce runs of the model showing the impact on projected tangible profitability over the planning horizon of minimum governments-to-assets ratios of 14%, 13%, etc. On the basis of the information thereby provided, management was able to make a reasoned judgment as to when increased intangible risks from lower governments-to-assets ratios were no longer compensated for by the projected increases in tangible profitability. The exact value ultimately chosen for the minimum acceptable governments-to-assets ratio was determined as a result of a series of dialogues involving executives, management scientists and the linear programming model. Ultimately, it was realized that the appropriate minimal value for the governments-to-assets ratio would change over time, as economic conditions and the policies of other banks change. The intangible effects that are of legitimate concern do not really depend upon the absolute magnitude of the governments-to-assets ratio; rather, they depend upon how the value of this ratio for your bank compares with the ratios found in other banks.

The preceding discussion has revealed the manner in which bank executives can utilize their management scientists and the linear programming model in order to reach an improved understanding of what initially appeared to be a hazy, ill-structured area. Similar situations arose in many other areas of dynamic balance sheet management during the 1962-1967 period at Bankers Trust Co. The types of dialogues that were thereby established helped bank management formulate new policies towards CDs, investments in municipal securities, capital notes and Eurodollars. In the following three subsections, more detailed information is provided concerning the manner in which these types of financial policies were analyzed with the aid of the model.

Certificates of Deposit. The initial motivation for developing the linear programming model for dynamic balance sheet management arose in 1962 in order to help formulate a new policy towards CDs. Although Bankers Trust was not the first bank to initiate the CD market, it was reasonably active in it during early 1962. Unfortunately, the bank's policy at that time regarding how to use the funds generated by the CDs did not permit a satisfactory rate of profit to be earned on those funds. Hence, by mid-1962 the bank began to wonder whether the establishment of the CD market had not been a mistake.

The bank's initial policy was to invest the net funds generated by a CD (after reserve requirements had been met) into assets of comparable maturity as the CD. Since the CD was in effect a fixed maturity time deposit, it was reasoned that the CD would be withdrawn upon its maturity. Hence, the net funds resulting from the CD should be invested in assets of the same (or shorter) maturity so that these funds would be available to repay the CD on maturity. While this reasoning at first seemed to be plausible, unfortunately the resulting policy did not prove to be profitable.

One of the first projects undertaken by the newly formed Management Science Division at Bankers Trust Co. in 1962 was a more fundamental analysis of CDs, in the hope that a more profitable policy could be formulated. We quickly realized that in order to determine how aggressively the bank should bid for CDs and how the net funds generated should be utilized, a rather comprehensive, systemwide view of the bank would need to be developed. In effect, the first version of the linear programming model for dynamic balance sheet management was developed in order to analyze CDs.

The fundamental error made in the previous analysis was the assumption that one needs to consider only the subsystem consisting of a single source of funds (CDs) and the particular assets into which the funds could be invested (assets of comparable or shorter maturity). By taking a more comprehensive viewpoint of the bank's entire balance sheet, both currently and over time, we discovered that there were some important system-wide interactions that could make CDs highly profitable to the bank if they were properly utilized. In particular, we discovered that because of some hitherto unsuspected secondary effects, the gross return on CDs could often be higher than the rate of return on any single asset into which the funds generated by the CD could be invested.

Such a result appeared, of course, to be a paradox. In effect, the model was stating that the bank could earn a gross return of 8% on CDs, even though the rates of return on all of the assets into which the CD funds could be invested ranged from 3% to 6%. While management's initial reaction was to feel that a logical inconsistency in the model had been discovered, after further dialogues we were able to convince management that the model was indeed correct and that CDs, if properly utilized, could be far more profitable than hitherto believed. In doing so, we did not ask management to accept these paradoxical results on blind faith; rather, we were able to get management to understand the underlying banking and economic reasons for these results.

The following type of explanation helped management gain new insights into the CD area. The key factor was the modified capital adequacy formula which provides the basis for the risk constraints in the model. As already indicated, management understood and accepted this modified capital adequacy formula as a meaningful internal guideline towards risk (and some associated aspects of liquidity).

Since a CD is a fixed-maturity time deposit, increasing the amount of CDs in the bank will, according to the modified capital adequacy formula, result in some specified increase in the potential liquidity needs of the bank. When the funds generated by the CD (net of reserve requirements) are directly invested in earning assets in an optimal manner, more liquidity may be generated than the potential liquidity needs specified by the modified capital adequacy formula. Since the reason for the bank to increase its CDs is to become more profitable, rather than to become more liquid, it would then be possible for the bank to make some secondary shifts of funds

from more liquid but lower yielding assets into less liquid but higher yielding assets. This indeed proved to be the case in late 1962. At that time, in fact, the incremental return earned on the shifted funds proved to be higher than the return earned on the initially invested funds. This discovery helped management to adopt a new and more profitable policy toward CDs at Bankers Trust Co.

Capital Notes. The preceding analysis of the manner in which new and highly profitable policies may be suggested by appropriate analyses of the linear programming model focused on the secondary effects associated with the modified capital adequacy formula incorporated in the risk constraints. These secondary effects are even more profound and easier to comprehend in connection with another major policy decision that was extensively analyzed with the aid of the model. This was the new policy adopted in 1964 when Bankers Trust Co. became the first major U.S. commercial bank to float a large, fully underwritten public issue of capital notes (i.e., of borrowed long term capital funds). The face amount of the capital notes initially issued was $100 million, and they carried an annual coupon rate of 4½%. This was a straight debt (rather than a convertible) issue, and it carried a mandatory sinking fund provision.

Let us now consider the type of insights that the linear programming model provided in 1964 concerning this issue of capital notes. We can usefully begin by asking what the bank would do with the funds provided by the $100 million of capital notes. To the extent that there was sufficient loan demand, the bank would use these new funds to increase its commercial loans. If the loan demand was not sufficient to absorb all of these new funds, then the remaining funds would be invested in long-term municipal securities. In either event, all of the $100 million in new funds provided by the new capital notes would be fully utilized to support earning assets.

Next, let us consider the implications of the above transactions for the bank's capital position, as measured by the modified capital adequacy formula. According to this formula, only 10% capital backing is required to support such earning assets as commercial loans or long term municipals. Hence, even though the bank had utilized all $100 million of the *funds* provided by the capital notes, it had absorbed only $10 million worth of the *risk-backing power* provided by the capital notes. Management had not been previously dissatisfied with the degree of risk that was being assumed by the bank; therefore the reason to consider issuing capital notes was to make the bank more profitable rather than less risky. Hence, there was an additional $90 million worth of risk-backing power provided by the capital notes that should be utilized in order to increase the bank's profitability.

The way in which this additional $90 million of risk-backing power could be utilized without requiring any additional funds is, of course, to shift some funds that had been previously allocated to lower risk and lower yielding assets into higher risk and higher yielding assets. In particular, the model indicated that large amounts of funds should be shifted from short term governments into commercial loans and long term municipals. Depending upon the particular set of economic forecasts utilized, somewhere between $500 million and $700 million of funds could be shifted in this manner. Thus, in effect, issuing $100 million of capital notes in 1964 permitted Bankers Trust Co. to put between $600 million and $800 million into new commercial loans and long term municipals. This was accomplished without changing the overall capital adequacy of the bank, i.e., without any deterioration in its risk or liquidity positions. The incremental return earned on the shifted funds proved to be much greater than the direct return earned on the initially invested funds. Again, the secondary effect was at work, and the exact impact that it had was sharply and convincingly revealed by analyses carried out with the aid of the linear programming model. In effect, the model was able to suggest to management new financial strategies for the bank which would otherwise have probably gone unnoticed.

Other Policy Considerations. We shall mention only briefly two additional policy considerations which were usefully analyzed at Bankers Trust Co. with the aid of the linear programming model during the 1962-1967 period. One policy concerned the extent to which funds in the investment portfolio should be shifted out of government securities and into municipal securities. The other policy concerned the extent to which Eurodollars should be used to support domestic loans during periods of tight money. Each of these policy considerations could be analyzed within a comprehensive, systemwide framework because of the availability of the model. Many indirect effects and interactions were discovered that made the resulting policies more appropriate than they were otherwise likely to be. Furthermore, the use of the model made it possible to adopt sophisticated policies that were readily modified over time as economic circumstances changed, instead of the simpler but overly rigid policies that were likely to result from more traditional approaches to financial planning.

Conclusions

In reviewing the various policy considerations for which analyses conducted with the aid of the linear programming model proved to be most helpful to Bankers Trust Co. management during 1962-1967, one striking characteristic emerges. Most of the examples discussed in the preceding section involved circumstances in which important institutional changes occurred in the marketplace. These changes were of such a profound nature that the long years of judgment, wisdom and experience which traditionally trained bankers had accumulated were inadequate to suggest the new policies which were most appropriate in the changed circumstances. CDs, for example, were a new money market instrument that entered the banking scene in the early 1960s. The ordinary intuition of bankers was less capable than the model to discover how best to utilize CDs. Similar considerations apply to capital notes and to the use of Eurodollars to support domestic loans. Although the market for municipal securities did exist much earlier, it was only during the 1960s that it acquired the great degree of depth, breadth and resiliency that made it possible for banks to buy and sell large amounts of municipals without causing great changes in market yields.

I believe that management science approaches to planning and decision making prove to be most fruitful when they are applied to new types of developments with which executives have not had extensive previous experience. When the environment remains relatively unchanged for long periods of time, executives will generally learn to operate effectively in such a stable environment on the basis of their judgment, wisdom and experience. When extensive environmental changes occur, however, then the unaided judgment, wisdom and experience of executives cannot be relied upon to lead to good decisions. In such circumstances, management scientists and the appropriate types of models can be of great aid to executives. This does not mean, of course, that the judgment, wisdom and experience of executives will be ignored. Quite the contrary, for the contents of the management science models will very much reflect the knowledge, attitudes and policies of executives. Furthermore, as has already been indicated, when decisions are ultimately made, they are made by executives rather than by management scientists or by models. In the last analysis, executives have to apply their judgment, wisdom and experience in balancing tangible against intangible effects, in analyzing the implications of uncertainties, in choosing the proper risk-return tradeoffs, etc. While the interactions that executives have with management scientists and models will lead to a more rational process of reaching decisions, the ultimate decision responsibility lies with executives.

Any attempt to develop a useful management science model for dynamic balance sheet management necessitates a great deal of time and commitment from senior executives. Traditionally trained bankers must be willing to work closely with management scientists in order first to formulate, and then to implement, a relevant model to improve the planning and decision-making process.[3] Senior bank executives must enter into serious, soul-searching discussions concerning what the long term goals and objectives of the bank should be, how to measure the degree of success in meeting these goals and objectives, what is the nature of the banking marketplace, how does the bank interact with its customers and with other banks, how does the state of the economy affect the bank, how can future states of the economy be predicted, what are the relevant institutional factors that impinge on the bank, etc.

Before concluding this paper, let me be sure that no reader misinterprets what I have said. I do not want to be understood as implying that there now exists a perfect model for bank financial planning, let alone that the linear programming model under discussion represents such a perfect model. Nonetheless, it definitely is the case that this particular model proved to be extremely valuable in a number of ways for at least a five-year period (1962-1967) at Bankers Trust Co. In the preceding section, I have tried to highlight some of the major applications that were made of this model during that period. The model itself, although it can be of great help in the dynamic balance sheet management process if properly utilized, does not possess any magical properties. The naive and passive use of this very same model (and its accompanying computer program) in a different bank (or even in Bankers Trust Co. during more recent years) is unlikely to result in improvements in the dynamic balance sheet management process. For such a model to be really useful, an extensive series of dialogues must be established involving senior bank executives, their management scientists and the model. Where such a dialogue is lacking, few, if any, benefits will result from the model.

In the above section, I have reviewed some examples of major dynamic balance sheet management policy decisions that were usefully analyzed with the aid of the linear programming model at Bankers Trust Co. during 1962-1967. It is not possible to prove that similar bank policies could not have been adopted without the aid of the linear programming model. In fact, however, I suspect that they would not have been adopted (at least not as early as they were) had it not been for the management science efforts at Bankers Trust Co. in the dynamic balance sheet management area. Moreover, I definitely believe that these new policies were adopted as part of a rational management process and that bank executives were able to exercise the courage of their convictions in an informed, analytical manner because of their interaction with management scientists and the linear programming model. The exact nature of this interaction is sufficiently imprecise, however, and it involves such an extended series of dialogues over a period of several years that it is impossible to state conclusively that the actual policies which were adopted could not have been arrived at in a different manner. The fundamental policy changes that were discussed in the previous section resulted from a complicated process of organizational decision making. Traditional bank executives, management scientists and the linear programming model all played a role in it. While similar policy decisions might eventually have been made without the aid of the management scientists and the model, it is clear that using traditional approaches a very different management process would have been required to reach these decisions. Furthermore, I suspect that bank management would have had far less confidence in the correctness of these new policies had they been reached in any other manner. ☐

---

3 For an extensive discussion of the way in which traditional executives and "management oriented" management scientists should jointly work together in order to formulate and effectively implement management science models, see [1].

[1] Cohen, Kalman J., "A Realistic Approach to Implementing Management Science," The Magazine of Bank Administration, Vol. 45, No. 9 (September, 1969), pp. 28 ff.

[2] Cohen, Kalman J., "Improving the Capital Adequacy Formula," Journal of Bank Research, Vol. 1, No. 1 (Spring, 1970), pp. 13-16.

[3] Cohen, Kalman J. and Frederick S. Hammer, "Linear Programming and Optimal Bank Asset Management Decisions," Journal of Finance, Vol. 22, No. 2 (May, 1967), pp. 147-165.

[4] Cohen, Kalman J. and David P. Rutenberg, "Toward a Comprehensive Framework for Bank Financial Planning," Journal of Bank Research, Vol. 1, No. 4 (Winter, 1971), pp. 41-57.

[5] .Cohen, Kalman J. and Sten Thore, "Programming Bank Portfolios Under Uncertainty," Journal of Bank Research, Vol. 1, No. 1 (Spring, 1970), pp. 42-61.

Chapter 17

FORECASTING VS. ALLOCATIONAL EFFICIENCY IN BANK ASSET PLANNING: AN INTEGRATED EVALUATION*

By Michael E. Echols and J. Walter Elliott

*This article is reprinted, with permission, from *Journal of Bank Research*, Vol. 6, No. 4 (Winter, 1976), pp. 283-295.

The management teams of banks are charged with the responsibility of making profits for their shareholders. In this fundamental duty, managers essentially structure and continually adjust the bank's portfolio of earning assets to maintain risk at acceptable levels while maximizing the present value of the portfolio and maintaining a growing flow of realized earnings. Efficient execution of this task requires predictions of the future economic environment and the integration of such predictions into portfolio allocation decisions.

Several recent studies in the *Journal of Bank Research* have discussed the forecasting problem facing bank management. Thomson [1973] has considered prediction of loan demand, deposit inflow and to a brief extent interest rates, and has offered a model structure for this purpose. Cramer and Miller [1973] have considered the specific problem of deposit prediction. Bradley and Crane's [1973] paper shows the structural role of yield curves in multi-period optimization models. Other recent studies have been concerned with the development of more sophisticated techniques for investment allocation decisions. These include dynamic approaches by Chambers and Charnes [1972] and Cohen [1972]; chance-constrained models by Charnes and Littlechild [1968] and Charnes and Thore [1966]; limited-scope dynamic models under uncertainty by Eppen and Fama [1968]; Dallenbach and Archer [1969] and Booth [1972]; a decision-theoretic formulation by Wolf [1969]; and a two-stage programming model under uncertainty by Crane [1971] which has been applied by Cohen and Thore [1970]. In a more applied context, Lifson and Blackmarr [1973] have recently been concerned with the response of bank asset deployment to sharp shifts in loan demand, deposit runoff and current and unrealized profit loss in the context of a simulation and optimization structure. In these studies, discussions of forecasting models have proceeded independently of discussions of allocation models. Accordingly, evidence has not been developed on the importance of forecasting accuracy in efficient allocational model solutions. In this paper, we

address this need by exploring the implications of predictive accuracy relative to allocational efficiency in the overall bank allocational framework.

To do this, a single period programming model for the allocational decisions is combined with an econometric model of the predicted inputs and applied to the portfolio decisions of a medium-sized bank. Portfolio results are obtained both assuming perfect forecasts and using the predictive model forecasts. A comparison of the performance obtained under these results enables conclusions as to the economic magnitude of the prediction problem compared to the allocational problem in short-term bank planning.

The Allocational Framework

Many of the recently-proposed mathematical programming bank allocational models have emphasized multi-period structures that imply some aspects of portfolio decisions in future periods are influenced by current-period portfolio decisions. It is by now generally accepted that multi-period models are conceptually superior to single-period models in that they account for this condition of temporal dependence.

Only under institutional circumstances where a structure of completely liquid secondary markets in all earning assets exists, coupled with an unrestricted level of asset holdings by bank investors (subject to available funds) at zero transactions costs, does complete temporal independence occur in portfolio choice. If levels of each asset can be reduced to zero by being sold in secondary markets at the "going rate" or increased to the limit of funds in each period through secondary market purchases, then current and future portfolio decisions are independent. Generally speaking, under these conditions, a single-period model will do as well as its multi-period counterpart.

In the real world of U.S. banks, these secondary market and unrestricted asset level assumptions are not strictly met. However, they are approximated to a degree for many medium-sized and large banks. Secondary markets do exist in many if not all of the asset categories on the balance sheet of such banks.[1] Although these markets are not perfect, they do as a matter of practice allow a bank to increase or decrease its position in most if not all of its earning assets over some finite range. In addition, many banks can increase or decrease their asset position in many if not all categories with little policy repercussions. The biggest exception to this flexibility is the commercial loan category where line of credit and other business relationships create an obligation to maintain a certain level of outstanding loan commitments. Finally, transactions costs in real markets are not zero as required for complete temporal independence, but they are relatively low for most asset categories, particularly when considered in relation to a policy-dictated minimum asset holding period of say one month or one quarter. Thus, a degree of temporal independence is obtained in bank investment and loan portfolios as a result of modern secondary markets, partial asset flexibility and low transactions costs. Allocational solutions obtained from a single-period model structure under conditions of modern secondary market structure accordingly should not be vastly different than otherwise-comparable multi-period structures. Because of this, a single-period model structure has been selected for this study due to its considerable simplicity compared to the multi-period structure and its capability to generate useful evidence on the relative efficiency of predictive and allocational model components.

Allocational Model Structure

The allocational mechanism chosen for the present study is a single period linear programming model. Its detailed structure is shown in Figure 1. The variables in the program identify the active decision categories available to banks. The three variables labeled discretionary liabilities define activities that may be used to increase the pool of funds available for investment. All the remaining variables deal with asset accounts.

The activities defining bond alternatives are partitioned along time to maturity and coupon level. Both dimensions are motivated by the nature of the constraint set. The examiners of the Federal Reserve Board define the riskiness of a bond in terms of the time to maturity; thus the weight assigned to each bond in the aggregate risk function depends upon that bond's location in the intervals shown in Figure 1. The second dimension used to classify bonds is their relative coupon. This dimension is required in order to deal with the real-

world problem faced by bankers of reporting acceptable levels of realized income on a continuing basis. When realized income is a limiting factor, bonds with high coupons must be given consideration over potential capital gains. This is accomplished in the model by the addition of a realized income constraint to be discussed below.

Specific loan activities are covered by activities X_{17} through X_{25}. As seen, each of the four major lending categories is partitioned into new loans and existing loans. This is necessary to operationalize the secondary market framework of the model as it applies to changes in holdings of loans. Unlike bond investment activities, loans may in general not be reduced to zero or added in large quantities over the course of a single planning period. Instead, new loans may be acquired only up to the limits of market demand, while existing holdings of loans be reduced only to the limit associated with their sale at approximately unchanged or "going" prices. Accordingly, the activities of acquiring new loans must be separated from reducing existing loans so that appropriate constraints can be applied to each.

The model's objective function maximizes the sum of realized and unrealized tax adjusted gross revenue associated with the model activities. The objective function coefficients ($P_1 \ldots P_{32}$) contain the per-unit gross revenue consequences of each activity.[2] Maximizing gross rather than net revenue offers the obvious advantage of simplicity and ease of application. Moreover, the loss in allocational efficiency appears to be low, due to the high degree of costs that appear to be substantially independent of activity levels. For example, the cost of bond management to banks is generally not greatly influenced by an increase or decrease in the dollar value of bond holdings. The same proposition is reasonable for loans. Within the model limits imposed by demand and by secondary market disposal, fluctuations in loan levels do not appear to create significant variable costs for most banks.[3] Under these circumstances where costs that vary with activity levels are low, the model solution that maximizes gross revenue approximates the optimal net revenue solution. Thus, the simpler gross revenue formulation is the more attractive alternative.

The 28 constraints shown in Figure 1 fall into three general categories: 1) Those imposed by governmental agencies, 2) those imposed by mar-

[1]Several authors have explored detailed strategies for continuing use of secondary market channels in the U.S. For examples, see Beazer [1965], Parks [1958], and Kane and Malkiel [1965].

[2]The special tax-exempt status of income from municipal bonds necessitates a special treatment of P_{14} through P_{16}; whereas $P_2 \ldots P_{13}$ are market rates of return on various bonds; P_{14} through P_{16} are adjusted to an equivalent non-tax-exempt rate.
[3]However, there are definite limits to the applicability of this statement. A bank that doubles its level of lending will usually have to hire additional loan officers.

Figure 1. Model Structures

			Activities											Asset
				U. S. Government Securities										Securities of U. S. Govt. Agencies
			Short Term		Low Coupon				High Coupon					
	Row ID	Cash & Due From Banks	U. S. Treasury Bills	Maturing Within 90 Days	Maturity 0-1 Years	Maturity 1-2 Years	Maturity 2-5 Years	Maturity Over 5 Years	Maturity 0-1 Years	Maturity 1-2 Years	Maturity 2-5 Years	Maturity Over 5 Years	Low Coupon	High Coupon
		X_1	X_2	X_3	X_4	X_5	X_6	X_7	X_8	X_9	X_{10}	X_{11}	X_{12}	X_{13}
Objective Function (Max.)	Cost	P_1	P_2	P_3	P_4	P_5	P_6	P_7	P_8	P_9	P_{10}	P_{11}	P_{12}	P_{13}
Realized Revenue	R_1	C_1	C_2	C_3	C_4	C_5	C_6	C_7	C_8	C_9	C_{10}	C_{11}	C_{12}	C_{13}
Reserve Requirement	R_2	1.0												
Collateral Requirement	R_3		-1.0	-1.0	-1.0	-1.0	-1.0	-1.0	-1.0	-1.0	-1.0	-1.0	-1.0	-1.0
Liquidity Buffer	R_4	1.0	1.0	1.0	1.0	1.0	1.0	1.0	1.0	1.0	1.0	1.0	1.0	1.0
Risk Constraint As	R_5	1.0	.995	.96	.96	.96			.96	.96			.96	
Defined By	R_6	1.0	.995	.96	.96	.96	.90		.96	.96	.90		.96	.90
Federal Reserve	R_7	1.0	.995	.96	.96	.96	.90	.85	.96	.96	.90	.85	.96	.90
Examiners	R_8		.005	.005	.04	.04	.04	.06	.04	.04	.04	.06	.04	.04
Balance Sheet Equation (R_{23})	R_9	1.0	1.0	1.0	1.0	1.0	1.0	1.0	1.0	1.0	1.0	1.0	1.0	1.0
Max. Existing Loans & Discounts	R_{10}													
Min. Existing Loans & Discounts	R_{11}													
Max. New Loans & Discounts	R_{12}													
Max. Existing Instalment Loans	R_{13}													
Min. Existing Instalment Loans	R_{14}													
Max. New Instalment Loans	R_{15}													
Max. Existing Mortgages	R_{16}													
Min. Existing Mortgages	R_{17}													
Max. New Mortgages	R_{18}													
Min. Ratio Govt. Securities	R_{19}	a_1	a_2	a_2	a_2	a_2	a_2	a_2	a_2	a_2	a_2	a_2	a_2	a_2
Max. Ratio Govt. Securities	R_{20}	a_3	a_4	a_4	a_4	a_4	a_4	a_4	a_4	a_4	a_4	a_4	a_4	a_4
Min. Loan to Deposit Ratio	R_{21}													
Max. Risky Assets to Capital Ratio	R_{22}													
Max. Controllable Liabilities	R_{23}													
Max. Federal Funds Bought	R_{24}													
Min. Federal Funds Bought	R_{25}													
Max. Funds from CD's over $100,000	R_{26}													
Max. Funds Borrowed from Federal Reserve	R_{27}													
Max. Credit Card Lending	R_{28}													

ket limitations and 3) those established by bank management. The constraints in Figure 1 imposed by governmental agencies include numbers $R2$-$R8$. They insure that allocational solutions meet legal reserve requirement and collateral conditions, as well as the guidelines for balanced-risk portfolio composition as laid down by Federal Reserve examiners. The specific structure and coefficients in these constraints are essentially fixed for banks in particular classes. They are given in specific numerical form in Figure 1 for banks in the class of the sample bank discussed below.

Constraints $R12$, $R15$, $R18$ and $R28$ define demand constraints on credit card lending, loans and discounts, new instalments and new mortgages, while constraints $R11$, $R14$ and $R17$ express re-

spectively the market limitations on the take-down of existing levels of these loans. In addition, external influences largely govern the level of new deposit inflows, which constrain the total level of deposit liabilities. These influences are represented by constraint $R9$ that equates asset and liability totals in a balance sheet format.[4]

The third group of constraints are managerial in nature and arise out of a general tendency of bank managers to consider the balance sheet and income statement appearance of their resource allocation strategies. Certain key financial statement relationships are commonly thought to reflect on

[4]In other words, increases in deposit inflows increase B_9 which enables greater asset expansion before constraint $R21$ applies. See the Appendix for a specific definition of B_9.

Activities

Variable definitions:

- X_{14} — General Obligation Municipals Maturity Less Than 2 Years: Low Coupon
- X_{15} — General Obligation Municipals Maturity Less Than 2 Years: High Coupon
- X_{16} — All Other Municipals & Loans Held
- X_{17} — Commercial Loans: New Loans This Period
- X_{18} — Commercial Loans: Existing Loans
- X_{19} — Personal Loans: New Loans This Period
- X_{20} — All Other Personal Banking Loans
- X_{21} — Mortgages: Existing
- X_{22} — Mortgages: New
- X_{23} — Instalment Loans: New This Period
- X_{24} — Instalment Loans: Existing
- X_{25} — Credit Card Loans
- X_{26} — Federal Funds Sold
- X_{27} — Federal Funds Bought & Repurchase Agreement Sold
- X_{28} — Discretionary Liabilities: Funds Borrowed by CD's Over \$100,000
- X_{29} — Discretionary Liabilities: Funds Borrowed From Federal Reserve
- X_{30}, X_{31}, X_{32} — Dummy Variables For Risk Constraints

	X_{14}	X_{15}	X_{16}	X_{17}	X_{18}	X_{19}	X_{20}	X_{21}	X_{22}	X_{23}	X_{24}	X_{25}	X_{26}	X_{27}	X_{28}	X_{29}	X_{30}	X_{31}	X_{32}	
	P_{14}	P_{15}	P_{16}	P_{17}	P_{18}	P_{19}	P_{20}	P_{21}	P_{22}	P_{23}	P_{24}	P_{25}	P_{26}	P_{27}	P_{28}	P_{29}	P_{30}	P_{31}	P_{32}	
	C_{14}	C_{15}	C_{16}	C_{17}	C_{18}	C_{19}	C_{20}	C_{21}	C_{22}	C_{23}	C_{24}	C_{25}	C_{26}	C_{27}	C_{28}	C_{29}	C_{30}	C_{31}	C_{32}	$\geq B_1$
													−1.0	1.0	−.05					$\geq B_2$
	−.90	−.90		−.80	−.80								1.0		1.0					$\leq B_3$
	1.0	1.0	1.0													−1.0				$\geq B_4$
													.995	−1.0	−1.0	−1.0	1.0			$\geq B_5$
	.90	.90											.995	−1.0	−1.0	−1.0		1.0		$\geq B_6$
	.90	.90	.85										.995	−1.0	−1.0	−1.0			1.0	$\geq B_7$
	.04	.04	.06	.10	.10	.10	.10	.10	.10	.10	.10	.005					.065	.04	.095	$\leq B_8$
	1.0	1.0	1.0	1.0	1.0	1.0	1.0	1.0	1.0	1.0	1.0	1.0			−1.0	−1.0				$= B_9$
				1.0		1.0														$\leq B_{10}$
				1.0		1.0														$\geq B_{11}$
				1.0		1.0														$\leq B_{12}$
										1.0										$\leq B_{13}$
										1.0										$\geq B_{14}$
										1.0										$\leq B_{15}$
								1.0												$\leq B_{16}$
								1.0												$\geq B_{17}$
									1.0											$\leq B_{18}$
	a_1	a_1	a_1	a_1	a_1	a_1	a_1	a_1	a_1	a_1	a_1	a_1								$\geq B_{19}$
	a_3	a_3	a_3	a_3	a_3	a_3	a_3	a_3	a_3	a_3	a_3	a_3								$\leq B_{20}$
				1.0	1.0	1.0	1.0	1.0	1.0	1.0	1.0	1.0								$\geq B_{21}$
				a_5	a_5	a_5	a_5	a_5	a_5	a_5	a_5	a_5								$\leq B_{22}$
														1.0	1.0	1.0				$\leq B_{23}$
															1.0					$\leq B_{24}$
															1.0					$\geq B_{25}$
																1.0				$\leq B_{26}$
																1.0				$\leq B_{27}$
												1.0								$\leq B_{28}$

the soundness of bank management. These relationships effectively constrain resource allocation decisions since their serious violation constitutes a disposition of assets that most bankers would find unacceptable. Constraints $R1$, $R19$-$R27$ express generally applicable managerial constraints. Several of these, namely $R19$-$R22$, $R24$ and $R27$ have been previously offered by Cohen and Hammer [1972] in the context of a multi-period, no-secondary-market structure. They represent acceptable ratios of government securities vis-a-vis other assets ($R19$-$R20$), acceptable ratios of loans-to-deposits ($R21$), acceptable ratios of risky assets to capital ($R22$) and maximum prudent levels of federal fund purchases and borrowings from the Federal Reserve ($R24$, $R26$). To these the present model adds constraints on the total level of discretionary liabilities acquired to support asset expansion ($R23$) and the level of large-denomination certificates of deposit ($R26$). Discussions with bankers suggest that clear managerial limits on these two means of expanding assets may be expected to generally characterize prudent bank management.

The present model recognizes the need for bank managers to produce stable flows of realized income (constraint $R1$) on their income statement. The programming constraint stipulates that realized revenue must be an acceptable fraction of the previous period's realized revenue. This approach contrasts with previous bank programming formulations that take realized revenue as the magnitude to be maximized in the objective function and, by doing so, ignore the capital gains or losses associated with model solutions. Since the wealth position of a bank at a point in time consists of both realized income and unrealized gains and losses, focusing on realized income in the objective function is in general inconsistent with overall wealth maximizing behavior. The use of realized income in previous formulations may be tied to the lack of a prediction of conditional expected market values of the associated assets. The present work incorporates a predictive sector, enabling solutions to be based on the expected total wealth consequences of alternative asset allocations. By constraining solutions to produce acceptable realized revenue flows, it is necessary to decompose the expected return on alternative investments into the realized portion and the capital gains portion. This has been done by making the coefficients ($C_{j's}$) of $R1$ the realized revenue portion and the coefficients of the objective function ($P_{j's}$) contain both the realized and capital gains portions.

The data required to determine the optimal solution to the programming model fall into three distinct categories. First there are the managerial parameters ($a_{i's}$ of appendix and Figure 1) which must be defined by the individual bank management. These parameters reflect their managerial inputs. Second, there are those inputs that are known with certainty at the beginning of the analysis period. These include the level of last period's loans, discounts, mortgages, etc., the rate of return on last period's loans and the coupon value ($C_{j's}$) of the various bonds available in the bond market. Third, predictions of future levels are necessary for a number of data entries.

The required predictions deal with the future conditions of the various markets in which the bank is active. In Figure 1, the coefficients P_4-P_{16} are all expected one-period rates of returns on bonds, P_{17}, P_{19}, P_{22}, P_{23} and P_{25} are expected one-period rates of interest on the various loans shown and P_{26} and P_{27} are expected rates of return on federal funds. In addition, several of the constraint parameters must be predicted. Parameters B_2-B_7, B_9 and B_{21} in Figure 1 are predicted values of various levels of deposit (see Appendix for detailed descriptions). The parameters B_{12}, B_{15} and B_{18} are all predicted levels of new loan demand.

Predictive Model Structure

The 14 specific predictions required are shown in Figure 2 along with influences expected to be of general importance in explaining fluctuations in these variables. The first category includes the

predicted demand for loans. For most non-rural banks, the largest part of such loans are seasonal and made to business firms for short-term periods. Current business conditions may be expected to influence this requirement along with a variety of influences impacting upon business inventory and other current asset investment decisions. The theory of corporation finance provides suggestions as to fundamentally influential variables in loan demand. Factors (a) and (b) in Figure 2 relate to formulation of expected profitability of new investments; while factors (c), (d) and (e) measure influences on the weighted average use-cost of capital for corporations. In addition, (e) measures the need for external funding to finance a given investment program, since larger cash flows reduce the demand for external capital by corporations.

Demand deposit levels represent transactionary balances that generally respond to income flows and earnings rates on near-money financial assets. Shifts in short-term interest rates presumably lead money holders to alter their level of transactions balances by substituting short-term financial assets for cash when earnings rates rise.[5]

Predicting one-period rates of return on the bond categories is necessary to correspond to the single-period allocational model. This prediction requires a restructuring of normally-available data. Available historical data on returns is expressed in yield to maturity rather than one-period rates of return. To obtain predictions of one-period rates of return, we can either 1) build models to predict yield, then use predicted yields to solve for one-period returns or 2) translate historical data into one-period returns and build models to predict return directly.

Models to explain and predict yields on bonds of varying maturities have been investigated extensively in both theoretical and predictive contexts. Explicit prediction models have been developed by Sargent [1969], Yohe and Karnosky [1969] and Anderson and Carlson [1970]. Their work leads to an empirical model for yields which is based on the monetarist view that yield fluctuations respond to three general classes of influences. Those influences are 1) current money supply changes, 2) a distributed-lagged effect of real output changes and 3) a distributed-lagged effect of price changes. The latter two influences are perceived as surrogates for expectations. Accepting the Sargent, Yohe and Karnosky, and Anderson and Carlson framework suggests that factors j through l in Figure 2 are important. The existence of imperfections in the operation of money and capital markets in the U.S. suggests that factor

Figure 2. Structure of Predicted Inputs

Variable	Fundamental Influences
Predicted Demand for Loans	a) Expected and actual area and aggregate economic growth
	b) Expected wage-price-profit climate
1. New mortgages	c) Cost of debt
2. New instalment loans	d) Cost of equity
3. New loans and discounts	e) Business cash flow
Predicted Deposit Inflows	f) Treasury cash management policies and Federal government budgetary position
4. Government demand deposits	g) Area and aggregate income, production levels
5. Other demand deposits	h) Earning rates on near monies
6. Time deposits	i) Earning rates on time deposits
Predicted One-Period Rates of Return	j) Money supply
	k) National output patterns
7. Federal funds	l) Inflationary patterns
8. 6-month U.S. Treasury issues	m) Reserve position of banking system
9. 9-12 month U.S. Treasury issues	
10. 9-12 month other government issues	
11. 2-5 year U.S. Government issues	
12. Over 5 year U.S. Government issues	
13. Aaa municipal bonds	
Bank Lending Rates	n) Money market rates
	o) Reserve position of banks
14. Prime rate of the banking system	p) Financial expectations

m should be added as a measure of this effect.

The prime rate is usually viewed as a direct product of current money market conditions. Accepting that view leads to the recursive prediction of this rate from the predictions obtained on money market rates (7-10 in Figure 2) as well as from exceptional measures and measures of money market imperfections.

The correct construction of demand functions from market equilibrium data requires solution of the identification problem. Fortunately, in the case of loan demand functions, it appears that most bankers service nearly all qualified loan requests received under all but stressful monetary conditions. With the exception of rationing periods such as 1969-70, the usual response of loan supply to loan demand means that historical data lies substantially along the demand function. Thus, regressions fit to these data usually are properly interpreted as demand relations.

The structures of the 14 econometric equations used in the predictive structure are shown in Figure 3. The specific variables in equations 1-6 are the result of the fundamental factors summarized in Figure 2 along with the particular circumstances associated with the sample bank. Equations 7-13 conform to the specific structure of Anderson and Carlson [1970] with three exceptions. First, net free reserves are added as an explanatory variable to account for interest rate impacts of money and capital market imperfections. Second, the distributed lag periods are shortened from 12 to 8 quarters and from 16 to 12 quarters in the short-run and long-run equations due to the length of the data period used in this study. Third, an alternative to the Almon technique for fitting the lag distribution is used. This technique is due to Shiller [1971] and is superior to the Almon technique in that it does not constrain the lag distribution to a polynomial but breaks multicollinearity to the same degree.[6] Ordinary least-squares may be used to obtain coefficient estimates in all 14 equations, since the first 13 are structurally tied to exogenous variables only and the 14th is recursive on the 7th.

An Evaluation

To evaluate the scope of the allocation versus prediction problem, the model now presented has been applied to the quarterly data of a national bank with total deposits in the interval of $100 million to $500 million. The test period is from the first quarter of 1971 through the first quarter of 1972. In applying the model over this period,

---

[5]Government-held deposits constitute an exception, responding to influences described by factor (f) in Figure 2.

[6]Shiller [1971] also contains a demonstration of this property.

several results are obtained. The actual performance of the bank compared with the performance associated with the model allocations that result from using predictive model inputs enables measurement of the efficiency of the econometric predictions. A separate mode of evaluation is based on a certainty data structure. In this certainty model, each of the required predictions are inputed at their true historical values and an allocational solution obtained. This solution shows bank performance under perfect forecasting, and provides a measure of the potential gain from improvements in forecasting performance when contrasted with the predictive model results.

By applying the model over several time periods, the operational requirements for implementing the model are identified. In this process, a number of new features appear. One such operational feature made clear in the comparison is the feed forward effects of revenue flows. Revenue flows in one quarter represent a source of funds for the next quarter. In comparing model solutions with actual results, higher model revenue flows in early

quarters thus have a compounding effect in later quarters. Another unique facet is the treatment of predicting errors in deposit inflows and demand constraints. If demand for loans is under-predicted, the initial model solution is constrained to the smaller predicted level. Under circumstances where the optimal solution involves supplying the entire demand (i.e., where the bank does not find it profitable to ration loans), this is an inappropriate result since the bank would quite probably service the additional loans as they evolved over the quarter. The reverse is true for over-predictions of demand. The bank could not make more loans than the level actually demanded. Thus, a two-step solution procedure has been employed in which under-predicted or over-predicted loans are adjusted to the level of actual demand. Funds for this adjustment are obtained by drawing down holdings of either short-term government notes or federal fund balances depending on the profit rate in the under-prediction case, and funds are added to these accounts in the over-predictions case.

A similar situation accompanies prediction

Figure 3. Equation Structure Econometric Section

Equation	Explanatory Variables
1. New mortgages	S, RC, QD, DD
2. New instalment loans	A, U, QD, DD
3. Loans and discounts	PD, U, QD, DD
4. Government demand deposits	i_{TB}, U, QD
5. Other demand deposits	DPI, i_{TB}, QD
6. Time deposits	DPI, U, QD
7. Federal funds	
8. 6-month U.S. Treasury issues	
9. 9-12 month U.S. Treasury issues	$\dot{MS}, NFR, \sum_{i=0}^{8} \dot{X}_{t-i}, \sum_{i=0}^{8} \left[\frac{\dot{P}_{t-i}}{U_{t-i}} \right]$
10. 9-12 month other government issues	
11. 2-5 year U.S. Government issues	
12. Over 5 year U.S. Government issues	$\dot{MS}, NFR, \sum_{i=0}^{12} \dot{X}_{t-i}, \sum_{i=0}^{12} \left[\frac{\dot{P}_{t-i}}{U_{t-i}} \right]$
13. Aaa municipal bonds	
14. Prime rate of banks	$FDR, r_{FF}, NFR, \dot{MS}$

where:
S = personal saving rate; RC = residential construction expenditures; QD = quarterly seasonal dummies; DD = credit rationing dummy, 0 for non-rationing periods and 1 for rationing periods; A = expenditures on new automobiles and parts; U = National Unemployment rate; PD = producer's durable goods expenditures; i_{TB} = Treasury Bill rate; DPI = disposable personal income; $\dot{MS}$ = per cent change in the money supply, narrowly defined; NFR = Net Free Reserves; $\dot{X}$ = per cent change in real GNP; $\dot{P}$ = per cent change in GNP deflator; FDR = Federal Reserve discount rate; r_{FF} = Federal Funds rate (eq. 7).
Note: All equations are linear and additive in nature.

errors in deposit inflows. Under-predicted deposits lead to allocation of smaller total pools of funds than are actually available while over-predicted deposits produce planned over-allocation. As before, the excess or deficiency is eliminated by adjustments in short-term U.S. securities and/or federal funds holdings, with the choice based on the relative profitability of these holdings.

The results of actual, certainty and prediction model allocations appear in Figures 4, 5 and 6. Figure 4 shows the actual asset allocations made by the sample bank over the 5-quarter period compared to the allocations made by the certainty and prediction models. The entries in Figure 4 are normalized for presentation purposes by dividing through by the 1971.1 total asset level, then multiplying by 100. Figure 4 reveals the optimal cer-

tainty response to a whip-saw pattern that characterized municipal and other bonds during 1971.2 and 1971.3. The decline in these prices in 1971.2 resulted in municipal holdings being eliminated from the certainty portfolio in 1971.2 in favor of higher yielding alternatives and added back in 1971.3 at lower purchase prices. The actual bank strategy was to hold an approximately constant volume of municipals through both periods, thus missing the dual advantages of higher 1971.2 alternative returns and lower purchase price (higher return re-purchases) in 1971.3. By contrast, the prediction model solution avoided the municipal category entirely during the first four periods due to the low predicted returns throughout this period. Consequently, the predictive solution failed to capitalize on the highly profit-

Figure 4. Normalized Allocation of Funds

Assets	First Quarter			Second Quarter			Third Quarter			Fourth Quarter			Fifth Quarter		
	A	P	C	A	P	C	A	P	C	A	P	C	A	P	C
Cash and Due	23.8	23.8	23.8	23.7	23.7	23.7	23.3	23.3	23.3	21.7	21.7	21.7	22.5	22.5	22.5
U.S. Gov't Securities															
90 Day Treasury	0	0	0	0	0	0	0	0	0	0	0	0	0	0	0
Maturity 0-1 yr.	4.1	0	0	4.4	0	7.9	4.2	0	0	3.5	0	0	2.3	0	4.8
Maturity 1-2 yrs.	0	0	0	0	0.2	0	0	0	0	0.4	0	0	0.3	0.5	0
Maturity 2-5 yrs.	2.4	0	6.7	2.3	0	0	0.3	0	0	0	0	0	0	0	0
Maturity over 5 yrs.	0	0	0	0	0	0	0	0	0	0	0	0	1.7	0	0
Other Securities	0.2	0	0	0	0	0	0	8.0	0	0	8.4	4.7	0	0	0
Municipal Securities	8.3	0	20.9	9.4	0	0	11.2	0	26.7	13.2	0	26.1	13.5	25.7	27.4
Bond Department	2.4	2.0	2.0	2.1	1.9	1.9	2.0	1.9	1.9	2.0	1.9	1.9	1.9	1.9	1.9
Loans & Discounts	31.5	31.5	29.0	32.1	30.7	30.8	33.1	32.5	29.1	32.7	32.4	25.0	22.4	25.1	24.6
Mortgage Loans	12.4	12.4	12.4	12.7	12.6	12.6	13.1	13.2	13.8	14.0	14.1	15.4	15.1	15.8	16.3
Instalment Loans	8.5	8.6	8.6	8.6	8.6	8.6	8.7	8.7	8.8	9.2	9.3	9.3	9.3	9.4	9.4
Bank Credit Card	0	0	0	0	0	0	0	0	0	0	0	0	0.5	0.6	0.6
Fed. Funds Sold	6.4	18.9	3.0	10.7	21.1	13.7	7.8	11.2	0.6	2.9	7.3	0	2.3	0	0
Discretionary Liabilities															
Fed. Funds Bought	6.7	3.3	12.9	7.6	3.3	3.3	7.6	3.3	12.8	9.3	3.3	11.6	11.3	6.5	11.9
CD's over $100,000	0	0	0	0	0	0	0	0	0	0	0	0	0	0	0
Borrowed from Fed.	0	0	0	0	0	0	0	0	0	0	0	0	0	0	0

A = Actual
P = Predicted
C = Certain
Base number is: (First Quarter actual total)/100

Figure 5. Certainty Model Comparisons (1971-I Actual = 1.00)

| | Realized Gross Revenue | | | | | | Gross Change in Asset Value | | | | | |
| | Quarterly | | | Cumulative | | | Quarterly | | | Cumulative | | |
	A	M	% MD	A	M	% MD	A	M	% MD	A	M	% MD
71-I	1.00	1.15	+14.67	1.00	1.15	+14.67	1.00	1.16	+16.03	1.00	1.16	+16.03
II	.99	1.05	+ 5.90	1.99	2.20	+10.30	.54	.84	+56.14	1.54	2.00	+30.10
III	1.12	1.15	+ 2.67	3.11	3.34	+ 7.56	1.23	1.78	+44.78	2.77	3.78	+36.61
IV	.99	1.14	+15.45	4.10	4.48	+ 9.46	.90	1.21	+35.53	3.67	5.00	+36.35
72-I	1.01	1.15	+13.77	5.11	5.63	+10.32	.85	1.10	+29.64	4.51	6.10	+35.09

A = Actual
M = Model
MD = Model Difference is per cent increase of model over actual

Figure 6. Prediction Model Comparisons (1971-I Actual = 1.00)

| | Realized Gross Revenue | | | | | | Gross Change in Asset Value | | | | | |
| | Quarterly | | | Cumulative | | | Quarterly | | | Cumulative | | |
	A	M	% MD	A	M	% MD	A	M	% MD	A	M	% MD
71-I	1.00	.95	−4.66	1.00	.95	−4.66	1.00	.80	−19.67	1.00	.80	−19.67
II	.99	1.03	+3.72	1.99	1.98	−0.49	.54	.83	+53.97	1.54	1.64	+ 6.17
III	1.12	1.09	−2.80	3.11	3.07	−1.32	1.23	.94	−23.29	2.77	2.58	− 6.90
IV	.99	1.04	+5.73	4.10	4.11	+0.38	.90	.99	+10.11	3.67	3.56	− 2.75
72-I	1.01	1.10	+8.68	5.11	5.21	+2.08	.85	.93	+ 9.33	4.51	4.49	− 0.47

A = Actual
M = Model
MD = Model Difference is per cent increase of model over actual

able opportunities during the 1971.1, 1971.3 and 1971.4 periods, although it did avoid the significant capital losses on municipals in period 1971.2.

Figures 5 and 6 show gross revenue comparisons for the certainty and prediction-solutions respectively. Data in the figures are a ratio of the model value to the value that resulted from the actual bank allocation for both the certainty and predictive solutions. These data include both realized gross revenue comparisons and comparisons of the change in gross asset value. Gross asset value change includes the current period capital gain or loss in addition to realized revenue flows. Data have been normalized for presentation purposes by setting the 1971.1 value equal to 1.00. Both quarterly and cumulative results are shown along with percentage comparisons. Figure 5 shows that gains in the growth of asset value of 35.09% and gains in realized income of 10.32% would have

been possible over the analysis period due to increased allocational efficiency if forecasts had been perfect. For banks of any size, these are tantalizing figures. However, Figure 6 shows these gains would have largely been eliminated due to the differing asset allocations resulting from predicted rather than actual values of the predictive parameters.

It is important to observe that in Figures 5 and 6 both certainty and predicted model solutions lead to a more stable pattern of growth in gross asset value than that associated with the actual bank performance. In particular, the certainty portfolio moved out of municipal securities in 1971.2 and into federal funds sold. The net effect was to stabilize asset value. To a lessor degree, this pattern characterized the entire 5-quarter period by reducing the effects of market value declines in securities.

The comparison of the certainty model with the actual results in Figure 5 gives an indication of the magnitude of the economic opportunity lost by not having perfect forecasts in bank decision making. On both realized and total gross revenue dimensions, the potential returns associated with complete knowledge of the predicted input provide ample motivation for the continued development of bank forecasting techniques. The results shown give a clear suggestion that the monetary reward from substantial improvements in forecasting efficiency can be multi-million dollar in magnitude for even medium-sized banks. On the other hand, comparing the results from the predictive model in Figure 6 with the actual results indicates that most of the potential gains in profit possible under perfect predictions remain untapped by our currently-specified forecasting model, as the forecast results did not outperform the actual results. This indicates that the gains in revenue due to the allocational efficiency of the programming structure are entirely offset by the incorrect decisions associated with predictive inefficiency.

Implications

Our results suggest that the scope of the predictive problem is large compared to the allocational problem in bank resource allocation. In our experiment, the value of the optimizing logic of our programming structure is reduced due to the predictive errors in future interest rate, loan demand and deposit levels. This suggests that substantial dollar and cents gains in results can be obtained through application of existing programming models if the predicted inputs can be forecast with greater accuracy, particularly with regards to the prediction of interest rate levels on both short-term and long term government and other securities. Although further development and refinement of programming models is likely to lead to further improvement in the allocational efficiency of bank planning structures, our results suggest that the biggest unrealized gain in bank planning efficiency associates with improvements in forecasting accuracy. □

APPENDIX

Definition of Variables

Account Variables

TDP – Total time deposits
DDG – Total government demand deposits
DDO – Total demand deposits other than government
CDB – Total of 90 day over \$100,000 certificates of deposit
CD – Total certificates of deposit minus CDB
K – Capital

Managerial Parameters

a_1 = Minimum ratio of government securities to total assets
$a_2 = (1 - a_1) \times (-1)$
a_3 = Maximum ratio of government securities to total assets
$a_4 = (1 - a_3) \times (-1)$
a_5 = Minimum ratio of capital to risky assets
a_6 = Minimum acceptable fraction of last period's realized revenue
a_7 = Minimum loan to deposit ratio
a_8 = Maximum total level of controllable liabilities acceptable to management
a_9 = Maximum total level of federal funds bought acceptable to management
a_{10} = Minimum level of federal funds bought
a_{11} = Maximum level of CDB acceptable to management
a_{12} = Maximum level of funds borrowed from the Federal Reserve System acceptable to management
a_{13} = Maximum level of credit card lending acceptable to management

Constraint Variables

$B_1 = (a_6) \times$ Realized revenue last period
$B_2 = (.03) \cdot (TDP) + (.05) \cdot (CD + CDB) + (.175) \cdot (DDG + DDO)$
$B_3 = -[DDG +$ Collateral required for trust department]
$B_4 = (TDP + CD + CDB + DDO) \cdot (.20) + DDG + B_2$
$B_5 = (.47) \cdot (DDG + DDO) + (.36) \cdot (TDP + CD)$
$B_6 = (.47) \cdot (DDG + DDO) + (.36) \cdot (TDP + CD)$
$B_7 = (.47) \cdot (DDG + DDO) + (.36) \cdot (TDP + CD)$
$B_8 = K$ plus capital required against trust department operations
$B_9 = TDP + DDO + DDG + K$
$B_{10} =$ Total loans and discounts last period minus runoff
$B_{11} =$ (Total loans and discounts last period) $\times$ (fraction of loans and discounts that cannot be sold in the secondary market)
$B_{12} =$ Total demand for new loans and discounts this period
$B_{13} =$ Total instalment loans last period minus runoff
$B_{14} =$ (Total loans and discounts last period) $\times$ (fraction of instalment loans that cannot be sold in the secondary market)
$B_{15} =$ Total demand for new instalment loans this period
$B_{16} =$ Total mortgages last period minus runoff
$B_{17} =$ (Total mortgages last period) $\times$ (fraction of mortgages that cannot be sold in the secondary market)
$B_{18} =$ Total demand for new mortgages this period
$B_{19} =$ Total level of bonds used exclusively for trading
$B_{20} =$ Total level of bonds used exclusively for trading
$B_{21} = (a_7) \times (TDP + CD + DDG + DDO)$
$B_{22} = K$
$B_{23} = a_8$
$B_{24} = a_9$
$B_{25} = a_{10}$
$B_{26} = a_{11}$
$B_{27} = a_{12}$
$B_{28} = a_{13}$

REFERENCES

Anderson, Leonall C., and Keith M. Carlson, "A Monetarist Model for Economic Stabilization," *Federal Reserve Bank of St. Louis Review*, Vol. 52 (April, 1970), p. 7-21.

Beazer, William F., "Tax Law, Lock-ins, and Bank Portfolio Choice," *Journal of Finance*, Vol. 20 (December, 1965), pp. 665-678.

Booth, G. Geoffrey, "Programming Bank Portfolios Under Uncertainty: An Extension," *Journal of Bank Research*, Vol. 2, No. 4 (Winter, 1972), pp. 28-40.

Bradley, Stephen P., and Dwight B. Crane, "Management of Commercial Bank Government Security Portfolios: An Optimizing Approach Under Uncertainty," *Journal of Bank Research*, Vol. 3, No. 1 (Spring, 1973), pp. 18-30.

Chambers, D., and A. Charnes, "Inter-temporal Analysis and Optimization of Bank Portfolios," *Management Science*, Vol. 7, No. 4 (Winter, 1972), pp. 393-410.

Charnes, A., and S. C. Littlechild, "Inter-temporal Bank Asset Choice with Stochastic Dependence," Systems Research Memorandum No. 188 The Technological Institute, Northwestern University, (April, 1968).

Charnes, A., and Sten Thore, "Planning for Liquidity in Financial Institutions: The Chance Constrained Method," *Journal of Finance*, Vol. 21, No. 4 (December, 1966), pp. 649-674.

Cohen, Kalman J., "Dynamic Balance Sheet Management: A Management Science Approach," *Journal of Bank Research*, Vol. 2, No. 4 (Winter, 1972), pp. 9-19.

Cohen, Kalman J., and Frederick S. Hammer, "Linear Programming and Optimal Bank Asset Management Decisions: Some Preliminary Notes, Equations, and Exhibits" (unpublished paper, Carnegie-Mellon, 1966)

Cohen, Kalman J., and S. Thore, "Programming Bank Portfolios Under Uncertainty," *Journal of Bank Research*, (Spring, 1970), pp. 43-61.

Cramer, Robert H., and Robert B. Miller, "Development of a Deposit Forecasting Procedure for Use in Bank Financial Management," *Journal of Bank Research*, Vol. 3, No. 2 (Summer, 1973), pp. 122-138.

Crane, Dwight B., "A Stochastic Programming Model for Commercial Bank Bond Portfolio Management," *Journal of Financial and Quantitative Analysis*, Vol. 6, No. 3 (June, 1971), pp. 955-976.

Dallenbach, Hans G., and Stephen H. Archer, "The Optimal Bank Liquidity: A Multi-Period Stochastic Model" *Journal of Financial and Quantitative Analysis*, Vol. 4, No. 3 (September, 1969), pp. 329-343.

Eppen, Gary D., and Eugene F. Fama, "Solutions for Cash Balance and Simple Dynamic Portfolio Problems with Proportional Costs," *Journal of Business*, Vol. 41 (January, 1968), pp. 94-112.

Kane, Edward J., and Burton G. Malkiel, "Bank Portfolio Allocation, Deposit Variability, and the Availability Doctrine," *Quarterly Journal of Economics*, Vol. 79 (February, 1965), pp. 113-34.

Lifson, K.A., and Brian R. Blackmarr, "Simulation and Optimization Models for Asset Deployment and Funds Sources Balancing Profit, Liquidity, and Growth," *Journal of Bank Research*, Vol. 3, No. 3 (Autumn, 1973), pp. 239-255.

Parks, Robert H., "Income and Tax Aspects of Commercial Bank Portfolio Operations in Government Securities," *National Tax Journal*, Vol. 11 (March, 1958), pp. 21-34.

Sargent, Thomas, "Commodity Price Expectations and the Interest Rates," *Quarterly Journal of Economics*, February, 1969), pp. 127-140.

Shiller, Robert J., "A Distributed Lag Estimator Derived from Smoothness Priors," unpublished paper, Massachusetts Institute of Technology, 1971.

——————, "Estimation of the Investment and Price Equations of a Macroeconometric Model," *Staff Economic Study 61, Board of Governors of the Federal Reserve System*, 1971.

Thomson, Michael R., "Forecasting for Financial Planning," *Journal of Bank Research*, Vol. 3, No. 3 (Autumn, 1973), pp. 225-231.

Wolf, Charles R., "A Model for Selecting Commercial Bank Government Security Portfolios," *The Review of Economics and Statistics*, Vol. 51. No. 1 (February, 1969), pp. 40-52.

Yohe, William P., and Denis S. Karnosky, "Interest Rates and Price Level Changes, 1952-1969," *Federal Reserve Bank of St. Louis Review*, (December, 1969), pp. 18-38.

Chapter 18

SMALL BANK BALANCE SHEET MANAGEMENT: APPLYING TWO-STAGE PROGRAMMING MODELS*

By Parvis Aghili, Robert H. Cramer,
and Howard E. Thompson

*This article is reprinted, with permission, from *Journal of Bank Research,*
Vol. 5, No. 4 (Winter, 1975), pp. 246-256.

In approaching the problem of bank asset and liability management, Cohen and Thore [1970] suggest that two-stage programming under uncertainty has certain advantages for ". . . bridging the gap between what is practically feasible and what is theoretically desirable . . ." since it brings ". . . some of the essential features of the uncertainties within which the bank dynamic balance sheet process has to be carried out, without invoking the full complexity of an intertemporal continuous joint probability distribution" [p. 44].

The purpose of this paper is to make some observations on the ability of two-stage models to bridge the gap between theoretical desirability and practical feasibility and to judge in a limited way the potential import of these types of models. In particular we will discuss the following questions: Is the two-stage model a conceptually reasonable approach to bank balance sheet management? Are data available that can be used to develop the necessary parameters and probability distributions for the model? Can these data be organized in a manner consistent with management's way of thinking about them? Can a model of reasonable size and complexity be formulated in such a way as to capture the essence of the decision problem? Does the two-stage model do away with the need to use "rules of thumb?" Does the two-stage model have any potential indirect effects on the management decision-making process?

Our conclusions with respect to the questions posed above should be useful to bank management, which will employ the results of the two-stage models, and management scientists, who have the technical job of implementing the models. Our comments should also prove useful in indicating directions for future research efforts.

In order to develop a realistic reference base for our analysis, we introduced the two-stage model into the budgeting process of a small midwestern bank. The goal in applying any mathematical programming model to bank financial management is to improve the planning and decision-making process. In order to accomplish this goal it is necessary to involve the bank's management directly in the formulation of the model. Management input on the following questions is essential:

1) What are the goals of the bank and how can they be stated as explicit objectives? 2) What are the legal and managerial constraints under which the bank operates? 3) What is the planning or budgeting horizon for the bank? 4) What are the costs and revenues associated with the basic activities of the bank? The answers to these questions were provided in numerous meetings with the bank's management and thus shaped the specific structure of the programming model.

Our role in the implementation of two-stage programming is to develop a computational form of the programming model that represents a conceptually reasonable approach to bank balance sheet management.

A REASONABLE APPROACH

In this section we discuss the question of whether or not the two-stage model adequately captures the essential management features of the bank balance sheet decision problems.

The Effect of Future Decision Environments on Present Decisions

One of the important conceptual features of two-stage programming is the allowance for a second chance, which is the ability to recover from a "bad" first period decision by making another decision in the second stage. This aspect of two-stage programming has a correspondence with a real life problem.

To dramatically illustrate this point let us use an extreme example. Suppose a bank has an opportunity to invest in a very speculative long-term commercial loan to the extent of $1,000,000. The alternative investment is in short-term Treasury bills. Assume the return on the commercial loan is 10% and the return on the Treasury bill is 5%. If there is a high probability of default on the commercial loan if a recession results, the bank may find itself in a position, in the future, of not being able to take advantage of opportunities which present themselves. On the other hand, the Treasury bill may have such a small probability of capital loss that the bank would be sure to find all of its options open even if a recession results. Thus, the decision on which to choose depends heavily on the ability to recover from each choice.

Clearly, from the above example, it can be seen that present decisions must be made with careful reference to the types of decision environments that will exist in the future, as well as the probabilities associated with these environments. It is precisely this concept that is incorporated into the idea of two-stage programming under uncertainty. Thus two-stage programming does systematically what bank management should do intuitively. For this reason it is an appealing approach.

Separation of Time and Decision Making into Discrete Stages

In forming a programming model that is computationally efficient, it is necessary to separate time and decision making into discrete stages. The question to be asked is whether the formulation of the model with an eye toward computational efficiency leads to a distorted picture of reality that is not practically useful.

Using discrete time intervals is done in order to employ standardized linear programming codes in solving the programming problem. The two-stage model has appeal over the multi-stage model in that the linear programs derived are of a smaller size and therefore can be more easily solved with existing codes.

Characterization of the real world into discrete stages does have some appeal. Empirical studies of many economic time series and especially interest rates reveal an ability to forecast well only over a very short horizon. As the forecast horizon lengthens, the probability limits of the forecast increase rapidly. Thus, when formulating the programming model, it is appropriate to specify a relatively short time period for the first stage. The second stage, which in the model corresponds to the more uncertain portion of the planning horizon, would correspond to the point in time where the probability limits of the forecast begin to widen rapidly.

Approximating Economic Events By a Finite Set

In addition to separating time and decision points into discrete periods, it is necessary to characterize future economic events with a finite set (e.g. interest rates can take on the values 6.1%, 6.2%, 6.3%, 6.4%). Since statistical forecasting methods produce continuous probability distributions this step involves approximating a continuous function with a discrete distribution.

To assess the reasonableness of a finite set of events and their associated probabilities as compared to a continuous set is not particularly difficult if one merely argues that a continuous distribution can be approximated by a discrete set of probabilities to any degree of accuracy desired. But this essentially begs the question. The key issue is whether one captures the entire range of events from a discrete set of future events with associated probabilities. We speculate that it is the extremes that are significant rather than the characterization of the events between extremes. To further understand this point one can look more closely at what will be done with a two-stage model when it is applied.

The solution of the two-stage model yields a set of optimal first-stage decisions plus a set of rules for responding to the stochastic events of the second stage. What happens in practice is that the model is solved and the first-stage solutions put into effect. As the first stage ends instead of an application of the computed rules determined from the first calculation, the model is repositioned in time and a new two-stage problem solved from which the first-stage solutions are again determined and put into effect. In other words, as is done with so many "horizon"-type problems a moving horizon is adopted in practice.

Since the moving horizon is used in practice, the only use of the second-stage rules is to make sure that the future is considered in making first-stage decisions. With this in mind it is clear that the answer to the question of whether a finite set of events is adequate depends on the sensitivity of the first-stage decisions to the characterization of the second-stage events. We will speculate at this point —although we have no formal analysis to call upon—that one need only roughly capture the second stage of the model in order to provide useful calculations of first-stage variables. Hence we now turn to the more specific problem of determining future eventualities and their associated probabilities for a specific bank.

DATA AVAILABILITY

As Cohen and Thore recognize, to express ". . . a continuous joint intertemporal probability distribution for all uncertain variables . . ." would be theoretically desirable but would in no way be empirically feasible or practically reasonable. Rather it would be reasonable from a management point of view to express the uncertainty in the form of a finite set of "economic scenarios." These should then possess the characteristics that they cover a sufficient range of possibilities so that they will produce all of the influence necessary on the first-stage decisions and will be an acceptable reference point for management's thinking about the future.

In the small midwestern bank, the alternative economic scenarios are developed by statistical forecasting methods. Time series methods developed by Box and Jenkins [1969] and applied to bank data by Cramer and Miller [1973] are used to forecast returns on assets, demand for loans and the levels of time and demand deposits. Since these methods not only produce forecasts but also allow calculation of the probability distributions of the forecast errors, approximate distributions of future interest rates, returns on other assets, demands for loans and deposit levels are developed. These estimates and their approximations are grounded in the past experiences of the bank in question.

In order to keep our problem to reasonable size for computing purposes we limited the future events on any rate of return to an expected value, a high value and a low value. Interest or yield variations of different investments, short-term and long-term, are assumed to be perfectly positively correlated. That is, one economic eventuality would allow for all yields and returns to be at their high values. Another eventuality would allow for all to be at their low values and finally for all to be at their expected values. In addition, based on the generally accepted theory of the relationship between money supply and interest rates, demand and time deposits are assumed to be perfectly negatively correlated with interest rates.

Based on the above results three economic scenarios are specified: e_2, the "expected outcome"; e_1, the "easy money" eventuality where low

yields and high values sources of funds obtain; e_3, the "tight money" eventuality where high yields and low demand and time deposits are combined. These outcomes are obtained from the discretization of probability distributions developed from available historical data. An important feature of characterizing uncertainty with scenarios is that communication with management about future events is facilitated.

We must now turn to the question of whether a model of reasonable size and complexity can be formulated for a real-life problem.

CAN A MODEL OF MODERATE COMPLEXITY CAPTURE THE ESSENCE OF A REAL-LIFE SITUATION?

In this section we discuss the formulation of the model for the small midwestern bank

The Objective Function

The objective function for the model was determined in discussions with bank management to be the maximization of the expected value of stockholders' equity at year end which turns out to be the end of the model's second stage. Market value maximization was ruled out because of the limited market for the bank's stock. Also, because of the short horizon specified by bank management the use of a discounted value was presumed to have no special benefits.

Two additional points on the objective function are worth noting briefly at this point. First, because of the short horizon there is a likelihood that the objective function will lead to "short-sighted" decisions. Second, because of expected value maximization it appears that risks are not being adequately considered. In both instances the adverse

Figure 1. Balance Sheet Variables

Financial Assets	Liabilities and Net Worth
X_1 – Cash	DD – Demand Deposits
X_2 – Federal Funds and Daily Investments	SD – Savings Deposits
X_3 – Government Agencies	CD – Certificate of Deposit
X_4 – Short-term Government Bonds	OL – Other Liabilities
X_5 – Long-term Government Bonds	D – Long-term Debt
X_6 – Short-term Municipal Bonds	V – Valuation Reserves
X_7 – Long-term Municipal Bonds	SE – Stockholders' Equity
X_8 – Residential Mortgages	
X_9 – Commercial Mortgages	
X_{10} – Short-term Commercial Loans	
X_{11} – Long-term Commercial Loans	
X_{12} – Installment Loans	

Figure 2. Definitional, Accounting, Legal and Financial Constraints: Assets

Balance Sheet Constraints

(A) $\quad \sum\limits_{j} X_j = DD + SD + CD + OL + V + SE$

(A) $\quad \sum\limits_{j} X_j(e_i) = DD(e_i) + SD(e_i) + CD(e_i) + OL(e_i) + V(e_i) + SE(e_i), i=1,2,3$

Primary Reserve Constraints

(L,F) $\quad X_1 \geq (a_1 + d_1)DD + (a_2 + d_2)SD + (a_3 + d_3)CD$

(L,F) $\quad X_1(e_i) \geq (a_1 + d_1)DD(e_i) + (a_2 + \dot{d}_2)SD(e_i) + (a_3 + d_3)CD(e_i), i=1,2,3$
$\qquad a_j$ – legal reserve requirement
$\qquad d_j$ – self-imposed additional reserve requirement

(D) $\quad X_2 = X_1 - (a_1 + d_1)DD - (a_2 + d_2)SD - (a_3 + d_3)CD$

(D) $\quad X_2(e_i) = X_1(e_i) - (a_1 + d_1)DD(e_i) - (a_2 + d_2)SD(e_i) - (a_3 + d_3)CD(e_i), i=1,2,3$

Secondary Reserve Constraints

(A) $\quad X_3(e_i) = (1-m_3)X_3 + P_3(e_i) - S_3(e_i), i=1,2,3$
$\qquad m_3$ – fraction of agency bonds which mature during stage 1

(L) $\quad S_3(e_i) \leq (1-m_3)X_3$

(L) $\quad X_4 \geq a_1'DD + a_2'SD + a_3'CD$
$\qquad a_j'$ – fraction of liability type j allowed to be invested in treasury bills

(A,L) $\quad X_4(e_i) = (1-m_4)X_4 + P_4(e_i) - S_4(e_i) + m_5X_5 - S_{4,5}(e_i) + a_1'DD(e_i) + a_2'SD(e_i) + a_3'CD(e_i), i=1,2,3$
$\qquad m_4$ – fraction of short-term bonds maturing
$\qquad m_5$ – fraction of long-term bonds becoming short

(L) $\quad S_4(e_i) \leq (1-m_4)X_4, i=1,2,3$

(L) $\quad S_{4,5}(e_i) \leq m_5X_5, i=1,2,3$
$\qquad S_{4,5}(e_i)$ – sales of long-term bonds becoming short-term

(A) $\quad X_5(e_i) = (1-m_5)X_5 + P_5(e_i) - S_5(e_i), i=1,2,3$

(L) $\quad S_5(e_i) \leq (1-m_5)X_5, i=1,2,3$

Municipal Bond Constraints

(A) $\quad X_6(e_i) = (1-m_6)X_6 + P_6(e_i) - S_6(e_i) + m_7X_7 - S_{6,7}(e_i), i=1,2,3$

(L) $\quad S_6(e_i) \leq (1-m_6)X_6, i=1,2,3$

(L) $\quad S_{6,7}(e_i) \leq m_7X_7, i=1,2,3$

(A) $\quad X_7(e_i) = (1-m_7)X_7 + P_7(e_i) - S_7(e_i), i=1,2,3$

(L) $\quad S_7(e_i) \leq (1-m_7)X_7$

Loan Constraints

(A) $\quad X_8(e_i) = (1-m_8-L_8)X_8 + P_8(e_i), i=1,2,3$
$\qquad m_8$ – fraction of residential mortgages maturing
$\qquad L_8$ – fraction of expected bad loans

(A) $\quad X_9(e_i) = (1-m_9-L_9)X_9 + P_9(e_i), i=1,2,3$

(A) $\quad X_{10}(e_i) = (1-m_{10}-L_{10})X_{10} + m_{11}X_{11} + P_{10}(e_i), i=1,2,3$

(A) $\quad X_{11}(e_i) = (1-m_{11}-L_{11})X_{11} + P_{11}(e_i), i=1,2,3$

(A) $\quad X_{12}(e_i) = (1-m_{12}-L_{12})X_{12} + P_{12}(e_i), i=1,2,3$

effects of these problems are mitigated to a large extent by management policy constraints. The role of these constraints will be discussed later.

The objective function is then expressed as

$$\text{Max}\{p_1 SE(e_1) + p_2 SE(e_2) + p_3 SE(e_3)\}$$

where p_1, p_2 and p_3 are the probabilities of economic eventualities e_1, e_2 and e_3 respectively, and $SE(e_1)$, $SE(e_2)$ and $SE(e_3)$ are the values of stockholders' equity under each of the economic eventualities.

Generic Description of Constraint Set

Before describing the constraints specifically, it is worthwhile to indicate the variables that are used in the analysis. In Figure 1 the balance sheet variables are listed. Each of the asset variables, which are specified for the first stage only in the table, represents a set of variables. For example, X_5 which represents the balance sheet amount of long-term government bonds has associated with it the variables $X_5(e_1)$, $X_5(e_2)$, $X_5(e_3)$, $P_5(e_1)$, $P_5(e_2)$, $P_5(e_3)$, $S_5(e_1)$, $S_5(e_2)$, $S_5(e_3)$ representing the balance sheet amounts, purchases and sales of long-term government bonds under the three economic eventualities. Some liability variables are exogenous such as SD, OL and D. Demand deposits are only partially exogenous because of the interaction between compensating balances and loans.

There are basically two sets of constraints included in structuring the model for the small midwestern bank. The first set involves definitional, accounting, legal and financial constraints. These are shown in Figures 2 and 3. The second set listed in Figure 4 is constraints which reflect policy decisions by management. Each constraint is given a designation D, A, L or F referring to whether it is

a definitional, accounting, legal or financial constraint.

Definitional, Accounting, Legal and Financial Constraints

The initial constraint set shown in Figure 2 is the balance sheet equation which assures that all the funds available through liabilities and capital are allocated to assets. The next two sets of constraints pertain to the primary and secondary reserves. The primary reserve constraints insure that sufficient funds are allocated to cash assets to satisfy the legal as well as any self-imposed reserve requirements. The secondary reserve equations account for the purchasing, selling and maturing of bonds. They also prevent short selling of bonds. The remaining constraints serve a similar function. The deposit constraints in Table 3 serve similar

Because of the inclusion of policy constraints, it was expected that Model II results would be more comparable to the bank's actual position. Even here there is substantially more allocated to municipal bonds and commercial loans resulting in a reduction in residential mortgages and an elimination of instalment loans. Before evaluating the reasonableness of Model II, it is helpful to look at the contingent allocation of the second stage.

Figure 6 shows the second stage balance sheet allocations produced by Model I and Model II under "expected" conditions and under conditions of "tight" and "easy" money. As in the stage one allocations, long-term municipal bonds play the predominate role. During periods of tight money and high interest rates, municipals receive the largest allocation of funds. During periods of normal credit conditions, commercial lending plays an increased role in Model II and during easy money situations while long-term municipals

Figure 3. Definitional, Accounting, Legal, and Financial Constraints: Liabilities

Deposit Constraints

(D) $DD = DD' + b(X_{10} + X_{11})$

(D) $DD(e_i) = DD'(e_i) + b(X_{10}(e_i) + X_{11}(e_i))$, $i=1,2,3$
DD', $DD'(e_i)$ exogenous demand deposits
b – compensating balance requirement

(A) $CD(e_i) = (1 - m_{15})CD + P_{15}(e_i)$, $i=1,2,3$
m_{15} – fraction of CDs maturing

Valuation Reserve Constraints

(D) $V(e_i) = V$, $i=1,2,3$

Figure 5. Balance Sheet, December 31, 1972

	Actual	Model I	Model II
Assets:			
Cash and Cash Equivalents	10.8%	7.8%	8.0%
Government Agencies	3.1		
Short-Term Government Bonds	4.2	3.0	3.0
Long-Term Government Bonds	7.4	1.0	
Long-Term Municipal Bonds	15.2	88.2	33.8
Residential Mortgage	19.5		12.8
Commercial Mortgage	3.9		2.6
Short-Term Commercial Loan	25.0		34.5
Long-Term Commercial Loan	2.0		5.3
Instalment Loan	8.9		
Total Assets	100.0%	100.0%	100.0%
Liabilities and Capital:			
Demand Deposits	47.3%	47.0%	49.2%
Saving Deposits	17.4	21.4	19.7
Certificates of Deposits	28.1	22.8	23.0
Other Liabilities	1.2	1.4	1.3
Valuation Reserve	.8	1.0	.8
Stockholders' Equity	5.2	6.4	6.0
Total Liabilities and Capital	100.0%	100.0%	100.0%

still are a significant factor, and commercial mortgages play an increased role.

The results shown in Figure 6 and described in the preceding paragraph are to be expected. During periods of high interest rates, assets presenting high yields are preferred. Hence, municipal bonds absorb all funds not required elsewhere by constraint relationships. Thus, in Model I about 90% of the assets are placed in long-term municipals. In Model II nearly 35% of the assets are so placed. In the expected and easy credit conditions, deposits are more plentiful and relatively more assets are devoted to loans and mortgages in Model II.

One of the apparent discrepancies between Model II and the actual balance sheet of the bank as of December 31, 1972 is with regard to instalment loans. Model I, stage 1 shows no assets in the instalment loan category. It is only under the easy money condition that instalment loans enter the model's balance sheet. Since gross yield on instalment loans has a narrow range relative to other components of the loan portfolio, it has become a good investment under the easy money environment. In other words, only in a declining interest rate situation does instalment lending have the potential of producing a reasonable return per dollar of investment. This result is consistent with the fact that most banks are reconsidering their instalment loan portfolio under the continuing high interest rate environment of today's market.

Recapping this section we can conclude that Model II does a reasonable job of capturing the types of constraints under which the small midwestern bank operates and thus represents a reasonable approach to asset management. Let us hasten to add, however, that Model I does not come close to duplicating the bank's asset structure. The addition of the management policy constraints which reflect the bank's attitude toward risk as well as an approximation to more complicated cost and opportunity cost structures is essential to the success of the model.

In this regard another observation is significant. There are two ways of dealing with the potential failure of myopic types of decision rules. One way is to expand the horizon as Booth did. This leads inevitably to complications in computing and a costly estimating procedure. More parameters must be determined. The order of magnitude of the difference in the number parameters is tremendous as one changes the length of the horizon by adding more stages to the programming problem. The second way is to insert management constraints which, although not theoretically appealing, capture the essence of the problem in an efficient manner.

OBSERVATIONS ON TWO-STAGE PROGRAMMING MODELS IN BANK ASSET MANAGEMENT

At the present point we have concluded that two-stage models offer a logical procedure for ap-accounting and definitional functions. However, it should be noted that the demand deposit constraints specify that demand deposits are divided into "regular deposits" and "commercial deposits" · arising from required compensating balances. The regular deposits are assumed to follow a stochastic process based on historical data.

Policy or Management Constraints

Figure 4 shows the policy constraints developed in conjunction with management. The areas covered are loan level and composition, deposit mix, capital adequacy and minimum earnings or loss level.

Formulating loan policy has traditionally been the central concern of bank management. To reflect bank policy, three types of constraints are specified. The loan limit constraints place upper limits on the amount of new loans that can be made in the planning period. This insures that loan activities will be kept within the capacity of staff and facilities. The loan composition constraints place upper and lower limits on the fraction of residential mortgage loans in the loan portfolio as well as relating the commercial, residential and instalment loans. These constraints assure a balanced portfolio.

The loan portfolio limits relate the loan portfolio to the deposit volume. The upper limit prevents the bank from committing funds to loan customers beyond a point that management feels is too risky. The lower limit forces enough loan activity so that continuity can be retained in the lending function. Even though residential mortgage lending may be sharply curtailed during periods of tight money, some mortgages will be granted to maintain the bank's reputation as a lender in this field.

The above model essentially operates to maximize the expected value of stockholders' equity. It is well known in risk theory that maximizing the

Figure 6. Balance Sheets Stage 2, December 31, 1973

	e_1: Easy Money		e_2: Average Conditions		e_3: Tight Money	
	Model		Model		Model	
	I	II	I	II	I	II
Assets:						
Cash and Cash Equivalents	7.7%	7.9%	7.6%	7.9%	7.5%	7.9%
Government Agencies						
Short-Term Government Securities	3.0	3.0	3.1	3.0	3.1	3.0
Long-Term Government Securities						
Short-Term Municipals	8.1	3.2	8.9	3.5	.1	.6
Long-Term Municipals	81.2	31.2	80.4	31.3	89.3	34.8
Residential Mortgage		12.6		12.5		13.9
Commercial Mortgage		6.7		3.7		2.6
Short-Term Commercial Loan		29.8		33.8		29.7
Long-Term Commercial Loan		3.9		4.3		7.5
Instalment Loan		1.7				
Total Assets	100.0%	100.0%	100.0%	100.0%	100.0%	100.0%
Liabilities and Capital:						
Demand Deposits	45.6%	48.2%	45.0%	47.7%	44.0%	46.7%
Savings Deposits	21.2	20.1	21.6	20.2	22.0	20.6
Certificate of Deposits	22.3	22.8	22.2	22.6	22.0	22.4
Other Liabilities	1.3	1.3	1.5	1.4	1.6	1.5
Valuation Reserves	.9	.8	.9	.9	1.0	1.0
Stockholders' Equity	8.7	6.8	8.8	7.2	9.4	7.8
Total Liabilities and Capital	100.0%	100.0%	100.0%	100.0%	100.0%	100.0%

Figure 4. Management-Policy Constraints

Loan Portfolio Limits

(P) $X_8 + X_9 + X_{10} + X_{12} \leq K_1 (DD + SD + CD)$

(P) $X_8 + X_9 + X_{10} + X_{11} + X_{12} \geq K_2 (DD + SD + CD)$

(P) $X_8(e_i) + X_9(e_i) + X_{10}(e_i) + X_{11}(e_i) + X_{12}(e_i) \leq K_1 (DD(e_i) + SD(e_i) + CD(e_i))$

(P) $X_8(e_i) + X_9(e_i) + X_{10}(e_i) + X_{11}(e_i) + X_{12}(e_i) \geq K_2 (DD(e_i) + SD(e_i) + CD(e_i))$

Loan Composition Constraints

(P) $X_8 \geq K_3 (X_8 + X_9 + X_{10} + X_{11} + X_{12})$

(P) $X_8 \leq K_4 (X_8 + X_9 + X_{10} + X_{11} + X_{12})$

(P) $X_8(e_i) \geq K_3 (X_8(e_i) + X_9(e_i) + X_{10}(e_i) + X_{11}(e_i) + X_{12}(e_i)), \ i=1,2,3$

(P) $X_8(e_i) \leq K_4 (X_8(e_i) + X_9(e_i) + X_{10}(e_i) + X_{11}(e_i) + X_{12}(e_i)), \ i=1,2,3$

(P) $X_9 \leq K_5 X_8$

(P) $X_{11} \leq K_6 X_{10}$

Loan Limits

(P) $P_8(e_i) \leq V_8(e_i)$ $, i=1,2,3$

(P) $P_9(e_i) \leq V_9(e_i)$ $, i=1,2,3$

(P) $P_{10}(e_i) \leq V_{10}(e_i)$ $, i=1,2,3$

(P) $P_{11}(e_i) \leq V_{11}(e_i)$ $, i=1,2,3$

(P) $P_{12}(e_i) \leq V_{12}(e_i)$ $, i=1,2,3$

Certificate of Deposit Limits —

$CD \leq K_7 (DD + SD + CD)$

$CD(e_i) \leq K_7 (DD(e_i) + SD(e_i) + CD(e_i)), \ i=1,2,3$

Capital Adequacy

$SE(e_i) + V(e_i) + D(e_i) \geq K_8 DD(e_i) + K_9 SD(e_i) + K_{10} CD(e_i), \ i=1,2,3$

Loss Constraints

$SE(e_i) \geq SE(1 + g_i), \ i=1,2,3$

g_i – minimum required equity growth rate

expected value of wealth does not maximize the expected utility of the decision maker. If the decision maker is risk averse he may prefer a smaller "more" certain return to a larger "less" certain return. Risk preferences and indeed loss tolerances are expressed through the utility function when dealing theoretically with decision issues. In practice, however, utility functions are illusive and indeed may be unstable. To avoid this problem it has been the practice of decision analysts to suggest the maximization of expected value subject to a constraint limiting the probability of large adverse returns. It is this conceptual approach to risk that makes the management policy constraints logically consistent with the whole intent and purpose of two-stage programming under uncertainty.

Another use of management policy constraints is to deal with cost and profit situations that are too difficult to model or would cause a vast increase in the computational burden of the model. The lower limits on the loan portfolio serve this purpose. To explicitly incorporate the costs of changing levels of loan portfolios would be difficult. The costs would involve the estimation of the opportunity costs of losing potential customers when the loan portfolio falls to such a level as to discourage future inquiries. It would also involve the costs of laying off and hiring employees in the loan department. Both of these costs are difficult to estimate. In addition incorporation of these dynamic costs would lead to nonlinearities in the programming model that would present serious problems for computation.

Management policy constraints then allow constraining out potential solutions from the shortened horizon problem that would definitely be nonoptimal if the horizon were lengthened. They allow a shortened horizon problem to be solved in such a way as to limit the deleterious effects of short-sighted decision making and in so doing they allow solution of a much smaller programming problem than that which would have to be solved if a many-period horizon were used. This is done, of course, by limiting the extent of the feasible set of decision alternatives.

It can be concluded at this point that management policy constraints, although not perfect, are very useful in developing a reasonable model that is a cross between what is theoretically desirable and what is practically reasonable.

Is The Model Reasonable?

In order to judge the reasonableness of the model discussed in the previous sections we compare two runs of the model with the actual operations of the bank. First, the model was run with just the accounting, legal and financial constraints; second the model was run with both the aforementioned constraints and the management policy constraints. The influence of the policy constraints is clearly demonstrated on the first-stage opening balance sheet as well as the financial statements resulting in the three economic scenarios.

Figure 5 shows the actual 1972 balance sheet for the small midwestern bank on a percentage basis along with the first-stage opening balance sheet for both Model I with accounting, legal and financial constraints and under Model II with policy constraints added. Model I's proposed asset structure for December 31, 1972 represents a rather extreme allocation of funds. Although bankers are not particularly interested in very long-term municipal bonds, the average yield on these securities was in excess of their historical relationship with other securities. As a result, the model finds long-term municipals the highest yielding asset and allocates all of the available investment funds to it. This action has the effect of reducing demand deposits since existing compensating balances are no longer needed without loan activity.

The allocations in Model I are quite different than the actual distribution of funds used by the bank. For example, since the loan portfolio does not produce sufficient returns, Model I suggests that it should be liquidated. However, to provide for continuity of services in the expectation that lending may again prove profitable, Model II enforces a minimum level of lending.

proaching the bank asset management problem. Recapping we find:

>The process of two-stage programming—fre-

quently called programming with recourse—shows the decisions for the first stage must be made with reference to the ways one can recover from decisions which turn out to be "bad" in retrospect. This is the essence of the process used by any reasonable bank management.

>The approximation of joint continuous intertemporal probability distributions by discrete distributions need not cause problems in application. The main issue to be resolved is whether the first-stage decisions are sensitive to this "discretization." One conjecture is that the range of future eventualities is probably more important than the accurate characterization of the probability distribution.

>The most important constraints in a formulation of the bank management problem are the so-called policy constraints which deal with management's attitude toward risk as well as capturing the essence of very complicated time dependent dynamic opportunity cost structures that would be difficult to formulate and would lead to computational difficulties.

>Applying the model to a small midwestern bank produced results very similar to the bank's actual balance sheet.

But to be practically reasonable we must ask the question of what potential use is the model to a bank? Perhaps the best framework to adopt when incorporating model results in the planning procedure is the bank's budgeting or profit planning process. An opportunity is presented for mapping out a strategy for the coming year and the model results can help in formulating activities within an overall planning strategy.

One of the key features of the two-stage model that can improve the bank's budgeting procedure is the use of various economic scenarios. Previously the midwestern bank of our study adopted one set of budget figures for a set of forecasted economic conditions and hence, the actual financial statements turned out to be far different than anticipated. The two-stage model in essence provides a "budget for all seasons." Whether easy money, tight money or average credit conditions prevail, an appropriate set of planning figures exists. Thus in reviewing progress or in the control function, the variations of actual figures from those budgeted are more helpful in separating the assignable causes and directing control actions.

It was most interesting to apply this concept to the situation faced by the bank during 1973. The economic scenario for tight money quite accurately portrayed the conditions which were obtained. Although there was no way of knowing in advance that this would be the scenario to unfold, management became alert to this possibility and was in a position to curtail commercial lending and acquire longer term bonds.

As previously mentioned the model virtually eliminated instalment lending. Although the bank is currently making instalment loans, management has instituted a study of this area, especially credit card activities. A major alteration of operations may lead the way to profitability in this area.

Finally, we conclude that the two-stage programming model can be put to practical use for bank management. It not only can be used to calculate optimal policies but can be used to "jog" the thinking of management on many practical issues. Indeed it is our opinion that it does bridge the gap between the theoretically desirable and practically reasonable, and above all can lead to better bank management. □

REFERENCES

Booth, G. G., "Programming Bank Portfolios Under Uncertainty," *Journal of Bank Research*, Winter 1972.

Box, G. E. P. and G. M. Jenkins, *Time Series Analysis: Forecasting and Control*, Holden Day, 1969.

Bradley, S. P. and D. B. Crane, "A Dynamic Model for Bond Portfolio Management," *Management Science*, October 1972.

————, "Management of Commercial Bank Government Security Portfolios: An Optimization Approach Under Uncertainty," *Journal of Bank Research*, Spring 1973.

Chambers, D. and A. Charnes, "Inter-Temporal Analysis and Optimization of Bank Portfolios," *Management Science*, July 1961.

Charnes, A. and W. W. Cooper, "Chance-Constrained Programming," *Management Science*, Vol. 6 (1959), pp. 73-79.

————, "Deterministic Equivalents for Optimizing and Satisficing Under Chance Constraints," *Operations Research*, Vol. 11 (1963), pp. 18-39.

———— and G. H. Symonds, "Cost Horizons and Certainty Equivalents: An Approach to Stochastic Programming of Heating Oil," *Management Science*, April 1958.

Cohen, K. J. and S. Thore, "Programming Bank Portfolios Under Uncertainty," *Journal of Bank Research*, Spring 1970.

Cramer, Robert H. and Robert B. Miller, "Development of a Deposit Forecasting Procedure for Use in Bank Financial Management," *Journal of Bank Research*, Summer 1973.

Dantzig, G. B. and A. Madansky, "On the Solution of Two-Stage Linear Programs Under Uncertainty," *Proceedings of the Fourth Berkeley Symposium on Mathematical Statistics and Probability*, Vol. I, University of California Press, 1961.

Dantzig, G. B. and A. R. Ferguson, "The Allocation of Aircraft to Routes," *Management Science*, October 1956.

El Agizy, M., "Two-Stage Programming Under Uncertainty with Discrete Distribution Function," *Operations Research*, January-February 1967, pp. 55-70.

Wagner, H. M., *Principles of Operations Research*, Prentice-Hall, 1969.

Chapter 19

SHORT TERM MONEY MANAGEMENT FOR BANK PORTFOLIOS*

By Morton Lane

*This article is reprinted, with permission, from *Journal of Bank Research*, Vol. 5, No. 2 (Summer, 1974), pp. 102-119.

In the United Kingdom there is an extensive branch banking network, and the head office of a bank must coordinate and direct the actions of many individual branches. This involves a high degree of decentralization, and the treasurer's office employs two basic methods to synchronize independent actions. These are the setting of "base rates," which provide the ground rules for the individual activities of the branches, and short-term financing, used to smooth out any discrepancies between the aggregate levels of advances, deposits and reserve assets. Thus, for example, if the aggregate rate of advances suddenly moves ahead of deposits, this may be temporarily funded by short-term borrowing. If this effect is persistent, base rates may be adjusted to encourage deposits and slow the rate of advances. At what point does it become appropriate for head office to switch from short-term financing to changes of base rates, and vice versa?

In this paper a model is presented which provides the ingredients necessary to answer this critical question. It characterizes the decisions facing a particular department within the treasurer's office, i.e., the department responsible for short-term financing, primarily in terms of Certificates of Deposit. It receives information about the projected level of aggregate advances and deposits (over which it has no direct control) and deduces the projected cash flows for the bank as a whole. This information, together with forecast interest rates, is fed into the model and the model chooses the optimal levels of short-term borrowing and lending necessary to finance these projections. More importantly, the model determines the opportunity costs associated with the optimal financing plan and deduces the marginal benefits to be derived from extra deposits or advances. Armed with this information it is possible to compare the cost of short-term financing with the cost of gaining extra deposits, and hence decide whether it is optimal to maintain current base rates.

The model also explicitly incorporates some of the uncertainties faced by the bank. In deriving the projected rates of advances and deposits, it is necessary to make assumptions, implicitly or explicitly, about the future course of environmental events. For example, a forecast may be based on the assumption that government policy will remain unchanged or, alternatively, several government policies may be postulated. In the latter case, a set of forecasts is necessary, each contingent upon the occurrence of a particular policy. The model simultaneously evaluates all contingent forecasts and determines those transactions to be enacted immediately, before the future is known, as well as those transactions to be enacted when particular futures are revealed. Complimenting this, the opportunity costs associated with the optimal plan may be derived as expected values, as well as conditional on particular futures.

The manner in which the model handles the multiple contingent futures follows the methodology set in motion by K. J. Cohen and S. Thore [1970] utilizing linear programming under uncertainty, but with one significant extension of that methodology: The separation of stages and decision periods. Previous models have assumed that uncertain events take place in each period, and, thus, stages of uncertainty were synonomous with time periods. This model assumes that major uncertainties will arise which have persistent effect over several time periods. This assumption enables the major components of uncertainty to be examined in conjunction with multiperiod considerations. The resulting characterization is particularly appropriate for uncertainty in environmental parameters which have long lasting effects. This may be referred to as "strategic uncertainty" and is the sort of uncertainty to which this model is addressed.

Presentation of the model begins with a general statement of the problem and its algebraic characterization, followed by a description of input requirements and the character of the outputs of the model, each illustrated by a numerical example. The model output is in two parts, the first being the optimal set of plans and contingency plans, and the second being the corresponding opportunity costs and conditional costs. It is shown how each of these costs can be used to derive the expected value of each of the instruments. The paper concludes with comments on the sensitivity of the model and the most appropriate circumstances for its use.

MODEL DEVELOPMENT

A general statement of the model is presented and illustrated by a particular numerical example. Notation is introduced as each of the elements of the model are discussed. Each time period used in the model is one month long. The short-term financing problem may be described as follows.

Over the next $t = 1 \ldots T$ months, projected aggregate advances (A_t) and projected aggregate deposits (D_t) may result in excess funds in some periods and a deficit of funds in others. Excess funds may be lent out for varying short periods of time, and deficits may be financed using various short-term instruments. In this model it will be assumed that four maturities (τ) are available for borrowing and lending, namely one, three, six and nine month Certificates of Deposits (i.e. $\tau = 1, 3, 6, 9$). Certificates of Deposits (CDs) are negotiable but it will be assumed for the purposes of the model that they are kept until maturity. The opportunity cost of premature retirement may then be calculated, if desired, after the model is solved.

The use of CDs is limited in a number of ways. First, total borrowing and lending must balance, i.e., sources of funds must equal uses in each period. A second, institutional, requirement is imposed by the Bank of England: A fixed percentage (⅛) of "eligible liabilities" must be held on reserve each month. Eligible liabilities are defined as deposits plus CDs issued less any CDs held by the bank. Reserve assets are liquid assets, i.e., cash in the till, money at call or balances at the Bank of England. In general these reserve assets earn a lower return than could be obtained on other instruments. Unlike the Federal Reserve requirements, this restriction of ⅛ % remains fixed. When the Bank of England wishes to dry up excess liquidity it can, among other options, require "special deposits" to be placed with it for some unspecified period of time. The uncertainty about government policy with regard to special deposits and credit control is one of the major considerations confronting the short-term financing department and one of the major issues taken up in the model developed.

Another restriction on the amount of borrowing that can be undertaken at the projected interest rates is the size of the market in short funds. Individual CDs of maturity τ are restricted by an upper borrowing limit of $B_{t\tau}$ in period t. In addition, the total market for borrowed funds, of all maturities τ is restricted by a limit of B_t in period t. (Note that $\Sigma_\tau B_{t\tau}$ may be greater than B_t).

Given these limitations, the objective of the bank is to maximize wealth at the end of the planning horizon. It is assumed that all CDs are retired at the end of the horizon and that the retirement value is equal to the accrued value of the appropriate interest, plus repayment of principal. Thus, the terminal value of a "τ" month CD, issued in period t will be denoted $b_{t\tau}$ or $d_{t\tau}$ depending on whether it is borrowed or lent by the bank. $b_{t\tau}$ and $d_{t\tau}$ are respectively defined as

$$\left[1 + \left(\frac{T-t+1}{12} \right) r_{t\tau} \right] \text{ and } \left[1 + \left(\frac{T-t+1}{12} \right) r_{t\tau}^\varepsilon \right],$$

where $r_{t\tau}$ and $r_{t\tau}^\varepsilon$ are the borrowing and lending rate of τ-month CDs issued in period t.

Several future courses of events may affect the bank's deposit and advance pattern. A call for special deposits is one such possibility. In the numerical example that follows two possible futures are foreseen, each contingent on the outcome of some unspecified event in period 2. More generally it will be assumed that $k = 1 \ldots K$ futures are foreseen and that forecasts and decision variables that are particular to each future k will be denoted by a superscript k. Thus, for example, the forecast level of deposits and advances in period t, given that future k occurs, are respectively D_t^k and A_t^k. In the event that only one future is foreseen, then $k = K = 1$.

With these elements of the problem now made explicit, it is possible to develop algebraically the various constraints.

Sources and Uses of Funds
Sources:

In period t, funds may be generated from any one of four sources. These are:

1) Additional Deposits. This is represented by the increment in deposits predicted for each period t, in each future k. In the event of a drop in deposits, this term is negative and represents a cash outflow. $[D_t^k - D_{t-1}^k]$

2) Short-term Borrowing. Denote $x_{t\tau}^k$ as the amount of borrowing done in period t, future k, of CDs of term τ. Then the actual borrowing done in any period t, future k, is the sum over all possible maturities. $\sum_\tau x_{t\tau}^k$

3) Repayment of Previous Lending. Cash is generated by the repayment of previous lending done by the bank. The lending done in period t, future k, of τ month CDs is denoted $y_{t\tau}^k$. This, plus accumulated interest, is repaid in period $t + \tau$. If the borrowing rate in period t is denoted $r_{t\tau}^k$, then

the lending rate is r_{tt}^k less a "turn" (perhaps of 1/16%). The lending rate for future k is denoted r_{tt}^{ke}. Then repayment of previous lending is,

$$\sum_\tau \left[1 + \left(\frac{\tau}{12}\right) r_{t-\tau,\tau}^{ke} \right] y_{t-\tau,\tau}^k$$

4) Holding of Reserve Assets. Funds committed to reserve assets in period $t-1$ represent a use of funds in that period. Their repayment, plus accumulated interest, represents a source of funds in period t. Denoting the volume committed to reserve assets in period $t-1$, future k, as a_{t-1}^k, and the corresponding rate of return as r_{t-1}^k, then the cash available from this source is equal to reserve assets plus accumulated interest.

$$\left[1 + \left(\frac{1}{12}\right) r_{t-1}^k \right] a_{t-1}^k$$

Total funds available each period is therefore equal to:

$$\left[D_t^k - D_{t-1}^k \right] + \sum_\tau x_{t\tau}^k + \sum_\tau \left[1 + \left(\frac{\tau}{12}\right) r_{t-\tau,\tau}^{ke} \right] y_{t-\tau,}^k$$

$$+ \left[1 + \left(\frac{1}{12}\right) r_{t-1}^k \right] a_{t-1}^k .$$

Uses of Funds (in period t):

There are four corresponding uses to which funds can be devoted. These are:

1) Increased Advances. This is represented by the increment in projected advances in period t. In the event of a fall in advances, this may result in an effective inflow of funds. $[A_t^k - A_{t-1}^k]$

2) Lending. CDs may be lent by the bank in four different maturities. In period t, future k, total lending is denoted. $\sum_\tau y_{t\tau}^k$

3) Repayment of Borrowing. Borrowing done by the bank must be repaid and this incurs a net cash outflow.

$$\sum_\tau \left[1 + \left(\frac{\tau}{12}\right) r_{t-\tau,\tau}^k \right] x_{t-\tau,\tau}^k$$

4) Commitment to Reserve. A fixed proportion of funds must be committed to reserve. a_t^k

Total use of funds is therefore

$$[A_t^k - A_{t-1}^k] + \sum_\tau y_{t\tau}^k + \sum_\tau \left[1 + \left(\frac{\tau}{12}\right) r_{t-\tau,\tau}^k \right]$$

$$x_{t-\tau,\tau}^k + a_t^k .$$

Rearranging terms and setting sources equal to uses of funds, the first constraint is:

$$\sum_\tau x_{t\tau}^k - \sum_\tau \left[1 + \left(\frac{\tau}{12}\right) r_{t-\tau,\tau}^k \right] x_{t-\tau,\tau}^k - \sum_\tau y_{t\tau}^k$$

$$+ \sum_\tau \left[1 + \left(\frac{\tau}{12}\right) r_{t-\tau,\tau}^{ke} \right] y_{t-\tau,\tau}^k$$

$$+ \left[1 + \left(\frac{1}{12}\right) r_{t-1}^k \right] a_{t-1}^k - a_t^k$$

$$= [A_t^k - A_{t-1}^k] - [D_t^k - D_{t-1}^k] \quad \ldots\ldots\ldots\ldots(1)$$

all t, all k.

The Reserve Requirement

The second constraint is of an institutional character requiring that (1/8) of eligible liabilities be held as reserve assets. The eligible liabilities are:

1) Current Level of Deposits D_t^k

2) Borrowed Funds Outstanding (i.e., CDs issued). These must be summed over all previous issues made by the bank. $\sum_\tau \sum_{v=t-\tau+1}^t x_{vt}^k$

3) Lending Outstanding (i.e., CDs held). Again these must be summed over all previous transactions. $\sum_\tau \sum_{v=t-\tau+1}^t y_{vt}^k$

The liquidity constraint may therefore be stated as

$$a_t^k \geq \tfrac{1}{8}[D_t^k + \sum_\tau \sum_{v=t-\tau+1}^t x_{vt}^k - \sum_\tau \sum_{v=t-\tau+1}^t y_{vt}^k]$$

and, transposing the variables to the left, this is equivalent to

$$- \sum_\tau \sum_{v=t-\tau+1}^t x_{vt}^k + \sum_\tau \sum_{v=t-\tau+1}^t y_{vt}^k + 8a_t^k \geq D_t^k \quad ..(2)$$

Borrowing Limits

Two sorts of borrowing limits are imposed. The first applies to individual securities in each period t and future k. This may be denoted simply as

$$x_{t\tau}^k \leq B_{t\tau}^k \qquad \text{all } t, \tau \text{ and } k \ldots\ldots(3)$$

The second limit restricts the total borrowing that may be undertaken in any time period t, future k. Thus

$$\sum_\tau x_{t\tau}^k \leq B_t^k \qquad \text{all } t, \text{ all } k \ldots\ldots\ldots(4)$$

The Objective Function

Since any one of several futures can occur, depending upon the outcome of some random event, several values for terminal wealth may arise. The objective of management is assumed to be the maximization of the expected terminal wealth. Let the probability of future k occurring be p^k. Then, remembering that $b_{t\tau}^k$ and $d_{t\tau}^k$ represent the terminal value of borrowing and lending respectively, the objective of management may be represented by;

$$\sum_k p^k \left\{ \left(1 + \left(\frac{1}{12}\right) r_T^k \right) a_T^k + \sum_{v=T-\tau+1}^T d_{v\tau}^k y_{v\tau}^k \right.$$

$$\left. - \sum_{v=T-\tau+1}^T b_{v\tau}^k x_{v\tau}^k \right\} \quad \ldots(5)$$

Figure 1a. Projected Levels of Advances and Deposits

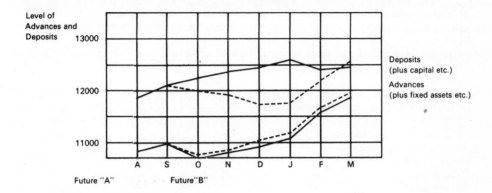

Future "A"   Future "B"

Figure 1b. Implied Net Cash Inflow Each Period.

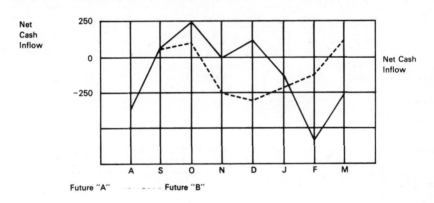

Future "A"   - - - - - Future "B"

Figure 2. Initial Input Data

Partial Balance Sheet (end–June)

Borrowed Funds (CDs issued)		Reserves	1,700
1 month funds	125	Funds Lent Out (CDs held)	
3 month funds (maturing in Oct.)	125	1 month funds	—
6 month funds (maturing in Jan.)	125	3 month funds	—
9 month funds (maturing in Apr.)	125	6 month funds	—
Deposits (plus capital etc.)	11,600	9 month funds	—
		Advances (Plus Fixed Assets etc.)	10,400
	12,100		12,100

Note: This is only a partial balance sheet of the bank. The various components of assets and liabilities are not detailed in full because they are outside the control of the department concerned with CDs. It is solely concerned with the aggregate levels of liabilities and assets and the way these change over time. For convenience, we have referred to these aggregate amounts as "Deposits" (plus capital etc.) and "Advances" (plus fixed assets etc.) since Deposits and Advances are the major and most volatile part of these totals.

Figure 3. Input Data For Both Futures

Future "A"

Probability of occurrence 0.60	A	S	O	N	D	J	F	M
Projections								
Advances (plus Fixed Assets)	10900	11000	10800	10900	10950	11100	11550	11850
Deposits (plus Capital)	11900	12050	12200	12300	12450	12600	12450	12500
Interest Rates								
Reserves								
1 month funds	8.75	8.75	8.00	8.00	8.75	8.75	10.50	10.50
3 month funds	8.75	8.75	8.25	8.25	9.25	9.25	10.25	10.25
6 month funds	9.00	9.00	8.75	8.75	9.50	9.50	9.50	9.50
9 month funds	9.00	9.00	9.00	9.00	9.50	9.50	9.50	9.50
Availability of Funds								
1 month funds	100	100	100	100	100	100	100	100
3 month funds	100	100	100	100	100	100	100	100
6 month funds	100	100	100	100	100	100	100	100
9 month funds	100	100	100	100	100	100	100	100
Total Availability	250	250	250	250	250	250	250	250

Future "B"

Probability of occurrence 0.40	A	S	O	N	D	J	F	M
Projections								
Advances (plus Fixed Assets)			10800	10900	11050	11175	11625	11925
Deposits (plus Capital)			12075	11925	11775	11825	12175	12575
Interest Rates								
Reserves								
1 month funds	AS IN	AS IN	8.75	8.75	8.25	8.25	8.50	8.50
3 month funds	"A"	"A"	8.75	8.75	8.25	8.25	8.50	8.50
6 month funds			8.75	8.75	8.50	8.50	8.50	8.50
9 month funds			8.75	8.75	8.50	8.50	8.50	8.50
Availability of Funds								
1 month funds			160	160	120	120	120	120
3 month funds			160	160	120	120	120	120
6 month funds			160	160	120	120	120	120
9 month funds			160	160	120	120	120	120
Total Availability			400	400	300	300	300	300

THE MODEL

Using the elements (1) .... (5) defined above, the model for the short term money management problem is as follows.

$$\text{Max } \Sigma_k p^k \left\{ \left(1 + \left(\frac{1}{12}\right) r_t^k \right) a_T^k + \Sigma_{v=T-\tau+1}^{T} d_{v\tau}^k y_{v\tau}^k \right.$$

$$\left. - \Sigma_{v=T-\tau+1} b_{v\tau}^k x_{v\tau}^k \right\}$$

s.t.

$$\Sigma_\tau x_{t\tau}^k - \Sigma_\tau \left[1 + \left(\frac{\tau}{12}\right) r_{t-\tau,\tau}^k \right] x_{t-\tau,\tau}^k - \Sigma_\tau y_{t\tau}^k$$

$$+ \Sigma_\tau \left[1 + \left(\frac{\tau}{12}\right) r_{t-\tau,\tau}^k \right] y_{t-\tau,\tau}^k$$

$$+ \left[1 + \left(\frac{1}{12}\right) r_{t-1}^k \right] a_{t-1}^k - a_t^k$$

$$= [A_t^k - A_{t-1}^k] - [D_t^k - D_{t-1}^k]$$

all t, all k,

$$- \Sigma_\tau \Sigma_{v=t-\tau+1}^{t} x_{v\tau}^k + \Sigma_\tau \Sigma_{v=t-\tau+1}^{t} y_{v\tau}^k + 8a_t^k \geq D_t^k$$

all t, all k,

$$x_{t\tau}^k \leq B_{t\tau}^k$$

all t, all k, all τ

$$\Sigma_\tau x_{t\tau}^k \leq B_t^k$$

all t, all k

$$x_{t\tau}^k, y_{t\tau}^k, a_t^k \geq 0.$$

236

Despite the fact that there are multiple futures that extend over several periods, the model is a straightforward linear programming problem. Rather than dwelling on its structure and particularities, its power is best revealed by proceeding to an illustration of its use (Figures 1a and 1b).

A NUMERICAL ILLUSTRATION—
THE INPUT

In this example a planning period of eight months, from August to March, is chosen. After two months, August and September, an unspecified event is anticipated which will result in quite different future projections. Two outcomes to the unspecified event are possible and each will generate different future behavior. These alternative futures will be denoted "A" and "B" and the corresponding forecast levels of advances, deposits and interest rates are listed in Figure 3. The advances-deposits pattern is also illustrated graphically in Figures 1a and 1b.

In future "A," the level of advances drops slightly during October and then rises steadily during the remaining months of the planning horizon. Deposits climb steadily during the early part of the horizon but reach a peak in January and fall slightly in February and March. More important perhaps is the fact that the rise in advances is faster than that of deposits and that there is an increasingly large net outflow of funds. This is illustrated in Figure 1a. The outflow reaches its maximum during February and eases only slightly in the last month of the horizon. The interest rates which correspond to these movements drop slightly in October, then rise steadily. The significant feature of the interest rates in this scenario is that short funds become very scarce towards the end of the horizon and their interest rates move ahead of the medium-term rates.

In contrast, the predicted interest rates for future "B" are stable for the first few months, dip during December and January and level out during February and March. Advances corresponding to this follow the same basic pattern as in future "A," but begin to move ahead faster in the last months of the horizon. Deposits on the other hand drop much sooner and much more dramatically than they do in future "A." The drop takes place in December rather than in February and eases continually after that. The net cash effect, shown in Figure 1b, is a maximum cash outflow during November which returns gradually to a net inflow during March.

Clearly, the scenarios are quite different and investment policy must make best allowance for either occurrence. It is estimated, in this example, that the probability of either future is 60% and 40% for "A" and "B" respectively. This data plus the initial balance sheet, shown in Figure 2, is all the necessary input to the model.

A NUMERICAL ILLUSTRATION—
THE OUTPUT (PART I)

The optimal solution corresponding to the numerical problem posed is listed in Figure 4. This table details the amount that should be borrowed in each maturity in each future time period, the corresponding lending, and the volume that must be held on reserve. Thus, for example, the table lists the optimal decisions for August as

Borrow: 50 of 1 month CDs
100 of 3 month CDs
100 of 9 month CDs
Lend: 67.86 as a 6 month CD
Hold: 1557.14 in reserve assets.

Notice that it is optimal to lend for six months, but not to borrow for that term. A glance at Figure 1 indicates why. In February, whether "A" or "B" materializes, a net outflow of funds is predicted. This outflow is particularly large if future "A" occurs. Clearly, a commitment to borrow funds now for six months would involve their repayment at the very time when funds were most needed. On the other hand, lending for six months will result in an inflow during February. Apparently, it is worth lending out 67.86 as a six month CD now, despite the fact that this will have to be financed out of shorter term borrowing. Exactly how this sort of decision is evaluated will be illustrated presently. For the moment, however, it is worth observing some other aspects of the solution.

In August and September it is optimal to undertake short (one month) and long (nine month) borrowing and use part of this to finance medium term lending in three and six month CDs. The reason, once again, appears to be the need for a cash inflow in the medium term, irrespective of which future materializes.

Notice that in August and September no information is available concerning which future will occur, and so a single decision is recommended. In October however, the first information characterizing the likely course of events becomes available and different actions are recommended depending on the outcome. If future "A" occurs then a large volume of borrowing takes place to finance the net outflow of funds that arises. Most of this borrowing takes place in long term CDs and any surpluses are lent out on a month to month basis. Because of the increasing value of short-term funds, these are accumulated by extra borrowing.

In future "B," despite the earlier and more dramatic fall off in deposits, no such persistent pattern of borrowing and lending exists. Some borrowing does take place but this fluctuates in both volume and maturity. Apparently, it is only worth lending out funds on two occasions and then only on a monthly basis.

The monthly balance sheets corresponding to the above set of optimal actions are shown in Figure 5. Notice again that only one set of balance sheets are shown for immediate periods, but subsequently two sets are detailed, each of which corresponds with one set of contingent plans. The balance sheets display the fact that minimum reserve requirements are met at the desired level for both future "A" and future "B." This is precisely what was wanted, i.e., a set of decisions that would not violate the requirements in any foreseen eventuality. The balance sheets also reveal the net profit gained from the short-term transactions. In future "A" and "B" this profit rises steadily during the course of the planning horizon, although at a faster rate in future "A."

THE OUTPUT — (PART II)

In addition to prescriptions concerning the actions that the bank should employ to optimize its return from short transactions, the model also provides a set of economic information concerning adjustments to the optimal plan. In its raw form, this information is presented as the dual variables associated with each of the constraints of the linear program. Suitably distilled, however, this data can provide the basis for interest rate changes and other "base rate" directives issued to the branches of the bank network. In order to understand the basis for such information, it is worth spending a little time on the dual variables in their raw form, since very little has appeared in the literature concerning the interpretation of dual values in stochastic models.

The variables listed in Figure 6 are the dual figures corresponding to the cash equations and

the liquidity constraints. In period 1 the figure of 1.06355 represents the expected value of an extra unit of cash if it is available in August and optimally invested until March. Thus, an extra unit of cash in August results in an expected extra 1.06355 in March, i.e., an annual equivalent increase of 9.53325% over the eight month horizon.

Similar interpretations apply to the extra cash made available in other months during the planning period. However, these interpretations depend on which future occurs. For December, future "A," the dual value is 0.62011. Thus, if an extra unit of funds is available in December, but only in future "A," the expected value of this in March is 0.62011. Since the probability of future "A" occurring is estimated to be 0.6, if "A" actual-

Figure 4. Optimal Borrowing, Lending and Contingent Plans

Borrowing	A	S
1 month	50.00	100.00
3 month	100.00	—
6 month	—	—
9 month	100.00	100.00
Lending		
1 month CD	—	—
3 month CD	—	195.67
6 month CD	67.86	—
9 month CD	—	—
Reserves	1557.14	1570.18

ly does occur, the value of that extra unit in December is $0.62011 \div 0.6 = 1.03351$, i.e., an annual equivalent increase of 10.0153%. If the extra unit of cash is available in December irrespective of which future ultimately occurs, its expected value in March is $0.62011 + 0.41162 = 1.03173$, i.e., an annual equivalent increase of 9.519%. Clearly, the value of cash conditional on the occurrance future "A" (10.05%) is greater than the value of funds conditional on the occurrance future "B" (8.37%). The expected value of extra funds, available in either future, lies between these two, at 9.519%.

The important point to notice about the value of funds in any period is that it is possible to derive both the conditional value of funds as well as the expected value of the funds. In situations where estimates of profitability may change quite quickly,

these figures can be used to establish first estimates of new expected values. Also, on those occasions where contingent contracts can be negotiated, such information is of vital importance. Thus, for example, if a bank customer wishes to make a forward contract to borrow funds, when and if a particular event happens, the real cost of a commitment to lend on the part of the bank may be evaluated using the contingent opportunity cost of funds obtained from the dual. Of course, the exact cost of such a commitment will depend on the exact form of instrument specified in the contract. Thus, it is valuable to have the opportunity cost of each of the instruments, rather than the opportunity costs of funds that have been derived from some arbitrary source. These may be obtained by suitable manipulation of the dual variables in their raw form. In the model, four classes of instru-

Future "A"

O	N	D	J	F	M
—	—	—	—	—	—
—	50.00	50.00	100.00	50.00	50.00
100.00	100.00	100.00	100.00	100.00	100.00
100.00	100.00	100.00	50.00	100.00	100.00
363.20	509.42	1067.01	1189.79	816.00	740.85
—	—	—	—	—	—
—	—	—	—	—	—
—	—	—	—	—	—
1540.41	1553.38	1558.14	1577.17	1638.62	1679.27

Future "B"

O	N	D	J	F	M
—	160.00	—	120.00	—	—
118.01	—	120.00	120.00	—	—
38.69	—	60.00	—	83.31	. 54.67
—	— •	120.00	60.00	120.00	—
194.91	—	28.12	—	—	—
—	—	—	—	—	—
—	—	—	—	—	—
—	—	—	—	—	—
1540.41	1553.52	1573.22	1590.10	1652.75	1694.58

Figure 5. Conditional Balance Sheets (Aug.-Mar.)

	A	S
Deposits Borrowing	11900.00	12050.00
1 month	50.00	100.00
3 month	225.00	225.00
6 month	125.00	125.00
9 month	225.00	325.00
Return		+ 8.71
	12525.00	12833.71
Advances Lending	10900.00	11000.00
1 month	—	—
3 month	—	195.67
6 month	67.86	67.86
9 month	—	—
Reserves	1557.14	1570.18
	12525.00	12833.71

Note: These Balance Sheets are only partially specified for the same reason
as that given in Figure 2.

Future "A"

O	N	D	J	F	M
12200.00	12300.00	12450.00	12600.00	12450.00	12500.00
—	—	—	—	—	—
100.00	50.00	100.00	200.00	200.00	200.00
225.00	325.00	425.00	400.00	500.00	600.00
425.00	525.00	625.00	675.00	775.00	875.00
+ 17.14	+ 26.33	+ 43.01	+ 59.82	+ 79.62	+ 95.27
12967.14	13226.33	13643.01	13934.82	14004.62	14270.12
10800.00	10900.00	10950.00	11100.00	11550.00	11850.00
363.20	509.42	1067.01	1189.79	816.00	740.85
195.67	195.67	—	—	—	—
67.86	67.86	67.86	67.86	—	—
—	—	—	—	—	—
1540.41	1553.38	1558.14	1577.17	1638.62	1679.27
12967.14	13226.33	13643.01	13934.82	14004.62	14270.12

Future "B"

O	N	D	J	F	M
12075.00	11925.00	11775.00	11825.00	12175.00	12575.00
—	160.00	—	120.00	—	—
218.01	118.01	238.01	240.00	240.00	120.00
163.70	163.70	223.70	98.70	182.01	236.68
325.00	325.00	445.00	505.00	625.00	625.00
+ 16.73	+ 25.34	+ 37.49	+ 44.26	+ 55.74	+ 62.90
12798.44	12717.05	12719.20	12832.06	13277.75	13619.58
10800.00	10900.00	11050.00	11175.00	11625.00	11925.00
194.91	—	28.12	—	—	—
195.67	195.67	—	—	— '	—
67.86	67.86	67.86	67.86	—	—
—	—	—	—	—	—
1540.40	1553.52	1573.22	1590.10	1652.75	1694.58
12798.44	12717.05	12719.20	12832.06	13277.75	13619.58

Figure 6. The Value of the Dual Variables Associated with the Cash Equation and Liquidity Constraints.

	The Cash Equation (u_t^k)	The Reserve Requirement (v_t^k)		
$t = 1$	1.06355	−.00033		
2	1.05474	−.00028		
	"A"		"B"	
$t = 3$	0.62847	−.00007	.41796	−.00008
4	0.62428	−.00007	.41488	−.00011
5	0.62011	−.00012	.41162	−.00006
6	0.61553	−.00012	.40878	−.00008
7	0.61098	−.00025	.40581	−.00007
8	0.60547	−.00025	.40290	−.00007

ments are described—advances, deposits, lending and borrowing. The opportunity costs of each of these will be derived in turn.

The Marginal Value of Deposits

Advances may be issued in different months and for different lengths of time. Thus the banker may be interested in the marginal value of many different forms of advance arrangements. In this section three types of advance are evaluated. These are: 1) The value of a permanent advance, i.e., made in period t until after the planning horizon; 2) the value of an advance made for one month, i.e., placed in period t and repaid in $t + 1$; and 3) the value of advances made in August for differing terms.

In the model, the projected stream of advances is $A_t^k, A_{t+1}^k \dots A_T^k$. If now an extra advance is made in period t until after the horizon, the new stream of advances will be $A_t^k + 1, A_{t+1}^k + 1, \dots, A_T^k + 1$. Taking first differences to derive the appropriate right hand side values for the linear program results in the following coefficients $[A_t^k + 1 - A_{t-1}^k]$, $[A_{t+1}^k - A_t^k] \dots [A_T^k - A_{T-1}^k]$. Clearly, only the right hand side coefficient for the cash equation in period t is increased by one unit. The dual variable associated with this constraint, which is denoted u_t^k, therefore represents the expected value of permanent advances made in period t. Dividing this, where appropriate, by the probability of future k gives the conditional value of advances for period t. This term is then multiplied by $\left(\dfrac{12}{9-t}\right)$ to convert the cost over the period month t to month 8, into an annual equivalent rate of interest. Performing this calculation for each period, and future, results in the figures listed in Figure 7.

To illustrate these, consider a marginal advance

made in November until the end of March. By November, future "A" or "B" will have occurred. Thus we may calculate the value of the permanent advance conditional on either "A" or "B" occurring. Assume we are interested in the cost conditional on event "A". The dual variable associated with the cash constraint in future "A", from Figure 6, is 0.62428 and the probability of "A" is 0.6. Therefore the cost of the advance over the period Nov.-Mar. when we know that "A" will occur is $(0.62428 \div 0.6) - 1 = 0.04046$. Annualizing this, i.e., multiplying

Figure 7. The Marginal Value of Permanent Advances, i.e., made in period t until the end of the horizon (percentages quoted in annualized equivalent).

Advances			
	Conditional Values		Expected Values
$t = 1$	9.53248		
2	9.38331		
	"A"	"B"	
$t = 3$	9.48997	8.97999	9.28597
4	9.71197	8.92799	9.39838
5	10.05500	8.71503	9.51901
6	10.35330	8.78000	9.72397
7	10.98000	8.71496	10.07400
8	10.93970	8.70008	10.04390

by $\left(\dfrac{12}{9-4}\right)$, gives an equivalent rate of interest of 9.71%. If "B" occurs, similar calculations give a rate of 8.93%. Thus the expected cost of a November

242

advance, if it is committed now, before either eventuality is known, is equal to 9.40%.

Two points about these interest rates must be borne in mind. First, they represent only the incremental costs of the marginal advance. The direct interest revenue received from the advance is not detailed here. The incremental cost computed must be compared with the interest charged to evaluate whether or not the advance is worthwhile. A second point is that these interest rates are not the rates that will actually occur in November. Rather, they are the current (August) estimates of the opportunity cost of advances contracted in August for issue in November. In this sense, the opportunity costs to be quoted in this paper are really forward rates. They represent the current value placed on future commitment.

If future advances are made in period t for only one month, then the right hand side coefficients of the linear program are

$$[A_t^k + 1 - A_{t-1}^k], [A_{t+1}^k - A_t^k - 1]$$
$$[A_{t+2}^k - A_{t+1}^k] .... [A_T^k - A_{T-1}^k]$$

Thus, the coefficient associated with period t is increased by one unit and that associated with $t + 1$ is decreased by one unit. Accordingly the term $(u_t^k - u_{t+1}^k)$ represents the marginal value of an advance made in period t for one month, dividing, where appropriate, by the probability of future k, and annualizing results in the figures listed in Figure 8. It is noticeable that the most expensive one-month advances for future "A" occur in February, whereas those for future "B" occur in November. These are the months when the greatest net cash outflow is experienced. Thus it is predictable that these months should incur the greatest real cost. However, the point of the present analysis is to gauge precisely what that real cost is so that it may be compared with actual rates of interest. This is not possible without some model of the sort described here.

Another valuation that may be placed on advances is to consider the effect of an extra advance made in August for τ periods. The effect on the right hand side values of the linear program is $[A_1 - A_0 + 1], [A_2 - A_1], ... [A_{t+1}^k - A_t^k - 1]$ .... $[A_T^k - A_{T-1}^k]$. Thus, only the constraints in period 1 and period τ are effected. Notice however, that the effect in period τ occurs in both futures k. Therefore the term $(u_1 - u_t^A - u_t^B)$ represents the expected value of an advance of term τ. It is also possible to derive conditional values, and these are listed, together with the expected values, in Figure 9. Notice that the most expensive maturity is for one and two months lending. Evidently, this is because of the large outflow of funds that is experienced during August, as well as the effect of

Figure 8. The Marginal Value of Single Period Advances, i.e., made in period t and repaid in period $t + 1$ (percentages quoted in annualized equivalent).

Advances

	Conditional Values		Expected Values
$t = 1$	10.57670		
2	9.96730		
	"A"	"B"	
$t = 3$	8.37994	9.24003	8.72397
4	8.33988	9.77987	8.91588
5	9.16004	8.52013	8.90408
6	9.09996	8.90994	9.02395
7	11.02020	8.73005	10.10410
8	10.94000	8.70000	10.40000

Figure 9. The Marginal Value of Advances made in period 1 for τ periods (percentages quoted in annualized equivalents).

Advances

	Conditional Values		Expected Values
$\tau = 1$	10.57670		
	"A"	"B"	
$\tau = 2$	9.66001	11.19000	10.27200
3	9.23332	10.54000	9.75599
4	9.00996	10.35000	9.54596
5	9.03997	9.98400	9.41759
6	9.04997	9.80499	9.35198
7	9.33143	9.65143	9.45943
8	9.53246	9.53250	9.53248

high rates of interest in August and September. If advances are made in August for longer periods of time however, the opportunity cost falls. Only if the extra advances are still outstanding in February and March does the real cost of the advances begin to rise again.

The calculations undertaken for Figures 7, 8 and 9 ignore any advance-deposit effect of the issue of an advance. In the U.K., banks very rarely impose deposit requirements on borrowers. However, in American banks compensating balance requirements are often attached to issued loans. If this were the case the above calculations would have to be amended to gauge the precise effect of such procedures. It would then be possible to compare the opportunity cost of pursuing one compensating balance requirement with another, or, alternatively, to design requirements more suited to the time the loan is issued.

The Marginal Value of Deposits

An exactly similar analysis may be performed to gauge the marginal value of deposits. Thus, in this section the value of permanent deposits, one month deposits and deposits placed currently for differing time periods will be estimated. The bank may have less discretion over its exact deposit position than it does over advances; nevertheless the implied economic costs of the various alternatives can be just as enlightening as is the case for advances.

An extra unit of deposits placed in period t until after the end of the planning horizon has much the same effect as a drop in the level of advances over the same period. There is, however, a single important difference. Some of the extra deposits generated in each period must be placed as reserve assets in order to fulfill the statutory liquidity requirements. This must be done for each period in which the deposits are held. The effect of this can be seen by examining the right hand side of the linear program. Deposits affect both the cash constraint and the reserve constraints. Thus, if extra deposits are permanently placed in period t, future k, the effect on the cash constraint is $[D_t^k + 1 - D_{t-1}^k]$, $[D_{t+1}^k - D_t^k]$ .... $[D_T^k - D_{T-1}^k]$ and the effect on the reserve constraint is $D_t + 1$, $D_{t+1} + 1$, ... $D_T + 1$. If the total dual value associated with the reserve constraint is denoted v_t^k, then the value of extra permanent deposits is

$$(u_t^k + \sum_{\tau=t}^{T} v_\tau^k).$$

This is calculated for each time period and converted to an annual equivalent interest rate in the usual manner. The result is listed in Figure 10.

Once the essential difference between the evaluation of advances and deposits is understood, it is easy to derive the effect of one month deposits and deposits of differing maturities. Thus in period t, future k, an extra deposit placed for one month results in an adjustment of $(u_t^k - u_{t-1}^k + v_t^k)$. Similarly, if a deposit is placed in period 1 for τ periods, the expected margin value is given by

$$[u_1 - \sum_k (u_\tau^k - \sum_{t=1}^{\tau} v_t^k)].$$

Notice that in this the expected value of the deposits must be summed over both possible futures. The results of these two calculations, appropriately annualized, is shown in Figures 11 and 12.

A quick comparison of Figures 10, 11 and 12 with Figures 7, 8 and 9 reveals the same basic intertemporal pattern of interest rate movements. This is to be expected. Much more illuminating are the differences that exist between the respective rates for advances and deposits. On one month advances in August, the opportunity cost is 10.5767%. In other words, the minimum charge that should be made for such an advance is 10.5767%. On the other hand, the value of extra one month deposits is 10.1807%, and this represents the maximum payment that the bank can offer to induce such deposits. The difference between the two (0.396%) represents the minimum margin that should exist between the costs of borrowing and lending. In October the minimum margin between the two expected rates drops to (0.18%). Of course, the actual margin charged may differ somewhat from this. However, fluctuations in these opportunity cost margins can be used to indicate how the actual margins might also change.

Borrowing and Lending

In the numerical illustration under discussion it is optimal to borrow three months funds during August and pay a rate of interest of 8.75%. It is not optimal to lend out at that rate of interest over the same period. If interest rates move slightly after the first estimates are provided, how much more can the bank afford to pay and still make three month borrowing worthwhile, and what change in the lending rate would induce it to lend in that period? These questions can again be answered by suitable manipulation of dual variables.

The short-term borrowing that is done in the model is limited by upper bounds on each instrument. If borrowing is undertaken to the limit and the dual variable associated with that limit is zero, then it is just worth paying the predicted rate of interest. If the dual variable is positive, then the bank could afford to pay a higher rate. Correspondingly, if no borrowing is undertaken and the slack variable of the dual constraint is positive, the rate will have to drop to induce some use of this particular instrument. If the dual variable, or dual slack, associated with each borrowing constraint is then divided by the marginal value of funds in the repayment period, it is possible to calculate the change in the rate of interest which would just make borrowing a marginal activity. This is done, after annualizing, and the results are listed in Figure 13.

In September, one month funds are borrowed at a rate of interest of 8.75%. Figure 13 indicates that it would still be optimal to undertake this borrowing even if the rate of interest rises to 9.2087%. On the other hand, in January, in future

Figure 10. The Marginal Value of Permanent Deposits, i.e., placed in period t till the end of the horizon (percentages quoted in annualized equivalents).

Deposits

	Conditional Values		Expected Values
$t = 1$	9.23938		
2	9.10492		
	"A"	"B"	
$t = 3$	9.19662	8.74500	9.01597
4	9.38799	8.69402	9.11040
5	9.68499	8.50503	9.21301
6	9.93996	8.55999	9.38797
7	10.48010	8.50496	9.69003
8	10.43990	8.49009	9.65996

Figure 11. The Marginal Value of Single Period Deposits, i.e., placed in period t and withdrawn in period $t + 1$ (percentages quoted in annualized equivalents).

Deposits

	Conditional Values		Expected Values
$t = 1$	10.18070		
2	9.63850		
	"A"	"B"	
$t = 3$	8.23994	9.00003	8.54397
4	8.19988	9.44987	8.69988
5	8.92004	8.34013	8.68808
6	8.85996	8.66994	8.78395
7	10.52020	8.52005	9.72013
8	10.44000	8.49000	9.66000

"A," a rate of 8.75% is predicted, and this would have to drop 1.355% to 7.395% to induce borrowing of one month money at that time.

No limits exist on the amount of lending that is undertaken each period and so it is either optimal to lend at the predicted rate of interest or it is not. As far as the lending options in this model are concerned, it is only possible to determine the increase in the rates of interest which would make lending a profitable alternative, if it is not already one. This is derived in a similar manner to the marginal borrowing costs. The dual slack associated with each lending option is divided by the

opportunity costs of funds in the repayment period. This is then adjusted by the appropriate probability, annualized, and the results are listed in Figure 14. The rates would apparently have to increase quite a lot to justify any lending in unused CDs. Thus the one month August rate of 8.75% must increase to 9.6943% before it is worth undertaking this alternative.

Reviewing the Solution

The solution clearly displays many of the features one would anticipate from a realistic resolution of the problem posed. For example, one month advances are most expensive in February if "A" occurs and in November if "B" occurs. Similarly the most valuable one month deposits occur

Figure 12. Marginal Value of Deposits placed in period 1 for τ periods (percentages quoted in annualized equivalents).

Deposits

	Conditional Values		Expected Values
Maturity			
$\tau = 1$	10.18070		
	"A"	"B"	
$\tau = 2$	9.30000	10.82400	9.90960
3	8.94665	10.21600	9.45439
4	8.75996	10.02450	9.26576
5	8.79198	9.68761	9.15023
6	8.80331	9.51799	9.08918
7	9.04857	9.37543	9.17932
8	9.22247	9.26474	9.23938

in August. These results provide a superficial validation of the model which is encouraging.

However the value of the model lies not in the predictability of its results, but in their unpredictability and precision. Whereas it may have been obvious that six month borrowing in August was unlikely to be profitable, it may not have been so clear that six month lending was an optimal action. Nor, perhaps, that it would be optimal to finance this lending with short borrowing to the amount of 67.86. The advantage of the model is not that it duplicates intuitive judgment, but rather that it extends that judgment. Again, it was clear that funds were scarce during August but it was not obvious that the opportunity cost of an eight month advance was exactly 9.53% p.a.

Figure 13. Increases in the Predicted Interest Rates Which Would Make Borrowing a Marginal Activity. (Increased percentages quoted are in annualized equivalents).

Borrowing			τ = 1	τ = 3	τ = 6	τ = 9		
t = 1				0.04619	0.21636	0.12150		
2			0.45870	−0.05815	−0.05950	0.10628		
		"A"				"B"		
t = 3	−0.07688	−0.00649	0.44666	0.19666	−0.05784			
4	−0.81275		0.48400	0.23600	0.43729	−0.04928	0.05400	0.05400
5	−0.35091		0.11000	0.11000	−0.11742	0.18863		
6	−1.35520	0.25333			0.11828	0.25000		
7	−0.53512		0.75000	0.75000	−0.05950			
8	−0.26000		0.74000	0.74000				

Figure 14. Increases in the Predicted Interest Rates Which Would Make Lending Worthwhile. (Increased percentages quoted are in annualized equivalents).

Lending		τ = 1	τ = 3	τ = 6	τ = 9		
t = 1		0.94430	0.40802		0.30300		
2		0.52750		0.00198	0.16971		
	"A"				"B"		
t = 3	0.05198	0.51000	0.26000		0.05871	0.06000	0.06000
4	0.30770	0.70000	0.44800	0.49560	0.00985	0.01200	0.01200
5	0.15855	0.24500	0.24500		0.26805	0.07500	0.07500
6	0.75333	0.50666	0.50666	0.35484	0.37000	0.12000	0.12000
7	0.30000	1.05000	1.05000		0.06000	0.06000	0.06000
8	0.26000	1.00000	1.00000	0.06000	0.06000	0.06000	0.06000

NB: It should be remembered that all lending is subject to a "turn" of 1/16%.

Provided with these costs the manager may compare the opportunity cost of an eight month advance (9.53% p.a.) with the actual charge that would be made using current base rates. If the difference is lower than expected he may then choose to readjust rates. On the other hand, in this example he may decide that the phenomena is temporary and that current policy should be maintained. He may also note that if future "B" occurs there will be some cause for drop in base rates.

It is worth asking how sensitive the model is to changes in data, particularly to estimates of probabilities. In this example the answer can be stated quite simply. The actions prescribed are insensitive to reasonable changes in probability estimates but are affected by larger changes. It turns out that if future "A" were to occur with certainty, only short-term borrowing in August would be encouraged, but if future "B" were certain then only longer borrowing would be optimal. In neither case would lending be recommended. For quite large ranges of probability between these two extremes the solution detailed is encouragingly stable and therefore forms a good basis for action.

Extending the Model

This model is still in the development stage, and a number of refinements have still to be made. At the moment, the constraints are at their most rudimentary. They contain just those elements that

246

are likely to apply to any bank. Superimposed on this are those constraints that may be placed by management's own operating policy. For example, management may require that additional borrowing always be spread across the spectrum of possible instruments. Or, analogously, it may require that the holdings of CDs be evenly balanced. These issues will have to be resolved by the individual banks in co-operation with the modeller. This resolution will have its advantages, as it is now possible to evaluate the cost of such policies and enable interested management to decide whether they are worth pursuing.

Another issue which will have to be faced by all modellers concerns the terminal assumptions. The world does not end in period T, as assumed in the proposed model. By assuming that all securities are retired at the end of period T and that nothing happens thereafter, one implies that management is indifferent to the character of the balance sheet at that time. Thus, it is possible for the model to switch all funds into the instrument gaining greatest return at the horizon date. Such a solution clearly will not correspond to management intentions at that time. It is therefore necessary to impose what has been called "horizon posture" constraints on the complexion of the terminal balance sheet. This forces the model to proffer solutions that are consistent with "reasonable" investment behavior over the entire course of the horizon. The exact impact of such "horizon posture" constraints on immediate decisions is not always easy to assess, but the impact on overall performance is easily gauged from the dual variables. The nature of these posture constraints again depends on the concern of individual managements, but it is important to remember that the model should be extended in this direction before practical use.

A final extension of the model is in terms of its facility to handle more scenarios and more stages of uncertainty. Given that the model will be used in the analysis of "strategic" uncertainties, the extra numbers involved need not be too great. Indeed, a limit to this expansion is likely to be the willingness of management to provide the necessary input data, rather than the excessive computational burden such models will provide for computers. This is important. It implies that the greatest attention must be paid to the input requirements in constructing such models. In this model, the major requirements are all listed in Figures 1-3. It is intended that any extension of the model's ability to handle multi-stage uncertainties will maintain this format in as simple a form as possible.

SOME CONCLUDING REMARKS

The model described in this paper was originally constructed to determine short-term financing policy given projected levels of advances and deposits. It was also constructed to take explicit account of the major uncertainties confronting the bank. Its ability to do this has been demonstrated using a relatively simple numerical example. It was shown that the model selects a set of transactions which maximize expected wealth, and which ensure the viability of the bank in any foreseeable future.

In many ways, however, the most exciting outputs from the model are the opportunity costs that can be derived for each of the instruments. It has been shown that these values provide vital information that can be used in policy evaluations.

It should be stressed that the model is intended for policy evaluation, and not presently for routine use. This caveat has appeared in most of the papers that have proposed bank portfolio models, although some of them have then gone on to describe uncertainties which were of a distinctly operational character and not really related to policy. In contrast, this paper had dealt squarely with uncertainties which are "strategic" rather than "tactical." These include changes in government policy, competitors' policies, international market realignments, as well as uncertainty about the timing of these events. The distinctive features of these "strategic" uncertainties is that their outcomes are recognizable, and their effects both pervasive and long lasting. The uncertainties that confront the routine financing decisions are both singular and short-lived. They affect particular instruments and are not recognizably the result of any special events. For these uncertainties other formulations of the model would appear desirable and proper. Until these are forthcoming it is not appropriate to recommend the routine use of the model described.

Having made this qualification of the model's use, it is worth considering what particular aspects of it may nevertheless be used as an aid for routine use. Here there is a great deal of room for experimentation and future research. It has been suggested, for example, that using the model with optimistic, pessimistic and most likely future predictions, rather like PERT, will result in a more realistic spread of investments than does the deterministic version of the model. This remains to be seen. Closer specification of its decision character will be necessary, and at the moment such a suggestion remains speculative. An alternative way of using the model to aid routine decisions is to utilize the opportunity costs already discussed.

The economic rates of interest associated with each of the borrowing and lending options may be used as bench marks to guide actual transactions. This use appears quite promising for a number of reasons. First, it is precisely these opportunity interest rates that should induce the optimal set of transactions. Secondly, the use of benchmarks as a guide to decisions allows the manager discretion over their actual use and avoids the "black box" reaction to prescribed solutions. Once again, it is not clear how such a scheme would work or how fast the opportunity costs would have to be updated. Work on these problems is progressing and it is hoped to report on this in the near future.

I have deliberately tried to limit US-UK language differences. However, the following definitions may prove helpful.

Advances: A general term describing the mainstream lending activities of UK banks, including, bill finance, overdrafts and loans to industrial and commercial customers. "Loans" are a particular form of advance for fixed periods and for fixed amounts. The major part of UK bank lending is done by overdraft.

Deposits: A general term describing the mainstream borrowing activities of the banks.

CDs: Certificates of Deposit. These instruments were introduced to the London market by the American banks in 1968. CDs issued are sometimes referred to as "bid money."   □

REFERENCES

Chambers, D. and A. Charnes, "Inter-Temporal Analysis and Optimization of Bank Portfolios," *Management Science*, July, 1961, pp. 393-410.

Charnes, A., J. Dreze and M. Miller, "Decision and Horizon Rules for Stochastic Planning Problems: A Linear Example," *Econometrica*, Vol. 34 (1966).

Charnes, A., and S.C. Littlechild, "Intertemporal Bank Asset Choice with Stochastic Dependence," Systems Research Memoranda No. 186, Northwestern University (1968).

Charnes, A., and S. Thore, "Planning for Liquidity in Financial Institutions," *Journal of Finance*, December, 1966, pp. 649-674.

Crane, D.B., "A Stochastic Programming Model for Commercial Bank Bond Portfolios Management," *Journal of Financial and Quantitative Analysis*, June 1971.

Cohen, Kalman J., "Dynamic Balance Sheet Management: A Management Science Approach," *Journal of Bank Research*, Winter 1972, pp.

Cohen, Kalman J. and Frederick S. Hammer, "Linear Programming and Optimal Bank Asset Management. Decisions," *Journal of Finance*, May 1967, pp. 147-168.

Cohen, Kalman J. and S. Thore, "Programming Bank Portfolios Under Uncertainty," *Journal of Bank Research*, Spring 1970, pp. 43-61.

Dantzig, G.B., "Linear Programming Under Uncertainty," *Management Science*, April-July 1955, pp. 197-206.

Dantzig, G.B. and A.R. Ferguson, "The Allocation of Aircraft to Routes," *Management Science*, October, 1956, pp. 45-73.

Lane, M.N., "Sequential Decisions and Systematic Risk in Capital Budgeting," Discussion Paper, London Business School (1972).

Littlechild, S.C., "A State Preference Approach to Public Utility Pricing and Investment Under Risk," *of Economics and Management Sciences*, Spring 1972, pp. 340-345.

Fried, J., "Bank Portfolio Selection," *Journal of Financial and Quantitative Analysis*, June, 1970, pp. 203-227.

Gray, Kenneth B., "Managing the Balance Sheet: A Mathematical Approach to Decision Making." *Journal of Bank Research*, Spring, 1970, pp. 35-42.

Walkup, D.W. and R. Wets, "Stochastic Programming With Recourse," *SIAM Journal of Applied Mathematics*, September, 1967, pp. 1299-1314.

Chapter 20

TOWARD A COMPREHENSIVE FRAMEWORK FOR BANK FINANCIAL PLANNING*

By Kalman J. Cohen and David P. Rutenberg

*This article is reprinted, with permission, from *Journal of Bank Research,* Vol. 1, No. 4 (Winter, 1971), pp. 41-57.

Abstract

The current and potential activities of a bank are depicted as a linear program. The objective is to maximize the present value of after-tax net income, where the discount rates reflect management's subjective time rates of preference. Among the constraints are those imposed on 11 accounting balance sheet items and 10 financial flows in each time period of the program. Any feasible solution produces a vector of dual evaluators that can be used to price out other bank activities. The intent is to use this vector of dual evaluators on a decentralized basis to screen new projects and to implement detail (e.g., decisions on specific loans) into aggregate decisions (e.g., overall volume of loans). Given the complex regulations and tax laws that govern cross-overs between the financial flows and balance sheet accounts of a bank, evaluation by pricing out is more appropriate than simpler project evaluation techniques, such as computing the present value of net after-tax cash flows. The deterministic linear program can be used as a subroutine within a stochastic programming with recourse formulation of bank planning in the face of risk.

In a commercial bank important problems of financial planning, decision making and control frequently arise. Typical examples would include analyses of the following:

Dynamic balance sheet management (which historically but erroneously has been called "asset management"), in which aggregate bank financial plans may be made over a several-year time horizon.

The investment account, especially in connection with tax switching decisions.

Trading decisions, especially as they affect the gross long or short portfolio positions in governments, municipals and foreign exchange.

Loans, especially setting interest rates, establishing repayment schedules, determining true yields, etc.

Capital budgeting problems internal to the bank, including the acquisition of assets such as real estate and computing equipment, the opening of new branches, etc.

Equipment leases, where the bank owns equipment for use by other parties.

Profit center accounting, which attempts to measure the profitability of various organizational units in the bank.

The procedures utilized in most banks for handling the financial problems that arise in these various areas generally leave a great deal to be desired. Even within any one bank, different approaches are typically utilized to address these various financial problem areas, and the different approaches are frequently mutually inconsistent. The purpose of this paper is to present a unified framework that can be utilized to analyze all of these various types of financial problem areas in an American commercial bank.

In Section A, a comprehensive linear programming (LP) model of the various financial planning and decision areas in a bank is advocated as the starting point. The interdependence of various types of financial plans and decisions is clearly addressed by this model. For such an LP model to be operationally implementable in any bank, a suitable degree of aggregation must be utilized. The most detailed version of this LP model which can reasonably be developed should be periodically run in a bank. One reason for doing so is to permit some types of financial plans and decisions that can feasibly be centralized in a bank to be made in a near-optimal manner. A second reason for doing so is to provide information for use when making in a satisfactory manner the remaining types of financial plans and decisions which for practical reasons cannot be directly analyzed with the LP model. This indirect use of the LP framework should result in better decentralized plans and decisions than those made using more conventional techniques.

In Section B, we show how any potential activity of the bank can be represented as a decision variable of the LP model. We also derive a figure of merit that indicates the relative desirability of that activity to the bank. The implications of this framework for decentralized financial planning and decisiőn making in a bank are presented in Section C. Some procedures for introducing considerations of risk and uncertainty into the analysis are discussed in Section D; these may prove to be of special importance for long-run strategic planning in a bank. Finally, the paper is summarized in Section E.

A. The Comprehensive Linear Programming Model

From a theoretical viewpoint, it would be desirable to develop an intertemporal linear programming model stretching over a long time horizon to permit the simultaneous optimization of all financial plans and decisions in an American commercial bank. Of course, we realize that it would be impractical to make and implement all decisions in a bank on a centralized basis. The LP model for financial planning and decision making, however, provides a conceptual bench mark against which to gauge the effect of simplifications that are required when financial decisions at a fashion.

The conceptually comprehensive LP model that we envision would assume that perfect forecasts can be made of all relevant future events. There are three reasons for assuming perfect certainty. First, there is still some disagreement over the approach to take in formulating the problem of risk, and none of the approaches have adequate computational techniques for handling large-scale problems.[1] Second, the interpretation of dual evaluators under risk is still being researched, and it clearly depends on the objective function chosen. In Section C we show that dual evaluators should play a crucial role when financial decisions are made one at a time. Third, in Section D, which is focused on risk, the deterministic model of Section A is used as a subroutine to be run repeatedly under different strategies and different scenarios about states of the world. Thus this deterministic model is a necessary stepping stone for a strategic stochastic model.

The types of decision variables that would be contained in such a comprehensive, long-term linear programming model would be suitably aggregated representations of:

The amounts of various types and maturities of investment securities to be purchased.

The amounts of various types and maturities of investment securities to be sold.

The amounts of various types of loans to be made.

The amounts of various types of deposits and other liabilities that the bank should obtain.

The amounts of investments in various fixed assets (e.g., new branches) by the bank.

The amounts of equipment leases that will be written.

Decisions directly affecting the bank's capital accounts such as paying dividends, issuing new common stock or capital notes, etc.

Strategic decisions that determine the product-market posture of the bank, e.g., should it issue a bank credit card, should it establish foreign branches, etc.

Each of the above decision variables is "dated." A decision variable in one time period is clearly different from the corresponding decision variable in another time period.

The objective function to be maximized is the present value[2] of after-tax[3] net income (NI) for the bank. Since all conceivably relevant decision

---

[1] Three major and distinct approaches to linear programming problems under conditions of uncertainty have been developed: Stochastic linear programming [35], chance-constrained programming [11] and two-stage (or, more generally, multistage) programming under uncertainty [17] [36].

[2] A present value criterion, based upon appropriate sequences of reinvestment rates, is always preferable to an internal rate of return criterion. This statement is valid even for evaluating investments in bonds, where institutional practice almost inevitably has led people to think in terms of internal rate of return (which is what market yield really is).

A major problem of the internal rate of return is its implicit assumption that all cash throw-offs from a project are reinvested at whatever rate the internal rate of return happens to be. If two alternative projects have different lifetimes, it is not necessarily the case that the project with the higher internal rate of return is to be preferred to the one with the lower rate of return; much depends upon the reinvestment rates that are anticipated when the shorter-lived project terminates. Furthermore, the internal rate of return for a project is not always uniquely defined; when there is more than one change of algebraic sign in the sequence of net cash flows associated with a project, multiple internal rates of return may exist.

The present value criterion is deficient if it ignores the time pattern of financing and investment opportunities that are anticipated. This defect can be removed by the use of reinvestment rates that differ from period to period. As is clear from this paper, however, the sequence of reinvestment rates that should be employed to evaluate individual projects cannot be determined without first solving an overall linear programming problem.

For further discussion of these points, see [1], [7], [9], [21], [28], [37] and [38].

Most existing LP models for financial planning are formulated entirely in terms of cash flows, and they pay no explicit attention to the accounting definition of earnings. One of the few exceptions is Lerner and Rappaport [24] who suggest that constraints on the minimum acceptable growth in accounting earnings be incorporated in an LP model of capital budgeting in which the objective function is the present value of net after-tax cash flows. While our modeling approach is similar, we prefer to formulate the objective function as the present value of accounting net income and to incorporate in constraints the effects of cash flows on the bank. Because it is net income, rather than cash flow, that is emphasized in reports to the public, we believe that bank executives are more interested in maximizing a function of the bank's net income than a function of the bank's cash flow.

TABLE 1. Balance Sheet Categories for Each Period of the LP Model

Assets	Liabilities and Capital
Cash	Demand deposits
Short-term securities	Savings deposits
Long-term securities	Certificates of deposit
Loans	Federal Reserve and money market borrowings
Fixed assets	Accruals and other liabilities
	Capital and retained earnings

variables are included (in some appropriate degree of aggregation) in the proposed intertemporal LP model, and since all endogenous changes in cash and in capital are explicitly incorporated into the constraints of the LP model, there is no reason to discount anything other than NI. Thus, for example, there would be no reason to separately calculate the present value of net after-tax capital flows or of net after-tax cash flows, because any profitable ways of taking advantage of these flows would already be seized upon by the optimal solution to the LP model.

Some people have suggested that the objective function should be the present value of dividends paid by the bank. Our main reason for rejecting this proposal relates to the current unfortunate state of financial theory. In particular, we feel that on the basis of financial theory we can neither determine 1) the proper discount rate to apply to this stream of future dividends nor 2) the effects on the bank's stock price of changes in its dividend policy. If only we had an acceptable model indicating how the various actions of the bank (not just its dividend policy) affect the price per

share of the bank's stock in the marketplace, then the best objective function to use in the LP model would be the market value of the stock held by the bank's present owners. As we are far from possessing this degree of objective knowledge, despite energetic work in asset valuation theory, the next best objective function to maximize in the LP financial planning model is the present value of NI. Until recently, many stock analysts, stockholders and managers paid attention to net operating earnings, and many probably still do. Now that the 1969 accounting rules for after-tax net income have been generally accepted[4] it seems appropriate to use the present value of net income as the objective function of the LP model.

The discount rates used to compute the present value of NI in the objective function would represent management's subjective preference for "NI now" rather than "NI later."[5] In principle management might have different marginal rates of subjective preference for NI across various adjacent time periods. Hence, rather than arbitrarily assuming a constant subjective time rate of preference for NI, a general vector of subjective time rates of preference should be incorporated in the objective function's calculation of the present value of NI.

---

[4] In July, 1969, the Federal banking agencies adopted new regulations which direct banks, starting with annual reports of 1969 activities, to report a net Income figure that will take into account both the actually realized capital gains and losses on securities and an average of recent loan losses [23]. Opposition to net income reporting developed among both bankers [20] and security analysts [2] [3] who offered alternate proposals.

[5] Conceptually, the most plausible candidates for determining the proper discount rates in the objective function are: a) the bank's cost of capital; b) the rate at which the stock market implicitly capitalizes NI in determining the market value of the bank's stock; or c) management's subjective time rates of preference for NI.

Many economists feel that on a theoretical basis, the bank's cost of capital should be used. There is a practical drawback to doing so, however, since few economists agree on an operational procedure for determining this rate. It would be a major project to try to develop such a procedure for any specific bank. Furthermore, the theoretical appropriateness of using the bank's cost of capital as a discount rate is open to question in the context of a comprehensive mathematical programming model in which all possible sources and uses of funds are considered.

It may be operationally possible to utilize econometric techniques in conjunction with a suitable bank equity valuation model (which is unfortunately not yet available) to estimate the implicit rate at which the stock market capitalizes a bank's NI. It should be noted, however, that employing any such rate implicitly assumes acceptance of the "traditional viewpoint" (in contrast to the Miller-Modigliani viewpoint) that, within conventionally accepted limits of leverage, raising additional debt capital does not change the cost of equity. (For a well-balanced discussion of these two different viewpoints regarding the effects of leverage on the cost of capital, see [31, Ch. 3].)

Finally, if no more objective basis for determining the proper discount rates can be agreed upon, one can always fall back upon management's subjective time rates of preference for NI. To determine these in a meaningful way, some management scientists would first need to help the relevant executives acquire a good understanding of the concept of time rates of preference. It would then be desirable to get some agreement within the management group concerning the numerical values of their time rates of preference for NI. In the absence of consensus, the LP model can be rerun to determine the sensitivity of the implied optimal decisions to the choice of discount rates.

---

[3] It is not correct to assume that the model can be formulated equally well on an after-tax basis, using appropriate after-tax reinvestment rates to compute the present value of after-tax net income, or on a pre-tax basis, using reinvestment rates which are twice as large (assuming a 50% income tax rate) to compute the present value of pre-tax income. These two approaches are not mathematically equivalent because the compound interest formulas are generally non-linear, rather than linear, transformations. Hence the set of decisions which optimizes the present value of after-tax net income will generally not be the same as the set of decisions which optimizes the present value of pre-tax income.

Furthermore, the relevant tax rate is not constant across all types of income. A bank is subject to a full panoply of taxes—Federal income tax, long-term capital gains tax (prior to 1969), state and local taxes and foreign taxes for which tax credits may or may not be granted. There are also complicated interactions of various types of taxes which can and should be modeled. Thus, for example, prior to the passage of the 1969 Revenue Act, some banks obtained investment tax credits by writing equipment leases; in total, however, investment tax credits and foreign tax credits cannot be used to offset more than 50% of the amount of U.S. income tax owed. Upper bounds of this nature can readily be incorporated in an LP model, but they prove troublesome in piecemeal analysis in that already accepted projects suddenly have to be dropped when it is realized that the previously anticipated tax credits cannot in fact be utilized.

TABLE 2. Relevant Categories of Flows for Each Period of the LP Model

Category	Type of Flow	Example
1	Taxable cash income	Interest received on U.S. Government securities*
2	Non-taxable cash income	Interest received on tax-exempt municipal securities*
3	Taxable non-cash income	Interest accrued on long-term single-payment loans
4	Non-taxable non-cash income	Accretion of the discounts on securities purchased below par
5	Tax-deductible cash expense	Payments for advertising
6	Non-tax-deductible cash expense	Interest paid on borrowed funds invested in tax-exempt municipal securities
7	Tax-deductible non-cash expense	Depreciation of fixed assets
8	Non-tax-deductible non-cash expense	Amortization of the premiums on tax-exempt municipal securities purchased above par
9	Cash receipt unrelated to net income	Repayments of loan principal
10	Cash expenditure unrelated to net income	Retirements of capital notes

*These examples assume that interest received on securities is accounted for (i.e., affects net income) on a cash basis, rather than on an accrual basis.

We do not suggest that the LP model should ignore dividends paid by the bank. On the contrary, we would include among the constraints of the model relations which require the bank to follow a clearly specified dividend payout policy. Such an approach allows the model to accurately reflect the impact of future net income on the dividends paid by the bank and, in turn, on the bank's future cash and capital positions.

We shall not now attempt to specify in detail all the constraints of the LP model. They have generally been described in [12] and [14], and as relevant they will be discussed further in Section B. For now, it is sufficient to note that the LP model will contain a large number of various types of intraperiod and interperiod constraints.

When such an LP model is formulated and solved, it generates optimal decisions and plans for the bank over an extended time horizon. Immediate attention would normally be focused on the first-period decision variables, since only these decisions must be implemented right now. However, the dual evaluators of the various constraints contain information pertinent to future years. These dual evaluators allow us to evaluate the desirability of a new project without rerunning the linear program, a property on which we shall elaborate further in Sections B and C.

B. Representing the Activities of the Bank

At the end of each year the state of the bank can be summarized by its balance sheet variables (other important elements, such as executive talent, customer goodwill, a bank credit card, etc., which could be depicted as additional relevant state variables will be omitted only for expository

simplicity). Let us conveniently suppose that the bank's balance sheet can be categorized into the 11 components shown in Table 1. We feel that this represents the bare minimum of detail that would need to be incorporated into any LP model implementing the approach being advocated in this paper. Additional disaggregation of the balance sheet variables, including the imposition of a more refined maturity structure than that implicit in Table 1, would probably be desirable in practice, at the expense, of course, of generating larger LP models. There are no conceptual limits to how much disaggregation can be accommodated, but at some point the additional computational costs imposed by the larger LP models resulting from further disaggregation would no longer be justified by the additional benefits stemming from more detailed models.[6] For expository convenience, we shall also suppose that each time period in the LP model is one year long (in practice, of course, the length of each time period is a parameter to be determined by the model builder, and it may be desirable to divide the total planning horizon into time periods of increasing length).

Any potential activity of the bank may, if undertaken, have some direct impact during one or more years on various ones of the 11 stock (i.e., balance sheet) categories shown in Table 1. As a result of the bank undertaking an activity, some flows will occur, and these flows may in

6 Choosing an appropriate level of detail remains an art. In industrial practice a linear program—once it runs and yields reasonable results—is usually enlarged and elaborated to detail particular activities. In academic theory it would seem proper to start with a highly detailed model, which is the bench mark against which to evaluate different degrees of aggregation; this assumes that the detailed LP can be debugged and run and that the cost of gathering the detailed data is negligible. In future years the aggregation theory of Ijiri [22] may provide helpful insight.

general have a different pattern in each year. There are ten relevant categories of different flow variables which may possibly be affected by any activity in any particular year, as shown in Table 2. The first eight of these flow variables will directly affect net income during the year, whereas the last two of these flow variables will directly affect the cash position of the bank without affecting its net income account. Although the degree of detail included in Table 2 may appear excessive, all ten of these flow categories are required in order correctly to portray the various ways in which any activity may affect the various balance sheet categories and the net income account of the bank.

For each year of the LP model, there will be one equality constraint corresponding to each balance sheet and flow variable shown in Tables 1 and 2. The year t constraint corresponding to a balance sheet variable is in effect an intertemporal linkage defining how that balance sheet account at the end of year t is determined by the values of relevant balance sheet accounts at the end of year t-1 and by the relevant flow variables during year t. The year t constraint corresponding to a flow variable defines the total amount of that type of flow during year t in terms of the direct impacts on that type of flow of all activities undertaken by the bank during year t and earlier years.

The general nature of these 21 equality constraints that (with suitable modification) are imposed on each year of the LP model is schematically illustrated in Table 3. A few of the bank's possible activities in years 1 and 2 are shown in Table 3, in order to partially illustrate how these activities generate relevant flows; in particular, only their impact on flows of taxable cash income and tax-deductible non-cash expenses are explicitly shown. In the constraint matrix portrayed in Table 3, the symbol a''_{ti} denotes the algebraic value of the flow category f ($f = 1,2, \ldots, 10$ as defined in Table 2) during year s directly resulting from undertaking activity i during year t. CB^0 is the cash balance at the end of year 0 (i.e., at the beginning of the planning horizon). b_x^{fs} is the algebraic value of the total flow of category f during year s resulting from exogenous activities (i.e., from activities of the bank other than those represented as decision variables in the LP model). The income tax rate applicable to the bank's pre-tax income is 1-τ, so that the bank's after-tax net income will be τ times its pre-tax income.

TABLE 3. Partial Illustration of the Constraint Matrix of the LP Model

Constraints	Activity 1 in year 1	Activity 2 in year 1	Activity 3 in year 1	Total taxable cash income in year 1	Total tax-deductible non-cash expense in year 1	Total after-tax net income in year 1	Cash balance at end of year 1	Activity 1 in year 2	Activity 2 in year 2	Activity 3 in year 2	Total taxable cash income in year 2	Total tax-deductible non-cash expense in year 2	Total after-tax net income in year 2	Cash balance at end of year 2	Right-hand side vector
Cash balance at end of year 1						1	−1								= −CB°
Cash balance at end of year 2							1						1	−1	= 0
Taxable cash income in year 1	a_{11}^{11}	a_{21}^{11}	a_{31}^{11}	−1											= −b_x^{11}
Taxable cash income in year 2	a_{11}^{12}	a_{21}^{12}	a_{31}^{12}					a_{12}^{12}	a_{22}^{12}	a_{32}^{12}	−1				= −b_x^{12}
Tax-deductible non-cash expense in year 1	a_{11}^{71}	a_{21}^{71}	a_{31}^{71}		−1										= −b_x^{71}
Tax-deductible non-cash expense in year 2	a_{11}^{72}	a_{21}^{72}	a_{31}^{72}					a_{12}^{72}	a_{22}^{72}	a_{32}^{72}		−1			= −b^{72}
After-tax Net income in year 1				τ	−τ	−1									= 0
After-tax Net income in year 2											τ	−τ	−1		= 0

As the LP model which is partially depicted in Table 3 has been formulated, most activities do not directly affect the bank's cash balance sheet account, even though they will generally give rise to various types of cash receipts or disbursements. The direct impacts of all activities on relevant cash flows will be accumulated into the corresponding types of total cash flow variables for each year. Each total cash flow variable in a year will then be appropriately entered into the intertemporal link defining the cash balance at the end of that year, as partially illustrated in Table 3. Similarly, most activities do not directly affect the bank's capital and retained earnings balance sheet account, even though they will generally have some direct impact on various components of net income. As with the cash flows, the direct impacts of all activities on relevant net income flows will be accumulated into corresponding total net-income-related flow variables for each year. In turn, these total net-income-related flow variables will be appropriately entered into the intertemporal link defining the balance sheet capital and retained earnings account at the end of the year. A few activities will, however, be modeled as having direct impacts on selected balance sheet accounts; e.g., as indicated below, the activity of opening a new branch will have a direct impact on the fixed assets account in its initial year to reflect the increase in fixed assets corresponding to expenditures on fixtures and equipment for the branch.

With the detailed categorization of relevant flows shown in Table 2, the LP model can accurately portray the exact timing of cash outflows for income tax payments. For this purpose, it will be convenient to introduce separate definitional variables to represent accrued taxes owed and taxes paid. Accrued taxes owed could be considered as part of the accruals and other liabilities balance sheet account, so that as accrued taxes owed build up through profitable operations, the accruals and other liabilities account would increase. Periodically, however, taxes are paid by the bank, thus reducing both the cash account and the accruals and other liabilities account on the balance sheet. Constraints can be introduced into the LP model reflecting the manner in which estimated income tax payments will be made. Appropriate lags can be incorporated to reflect the fact that a bank is not penalized for underestimating its current Federal income tax if it bases its payments of estimated income tax during any year on its actual net income during the previous year.

In order to provide a more concrete illustration of the somewhat abstract symbolism contained in Table 3, let us consider the manner in which the LP model would represent the activity of opening a new branch (assuming that the bank will lease, rather than own, the land and building). In the first year fixed assets will increase by the expenditures for fixtures and equipment in the branch. Flows of tax-deductible cash expenses are incurred for rent, promotional publicity, etc.; there is also a flow of cash expenditures to the vendor of the fixtures and equipment which has no direct effect on net income during the first year.

In the second year the new branch begins operation. The demand for new loans increases. Fixed assets begin to be depreciated, generating a flow of tax-deductible non-cash expense. Demand deposits and savings deposits increase. Tax-deductible cash expenses are incurred for rent, local advertising, wages and salaries, and some other branch operating costs. Similar effects occur in subsequent years. We must forecast each of these direct effects on stocks and flows, predicting their magnitude in each year of the new branch's lifetime. The indirect effects stemming from the new branch (e.g., how the new deposits will be utilized and whether loan demand will be met) need not be predicted; the linear program calculates them.

Each possible activity of the bank corresponds to a vector in the constraint matrix of the linear program. We have already mentioned in our discussion of Tables 1, 2 and 3 that 21 equality constraints will be imposed on each year of the LP model. In addition, for each year a number of intraperiod financial constraints will be imposed to reflect management policies and the economic and institutional realities of the marketplace (see [14] for a more complete discussion of these intraperiod constraints). Thus the amounts of new loans made by the bank cannot exceed the demand for new loans by the bank's customers on a category-by-category basis, e.g., with respect to loans for financing consumer durables, residential mortgages, industrial equipment or seasonal inventory accumulations by business firms. Management policy may dictate that the total loans outstanding may not exceed some stated percentage of total deposits. Pledging requirements may have been imposed on certain deposits, such as the requirement that at least 110% of a state government's deposits be collateralized by securities issued by that state or by the Federal government. Float considerations and legal reserves necessitate certain minimum cash requirements. These and other relevant constraints must be modeled.

Bank activities are represented by column vectors in the constraint matrix. Coefficients in such a column depict the impact of an activity on the various interperiod and intraperiod constraints that are imposed on the bank. In addition, each activity could conceivably also have an entry in the objective function of the LP model to represent the direct impact of that activity on the present value of the bank's after-tax net income. An alternative and preferable way of formulating the LP model has been adopted in Table 3, where additional equations (in the bottom portion of the constraint matrix) define the bank's after-tax net income, one equation for each year. Non-zero coefficients appear in this row only under the accumulation variables defining the totals of the eight net-income-related flows. In this way we can readily model the effects of tax credits, losses carried forward and other discontinuities in after-tax NI that could not otherwise be accurately represented. The accumulation variables of the after-tax NI equations are then the only variables with non-zero entries in the objective function.

Any potential project that the bank may undertake or any financial decision which the bank may make can be represented as an activity in the LP model and, hence, as a column in the constraint matrix of the LP model. Since we have formulated the model so that all real bank activities have zero coefficients in the objective function, the desirability of an activity depends entirely upon the impact that it has on the various constraints (i.e., the non-zero entries in the vector corresponding to that activity) and upon the opportunity costs associated with those constraints (i.e, their dual evaluators). In other words, a measure of the desirability of any bank activity is the figure of merit obtained by multiplying each non-zero coefficient in the vector representing that activity in the constraint matrix by the dual evaluator on the corresponding constraint, summing these products and then multiplying this sum by —1. Stated more simply, a figure of merit for any activity is the negative of the scalar product of the vector representing that activity in the constraint matrix and the vector of dual evaluators of the constraint matrix.

This method for determining a figure of merit for any bank activity is quite obvious when one thinks about linear programming by the revised simplex method [33]. Dual evaluators from one feasible solution are used to price out all the non-basic variables in the hope of finding one which prices out positively. When such a variable is increased, other basic (positive) variables have to adjust because the bank has limited resources. The adjustment ends when one of the basic variables is decreased to zero and, therefore, is con-

sidered non-basic. Note that it was the vector of dual evaluators that identified the non-basic variable to increase, but a knowledge of the existing basic variables was required to identify the variable that would drop from the basis. Note also that the dual variables remained unchanged while the basic variable was being increased (they changed only when the basis changed) so if the incoming variable was upper bounded to remain moderately small, the dual evaluators would have been left unchanged.

C. Implications for Decentralized Decision Making in a Bank

The linear programming model described in Sections A and B can be used directly to analyze those bank plans and decisions which are formulated on a centralized basis and which are represented with sufficient disaggregation as decision variables in the LP model. Some of the financial problem areas mentioned in the introduction (such as dynamic balance sheet management and capital budgeting problems internal to the bank) have these characteristics. Here the LP model will be immediately useful as a tool for the centralized decision makers responsible for these areas of bank planning.

For other financial problems in a bank it will be better to use the linear program indirectly. While some decisions could be made on a centralized basis, they should not be represented in sufficiently disaggregated form in the LP model. An example of this would be the detailed management of the bank's investment securities, in which specific issues of securities must be purchased and sold (rather than just broad types and general maturity classes of securities being purchased and sold, as the LP model would be formulated). Other financial decisions are made on a decentralized basis, and so the LP model is not directly applicable. For example, the LP model might be used to centrally plan the aggregate volume of loans of broad types which the bank will make, but actual loans must be made to specific customers by the bank's account officers. For a variety of practical reasons, the account officers must have authority to make loan commitments to their customers on a decentralized basis without referring each specific proposed loan to bank headquarters for centralized approval.

We feel that this same LP model can be of considerable benefit for these two types of decisions if properly utilized in an indirect manner. We shall now describe a procedure by which problem areas can be approached on a decentralized or a piecemeal basis and still lead to approximately the same decisions that would be reached if these problem areas were analyzed directly in the LP model. For expository convenience, we shall now use the word "project" to refer to any type of decision that is being contemplated in the bank which for practical reasons cannot be directly incorporated as an activity in the LP model formulated in Sections A and B (e.g., making a specific loan to a particular customer, executing a tax swap involving a specific pair of investment securities, etc.).

When a decentralized decision maker in the bank is considering a new project, he should first identify the various stock and flow variables delineated in Tables 1 and 2 that will be directly affected by the acceptance of that project during each year of its projected lifetime. Having defined the "relevant dimensions" of the project, the decentralized decision maker should then forecast the manner in which acceptance of the project will alter the yearly values of those dimensions for the bank. Each of these directly affected dimensions corresponds to a constraint in the LP model described in Sections A and B. Thus the decentralized decision maker in effect is constructing the column in the constraint matrix that would correspond to the project if it were represented as a decision variable of the LP model (see Table 3).

The dual evaluators from the most recent optimal solution to the LP model that has been obtained by the bank headquarters can then be used to determine a figure of merit for the project in the manner described in Section B. This will be the negative of the scalar product of the vector of the project (as constructed by the decision maker) and the vector of dual evaluators (which the bank headquarters provides). In effect, computing this figure of merit for a project, which can be done decentrally on the basis of information routinely supplied by headquarters, corresponds to pricing out a proposed project. A project with a positive figure of merit would appear in the optimal solution of the LP model if it were represented as a decision variable in that model. It should be clear that the figure of merit computed for the project indicates the change in the present value of the bank's net income that will result from acceptance of this proposed project. Proposed projects whose figures of merit computed in this manner are negative should generally be regarded as undesirable projects. Such projects will probably remain undesirable after other activities have been accepted; this corresponds to the linear programming result that activities which

price out as negative on one iteration will likely continue to do so after basis changes. Hence the use of this figure of merit as a decision criterion permits many decisions to be made on a decentralized basis, while still resulting in the same outcomes as if they had been made a centralized basis. The practical advantages of such a procedure should be self-evident; the disadvantage is that we cannot drop projects from the basis.

The decentralized decision maker would be instructed to accept all independent projects having positive figures of merit. If a set of mutually exclusive projects is being considered by him (e.g., alternative ways of packaging a loan deal to a corporate customer), he should accept that project from the set with the highest positive figure of merit. If such accepted projects are relatively small, we need not worry about changes in the dual evaluators; this corresponds to linear programming with upper-bounded variables. We can proceed to accept projects as ranked by their figures of merit until the accumulation of these projects becomes substantial. At this time the bank's headquarters staff group should rerun the LP model to obtain a new set of dual evaluators for subsequent use. If a periodic review by headquarters of the accepted projects with high figures of merit uncovers the fact that not all of them really should have been accepted because of some constraint that had not been included in the LP model (e.g., lack of available executive talent), a relevant restriction can be added as a constraint in the LP model so that later figures of merit can reflect this oversight; this corresponds to adding constraints to a partially solved linear program.

For the most part, decentralized decision makers have a great deal more responsibility and control over the column of the constraint matrix that they develop to represent a project (as an activity in the LP model) than they do over the vector of dual evaluators. In that an individual's performance evaluation should be congruent with this comprehensive LP framework, decentralized decision makers should be held more accountable for errors that they make in forecasting the impact of accepting a project on the future relevant changes in stock or flow variables describing the bank (e.g., the future loans and demand deposits that a particular customer relationship will generate for the bank) than for errors that were made in forecasting the future dual evaluators (e.g., the future loan interest rates and marginal worths of demand deposits). In essence, we are suggesting that dual evaluators arising from the LP model be utilized in developing decentralized profit-center accounting statements in a bank.[7]

Several articles have been published discussing the general relevance of the decomposition algorithm of linear programming to decentralized organizations (see, e.g., [6], [19], [27] and [40]). These have generally been concerned with how the flow of information between a headquarters group and decentralized divisions can be organized to permit the headquarters group to obtain an optimal solution to the overall LP model. There are two reasons why decomposition may be advantageous. First, the headquarters group under this formulation need not possess detailed knowledge of the technological relations relevant to each decentralized division. Second, the sizes of the multiple linear programs that are solved under this formulation are considerably smaller than the size of the overall linear program. In practice, however, one serious drawback to using the decomposition algorithm as a guide to the design of decentralized organizations is that it would require a great deal of "wheel spinning" behavior before actions are taken. Under decomposition, each decentralized division must solve its own LP submodel many times, each time using a specific set of transfer prices which it has been given by the headquarters group. When it has solved its own LP submodel, the division is not permitted to take any actions immediately. Instead, the division must merely report some properties of the solution to the headquarters group and await further instructions. This process may take place many times before the divisions are permitted to implement any solutions (or combination of solutions) that they have derived for their submodels. When the decomposition algorithm is applied in this manner in a changing world, the mathematical proof that an optimal solution to the overall LP model will be reached in this manner no longer is valid.[8]

The suggestions that we are making in this section concerning how the LP model sketched in Sections A and B can be used to improve upon the process by which decentralized decisions are made in a bank do not primarily concern themselves with the use of the decomposition algo-

rithm. We have not addressed the question of how the suitably aggregated LP model of Sections A and B will be solved by the bank headquarters group, although the decomposition algorithm may in fact turn out to be a useful approach (but for computational reasons, rather than for reasons of decentralized information flow). It should be noted that this LP model, which we assume that the headquarters staff group will be able to solve, is not at all the same as the "master" linear program which headquarters is supposed to solve under the decomposition algorithm.

As dual evaluators are to be used to guide decentralized decisions, it would be reassuring to know the ranges over which the dual evaluators hold without change. It is possible to find this region by parametric programming, but when many coefficients are being varied simultaneously the detail becomes overwhelming. A more conservative approach is to search for unconstrained sources and uses of resources (such as Eurodollars were until reserve requirements were imposed). These unconstrained activities establish bounds on the dual evaluators. If a project prices out attractively using these unconstrained sources of resources, then it most certainly should be accepted, since the same resources may be available even more cheaply within the bank.

When the dual evaluators are sensitive to the projects being accepted, it will be necessary to issue provisional project quotas. In implementing a decentralized decision making system with quotas, we should ponder the French national planning experience (summarized in [25, Ch. 7]). Several conceptual methods have been tried. In fact the traditional decomposition has been speeded up by the headquarters issuing both guideline quotas and dual evaluators. While quotas function as preemptive goals [10], they also permit the wisdom and experience of the planner to initiate the computer model at an attractive starting solution. Quotas also have an effect upon behavior [34], for they become levels

---

[7] For an academic discussion of how dual evaluators (often called "shadow prices") may be used in the development of decentralized profit-center accounting statements, see [16], [26], [27] and [40]. For a practical discussion based on a decade of LP experience in the oil industry, see Aronofsky [5]. Our suggestion that the dual evaluators on constraints of the suitably aggregated LP model be used as guidelines for decentralized decision making in banks is fully consistent with the proposals made by Whinston [40, pp. 426-427] for industrial firms. He has urged that when a cost-accounting system is developed for use in managerial decision making, it should not only include direct monetary costs but also indirect opportunity costs (which are measured by the dual evaluators of an LP model). When this is done, the transfer prices and costs which are developed as guidelines for the decentralized departments will reflect the benefits and penalties that will be incurred when particular activities are undertaken.

[8] The difference between the assumptions of the mathematical proof guaranteeing that the decomposition algorithm will result in an optimal solution to the overall LP model in a finite number of steps and the actual conditions which would prevail were this procedure attempted in the real world in decentralized organizations has been noted by Hass [19, p. B328]. He has indicated that in a real-time application, the decomposition algorithm may be an on-going process that never terminates. The underlying LP problem would be continually modified as changes occur in technology, market conditions, resource limitations or policies. Hence the divisional plans generated many iterations ago need not coincide with those which would be generated under currently existing conditions. Hass is more optimistic than we are, however, in concluding that these problems are of little practical importance. Hass states [19, p. B328]: "If the aforementioned changes are not extreme at any point, the algorithm should still track the optimal transfer prices and, therefore, the optimal solution quite well."

of aspiration to which decentralized managers will target their activities. These observations are quite congruent with our model; they merely warn that decentralized decision makers should be issued guidelines with care and have their performance monitored with vigilance. Adequate vectors of dual evaluators and a central LP in which to evaluate large projects should help attain these ends.

Our discussion of decentralized decision making has thus far implicitly assumed that the direct impact of any project on the various relevant constraints of the LP model will be small enough so that the set of dual evaluators is unchanged by the acceptance of the project. Some projects will be so large, however, that this assumption will be violated. Let us define as "major" any project of such a magnitude that its acceptance will change the set of dual evaluators of the LP model. The acceptance of a major project should ideally be made by the headquarters group with the aid of the LP model. When a major project is accepted, its presence in the basis of the linear program not only will change the dual evaluators, but it will consequently also change the figures of merit already computed for smaller projects by various decentralized decision makers in the bank. Although it may often be impractical to review previously made decisions on various projects, to the extent feasible the decentralized decision makers should recompute figures of merit (using the new set of dual evaluators) for all recently evaluated projects for which irrevocable decisions have not yet been made.

Although a major project may price out to have a large positive figure of merit, if this project is indivisible (so that it must either be entirely accepted or entirely rejected), it will not necessarily be optimal for the bank to accept it. One way of determining whether such an indivisible project should be undertaken is to compare the resulting values of the objective function from two different solutions to the LP model. The first solution is that obtained when the decision variable representing this indivisible project is constrained to equal unity (i.e., the project will be entirely accepted), and the second solution is that obtained when the decision variable representing the project is constrained to equal zero (i.e., the project will be entirely rejected). It is then optimal to accept or to reject this indivisible project according to whether the value of the objective function is higher for the first or the second solution.

The reason why the incremental approach inherent in computing the figure of merit cannot always be used with an indivisible major project is that several activities will probably be dropped from the basis as the activity representing the indivisible major project is increased from zero to unity. Since this project originally priced out with a high figure of merit, the objective function of the LP model will initially improve as small fractions of the project are accepted. But as the corresponding activity is forced towards unity, the objective function may pass through its maximum and start to decrease. If there are several major and indivisible projects to be analyzed, each and every combination of projects should be evaluated. To do this systematically (it rapidly becomes tedious), one could follow Weingartner's [37] recommendation and use mixed integer programming.

When a divisible major project is under consideration, we can predict what the dual evaluators will become if it is accepted. The linear program does not need to be rerun so long as we can predict which previously accepted project will now be eliminated and, hence, dropped from the basis. The mathematics of pivot matrices [33, p. 364] can then be applied. Let us depict the project under consideration as the column vector $A_{\cdot s}$. By knowing which project will be eliminated from the basis, we know which element A_{rs} of this vector will bind first, and hence necessitate a pivot on A_{rs}. Let us calculate a constant for the pivot; let k equal the reciprocal of A_{rs} multiplied by its corresponding dual evaluator π_r. Multiply the vector $A_{\cdot s}$ by this constant k, and add their product to the old dual evaluators. The new dual evaluator for row r is, however, merely k.

As already indicated at the beginning of this section, some types of financial problem areas in a bank will be analyzed on a centralized basis with the aid of the LP model described in Sections A and B. A staff group at the bank's headquarters will be responsible for initially formulating the LP model, updating and improving it whenever possible and periodically running it to provide a variety of useful information for both centralized and decentralized decision makers in the bank. Each decentralized decision maker in the bank will not only receive information concerning the latest set of dual evaluators, but he will also receive minimal targets that he should strive to attain for particular types of activities and maximum bounds for some activities which he should not exceed without permission from the bank's headquarters.

The use of large LP models of the type described here is most advanced in the petroleum industry. Large linear programs detailing operations of single or double refineries were put into regular use with the introduction of large computers in 1960. For over a decade managers have used dual evaluators as a routine tool for decentralized decision making, particularly attractive because there is no need to negotiate continuously over transfer prices—it is simpler to accept the dual evaluators. Some managers who planned refineries in 1960 have since moved to more responsible positions, and most appear to still find LP models useful—so much so that Aronofsky [5] (then at Mobil Oil) believed they used overly detailed models.

D. Long-Run Strategy in the Face of Risk

The LP model we have been discussing in the preceding sections is deterministic and of a given bank strategy. This "tunnel vision" is somewhat limiting in that a long-range planning model ought to be concerned with planning for flexibility —with the impact of this year's actions on the decision space available decades into the future.

Perhaps an example will help to clarify the point. Suppose two major projects will have identical effects on the bank's flows and balance sheet during the next thirty years. But the contract of the second project contains a clause giving the bank power to liquidate this project in the tenth year at a reasonable (though not attractive) return. The LP model would be indifferent between the two projects, yet we know that an option is a valuable right. Somehow we would like a framework sufficiently comprehensive to include the valuation of options, risk/return tradeoffs and planning with an eye to flexibility.

The fact that the problem of decision making under risk and uncertainty is complicated is attested by the persistence of simple rules of thumb which seem clearly obsolete. As Weingartner [39, p. B594] observed, "The Payback Period has been dismissed as meaningless and worthless by most writers on capital budgeting at the same time that businessmen continue to utilize this concept." He then proceeded to explore payback as a concern for liquidity, as a measure that is robust and as the rate at which a project's uncertainty is expected to be resolved. Weingartner did not argue that payback itself be used, for more sophisticated measures exist, but rather that these considerations should not be ignored. In this section we shall not use payback, but rather we will attempt to model appropriate considerations of flexibility in the face of uncertainty.

The preceding sections of this paper have discussed an approach to bank financial planning which is currently implementable with existing

computer programs. New developments in decision making under risk are not yet commercially applicable, but we would be remiss if we failed to describe what will likely become available in the next decade.

Let us formulate the problem of planning for flexibility as a decision tree [29]. The bank faces a number of environmental scenarios such as those depicted by Booz, Allen and Hamilton [4]; its management can pursue several fundamental strategies. We shall use our linear program to evaluate each node of the decision tree, modifying the LP model for the environmental scenario and managerial strategy of the particular node. Thus experience with the deterministic model would be used, not discarded, while planning in the face of risk.

A bank is a complicated institution, so our decision tree will also be complicated. The state of the bank cannot be described in one variable, so our decision tree will have to encapsule several variables. In that a decision tree is a simple dynamic program, let us use dynamic programming language to better handle these several variables.

We enter each time period (and it would appear sensible to formulate the model so that the lengths of time periods increase as we move further into the future) with the bank in a particular state. During the period we will run the bank as best we can considering how the state of the bank at the end of the period will constrain activity in the next period. Since we do not know which of several environmental scenarios will occur as we move to the next period, we shall have to see how activities would be constrained for each relevant scenario.

This dynamic program is not easy to solve. Let us use backward induction. Assume that decisions have been made for all periods but the last, so that we know the state of the bank at the beginning of the last period. Then solve a one-period linear program for the last period. The dual evaluators of this LP model reveal the value of each element of the state of the bank. Thus when we go to solve for the next-to-last period's decisions, we will know what values to assign to the slack variables that describe the end-of-period state of the bank. Before getting into computational details, let us note that the problem of achieving congruence between dual variables and assumed state of the bank becomes harder as the number of state variables increases.

Computation will become burdensome unless we describe the state of the bank in as few variables as possible. There are many possible descriptors of the state of a bank. We shall focus on attributes that cannot easily be sold—they represent decisions that are not reversible except at a penalty. For example, one element of the state of a bank is the number of branches; the decision to build branches is not cheaply reversible because bank buildings (like churches) have few alternate uses. Another example of the state of a bank is whether or not it issues credit cards; the expense of persuading stores to honor a new credit card cannot be recouped if the bank later decides to abandon its credit-card strategy. On the other hand, the detailed composition of the bank's portfolio of investment securities, being easily reversible, does not deserve many state variables. It is impossible to provide *a priori* bounds on the number of state variables, for what is involved is a trade-off between computational time and accuracy of modeling.

The problem we face is a multi-stage stochastic program with recourse [36]. So long as the one-period linear programs are feasible for any state vectors, the objective function of the entire problem is convex.

In the illustrative formulations below (which could be extended to more periods), x is the vector that describes the bank's operations during the first period, y describes operations during the second period and z during the third period. The constraint matrix appropriate to each of the three periods is A^1, A^2 and A^3. T is a matrix (usually -1) that transfers the state of the bank from one period to the next. If certain elements of the state of the bank are stochastic, T will be stochastic as indicated by T_ξ or T_ζ. The actual environmental scenario cannot be forecast with certainty. Hence b^2_ξ and b^3_ζ are stochastic to indicate probability distributions, e.g., over the willingness of the public to make deposits, as are c^2_ξ and c^3_ζ to indicate probability distributions over the amount of net income to be received.

A two-period problem may be written as:

$$\underset{x}{\text{Maximize}} \left\{ c^1 x + E_\xi \left[\underset{y}{\text{Max}} (c^2_\xi y) \right] \right\}$$

$$
\begin{aligned}
\text{subject to} \quad & A^1 x && = b^1 \\
& T^{12}_\xi x + && A^2 y && = b^2_\xi \\
& x, y \geqq 0
\end{aligned}
$$

A three-period problem may be written as:

$$\underset{x}{\text{Maximize}} \left\{ c^1 x + \left\{ E_\xi \left[\underset{y}{\text{Max}} (c^2_\xi y) \right. \right. \right.$$

$$\left. \left. \left. + E_{\zeta|\xi} \left(\underset{z}{\text{Max}} (c^3_\zeta z) \right) \right] \right\} \right\}$$

$$
\begin{aligned}
\text{subject to} \quad & A^1 x && && = b^1 \\
& T^{12}_\xi x + && A^2 y && = b^2_\xi \\
& && T^{23}_\zeta y + A^3 z && = b^3_\zeta \\
& x, y, z \geqq 0
\end{aligned}
$$

Let us discuss the solution procedure for the three-stage problem. The vector x is specified, as is a separate y for each possible value that the ξ stochastic variables may take. We now solve the third-period problem for an optimal z, except that there will be a separate third-period problem for each possible environmental scenario (there are as many possible scenarios as there are elements in the joint probability distribution of ξ and ζ). As part of the optimal solution to third-period z problems we obtain vectors of dual evaluators. We must now prepare for the y second-period decisions. For each value of the first-to-second period ξ stochastic variables, we take the ζ weighted average of the dual evaluators associated with the third-period state-of-the-bank constraints.

The state of the bank at the end of the second period is unknown, but it is to be priced at the weighted average of the dual evaluators from the third-period z decisions. We go ahead and solve the second-period problem (with input x assumed and using the ζ weighted average dual evaluators to value the output). A separate problem is to be solved for each environmental scenario that ξ can represent. It is likely that these calculated y decisions yield period-ending states of the bank different from those assumed in calculating z, so we must return to repeat the third-period calculations. Then we again repeat the second-stage y calculations, and cycle back and forth between second- and third-period calculations until the state of the bank is congruent between these two periods. (Details of such a two-period calculation are explained in [18] and illustrated for a bank dynamic sheet management model in [15].) Now we turn to the first-stage decisions.

The dual evaluators associated with state-of-the-bank constraints at the start of the second period must be averaged using probabilities of each ξ first-to-second-period environmental scenario. These now enter the objective function of the first-period problem, for they represent the mean value of the state of the bank at the end of the first period. The calculated optimal state of the bank at the end of the first period will probably differ from the value that was assumed in calculating the second- and third-period decisions. So we select a new vector of the state of the bank at the end of the first period, a new set of values for the end of the second period and then return to reoptimizing the third period. The solution to the deterministic model of Sections A and B is extremely valuable as a computational starting point around which perturbations will be explored. The initially assumed values of x and all y are vitally important to speed computation. Two areas remain a black art where computational experience and theory are underdeveloped. First, what degree of interperiod congruence should be achieved between later periods before earlier periods can be evaluated? Second, when there is incongruence between the assumed state of the bank (used to calculate dual evaluators) and the economical state of the bank (using these weighted evaluators), what new state of the bank should be assumed to achieve fastest convergence?

In Section C of this paper, we stressed the importance of knowing dual evaluators which could be used to develop guidelines for decentralized decision makers. Although in a stochastic world the next environmental scenario is unknown, we should use similar decentralized decision rules based on the weighted average of the dual evaluators. Should it prove to be feasible to reformulate the aggregative LP model sketched in Sections A and B as a multi-stage LP model under uncertainty, there would be no conceptual difficulties in using this more complex model as the basis for the analysis of financial decisions described in Section C of this paper. The major difference is that when analyzing projects whose activity vectors in the constraint matrix are not directly affected by the states of the world, the vector of dual evaluators of various constraints would be replaced by the mathematical expectation of the vector of dual evaluators. When the activity vectors of projects do depend on the states of the world, there appears to be no alternative but to evaluate all relevant branches using the appropriate dual evaluators for each branch.

Stochastic programming with recourse is not the only approach we could have taken to decision making in the face of risk. One alternative approach would be sensitivity analysis or parametric programming as formalized by Tintner [35]. This provides a mapping from a probability distribution on the coefficients of the LP model to a distribution of the value of the objective function. This is particularly helpful in selecting coefficients to be firmed up before making a decision that will be costly to revise.[9] However, insofar as planning for flexibility is conceivable in the strategic planning process, it cannot be incorporated in Tintner's approach.

Another approach, chance-constrained programming,[10] becomes useful once certain critical years have been identified. It then becomes sensible to specify probabilities of being unable to meet loan demand (or even probabilities of going bankrupt). At such times we are interested in the left-tail areas of stochastic variables, not the entire distributions, and we wish to select decisions that will have the highest expected profit subject to probabilistic constraints.

E. Summary

This paper has developed an approach to bank financial planning which starts from the premise that financial planning and decision making should ideally be conducted in a portfolio (i.e., a comprehensive, system-wide) context. In centralized dynamic balance sheet management this philosophy can be directly implemented by means of a suitable intertemporal linear programming model. Where it is preferable to make decentralized decisions, one can still utilize a conceptually correct financial portfolio framework to derive a procedure by which piecemeal financial decisions should be made. This approach can feasibly be applied to most types of decision situations commonly found in commercial banks.

Sections A and B of this paper outlined a suitably aggregated long-term linear programming model designed to permit the simultaneous optimization of all financial plans and decisions in a bank. Unfortunately, it is not feasible to utilize such a model as a tool for directly making all possible financial decisions in a bank. One reason is that some decisions which can in fact be made on a centralized basis are represented in the LP model in too highly aggregated a form to permit definite conclusions to be drawn concerning their desirability on the basis of the LP model's direct solution. A second reason is that many decisions in a bank must in fact be made on a decentralized basis, and it would be impractical for the LP model to be run each time a decentralized decision is made. We showed in Section C, however,

---

9 Instead of mapping the exact probability distribution [35], it is appreciably quicker and simpler to use Monte Carlo techniques and repeatedly run the problem as a simulation in order to construct an approximate mapping.
   This method of appraising project risk in a piecemeal fashion is consistent with the Cohen-Elton [13] portfolio approach which carefully separates the time and the risk discounts. During the proposed simulation runs, each cash flow is discounted for time, but not for risk. The discounting for risk is implicitly done later, when one decides on the most appropriate risk-return combination, i.e., when a specific point on the efficient frontier is selected. (For further discussion of why the risk and time discounts should be separated, see [31, Chs. 5, 6] and [32].)

10 Charnes and Cooper [11] and those who have followed them such as Raike [30] and Byrne and Kortanek [8], have been prolific in developing different approaches to chance-constrained programming. For this problem the most relevant is their P-type, which focuses attention on the left-tail area:

$$\text{Maximize} \quad cx$$
$$\text{such that} \quad \text{Probability}(Ax \leq b) \geq \alpha$$
$$x \geq 0$$

that the LP model can be indirectly utilized to improve the decision analyses in both of these types of situations. The paper concluded by discussing in Section D some procedures for incorporating considerations of risk and uncertainty into the financial planning framework. ☐

REFERENCES

1. Alchian, A. A., "The Rate of Interest, Fisher's Rate of Return over Cost, and Keynes' Internal Rate of Return," *American Economic Review*, Vol. 26 (December, 1955), pp. 938-943.

2. Anonymous, "Bank Reporting: The Full Story?" *Bank Stock Quarterly*, M. A. Schapiro and Company, Inc., New York, March, 1969, pp. 18-24.

3. Anonymous, "Closer to Full Disclosure," *Bank Stock Quarterly*, M. A. Schapiro and Company, Inc., New York, September, 1969, pp. 1-10.

4. Anonymous, "The Challenge Ahead for Banking: A Study of the Commercial Banking System in 1980," Booz, Allen & Hamilton, Inc., New York, 1970.

5. Aronofsky, J. S., "Linear Programming Models for Business Systems," *Chemical Engineering Progress*, Vol. 64, No. 4 (April, 1968), pp. 87-92.

6. Baumol, William J. and Tibor Fabian, "Decomposition, Pricing for Decentralization and External Economies," *Management Science*, Vol. 11, No. 1 (September, 1964), pp. 1-32.

7. Bierman, Harold, Jr., and Seymour Smidt, "Capital Budgeting and the Problem of Reinvesting Cash Proceeds," *Journal of Business*, Vol. 30 (October, 1957), pp. 276-279.

8. Byrne, Robert F., A. Charnes, W. W. Cooper and K. O. Kortanek, "A Chance-Constrained Approach to Capital Budgeting with Portfolio-Type Payback and Liquidity Constraints," *Journal of Financial and Quantitative Analysis*, Vol. 2, No. 4 (December, 1967), pp. 339-364.

9. Carleton, Willard T., "Linear Programming and Capital Budgeting Models: A New Interpretation," *Journal of Finance*, Vol. 24, No. 5 (December, 1969), pp. 825-833.

10. Charnes, A., R. W. Clower and K. O. Kortanek, "Effective Control through Coherent Decentralization with Preemptive Goals," *Econometrica*, Vol. 35, No. 2 (April, 1967), pp. 294-320.

11. Charnes, A. and W. W. Cooper, "Chance-Constrained Programming," *Management Science*, Vol. 6, No. 1 (October, 1959), pp. 73-79.

12. Cohen, Kalman J., "Improving the Capital Adequacy Formula," *Journal of Bank Research*, Vol. 1, No. 1 (Spring, 1970), pp. 13-16.

13. Cohen, Kalman J. and Edwin J. Elton, "Inter-Temporal Portfolio Analysis Based on Simulation of Joint Returns," *Management Science*, Vol. 14, No. 1 (September, 1967), pp. 5-18.

14. Cohen, Kalman J. and Frederick S. Hammer, "Linear Programming and Optimal Bank Asset Management Decisions," *Journal of Finance*, Vol. 22, No. 2 (May, 1967), pp 147-165.

15. Cohen, Kalman J. and Sten Thore, "Programming Bank Portfolios Under Uncertainty," *Journal of Bank Research*, Vol. 1, No. 1 (Spring, 1970), pp. 42-61.

16. Colantoni, Claude S., Rene P. Manes and Andrew Whinston, "Programming, Profit Rates and Pricing Decisions," *The Accounting Review*, Vol. 44, No. 3 (July, 1969), pp. 467-481.

17. Dantzig, G. B., "Linear Programming under Uncertainty," *Management Science*, Vol. 1, Nos. 3-4, (April-July, 1955), pp. 197-206.

18. Gartska, Stanley and David P. Rutenberg, "Efficient Computation in Stochastic Programs with Recourse," *Operations Research*, forthcoming.

19. Hass, Jerome E., "Transfer Pricing in a Decentralized Firm," *Management Science*, Vol. 14, No. 6 (February, 1968), pp. B310-B331.

20. Heinemann, H. Erich, "Banks Test New Role in Finance," *New York Times*, Sunday, August 24, 1969, Section 3, pp. 1 and 8.

21. Hirshleifer, Jack, "On the Theory of Optimal Investment," *Journal of Political Economy*, Vol. 66, No. 4 (August, 1958), pp. 329-352.

22. Ijiri, Yuji, "Fundamental Queries in the Aggregation Theory," *Journal of the American Statistical Association*, forthcoming (in December, 1971).

23. Larkin, Eugene L., Jr., "Accounting for the Realities of Bank Portfolio Management," Haskins and Sells, New York, February, 1970.

24. Lerner, Eugene M. and Alfred Rappaport, "Limit DCF in Capital Budgeting," *Harvard Business Review*, Vol. 46, No. 5 (September-October, 1968), pp. 133-139.

25. Malinvaud, Edmond and M. O. L. Bacharach, *Activity Analysis in the Theory of Growth and Planning*, St. Martins, New York, 1967.

26. Manes, Rene P., "Birch Paper Company Revisited: An Exercise in Transfer Pricing," *The Accounting Review*, Vol. 45, No. 3 (July, 1970), pp. 565-572.

27. Onsi, Mohamed, "A Transfer Pricing System Based on Opportunity Cost," *The Accounting Review*, Vol. 45, No. 3 (July, 1970), pp. 535-543.

28. Quirin, G. David, *The Capital Expenditure Decision*, Richard D. Irwin, Inc., Homewood, Illinois, 1967, Chapters 3 and 9.

29. Raiffa, Howard, *Decision Analysis: Introductory Lectures on Choice Under Uncertainty*, Addison-Wesley, Reading, Massachusetts, 1968.

30. Raike, William M., "Dissection Methods for Solutions in Chance-Constrained Programming Problems with Discrete Distributions," *Management Science*, Vol. 16, No. 11 (July, 1970), pp. 708-715.

31. Robichek, Alexander A. and S. C. Myers, *Optimal Financing Decisions*, Prentice-Hall, Inc., Englewood Cliffs, New Jersey, 1965.

32. Robichek, Alexander A. and S. C. Myers, "Valuation of the Firm: Effects of Uncertainty in a Market Context," *Journal of Finance*, Vol. 21, No. 2 (May, 1966), pp. 215-228.

33. Simonnard, Michael, *Linear Programming*, Prentice-Hall, Inc., Englewood Cliffs, New Jersey, 1966.

34. Stedry, Andrew, *Budget Control and Cost Behavior*, Prentice-Hall, Inc., Englewood Cliffs, New Jersey, 1960.

35. Tintner, Gerhart, "A Note on Stochastic Linear Programming," *Econometrica*, Vol. 28, No. 2 (April, 1960), pp. 490-495.

36. Walkup, David W. and R. J-B. Wets, "Stochastic Programs with Recourse," *SIAM Journal of Applied Mathematics*, Vol. 15, No. 5 (September, 1967), pp. 1299-1314.

37. Weingartner, H. Martin, *Mathematical Programming and the Analysis of Capital Budgeting Problems*, Prentice-Hall, Inc., Englewood Cliffs, New Jersey, 1963.

38. Weingartner, H. Martin, "The Excess Present Value Index —A Theoretical Basis and Critique," *Journal of Accounting Research*, Vol. 1 (Autumn, 1963), pp. 213-224.

39. Weingartner, H. Martin, "Some New Views on the Payback Period and Capital Budgeting Decisions," *Management Science*, Vol. 15, No. 12 (August, 1969), pp. B594-B607.

40. Whinston, Andrew, "Price Guides in Decentralized Organizations," in *New Perspectives in Organization Research*, edited by W. W. Cooper *et al.*, John Wiley and Sons, New York, 1964, pp. 405-448.

Part V

THE BOND PORTFOLIO

Most commercial banks allocate a substantial portion of their resources to bond investment. We examined this allocation decision in the discussions in Part IV on balance sheet management. Part V examines the security holdings of commercial banks in more detail.

Banks invest in securities to provide an income stream with risk levels substantially below those of their loan portfolios. Government bonds, short-term treasury notes, and municipal issues are the principal holdings, partly for tax advantages, but also because the composition of bank investment accounts is regulated. Most of the regulation limiting bank investment grew out of the Great Depression and the collapse of numerous banks. Since World War II, loans have constituted an increasing percentage of total bank assets, while securities have declined as a percentage of assets. Despite this fact, the investment accounts of U.S. banks had grown to $190 billion by 1974. Fastest growing among bank-held securities has been the municipal bond, with its high yield and significant income tax advantages.

Because municipals are somewhat less marketable and represent a greater credit risk than other government bonds or treasury bills, bank portfolios have become less liquid and more risky as municipal holdings have increased. In 1974 municipals represented over 50% of all holdings in bank investment accounts. Since bank portfolios provide some protection against bank failure, regulatory authorities have expressed concern over the decreasing liquidity of investment accounts. However, because of government safeguards against bank failure, this concern has not gained widespread support.

Because municipals are the most risky element in bank investment accounts, bank management continually evaluates the quality and characteristics of municipal holdings. Bond rating services are a principal source of bond evaluation information, but they do not rate all bonds. As a result, understanding the key rating variables and their interrelationships is necessary to evaluate unrated issues. Additionally, bank management may wish to evaluate the validity of the ratings. In Chapter 21, "Statistical Classification of Municipal Bonds," Joseph J. Horton, Jr. points out that only 20-25% of all municipals are rated. A substantial portion of a bank's portfolio may, therefore, be unrated. Horton's article examines several attempts to determine key rating variables. If variables could be isolated and their interrelationships analyzed using statistical techniques, then banks could easily rate issues being considered for purchase as well as their current holdings of unrated bonds.

Modern investment managers have shifted their attention away from individual bonds toward a broader view of the entire investment portfolio. This shift to a portfolio approach has led to new applications of management science techniques to the problems of managing the bond portfolio.

Several factors affect the performance of securities in bank investment accounts. Among them are economic conditions, tax rates, deposit flows, coupon levels, and maturities. These are combinations of internal and external factors. Internally, such variables as the bank's tax rate, deposit flow, and loan demand are important considerations. Externally, changing interest rates, risk levels, and marketability impact on the performance of portfolios and a desirable portfolio strategy.

Much of the research in bond portfolio management has dealt with maturity structure characteristics. There is a clear trade-off between liquidity and long-term yield which must be carefully evaluated in developing a long-range bond investment strategy. Two maturity structures have been widely recommended and used by commercial banks. The first might be referred to as a "dumbbell" strategy; it consists of a relatively equal distribution between short and long maturity securities, with no intermediate maturity securities. The short-term securities provide liquidity, while the long-term securities provide high return. The second commonly employed strategy is a "laddered" maturity structure, in which distribution of maturity over time is relatively even.

Stephen P. Bradley and Dwight B. Crane have examined the maturity structure of bond portfolios, and two of their relevant articles are presented in Part V. They employ two techniques to develop an "optimal" strategy. First, Chapter 22, "Management of Commercial Bank Government Security Portfolios: An Optimization Approach Under Uncertainty," evaluates the application of a dynamic programming model to portfolio decisions whether to buy, hold, or sell. The resulting "optimal" strategy leads to a maturity structure that differs from the traditional structures described above. In this structure, maturities are laddered at both ends, but there are few intermediate securities. This result does not automatically answer the day-to-day questions of the portfolio manager, however, since it is difficult to decide how to replace long-term issues to maintain the dumbbell structure, while also selecting sufficient short maturities to maintain some laddering.

In Chapter 23, "Simulation of Bond Portfolio Strategies: Laddered vs. Barbell Maturity Structure," Bradley and Crane examine the portfolio problem using Monte Carlo simulation techniques. The conclusions are similar to those derived in Chapter 22. The results in Chapter 23 point more toward a barbell strategy for banks that want to actively manage their portfolios. Although interest income is somewhat more erratic, the increased liquidity is often desirable. Together, the two articles by Bradley and Crane provide an extensive look at critical issues in determining a long-range bond portfolio management strategy.

Most banks hold substantial amounts of U.S. government securities in their investment accounts. Banks are the largest traders of U.S. government bonds. This trading is carried out through various dealers on an "over the counter" basis; for this reason, prices may vary from dealer to dealer. Often such price differentials may appear abnormal or irrational, but they frequently provide an opportunity for a profitable maneuver known as "arbitrage." Through this maneuver, dealers and traders attempt to sell short securities that are relatively overpriced and to buy securities that are relatively underpriced. By going long in one security and short in another, traders can potentially net a significant profit in large transactions. Robert L. Kramer's article in Chapter 24, "Arbitrage in U.S. Government Bonds: A Management Science Approach," provides a framework for evaluating arbitrage opportunities. Generally, traders have established arbitrage transactions on the basis of intuition or past experience. Kramer's model offers a more systematic approach to the decisions involved in arbitrage. It has been successfully implemented in a large commercial bank that is a major dealer in U.S. government securities. Kramer describes the benefits that this dealer-bank has obtained from use of the arbitrage model.

We examine in Part V numerous aspects of managing the bond portfolio. Management science techniques can contribute significantly to effective investment management by systematizing decision making and structuring decision variables. While some management science techniques are aimed at directly improving investment decisions, others are more useful in structuring the critical variables which should be analyzed as a basis for decision making. Effective management of the bond portfolio is important for potential profitability and stability of banks.

Chapter 21

STATISTICAL CLASSIFICATION OF MUNICIPAL BONDS*

By Joseph J. Horton, Jr.

*This article is reprinted, with permission, from *Journal of Bank Research,* Vol. 1, No. 3 (Autumn, 1970), pp. 29-40.

Commercial banks are perhaps the largest investors in municipal bonds, yet a major problem exists in attempting to determine the quality of individual issues. Although 92,000 governmental units issue municipal bonds, the rating services rate the issues of only 20,000 [6], and thus investors have no authoritative standard of quality for the remaining 72,000 issuers of debt. Banks hold about 40% of the outstanding state and local securities [5]. The quality of these securities is of interest to bank regulatory agencies because of the large investment in them by banks. The bank supervisory agencies classify municipal bonds in a bank's portfolio as being in one of two groups, those that are of suitable quality for bank investment and those that are not. Bonds with a rating in one of the four highest ranks given by *Moody's* or *Standard and Poors* rating services, or that are of comparable quality, are considered to be suitable for banks to include in their portfolios. Bank examiners and security analysts from the supervisory agencies are responsible for determining if unrated bonds meet this standard. Banks investing in unrated municipals must also make the determination. The large number of unrated bonds and lack of data on many of them make comprehensive evaluation of municipal bonds in which banks have invested or might wish to invest a particularly difficult problem. The use of ratings by investors and regulators as a guide to quality is taken as given in this paper; the question of whether the ratings accurately reflect or are intended to reflect only risk of default is not considered. The purpose of this study is limited to developing a means of assigning bond issues to one of these two groups and to improving our knowledge of objective variables that influence ratings.

The FDIC recently supported a statistical study that attempted to reproduce *Moody's* ratings utilizing relatively accessible data [1]. A brief summary of the findings will be useful as background and as an explanation of the reason for this additional study. Although state bonds are often included in the municipal category, they were excluded from the earlier research and from this study. *Moody's* was selected because it is used as a standard for bonds that it rates and because data are relatively available for these bonds. The variables which Carleton and Lerner considered were 1) school district, 2) debt/assessed value, 3) debt/population, 4) log population, 5) log debt and 6) average tax collection rate. They used a sample of 491 bonds to estimate equations that would classify bonds into the grades used by *Moody's*. A hold-out sample of 200 bonds was used to evaluate the equations. Discriminant analysis was used to estimate the equations. This method insures, subject to certain assumptions, that the equations will do the best possible job of classifying the bonds correctly, given the variables and the sample of bonds used. On the hold-out sample the equations performed quite well in classifying the bonds into five groups.

Carleton and Lerner were less successful in separating bonds into two groups—those rated above Ba and those rated Ba and below. There were only six bonds rated Ba and lower in their hold-out sample. Using five rating groups, two of these were correctly classified. One was rated Baa, two were rated A and one was rated Aa; three A bonds and 10 Baa bonds were incorrectly classified Ba. Using only two groups, two of the Ba bonds were correctly classified but 20 of the investment quality bonds were classified as Ba. Even though this means that overall 88% were correctly rated, only ⅓ of the very small sample of Ba bonds was correctly rated. When knowledge of the relative occurrence of each rating in the total population was used, none of the Ba or lower bonds were correctly rated and from two to four of the better than Ba bonds were rated Ba depending upon the number of discriminant functions and classifications used.

It is this problem of dividing bonds into two groups that is of primary importance to the bank supervisory agencies. Carleton and Lerner's success, on the other hand, was greatest in classifying bonds into five groups. Three ways of improving upon their success for the two group case were considered. First, the number and proportion of

TABLE I. Table of Means and Standard Deviations of Variables.

Variables	Noninvestment Quality Group		Investment Quality Group	
	Mean	Std. Deviation	Mean	Std. Deviation
Debt/Assessed Value	0.42064	0.526292	0.131018	0.167314
Debt/Population	714.215	1333.56	187.454	139.117
Log Population	3.99267	0.515212	4.47107	0.58003
Log Debt	6.52707	0.331503	6.61477	0.425879
Tax Collection Rate	94.10800	4.40965	94.91070	7.08259
Debt/Capacity	189.06600	714.89100	33.3311	34.6227
Percent Increase in Income of the District	1.43453	0.287168	1.34491	0.282595
Percent Increase per capita Income of the District	1.22480	0.11277	1.23513	0.29789
School District	0.5333	0.4994	0.6000	0.4898
Water-Sewer Purposes	0.2133	0.6984	0.0533	0.2237
Poorer States	0.7467	0.4350	0.2667	0.4422
Better States	0.0400	0.1960	0.4400	0.4964
Per capita Income of the District	2.4855	0.8194	2.6814	1.1870
Total Income of the District	1523.5300	3648.65	1735.8400	3246.95
State per capita Income	2.8819	0.3913	2.9129	0.4010

bonds rated Ba and lower were increased. There were only 12 bonds of noninvestment quality in their sample of 491 bonds and only six in their hold-out sample of 200. The second change was to consider additional variables. These two changes resulted in an equation that performed better in classifying the bonds into two groups. The third change in method was to use only data which was available to *Moody's* when the bonds in the sample were rated. This seems to have had only a minor effect on the results.

The results obtained should be of general interest in that they shed light on which variables influence the classification of municipal bonds by analysts. The immediate problem of bond rating is, of course, important to bank supervisory agencies and to banks themselves because both attempt to determine if particular unrated bonds are suitable for bank investment. Some attention will be given to the methodology of the research and to the variables that seem to influence ratings as well as to the specific output of the research. This output is an equation that relates the rating of each bond to certain characteristics of the district issuing the bond. It assigns a quality index number to the bonds. In general, the higher the index the higher the quality of the bond.

The Model

Carleton and Lerner used discriminant analysis in their study. However, in the two group case a linear probability function produces an identical ordering of the bonds that are rated [3]. A linear probability function is a regression equation estimated using a dummy dependent variable that takes on the values zero and one. The predicted values of the dependent variable are not, however, constrained to produce values of zero and one. The predicted values are not interpreted in the sense of a probability that the bond is in a given classification. Only the correspondence between the ordering produced by discriminant analysis and regression analysis is important for this case; the problem of heteroskedasticity common to the use of a dummy dependent variable is not a matter of concern for this application. Regression analysis was, therefore, used in this case. A number of equations using different explanatory variables were estimated, and some are listed in Table V.

The best of these equations is equation V. It requires data on only five variables: Debt, assessed value, population, average tax collection rate and the state in which the district issuing the bond is located. These are discussed more fully

271

below. The simplicity of the equation is a computational advantage when it is to be used for small numbers of bonds that do not warrant a computer run. It could, for example, be used by examiners in the field. A number of other variables were considered; these are listed in Table I and various of their statistical characteristics are provided in Tables I through IV. Those not included in equation V failed to improve the predictive ability of the equation when they were considered in addition to or in place of the five variables that were included in equation V.

The equations were estimated on the basis of a sample of 150 general obligation municipal bonds that had been rated by *Moody's*. State bonds and housing authority bonds were excluded because of the special characteristics of these bonds and because virtually all such issues are rated by the rating services. They do not constitute a problem for banks or the supervisory agencies. The sample was stratified to include 75 bonds of investment quality and 75 of noninvestment quality. The bonds were selected by use of a table of random numbers to insure a random sample. A hold-out sample of 50 bonds, 25 of investment quality and 25 of non-investment quality as rated by *Moody's*, was used to evaluate the equations.

Equation V relates the ratings of bond issues to variables that measure the economic characteristics of the issuing districts. The expected influence of each of the five variables will be considered. The population of a community is likely to influence the rating of its bonds in a number of ways. Larger communities tend to have more specialized and experienced financial staff and management, and a larger community is likely to have greater economic diversity than a small one and thus is able to better withstand fluctuations in economic conditions. Size in itself may allow a larger municipality to withstand financial difficulties which a smaller community could not. There is also the consideration that the larger community may be more able to depend upon being bailed out of financial difficulties by higher levels of government.

The ratio of a community's debt to its assessed value was used to measure its ability to carry debt. A better measure of the income available for taxation would be preferable, however, often none is available. Thus no correction was made for differences in assessed value relative to market value; only the debt of the district itself was considered. The debt of districts that overlap the community in question was not considered. Often,

TABLE II. Table of Tests of Significance of Relationship Between Variables and Investment Quality of Bonds.

Variable	R^2	t	Chi Square	Level of Significance
School District	.0065	0.983	1.4607	Not Significant at 10%
Debt/Assessed Value	.1209	4.5156		Significant at 1%
Debt/Population	.0700	3.3063		Significant at 1%
Log Population	.1598	5.3293		Significant at 1%
Log Debt	.01304	1.4099		Not Significant at 10%
Tax Collection Rate	.0046	0.8280		Not Significant at 10%
Water-Sewer	.0554	2.9785	7.4773	Significant at 1%
Poorer States	.2304	6.6667	34.5660	Significant at 1%
Better States	.2193	6.5042	32.8950	Significant at 1%
Debt/Capacity	.0231	1.9253		Significant at 10%
% Income Increase of District	.0242	1.9185		Significant at 10%
% per capita Income Increase of District	.0005	0.2793		Not Significant at 10%
Per capita income of District	.0091	1.1422		Not Significant at 10%
Total Income of District	.0009	0.3744		Not Significant at 10%
State per capita Income	.0015	0.4827		Not Significant at 10%

R^2 is the coefficient of determination between each variable and the dependent variable. The dependent variable takes on the value 1 if the bond in question is of investment quality and the value 0 if it is not investment quality. The t column shows the value of t associated with the R^2 for each variable. Chi square is the value of chi square associated with the contingency matrix of each dummy variable and the dependent variable.

communities allow unpaid taxes to accumulate without instituting action to force payment; in some cases taxpayers go for years without paying local property taxes. Thus, the ratio of taxes actually collected to those charged is a measure of the community's ability and willingness to support its debt. The tax collection rate is expressed as a percentage. In order to obtain a more representative figure the average of the rates for the most recent available year and the year prior to it was used. If this resulted in an unreasonably low rate in the light of past rates so that additional payments on the most recent year's taxes were to be expected, the rates were lagged one year. The expectation was that the higher the tax collection rate, the greater is the community's willingness to fulfill its financial obligations, and hence the better is the rating received by its bonds.

The bonds of municipalities located in the Southeast tend to receive lower ratings than those of other areas that are similar in terms of the other variables used in this study. To some extent this may be a marketability factor that reflects the preferences of bond buyers. This variable may also be a proxy for complex economic, social, historical and demographic factors not included among the variables tested. This group of states includes Alabama, Arkansas, Florida, Georgia, Louisiana, Mississippi, North Carolina, South Carolina and Tennessee. Minnesota and cities and school districts in New Jersey are included in this group because of limitations on taxing and assessing powers. Villages, towns and other designations of communities that are limited in their taxing powers are included in the term "city." These two states were included in this group even though the cause of the lower ratings received by their communities differs from those of the other states in the group. In discussions with bond analysts these two states were mentioned as being like the Southern states in having some characteristics which lowered their ratings; in these two cases specific legal restrictions rather than more general factors were given as a cause for the generally lower ratings received by the communities. The variety of factors mentioned for the Southeast was too great for individual testing given available data. Suggestions ranged from a history of higher rates of default in the 1930s in this region to prejudice of bond rating analysts most of whom live in the Northeast. Maine, Vermont, New Hampshire, Massachusetts, Rhode Island, Connecticut, New York, Pennsylvania, Wisconsin, Michigan, Ohio, Illinois, Indiana and (except for cities and school districts) New Jersey constitute a second group. They are designated

TABLE III. Table of Actual and Expected Occurrence of Dummy Variables (Contingency Matrices)

	School District	
	1	0
Noninvestment Quality	39(42)	36(33)
Investment Quality	45(42)	30(33)

	Water-Sewer Purposes	
Noninvestment Quality	16(10)	59(65)
Investment Quality	4(10)	71(65)

	Better States	
Noninvestment Quality	3(18)	72(57)
Investment Quality	33(18)	42(57)

	Poor States	
Noninvestment Quality	56(38)	19(37)
Investment Quality	20(38)	55(37)

The 1 column indicates the number of observations in which the indicated variable occurred. The 0 column indicates the number in which it did not occur. The number in parentheses are the numbers of occurrences (1 column) and nonoccurrences (0 column) which would be expected if there were no relation between the quality of bonds and the variable.

the "better group," as bonds issued by communities located in those states tend to have higher ratings. This reflects economic and social factors as well as a long history of financial responsibility. The use of these two groups of municipalities implicitly defines a third group consisting of those located in all other states.

Equation V was the most successful predictor of bond ratings although there is relatively little difference in predictive ability and statistical characteristics among the five equations. Nine other equations that exhibited less satisfactory performance were estimated but are not described here. The five are listed in Table V. In a sense, the basic equation is equation I to which additional variables are added to form equations II through V. It may be noted that no equation, including variables other than those used in these five equations, had as good a predictive performance as these equations. The rather small improvement in predictive ability as a result of adding variables to equation I suggests that the variables included in it are the more important ones for determination of the investment quality of municipal bonds.

It is, therefore, rather surprising to find that equation I contains no financial variables. The only data it uses are the population of the municipality issuing the bond and the state (New

TABLE IV. Analysis of Variance Test of Relationship between Variables and Investment Quality of Bonds.

Variable	Mean Square (Between Samples)	Mean Square (Within Samples)	F Ratio	Probability F of this large by Chance
School District	.2400	.2481	.9673	.3290
Debt/Assessed Value	3.1456	.1454	20.3535	.0000
Debt/Population	10,039,900.0000	911,894.0000	11.0100	.0010
Log Population	7.6524	.3444	22.2193	.0000
Log Debt	.2884	.1476	1.9541	.1600
Tax Collection Rate	24.0800	35.2688	.6828	.4150
Water-Sewer	.9600	.1106	8.6775	.0040
Poorer States	8.6400	.1950	44.3179	.0000
Better States	6.0000	.1443	41.5730	.0000
Debt/Capacity	909,500.0000	259,595.0000	3.5035	.0600
% Income Increase of District	.3012	.0823	3.6614	.0550
% Per Capita Income Increase of District	.0040	.0514	.0779	.7720
State Per Capita Income	.1133	.1585	.7148	.4040
Per Capita Income of District	1.4392	1.0543	1.3652	.2430
Total Income of District	1,669,400.0000	12,088,300.0000	0.1381	.7100

Jersey municipalities being divided into two "states") in which the municipality is located. Both state and population are proxies for financial variables as discussed above. Therefore, the success of this equation may, to some degree, be attributed to these hidden financial factors which are highly correlated with location and population. From the point of view of its practical application the simplicity of this equation, given its generally good predictive results on the hold-out sample of 50 bonds, is a virtue. The required information is available for almost all municipalities and bank examiners could use it with great ease. Indeed a statistical clerk could classify most bonds with only a glance at the data. Ninety-three per cent of the noninvestment quality bonds and 65% of the investment quality bonds in the sample of 150 are correctly classified by this equation. Of course, the sample used to estimate the parameters of the equation would more nearly fit the "predictions" of the equation than would another sample. That these results are not merely artifacts of the particular sample chosen is indicated by its performance on the hold-out sample. Using the same cut-off point 88% of the noninvestment quality bonds and 60% of the investment quality bonds in the hold-out sample were correctly classified.

Equation II requires, in addition to the data called for by equation I, knowledge of whether the bond was issued for water or sewer purposes. Water and sewer districts are highly correlated with low bond quality. It was, therefore, believed that they might be an important variable for use in the equation. The lower rating of bonds of municipalities located in the poor states is not attributable to a disproportionate number of water and sewer bonds from them. Indeed, they have proportionately fewer such bonds. The regression coefficient of the water-sewer variables has a very low t value. The value of the t statistic can not be used to indicate the significance level of the coefficient. However, larger values of t are, nonetheless, preferable to smaller ones and the t statistic is here used as a heuristic screening device.

Equation III adds to equation I the debt/assessed value variable. This is a financial variable that receives frequent mention in the literature as an important determinant of bond quality. It is to some degree a measure of the ability of the municipality to support its debt. It is highly correlated with bond quality. However, when considered in addition to the variables of equation I, its regression coefficient has a very low t value. This additional variable reduces the level of significance of the correlation coefficient although raising the correlation coefficient itself only slightly. Since there is no consistent increase in the predictive power of the equation, the addition of this

TABLE V. Table of Estimated Equations.

Variable		I	II	III	IV	V
Debt/	A			-0.14551	-0.12790	-0.18281
Assessed	B			0.08643	0.08733	0.08820
Value	C			-0.12120	-0.10654	-.015228
Log	A	0.24634	0.21483	0.21068	0.18828	0.20462
Population	B	0.05622	0.05966	0.05975	0.06213	0.05938
	C	0.29485	0.25713	0.25217	0.22536	0.24491
Tax	A					0.01019
Collection	B					0.00564
Rate	C					0.12055
Water-	A		-0.16248		0.13771	
Sewer	B		0.10655		0.10747	
Purposes	C		-0.11046		-0.09362	
Poorer	A	-0.24821	-0.28565	-0.24163	-0.27416	-0.22253
States	B	0.08125	0.08453	0.08084	0.08456	0.08091
	C	-0.24812	-0.28565	-0.24163	-0.27415	-0.22252
Better	A	0.34374	-0.29623	0.31957	0.28222	0.33602
States	B	0.09199	0.09674	0.09254	0.09683	0.09227
	C	0.29635	0.25539	0.27551	0.24331	0.28969
Intercept		-0.50314	-0.31764	-0.30939	-0.17564	-0.25060
Adjusted R^2		.37398	.37963	.38177	.38452	.39134
F, Degrees of		30.13020	23.38400	23.59026	19.28391	19.82237
Freedom		3 & 146	4 & 145	4 & 145	5 & 144	5 & 144

A is the regression coefficient; B is the standard error of the regression coefficient; C is the beta weight.

TABLE VI. Maximum Correct Classification (Cut Off Determined on Basis of the Sample of 150)*

	Original Sample of 150			Hold Out Sample of 50		
Equation	Percent of Noninvestment Quality Bonds Correct	Percent of Investment Quality Bonds Correct	Percent of Total Correct	Percent of Noninvestment Quality Bonds Correct	Percent of Investment Quality Bonds Correct	Percent of Total Correct
I	91	72	82	88	68	78
II	93	71	82	92	60	76
III	91	72	82	88	72	80
IV	92	71	82	88	68	78
V	92	75	84	88	72	80
VI	74	53	64	88	52	70

*In cases in which more than one cut-off point would result in the same percent of total correct, the point chosen was the one with the larger percent of non-investment quality bonds rated correctly. Equation VI represents the best results obtained using Carleton and Lerner's equations and is included here for comparison with the other equations.

variable alone is not warranted. On balance, neither it nor equation II is superior to equation I as a predictive or screening device and equation I had the advantage of extreme simplicity.

Equation IV contains both variables of equations II and III added to equation I. The significance of the correlation coefficient declines further and its value increases slightly. There is no increase in predictive value as a result of the additional variables.

The other equations using combinations of the debt/assessed value, water-sewer and tax collection rate variables, and the variables of equation I, failed to improve the predictive ability or statistical properties of the equation except equation V. Equation V includes debt/assessed value

275

and the tax collection rate variables. The coefficient of correlation is increased although its significance is less than for equation I. The significance is still well above the 1% level. This equation has the best prediction record of any tried and there is a priori reason for inclusion of the two financial variables. The debt/assessed value variable has been considered above. The tax collection rate alone is not a good guide to the quality of the bond offered but when considered with other factors is of some importance as indicated by the improved predictive value of this equation. There are probably relatively few cases in which it would be a deciding factor; hence its relatively small weight in equation V is in accord with expectations.

As a result of the new variables used and the higher proportion of noninvestment quality bonds included in the sample, equation V did a better job of classifying bonds into two groups than did any of Carleton and Lerner's. This is shown in tables VI and VII. Using the original sample of 150 bonds, it correctly classified 75% of the investment quality bonds and 92% of the noninvestment quality bonds. This was using a cut-off point that maximized the total number of bonds correctly classified. On the hold-out sample of 50 bonds, 72% of the investment quality bonds and 88% of the noninvestment quality bonds were correctly classified. An attractive feature of the index is that any cut-off point that one desires may be used. A cut-off point that should, on the average, correctly classify 90% of the noninvestment quality bonds was tried. On the original sample of 150 bonds, 67% of the investment quality bonds and 93% of the noninvestment quality bonds were correctly classified. The corresponding percentages for the hold-out sample

are 72% and 88%. The close nature of the decision for the Ba bonds that were incorrectly classified by our equation is indicated by the fact that all of them were judged to be of investment quality by *Standard and Poors. Standard and Poors'* ratings are higher than *Moody's* for about 20% of the municipal bonds rated by both and lower for 10% [2].

Suppose the equation were applied to bonds like those rated by *Moody's*. What sort of results could be expected? A "typical" sample of 1,000 general obligation municipal bonds rated by *Moody's* would contain about 980 bonds rated above Ba and 20 rated Ba or lower. If our equation were applied to the 1,000 bonds with a cut-off to insure, on the average, correct classification of 90% of the lower than Baa bonds, the group above the cut-off point would contain about 653 bonds rated above Ba and two rated Ba or lower. The other group would contain about 327 bonds rated above Ba and 18 rated Ba or below. If the population of bonds with which the FDIC is concerned were like *Moody's*, the equation could screen out about ⅔ of them (655) as being of investment quality with an error rate of only $\frac{3}{10}$ of 1% (2 incorrectly classified).

We do not, however, know the proportion of noninvestment quality bonds in the population of unrated bonds. The error rate in the group screened out as being of investment quality depends on the proportion as shown in the above example. Thus, it is impossible to tell what the error rate would be if the equation were applied to them. It is, nonetheless, clear that the equation tends to assign higher numbers to investment quality bonds and lower ones to noninvestment quality bonds. This was verified by using the equation to assign an index to 71 North Carolina

TABLE VII. 90% Noninvestment Quality Bonds Correctly Classified*

	Original Sample of 150			Hold Out Sample of 50		
Equation	Percent of Noninvestment Quality Bonds Correct	Percent of Investment Quality Bonds Correct	Percent of Total Correct	Percent of Noninvestment Quality Bonds Correct	Percent of Investment Quality Bonds Correct	Percent of Total Correct
I	93	65	79	88	60	74
II	93	67	80	92	60	76
III	93	64	79	88	56	72
IV	93	65	79	88	60	74
V	93	67	80	88	72	80
VI	91	29	60	88	52	70

*Cut-off point selected, on the basis of the sample of 150, to correctly classify 90% of the noninvestment quality bonds. Equation VI represents the best results obtained using Carleton and Lerner's equations and is included here for comparison with the other equations.

bonds. It performed better at this than any of the other equations, including Carleton and Lerner's, that were tried. Thirty-five of the bonds had been classified as investment quality bonds and 36 as noninvestment quality bonds by the FDIC Securities Unit. The 13 bonds with the highest rating by our equation were all bonds that had been classified as investment quality bonds. The 11 with the lowest rating by the equation had been classified as noninvestment quality bonds. Of the 28 bonds with the highest scores according to the equation, 24 had been classified as investment quality bonds and only four had been considered of noninvestment quality. Of the bottom 28 bonds as rated by the equation, 24 had been classified noninvestment quality and only four were investment quality bonds. The quality index scores of the bonds that had been rated investment quality by our Securities Unit were lower than would have been expected on the basis of the scores achieved by bonds rated by *Moody's* as being of investment quality. Analysis of the two groups of bonds suggests that our Securities Unit gave much less weight to the fact that the bonds are from a Southern state and somewhat less weight to the population variable (or to the complex of variables that these two elements represent) than *Moody's* does. This result is in accord with the view that *Moody's* includes a significant marketability factor in its ratings that is generally absent in the FDIC's evaluation of bonds. In any event, larger numbers were assigned to investment quality bonds and smaller ones to noninvestment quality bonds by the equation.

Other Variables

It was hypothesized that the state variable primarily reflected income or income related factors. Moreover, it was expected that income and rate of increase in income should be important in the determination of bond quality. Several measures of income and its rate of change were, therefore, investigated. None was adequate as a substitute for or as a supplement to the state variable. The state per capita incomes used were the 1966 Department of Commerce estimates. The total income of the districts and their per capita incomes were based on *Sales Management's* effective buying income that is comparable to disposable personal income. Estimates were made by weighting counties and parts of counties that made up districts on the basis of their population. This data was directly available for districts that were counties or cities listed in *Sales Management*. The rate of growth of per capita income is the percentage increase in the last five

years. The percentage increase in total income in the last five years was also used. It had been expected that higher levels of income and more rapid rates of increase would tend to result in higher bond ratings. None of these variables improved the predictive power of the equation and all had very low *t* values.

The school district variable takes on the value of one if the district issuing a bond is a school district and a value of zero otherwise. It was found that this variable is not significantly related to the rating of investment or noninvestment quality received by the municipal bonds included in our sample. It may be that the greater relationship found by Carleton and Lerner is a result of the characteristics of their sample which apparently contained a number of bonds for New Jersey school districts.

Log debt and debt/population were not used for the reasons cited by Carleton and Lerner. Moreover, they were less significantly related to bond quality than log population and debt/assessed value especially when the other variables of equation V were used.

A more sophisticated measure than debt/assessed value of the debt burden of the district issuing a bond seemed desirable. Mitchell's debt capacity index was used [4]. It weights income more heavily than population as income is the more important determinant of ability to support debt. See Mitchell [4] for further discussion of the index and references as to the appropriateness of this weighting. His index is:

$$C = \frac{D/Y}{Y/P}$$

where:

C = debt capacity index
D = debt outstanding
Y = personal income
P = population

Sales Management's estimate of effective buying income was used here as the measure of personal income. The data is, therefore, different from that which Mitchell used in constructing the index and, of course, prediction of bond ratings was not the original purpose of the index. Nonetheless, it is rather disappointing that this more sophisticated measure of capacity to support debt is less highly correlated with bond quality than is the debt/assessed value or debt/ population ratio. It also has less explanatory power as a variable in any of the multivariate equations tested.

Summary and Conclusions

The purpose of this study was to improve our knowledge of the objective variables that have an important influence on bond quality. Its primary output is an equation that provides an index of the quality of municipal general obligation bonds. By using an appropriate cut-off point on this index bonds may be classified into one group that contains predominantly bonds of suitable investment quality for banks and another group most of which are not of bank investment quality. The method used to estimate the quality index equation was least squares regression that is equivalent to discriminant analysis in the two group case. The project is an extension of a study by Carleton and Lerner. It differs from theirs in that only separation into investment and noninvestment groups rather than separation into several groups was attempted. A sample containing a higher proportion of noninvestment quality bonds was used. Additional variables also were tried. Contrary to their results, whether a bond was issued by a school district was not found to add to the predictive power of the equation. The state from which the bond was issued was found to be important. Indeed, rather surprisingly good results were obtained when the only data used was the state in which the district issuing the bond was located (and for only one state the type of district) and the population of the district. An objective of the selection of variables was to use readily available data and to minimize the number of variables used, thus facilitating the practical application of the equation. The standard used in estimating the equation was *Moody's* bond ratings. A random sample of 75 investment quality bonds and 75 noninvestment quality bonds was used to estimate the equations. A random sample of 25 of each was used to evaluate these equations and to compare them with Carleton and Lerner's results. For purposes of evaluation several cut-off points were considered. One cut-off point, expected to correctly classify 90% of the noninvestment quality bonds on average, was used with the results shown below. Equation I uses only the

state (and for one state the type of district) and population of the issuing district to determine the value of its index. Equation V uses the ratio of debt to assessed value, population, tax collection rate and state of issuing district. Equation VI shows the best result using one of Carleton and Lerner's functions. The results are as follows for the hold-out sample of 50 bonds.

Equation	% Noninvestment Bonds Correct	% Investment Bonds Correct	% of Total Correct
I	88	60	74
V	88	72	80
VI	88	52	70

All noninvestment quality bonds that were incorrectly rated in the above test were the same regardless of the equation used. Incidentally, all were rated as being of investment quality by *Standard and Poor's* which indicates the close nature of the decisions. *S & P* ratings are higher than *Moody's* in about 20% of the cases and lower in about 10% for municipals rated by both.

All in all, equation V is more in accord with economic expectations as to the variables that would influence bond quality and has sufficiently desirable statistical characteristics that it is probably the best equation to use as a rating device although its superiority to equation I is not clear cut.

REFERENCES

1. Carleton, W. T., and E. M. Lerner, "Statistical Credit Scoring of Municipal Bonds," *Journal of Money, Credit, and Banking*, I, No. 3 (November, 1969).
2. Goodman, R. M., "Prepared Statement," in U.S. Congress, Subcommittee on Economic Progress of the Joint Economic Committee, *Hearing, Financing Municipal Facilities*, 90th Cong., 1st Sess., 1967, p. 18.
3. Ladd, George W., "Linear Probability Functions and Discriminant Functions," *Econometrica*, XXXIV, No. 4 (October, 1966), pp. 873-885.
4. Mitchell, W. E., "The Effectiveness of Debt Limits on State and Local Government Borrowing," *The Bulletin of the Institute of Finance of New York University*, No. 45 (October, 1967), pp. 7-54.
5. Staats, W. T., "The Municipal Bond Market and Tight Money," *Federal Reserve Bank of Philadelphia Business Review*, (June, 1968), p. 4.
6. U.S. Congress, Subcommittee on Economic Progress of the Joint Economic Committee, *Hearing, Financing Municipal Facilities*, 90th Cong., 1st Sess., 1967, p. 3.

Chapter 22

MANAGEMENT OF COMMERCIAL BANK GOVERNMENT SECURITY PORTFOLIOS: AN OPTIMIZATION APPROACH UNDER UNCERTAINTY*

By Stephen P. Bradley and Dwight B. Crane

*This article is reprinted, with permission, from *Journal of Bank Research*, Vol. 4, No. 1 (Spring, 1973), pp. 18-30.

1. Introduction

This paper reports on the nature of bond portfolio strategies suggested by the application of a multi-period optimization model. The problem definition focuses on management of U.S. Government securities in a commercial bank environment, but the model structure and results are potentially applicable to other types of bonds and institutions. The portfolio manager starts with an initial portfolio and then makes a series of buy, sell and hold decisions over a sequence of time periods. Each of these decisions is made in the face of uncertainty about future interest rates and about possible needs to liquidate some of the portfolio to meet a cash outflow. Possible future events and portfolio responses to them must be taken into consideration in each decision, since transaction costs make it too costly to frequently turn over the portfolio as conditions change.

Portfolio problems of this type have been receiving an increasing amount of attention, but until recently optimization models have not been capable of dealing with realistic descriptions of the problem. Most approaches have lost realism by trying to limit the size of the problem by ignoring its dynamic structure, excluding or restricting the uncertainty, limiting the number of assets, and/or considering only one or two time periods. Linear programming models, such as those of Chambers and Charnes [1961] and Cohen and Hammer [1967], ignore both the dynamic structure and the uncertainty. The chance-constrained models of Charnes and Littlechild [1968] and Charnes and Thore [1966] do not incorporate the dynamic structure, nor does the mathematical programming approach proposed by Cheng [1962]. Dynamic models under uncertainty have been structured and solved for only a limited number of assets, such as the two and three-asset models of Eppen and Fama [1968 and 1971] and the two-asset and one-liability model of Dallenbach and Archer [1969].

Wolf [1969] tackled the bond portfolio problem directly with a decision theoretic formulation which incorporated several bond maturity categories, uncertainty in interest rates and multiple time periods. His solution procedure though, provided an optimal solution for only one period. Crane [June 1971] used two-stage programming under uncertainty to solve an expanded two-period bond portfolio problem, and Cohen and Thore [1970] applied this approach to a two-period bank asset and liability management problem. In theory, mathematical programming under uncertainty could also be used to solve general multi-period problems, but the problem size grows enormously when more than two periods are considered.

Our ability to solve general multiple-period bond problems under uncertainty was greatly improved by the development of a new modeling approach and solution technique reported in Bradley and Crane [1972]. The new solution procedure utilizes the decomposition algorithm of mathematical programming with an extremely efficient technique developed to solve subproblems of the over-all portfolio model. This procedure is capable of solving bond portfolio problems which are large enough to make use of as much information as managers can reasonably be expected to provide. As shown in the discussion of optimal portfolios in later sections, the ability to handle many assets over more than one or two time periods is important. The addition of more time periods changes the nature of optimal portfolio strategies and provides insights as to why some banks maintain "laddered" or even spreads of bond maturity distributions and suggests how they might do better.

In related work, Watson [1972] has studied alternative maturity structures for commercial bank government securities portfolios via Monte Carlo simulation. His problem is similar to ours in that there are uncertainties in the future interest rates and cash flows, but his approach is to study the efficiency, in a Markowitz mean-variance [1970] sense, of portfolio strategies which are fixed over time. The optimization approach, on the other hand, explores a richer set of strategies since it selects a strategy which dynamically adjusts over time for the uncertain interest rates and cash flows which might occur. Although there are some interesting differences in results which will be discussed, the optimal portfolio structures suggested by the dynamic model are of the same general class as those shown to be efficient by Watson.

The following section of the paper describes the structure of the interest rate uncertainty and reviews the model formulation used to analyze optimal strategies. Then we discuss the nature of optimal portfolio strategies in a "base case." This is followed by a report of the results of experimentation with the model under a variety of assumptions. In the last section, some conclusions are drawn about the nature of desirable portfolio strategies.

2. Formulation of the Model

Each time period the portfolio manager is faced with the difficult problem of deciding which securities to sell or hold in the portfolio and which to buy. This decision is difficult for two important reasons. First, he faces an uncertain future in that interest rates on securities may rise or fall and that funds may be made available to or withdrawn from the portfolio depending upon external economic conditions and other exogenous factors. The uncertainty in future periods and the response of the portfolio manager to interest rates and exogenous cash flows which might occur should be taken into account in deciding upon current portfolio actions. This leads to the second problem, a very large number of possible portfolio actions which must be evaluated.

To approach the first problem we assume that the portfolio manager is able to specify a collection of economic scenarios consisting of a sequence of specific yield curves and exogenous cash flows which might occur. Associated with each sequence is its probability of occurrence. The scenarios are complicated by the fact that the yield curve which might occur in a specific period is conditional upon the sequence of yield curves which preceded it. After the first decision, for example, interest rates might rise, remain the same or fall. Given that one of these uncertain events has occurred, rates might then rise from the new level, remain the same or fall. Thus, a scenario is not simply a sequence of continuously rising or falling rates.

A sample set of yield curve sequences is shown in Figure 1. Other than the initial yield curve which is known, we assume in this example that there are three possible yield curves which can occur in each period, given the curve which prevailed in the previous period. The probability of each set of interest rates, conditional upon the previous sequence of rates, is shown in parentheses. Associated with each of these curves might be an exogenous cash flow.

The large number of portfolio actions to be evaluated results from the need to make a decision at the start of each period for each of the possible yield curves. Except for the initial decision, each portfolio action is conditional upon the sequence of uncertain events and portfolios which precede it, and the decision takes into account future uncertainties and decisions. The model formulation and computational approach used to optimally determine these portfolio strategies has been discussed in detail in Bradley and Crane [1972], so only the basic formulation will be reviewed here.

We assume that the portfolio manager is able to aggregate the securities available for him to purchase into a number of security classes $k = 1, 2, \ldots, K$. These security classes might represent maturity categories of securities e.g., 3 months, 6 months, 1 year, etc. and types of bonds, such as U.S. Governments or municipals and deep-discount or current coupon bonds. Further, there may be an initial portfolio of holdings of some security classes as well as cash available for investment, or even an initial requirement for cash that must be withdrawn from the portfolio. Finally, we assume that there are a finite number of time periods and a finite number of future economic scenarios, each defined by a particular sequence of yield curves and exogenous cash flows either into or out of the portfolio. Associated with each such scenario is the probability of that scenario occurring.

At the beginning of each period, assuming that a particular portfolio is currently held and cash is either available to or required from the portfolio, the portfolio manager must decide how much of each security class to buy $b_n^k(e_n)$ and how much of each security class that he is currently holding to sell $s_{m,n}^k(e_n)$ or continue to hold $h_{m,n}^k(e_n)$. The subscript n identifies the current period and m indicates the period where the security is purchased. Since the amount of capital gain or loss on a security class sold will depend on the difference between the purchase price and sales price,

Figure 1. Distribution of Future Yield Curves.

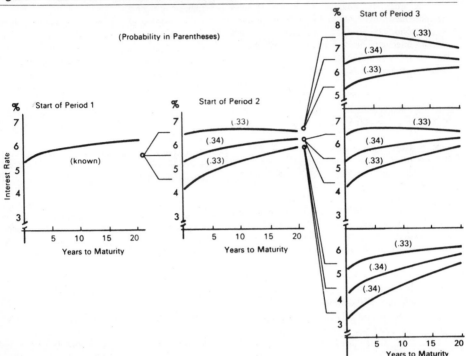

the portfolio manager must keep track of the amount of each security class held by its date of purchase. Further, the variables which represent decisions at the start of period n are conditional on the sequence of uncertain events, e_n, which precede the start of period n since the model computes the optimal policy for every uncertain event sequence. More precisely, the decision variables are defined as follows:

$b_n^k(e_n)$ = amount of security class k purchased at the beginning of period n conditional on event sequence e_n; in dollars of initial purchase price.

$s_{m,n}^k(e_n)$ = amount of security class k, which had been purchased at the beginning of period m, sold at the beginning of period n conditional on event sequence e_n; in dollars of initial purchase price.

$h_{m,n}^k(e_n)$ = amount of security class k, which had been purchased at the beginning of period m, held (as opposed to sold) at the beginning of period n conditional on event sequence e_n; in dollars of initial purchase price.

It is useful to explain the notation used for event sequences.[1] The symbol e_n refers to a

particular sequence of events starting after period 1 decisions and leading to the beginning of period n. The set of all such event sequences is E_n. For example, e_4 might refer to the event sequence in which interest rates rise in period 1, rise again in period 2 and remain unchanged in period 3. Note that there is only one event in E_1 since the yield curve at the start of period 1 is known with certainty.

The model has four types of constraints: Non-negativity, cash flow, inventory balance and net capital loss. Each of these will be explained in turn. The variables are first required to be nonnegative,

$$(2.1)\ b_n^k(e_n) \geqq 0,\, s_{m,n}^k(e_n) \geqq 0,\, h_{m,n}^k(e_n) \geqq 0$$
$$m = 1,2,\ldots n-1$$
$$\forall e_n \varepsilon E_n,\, n = 1,2,\ldots,N\ \ k = 1,2,\ldots,K$$

which merely implies that short sales are not permitted. As a practical matter short sales are uncommon in the investment portfolios of financial institutions.

[1] It should be pointed out that the notation used for event sequence here differs from that used in Bradley and Crane [1972].

The model is designed on a cash accounting basis in order to accurately reflect when cash is actually made available to or withdrawn from the portfolio. The cash flow equations require that the cash used for purchasing securities be equal to the sum of the cash generated from the coupon income on holdings during the previous period, cash generated from sales of securities, and exogenous cash flow. We can define the coupon yield $y_m^k(e_n)$ from holding a security, the capital gain or loss $g_{m,n}^k(e_n)$ from selling a security, and the exogenous cash flow $f_n(e_n)$ as:

$g_{m,n}^k(e_n)$ = capital gain on loss on security class k, which had been purchased at the beginning of period m and was sold at the beginning of period n conditional on event sequence e_n; in per cent of initial purchase price.

$y_m^k(e_n)$ = income yield from interest coupons on security class k, which was purchased at the beginning of period m, conditional on event sequence e_n; in per cent of initial purchase price.

$f_n(e_n)$ = incremental amount of funds either made available to or withdrawn from the portfolio at the beginning of period n conditional on event sequence e_n; in dollars.

Hence, we have the following cash flow equations:

$$(2.2) \quad \sum_{k=1}^{K} b_n^k(e_n) - \sum_{k=1}^{K} \left[\sum_{m=0}^{n-2} y_m^k(e_m) h_{m,n-1}^k(e_{n-1}) \right.$$
$$\left. + y_{n-1}^k(e_{n-1}) b_{n-1}^k(e_{n-1}) \right]$$
$$- \sum_{k=1}^{K} \sum_{m=0}^{n-1} \left(1 + g_{m,n}^k(e_n) \right) s_{m,n}^k(e_n) = f_n(e_n)$$

$$\forall e_n \varepsilon E_n, \ n = 1,2,\dots,N$$

The coupon yield is defined as after-tax and the capital gain or loss is defined as after-tax and after transaction costs, where transaction costs are measured as the spread between bid and asked prices. The index $m=0$ refers to holdings of the security classes in the initial portfolio. The exogenous cash flow $f(e_n)$ may be either positive or negative depending upon whether cash is being made available to or withdrawn from the portfolio respectively. Finally, these relationships (2.2) hold with equality, implying that the portfolio is at all times fully invested since it is assumed that there is always a risk free asset to purchase which has no transaction cost.

The model has what is referred to as inventory balance constraints. The commodities which need to be accounted for are the holdings of each security class purchased in a particular period. Hence, these equations state that the amount of a commodity sold plus the amount of that commodity held at the beginning of a period must equal the amount of that commodity on hand at the end of the previous period,

$$(2.3) \quad -h_{m,n-1}^k(e_{n-1}) + s_{m,n}^k(e_n) + h_{m,n}^k(e_n) = 0$$
$$m = 0,1,\dots,n-2$$
$$-b_{n-1}^k(e_{n-1}) + s_{n-1,n}^k(e_n) + h_{n-1,n}^k(e_n) = 0$$
$$\forall e_n \varepsilon E_n; n = 1,2,\dots,N; k = 1,2,\dots,K$$

The amount on hand at the end of the previous period* is either the amount purchased or the amount held at the beginning of the previous period.

In order to reflect bank practice and to represent the portfolio manager's attitude toward risk, constraints are put on the allowable net realized capital loss during any year. This use of loss constraints to express risk aversion is similar to the "safety first principle" which Telser [1955-56] and others have used in portfolio models.

If we define the allowable losses as:

$L_n(e_n)$ = upper bound on the realized net capital loss (after taxes) from sales during the year ending with period n conditional on event sequence e_n; in dollars

we can write the constraints on net realized capital loss in the following form:

$$(2.4) \quad -\sum_{k=1}^{K} \sum_{m=n}^{n} g_{m,n}^k(e_n) s_{m,n}^k(e_n) \leqq L_n(e_n)$$

$$\forall e_n \varepsilon E_n, \forall n \varepsilon N'$$

These loss constraints sum over the periods contained in a particular year the gains or losses from sales of securities in that year and limit this value. N' is the set of indices of periods which correspond to the end of years and n' is the index of the first period in a year defined by an element of N'. Usually, the loss constraints are applied so as to limit the unrealized losses in the portfolio at the horizon as well as realized losses each year. The limiting of unrealized losses at the horizon is important to insure that current coupon income and capital gains are not achieved at the expense of large holdings of unrealized losses at the horizon of the model.

Finally, the objective function of the model is to maximize the expected value of the portfolio at the horizon. In order to formalize this we need to define the probability $p(e_n)$ of each event sequence and the value of the holdings in the final period. For simplicity, the value of securities at the horizon is taken to be the expected "bid" price, the market price at which the securities could be sold. The total value at the horizon is the sum of this expected value plus the coupon income received in the final period. More precisely we have:

$\bar{v}_{m,N}(e_N)$ = expected (over period N) cash value per dollar of initial purchase price of security class k which had been purchased at the beginning of period m and held at the end of the last period in the model.

$p(e_N)$ = probability that event sequence e_N obtains

which allows us to write the objective function as follows:

$$(2.5)\ \text{Maximize}\ \sum_{e_N \varepsilon E_N} p(e_N) \sum_{k=1}^{K} \left[\sum_{m=0}^{n-1} \left(y_m^k(e_m) \right. \right.$$

$$+ \left. \bar{v}_{m,N}^k(e_N) \right) h_{m,N}^k(e_N)$$

$$+ \left. \left(y_N^k(e_N) + v_{N.}^k(e_N) \right) b_N^k(e_N) \right]$$

The value of the portfolio at the horizon is merely the cash generated from the coupon income of the final period holdings plus the expected final period cash value of these holdings.

3. Optimal Portfolios in the Base Case

Experiments with the model were conducted to explore the impact of several factors on portfolio strategies. These factors included liquidity requirements, willingness to accept realized and unrealized losses on securities, the shape of yield curves and the number of periods considered in the model. Before discussing these results it is helpful to define a basic portfolio problem. This "base case" will illustrate the nature of solutions produced by the model. In additon, it will provide a basis for comparison among the experimental results, since the experiments were designed as variations of the base case.

The problem structure for the base case assumes a three-year planning horizon which is divided into three one-year periods. Buy, sell and hold decisions are made at the start of each year. Each decision is made in the context of a particular yield curve and amount of funds available to the portfolio, but at the time of the first decision only the current yield curve and amount of

funds are known with certainty. After the first decision one of three equally likely random events occurs, where each possible event is defined by a yield curve and a cash flow made available to or subtracted from the portfolio. After the random event, a new decision is made at the start of year two. Then another one of three possible events occurs and a decision is made at the start of year three. Finally, an uncertain event occurs during year three which determines the value of the portfolio at the horizon.

For the base case it is assumed that the portfolio starts with $100,000 in cash. This cash can be invested in any of nine "securities" which represent different maturity categories of U.S. Government securities. The maturities available for purchase in the first period and all subsequent periods are 1, 2, 3, 4, 5, 10, 15, 18 and 20 years. All securities are purchased at par and the coupon yield on each maturity at the start of the first period lies along a rising yield curve as shown by the initial yield curve in Figure 1.

The yield curve which prevails for the second decision is uncertain. This uncertainty is represented by a random shift in the initial yield curve. With equal probabilities the yield curve may shift up, stay the same or decline. The size and nature of these shifts were chosen to approximate the distribution of actual 12 month changes in the Government yield curve which has occurred over the past several years. Analysis of these data suggests that the three month rate will increase 120 basis points, not change or decrease 120 basis points with approximately equal probability. In addition, changes in the three year yield average about 80% of changes in the three month rate and changes in the 12 year rate average about 30% of the change in short rate. These parameters determine three points on each possible yield curve. Yields for all other maturities are then computed from a form of the Pearson "Type III" frequency curve,

$$R_t = at^b e^{ct}$$

where t = time to maturity. A more complete description of the statistical analysis and data generation technique are provided in Crane [Dec. 1971].

The yield curves which are possible at the decision points at the start of each period are shown in Figure 1. Note that as the yield curve moves upward it becomes flatter and then inverted. As it moves down the slope rises more steeply. Both of these trends occur in actual security markets as monetary conditions tighten or become easier.

Figure 2. Optimal Portfolios for Each Period and Interest Rate Sequence

	Sequence of Interest	Amounts in Each Maturity							
Period	Rates	1 year	2 years	3 years	. . .	18 years	19 years	20 years	Total
1	Initial Curve	7,108	44,383	32,085				16,424	100,000
2	Rise	44,383	32,085				16,424		92,892
3	Rise	69,164				16,424			85,588
1	Initial Curve	7,108	44,383	32,085				16,424	100,000
2	Rise	44,383	32,085				16,424		92,892
3	No Change	32,085	22,889	23,190		16,424			95,588
1	Initial Curve	7,108	44,383	32,085				16,424	100,000
2	Rise	44,383	32,085				16,424		92,892
3	Fall	32,085	29,577			16,424			105,588
1	Initial Curve	7,108	44,383	32,085				16,424	100,000
2	No Change	44,383	33,970				16,424	8,115	102,892
3	Rise	71,358				16,424	8,115		95,897
1	Initial Curve	7,108	44,383	32,085				16,424	100,000
2	No Change	44,383	33,970				16,424	8,115	102,892
3	No Change	33,970	27,520			16,424	8,115	19,868	105,897
1	Initial Curve	7,108	44,383	32,085				16,424	100,000
2	No Change	44,383	33,970				16,424	8,115	102,892
3	Fall	33,970				16,424	8,115	57,388	115,897
1	Initial Curve	7,108	44,383	32,085				16,424	100,000
2	Fall	46,762	32,085				16,424	17,621	112,892
3	Rise	72,119				16,424	17,621		106,164
1	Initial Curve	7,108	44,383	32,085				16,424	100,000
2	Fall	46,762	32,085				16,424	17,621	112,892
3	No Change	41,779				16,424	17,621	40,340	116,164
1	Initial Curve	7,108	44,383	32,085				16,424	100,000
2	Fall	46,762	32,085				16,424	17,621	112,892
3	Fall	32,085				16,424	17,621	60,034	126,164

In keeping with the notion that rising yields imply tighter credit conditions and vice versa, the base case assumes that a part of the portfolio will need to be liquidated if rates rise to finance a cash outflow. A fall in the yield curve implies that extra cash is available for investment. This phenomenon is represented by a $10,000 reduction in funds available to the portfolio if rates rise, no change if rates remain stable and a $10,000 increase in investable funds if rates fall. In effect, this means that the portfolio strategy must take into account the possibility of approximately a 10% change in the amount of funds available in each future decision period.

Aversion to risk in the portfolio is expressed by limits on losses resulting from sale of securities. The base case adopts a conservative approach by limiting net realized losses on sales in each year of the model to zero. At the end of the third period there is an upper limit on unrealized losses of $1000, or 1% of the original value of the portfolio.

Securities are bought for the model at the market "asked" price and sold at the "bid" price. The spread between these two prices is the trans-

action cost associated with trades. It typically increases in discrete steps as a function of maturity. In the base case the spread is ⅛% for maturities up to two years, ¼% from two to eight years and 1% for longer maturities. When securities are held to maturity, the portfolio receives the par value of the bond without a deduction for transaction costs.

It is assumed that the tax rate on income and capital gains is 50%. In determining the funds available for reinvestment and in valuing the portfolio, interest income is computed as after-tax and capital gains and losses are measured as after-tax and transaction costs.

The optimal decisions computed by the model for the base case are shown in Figure 2. These decisions include not only an initial portfolio, but also a set of portfolio actions for each decision period. Thus, there are three sets of portfolio actions for period two and nine for period three, Although the initial portfolio is the same for all interest rate sequences it is repeated in the figure for all sequences to show the transition of portfolios over time. Optimal actions at the start of period two are conditional upon the uncertain events which precede the period so there are three possible actions. Similarly, optimal period three decisions are conditional upon the nine possible sequences of interest rates which can occur. For example, the first set of portfolios shown in Figure 2 indicates optimal portfolios for each of the three periods under the assumption that interest rates rise and then rise again.

The optimal initial portfolio for the base case tends to be "dumbbell" shaped with maturities concentrated at the short and long end of the maturity range. However, the maturities at the short end are "laddered" in the sense that there is a spread of maturities with some bonds maturing at the end of each decision period of the model. If rates rise and there is a cash outflow in the first year, this outflow is financed by the cash received from maturing securities and interest income. If rates rise again, the outflow is financed by maturities of the two-year bonds which were originally purchased for the initial portfolio. These maturities provide more than enough cash so the extra is invested in new one year securities. Thus, the final portfolio is split between one and 18-year maturities. The one year matures at the horizon with no loss and the 18-year securities (17-year at the horizon) will incur the maximum $1000 loss if rates rise again.

The pattern of optimal portfolios differs over time, depending upon the sequence of interest rates which occurs. If rates do not change, for example, proceeds from the original one-year maturity are reinvested in a new 20-year bond at the start of year two. If rates are again stable, proceeds from bond maturities are then invested in a mixture of new two and 20-year bonds. After this interest rate sequence the portfolio enters the final year of the model with bond maturities of 1, 2, 18, 19 and 20 years. The portfolio is laddered at the short and long end of the maturity range, but it includes no intermediate maturities.

In the base case the initial and all subsequent portfolios have a dumbbell shape, but they have clusters of maturities at the short and/or long end of the maturity range. This result is in effect a combination of two more extreme portfolio strategies which have been recommended to or used by banks. At one extreme is a pure dumbbell portfolio strategy which contains only the shortest and longest maturities. At the other is a completely laddered portfolio which contains securities spread throughout the maturity range. The dumbbell strategy has been largely recommended in the academic literature (e.g., Wolf [1969] and Crane [June 1971]) as an efficient means of achieving maximum return for a given level of risk. The laddered portfolio approach is much more commonly used by banks as they consider it to be a practical means of achieving high average yields with liquidity provided by a continuing stream of maturities.

4. Further Exploration of Optimal Portfolios

Variations on the base case were studied to explore the effect of several factors on the structure of optimal portfolios, particularly their impact on the mixture of dumbbell and laddered portfolios. How do strategies change as the number of future periods taken into consideration is varied? How are portfolios affected by a greater willingness to realize losses on security trades? By a greater or lesser willingness to experience unrealized losses at the horizon? Is the nature of optimal portfolios the same if there are no exogenous cash flows associated with the uncertain event sequences?

The amount of laddering on the short end of the initial portfolio is significantly affected by the number of periods included in the model. In the three period base case, the initial portfolio contained some one, two and three year maturities. As shown in Figure 3, though, the number of short maturity categories decreases with smaller numbers of periods. The optimal initial portfolio for the one period case is a pure dumbbell portfolio which contains only one and 20 year bonds. When the model is extended to two periods, the laddering appears with maturities of both one and two years. It expands to include a three year maturity with the addition of a third period, but the laddering stops at this point. The addition of a fourth time period does not lead to a four-year bond in the initial portfolio.

The structure of one and two-period models was exactly like the three-period base case except that the horizons were only one and two years, respectively. To save computation time, however, the four-period case did not contain the same number of uncertain events in years three and four. As in the base case, there were three possible events which could occur after period one and two decisions, but in periods three and four the distribution of interest rates was approximated by two random events rather than three. Thus, yield curves could rise or fall with equal probability following each of the last two decisions.

Although the number of uncertain events in the last two periods is smaller in the four period case, there is still a need to plan for the possibility of rate increases and cash outflows after each decision. This is reflected partially in the reduction of dollars allocated to the 20-year bond as the

Figure 3. Effect of Number of Model Periods

Number of Model Periods	Maturities in Optimal Initial Portfolios				
	1 year	2 years	3 years	. . .	20 years
1	$49,495				$50,505
2	$43,612	31,568			24,820
3	7,108	44,383	$32,085		16,424
4	7,102	20,770	57,528		14,600

Figure 4. Effect of Limits on Annual Realized Losses

Maximum Annual Losses (A/T)	Maturities in Optimal Initial Portfolios				
	1 year	2 years	3 years	. . .	20 years
$ 0	$ 7,108	$44,383	$32,085		$16,424
200	11,911	44,628	23,621		20,840
400	17,096	46,767	10,881		25,256
600	23,291	47,047			29,672
800	30,220	37,166			32,614
1000	38,672	28,714			32,614

number of periods is increased and the planning horizon is extended. The addition of periods increases the number of upward shifts in the yield curve which can occur before the horizon and hence raises the potential loss on the long bond. As a result fewer dollars are allocated to the 20 year bond as the number of periods is increased from three to four, but the funds are shifted to a mixture of the one, two and three year bonds. A four-period bond was not purchased because it was too costly to prepare for the uncertainty in the fourth year in the initial portfolio. In effect, there were a sufficient number of periods and length of time for the model to maneuver after the first-period decisions.

Room for maneuvering is also increased by a greater willingness to realize losses on trades each period and to experience unrealized losses at the horizon. The model results reported in Figure 3 were based on the assumption that no realized losses were allowed and that $1000 in after-tax losses were permitted at the horizon. Figure 4 extends the results of the three period base case to explore the impact of greater willingness to have trading losses. It indicates that if annual after-tax losses of $600 or greater are acceptable the optimal initial portfolio does not contain any of the three year maturity. In effect, losses of this magnitude give the portfolio manager enough

room to maneuver so that it is not necessary to build in a maturity in the initial portfolio for the period three uncertainty.

A similar phenomenon occurs with increases in the maximum losses allowed at the horizon in the three period model. As shown in Figure 5, there is no need to hold a three-period bond in the initial portfolio if after-tax horizon losses of $1500 or greater are allowed. Other than the variation in horizon losses, this figure is based upon the assumptions of the base case including the restriction against realized losses at the decision periods.

Although laddering of the portfolio provides maturities at the time of possible cash outflows, liquidity needs are not an essential condition to laddered portfolios. Even when no random exogenous cash flows are associated with the portfolio, some laddering occurs in the short maturities of the initial portfolio. This is illustrated in Figure 6 which shows optimal initial portfolios for a variation of the base case which has no exogenous cash flows. The pattern of initial portfolios for a variety of limits on realized losses is very similar to those shown in Figure 4 which incorporates random cash flows. Thus, even when there is no liquidity need it is optimal to have a distribution of short maturities to reduce risk and put the portfolio manager in a flexible position to take advantage of interest rate changes.

Figure 5. Effect of Limits on Book Losses at the Horizon

Limits on Losses at the Horizon (A/T)	Maturities in Optimal Initial Portfolios			
	1 year	2 years	3 years	20 years
$ 500	$ 7,118	$15,712	$68,958	$ 8,212
1000	7,108	44,383	32,085	16,424
1500	13,533	61,831		24,636
2000	22,323	44,829		32,848
2500	31,114	27,826		41,060
3000	39,905	10,823		49,272

Figure 6. Effect of Realized Loss Limits with No Exogenous Cash Flow

Maximum Annual Losses (A/T)	Maturities in Optimal Initial Portfolios			
	1 year	2 years	3 years	20 years
$ 0	$14,743	$54,391	$14,442	$16,424
200	20,928	54,638	3,595	20,840
400	27,109	47,635		25,256
600	33,289	37,039		29,672
800	40,230	27,159		32,614
1000	48,679	18,707		32,614

All of the results shown in Figures 2 through 6 are based upon the same set of transaction costs, the same initial yield curve and the same assumption that the uncertain events have equal probabilities. These assumptions, of course, have an important impact on the selection of portfolios by the model. Lower costs of selling securities would lead a larger share of the portfolio to be placed in longer term bonds. Differently shaped yield curves would lead to very different investment strategies. For example, experiments conducted with "humped" yield curves, i.e., yield curves which peak at an intermediate maturity, indicated some tendency to buy maturities at the peak rather than combinations of long and short bonds. Even with normally rising yield curves, it is possible to find curves which rise steeply enough as a function of maturity that the optimal portfolio might not contain a one year bond. The extra coupon income from a slightly longer maturity more than compensates for the additional capital loss potential. With normal yield curves, though, there is a strong tendency to hold dumbbell shaped portfolios with clusters of maturities at the short and/ or long end.

5. Conclusions and Implications

Our experimental results suggest that optimal portfolios in a multiperiod environment with normally shaped yield curves tend to be laddered on both the long and short ends of the maturity range, with an absence of intermediate maturities. In the results reported, optimal first period decisions led to a spread of short maturities and a single long term bond. With the passage of time, however, the new purchases of long bonds resulted in a laddering of maturities at both ends of the spectrum. This result has been confirmed by preliminary experiments in the more realistic situation in which the model is given an initial portfolio of securities to deal with rather than cash. In this situation the model tends to replace intermediate maturities with short and long term purchases, moving toward the dumbbell shape with laddering at both ends.

This basic conclusion is at variance with two extreme portfolio strategies which have been recommended. At one extreme is the completely laddered portfolio which contains some holding in each maturity category. At the other extreme is the pure dumbbell portfolio strategy which contains only the shortest and longest maturities.

The completely laddered portfolios contain a spread of maturities from the shortest to the longest with the amount of short maturities depending upon the liquidity needs facing the portfolio. This kind of portfolio has been recommended in the traditional banking literature and is used by many banks, although some large banks have moved away from the practice in recent years. One virtue of this strategy is its simplicity. As the short bonds mature with the passage of time, the cash generated is available for liquidity needs or for reinvestment in long term bonds to maintain the laddered structure. Since the cash is obtained from maturities rather than sales, there is no cost resulting from the spread between bid and asked prices. Furthermore, if the yield curve has its normal upward slope, funds used to purchase long· term securities are invested in the highest yield available at the time. Thus, it is argued that laddered portfolios combine high average return with substantial liquidity.

At the other extreme, the rational for the pure dumbbell portfolio is that it provides the most efficient way of obtaining maximum return for a given level of risk. If the initial yield curve is upward sloping and if rates subsequently fall, the 20-year bond provides the highest interest income and the largest capital gain. On the other hand if rates rise, the shortest maturity provides the least risk of capital loss. Thus, combinations of the short and long maturities tend to provide a more efficient means of obtaining income at a given level of risk than does the purchase of an intermediate length maturity. It is easiest to believe that the dumbbell portfolio is sound in a world of no transaction costs. In this situation, the portfolio manager has to look only one period ahead as in the one period model reported above. At the end of the period the entire portfolio is liquidated at no cost and reinvested in a new dumbbell portfolio. In the presence of transaction costs the portfolio cannot be turned over at will since the losses resulting from the transaction costs will tend to outweigh the potential gains resulting from selecting a new dumbbell portfolio each time period.

Our results tend to reject the two extreme strategies and support an intermediate one which is laddered both at the long and short ends but containing no medium maturity classes. Intuitively such a strategy is appealing since the laddering on the short end provides a continuous stream of maturities to provide liquidity and flexibility while the laddering on the long end provides a high average yield assuming that the yield curves which generally occur are rising with the longer maturities. However, intermediate maturities might be more attractive for a particular set of assumptions about the shape of initial and future yield curves, their probability of occurrence and the length of the planning horizon. As an example, if the initial yield curve rises steeply to some intermediate

maturity before flattening and the curve is expected on average to maintain its original shape, the intermediate maturity is an attractive investment. It has both a relatively high initial yield and built-in capital gains as it "slides down the yield curve" with the passage of time, i.e., becomes a shorter maturity.

Watson [1972] studied a number of portfolio strategies via Monte Carlo simulation and also concluded that an intermediate strategy was best. The strategy which was found to be efficient in the Markowitz sense was one which consisted of a spread of maturities on the short end, with decreasing percentages from three month to 2½ year maturities, and the longest maturity (15 year) on the long end. The dumbbell portfolios using only the shortest and longest maturities were shown to be inefficient. Results were not reported for a completely laddered portfolio.

The most important difference between Watson's simulation results and those of the optimization model is that his efficient portfolios contain no laddering at the long end. This difference probably results from his assumption that the long term bond can be sold at the end of each period and a new one purchased at no cost. Thus, there is a constant turnover of the long bond with no chance for laddering to occur. If this unrealistic assumption of no trading cost were removed, his analysis would in all likelihood show that efficient portfolios would be laddered on both the long and short end of the maturity range.

Although the experimentation suggests that the nature of optimal portfolios will tend to be dumbbell shaped with some laddering at both ends of the maturity spectrum, these results do not tell the manager what to do in the day-to-day managing of his portfolio. A strategy of maintaining a complete laddering of maturities is relatively easy to implement since the cash from maturities of short bonds is simply reinvested in long term bonds. With dumbbell shaped portfolios the problem is more difficult since the portfolio loses its dumbbell characteristic with the passage of time unless the longer maturities are periodically replaced by new long term bonds. When should the bonds be taken long again? Furthermore, what proportion of the portfolio should be concentrated at each end of the maturity spectrum? How should these proportions be altered over time as new economic environments are encountered and new expectations are formed? How should the portfolio manager move from his present portfolio to the more desirable clustering of maturities at the short and long end?

The multiperiod optimization model can be

used in an operational mode to help answer such questions and assist in managing a portfolio over time. Input to the model would include information about the securities currently held and the portfolio manager's probability assessments of short and long term economic conditions. The model would then suggest portfolio trading strategies over time which adjust for the uncertainties in the future economic environment. After some portfolio decisions have been made and a period of time has passed, the model would be run again with updated information about the portfolio and assessments of future environments. ■

REFERENCES

Bradley, Stephen P. and Crane, Dwight B., "A Dynamic Model for Bond Portfolio Management," *Management Science*, Vol. 19, No. 2 (October 1972).

Chambers, D., and Charnes, A., "Intertemporal Analysis and Optimization of Bank Portfolios," *Management Science*, Vol. 7, No. 4 (July 1961), pp. 393-410.

Charnes, A. and Littlechild, S. C., "Intertemporal Bank Asset Choice with Stochastic Dependence," Systems Research Memorandum No. 188, The Technological Institute, Northwestern University, April 1968.

——————— and Thore, Sten, "Planning for Liquidity in Financial Institutions: The Chance-Constrained Method," *The Journal of Finance*, Vol. XXI, No. 4 (December 1966), pp. 649-674.

Cheng, Pao Lun, "Optimum Bond Portfolio Selection," *Management Science*, Vol. 8, No. 4 (July 1962), pp. 490-499.

Cohen, Kalman J. and Hammer, Frederick S., "Linear Programming and Optimal Bank Asset Management Decisions," *The Journal of Finance*, Vol. XXII, No. 2 (May 1967), pp. 147-165.

Cohen, Kalman J. and Thore, Sten, "Programming Bank Portfolios Under Uncertainty," *Journal of Bank Research*, Vol. 1, No. 1 (Spring 1970), pp. 42-61.

Crane, Dwight B., "A Stochastic Programming Model for Commercial Bank Bond Portfolio Management," *Journal of Financial and Quantitative Analysis*, Vol. VI, No. 3 (June 1971), pp. 955-976.

———————, "Assessment of Yields on U.S. Government Securities," Graduate School of Business Administration, Harvard University, Working Paper No. 71-18, December 1971.

Daellenbach, Hans G. and Archer, Stephen H., "The Optimal Bank Liquidity A Multi-period Stochastic Model," *Journal of Financial and Quantitative Analysis*, Vol. 4, No. 3 (September 1969), pp. 329-343.

Eppen, Gary D. and Fama, Eugene F., "Solutions for Cash Balance and Simple Dynamic Portfolio Problems with Proportional Costs," *Journal of Business*, Vol. 41 (January 1968), pp. 94-112.

Eppen, Gary D. and Fama, Eugene F. "Three Asset Cash Balance and Dynamic Portfolio Problems," *Management Science*, Vol. 17, No. 5 (January 1971), pp. 311-319.

Markowitz, Harry M., *Portfolio Selection: Efficient Diversification of Investments*, Monograph 16, Cowles Foundation for Research in Economics at Yale University, Yale University Press, New Haven, Connecticut, 1970 (second printing).

Telser, Lester, "Safety First and Hedging," *Review of Economic Studies*, Vol. 23 (1955-1956).

Watson, Ronald D., "Tests of Maturity Structures of Commercial Bank Government Securities Portfolios: A Simulation Approach," *Journal of Bank Research*, Vol. 3, No. 1 (Spring 1972), pp. 34-46.

Wolf, Charles R., "A Model for Selecting Commercial Bank Government Security Portfolios," *The Review of Economics and Statistics*, Vol. LI, No. 1 (February 1969), pp. 40-52.

Chapter 23

SIMULATION OF BOND PORTFOLIO STRATEGIES: LADDERED VS. BARBELL MATURITY STRUCTURE*

By Stephen P. Bradley and Dwight B. Crane

*This article is reprinted, with permission, from *Journal of Bank Research*, Vol. 6, No. 2 (Summer, 1975), pp. 122-134.

The great majority of commercial banks utilize laddered maturity structures for their investment portfolios. In these portfolios, the maturities are spread relatively evenly over some range considered appropriate for the bank. An investment portfolio of state and local government securities might, for example, have its maturities spread evenly out to a maximum maturity of 15 years.

Banks believe this kind of structure has a number of important advantages. As time passes there is a continuing stream of maturing securities which provides liquidity if needed to fund deposit outflows or loan increases. This has become a less important reason for laddered structures in recent years as banks now rely less on their portfolios for liquidity, but these portfolios still have the desirable characteristic of being easy to manage over time. The maturity structure can be maintained by simply reinvesting the proceeds from maturing securities in new 15-year bonds, or the longest maturity allowed. Bankers believe that this policy will also provide relatively high interest income since in normal times the yield to maturity of bonds tends to be higher for longer maturities. Thus, the regular purchase of relatively long-term securities will lead to a portfolio with a high average interest rate.

The research literature has tended to recommend, and a few large banks have adopted, an alternative maturity structure in which bonds are concentrated in short and relatively long-term securities with little or no securities with maturities in between. The essence of the argument given for this kind of policy, commonly referred to as a barbell maturity structure, is most clearly seen if a one-period investment horizon is assumed as in the paper by Hempel and Yawitz [1974]. With this assumption, the total return from a bond which matures in one period is risk free in the sense that the interest income and the market value at the end of the period are known. Longer term bonds offer potentially higher return at the cost of more variability, or risk, in their total return. If one of the longer maturities offers a higher return relative to its variability than the

others, then optimal portfolios should contain combinations of the risk free maturity and the longer maturity that offers the highest return relative to its risk. Including any other maturities would either add to the risk of the portfolio without increasing return or would provide lower return at the same level of risk, i.e., it would lead to a less efficient portfolio.[1] This suggests that desirable portfolios should contain a mixture of short and long bonds, although the maturity of the long bonds depends upon the shape of the current yield curve and the investor's expectations about future interest rates. If the investor expects rising interest rates, the "long" bonds could have a short maturity.

While the logic of a barbell type portfolio is correct for a single-period horizon, it is not necessarily applicable to the multi-period investment problem faced by a bank portfolio manager. There is a significant transaction cost involved in maintaining a barbell portfolio. As time passes the long bonds become shorter so they must be sold and reinvested in a new long-term bond. In addition, the one-period bond is not risk free since proceeds from its maturity must be reinvested in a new security at an uncertain interest rate. Thus, the question of whether a laddered or a barbell portfolio works best in a real world environment must be resolved empirically.

In Bradley and Crane [1973] we used a multi-period optimization model under uncertainty to study this question. Portfolios of U.S. Treasury securities selected by the model tended to have the barbell structure with maturities clustered at both ends of the maturity range The model was also used to manage a hypothetical portfolio of state and local government bonds during the period of 1964 to 1973, as reported in Bradley and Crane [1975]. Portfolio decisions made by the model each year tended to maintain the barbell structure over time. The model's performance

---

[1] This conclusion also requires an assumption that the shortest maturity available is a one-period bond as might be the case with a short planning period. As discussed later in the paper, bonds maturing before the planning horizon can be combined with securities maturing after the horizon to reduce the variance of total return.

over the 10-year period was better than those of naive laddered and barbell strategies simulated over the same period.

One of the criticisms of the barbell maturity structure is the difficulty of managing it over time. The laddered approach involves very simple investment rules and it can be managed without making assessments about future rate movements. When the barbell approach is used, periodic trading decisions must be made to maintain the structure. It would be possible to make these decisions mechanically in a manner similar to the automatic reinvestment procedure of laddered portfolios. For example, a rule might be to sell a bond whenever its maturity shortens to 20 years and reinvest the proceeds in a new long-term bond. An unresolved issue is whether a mechanically managed barbell performs better or worse than a similarly managed ladder portfolio. The purpose of this paper is to help answer this question through the use of a Monte Carlo simulation model.

Some earlier studies with simulation models have been reported, but they have not provided complete answers to the question. Watson [1972] used a Monte Carlo simulation model to study alternative maturity structures. He concluded that the best structure contained a spread of short maturities and a single long maturity bond. Unfortunately his study did not include laddered portfolios with maturities longer than two years and he ignored the cost of trading to maintain the barbell structures considered. Hempel and Kretschman [1973] used a deterministic simulation model to study the performance of laddered and barbell portfolios over a historical period (1950-70) and over four different scenarios of future rate movements. It is difficult to draw definitive conclusions about risk and return characteristics with their limited number of scenarios,[2] but the historical analysis illustrated the problems posed by holding long-term bonds in a period of secularly rising interest rates. The performance of both the laddered and barbell strategies was hurt by the decline in value of long-term bonds during the period. As a result, laddered portfolios that did not contain long-term bonds tended to outperform barbell portfolios that did have some long-term securities.

In this paper a Monte Carlo model is used to simulate various laddered and barbell structures over both short and long investment horizons. The portfolios are assumed to consist of municipal securities. For each simulation, a portfolio strategy is specified, such as a laddered portfolio with maturities spread evenly from one to ten year maturities. An initial portfolio is randomly selected and updated each year of the simulation at the prevailing interest rates. These rates are selected randomly by a Markov process based upon the behavior of "good grade" municipal interest rates as reported by Salomon Brothers, during the period of 1966 through 1972.

In the next section of the paper we describe the simulation model, including definitions of the portfolio strategies and the process for generating interest rates. Then the results of the model are presented for both 10-year and three-year investment horizons. An important part of this discussion is the definition and measurement of risk since the selection of a portfolio strategy is critically affected by the way a bank views risk. Finally, the implications of these results for management of bank portfolios are discussed.

DESCRIPTION OF THE MODEL

Definition of Portfolio Strategies

The laddered maturity structures studied are all assumed to have their maturities spread evenly from one year out to a specified maturity. For example, the 10-year laddered portfolio is assumed to contain equal amounts of one-year, two-year, etc. out to a 10-year maturity. At the end of each year of the simulation the proceeds obtained from the maturing one-year bond are reinvested in a new 10-year bond. The interest obtained each year is reinvested in new securities to maintain the maturity distribution under study. In the example of the 10-year ladder, 10% of the interest received each year is used to buy a new one-year bond, a new two-year bond, etc.

The barbell portfolios studied have clusters of maturities at the short and long end of the maturity range. Specifically, we assumed that all of the short maturities in each barbell were spread equally from one to seven-year maturities, while the long-term securities were divided equally among 24 to 30-year maturities. We varied the proportion of funds allocated to the short and long ends of the distribution, but the amount of funds within each category were always spread from one to seven and 24 to 30 respectively. The short end of the barbell is maintained in the same manner as the laddered portfolios, i.e., funds from

---

[2] In the future interest rate patterns used by Hempel and Kretschman [1973], it was assumed that yield curves would move up and down in parallel. In other words, long-term rates rose and fell by the same magnitude as short. This assumption tends to overstate long-term rate movements and the gains and losses that would result from holding long-term securities. In more recent work, Hempel and Yawitz [1974] show why longer-term rates tend to be less volatile than short.

maturing one-year securities are reinvested in new seven-year bonds. The long end is maintained by selling the 24-year bond when it becomes a 23-year maturity at the end of each period. Proceeds from this sale after taxes and transaction costs are used to buy a new 30-year bond. The transaction cost is assumed to be 1% of book value which approximates the spread between bid and asked prices on long-term municipal securities. Capital gains on the sale are taxed at a 50% rate while losses generate a 50% tax saving that adds to funds available for reinvestment. Finally, interest received from the barbell portfolio is reinvested in new securities in the same proportion as the original maturities in the portfolio.

There is an initial portfolio at the start of each simulation which contains a set of securities with a book value of $100 and a maturity structure similar to the portfolio strategy under study. Thus, if the strategy to be studied is a laddered portfolio with maturities spread from one to 10 years, the starting portfolio would contain $10 each of one-year, two-year, etc., securities. There is a question, though, on how the interest rates on the initial portfolio should be selected. One approach would be to assume that the initial portfolio is purchased with cash at the start of the simulation. For example, the one-year bond in the starting portfolio would be a new bond which carried the one-year coupon rate from the initial municipal yield curve. In practice a laddered or a barbell portfolio would be started in this way, but after a time the interest rate on one-year bonds in the

portfolio would be the rate which prevailed on a longer-term security. One of the alleged advantages of laddered portfolios is that new money is being regularly invested in some maturity, say 10 years, and that after a while all of the bonds contain coupon rates that were the 10-year rate which prevailed at the time of purchase.

To conform to this characteristic of laddered portfolios, we in effect assume that our initial portfolios have reached a steady state. When simulating a 10-year ladder, the one-year bond included in the initial portfolio represents a 10-year bond purchased nine years ago, the two-year bond was purchased eight years ago, etc. The same convention is used with the barbell portfolios. For example, the three-year bond in the initial portfolio represents a seven-year security purchased four years earlier and the 26-year bond was originally a 30-year security, also purchased four years earlier.

Process for Generating Sequences of Yield Curves

The general assumption we have made in the process used to generate sequences of municipal yield curves is that the volatility of interest rates will be about the same as it was in the period 1966 through 1972. This period contained two major interest rate cycles, including the credit crunch of 1966 and the tight money period of 1969-70. At the end of this period short-term municipal rates were about the same as at the beginning. Years prior to this period were excluded because rates moved within a much narrower range which most observers feel will not be typical of the future.[3]

A Markov process in which the yield curve for period $t+1$ depends upon the yield curve which occurred in period t was used to generate sequences of rates. The magnitude of the shift in the yield curve each period and its probability was based upon the distribution of changes in municipal yield curves during the 1966-72 period. We used the one-year "good grade" municipal rate as the basis for changes in all rates. Specifically, we assumed that the one-year rate had equal probabilities of increasing 100 basis points (one percentage point), staying the same or decreasing 100 basis points from one period to the next, except at boundaries as described below. These

Figure 1. Cumulative Distribution of Changes In the One-Year Municipal Rate

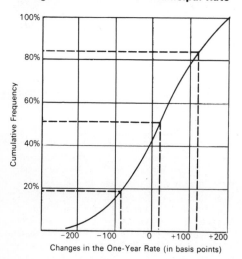

Changes in the One-Year Rate (in basis points)

[3] This time period encompasses the enactment of the Tax Reform Act of 1969 which eliminated the low capital gains tax on security sales by commercial banks, except for a transitional period. Although this change in bank tax rates may have some impact on the behavior of municipal rates, our estimates of the relationship among rates for the four years following the tax change were very similar to the parameters estimated for the 1966-72 period.

Figure 2. Changes of Other Municipal Rates Relative to Changes in the One-Year Rate: 1966-72

Maturity (years)	Regression Coefficient (stated as a % of the one-year rate change)	Percent of Variance Explained[4]
2	96.0%	99.4%
5	89.2	96.2
10	80.5	90.1
20	67.0	71.1
30	61.2	62.1

Figure 3. Yield Curves Used In Monte Carlo Simulation

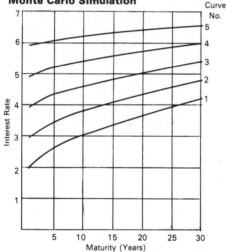

Figure 4. Yield Curve Transition Probabilities

		Yield Curve in Period $t+1$			
		I	II	III	IV	V
Yield Curve in Period t	I	.1	.9	—	—	—
	II	.333	.333	.333	—	—
	III	—	.333	.333	.333	—
	IV	—	—	.333	.333	.333
	V	—	—	—	.9	.1

magnitudes approximate the medians of three equally likely brackets of the distribution of one year changes in the one-year rate as shown in Figure 1.

Changes in yields for other maturities were tied to changes in the one-year rate. Generally longer-term interest rates tend to move in the same direction as the one-year rate, but the magnitude of the shift decreases as maturity increases. These magnitudes were estimated with regression equations and the results are shown in Figure 2.

The yield curves which were used in the simulation model are shown in Figure 3. Curve 3, the middle curve, was selected to represent an average or normal curve for the period with a 150 basis point spread between the 30-year and one-year rates. The other curves are based upon changes from curve 3. Increments between the one-year rates are 100 basis points, while increments between rates of other maturities are based upon the regression results of Figure 2. Points on the yield curves not specified by the regression equations were filled in to obtain smooth curves. Note that the yield curves flatten as rates rise and they become more steeply sloped as rates fall which is the typical behavior of yield curves.

The probabilities of moving from one yield curve to another are shown in the transition matrix of Figure 4. If the current yield curve is one of the intermediate curves 2, 3 or 4, we assumed that there are equal probabilities of moving up to the next higher curve, staying the same or falling to the next lower curve. This is consistent with the historical distribution of municipal rate changes, but it does not seem appropriate to assume that the probabilities will remain unchanged when very high or low interest rate levels are reached. Thus, we assumed that there was a high probability, .9, of rebounding from the high and low boundaries, curves 5 and 1.[5]

After randomly selecting an initial curve, the transition matrix was used to randomly select 400 sequences of municipal yield curves. In our experiments we selected 10 years as the maximum

---

[4] The coefficients were developed from regression equations in which the independent variable was the change in the one-year rate and the constant term was forced to zero. Because the constant term was zero, the R^2 is not strictly defined. However, we computed "per cent variance explained" using the standard formula for R^2 to give a reasonably accurate measure of how well the equation fit.

[5] The structure and behavior of the Markov model are consistent with work by Malkiel [1962] and Pye [1966]. Malkiel suggested that if interest rates appear to be near the extremes of their normal range, investors will assign a high probability to rates moving away from the extremes. Pye used a Markov model to describe investors' expectations about changes in the one-period rate. The expectation assumptions of both authors lead to yield curves which change their slope as interest rates rise and fall in the same manner as observed yield curves and the curves in our model.

planning horizon and we simulated each portfolio strategy over the 400 interest rate scenarios. The portfolio strategies were evaluated from the start of the simulation model, year one, to the end of the planning horizon, but it was necessary to also generate sequences of rates for time periods prior to the start of the model in order to obtain initial portfolios. As discussed above, we assumed that the portfolio policy being simulated contains an initial portfolio consistent with this policy. For example, a strategy that maintains a laddered portfolio with maturities from one to 10 years requires a rate sequence that was begun nine years earlier. At the start of the simulation the initial portfolio contains a 10-year bond purchased nine years earlier, a 10-year bond purchased eight years earlier, etc., so that its maturities are evenly distributed from one to 10 years. To handle this assumption each of the interest rate sequences generated by the model cover a 40-year period, the last 10 of which are used to evaluate the policy. Sequences of this length allow an initial portfolio laddered out to a 30-year maturity and this policy can then be tested for an additional 10 years. The same sequence of interest rates were used to test each portfolio strategy. The first 30 years of each sequence ($t = -29$ through $t = 0$) were available as needed to develop an initial portfolio, and the last 10 were available to evaluate the strategy.

Performance Measures

Measures of performance were selected to provide an indication of the expected or mean return and the risk of each portfolio strategy. The measure of total return used was the final market value of the portfolio at the investment horizon, including any cash received from interest or maturities at the horizon. Thus, the mean return from a strategy is the average horizon market value taken across the 400 trials of the simulation.

For analysis of the results later it is useful to transform this return into its components of interest income and capital gains. Each portfolio policy studied will produce some interest income and a net capital gain or loss. Since the laddered portfolio strategies involve no sale of securities their gain or loss will be an unrealized amount at the horizon, but the barbell portfolios might also have a net realized gain or loss from the trades necessary to maintain the maturity structure. The final market value is equal to the $100 initial book value plus the interest income and the total unrealized and realized capital gain or loss. Thus, an alternative measure of return is the sum of these two items and the mean return can be split

into these interest income and capital gain components.

$$M(R) = M(I) + M(G)$$

It should be noted that the performance of a barbell strategy can be improved by holding on to bonds which have an unrealized gain, thus avoiding the potential realized gain and payment of the gains tax. This is a procedure banks are likely to follow in practice, but we do not take advantage of it in our experiments. The 23-year bond is automatically sold even if a gain would be realized. Although this approach somewhat penalizes the return of barbell structures relative to laddered policies, we used the automatic sale assumption so that the maturities held in each barbell portfolio would be the same for all strategies studied.

Two measures of risk were computed by the model. One was the traditional measure of portfolio risk, the standard deviation of return which in this case is the standard deviation of the 400 final market values for each portfolio strategy. As with the mean it is useful to break this risk measure into its component parts. This can be done by computing the variance of total return in terms of its interest income and capital gain components:

$$\text{Var}(R) = \text{Var}(I) + \text{Var}(G) + 2 \times \text{Covar}(I,G)$$

While the standard deviation or variance of total return is a useful measure of risk, it makes the assumption that banks do not care whether the variability of return comes from the variation in interest income or in capital gains or losses. Many banks would argue that this is not a reasonable assumption since fluctuations in realized and unrealized gains and losses have special implications. Banks are reluctant to realize net losses on the sale of securities, in part because it is a very visable direct reduction in the earnings per share of the bank. In recent years banks have also limited their realized losses because of their small taxable income position. Realized losses on bond sales can be treated as a deduction from taxable income and reduce the bank's taxes. Most large banks, though, have relatively small taxable income positions and hence limited ability to use the tax deductions because of other activities which reduce their tax liability such as equipment leasing and foreign tax credits. Finally banks desire to limit their exposure to declines in the market value of their assets, even if they do not intend to realize the loss by selling the bonds. One of the reasons is that large potential losses tend to increase their need for equity capital as perceived by regulatory authorities. [6]

For these reasons, many banks consider the

"risk" of a portfolio strategy to be its potential for realized and unrealized losses in market value.[7] We have attempted to capture this aspect of risk by computing the total of realized and unrealized losses for each trial of the model. Then by looking at the 400 trials for each portfolio strategy we can compute a "maximum" loss position for this strategy. This maximum loss is selected so that the realized and unrealized losses on approximately 98% of the trials will be smaller, i.e., total losses will be worse than the "maximum" only 2% of the time.[8]

In computing the total of realized and unrealized gains and losses over the horizon of the model, we are assuming that banks are indifferent between accumulated realized losses and the unrealized loss at the end of the planning horizon. Banks actually plan for and consider these two aspects of portfolio management individually, but we adopted the simplification to obtain a combined measure of risk that would apply to both the laddered and barbell strategies. Use of realized losses by itself is not an appropriate measure of risk since all of the loss potential of a laddered portfolio is the unrealized amount at the horizon. Similarly, unrealized loss at the end of the horizon is a useful risk measure for some purposes, but consideration of this number alone ignores the ability of a bank to reduce unrealized loss potential by regular trading of securities. For example, the trading of the 23-year security in the barbell strategies reduces the potential buildup of unrealized losses. Thus, their unrealized loss potential tends to be less than the laddered policies.

IMPACT OF RISK MEASURE

As a first step laddered and barbell policies were studied using a 10-year planning horizon to look at the longer run implications of following a naive strategy. Figure 5 shows the risk-return characteristics of laddered portfolios of various maturity lengths. Each point in the exhibit represents a portfolio laddered from a one-year maturity out to the maturity identified in the label. For each of these portfolios, the figure shows the expected return as measured by the average mar-

ket value of the portfolio at the horizon. Risk is shown on the vertical axis and is measured by the standard deviation of the horizon market values. The plotting of the risk and return for each of the laddered portfolios forms a "frontier" in which return increases and variability declines as the longest maturity in the ladder increases from one to 30 years.

It is to be expected that longer maturity laddered portfolios would produce higher returns since they were constructed with longer term bonds. Portfolios laddered from one to 30 years, for example, consist of bonds which were all originally 30-year bonds. Since the 30-year rates are higher on average than other rates and there is no upward bias in the interest rate scenarios, these portfolios should produce the highest average return. It is somewhat surprising, though, to note that this higher return can be achieved at a lower rather than higher variability. Most portfolio managers regard longer term bonds more risky than short bonds. Some banks, even some very large ones, do not hold municipal securities with maturities longer than 10 to 15 years.

A large part of the reason that risk declines with longer maturities stems from the use of standard deviation of return as the measure of

Figure 5. Expected Return Vs Standard Deviation: Ten Year Horizon

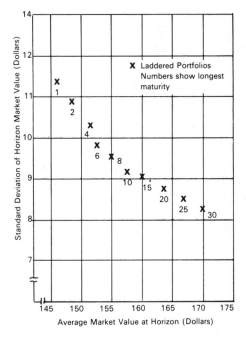

[6] Kane [1968] provides some empirical evidence for banks' reluctance to realize losses. Using cross-section data for 1966 he showed that realized losses were positively correlated with the amount unrealized loss in the portfolio and to the bank's amount of capital, among other variables.

[7] Use of potential losses as a measure of risk is analogous to the "safety first principle" which has been used in portfolio theory and models. An example is provided by Telser [1955-56].

[8] The 98th percentile of total losses was estimated by assuming that the distribution of total net gains (losses) is normal and computing the loss represented by the mean less two standard deviations, i.e., the .023 point on the cumulative distribution.

risk. Lengthening the maturity structure of a laddered portfolio tends to reduce the variability of interest income over the horizon because it lowers the turnover of the portfolio and because longer rates are less volatile than shorter rates. As an example, compare a portfolio laddered from one to 10 years with a portfolio laddered out 20 years. Over a 10-year horizon all of the initial securities in the 10-year ladder are completely replaced with new securities, but only 50% of the 20-year ladder turns over. Moreover, the fluctuations in the 20-year interest rate are only 83% as large as those of the 10-year municipal rate, based upon the volatility of interest rates reported in Figure 2.

Although the variability of unrealized gains and losses grows when the portfolio ladder is lengthened from 10 to 20 years, this increase is more than offset by the reduction of interest income variability. The variance components for the 10- and 20-year ladder are shown in Figure 6.

When the definition of risk is changed to be the maximum realized plus unrealized losses, the risk-return frontier of laddered portfolios behaves more as expected. As shown in Figure 7, the riskiness of the portfolios increases as the length of the ladder is increased to include longer term bonds. Thus, one reason a bank might not include longer term municipals in a laddered portfolio would be its desire to limit the unrealized loss potential of the portfolio.

One of the major purposes of experimentation with the simulation model is to see how barbell portfolios would perform in comparison with laddered portfolios, if both were managed mechanically. All of the barbell portfolios studied contained an equal spread of one- to seven-year maturities on the short end and an equal spread of 24- to 30-year maturities at the other end of the range. Various mixes of these two maturity groups were tried, ranging from 100% short to 100% long.

Figure 8 illustrates the risk return profile of barbell portfolios when the standard deviation of return is used as the measure of risk. It can be seen that the standard deviation increases along with return as the proportion of the portfolio allocated to the long bonds is increased above 20%. Of more interest is the result that laddered portfolios are more "efficient." For a given level of return, the laddered portfolios tend to have less variability than the barbell structure. This results from the lower volatility of interest income when laddered portfolios are used. For example, the portfolio laddered from one to 15 years and the barbell portfolio with 70% allocated to short maturities provide about the same return. The total variance and its components for each of these two portfolio policies are shown in Figure 9. These two policies have similar variances of net capital gains, but the barbell portfolio has a significantly larger variance of the interest income. This stems partly from the higher turnover of the barbell portfolio which has one-seventh of its bonds maturing or traded each year as compared to the one-fifteenth of the laddered portfolio which matures. In addition, proceeds from maturities in the barbell portfolio are reinvested at the relatively volatile seven-year rate.

Figure 6. Components of Variance of Total Return: 10- and 20-Year Laddered Portfolios

	Total Variance[9]	Variance of Interest Income	Variance of Net Capital Gain (Loss)
10-Year Ladder	$87.11	$71.80	$ 5.62
20-Year Ladder	76.23	44.00	18.27

[9] The columns do not add to total variance since two times the covariance has not been shown.

Figure 7. Expected Return Vs Maximum Loss: Ten Year Horizon

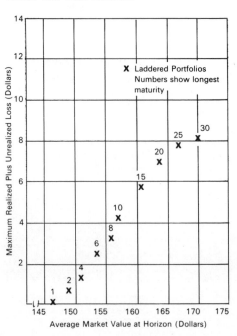

Figure 8. Expected Return Vs Standard Deviation: Ten Year Horizon

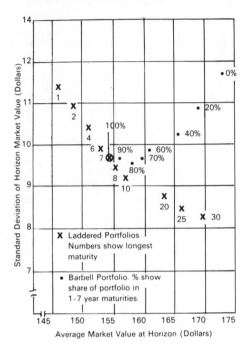

Average Market Value at Horizon (Dollars)

Figure 10. Expected Return Vs Maximum Loss: Ten Year Horizon

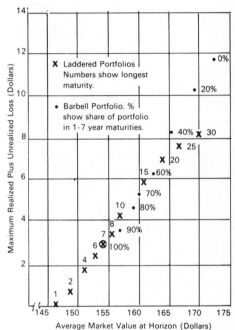

Average Market Value at Horizon (Dollars)

Figure 9. Variances for Laddered and Barbell Portfolios

Portfolio Strategy	Total Variance	Variance of Interest Income	Variance of Net Capital Gain (Loss)
15-Year Ladder	$80.49	$55.75	$11.76
Barbell with 70% Short	93.87	71.81	11.14

If risk is defined to be maximum total loss rather than the standard deviation of return, the performance of barbell portfolios relative to laddered maturities improves. In fact, the barbell portfolios perform slightly better than the ladder portfolios over some maturity ranges, as shown in Figure 10. For example, the barbell with 70% allocated to short maturities had a maximum loss of $5.22 as compared to the $5.79 maximum loss of the one to 15-year laddered portfolio which provides a similar return. This may or may not be a significant improvement, but the pattern in Figure 10 does suggest that if banks are concerned

about the potential for realized and unrealized losses, mechanically managed barbell portfolios perform competitively with laddered structures over a wide range of policies.

The barbell portfolios perform even better if the measure of risk is taken to be maximum unrealized losses only. Most, if not all, banks want to limit realized losses each year, but some may be willing to tolerate modest losses from their trading activity. So long as realized losses are within some policy limit, the bank's major concern of a risk nature is the unrealized losses that might build up. If so, the barbell portfolio has an advantage over a mechanically managed ladder because of the regular sales necessary to maintain the structure. In the example of the previous paragraph, the 15-year ladder had a maximum unrealized loss of $5.79 while the maximum unrealized loss of the barbell with a comparable total return was $4.08. Although the annual trading activity exposed the portfolio to realized losses, the 98th percentile of the distribution of realized losses per year was a relatively modest $.60 or .6 of 1% of the initial book value of the portfolio.

IMPACT OF PLANNING HORIZON

The risk-return profile of laddered portfolios in Figure 5 suggests that banks can lower variability of returns and increase expected return over relatively long investment horizons by maintaining a laddered structure with longer maturities. Since many banks maintain ladders with relatively short maturities, this suggests that maximum loss is a more relevant measure of portfolio risk. Although there is a rationale to support this position, there is a complementary explanation of the short maturity ladders which depends upon the length of the bank's investment horizon.

Roll [1971] has pointed out that the variability of returns can be reduced in bond portfolios by holding bonds which mature both before and after the investor's horizon. The reduction in total standard deviation results from the negative correlation between the returns on bonds that mature before the horizon and the returns on those that mature after. If interest rates move in a direction that will increase the return from the "shorter" bonds, the return on the bonds longer than the horizon will fall, lowering the impact of this rate movement on total return. This can be seen by considering a situation in which interest rates rise over the planning horizon. The bonds maturing before the horizon provide cash that can be reinvested at higher rates. On the other hand, the longer bonds will decline in value reducing the return from this part of the portfolio. If rates were to fall, the longer securities would increase in value, but the return from the short end of the portfolio is reduced because the maturing short bonds must be reinvested at lower rates.

This negative correlation between the returns of bonds maturing before and after the investment horizon indicates that the riskiness of a particular maturity structure is dependent upon the length of the investor's planning horizon. Fisher and Weil [1971] have identified an important relationship between risk, maturity structure and investment horizon by using the concept of duration.[10] They showed that under some assumptions about

the behavior of interest rates, the variability of returns from a portfolio can be minimized if the duration of the portfolio is kept equal to the time remaining to the end of the investment horizon. Actual interest rates do not behave exactly as assumed, but they tested their portfolio strategies using actual corporate bond rates and found that the standard deviation of returns was kept small by equating duration and the horizon length.

Duration is an important measure of the "maturity" of a portfolio because it recognizes that not all the cash flow from a typical bond occurs at its maturity. Consider, for example, a typical 6% bond with semi-annual coupons and a 10-year maturity that was purchased at par. A substantial share of the cash that will be obtained from this bond will be received before maturity so that its duration is about 7.7 years. If the bond had no coupons, but was purchased at a discount to yield 6% at maturity, there would be no interim cash flows and the duration of the bond would be 10 years. For an investor with a fixed 10-year horizon, the second bond is risk free in the sense that there is no variability in its return. The bond with semi-annual coupons is not risk free since it will be generating cash before the horizon which must be reinvested at rates that are uncertain.

If banks had fixed investment horizons and if bonds without coupons were available, it would be relatively easy to select a portfolio of non-coupon bonds with maturities equal to the horizon so that there would be no variability of returns. Even though these bonds are not normally available, Fisher and Weil have shown that there is a comparable strategy of coupon bonds that has a small variability of total return. Their suggested strategy is to select coupon bonds so that the duration of the portfolio as a whole is equal to the investment horizon. To obtain this duration, at least some of the bonds will have to have maturities longer than the horizon. Although this portfolio will generate some cash before the horizon which will have to be reinvested at uncertain rates, the variability of total return is still kept small. This results from the negative correlation of returns from maturities before and after the investment horizon, a situation pointed out by Roll.

The concept of duration helps explain the relationship between average return and standard deviation of return from laddered portfolios over the 10-year investment horizon discussed in the previous section. As shown in Figure 5 increases in the maturity of the laddered portfolios led to higher average returns, but also to lower varia-

---

[10] The duration of a portfolio is based upon the present value of future cash flows from interest and maturing bonds. Let P_t be the present value of the cash flows that will occur at the end of the period t and assume that n is the last period in which a cash flow occurs. Then the duration equals:

$$D = \frac{\sum\limits_{t=1}^{n} t \, P_t}{\sum\limits_{t=1}^{n} P_t}$$

The duration for a portfolio is affected to some extent by the choice of the discount rate used to calculate present values. In the durations for the portfolios presented we use the average yield-to-maturity of the portfolio as the discount rate.

bility of returns. This reduction in variability occurred because the duration of the laddered portfolios moved closer to the length of the investment horizon as longer maturities were added to the portfolios. When the portfolio was laddered out to 30-year maturities, the duration of the portfolio finally reached 10 years since the average duration of these portfolios was about 10.4 years.

If the duration concept has validity, we would not expect long-maturity laddered portfolios to be the lowest risk portfolio when the investment horizon is relatively short. This is illustrated in Figure 11 which shows the relationship between average return and standard deviation for a laddered portfolio over a three-year investment horizon. The portfolio with the least variability is the one laddered out to a six-year maturity. This portfolio has an average duration of about 3.25 years which is close to the length of the investment horizon. As longer bonds are added to the ladder, the average return can be increased, but only at the cost of more variability of returns.

The concept of duration does help explain the results obtained with our simulation model, even though the portfolio strategies we tested are different from the strategies studied by Fisher and Weil. They held the investment horizon fixed at some future point in time. An initial portfolio was selected so that its duration would be equal to the horizon. Then at the end of each year the portfolio was adjusted so that the duration would be one year shorter. In this manner, the duration of the portfolio was kept equal to the time remaining to the fixed horizon.

In both our laddered and barbell strategies, the duration of each portfolio was kept approximately constant over time, even though we evaluated the strategy at the end of a fixed horizon. The exact duration of the six-year laddered portfolio, for example, varied because of the variability in the interest rate on new six-year bonds added to the portfolio. However, the basic maturity structure was not altered over time. We believe this is in keeping with the way banks manage their portfolios. Although there should be a specific planning horizon in mind when a portfolio strategy is selected, this horizon is moved forward as time passes rather than held fixed.

In addition to the performance characteristics of laddered portfolios, we are also interested in the performance of barbell strategies over the three-year investment horizon. Thus, Figure 11 includes average return and standard deviation results for barbell portfolios. The conclusion remains the same as it was with the 10-year horizon. Laddered portfolios appear to be more efficient

Figure 11. Expected Return Vs Standard Deviation: Three Year Horizon

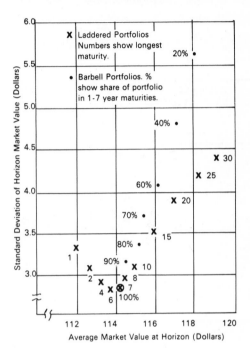

than mechanically managed barbell portfolios, providing a higher average return for the same level of variability.

As a final experiment the performance of laddered portfolios was compared to barbells over the three-year investment horizon using maximum loss as the measure of risk. These results, shown in Figure 12, suggest that barbell and laddered portfolios perform comparably for portfolios with moderate to low risk. However, the maximum loss of barbells tends to increase more rapidly than that of laddered portfolios as the average maturity is increased.

IMPLICATIONS FOR MANAGEMENT OF INVESTMENT PORTFOLIOS

The major question explored was whether barbell or laddered municipal portfolios performed better if managed mechanically over multiple time periods. This question cannot be answered unambiguously, but the results of the Monte Carlo simulation model do suggest some conclusions.

If a bank wished to adopt a mechanical trading rule, laddered portfolios appear to work relatively well. The reinvestment of funds from maturing bonds into new intermediate or long-term securities provides relatively high interest income. At the same time, the relatively slow turnover of the portfolio and the low volatility of intermediate or long-term rates leads to low variability in the return from the portfolio, particularly in interest income.

Figure 12. Expected Return Vs Maximum Loss: Three Year Horizon

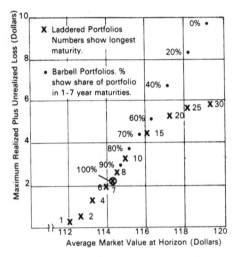

Average Market Value at Horizon (Dollars)

The appropriate length of the laddered portfolio depends critically upon two factors—the length of the bank's investment horizon and its willingness to have unrealized losses build up in the portfolio. If the bank has a long investment horizon and a high tolerance for capital losses, long maturity ladders perform well since they have a high return with a low variability. It is more likely that banks, particularly small to medium size banks, would not find themselves in this position. Most banks are concerned about managing their potential capital loss position to make sure that it does not become too large. In addition, it is likely that banks have a relatively short investment horizon since their liabilities have a very short average maturity. For either or both of these reasons, banks which use laddered portfolios are not likely to maintain a long maturity structure.

Although laddered portfolios appear to perform better than barbells when the standard deviation of return is used as the measure of risk, there are several reasons why a bank might wish to use a barbell portfolio strategy. Banks may be more concerned about capital loss position than they are about the variability of total return. Few, if any, banks even measure the variability of total return on their investment portfolios. If "maximum loss" is the more important or binding measure of risk, then barbell portfolios appear to perform about as well as laddered structures when managed mechanically. They perform even better relative to laddered portfolios if a bank is primarily concerned about the potential buildup in unrealized losses and is willing to tolerate up to modest amounts of realized losses each year. Furthermore, the performance of barbell portfolios can be improved in practice by avoiding or postponing realized gains, a tactic we did not use in this study.

Barbell portfolios also offer the advantages of more liquidity and more flexibility. The higher turnover rate of barbell portfolios does lead to more volatility of interest income, but it also provides more liquidity in that a larger per cent of the portfolio is in "short" bonds and a larger volume matures each year. In an example discussed above, a portfolio laddered from one to 15 years provides about the same return as a barbell with 70% of its funds in the one to seven-year range. The barbell portfolio, however, leaves the bank in a much better position if part of the portfolio must be liquidated to meet loan demand or deposit withdrawals. Ten per cent of this barbell portfolio matures within one year and 50% matures within 5 years. The laddered portfolio runs off at the rate of 6.67% per year and only one-third matures within five years.

The barbell portfolio also provides more flexibility for a bank that wishes to manage its portfolio more actively. With the higher turnover rate of a barbell portfolio, it is relatively easy for the portfolio manager to change the average maturity structure significantly if he wants to alter the bank's portfolio posture or to take advantage of the expected interest rate swings. A comparable change in the maturity structure of a laddered portfolio requires either a longer period of time or a larger trading program, neither of which may be feasible at the time the change is desired.

The performance of barbell portfolios is affected to a slight extent by the transaction costs involved in the trades and the marginal tax rate of the bank. In the barbell portfolio, with 70% of its funds allocated to short maturities, for example, elimination of the transaction cost would have improved performance by about 2 basis points per year. Small changes in the marginal tax rate would have very little impact on expected return. To the extent it had some impact, a lower marginal tax rate would increase expected return, but it would also increase the variability of returns since the tax payments and tax savings would absorb less of the capital gains and losses.

In summary, barbell maturity structures do offer some significant advantages to banks that wish to manage their portfolios actively. They provide more liquidity and flexibility than laddered portfolios with the same level of expected return. The total return of barbell portfolios may be more volatile, but this may not be an important price to pay for some banks. On the other hand, banks that do not want to actively manage their municipal portfolio may find laddered portfolios very attractive. They can provide a comparable return with less uncertainty that the return will be achieved. □

REFERENCES

Bradley, Stephen P. and Dwight B. Crane, "Managing a Bank Bond Portfolio Over Time," in M.A.H. Dempster, *Stochastic Programming*, (London: Academic Press), 1975 (forthcoming).

Bradley, Stephen P. and Dwight B. Crane, "Management of Commercial Bank Government Security Portfolios: An Optimization Approach Under Uncertainty," *Journal of Bank Research*, Vol. 4, No. 1 (Spring 1973), pp. 18-30.

Fisher, Lawrence and Roman L. Weil, "Coping with the Risk of Interest-Rate Fluctuations: Returns to Bondholders from Naive and Optimal Strategies", *The Journal of Business*, Vol. 44, No. 4 (October 1971), pp. 408-431.

Hempel, George H. and Stephen R. Kretschman, "Comparative Performance of Portfolio Maturity Policies of Commercial Banks," *Mississippi Valley Journal of Business and Economics*, Vol. IX, No. 1 (Fall 1973), pp. 55-75.

Hempel, George H. and Jess B. Yawitz, "Maximizing Bond Returns," *The Bankers Magazine*, Vol. 157, No. 3 (Summer 1974), pp. 103-114.

Kane, Edward J., "Is There a Predilected Lock-In Effect?", *National Tax Journal*, Volume XXI, No. 4 (December 1968), pp. 365-385.

Malkiel, Burton G., "Expectations, Bond Prices, and the Term Structure of Interest Rates," *Quarterly Journal of Economics*, Vol. LXXVI, No. 2 (May 1962), pp. 197-218.

Pye, Gordon, "A Markov Model of the Term Structure," *Quarterly Journal of Economics*, Vol. LXXX, No. 1 (February 1966), pp. 60-72.

Roll, Richard, "Investment Diversification and Bond Maturity," *Journal of Finance*, Vol. XXVI, No. 1 (March 1971), pp. 51-66.

Salomon Brothers, *An Analytical Record of Yields and Yield Spreads*.

Telser, Lester, "Safety First and Hedging," *Review of Economic Studies*, Volume 23, 1955-56.

Watson, Ronald D., "Tests of Maturity Structures of Commercial Bank Government Securities Portfolios: A Simulation Approach," *Journal of Bank Research*, Vol. 3, No. 1 (Spring 1972), pp. 34-46.

Chapter 24

ARBITRAGE IN U.S. GOVERNMENT BONDS: A MANAGEMENT SCIENCE APPROACH*

By Robert L. Kramer

*This article is reprinted, with permission, from *Journal of Bank Research,* Vol. 1, No. 2 (Summer, 1970), pp. 30-43.

The market in U.S. Government bonds[1] is conducted much like the over-the-counter market in common stocks. It is maintained by 21 "primary dealers," mostly commercial banks, investment bankers and bond houses. Primary dealers maintain trading positions in most of the issues outstanding and quote bid and asked prices on all issues. Many publish a daily "quote sheet," showing the bid and asked prices for each issue, as of the close of trading on the preceding business day, expressed as a per cent of face value, with fractional per cents given in 32nds (e.g. a quote of 98 8/32 means $98.25 per $100 of face value, or a price of $982.50 for a $1000 bond, see Exhibit I. The dealer's spread—the difference between the bid and asked prices—may range from 2/32 on short maturities to 12/32 or more on longer maturities. Bonds are bought and sold by a variety of firms, both financial and non-financial, by governmental bodies and by individuals. The largest single group trading in the U.S. Government bond market is commercial banks. (Dealers also frequently trade among themselves, usually in larger transactions and at smaller price spreads.)

Arbitrage may be defined as 1) the simultaneous purchase and sale of the same security in different markets in order to profit from price differences, or 2) the simultaneous purchase of one security and sale of a similar security in order to profit from abnormal price differences between them. In this application, it is the second sense which is relevant. As bond prices fluctuate, often in a "non-rational" manner, there are frequent oppotunities for arbitrage. However, because of the dealer's spread (i.e., because customers must buy at the asked price and sell at the bid price), transaction costs become a significant consideration. Many arbitrage situations do not offer enough profit to justify the effort and risk involved: The usual potential

[1]In this paper, the phrase "U.S. Government bond" is used to devote any coupon-bearing U.S. Government security, regardless of whether it is technically referred to as a certificate, note or bond. The distinctions among these categories have no direct relevance for arbitrage purposes. Possible arbitrage opportunities involving U.S. Government bills are not being considered.

profit ranges between 6/32 and 16/32 per transaction. Obviously, in order to be worthwhile, arbitrages must involve reasonably large amounts —usually $1 million or more. The potential profit to a dealer on a $1 million trade may be from $2,000 to $5,000; for a customer, it would usually be between $500 and $3,000. Thus, worthwhile arbitrage opportunities are available more often to dealers than to their customers, and at lower transaction costs. Nevertheless, many customers do engage in such transactions.

The possibility of arbitraging in the U.S. Government bond market has long been recognized and exploited. At least as far back as 1933, banks and other financial institutions have been engaging in and advising customers of arbitrage transactions (see bibliography). With rare exceptions, these analyses have been based upon frequency distributions of historical price spreads between specific pairs of very similar issues. Sometimes, trends in these spreads were also taken into account. As will be seen, other explanatory factors should also be considered.

In practice, an arbitrage is set up by 1) buying a given number of bonds of one issue and 2) selling short an equal number of bonds of another issue. The latter is accomplished by "borrowing" the bonds from another firm, in return for payment of interest, usually 1/2 of 1% per year, on the par value involved. When the prices return to their normal differential, the transaction is reversed, i.e. the purchased bonds are sold and the borrowed bonds are bought and returned to the lender. (This does not imply that the total *market* value of bonds purchased equals that of bonds sold. Only the *face* values are equal. Any difference in market value must be included when computing the return on the arbitrage operation.)

At any given time, there may be anywhere from 35 to 60 bond issues outstanding, due to mature in from one day to 40 years. Theoretically, it is possible for an arbitrage opportunity to exist between any pair of issues. The number of such combinations is given by $N(N-1)/2$ where N is the number of issues outstanding.

Exhibit 1. Typical Bond Quote Sheet

CTFS. – NOTES – BONDS (1) (2)

Out-standing (Millions)	RATE	MATURITY	SEE FOOTNOTES	BID	ASKED	CHANGE PREVIOUS DAY	YIELD (a)	YIELD AFTER CORPORATE TAXES	TAXABLE EQUIV.	YIELD VALUE 1/32	MEMORANDA	HIGH 1969	LOW 1969
4,381	4	2/15/70	b	99-15	99-17	+1	8.12	3.83	8.12	.279		99- 5	97-14
2,281	2 1/2	3/15/70-65	b f	98-25	98-27	+1	8.61	4.06	8.61	.166		98-11	96- 4
7,793	5 5/8	5/15/70	n	98-31	99- 1	..	8.34	3.93	8.34	.090		99-22	98- 6
8,759	6 3/8	5/15/70	n	99- 8	99-10	+1	8.27	3.90	8.27	.089		100-10	98-26
2,329	6 3/8	8/15/70	n	98-27	98-29	+2	8.23	4.35	9.22	.055		100- 3	98-23
4,129	4	8/15/70	b	97- 9	97-11	..	8.51	5.15	10.92	.055		97-20	96- 6
7,675	5	11/15/70	n	97- 3	97- 5	..	8.48	4.88	10.34	.039		98-10	96-12
2,931	7 3/4	2/15/71	n	99-20	99-24	+2	7.98	3.82	8.10	.031		100-25	99-17
2,509	5 3/8	2/15/71	n	96-31	97- 3	..	8.16	4.55	9.65	.031		98-29	96-16
1,221	2 1/2	3/15/71-66	b f	93-20	93-24	+2	8.09	5.23	11.08	.030		94-28	92-16
4,265	5 1/4	5/15/71	n	96- 7	96-11	+1	8.14	4.57	9.68	.025		98-20	95-30
4,173	8	5/15/71	n	100- 6	100- 6	+4	7.84	3.70	7.84	.025		101-11	99-23
2,806	4	8/15/71	b	93-23	93-27	+3	8.15	4.89	10.37	.022		96-21	93- 2
2,760	3 7/8	11/15/71	b	92-13	92-17	+5	8.28	5.02	10.64	.019		95-10	91-24
1,734	5 3/8	11/15/71	n	95- 7	95-11	-1	8.11	4.51	9.57	.019		98-19	95- 2
2,344	4	2/15/72	b	91-16	91-24	+2	8.34	5.03	10.66	.017		95- 7	91- 4
2,006	4 3/4	2/15/72	n	93- 2	93-10	+4	8.27	4.79	10.15	.016		96-29	92-24
5,310	4 3/4	5/15/72	n	92- 6	92-14	+2	8.33	4.83	10.24	.015		96-16	91-30
1,242	2 1/2	6/15/72-67	b f	87-14	87-22	+6	8.15	5.27	11.37	.015		94- 6	86-20
2,578	4	8/15/72	b	90-	90- 8	+2	8.22	4.94	10.48	.014		94-16	89-20
1,951	2 1/2	9/15/72-67	b	86-	86- 8	+6	8.30	5.38	11.40	.014		91-12	85-20
2,587	2 1/2	12/15/72-67	b f	85- 2	85-10	+12	8.22	5.32	11.28	.013		90-19	84-16
1,158	7 3/4	5/15/73	n	101- 2	101-10	+10	7.30	3.44	7.30	.011		102-24	99-18
3,894	4	8/15/73	b	86-12	86-20	..	8.36	5.04	10.68	.011		93-16	86-
4,348	4 1/8	11/15/73	b f	86- 4	86-12	..	8.31	4.95	10.55	.010		93-12	85-24
3,128	4 1/8	2/15/74	b f	85-16	85-24	+4	8.29	5.26	10.13	.010		93- 6	84-30
3,585	4 1/4	5/15/74	b f	85- 4	85-12	+4	8.30	5.24	10.09	.009		93-18	84-20
10,283	5 5/8	8/15/74	n	89-24	90-	+4	8.26	4.90	9.42	.008		97-18	89-14
2,240	3 7/8	11/15/74	b f	83-	83- 8	+8	8.10	5.18	9.96	.008		91- 8	82-J 6
3,981	4 1/4	11/15/74	n	90- 4	90-12	+6	8.18	4.81	9.25	.008		98-14	89-20
5,148	5 3/4	2/15/75	n	90- 2	90-10	+6	8.09	4.74	9.12	.008		98-14	89-14
6,760	6	5/15/75	n	91- 8	91-16	+6	7.97	4.59	8.84	.008		100-16	90-20
3,726	6 1/4	2/15/76	n	93-	93- 8	+8	7.66	4.30	8.28	.008		100-26	92- 6
2,697	6 1/2	5/15/76	n	94- 6	94-14	+6	7.61	4.21	8.10	.007		100- 7	93- 8
1,681	7 1/2	8/15/76	n	100- 4	100-12	+14	7.43	3.50	7.43	.006		103-24	98-22
2,598	4	2/15/80	b f	72- 8	73-	+24	7.93	5.02	9.66	.005		85- 8	71-
1,906	3 1/2	11/15/80	b f	68-16	69- 8	+24	7.71	4.97	9.57	.005		80-20	67- 8
1,557	3 1/4	6/15/83-78	b f	64-12	65- 4	+16	7.38	4.78	9.20	.004		76-12	63-
1,095	3 1/4	5/15/85	b f	64- 4	64-28	+20	7.02	4.51	8.68	.004		74-24	62-24
1,214	4 1/4	5/15/85-75	b f	72- 8	73- 8	+6	7.15	4.38	8.43	.004		84-	70-24
4,841	3 1/2	2/15/90	b f	64-12	64-28	+16	6.70	4.22	8.11	.004		74- 4	62-20
3,815	4 1/4	8/15/92-87	b f	69-28	70-12	+20	6.83	4.14	7.97	.003		80- 4	67-28
249	4	2/15/93-88	b f	66-24	67-24	+24	6.78	4.16	8.00	.003		77-24	65-24
1,558	4 1/8	5/15/94-89	b f	67- 8	68- 8	+24	6.81	4.15	7.99	.003		78-	65-24
1,459	3	2/15/95	b f	64- 8	64-24	+16	5.62	3.52	6.77	.003		74- 4	62-16
4,249	3 1/2	11/15/98	b f	64-12	64-28	+16	6.10	3.77	7.25	.003		74-	62-20

(1) The 10% surcharge is being used in computing yields on maturities through 1973.
As the effect of the surtax becomes minimal beyond that date, it has been disregarded.
(2) 52.8% Taxable Equivalent through 1973.
Quotation on Treasury 1 1/2% notes and Agency issued not listed on reverse side will be furnished on request.

DECIMAL EQUIVALENTS OF 64ths (+) and 32nds per $100.

+$.015625	4 $.125000	7+$.234375	11 $.343750	14+$.453125	17+$.546875	20+$.640625	23+$.734375	26+$.828125	29+$.921875
1 .031250	4+ .140625	8 .250000	11+ .359375	15 .468750	18 .562500	21 .656250	24 .750000	27 .843750	30 .937500
1+ .046875	5 .156250	8+ .265625	12 .375000	15+ .484375	18+ .578125	21+ .671875	24+ .765625	27+ .859375	30+ .953125
2 .062500	5+ .171875	9 .281250	12+ .390625	16 .500000	19 .593750	22 .687500	25 .781250	28 .875000	31 .968750
2+ .078125	6 .187500	9+ .296875	13 .406250	16+ .515625	19+ .609375	22+ .703125	25+ .796875	28+ .890625	31+ .984375
3 .093750	6+ .203125	10 .312500	13+ .421875	17 .531250	20 .625000	23 .718750	26 .812500	29 .906250	32 1.000000
3+ .109375	7 .218750	10+ .328125	14 .437500				

(a) Callable bonds offered above 100 computed to earliest call.
(b) Bonds
(c) Certificates
(d) A combined Federal normal and surtax of 48% is figured on yield for bills and issues offered at and above 100. For issues offered below 100, other than bills, tax is figured on coupon plus 25% long term capital gains tax on difference between coupon and gross yield.
(e) Tax anticipation series
All transactions are subject to confirmation by us in New York. Interest accrued to date of receipt of funds by us to be added to sale price. Statements contained herein while not guaranteed as to accuracy, completeness, or otherwise, are based on information we believe to be reliable.

(f) Redeemable at par in payment of Federal Estate Taxes
(g) Interest payable at maturity
Minimum denomination of Agency issues is $5,000 except for issues marked:
(h) $100.
(i) $1,000.
(j) Notes

Abbreviations:

COOP — Banks for Cooperatives
EXIM — Export-Import Bank
FHLB — Federal Home Loan Banks
FICB — Federal Intermediate Credit Banks
FLB — Federal Land Banks
FNMA — Federal National Mortgage Association
PC — Participation Certificates
CD — Capital Debentures

Coupon Rate %	Nbr. Days* to Equal 1/32nd
1½	7.6
2	5.7
2½	4.6
3	3.8
3½	3.3
4	2.9
4¼	2.7
4½	2.6
4¾	2.5
5	2.3
5½	2.0

*365 DAY BASIS

Thus, on any given day, arbitrage opportunities might exist between one or more of approximately 500 to 1,800 pairs of issues.

Practically, however, a number of these combinations are normally eliminated from consideration. Issues maturing in less than two years are disregarded because there may not be sufficient time to reverse the transaction and because price fluctuations in this maturity range are usually quite small. Issues differing significantly in coupon rate are eliminated because arbitrages will only be undertaken in one direction i.e., when the high-coupon issue is underpriced relative to the low-coupon issue, since the difference in coupon rates would usually offset the profit made on the arbitrage in the other direction. (Perhaps, though, they should be considered for arbitrage purposes, since some of the time the coupon difference as well as the price difference will be favorable.) Finally, comparisons of issues separated widely in maturity are affected by different factors and may tend to diverge from any established ralationship. This is virtually the only risk involved in arbitrage operations (in government bonds) i.e., that the price spread will remain "abnormal" too long.[2] The carrying cost of the borrowed bonds for such an extended period will usually offset much if not all of the potential profit (see Exhibit II).

For these reasons, the search for arbitrage opportunities is usually conducted only among issues of at least intermediate maturity with "similar" coupon rates, say within 3/4 of 1%, and similar maturities, say within two to three years in the intermediate maturities, and five to eight years in the longer maturities. However, these restrictions would still permit consideration of from 150 to 300 pairs of issues.

The usual method is to study only a few (20-60) of the more obvious comparisons, then set up an arbitrage only when the spread between a pair of issues has exceeded some intuitively-determined maximum difference from the historical average This method has several obvious faults:

> Since only 10-20% of the possible "arbitragable" pairs of issues are studied, a large fraction of the potential arbitrages are necessarily overlooked.

> By using subjective limits, the process is prone to errors in intuition, in addition to the ever-present statistically random movements of the price spreads.

> Because the criteria are not clearly stated or even recorded, the process cannot be replicated by others.

> The historical average introduces bias because it does not correct for the time trend of the spreads.

> This approach ignores the market level at which each spread was observed.

These shortcomings of the traditional method, then, were the *raison d'etre* for the investigation reported in this paper. The approach to this problem had four primary attributes: (1) Use of a computer; this was a prerequisite for the voluminous calculations and records involved; (2) examination of a greater number of "arbitragable" pairs of issues; (3) use of time trends of prices and spreads; (4) consideration of the market level at each point in time. These will be explained in greater detail below.

Early Phases of the Project

Before arriving at the final model, several alternative approaches were explored. The first of these was multiple regression analysis. Dependent variables investigated included prices and spreads for various issues and pairs of issues, respectively, for each day of a sample period. The independent variables investigated included various transformations of prices, spreads and yields for several preceding days; bond and stock market indices; and assorted economic indicators, such as industrial production, manufacturer's inventories, bank loans and new orders. Although reasonably large correlation coefficients were obtained, the resulting accuracy was not high enough for arbitrage purposes.

Another unsuccessful approach was the "random walk" or Markov Chain model. With this technique, only the magnitude and direction of daily changes in the spread are important. The implicit assumption is that a large change in either direction will be "corrected" shortly, while a small one will go "unnoticed" by market forces. However, despite the development of a theoretically workable heuristic, this method too was discarded, primarily because the resulting transactions would have to be executed more rapidly than is usually possible. Also it usually involved a greater risk of loss and less profit per transaction than existing approaches.

---

[2]There is no default risk, since the bonds are fully backed by the Federal Government. Nor does the market level affect profits significantly. As long as the bonds are similar enough to move together during a major market adjustment, the loss on the short sale (in an up market) will be offset by a gain on the purchased bond (or vice versa in a down market).

Exhibit 2. Number of days before net profit disappears – Difference in coupon rates

(Borrowing cost = 1/2% per year = $14/day/$MM)

EXPECTED TRADING PROFIT	+3/8	+1/4	+1/8	0	−1/8	−1/4	−3/8	−1/2
	(Bought higher coupon issue)				(Bought lower coupon issue)			
1/32	89	44	29	22	17	14	12	11
2/	178	89	59	44	35	29	25	22
3/	267	134	89	67	53	44	38	33
4/	357	178	119	89	71	59	51	44
5/	446	222	148	111	89	74	63	55
6/		267	178	134	107	89	76	66
7/		312	208	156	125	104	89	78
8/		357	238	178	142	119	102	89
9/		401	267	200	160	133	114	100
10/			297	222	178	148	127	111
11/			327	244	196	163	140	122
12/			357	267	214	178	148	133
13/			386	289	232	193	165	145
14/				312	250	208	178	156
15/				334	267	223	191	167
16/				357	285	238	204	178

After taking transaction costs into account, this method would have resulted in net losses.

Development of the Model

The model which finally evolved has some similarity to one used in the late 1930s. However, it contains some additional features lacking in the earlier approach.

The model is based on the theoretical price behavior of a "perfect" bond (i.e., no special features) in a "perfect" market (i.e., free of investor irrationality, government interference and taxes, and with no commissions or dealers spreads, etc.). Under such conditions, the price of the bond at any moment is completely determined by three factors:

1) The coupon rate of the bond.
2) The maturity date of the bond.
3) The annual yield, compounded semi-annually, if held to maturity.

Thus, the price for issue i at time t may be expressed mathematically as follows: [3]

(1) $P_{it} = [1/(1 + y/2)^{2(T_i - t)}]$
$$[100 - 100 \ c/y] + 100 \ c/y$$

where y and c are the yield and coupon respectively, expressed as decimal fractions, and $T_i - t$ is the number of years to maturity including fractional parts as decimals.

Use of Time Trends: If, over the entire life of a bond, it is always priced to yield a constant

[3] The derivation of this formula is shown in Appendix A.

y per cent to the investor, the price will follow a trend similar to one of the curves in Figure 1, depending on the relationship between the yield (y) and the coupon rate (c):

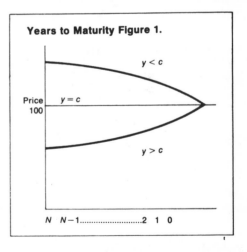

Years to Maturity Figure 1.

$y < c$

Price 100 $\quad y = c$

$y > c$

N N−1..........................2 1 0

The greater the difference between y and c, the greater will be the slope of the price trend line. Such curves could be drawn for every issue outstanding at any point in time. Then, by superimposing the price trend for one issue over that for another, moving it to the left or right to reflect the difference in maturity dates and subtracting each point on one curve from the vertically corresponding point on the other,

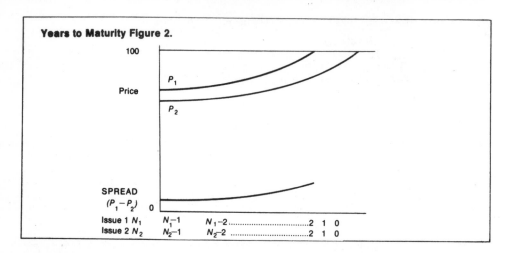

Years to Maturity Figure 2.

it is possible to plot the time trend of the spread between the two issues at a constant yield of y. (See Figure 2.)

This process can be stated mathematically as follows:[4]

$$(2) \quad S_t = 100\left[\frac{(1+y/2)^{2N_2}-(1+y/2)^{2N_1}}{(1+y/2)^{2(N_1+N_2)}}\right] - \frac{100}{y}\left[\frac{c_1}{(1+y/2)^{2N_1}}-\frac{c_2}{(1+y/2)^{2N_2}}-c_1+c_2\right]$$

where S_t is the theoretical price spread between the issues at time t

c_1 and c_2 are the coupon rates of the two issues

n_1 and n_2 are the times to maturity (equal to T_1-t and T_2-t, respectively)

y is the constant yield, effective for both.

Obviously, the above formula holds for any units of time to maturity, as long as the yield and coupon rate are expressed in consistent terms.

As stated, the foregoing analysis is based upon the assumption of a constant yield, y, over the life of the bonds. It is obvious that this condition never holds, in fact it does not usually hold for even a week at a time. This does not invalidate the equations. Similar computations can be made (or curves drawn) for any number of different yields, producing a table of theoretical spreads at every yield level for each pair of issues, for all times to maturity (of the earlier maturing issue, obviously). Graphically it would appear as shown in Figure 3.

This information tells what the spread between any two issues should be at a given point in time, and with a given yield, y, on both issues. However, the yield on both issues will very seldom be identical. This does not affect the validity of the approach; it simply makes the derivation more complicated.

Three different modifications of the model were investigated, in order to allow for the yield differences between issues:

1) The average of the yields on the two issues.
2) A "Market index," applicable to broad maturity ranges, similar to the S&P bond yield indices.[5]
3) Observations from a multiple regression-determined yield curve.

The two issue average has the disadvantage that it must be recalculated for each pair of issues examined, while the others need only be calculated once each day. Furthermore, the two issue average is distorted more by the price (or yield) of one of the issues being "out of line." This produces a negative "feedback" effect: The more out of line an issue is, the more distorted will be the yield index, and the less out of line it will appear.

The results of using each of these alternatives were compared via computer simulations. These showed that the S&P-type index provided more recommendations, greater profit per arbitrage and shorter periods outstanding than the two

[5] The three maturity ranges used by S&P are: short (up to five years to maturity), intermediate (five-ten) and long term (over ten years). Each index is calculated by deleting the highest and lowest yield in the maturity range and taking a straight arithmetic average of the rest.

[4] The derivation of this expression is shown in Appendix B.

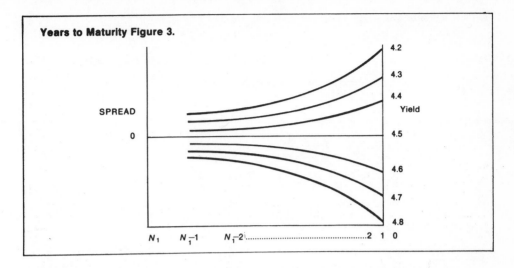

Years to Maturity Figure 3.

issue average. Not only is it easier to use, but it gave clearly superior results. The disadvantage of this procedure was that there were spurious "changes" when, with the passage of time, an issue moved from one maturity range into another. Also, yield differentials within a maturity range were not reflected. These defects were overcome by the use of the regression model.[6]

Given such a measure of the market level, it is possible to determine, graphically or analytically, the theoretical prices of any two issues and the spread between them on any date. On the average, the actual spread should be equal to this theoretical spread. Any time there is a large difference between the actual and theoretical spreads there exists an opportunity for arbitrage, since the two can be expected to return to equality (at which time the transaction would be reversed).

However, because the "real world" does not consist of "perfect" bonds in a "perfect" market, the actual spread is seldom equal to the theoretical spread, even when both are averaged over a long period. This is because the issues may differ in a variety of qualitative factors which are not taken into account in the idealized model:

> Call features
> Tax features (Many issues, selling at a discount, are acceptable at par in payment of federal estate taxes.)

[6]The yield curve regression model is:
$X_i = a + b\ Y_i + c\ Z_i$, where X_i is the estimated before-tax yield, Y_i is the square of days to maturity and Z_i is the square of the log of days to maturity. The derivation of this model is described in Kalman J. Cohen, Robert L. Kramer and W. Howard Waugh, "Regression Yield Curves for U.S. Government Securities", *Management Science*, Vol. 13, No. 4 (Dec. 1966) pp. B-168-B-175.

Exhibit 3. Sample Output

INPUT PRICES	8 25 65			
NO. COUPON	MATURITY		PRICE	YIELD
1	3.625	2 15 67	99.11	4.09
2	2.500	6 15 67	97.21	3.86
3	3.750	8 15 67	99.11	4.10
4	3.625	11 15 67	99.00	4.10
5	3.875	5 15 68	99.10	4.14
6	3.750	8 15 68	98.26	4.18
7	3.875	11 15 68	99.04	4.17
8	2.500	12 15 68	95.17	3.96
9	4.000	2 15 69	99.12	4.20
10	2.500	6 15 69	94.21	4.03
11	4.000	10 1 69	99.08	4.20
12	2.500	12 15 69	93.31	4.04
13	4.000	2 15 70	99.04	4.22
14	2.500	3 15 70	93.21	4.04
15	4.000	8 15 70	99.04	4.20
16	2.500	3 15 71	92.11	4.05
17	4.000	8 15 71	98.28	4.22
18	3.875	11 15 71	97.28	4.27
19	4.000	2 15 72	98.20	4.25
20	2.500	6 15 72	90.22	4.08
21	4.000	8 15 72	98.18	4.24
22	2.500	9 15 72	90.12	4.08
23	2.500	12 15 72	90.05	4.07
24	4.000	8 15 73	98.06	4.27
25	4.125	11 15 73	99.04	4.25
26	4.125	2 15 74	99.03	4.25
27	4.250	5 15 74	99.30	4.26
28	3.875	11 15 74	96.31	4.28
29	4.000	2 15 80	97.04	4.27
30	3.500	11 15 80	91.14	4.27
31	3.250	6 15 83	87.12	4.27
32	3.250	5 15 85	87.00	4.23
33	4.250	5 15 85	99.20	4.28
34	3.500	2 15 90	88.22	4.25
35	4.250	8 15 92	99.19	4.28
36	4.000	2 15 93	96.06	4.23
37	4.125	5 15 94	97.20	4.27
38	3.000	2 15 95	85.14	3.83
39	3.500	11 15 98	87.12	4.21

Exhibit 3. (continued)

DATE MO DA YR	PAIR CODE	ISSUE	NO.	COUPON	MO	YR	PRICE	SPREAD	POT.PRFT / $MM	FIRST REC.
SETUP RECOMMENDATICNS										
8 25 65										
	4	BUY	1	3.625	2	67	99.11			
		SELL	5	3.875	5	68	99.10	0.0313	8401.	7 27
	5	BUY	1	3.625	2	67	99.11			
		SELL	6	3.750	8	68	98.26	0.5313	8091.	7 27
	3	BUY	1	3.625	2	67	99.11			
		SELL	4	3.625	11	67	99.00	0.3438	7220.	7 27
	2	BUY	1	3.625	2	67	99.11			
		SELL	3	3.750	8	67	99.11	0.0000	6364.	7 27
	1	BUY	1	3.625	2	67	99.11			
		SELL	2	2.500	6	67	97.21	1.6875	5612.	7 27
	7	BUY	2	2.500	6	67	97.21			
		SELL	8	2.500	12	68	95.17	2.1250	3223.	7 27
	11	BUY	3	3.750	8	67	99.11			
		SELL	5	3.875	5	68	99.10	0.0313	2036.	7 27
	12	BUY	3	3.750	8	67	99.11			
		SELL	6	3.750	8	68	98.26	0.5313	1727.	7 27
	23	BUY	9	4.000	2	69	99.12			
		SELL	6	3.750	8	68	98.26	-0.5625	1652.	7-29
	6	BUY	1	3.625	2	67	99.11			
		SELL	7	3.875	11	68	99.04	0.2188	8161.	7 27
	13	BUY	3	3.750	8	67	99.11			
		SELL	7	3.875	11	68	99.04	0.2188	1797.	7 27
	25	BUY	9	4.000	2	69	99.12			
		SELL	7	3.875	11	68	99.04	-0.2500	1721.	7-27
	63	BUY	24	4.000	8	73	98.06			
		SELL	13	4.000	2	70	99.04	0.9375	1393.	8-11
	90	BUY	21	4.000	8	72	98.18			
		SELL	25	4.125	11	73	99.04	-0.5625	1292.	8 4
	71	BUY	21	4.000	8	72	98.18			
		SELL	15	4.000	8	70	99.04	0.5625	2188.	8-10
	37	BUY	9	4.000	2	69	99.12			
		SELL	15	4.000	8	70	99.04	0.2500	2085.	7 27
	21	BUY	9	4.000	2	69	99.12			
		SELL	5	3.875	5	68	99.10	-0.0625	1961.	7-29
	70	BUY	19	4.000	2	72	98.20			
		SELL	15	4.000	8	70	99.04	0.5000	1905.	8-16

> Coupon rate (The market values low coupon, deep discount issues somewhat differently from high coupon issues selling at a premium.)

> Amount outstanding (A thinly traded issue is likely to be higher priced than an identical but larger issue.)

> Government action (The treasury periodically offers exchanges, new issues or reopens sales of existing issues. This may affect the prices of the issues involved, or those most similar to them.)

> Investor preferences (Some investors, particularly banks, prefer issues maturing in just under five years or 10 years, bidding up prices of such bonds relative to similar issues.)

> Income tax structure (Since capital gains are taxed at a lower rate than current income, low-coupon bonds frequently exhibit slightly lower before-tax yields and slightly higher after-tax yields than high-coupon bonds with comparable maturity and other features.)

The effect of these factors is to cause the average of the actual spread between two issues to differ somewhat from the average of the theoretical spread. Thus the actual spread between an unusually attractive issue and an unusually unattractive issue which is similar in coupon and maturity may always be above the theoretical spread for the pair.

Obviously, this does not mean that arbitrage opportunities are always available between the issues involved. An adjustment must be made for such persistent historical differences. The device selected to accomplish this adjustment is an exponentially weighted moving average[7] of the difference between the actual and theoretical spreads between each pair of issues. The optimal weighting system was defined as that which, when comparing the profitability of recommended transactions with those using other weighting systems, produces the greatest net arbitrage profits.

Given a measure of the current difference between actual and theoretical spreads and a measure of the historical average difference, it still remains to select a measure of the significance of the current difference, i.e., whether it is sufficiently far away from the historical

average to be considered an arbitrage opportunity. The measure developed can be described as the "exponentially weighted moving standard deviation"[8] of the difference between actual and theoretical spreads. This was chosen because it "matches" the exponentially weighted moving average from which deviations are to be measured:

1) In exactly the same manner that recent observations are given greater weight in determining the average, recent variations are given greater weight in calculating the standard deviation.

2) It is updated the same way, i.e., by multiplying the existing value by a constant $(0 < \alpha < 1)$ and adding the product of the new observation times the term $(1 - \alpha)$.

The decision variables thus defined, the decision criteria are analogous to those used in statistical quality control: "Control limits" are expressed as some maximum "allowable" number of standard deviations from the mean. When the difference between the actual and theoretical spreads exceed this limit, an arbitrage is recommended. When the "process is back in control," i.e., when the actual difference returns to within some stated range of the average, the reversing transaction is recommended.

A computer program was written to perform these calculations and maintain historical records. The output of the program consists of three parts: (See Exhibit III)

1) A copy of the input data (closing bid prices for each outstanding issue), which can be used to verify the data used by the program.

2) A list of arbitrage recommendations, including identification of the issue to be purchased and its price, the issue to be sold short and its price, the price spread between them and an estimate of the potential profit to be achieved when the two prices return to their normal relationship. The recommendation also indicates whether or not the same set of transactions

---

[7]The exponentially weighted moving average is of the form:

$A = \sum_{n=1}^{\infty} X_{t-n} W_{t-n}$, where X_{t-n} is the nth observation previous to time t in the series and W_{t-n} is the weight assigned to the $t-n$th observation. The weights are determined by $W_{t-n} = \alpha W_{t-n}$, $\sum_{n=1}^{\infty} W_{t-n} = 1$, and $0 < \alpha < 1$. The value of α is determined experimentally, as described in the text.

[8]The exponentially weighted moving standard deviation is calculated using the exponentially weighted moving sum of the squares of observed values: $SS_t = \sum_{n=1}^{\infty} W_{t-n} X^2_{t-n}$. (Using the same notation as in the preceding footnote.) Thus, $SD_t = (SS_t - A^2)^{1/2}$. (Since $\sum_{n=1}^{\infty} W_{t-n} = 1$, there is no need to divide by the sample size.) Although the use of this measure is somewhat of a methodological innovation, it can be justified on theoretical grounds similar to those used to justify the use of exponentially weighted moving average, i.e., that if the variability of the process is changing over time, the more recent observations of the measure should carry greater weight. It is quite conceivable that the rate of change or the importance of change might differ between the moving average and the moving standard deviation, and therefore separate optimal exponential weighting factors should be derived. In this case, however, the same weight, α, that is used for the moving average is used for the moving standard deviation for both logical simplicity and computational efficiency.

has been recommended recently. If more than one arbitrage involving the same issue is recommended, all such pairs are arranged by descending profitability, with the best one considered the primary recommendation and the others listed as alternatives or secondary choices.

3) A list of reversal recommendations, if any, among currently outstanding arbitrages, along with all recordkeeping and accounting involved when the arbitrage has been completed.

Final Stages of the Project

A major part of the project was concerned with the determination of optimal, or at least acceptable, values for the "set up" and "reversal" criteria. This was accomplished by simulating the recommendations over a period of time, using various values for each criterion and comparing the resulting profits.

The "test run" program was a simulation of the bond department's behavior, given the recommendations produced by the computer. There were two primary purposes for this part of the study: 1) To test the criteria and parameters chosen in earlier phases, using a different trial period, a larger number of feasible pairs of issues and an "operational milieu;" and 2) to evaluate the potential profitability of the system under these more realistic conditions.

There were two distinct parts to this program: The "operational" program itself and a simulation of bond department decisions based on the output of the first part.

The simulation program was based on a number of "rules of thumb" developed through discussions with experienced bond department personnel. These heuristics were:

> Set up or reverse an arbitrage only if the transaction has been recommended at least twice within a short period (e.g., one week). (This minimizes the possibility of simulating action on a "freak" recommendation.)

> Undertake additional setups only up to certain limits, specified by the bond department. (This prevents setting up unrealistically large arbitrages and thus distorting the results.)

> Undertake additional setups only if the "new" spread is at a more favorable level than the best spread already achieved. (Such "averaging up" assured that the original potential profit will not be diluted.)

> Set up $2 million par value in the first transaction and $1 million in each succeeding one.

> On reversal recommendations, reverse the entire amount outstanding.

> Do not buy or sell more than specified amounts of any issue, even if it is involved in several arbitrages. (Certain issues are difficult to borrow or to sell, and this prevents simulating unrealistic volume in any such issue.)

> If an issue has been bought (sold) in one or more outstanding arbitrages, do not sell (buy) it in additional setups.

> If the potential profit of the newly recommended arbitrage is more than twice the remaining potential profit of the outstanding arbitrage with the smallest remaining potential, reverse the outstanding arbitrage so that the new one can be set up without violating the two preceding rules.

> If, for any reason, a "primary" recommendation cannot be set up try its subordinates. If these cannot be set up either, without violating one of the earlier rules, take no action.

Using these heuristics, the recommendations and decisions were simulated for the four year period from 1961 through 1964. Approximately 150 pairs were selected from among about 40 issues and were analyzed simultaneously for arbitrage possibilities each business day. Twenty different simulation runs were made, each using a different set of parameters in the "operational" program. Four different parameters were varied:

ALPHA — The weight used in the exponentially weighted moving average and standard deviations (values tested ranged from approximately .95 to .99).

P8 — The number of standard deviations from the "normal" that the difference between actual and theoretical spreads must reach before a "setup" recommendation is made (values from .8 to 1.2).

C15 — The multiple of P8 standard deviations which must be reached before an "urgent" setup recommendation is made (values from 1.0 to 1.5).

P6 — The fraction of the original profit goal (which is the number of standard deviations from the normal difference between the actual and theoretical price spreads at which the

EXHIBIT 4. Simulated Net Profits ($000's)

ALPHA		.954		.977		.989	
P6 P8 C15		.8	.8	1.0	.8	1.0	
.6	1.0	•	$935	•	$982	•	
.6	1.5	$757	$756	•	•	•	
.8	1.0	•	•	$596	•	$422	
1.0	1.0	$1193	$721	$668	$953	$252	

'These combinations were not run.

arbitrage was actually set up) which must be achievable before a reversal recommendation is made (values from .6 to 1.5).

The apparently restricted ranges of values used for these parameters were suggested by the results of earlier, less comprehensive test runs. To test many more values with the large simulation model would have been prohibitively expensive. As it was, each four year run required eight to 12 hours of IBM 7074 computer time.

The results exhibited a rather flat "response surface" with many "irregularities," i.e., total profits were roughly comparable over a moderate range for both setup and reversal criteria, with some values providing the greatest profits for specific time periods or pairs of issues, and other values giving better results for different periods or pairs.

Specifically, total profits generally appeared greatest (with relatively little variation) when 1) ALPHA was between .954 and .989, 2) the "setup" control limit was between .8 and 1.2 standard deviations and 3) the "reversal" limit was between .6 and 1.0 times the profit goal. The parameter values finally selected were: ALPHA = .977, setup limit = 1 standard deviation and reversal point = profit goal. (See Exhibit IV.)

Operational Program

The operational program incorporating the best parameter values found in the simulation runs went into daily use in a major dealer bank in August 1965. (A previous version, using slightly different parameter values and the "S&P-type" indices rather than the regression curve) had been operating daily since early 1964.)

At the close of each trading day, an assistant in the bond department key punches the closing bid price for each issue. These cards are then sent to the data center for overnight proces-

Exhibit 5. Indexes of Arbitrage Activity*

Year	# of Arbitrages	Total Par Value	Total Net Trading Profit
'60	138	178	230
'61	88	90	46
'62	75	31	27
'63	100	113	139
'64	278	256	298
'65	178	148	34
'66	150	148	418

* '60-'62 average = 100

sing. When the head of the department arrives at his desk the next morning, the output is waiting for him. Together with other tables, charts and his "feel for the market," the program's recommendations play an important role in deciding whether or not to arbitrage, which issues to buy and sell, how much par value of each to trade and how great a profit to look for.

As can be seen from Exhibit V, arbitrage profits have increased substantially since the program was installed. The number of arbitrage transactions, total par value traded and net trading profit all increased substantially over

315

the preceding four years. This was accomplished in a market not particularly favorable for arbitrage purposes. (Arbitrage opportunities arise and can be reversed most profitably in a volatile but level market. In 1965 and 1966, however, the bond market declined fairly steadily with fewer fluctuations than previously.)[9]

It is important to note that the arbitrage program was not intended to and does not function as the sole determinant of the bank's strategy in this area. The program recommends far more arbitrages than would be practical (or perhaps even possible) in the real world. (This is because when one issue "gets out of line," it presents arbitrage opportunities with every other "comparable" issue. But in practice, an arbitrageur would only set up one or at most two of these — the ones which offer the greatest potential profit.) Another reason for not following all recommendations is that when the shape of the yield curve (yield vs. time to maturity) changes, the "normal relationships" used in this system — or any other, whether adaptive or non-adaptive — will change also. The amount of time required for the system to stabilize depends upon the exponential weighting factors used and the magnitude of the change in the market. It may range between one and three months. During this period, many "spurious" recommendations may result.

In spite of these caveats and a few operational problems (such as keypunch errors or computer malfunctions) the bank's several years' experience has been generally favorable, both quantitatively and qualitatively.

APPENDIX A

The price of a bond is its present value, using the yield as the interest rate. It is composed of two parts: The present value of the semi-annual coupon payments (c/2) and the present value of the face amount (100) to be paid at maturity. Since interest is paid semi-annually, the appropriate time period is half-years and the proper discount rate is the semi-annual yield (y/2). For simplicity, the derivation is expressed in annual terms (using i,n,c and 100 for the interest rate, number of periods to maturity, coupon rate and principal amount, respectively. Appropriate substitutions are made in the final step.)

[9]Due to extreme abnormal conditions in the U.S. Government bond market arbitrage operations have been severely restricted since 1967. Thus, comparisons with earlier years would not be meaningful. Nevertheless, the program is still in daily operation and is used when arbitrages are considered.

Present value of an annuity factor: $\dfrac{1-(1+i)^{-n}}{i}$

Present value of an amount factor: $(1+i)^{-n}$

Present value of coupon stream:

$$100c\left(\frac{1-(1+i)^{-n}}{i}\right)$$

Present value of principal: $100\,(1+i)^{-n}$

Total present value of bond:

$$P = 100(1+i)^{-n} + 100c\left[\frac{1-(1+i)^{-n}}{i}\right]$$

$$= \frac{100i(1+i)^{-n} + 100c[1-(1+i)^{-n}]}{i}$$

$$= \frac{100i(1+i)^{-n} + 100c - 100c(1+i)^{-n}}{i}$$

$$= \frac{(1+i)^{-n}(100i - 100c) + 100c}{i}$$

$$= (1+i)^{-n}(100 - \frac{100c}{i}) + 100\frac{c}{i}$$

$$= (1+y/2)^{-2n}(100 - 100\frac{c/2}{y/2}) + 100\frac{c/2}{y/2}$$

$$= (1+y/2)^{-2n}(100 - 100c/y) + 100\,c/y$$

APPENDIX B

$$S = \frac{1}{(1+y/2)^{2n_1}}(100 - 100c_1/y) + 100c_1/y$$

$$- \frac{1}{(1+y/2)^{2n_2}}(100 - 100c_2/y) - 100c_2/y$$

$$= 100\left[(1-c_1/y)\,\frac{1}{(1+y/2)^{2n_1}} - (1 - c_2/y)\right.$$

$$\left.\frac{1}{(1+y/2)^{2n_2}}\right] + \frac{100}{y}\,(c_1 - c_2)$$

$$= 100$$
$$\left[\frac{(1-c_1/y)\,(1+y/2)^{2n_2} - (1-c_2/y)\,(1+y/2)^{2n_1}}{(1+y/2)^{2(n_1+n_2)}}\right]$$

$$+ \frac{100}{y}(c_1 - c_2)$$

$$= 100\left[\frac{(1+y/2)^{2n_2} - (1+y/2)^{2n_1}}{(1+y/2)^{2(n_1+n_2)}}\right] - \frac{100}{y}$$

$$\left[\frac{c_1(1+y/2)^{2n_2} - c_2(1+y/2)^{2n_1}}{(1+y/2)^{2(n_1+n_2)}}\right]$$

$$+ \frac{100}{y}(c_1 - c_2)$$

$$= 100\left[\frac{(1+y/2)^{2n_2} - (1+y/2)^{2n_1}}{(1+y/2)^{2(n_1+n_2)}}\right]$$

$$- \frac{100}{y}\left[\frac{c_1}{(1+y/2)^{2n_1}} - \frac{c_2}{(1+y/2)^{2n_2}} - c_1 + c_2\right]$$

BIBLIOGRAPHY:

Books

Porter, S.F., *How to Make Money in Government Bonds* (New York: Harper & Bros., 1931)

Weinstein, Meyer Hugh, *Arbitrage in Securities* (New York: Harper & Bros., 1939)

Evans, Morgan D. Jr., *Arbitrage in Domestic Securities in the United States* (New York: Parker Publishing Company, Inc.)

Journal Articles

Stoddard, Ralph G., "The ABC of Government Bond Arbitrage," *Bond Account,* July, 1940, pp. 5-10

Durand, D., "Comment," *American Economic Review,* 1959, pp. 641-2

Gardner, Robert Livingston, "Exploring Management Problems of U.S. Government Securities Portfolio – A Roundtable Discussion," *Savings Bank Journal,* April, 1940, pp. 888

Other

Stern, Richard M., "Government Bond Account Profits are Fictitious," *American Banker,* March 15, 1939 (Discussed reason for and advantages of arbitrage.)

Carney, Peter J., *Arbitrage in U.S. Government Securities,* unpublished master's thesis, New York University, 1966

————, "Price Spreads for U.S. Government Securities", Newsletter, published periodically in the late '30's and early '40's by Bankers Trust Company Bond Department, U.S. Government Division. (Early issues simply tabulated low, high and average price spreads among all combinations of 15-20 issues. Later issues recognized the exponential increase in spreads as the bonds approach maturity.)

————, "Record of Spreads for 1939 and the First 3 Months of 1940", C.F. Childs & Co., New York 1940 (Tabulated low, high and modal values for about 50 pairs of issues.)

————, "Arbitables", published monthly by Knight & Company, New York, circa 1939. (Tabulated low, high and 1-, 3-, 6- and 12-month averages for 120 pairs selected from among about 20 issues. Also showed control limits for setting up arbitrages.)

————, "Arbitrage Recommendations", published periodically by the First Boston Corporation, New York, circa 1939-40. (Showed graphically monthly low, high and average price spreads for about 18 months, for several selected pairs of issues. Made specific recommendations.)

————, "Newsletter", William E. Pollock & Co. Inc., New York, circa 1967. (Tabulated high and low spreads among all pairs among about 30 issues.)

————, "Monthly Price Spread Range of Selected Combinations of U.S. Treasury Securities", New York Hanseatic Corporation, circa 1964. (Tabulated monthly high and low spreads for about 18 months for about two dozen selected pairs of issues.)

————, Arbitrage in United States Government Bonds", Kimball & DeLima, New York (Defined and described arbitrage operations.)

————, "Range in Price Spreads United States Government Bonds 1933", Charles E. Quincey & Co. New York, circa 1934-5. (Showed, in bar graphs, frequency distributions of spreads between about 30 selected pairs of issues, along with highs, lows and their dates of occurrence.)

Part VI

THE LOAN PORTFOLIO

LENDING has traditionally produced the bulk of earnings of nearly all commercial banks. Generally, the loan portfolio constitutes the largest single item on a bank's balance sheet, and loans are increasing as a percentage of total assets. Effective management of the loan portfolio is crucial to the profitability and security of most commercial banks. The careful trade-off between default risk and potential return is the essence of loan portfolio management. On the one hand, credit worthiness, acceptable security, and minimal default risk are desirable to protect the bank from widely fluctuating performance as a result of loan losses. The concern in the mid-1970s over bank loans to the real estate and shipping industries and to foreign developing countries vividly demonstrated the need for effective lending policies. But, while banks should be prudent in making loans, they should also recognize that the most profitable loans often involve substantial levels of risk. Critics often overlook the fact that some risks are necessary and desirable.

To balance the trade-off between risk and return, banks generally diversify their loan portfolios by spreading loans over various industries with differing risk characteristics. This allocation among different borrowers can be critical in insuring maximum return at acceptable risk levels.

Effective management of the loan portfolio involves not only the evaluation of new applications, but also profitability analysis of present bank customers. Other factors influencing loan portfolio decisions are liquidity needs, alternative investment opportunities, maintenance of customer goodwill, and profitability differences among various lending terms.

The most difficult lending decision usually involves a new application from a person or firm with whom the bank has had little or no dealing in the past, because such an application cannot be reviewed on the basis of past account information. Management science models

319

for loan review have focused on present bank customers for whom a data base is available based on past experience. However, management science techniques can provide a useful framework for analysis of new applications as well. In many cases, the loan review models already developed can serve as a starting point for the development of models for evaluating new applications.

Detailed models have been developed for numerical credit evaluation of consumer loans, but the complexity and uniqueness of business loan applications have hampered efforts to develop similar models for evaluating these applications. Although substantial information is provided in financial reports, the accuracy and substance of these reports vary widely, rendering all but the most basic measures relatively useless. In fact, most commercial banks devote significant resources to long training periods to develop officers capable of business loan evaluation.

Management science tools are aimed at enhancing the capabilities of management by removing routinized and time-consuming tasks. In no sense are the discussions presented in Part VI meant to suggest that lending officers' decisions would be made by a computerized analysis system. What these models provide is an opportunity for the lending officer to spend more time on significant decisions which require thorough analysis. Management science can also provide a framework for comparison among similar situations and an alerting mechanism for problem loans in the portfolio. Models might also be valuable in establishing broad loan policies consistent with economic conditions and recognizing potential lending opportunities among existing accounts.

One of the most widely cited research efforts in the area of loan review is the model developed by Yair E. Orgler in Chapter 25, "A Credit Scoring Model for Commercial Loans." Orgler describes the development of a scoring model, including the methodology for determining critical review variables. Orgler's model is not highly complex and can be adapted for use in banks of widely varying sizes. In a smaller bank, a clerk might be able to carry out the computations by hand, while in a larger bank a simple computer program would probably be used. Indications are that the model is economically feasible in actual use. Since no effort is made here to critique the methodology underlying the model, it is advisable to carefully examine the cost factors and other practical aspects before implementing the model. Orgler does provide a framework for cost analysis of the model; its cost effectiveness is best evaluated if it is clearly defined as a tool for effectively allocating bank officers' time.

Profitability must be the underlying goal of bank lending. While it is quite true that banks perform a service to the community through the extension of credit, this service could not continue for long if profits did not result. As Daniel L. White indicates in Chapter 26, "The Present Value Approach to Selecting Bank Customers": "Banks lose money on loans made in a credit crunch because in order to honor their credit lines, they are forced to sell their bond portfolios at a loss and/or borrow funds at rates much higher than prime." White correctly points out that a customer who borrows only during tight money periods may be unprofitable for this reason. White provides a simple model for computing the long-run profitability of bank customers. The up and down nature of bank performance in terms of profitability may be traced to lending decisions, and profitability may be smoothed somewhat by developing long-run credit guidelines. The development of the "floating prime" is evidence of banks' increasing concern with fluctuating profitability. The threat of price controls in tight money periods could create a need for high selectivity of customers based on profitability.

Because bank loans constitute such a large percentage of a bank's total assets, a bank's sensitivity to shifts in economic conditions, interest rates, and loan demand is a critical concern in strategic planning. The ability to project the impact of economic shifts on a bank's performance is extremely valuable. In Chapter 27, "Method for Evaluation of the Economic Characteristics of Loan Portfolios," Wolfgang P. Hoehenwarter attempts to model the relationships among key economic variables and their impact on bank performance. The model described has been implemented at the National Bank of Tulsa and this application is examined in an accompanying comment by John Davis, presently a planning officer for that bank. The model, "COMLON," requires only readily available data. This enhances its practicality and general applicability. The model provides estimates of income by loan category as well as valuable sensitivity information related to movements in the prime rate. To the extent that the model provides information on lag time and reaction of earnings to key variables, it is a useful planning aid with practical implications for strategic policy formulation.

A great deal of current debate centers on the concept of fee based services versus the present system in which many bank services are paid for through compensating balances. The use of compensating balances has severely handicapped bank management in attempts at internal profit analysis. The return from offering services to customers is difficult to ascertain. Bernell K. Stone offers a basis for evaluating profit from compensating balances in Chapter 28, "The Cost of Bank Loans." This is an area of special interest to banks in highly competitive environments and in need of tighter pricing policies. Analysis similar to Stone's is being carried on in several major banks nationwide.

We examine the lending function of commercial banks in detail in Part VI. In most cases, a bank's success hinges on decisions involving the extension of credit. Banks will continue to be a major source of financing for most U.S. corporations. In addition, the foreign lending activities of most banks have increased. The usefulness of management tools that structure and simplify credit decisions and management of the loan portfolio is apparent. Banks must, however, approach the implementation of management science models with care. In most cases, the model will have to be tailored to fit the unique characteristics of the particular bank's loan portfolio and lending functions.

Chapter 25

A CREDIT SCORING MODEL FOR COMMERCIAL LOANS*

By Yair E. Orgler

*This article is reprinted, with permission, from *The Journal of Money, Credit and Banking,* Vol. 2, No. 4 (November, 1970), pp. 435-445. Copyright © 1970 by the Ohio State University Press.

An increasing number of credit scoring models have been developed in recent years as a scientific aid to the traditionally heuristic process of credit evaluation. With few exceptions these models are designed for screening consumer loan applications. The purpose of this paper is to present a credit scoring model for commercial loans. The model is limited to the evaluation of existing loans and could be used by bank loan officers for loan review and by bank regulatory agencies for loan examination.

INTRODUCTION

The loan review function is an important, though often neglected, part of the lending process: "The second major aspect of systems and procedures for business loans is loan review. Long experience has indicated that loan losses tend to be related to lack of attention as much as to inadequate credit standards or inadequate analysis at the outset" [2, p. 260]. The loan review function is very similar to loan examination by regulatory bank agencies which is a most difficult and time-consuming task in examining commercial banks. Both activities involve the evaluation of existing loan portfolios rather than screening new loan applications and, unlike other lending functions, have received little attention from management scientists despite their important role in bank management and bank supervision.

Analytical models have long been developed for screening consumer loan applications (e.g., [8]). Using multivariate regression or discriminant analysis, these studies tried to identify the variables which best distinguish between loans that are eventually paid-up and loans that are charged off as losses. The best discriminant function which is composed of these variables is then used to compute a score for each loan application. This score is compared with a certain cutoff rate to determine whether the application is accepted, rejected, or designated for further analysis. While the variables incorporated in the credit scoring formula vary somewhat among the different models, they are all based on personal data of the applicant such as age, sex, residential stability, occupation, and credit record.

A similar approach to credit scoring commercial loans would require the use of information contained in the financial statements of the applicants. For several reasons it is difficult to apply the methodology used in credit scoring consumer loans to commercial loans. First, commercial borrowers do not belong to large homogeneous populations as do customers for consumer credit.

This lack of standardization presents a problem in obtaining sufficient data for a statistically significant study. Second, there are substantial variations among commercial loans with respect to their size, terms, collateral types, and payment procedure, all of which are relatively uniform in the case of consumer loans. Finally, there is a lack of reliable up-to-date financial data cn small commercial borrowers and particularly on those who defaulted on their loans.

Because of these difficulties, it is impossible to develop a general scoring model for commercial loans. Instead, it is necessary to develop individual models for small commercial borrowers in each industry, provided that sufficient data are available. This limitation may be one of the reasons for the lack of analytical models in this area. There are, however, several related studies which should be analyzed briefly. Using discriminant analysis, Altman derived a discriminant function with only five variables, all of them financial ratios, and predicted corporate bankruptcy with a remarkable accuracy (4% error on a hold-out sample of 25 bankrupt firms) [1]. This prediction was performed with financial data one year prior to bankruptcy while longer lead times produced substantially higher error rates. Since commercial loans may result in a complete or partial loss several years prior to bankruptcy, or even without the borrower becoming bankrupt at all, Altman's model is not applicable to credit scoring commercial loans.

A model more directly related to the problem was derived by Ewert for screening trade credit applications by small firms, mostly one-owner retail stores [5]. These applicants, and the amounts involved, more closely resemble consumer credit than average bank loans to commercial customers. Nevertheless, the model provides a useful tool for reviewing new customers for trade credit. The model combines information on the owner with data on the financial position of the store as listed in the Dun and Bradstreet reports. Another interesting study was performed by Cohen, Gilmore, and Singer who developed a model which simulates the lending decisions of bank loan officers [4]. Consequently, the model is of a descriptive rather than a normative nature.

The objective of this study is to develop a general credit scoring model for evaluating existing commercial loans. While this goal is somewhat less ambitious than deriving a general model for screening new commercial loan applications, it does provide a useful tool for loan review and examination. A discussion of the dependent and independent variables in the model and the use of multivariate regression to derive the discriminating function appears in the next section. Section II briefly describes the data which were used to obtain the empirical results. Regression results and a comparison of model predictions with actual loan classifications appear in Section III. Implementation problems are discussed in Section IV followed by some concluding comments in the final section.

I. THE MODEL

The method used in deriving the model is similar to the approach of the credit scoring models mentioned in the previous section where a sample of good and bad loans are compared to find the key elements which discriminate between these two groups. The main difference between this model and previous studies lies in the selection of variables and in solving the particular problems which arise in developing a general model for a heterogeneous population of commercial borrowers.

Multivariate regression analysis, where the dependent variable is restricted to the values zero or one, was used to discriminate between good and bad loans. This technique provides the same results as discriminate analysis when only two groups are involved; and it has the advantages of being more readily available, better known, and normally containing more statistical information [7]. Regression analysis was performed on a sample of good and bad loans where independent variables represent various characteristics of each borrower, and the dependent variable (Y_i) is a dummy which equals one for bad loans and zero for good loans. After eliminating all the variables which do not add to the explanation of variation in Y_i and which are not significantly related to Y_i, we obtain the equation which discriminates best between good and bad loans.

The expected values of the dependent variable ($\hat{Y}_i$), which are obtained by applying the regression equation to new observations, are compared to two cutoff points C_1 and C_2 where $0 < C_1 < C_2 < 1$. When $\hat{Y}_i \geq C_2$, loan i is expected to result in a loss; and therefore it requires a thorough examination. All observations for which $\hat{Y}_i \leq C_1$ are considered good loans and are eliminated from review and examination. The remaining cases ($C_1 < Y_i < C_2$) are marginal loans which are reviewed briefly and segregated by the evaluator into the two other groups where potentially bad loans are carefully examined and good loans are not covered at all. The accuracy of this prediction depends, of course, on the selection of independent variables and the extent to which these variables, as a group, explain variations in the dependent variable. The determination of C_1 and C_2, which also have an important impact on the results, is discussed in the implementation section.

The dichotomous dependent variable expresses the loan quality. In this study the definition of quality, i.e., whether a loan is good or bad, was not based on actual payoff or charge-off. Instead, any loan which was criticized by a bank examiner was considered as bad while any loan which was evaluated but not criticized was classified as good. This definition was selected because of data availability and because of the fact that many loans which are eventually paid off are either not profitable or even incur a partial loss. Loan classification by bank examiners is considered, therefore, a better indicator of poor quality than actual default. Moreover, a study by Wu confirmed that examiner criticisms on business loans are a good *ex ante* measure of loan quality [9].

Independent variables were derived from the borrowers financial statements and from examination reports. In addition to standard financial ratios, a number of elements which do not appear in financial reports but which may be associated with the loan's quality were incorporated as independent variables. The information for calculating all these variables is available both to the loan officer and the bank examiner. Several important variables are not available when a loan application is first screened, and consequently the resulting model is applicable to loan review and loan examination but not to the approval or rejection of new loan applications.

A large number of relevant financial ratios and other elements appearing in financial reports were first incorporated in the model. A partial list of these variables appears below.

Liquidity: current assets/current liabilities; working capital; cash/current liabilities; inventory/current assets; quick ratio; working capital/current assets.

Profitability: net profit/sales; net profit/net worth; net profit/total assets; net profit $\geqq$ 0; net profit.

Leverage: net worth/total liabilities; net worth/fixed assets; net worth/long-term debt; net worth $\geqq$ 0.

Activity: sales/fixed assets; sales/net worth; sales/total assets; sales/inventory; sales/receivables.

These and many other ratios were derived from the last available financial statement prior to classification. Additional independent variables were based on the difference between the last (t) and next-to-last ($t - 1$) annual reports which should indicate a deterioration in the liquidity, profitability, or solvency of the borrower: current ratio (t)/current ratio ($t - 1$); net profit (t) − net profit ($t - 1$); net profit (t)/net profit ($t - 1$); [sales (t) − sales ($t - 1$)]/ sales ($t - 1$); total assets (t)/total assets ($t - 1$); net worth (t)/net worth ($t - 1$).

A third group of independent variables represents some additional information on the borrower which is expected to affect his financial position and eventual payoff of his debt. Some of these variables can be obtained from the firm's financial statements while others are incorporated in bank examination reports which are also available to the loan officer. Each of the following terms, for instance, can be answered positively or negatively, and this answer is the basis for a dummy variable:[1] Is the firm incorporated? Is the latest balance sheet available? Is the latest profit and loss statement available? Are the financial statements audited? A positive answer to each of these questions is considered an indication of a good loan and vice-versa. The answers on another set of dichotomous variables provide information on the loan and its past performance: Has the loan balance decreased, increased, or remained steady during the last year? Has the loan been criticized by a bank examiner during last examination? Is the loan secured or unsecured? Is it a demand or time loan? The data for deriving most of these variables are normally more readily available than financial statements from which the financial ratios are computed.

---

[1] While the explanatory variables are assumed to belong to multivariate normal populations, it has been shown that functions with dichotomous variables can be used efficiently for discriminant analysis [6].

II. The Data

The data were obtained from the files of bank examiners in a number of East Coast states. The two major problems in obtaining the data were the lack of complete financial statements and the small number of criticized or bad loans. In order to obtain a sufficient number of observations, thousands of loan reviews in 100 state non-member commercial banks were screened. Each observation had all the items mentioned in the previous section, including data from next-to-last financial statements. While earlier reports were generally not available, it turned out that they were unnecessary since none of the financial ratios with previous year $(t - 1)$ variables were significant.

Any bad loan for which all the necessary data were available has been incorporated in the study. The control group of good loans was randomly selected from a stratified population of all the good loans with adequate data that were listed in the observed files of bank examiners. Good loans were stratified by industry because of the large variety of borrowers, and for each bad loan in a certain industry several good loans were randomly selected from the appropriate stratum. Loans were not matched by the size of borrowing firms (neither by assets, sales, or other measures) since we were interested in examining the effect of size on the quality of commercial loans. Many types of industries were included, and total assets of individual firms ranged from $7500 to $11,623,900. This diversification served the purpose of developing a general credit scoring model.

The observations were randomly divided into two groups. The first group contained 75 bad loans and 225 good loans, i.e., each bad loan was matched with three good loans to the same industry. This group provided the data for the regression analysis and the derivation of the best discrimination function. The effectiveness of this equation was tested on the second group which served as a hold-out sample and included 40 bad loans and 80 matched good loans.

III. Empirical Results

The regression equation which provided the best discrimination between good and bad loans included only six independent variables which are listed in Table 1. Most of the independent variables originally incorporated in the model had insignificant coefficients and did not contribute to the explanation of the dependent variable variance (no addition to R^2). Another group of varibles was eliminated because of multicolinearity. While multicolinearity is acceptable when the main purpose of the regression results is to predict, all these variables improved only the prediction of the original sample and provided inferior results when tested on the hold-out sample. Moreover, the coefficients of all the variables rejected for multicolinearity had signs which could not be rationalized on a priori grounds.

The signs of the regression coefficients are consistent with our expectations about the effect of each variable on loan quality.

a. $X_1 = 0$ for unsecured loans and one for secured loans. Since the dependent variable is zero for good loans and one for bad loans, a positive coefficient means that secured loans are more risky than unsecured loans. This result is somewhat surprising at a first glance. However, the need for a security is an indication that such a loan was considered more risky when it was originally made.

b. $X_2 = 0$ for past-due loans and one for current loans. It is obvious that if an interest payment is overdue, the likelihood of a loss is larger and hence the negative coefficient.

c. $X_3 = 0$ for a firm which is *not* audited while $X_3 = 1$ for an audited firm. It is expected that examiners have more confidence in the reliability of audited statements than those submitted by a borrower without audit. A negative coefficient confirms this expectation.

d. $X_4 = 0$ for a net loss and one for a net profit. A negative coefficient for this variable is obvious. It is interesting that this variable provided better explantory and predictive results than any of the other profitability ratios whether independently or within the regression equation.

e. X_5 is the only independent variable which is not restricted to the values $(0; 1)$. Obviously, as the ratio of working capital (current assets less current liabilities) to current assets increases, the quality of the loan should increase and hence the negative coefficient. Slightly inferior results were

TABLE 1

REGRESSION RESULTS

Variable	Coefficient	t Value
1. Secured/Unsecured	.1017	1.83*
2. Past-Due	− .3966	−4.14
3. Audit	− .0916	−2.01
4. Net Profit $\gtreqless 0$	− .1573	−2.96
5. Working capital/Current assets	− .0199	−3.28
6. Criticized last examination	− .4533	−9.22
Intercept $= 1.1018$		
$R^2 = .364$		
$n = 300$		

* Significant at the 10 per cent level. All other variables are significant at 5 per cent or better.

obtained when X_5 was replaced with a dummy variable which, like X_4, applied only to the sign of working capital, i.e., whether it is negative or positive. The use of dummy variables has, of course, the advantage of simplicity and is less sensitive to inaccuracies in the financial reports.

f. $X_6 = 0$ for loans which were criticized last examination by a bank examiner and one for uncriticized loans. A previously classified loan is obviously of poor quality and hence the negative sign. Like past-due status, a previous classification normally stimulates a review and an evaluation during the next examination. It is important to note, however, that the regression equation provided a much better discrimination between bad and good loans than a simple rule which states that all past-due and previously classified loans are bad and *vice-versa*.[2]

While all the coefficient signs are consistent with prior expectations, the interesting aspect of the results is not so much the explanation of the dependent variable as the prediction of commercial loan quality. As explained in Section I, the prediction of loan quality is based on a comparison of the dependent variable's expected value with two cutoff points C_1 and C_2. The values of these points were determined according to an arbitrary decision rule which specified that the proportion of bad loans classified as good should be less than 5% of all bad loans and the proportion of bad loans classified correctly as bad should be at least 75% of total bad loans. The emphasis on bad loans is explained by the relatively high penalty cost associated with overlooking a potentially bad loan. The tradeoff for this cost is the gain from reducing the number of good loans subjected to evaluation. If this cost information is available, C_1 and C_2 can be determined so that total cost is minimized as will be discussed in Section IV. For practical purposes, however, the above decision rule has been applied to the original sample resulting in relatively low cutoff points:[3] $C_1 = .08$

TABLE 2

PREDICTION RESULTS—ORIGINAL SAMPLE

(In Number of Loans)

		Prediction			
		Bad	Marginal	Good	Total
Actual	Bad	60	12	3	75
	Good	46	123	56	225
	Total	106	135	59	300

and $C_2 = .25$. Prediction results based on these cutoff values are presented in Table 2.

The results indicate, for instance that three of the actually bad loans were classified as good, twelve as marginal, and sixty as bad. The implication for review and examination purposes is that three bad loans will not be evaluated at all, while twelve such loans will be examined briefly, assuming that such an evaluation will suffice to identify them as potentially bad loans and transfer them to the group of sixty loans designated for thorough analysis. On the other

---

[2] A few additional regression equations which differed from the selected function in one or two variables provided similar but slightly inferior results both in explaining Y_i and predicting loan classifications.

[3] Because of the low cutoff points and the small number of variables of which only one is continuous, part of the classification can be done by a simple set of decision rules. For instance, all unsecured ($X_1 = 0$) current ($X_2 = 1$) loans which have not been previously criticized ($X_6 = 1$) and which were made to profitable borrowers ($X_4 = 1$) with audited financial statements ($X_3 = 1$) are classified as good. The same loans ($X_1 = 0$; $X_2 = 1$; $X_4 = 1$; $X_6 = 1$) to borrowers with unaudited statements ($X_3 = 0$) and a working capital to current assets ratio of at least 75% ($X_5 \geq .75$) are the only other type of loans to be classified as good. Similar rules for marginal classifications are much more complex and hence impractical.

hand, this segmentation eliminates from consideration 56 good loans and requires only a brief evaluation of another 123 loans. A better presentation of these results is provided in terms of percentage points in Table 3.

It is important to note that the total time saving resulting from the reduction in loan evaluation are much higher than those listed in Table 3, since the normal ratio of good to bad loans is much higher than 1:3. Thus, the percentage of loans completely eliminated from examination is closer to 24.9% than 19.7%; and the proportion of loans briefly examined is approximately 54.7% rather than 45.0%. Assuming that the evaluation of marginal loans requires 10% of a normal evaluation, the total time saving will be about 65–75 per cent. Both adjustments are incorporated in a more general way in the total cost function (Section IV).

The prediction test of the original sample is biased since the regression equation is based on the same data. A more rigorous test is obtained by using the regression coefficients to classify the observations in the hold-out sample which includes forty bad loans and eighty good loans. The results are presented in Table 4 and are somewhat better than the prediction of the original sample. Good loans are classified more accurately in each of the three categories while the percentage of bad loans classified as good is reduced from 4

TABLE 3

PREDICTION RESULTS—ORIGINAL SAMPLE

(In Per Cent)

		Prediction			
		Bad	Marginal	Good	Total
Actual	Bad	80.0	16.0	4.0	100.0
	Good	20.4	54.7	24.9	100.0
	Total	35.3	45.0	19.7	100.0

TABLE 4

PREDICTION RESULTS—HOLD-OUT SAMPLE

(In Per Cent)

		Prediction			
		Bad	Marginal	Good	Total
Actual	Bad	75.0	22.5	2.5	100.0
	Good	17.5	47.5	35.0	100.0
	Total	36.7	39.2	24.1	100.0

per cent to 2.5 per cent.[4] Only the prediction of bad loans as bad is somewhat smaller, due to an increase in the marginal classification.

[4] In practice, the percentage of actual loss loans classified as good is expected to be even smaller. This is explained by the fact that bank examiners are more likely to criticize a good loan than define a bad loan as good. Thus, some of the bad loans in our sample, which are classified by the discrimination model as marginal or good, may actually be paid off without any loss.

IV. IMPLEMENTATION

An implementation of the credit scoring model depends on data availability and cost considerations. For review and examination purposes, the necessary information is readily available on any existing loan. Moreover, the model is very simple, and the credit score ($\hat{Y}_i$) can be easily computed by a junior clerk on an adding machine. In a large bank the computation can be performed by a computer; and if the loan portfolio is maintained on auxiliary storage, the credit score can be computed periodically. The output of such a program will include a listing of potentially bad and marginal loans together with additional information on each of the marginal cases for analysis purposes. But even if the scoring model is not automated, its main advantage is in releasing loan officers and bank examiners from routine evaluations of all loans and allocating their time to a small proportion of riskier borrowers.

The only major problem in implementing the model is the definition of C_1 and C_2. Assuming an objective of minimizing total evaluation cost, the values of these cutoff rates depend on several parameters which are very difficult to estimate.

a. The cost of eliminating from consideration a bad loan (F). This cost depends on the likelihood that the evaluator will actually classify the loan as bad and on the savings that will result from the classification.

b. The average evaluation cost per loan (E).

c. The proportion of time necessary to evaluate a marginal loan (p).

d. The a priori probability that a commercial loan will be criticized by a bank examiner (h).

e. The probability that a marginal loan will be transferred to tight examination (q_1 for actually bad loans and q_2 for good loans).

Given this information, the total evaluation cost per loan is

$$K = \{E(Y_{bb} + pY_{bm} + q_1Y_{bm}) + F[Y_{bg} + (1 - q_1)Y_{bm}]\}h/Y_b$$

$$+ E(Y_{gb} + pY_{gm} + q_2Y_{gm})(1 - h)/Y_g$$

where Y_{bb}, Y_{bm}, and Y_{bg} are the number of actually bad loans classified as bad, marginal, and good, respectively, and $Y_b = Y_{bb} + Y_{bm} + Y_{bg}$. Similarly, Y_{gb}, Y_{gm}, and Y_{gg} are good loans classified as bad, marginal, and good, respectively, and $Y_g = Y_{gb} + Y_{gm} + Y_{gg}$. By using trial and error, total cost can be empirically minimized for the original sample by varying C_1 and C_2. Since the regression results are obtained from the original sample, the values of C_1 and C_2 can also be derived from the same data and used in the credit scoring model. Moreover, if the above information is available, the cost of operating the model plus K can be compared with the current cost of loan review or examination to determine whether the model is economically justifiable.

Unfortunately, reliable cost information is practically not available. For this reason it is necessary to determine C_1 and C_2 subjectively or else use some rough estimates of the cost data. The empirical results seem to justify the use of this approach. Another alternative is to further simplify the model by eliminating the marginal state and to classify all loans as bad or good.

Instead of using trial-and-error methods, it is theoretically possible to define K as a function of the credit score and to derive analytically the optimal scores for which K is minimized. This approach is based on the assumption that the functional relationship between K and Y_i can be obtained empirically. Considering, however, the difficulties in estimating the cost coefficients, it is highly unlikely that the additional effort in deriving the functional form of K will be justified.

V. Concluding Comments

The credit scoring model can be considered a tool for allocating the time of bank officers and bank examiners in the review and evaluation of existing commercial loans. Because of its simplicity and generality, the model is applicable to most banks. The lack of standard review systems in many banks and the time pressure on examiners of bank regulatory agencies are two important reasons why such a model is necessary. Further developments in the credit scoring area should be directed to the evaluation of new loan applications. Such models could be developed, however, only for small borrowers in specific industries.

In addition to its normative value, the model provides some evidence on the relationship between loan classifications by bank examiners and information on the borrower. This result agrees with the expectations of Benston who tried unsuccessfully to predict loan classifications (substandard loans) by factors related to individual banks [3]. His main conclusion, which is confirmed by this study, is that the factors that influence substandard loans are related to the characteristics of the borrowers and not those of the bank.

Literature Cited

1. Altman, E. I. "Financial Ratios, Discriminant Analysis and the Prediction of Corporate Bankruptcy," *Journal of Finance,* XXIII (September, 1968).

2. Baughn, W. H. and C. E. Walker, eds. *The Banker's Handbook.* Homewood, Ill.: R. D. Irwin, Inc., 1966.

3. Benston, L. J. "Substandard Loans," *National Banking Review,* IV (March, 1967).

4. Cohen, K. J., T. C. Gilmore, and F. A. Singer. "Bank Procedures for Analyzing Business Loan Applications," in *Analytical Methods in Banking* eds. K. J. Cohen and F. S. Hammer. Homewood, Illinois: R. D. Irwin, Inc., 1966.

5. Ewert, D. C. "Trade Credit Management: Selection of Accounts Receivable Using a Statistical Model." Ph.D. dissertation, Stanford University, 1968.

6. Gilbert, E. S. "On Discrimination Using Qualitative Variables," *American Statistical Association Journal*, 63, (December, 1968).

7. Ladd, G. W. "Linear Probability Functions and Discriminant Functions," *Econometrica*, XXXIV (October, 1966).

8. Myers, J. H. and E. W. Forgy. "The Development of Numerical Credit Evaluation Systems," *American Statistical Association Journal*, 58, (September, 1963).

9. Wu, H. K. "Bank Examiner Criticisms, Bank Loan Defaults, and Bank Loan Quality," *Journal of Finance*, XXIV (September, 1969).

Chapter 26

THE PRESENT VALUE APPROACH TO SELECTING BANK CUSTOMERS*

By Daniel L. White

*This article is reprinted, with permission, from *Journal of Bank Research,* Vol. 5, No. 2 (Summer, 1974), pp. 96-101.

Many authors have argued that compensating balance requirements, the prime rate convention and the provision of services below cost are parts of a rational system that maximizes the long run profit to commercial banks from a customer relationship [Hodgman, 1963]. It has been shown that banks do charge lower rates for loans made to depositors [Murphy, 1967]. This paper will investigate the ability of a bank to discriminate between profitable and unprofitable customers in the long run.

Forty-eight months is arbitrarily chosen as a long run period. The period from January 1966 through December 1970 starts with the credit stringency of 1966 and ends in the trough of the 1968-1969 credit crunch, thus covering a complete business cycle.

It is important that account analysis be extended over at least one business cycle, because the cost to the bank of granting credit lines when money is plentiful and when the bank is seeking to expand loans is not known until these lines are used during periods of stringency. Banks lose money on loans made in a credit crunch because in order to honor their credit lines they are forced to sell their bond portfolio at a loss and/or borrow funds at rates much higher than the prime rate which they will receive on these loans.

Credit lines are often used by firms to back up their sales of commercial paper, which is usually a cheaper source of funds than bank loans. Whenever the commercial paper market dries up—as it did during the Penn Central crisis—these lines are desperately needed to maintain firms' working capital investment. However, sometimes in periods of stringency there will be a liquid commercial paper market with yields higher than the prime rate. Most astute treasurers will take advantage of this situation and borrow at the cheaper prime rate even though the bank, in order to make these loans, must borrow at rates above the prime.

Not every customer will use his line during periods of credit stringency. If these customers also increase deposits in this period, they are likely to be very profitable customers from the bank's point of view. But if the bank does not know who these desirable customers are, it may carelessly lose them to competing banks, and in seeking new customers cannot make special efforts to attract them. The converse may be even more important from the bank's point of view. A customer who only borrows during a credit crunch can be a very unprofitable customer to serve. These customers will remain a constant drain on bank profits until they are identified.

Consequently, commercial banks need a measure of long-run profitability that will be equitable to both customer and banker alike. Business customers will continue to demand that their banks guarantee their regular working capital loans at reasonable rates, and banks must be sure to charge each customer a fair price for that guarantee.

Traditional Practice

The central figure in a bank information system is the loan officer. Loan officers deal directly with the borrowing customers and generally assume a large share of the responsibility for the judgment made with respect to the extention of credit. These are the men who "bargain" with the customers on the level of required compensating balances and the interest rate charged on loans. They may also discover which services the customer needs. Usually, loan officers are also salesmen, who search the community for new profitable customers.

This role requires that the loan officer know the profitability of each of his accounts. He also needs information as to which activity provides each account's profit, and an algorithm to determine an estimated profitability of each new customer. The above information is crucial if the loan officer is to successfully bargain with and serve the bank's clients.

In practice, long run customer profitability is almost universally ignored. Instead, the account analysis form is based on the past month's activity and emphasizes the cost of holding reserves in order to be sure of clearing checks. There is no charge made for the opportunity cost of holding reserves in order to be sure of honoring that customer's lines.

In computing earnings, the bank gives the customer a credit for the worth of his balances on the basis of the value of money to the bank rather than the value of money in the money market. In the past few years the interest credit given to customers' balances has increased significantly. Yet this rate is more a function of what can be justified to customers than a function of money market rates. The value of the money which customers have borrowed is also determined in an arbitrary way.

Thus the conventional approach uses a subjective valuation of deposits coupled with an equally subjective costing of funds lent to customers. Because these two items dominate the other costs or benefits associated with serving any given customer, the conventional approach is also subject to serious errors in the short term.

Many have argued that the answer to the problem of pricing bank services is for banks to pay interest on demand deposits and to set fees for each of the services that banks perform [Jacobs, 1971]. This would have the effect of changing the bank services market from one in which prices are set by bargaining, to an organized market in which standardized commodities and services are sold, prices are publicly quoted and adhered to, and every buyer of a specific service pays the same price.

Since prices would be public, a large corporation with volume business could not be charged less than a local firm, so similar prices for bank services might become the norm for all banks in a given region. Also the tradition of using the costs to the bank of performing a customer's services as a means of explaining the bank's prices to the customer would fade. Thus local, regional or money market banks with differing services for their different proportions of customer classes, and hence different cost schedules, could no longer use these differences to justify different prices for identical services [Jacobs, 1971].

A Model for Computing
Long Run Customer Profitability

It has been shown that there are two major deficiencies in the traditional type of account analysis. First, there is no charge for the insurance given by the line of credit that funds will be available during periods of credit stringency. Reserves must be bought to honor these lines, and the opportunity cost of these investments are never computed. In other words, the conventional approach does not provide for the effect of net cash flows over the business cycle. Second, the conventional

approach uses a subjective valuation of deposits coupled with an equally subjective costing of funds lent to customers.

It is easy to correct the first deficiency. In any given period, each customer will cause either a net cash inflow or outflow of funds from its bank. This flow results from changes in a firm's demand or other deposit balances, changes in loan indebtedness or from fees charged by the bank for its services. If the factors used in servicing a customer's account (labor, plant and funds) are purchased at a constant price (or at a price independent of the amount purchased), then the cost of serving a customer can be deducted from the above net cash flow. In this case, each customer becomes an investment project, and his value to the bank is a sum of each period's discounted net cash flow.

The second deficiency must be corrected with a model that can value deposits and the cost of lent funds by matching available deposits with the opportunity to lend to customers. Thus the model should be able to compute the present value of each customer, given economies that result from interaction effects between customers.

One simple model that meets these requirements is an equivalent of Baumol and Quandt's [1965] basic linear programming model.

$$\text{Maximize} \quad \Sigma_t U_t W_t$$

$$\text{Subject to} \quad -\Sigma_i a_{it} C_i \times W_t \leq E_t$$

$$W_t, C_i \geq O$$

$$C_i \leq 1$$

Where U_t = the discount factor in each period

W_t = the withdrawals in each period

C_i = each customer

a_{it} = net revenue flow in each period for customer c_i

E_t = new equity invested in each period

Essentially all this model does is compute the present value of the cash flows, a_{it}, discounted at the rate U_t. However, if these cash flows can be invested at a higher rate than U_t, the cash is invested and the returns from this investment are added to the present value of the cash flows. This partially solves the second deficiency of the traditional approach. The discount rate is still subjective, but the investment opportunity rate is mathematically determined from the actual loan demands of other customers.

In order to adjust this model to handle the required information, an equivalent form of this model will be used [Chambers and Charnes, 1961].

Maximize $\quad \Sigma U_t W_t$
$\quad\quad\quad t$
$\quad\quad\quad -\Sigma a_{it} C_i \times W_t - BOR_t +$
$\quad\quad\quad INV_t \leq E_t$
$\quad\quad\quad C_i \leq 1$

Where $\quad U_t =$ the discount factor in each period
$\quad\quad\quad W_t =$ the withdrawals in each period
$\quad\quad\quad C_i =$ each customer
$\quad\quad\quad a_{it} =$ the net cash flow in each period for each customer C_i
$\quad\quad\quad Bor_t = 1 +$ the borrowing rate for funds in each period times the amount borrowed
$\quad\quad\quad Inv_t = 1 +$ the investment rate for funds in each period times the amount invested
$\quad\quad\quad E_t =$ new equity invested in each period

E_t has been assumed to equal zero in all cases, because it was viewed as undesirable to allow new equity investment either in the form of retained earnings or equity capital. This has been viewed as a worthwhile assumption, because to allow new equity investment would permit a factor exogenous to each individual customer's fund flow and subsequent income stream to have an impact on his long run profitability.

Although the unrealistic assumption of infinitely elastic factor prices is specified by this model, as opposed to a more realistic step-wise linear function for factor prices (i.e., stratified inelastic factor prices), the results should not suffer, given the objective of ranking various customers on the basis of their long run profitability. The reason this assumption, inherent in the model, is not detrimental is twofold. First, the assumption should not alter the relative results. Second, the assumption simplifies the mathematical complexity of the problem and, consequently, facilitates computer processing of data, as well as reducing the data collection burden.

A second weakness in this model is the omission of a number of real world constraints under which bankers must operate. No attempt was made to allow for required reserves or adequate capital ratios. Again this reduced the complexity of the model. But the major reason that these constraints were omitted is that these constraints exist because bankers operate in a world of uncertainty, and the above model is a certainty model. What this paper attempts to measure is the profitability of customers with known cash flows in a risk-free world. [1]

Both of these assumptions will tend to overvalue the profitability of customers. Assuming infinitely elastic factor prices will reduce the marginal cost of serving each customer, and assuming the cash flows of each customer are known with certainty eliminates the expense of providing reserves to meet unexpected cash outflows.

Unfortunately, there is one other assumption that may lower the profitability of certain customers. Data were not saved which measured the services that were paid by fees, or services paid by a spread between bid and asked prices. It was also impossible to measure the free services that the bank offered each customer. Thus, although this simple model is far superior to the traditional practice, there is still much room for improvement.

Computing Long Run Profitability

The 14 customers chosen for this project were selected from one national group in a major commercial bank. Commercial banks are very reluctant to provide information concerning their individual customers. These customers were among the largest firms to whom credit facilities were made available. As such, their demands for credit in large amounts may have produced a bias to the extent that the "pool of funds" was required to borrow from outside sources frequently.

The net cash flows were computed as follows: The difference between the average ledger balance and the average loans outstanding was computed for each customer for each of the 48 months. This gave a net balance for each month, which was subtracted from the following month's net balance to give the net change in balances. The interest earned on the average loans outstanding in each month was added to the net change in balances, and the total expense of handling the activity of each customer was subtracted from the net change in balances. The result was the net cash flows for each customer for each of the 48 months. A final, zero-out figure was computed which equaled the net cash flows that would result if the customer withdrew all his deposits and paid off all his loans. The sum of the net cash flows plus the zero-out figure gives the total cash revenues earned by the bank for serving a customer over the four-year period.

[1] There are two methods of including risk in the model. First one can use the ABC form of the Fed. This would involve separating the net cash flows into changes in account balances and then add the constraint set developed by Chambers and Charnes [1961] or Cohen and Hammer [1967]. Another approach is chance constrained programming. Chance constraints have been added to the Baumol model by Naslund [1966] and White [1970].

The bank's information system has established an account into which various functional areas may place any accumulated "excess" funds. By the same token, functional areas deficient in funds may borrow these "excess" funds in order to nullify their deficiency. When a functional area deposits its "excess" funds in this account it is given an earnings credit on these funds. This earnings credit has been used as the investment rate. These investment rates were low relative to the market rates of interest over the same time period, but these rates were actually used by the bank in its decision-making process. These investment rates are given in Figure 1.[2]

Figure 1[2]

Year	Annual Investment Rate	Annual Borrowing Rate	Cost of Capital	Prime Rate
1966	5.15	6.15	5.65	5.5-6
1967	5.29	6.29	5.79	5.5-6
1968	5.92	6.92	6.42	6-6.75
1969	7.06	8.06	7.56	7-8.5

The rates at which functional areas could borrow from this account were not available. Thus the borrowing rate has been arbitrarily defined as the investment rate plus one percent.

One of the limitations of assuming elastic factor prices is that one must define the cost of capital as a rate lower than the borrowing rate. In a more realistic model, the borrowing rate would increase in a stepwise linear fashion as the total funds borrowed increased. Thus in this simple model the cost of capital is defined as the investment rate plus one half of one per cent.

These annual rates were adjusted to monthly rates and the model was set up. The L-P has 63 rows and 119 variables. If a customer was accepted, the dual value of the constraint $C_i \leq 1$ can be used as a measure of the value of that customer to the bank. If the customer was not accepted, the opportunity cost accepting that customer gives a measure of the loss to the bank in accepting that customer's business. These marginal values or marginal costs are listed in Figure 2.

Figure 3. Actual Customer Profitability by the Bank's Accounting System

	Net Profits in Last Month		Net Profits in Last Month
Cust 9	$4773	Cust 3	$2558
Cust 2	4472	Cust 10	1793
Cust 14	3906	Cust 3	1244
Cust 5	3879	Cust 11	1243
Cust 77	3204	Cust 6	920
Cust 8	3073	Cust 1	904
Cust 4	2863	Cust 12	663

As expected, there was a wide difference in the profitability of customers. Two customers were very profitable indeed. Sixty-four per cent of the customers were profitable. But the bank lost money on over 28% of this group of 14 customers, and one customer cost the bank over half a million dollars a year to serve.[3] If the four unprofitable customers had not been served, the bank would have earned over one third more than by serving all 14 customers. By accepting all customers the bank earned $8,537,577.69. It could have earned $11,044,437.41.

Notice that the bank neither made nor lost money on customer 5. Usually a model of this type will accept a fraction of a customer, but in this case the model accepted all of customer 5, but its dual value was zero. Integer programming may be needed in cases where a fraction of a customer is accepted. The four unprofitable customers were not accepted by the model, and their dual values are the opportunity cost of acceptance.

Finally, it should be pointed out that the bank's information system provided no hint as to which customers were unprofitable. It did point out that

Figure 2. Dual Value of Customers from LP Model

Cust 9	$4,427,224.69	Cust 6	$105,555.16
Cust 8	4,403,360.21	Cust 3	76,920.18
Cust 2	589,458.29	Cust 5	0.00
Cust 14	525,866.31	Cust 12	-50,170.98
Cust 10	467,873.29	Cust 11	-65,271.55
Cust 13	284,618.00	Cust 1	-235,043.86
Cust 7	163,561.31	Cust 4	-2,156,373.33

[2] This model requires that the cost of external funds be measured by the actual money market rates that were in effect. What this model does avoid is the subjective valuation of internal funds (i.e., demand deposits and earnings) that can either be invested at money market rates or loaned in order to preserve a valuable customer relationship. In the theoretical financial literature, this problem is best described by Hirshleifer [1958].
[3] Some of the customers were not prime, and the bank earned prime +¼ or prime +½ on these loans. This extra interest was included in the net cash flows.

customers 12, 11 and 1 were among the least profitable; but it also ranked customer 4 right in the middle. Customer 5 was ranked among the most profitable, and customer 8 was not recognized as being unusually profitable. It is obvious that if the bank had realized that customer 4 was so unprofitable, it would have severed the customer relationship; so even though data on only one month's profitability was available, it is safe to assume that the bank had no idea of the magnitude of their loss. Again, it should be pointed out that this simple L-P model tends to overestimate the profits of a customer relationship.

New Trends and New Directions

Banks have known about their pricing dilemma for years, and after the credit crunch of 1969 they resolved to do something about it. Their solution was the floating prime rate which would fall and rise with money market rates. This would insure that banks could borrow money at rates cheaper than they charged for loans. The floating prime rate, coupled with the removal of Regulation Q ceilings on certificates of deposits, led bankers to believe that they were free of the business of guaranteeing credit at reasonable rates. No longer would they be forced to borrow Eurodollars at 13% to lend at 8%. Instead they could sell CDs and make loans at one percentage point higher.

Their customers were very happy to accept the low prime rate but were worried that in the event of a future credit crunch they would have to pay 11% or more on their working capital loans. So they asked for and received Cap loans, which were long-term loans made at prime but with a maximum of 8%. In making Cap loans, banks had returned to the business of guaranteeing loans at reasonable rates.

However, there is a more serious threat to the floating prime—price controls. In a political environment in which monetary policy is the principal tool used to combat inflation, interest rates will fluctuate. If the prime rate is fixed by price controls or by government jawboning, banks will bear the major costs of industry's share of credit restraint.

From a macro point of view, there is a good reason for banks to assume this expense. Banks have more expertise at forecasting future rates, so they will be more efficient at minimizing the cost of providing industry with sufficient liquidity than if each individual company used the money market to provide for its own liquidity needs. Also the method by which banks provide this liquidity reduces segmentation of money markets. Banks buy medium-term bonds when short-term rates are low, causing the rates on longer maturities to fall. When short-term rates are high, banks sell these bonds at a loss in order to make short-term loans. This increases the rates on medium-term bonds. This link between short-term and medium-term rates is important if we are to avoid further segmenting of our money and of capital markets.

Thus banks have tried to change their business in order to conform to the limits of their accounting system. It looks as if society will not allow banks to abandon the guarantee of loans at reasonable rates, so a new information system must be constructed in order for banks to continue performing this essential and traditional service. Even though the long-term customer relationship hypothesis is not yet built into the bank's information system, this hypothesis can serve to build a rational system to maximize the long-run profit to commercial banks from a customer relationship. □

REFERENCES

Hodgman, Donald R., *Commercial Bank Loan and Investment Policy* (Urbana: Bureau of Economic and Business Research, University of Illinois, 1963), Chaps. 9-12.

Murphy, Neil B., "A Test of the Deposit Relationship Hypothesis," *Journal of Financial and Quantitative Analysis*, March, 1967.

Jacobs, Donald P., *Business Loan Costs and Bank Market Structure*, Occasional Paper 115, National Bureau of Economic Research, 1971.

Baumol, William J., and Richard E. Quandt, "Investment and Discount Rates Under Capital Rationing—A Programming Approach," *Economic Journal*, June, 1965.

Chambers, D., and A. Charnes, "Intertemporal Analysis and Optimization of Bank Portfolios," *Management Science*, July, 1961.

Cohen, K. J., and F. S. Hammer, "Linear Programming and Optimal Bank Asset Management Decisions," *Journal of Finance*, May, 1967.

Naslund, B., "A Model for Capital Budgeting Under Risk," *Journal of Business*, April, 1966.

White, Daniel L., "Customer Allocation in Banking," Dissertation Submitted to Northwestern University Graduate School, June, 1970.

Hirshleifer, J., "On the Theory of Optimal Investment Decision," *Journal of Political Economy*, August, 1958.

Chapter 27

METHOD FOR EVALUATION OF THE ECONOMIC CHARACTERISTICS OF LOAN PORTFOLIOS*

By Wolfgang P. Hoehenwarter

And Accompanying Discussion:
A BANKING APPLICATION
By John Davis

*This article is reprinted, with permission, from *Journal of Bank Research,*
Vol. 6, No. 4 (Winter, 1976), pp. 257-267.

The loan portfolio of a commercial bank consists of groups of loans whose rates are related to a certain key rate, the prime rate, and groups that are more or less independent of this rate. This paper describes the functional relationships that tie average rates and contributions to income—of these groups or of the entire loan portfolio—to moves in these rates and fluctuations in loan balances outstanding. The application of these relationships can provide banks with a valuable planning tool and greater insight into the economic characteristics of the loan portfolio. They will be able to answer such questions as the following:

> What are the average rates, and their lag behind prime, for individual loan groups and for the entire portfolio?
> What is the total income produced from a certain group of loans, or of a department, over, say, the next year on a monthly basis, given forecasts of loans outstanding and prime rate?
> What are the income effects of changes in rates, particular the prime, and of changes in loan levels? Should more emphasis be placed on a certain group of loans?
> What is the sensitivity of the portfolio to moves in prime?
> What are the trade-offs of emphasizing fixed vs. variable time loans? This is particularly important with the greatly increased volatility of the prime rate.

Questions of this nature come up frequently during the preparation or periodic review of the budget-profit plan. Such questions do have ready answers, since the relationships involved are strictly deterministic, depending only on the proper input—forecast of levels and rates. But, many times these questions are never used, or they are answered only using guesses or rough approximations.

The difficulty is that many times the loan portfolios are not organized along mathematical principles, either missing information or lacking an ability to obtain it through the computer program.

That is, information might be part of the loan agreement but not of the computer record. Even if the necessary information can be obtained, the amount of data and calculations necessary to arrive at the exact answer is almost prohibitive for even a small sized loan portfolio.

The purpose of this paper is to point out what information is necessary and sufficient to answer the above questions. Thereafter a general model is proposed that could be used if all information was available. Finally, the paper proposes certain approximations to the general model, which should make the model easy to use, whether on computer or hand calculated, while still maintaining a reasonable level of accuracy.

Obviously the effect of loan-rate changes on income only represents half of the picture. Effects of deposit and other liability rate changes also have an impact and must be considered. Generally speaking, banks must buy money as efficiently (cheaply) as possible, and then sell it at prices (rates) allowing for sufficient profit margin. (Although in the short run, banks tend to meet loan demand independently of liability concerns, reflecting other policies than pure cost-considerations.) Management of the loan portfolio rate of return, therefore, has to take into consideration management of liabilities. But here again, an ever increasing percentage of liabilities has become subject to high cost volatility, leading to quite unstable profit margins.

The ways to react to rate changes may be unique to each bank, depending on the management goals, the composition of the balance sheet and the market environment. But banks do have to react, and to select the proper course has become more complex than ever. This paper does not describe a full asset and liability management model (like BAI's BANKMOD). It merely describes one facet within the overall planning context, which even by itself is complex enough: The relationship of loan rates to moves in certain key rates. It should allow banks to obtain more reliable answers, contributing to a more accurate overall planning procedure.

The Model

Generally, the income between $T1$ and $T2$ is (time unit 1 year):

$$\text{Income} = \int_{T1}^{T2} AVRAT_t * LBO_t * dt \qquad (1)$$

For purposes of this paper and particularly for the proposed algorithm, it is sufficient to consider a week as the smallest time increment. That is, within a week rates and balances remain constant, and the income for one week is just the product of this constant rate.

Let

t = week in consideration

Δ = time increment measured in years (i.e. 1 week = 1/52)

$AVRAT_t$ = average rate at week t

LBO_t = loan balance outstanding at week t

then

$$\text{Income}_t = AVRAT_t * LBO_t * \Delta \qquad (1A)$$

The major difficulty is to calculate $AVRAT$, since the loan balances that are written at t, at the rate prevailing at t, varies from period to period. In addition, the total portfolio is a composition of several loan categories with different characteristics. What is known is the functional dependency of the current rates to prime, or in the case of independent rates, the current rate (for new loans).

The second factor in (1A), total loan balance, presents few problems. LBO is either forecast as a total or the sum of forecasts for individual categories. But the amount LBO enters the calculation of $AVRAT$ indirectly, complicating the matter substantially.

At this point we can define precisely what attributes of loans are necessary and sufficient to these calculations. The average rate and income depends on the amount and rate of loans written at each period, in other words, the amount repriced and the repricing rate.

If we consider two successive periods (weeks) t and $t + 1$ then we have

(2) $LBO_{t+1} = LBO_t - ROFF_{t+1} + NEW_{t+1}$

or, more significantly

(2A) $LBO_{t+1} = LBO_t - AVAIL_{t+1} +$
                 $REPRIC_{t+1} + NEW_{t+1}$

where

$ROFF$ = balance running off from t to $t+1$

$AVAIL$ = balance available for repricing

$REPRIC$ = amount repriced of the available

NEW = new loans written

Naturally, $ROFF = AVAIL - REPRIC$. For example, a group of time loans with rates tied to prime might run off over a year, but is available for repricing almost instantaneously. Since income depends on the rates, the important number is the balance written at the new rate, that is

$$LBN = REPRIC + NEW$$

How much LBN is due to repricing or to new loans is insignificant, therefore equation (2) reduces to

$$LBO_{t+1} = LBO_t - AVAIL_{t+1} + LBN_{t+1} \qquad (3)$$

Also significant is the time span during which the new rate remains contractually unchanged, that is the time between possible repricings, L. It is exactly this number that strongly influences the dynamic behavior of the portfolio.

Summarizing, the important attributes for a loan group are: 1) Rate of new loans, either independent or as a certain function of prime and 2) length for which the new rate is applicable, that is length until repricing. Loan groups that differ in either of the two show different behavior over time. Loan groups with identical (or almost identical) parameters may be summed together without loss of generality.

Let

i = number (index) of loan group I

$R_{i,t}$ = rate of new loans of category I at time t (issued during week t)

L_i = length for which $R_{i,t}$ remains fixed, i.e. time to next repricing

$LBO_{i,t}$ = total balance outstanding for category I at time t

$AVAIL_{i,t}$ = amount available for repricing

$LBN_{i,t}$ = amount actually repriced

$PRIM_t$ = prime rate at t

$AVRAT_{i,t}$ = average rate of category I at t

$INCOME_{i,t}$ = interest income

Stated in these terms the income of one category for period t is the sum of all the incomes of those amounts that were repriced, taken over the past repricing time.

$$INCOME_{i,t} = \Delta * \sum_{t-L_i+1}^{t} R_{i,j} * LBN_{i,j} \qquad (1B)$$

Stated differently, if a loan was repriced five weeks ago, and its repricing time is three months, its rate today is still the one given to it five weeks ago, even if prime has moved.

The income of the total portfolio or of a group of categories is the sum of the income of individual categories.

$$INCOME_t = i\Sigma INCOME_{i,t} = \Delta * i\sum_j\sum_{t-L_i+1}^{t} R_{i,j*} \, LBN_{i,j} \tag{1C}$$

$R_{i,j}$ is either independent of prime or a certain function f_i (Prime), and

$$LBN_{i,j} = LBO_{i,j} - LBO_{i,j-1} + AVAIL_{i,j}$$

If we consider that each group has a renewal time of L_i, it can easily be seen that

$$AVAIL_{i,j} = LBN_{i,j-L_i} \tag{4}$$

which gives a recursive formula

$$LBN_{i,j} = LBO_{i,j} - LBO_{i,j-1} + LBN_{i,j-Li} \tag{5}$$

for all $j \geq L_i + 1$

The average rate for t now is

$$AVRAT_t = \frac{i\sum_j\sum_{t-L+1}^{t} R_{i,j} {}_* LBN_{i,j}}{i\Sigma LBO_{i,t}} \tag{6}$$

In order to calculate $INCOME$ and $AVRAT$ for several periods, say four weeks ($=$ 1 month), equations (1C) and (6) have to be summed up over t, giving

$$INCOME = t\sum_{T1}^{T2} i\Sigma INCOME_{i,t}$$

$$= \Delta * t\sum_{T1}^{T2} i\sum_j\sum_{t-L_i+1}^{t} R_{i,j} * LBN_{i,j}$$

and

$$AVRAT = \frac{t\sum_{T1}^{T2} i\sum_j\sum_{t-L_i+1}^{t} R_{i,j} * LBN_{i,j}}{t\sum_{T1}^{T2} i\Sigma LBO_{i,t}}$$

Plotting $INCOME$ or $AVRAT$ against the prime rate shows the dynamic characteristics of the loan portfolio, and how the "lag" behaves. Using the information contained in the balances LBN has one more informative feature—it is very easy to determine the sensitivity of the loan portfolio or selected parts, to changes in prime. That is, if the prime rate moves today, what percentage of the portfolio will move today, within a week or a month? And by what magnitude will the average rates be effected?

The LBN's are the balances that are written at the new rate. Thus, they are the only ones effected by a move in the current rate, be it prime or an independent rate. Keeping that in mind, the ratio of the total balance outstanding that is effected immediately by a move in rates is LBN divided by the total balance LBO. This ratio may be denoted $S^o_{i,t}$ the immediate sensitivity of the loan group i at the time t. The term immediate is important because it is also possible to look at those loans that follow with a delay, say one or more weeks. Using this notation

$$S^o_{i,t} = \frac{LBN_{i,t}}{LBO_{i,t}} \tag{7}$$

with proper summations for the whole portfolio or groups of categories, it can easily be verified that the effect of a rate change on the average rate is proportional this sensitivity.

$$\delta AVRAT_{i,t} = \delta R_{i,t} {}_* S^o_{i,t} \tag{8}$$

Similarly, a "delayed" sensitivity $S^r_{i,t}$ might be defined as that per cent of the portfolio that will follow a move in rate today (t) between the times $r = r_1 - r_2$. For example, a bank might ask: If the prime moves today, what per cent of the portfolio is effected immediately (i.e., within one week) and what per cent is effected from two to four weeks hence. Again, using the concept of LBN's, the answer can be found very easily:

$$S^r_{i,t} = \frac{j\sum_{t-r_1}^{t-r_2} LBN_{i,j}}{LBO_{i,t}} \tag{7a}$$

Care has only to be taken in cases where the range r is not totally within the renewal length L_i.

All formulas, (1C), (6), (7) and (8) contain only factors which are known. $R_{i,j}$ ($j \geq o$) is either forecast directly, or a function of a directly forecast rate (prime). $LBO_{i,t}$ is forecast directly, and LBN can be calculated with the help of formula (5), at least for all $j \geq o$.

Only the missing link of formula (5) for $j < o$, (equivalent to $t < L + 1$) remains—the start of the recursive procedure. But we know that what is available for repricing at t, has been a LBN at time $t - L$, at a rate R at time $t - L$ (equation (4)). Therefore, the start of the recursive procedure can be supplied by historical data from within the bank, going back exactly L_i weeks. $LBN_{i,j-Li}$ in (5) and the rates in (1) are substituted by the actually repriced loan balance L_i weeks before the current.

With the available data and above equations an exact projection model, (decision model) is possi-

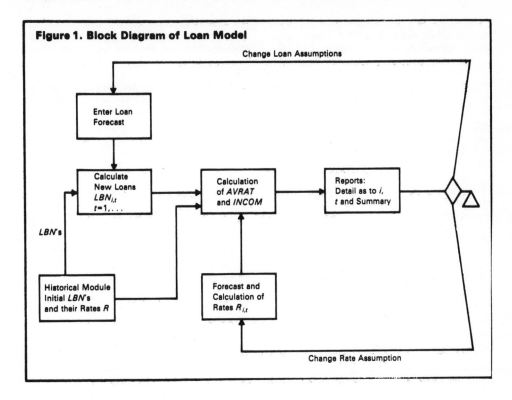

Figure 1. Block Diagram of Loan Model

ble. It might be structured as an interactive "what if" type model with the decision variables rates (prime and independent) and loan forecasts. In addition, some module has to inject historical data on *LBN*'s and their rates. Figure 1 outlines the structure of this model.

The output of such a model might not be only of immediate use when studying the questions mentioned previously. It can also be used as an input to various bank planning models. Most of them require as an input a forecast of average loan levels and average loan rates for periods within the planning horizon. The product of those forecasts is then applied to income. Since the economic environment has become increasingly volatile, it is very difficult to assess the impact of these strong movements in rates and levels on averages. This is particularly so if the base period of the model is one quarter or even a year. Using a model like that described above as a front-end could substantially increase the accuracy of a full-fledged bank planning model.

The inclusion of the attributes time to repricing (L_i) and repriced balance (LBN_i) into the loan description is most important since it allows for easy study of the economic characteristics of the

loan portfolio. If this information is available, questions on average rates, income contributions, lag behind price and sensitivity of the portfolio to moves in rates can easily be answered.

Simplified Model

The above general model has one weak point— the historical module that must supply *LBN*'s and their rates before the recursive formula (5) sets in. Generally a bank does not have the data readily available; it would be necessary to go through records years back for certain groups, and recalculate on a weekly basis *LBN*'s and rates for the various groups. This might involve, in the case of an automated loan portfolio system writing and adding to already existing and proven programs, or in a manual system an insurmountable task of file searching and hand-calculating. In either case, it is impractical.

It seems, therefore, desirable to devise an alternative of supplying the initial *LBN*'s. Obviously any other method would compromise accuracy. The method pointed out below is believed to be within tolerable limits.

345

When we enter the calculations, we have the starting balance outstanding, $LBO_{i,o}$ and the starting average rate $AVRAT_{i,o}$. In addition, we know L_i and $R_{i,o}$, the current rate. If $AVRAT_{i,o}$ is not equal to $R_{i,o}$, we know rates have varied within the span L_i in the past. (If $AVRAT_{i,o} = R_{i,o}$ we could not conclude that rates have remained at this level, and would have to consider the variance as well.) Similarly, in order to find the LBN's over the past L_i, we need more information.

While it is very difficult for most banks to obtain past LBN's, it is very easy for them to obtain past total levels, that is, LBO's. They may either be taken directly from accounting records or, for the purpose of his model, aggregated by proper summation into the various groups.

In order to develop the past LBN's from the past LBO's in a convenient fashion, the following "critical assumption" has to be introduced: The repriced levels have behaved similar to the total levels in the past; more precisely, if the LBO's have followed a straight line or a polynom, then the LBN's are assumed the same. From a practical point of view this assumption makes sense for several reasons:

1) We know if the total loan level has increased, the level of new loans has increased—total levels are the summation of new levels. Similarly, if total levels have decreased, new levels must have decreased. In addition, loan levels do not swing dramatically up and down, but change gradually with the rate of change only fractional.

2) This assumption applies to the less volatile loans only. Variable rate demand loans are considered to have a repricing time of one; that is the smallest time interval in the model. Therefore the new balances are always identical to the total balances, requiring no past history, since they do not enter the approximation routine. On the other side it is generally found the larger the repricing time on loans, the slower the rate of change on total balances.

3) A model like this is not an accounting program and must not be used as such. Smoothing out some erratic behavior in the past is acceptable. The model's main concern is future behavior and future trends (the value of a model, this or any other, lies in the new insight it gives management into a problem); that is, how are average rates and incomes affected by forecasted changes in rates and levels. In particular, how does the "lag" behave, and how sensitive is the portfolio to changes in rates.

4) The "proof" of a model lies in its capacity to provide useful and reasonably accurate information. What is considered reasonable depends on its use. If the accuracy is not sufficient, because the assumption does not fit the data, then the assumption cannot be used; one has to use historical data to use the model.

Let t be the time in the past. The assumption states, if LBO_t can be described as a polynom $P_1(t)$ then LBN_t can be described as a polynom $P_2(t)$. If LBO is a polynom of order r

$$LBO_t = e \sum_0^r \hat{A}_e t^e \tag{9}$$

then the LBN's are a polynom of the same order:

$$LBN_t = e \sum_0^r A_e t^e \tag{10}$$

Let k be the time in the past. At each point in time, the total balance LBO_t is the sum of all the individual balances that were repriced within the past repricing time. That is,

$$LBO_t = k \sum_t^{t+L-1} LBN_k \tag{11}$$

Inserting (10) into (11) and grouping with respect to the order of t leads to a polynom with the coefficient expressions in A_e. Since the equations hold for all t, those expressions have to equal the coefficients of equation (9), leading to a set of equations that can be solved to obtain the A_e.

The following discusses this approach with the polynom reduced to a straight line. The reasons for this simplification are that a straight line through current total balance and a previous total balance is very practical. Both balances can be obtained easily. If only qualitative studies are to be made, the straight line can even be simplified to a constant if the previous balance is set equal to current (see (12) and (13)). On the other hand, using a polynom of higher order does require more information. To develop the coefficients of a polynom of order r, $r+1$ total balances are required. While this does not pose theoretical problems it does present practical problems since too much information is required.

The author has developed, together with Tymshare Inc., a computer program that uses the straight line assumption. The program produces tables for average rates, incomes and sensitivities of the portfolios to rate changes. This program is currently being tested in a bank. A report on the findings appears on page 349.

Figure 2 outlines the assumption. A straight line is fitted through the past "true" total levels, giving us LBO, which is known, and an estimate of

LBO_4. Also, the LBN's are assumed to lie on a straight line. With this in mind, plus the total balances at two points, the LBN's can be calculated.

For point 1 we have, setting $LBO_{i1} = LBO_{i,t=o}$

$$k \sum_{1}^{L_i} LBN_{i,k} = LBO_{i,o} \qquad (11A)$$

and

$$LBN_{i,k} = LBN_{i,1} + (k-1) * A \qquad (10A)$$

Taking the difference between $LBO_{i,1}$ and $LBO_{i,k}$ under above assumptions, allows one to solve for A and $LBN_{i,1}$.

$$LBN_{i,1} = \frac{3LBO_{i,o} - LBO_{i,Li}}{2.Li} \qquad (12)$$

$$A_i = \frac{LBO_{i,Li} - LBO_{i,o}}{L_i * (L_i - 1)} \qquad (13)$$

A similar assumption is made for past rates. Lacking an exact method it may be postulated that rates have increased or decreased following a straight line.

$$R_{i,k} = R_{i,o} + (k-1) * B_i \qquad (14)$$

with B_i the constant rate increment for category i. This assumption appears more imposing than the one on levels—the rate environment is substantially more volatile than the level of loans outstanding. It may be that the prime rate changed within a few weeks by a significant percentage; for example, in Fall 1974, weekly changes amounted to about 2.5%.

However, examining the calculation method for $INCOME$ reveals that any errors on rates introduced by this assumption must work itself out of the system at $t - L_i$, and from here on the rate factor in the income calculation is exact. And, in fact, those rates that are furthest in the past and are least accurate, leave the system first.

The equation of average rates is

$$k \sum_{1}^{L_i} LBN_{i,k} * R_{i,k} = AVRAT_{i,o} * k \sum_{1}^{L_i} LBN_{i,k} \qquad (15)$$

Inserting (10A) and (14) into (15) leads to

$$k \sum_{1}^{L_i} \left[R_{i,o} + (k-1)B_i \right] * \left[LBN_{i,o} + (k-1)A_i \right]$$

$$= AVRAT_i * LBO_{i,t=0}$$

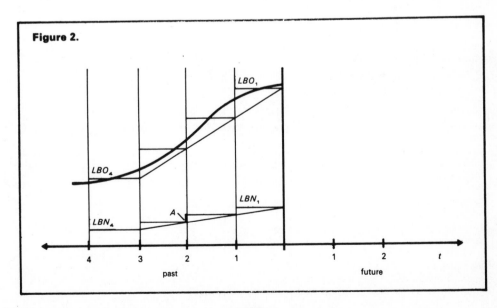

Figure 2.

347

which can be solved, resulting in   (16)

$$B_i = 12* \frac{LBO_{i,o} * (AVRAT_i - R_{i,o})}{LBO_{i,o} * (5L_i - 7) + LBO_{i,L_i} * (L_i + 1)}$$

Equations (12), (13) and (16) fully describe the past situation. All the parameters on the right side are known and can be obtained relatively easy from historical records.

In calculating income and average rates the following procedure is to be used: 1) For the beginning of the planning horizon, as long as $t < L_i$, formulas (12) to (16) supply the initial LBN's and R's; 2) as soon as $t = L_i$ the recursive procedure (5) together with the forecasted rates are used. Only in the case of totally erratic behavior coupled with the desire for complete accuracy, the approximation method may not be used, and one has to use the formulas of the general case (1) to (8). Then the LBN's must be supplied differently, for example, by an external table or a subroutine.

Conclusion

Questions on average rates, income contribution, their lag behind the prime rate and their sensitivity are always important to banks. A concise mathematical method for the general case often seems impractical. It is believed that the proposed approximation using a linear function and averages for past behavior of rates and levels strikes a reasonable compromise between practicality and accuracy.   □

A Banking Application

By John Davis
Planning Officer
National Bank of Tulsa
Tulsa, Oklahoma

The impact on the banking industry of key interest rate changes has scarcely been so significant as in the recent past. The frequency of these rate changes increased tremendously during 1973 and 1974. There is a clear need to properly assess these rate changes before they take place in terms of how they will affect bottom-line earnings. The National Bank of Tulsa's early attempts at this assessment were the manual projection of significant, rate-sensitive asset and liability accounts and the yields or rates on those accounts. Our own historical data on the rate-sensitive accounts enabled the formulation of a predictable impact to net income of changes in the prime rate and/or changes in the cost of funds. Thus, the bottom-line consequences of such an action could be tested and analyzed before it was ever put into effect. The major goal of being able to analyze the impact of these rate changes is to eventually reach that point where changes in the cost of funds to the bank will not affect the net interest spread. In other words, the managed net interest spread remains constant no matter what rate changes take place.

The NBT was approached by Wolfgang Hoehenwarter of Bank Administration Institute in October 1974, to evaluate the method defined in this accompanying article by testing a commercial loan model known as COMLON. My approach in testing and evaluating this program was three-fold: First, determine if the data necessary for input to the program was readily available in a banking environment. Second, determine the accuracy of the method. Could the program with its inherent straight-line assumptions closely approximate actual contributions to income with the actual prime rate and loan volume figures experienced by the bank during a defined time frame? Third, determine if the method was suitable for forecasting.

The time frame selected for testing was a six month period from July through December 1974. During this period, the prime rate at the National Bank of Tulsa changed eight times. A broad group of commercial loans whose yields are tied, in some fashion, to the prime rate was selected for the test. This group of loans was divided into four loan categories depending upon the following two criteria: 1) The dependence of the loan category upon one particular key rate (such as NBT prime) and 2) the length of time before which a change in that key rate is noticeable to the loan category. The four loan categories are defined as follows:

> Those commercial loans that are on an immediate, floating prime basis.
> Those commercial loans whose rates change either on the next interest payment date or on the first day of the following quarter.

> Those commercial loans whose rates are based on a New York prime rate.
> All other commercial loans whose rates move on an irregular basis.

With the loan categories so defined, the next step was to determine the historical data necessary for input into the program. The source of this historical data was as follows:

Prime Rate Change Review. This is a computer print-out listing the following information on each note for the bank's commercial loan portfolio: Issue and maturity dates, original and current principal, interest earned and outstanding, rate change and the effective date of the change, and pricing (i.e. NBT Prime + ½% floating, etc.).

The total loans tied to prime rate by responsibility center. These are both dollar and percentage figures and are determined monthly on a manual basis from the prime rate change review.

The summary of loans tied to a prime rate by the day that the rate will change. These are also both dollar and percentage figures and are determined monthly on a manual basis from the prime rate change review. (Personnel requirements for this and the category immediately above are three man-days.)

The yields on loans tied to a prime rate by the defined loan categories. This is determined manually from the prime rate change review upon request. (Personnel requirements are three man-days.)

It should be noted that personnel requirement figures were for the first usage of the model. Time requirements have since been reduced by 50%.

The preceding historical data provided all information required for testing the program. The historical yields on all loan categories allowed the determination of the spread over prime. The initial balance and initial average rate for each loan category was determined as of the last day of June 1974. All that remained was to forecast the expected loan levels and the expected key rates. Of course, for the test, these loan levels and rates were known and the actual data experienced was used.

The methodology employed by the program gave the following variances by month from the actual monthly average loan balances:

**Figure 1. Per Cent Variance
Actual vs. COMLON Projection
Monthly Average Loan Balance**

Month	Variance
July	.05%
August	.29%
September	1.01%
October	(.91%)
November	.21%
December	(1.58%)

The variance from the forecasted data from the actual loan volumes was very slight. In fact, the average monthly variance was only (.16%).

The variances in the average loan rates by month from the actual monthly average loan rates were as follows:

Figure 2. Per Cent Variance
Actual vs. COMLON Projection
Monthly Average Loan Rates

Month	Variance
July	(.40%)
August	(3.45%)
September	(2.28%)
October	(2.98%)
November	(3.08%)
December	(4.11%)

Figure 2 shows that the program was not as adept in accurately picking up rate changes as it was with loan volume changes. However, the variances were, by no means, severe; the average monthly variance for loan rates was (2.72%).

Variances in the COMLON program contributions to income by month from the actual contributions to income are as follows:

Figure 3. Per Cent Variance
Actual vs. COMLON Projection
Monthly Contribution to Income

Month	Variance
July	(.35%)
August	(3.16%)
September	(1.27%)
October	(3.89%)
November	(2.87%)
December	(5.69%)

Since the contribution to income is dependent upon the average loan levels and the average loan rates, the summation of the variances for the loan levels and the loan rates equal the variances experienced for the contribution to income. The average monthly variance for contribution to income was (2.88%).

These test results show that the historical data necessary to effectively use this mathematical method are available in the banking environment. The results of the program appear to be accurate to an acceptable variance level from the actual results over the test period. Therefore, predictions of rate changes (available through either research institutions or in-house economic research departments) and forecast of loan volumes (available from conscientious planning endeavors) enable the program to provide excellent insight into the income contributions of isolated loan categories and the sensitivity of those loan categories to changes in the key rates.

Chapter 28

THE COST OF BANK LOANS*

By Bernell K. Stone

*This article is reprinted, with permission, from *Journal of Financial and Quantitative Analysis,* Vol. 7, No. 5 (December, 1972), pp. 2077-2086.

I. Introduction

The interdependence of loan cost and tangible bank activity[1] is an aspect
of the cost of bank debt that has not been treated in the literature. Understanding this interdependence is important for banks in pricing their services,
especially as banks adopt more flexible pricing policies. This understanding is
crucial for a firm in establishing the true cost of bank borrowing, in comparing bank borrowing with other sources of funds, and in evaluating the firm's
banks. It is also important for understanding the firm-bank relationship in
general and the cost of capital in particular.

This paper investigates this interdependence and determines the effective
cost of bank borrowing as a function of useful loan size when banks: (1) impose
compensating balance restrictions in addition to interest charges in obtaining
compensation for loans, (2) allow the firm to earn credits on average net
collected balances in the firm's account that can be applied to payment for
tangible bank services, (3) allow the same balances that earn credits for
tangible services to be used to satisfy the compensating balance requirements
associated with borrowing, and (4) impose constraints on the percentage of
charges for tangible services that can be paid for by cash payments. Conditions
1 to 4 and the necessity of providing for transaction balances are typical of
most firms.

This paper (1) defines the concept of both the effective interest rate
and the effective rate of compensating balances, and (2) derives the effective
cost of bank borrowing as a function of useful loan size at a given bank. We
find that the marginal effective loan cost versus useful loan size is a step
function of three steps at a single bank and is a step function of many steps
for a firm with many banks.

---

[1] As in Calman [2], we use the term *tangible services* to refer to services
such as check cashing, deposit processing, bank wires, lock boxes, etc., for
which the bank levies an explicit charge. The term precludes loans and credit
services such as credit lines, credit agreements, and revolving credit arrangements.

II.   Effective Interest and Compensating Balance Rates

In the presence of compensating balance requirements, the interest rate *per se* does not completely reflect the cost of the loan when the firm must hold idle balances that it would not maintain otherwise. To determine the cost of maintaining compensating balances, we assume that these balances must also be borrowed *unless* the firm already has the balances available. Let i be the *nominal interest rate*[2] and I the *effective interest rate*. We need to distinguish between the *useful loan size*, the funds actually available to the firm for its own use, and the *total loan size*, which also includes any funds that the firm must borrow to meet compensating balance requirements. We denote useful loan size by X and total loan size by Y. The effective interest rate associated with a nominal interest rate i per period is:

$$(1) \qquad I = \frac{\text{total interest paid per period}}{\text{funds available for use}} = \frac{iY}{X} \; .$$

Let r_o be the rate of compensating balances quoted by the bank and let r_1 be the ratio of required balances to useful loan size under the assumption that *all* required balances will be provided by borrowing. We call r_o and r_1 the *nominal* and *effective* rates of compensating balances. By definition, we have $Y = (1 + r_1)X = X/(1 - r_o)$; hence

$$(2) \qquad r_1 = r_o/(1-r_o).$$

III.   Assumptions and Constraints

To study the interdependence of bank services and the implications of these interdependencies for the cost of bank loans, we assume:

A1. The allocation of tangible bank activity among the firm's banks has taken place; thus, total charges for tangible services at a given bank are fixed.

A2. The nominal interest rate i, the nominal compensating balance rate r_o, and the rate ρ at which credits are earned are all constants that do not vary as loan size changes.

A3. Lines of credit, credit agreements and revolving credit arrangements are all at the level of zero.

---

[2]As used in this paper, the *nominal interest rate* is not necessarily the quoted rate. Various loan features (discounting, periodic payments, etc.) can increase the interest charge above that quoted by the bank. In order to treat only the effect of compensating balances, we assume that the nominal rate already reflects all necessary adjustments in the quoted rate. See, for instance, Johnson [5, pp. 342-344] for a discussion of this problem.

A4. The same balances used to satisfy compensating balance requirements for loans can be used to earn credits to pay for tangible bank services.

A5. The firm is subject to the following constraints in its relations with a given bank:

(C1) $$NCB(X) \geq CBRL(X)$$

(C2) $$CPT + \rho \cdot NCB(X) \geq TCH$$

(C3) $$NCB(X) \geq MTB$$

(C3') $$CPT \leq \alpha \cdot TCH$$

where NCB is average net collected balances, CBRL is compensating balance requirements for loans, CPT is cash payments for tangible services, ρ is the rate at which credits are earned on average net collected balances, TCH is total charges for tangible services, α is the maximum fraction of tangible services that can be paid for by cash payments, and MTB is the minimum level of average transaction balances.

A6. The firm minimizes the cost of bank services subject to the constraints under which it operates, but the firm does not violate the constraints.

A7. The required transaction balances are not so large that the firm earns credits in excess of total charges for tangible services, i.e., MTB < TCH/ρ.

Assumption A1 means that the analysis of this paper specifies the cost of loans from a bank conditional on a given level of tangible services at that bank. A change in level will mean a change in TCH and a shift in the curve describing cost of loans versus useful loan size. Assumption A2 is realistic as long as the firm does not borrow so much that the nominal interest rate is raised to reflect increased default risk. Assumptions A3 and A7 are made to simplify analysis and can be easily relaxed. For instance, relaxing A3 would mean adding a constant to Constraint (C1) to reflect the additional balances required to support the line and possibly adding a constant to Constraint (C2) to reflect commitment fees. Assumption A4 represents generally accepted bank practice for major banks. The use of balances for dual purposes is the source of the link between the cost of bank loans and tangible services. Assumption A6 is a rationality assumption, which means that the cost-of-loans curve to be derived will be the cost *if* the firm minimizes the cost of its bank activity.

Constraint (C1) requires that average net collected balances be large enough to satisfy the compensating balance requirements associated with the firm's borrowing. Constraint (C2) requires that the combination of cash payments and credits be large enough to cover all charges for tangible services. The combination of (C1) and (C2) forces the firm to compensate the bank for its services. Constraint (C3) requires that average net collected balances be large enough to provide the minimum level required for transaction purposes. Constraints (Cl), (C2), and (C3) are typical of the restrictions on cash balances under which almost all firms operate. Some banks also impose limitations on the maximum percentage of cash payments that can be used to compensate the bank for tangible services. This restriction on the maximum percentage of compensation that may be made by cash payments is represented by (C3').[3]

The rationale for the existence of (C3') is that banks prefer deposits to cash payments. However, because the rate at which credits are earned is generally less than money market rates and is always less than a firm's cost of capital, a firm that acts optimally will prefer to pay for its tangible services via cash payments rather than via credits earned on balances *unless* these balances must be provided anyway for either transactions or the support of loans. For this reason a firm with no borrowing will maintain average net collected balances at MTB and use cash payments for tangible services in excess of $\rho \cdot MTB$. By imposing Constraint (C3'), a bank may force a firm to maintain a higher level of balances than it would maintain solely for transaction purposes.

Although (C3') is not always applicable, as are (Cl), (C2), and (C3), its inclusion in the system of constraints provides greater generality with no loss of descriptive accuracy. The case in which the bank imposes no restriction on the percent of compensation by cash payments can be treated by setting $\alpha = 1$. (A value of $\alpha < 1$ is probably most common between large firms and large banks.)

Another requirement sometimes imposed by banks to force maintenance of deposits is that the firm maintain a minimum level of average net collected balances to compensate the bank for tangible services in addition to the usual per item charge. This restriction can be treated by regarding MTB as the maximum of actual transaction requirements and the fixed minimum level required by the bank. With this convention, Constraints (Cl), (C2), (C3), and (C3') are adequate to describe the bank-firm interaction with fairly great generality.

Constraints (C3) and (C3') are mutually exclusive in that both do not hold simultaneously (except possibly at one value of TCH). The effect of (C3') is to require a minimum level of NCB. If this level is greater than MTB, then (C3) is inactive; if this level is less than MTB, then (C3) is active and (C3') has no effect.

To see how (C3') implies a minimum level of net collected balances if active, assume (C3') is binding. Then CPT = $\alpha \cdot$TCH; substituting into (C2) (which is also binding if (C3) is binding) and solving for NCB gives:

$$(3) \qquad\qquad NCB = \frac{(1 - \alpha) TCH}{\rho} .$$

---

[3] See Calman [2, p. 17] and Pogue, Faucett, and Bussard [6, p. 56] for further references to this constraint in the literature.

Since (C3) requires that NCB $\geq$ MTB, (C3) is active only if MTB $\geq$ (1 - α) TCH/ρ.
From the preceding, it is clear that the minimum possible level of net collected
balances is given by:

(4)   NCB' = max {MTB, (1 - α)TCH/ρ}.

When the firm has no borrowing from the bank, Constraint (C1) is inactive
since **CBRL** = 0.   As useful loan size X increases, CBRL increases; Constraint
(C1) becomes active when CBRL = NCB'. Let X' be the level of useful loan size
that makes Constraint (C1) become active, i.e., that makes CBRL = NCB'. As
borrowing increases beyond the level X', the level of net collected balances
must be increased to satisfy Constraint (C1). Neither Constraint (C3) nor (C3')
is binding; the cash payment CPT decreases as the level of net collected
balances increases until CPT = 0. At this point, all compensation for tangible
services is made by credits earned on balances.

Let X" be the level of useful loan size at which required compensating
balances for loans are such that CPT = 0, but at which no excess credits are
being earned. (For X > X", (C2) is inactive and there are excess credits.) If
NCB" is the level of net collected balances corresponding to X", then[4]

(5) $NCB" = \dfrac{TCH}{\rho}$.

IV.   The Cost of Loans Curve

Computation of Effective Interest Rates

The preceding section has described the behavior of a firm subject to
Constraints (C1), (C2), and either (C3) or (C3') as useful loan size increases.
We have defined the quantities X' and X" as critical values of useful loan size
at which different constraints become binding and the behavior of the firm
changes. The values of useful loan size given by X' and X" are the values at
which the cost of bank loans changes.[5] In particular:

1. For X $\leq$ X', no additional borrowing to provide compensating balances
is necessary since the balances are already required to support tangible bank
activity. The cost of the loan is the interest rate.

2. For X' < X $\leq$ X", the firm must provide compensating balances; however,

---

[4]If TCH/ρ $\leq$ MTB, then X' = X". This situation occurs if required transaction balances are so large that they earn more credits than are required to
compensate the bank for tangible services, i.e., if Assumption A7 does not
hold.

[5]We derive expressions for X' and X" in terms of given parameters in the
second part of Section 4.

these balances earn credits and therefore reduce the cost of providing compensating balances by the rate at which credits are earned.

     3. For X" < X, the firm has excess credits; therefore the compensating balances have no use other than to support the loan. Thus the entire cost of the compensating balances must be added to the cost of the loan.

     Let c be the cost of providing compensating balances per dollar of loan.
Then:

     1. $c = 0$ if $X \leq X'$ because the balances must be provided anyway;

     2. $c = r_1(i - \rho)$ if $X' < X \leq X"$ since the cost is reduced by the credits that offset cash payments;

     3. $c = i \cdot r_1$ if $X" < X$ since $i \cdot r_1$ is the cost of compensating balances per dollar of useful loans if there is no other use for the balances.

     To obtain the marginal effective loan cost, we add c to the nominal interest rate i. Writing I as a function of X, we have:

$$(6) \qquad I(X) = \begin{cases} i & 0 \leq X \leq X' \\ i \cdot (1 + r_1) - r_1 \rho & X' < X \leq X" \\ i \cdot (1 + r_1) & X" < X. \end{cases}$$

Thus, the marginal effective loan cost as a function of useful loan size at a given bank with fixed levels of tangible bank activity is a step function with three steps.

The Location of the Discontinuities in the Cost of Loans Curve

     We now specify X' and X" as a function of given parameters. When $X = X'$, we know that (C1) has just become binding and $NCB' = CBRL(X') = r_o X'$. From equation (4), we have:

$$(7) \qquad X' = \frac{NCB'}{r_o} = \frac{\max \{MTB, (1 - \alpha)TCH/\rho\}}{r_o}$$

     From our description of the firm's behavior and the definition of r_o and r_1, we know that $NCB(X)$ is given by:

$$(8) \qquad NCB(X) = \begin{cases} NCB' & 0 \leq X \leq X' \\ NCB' + r_1(X - X') & X' < X \end{cases} \quad .$$

To find X" in terms of given parameters, we let $X = X"$ in equation (8), solve for X", and simplify, giving:

(9) $X'' = \dfrac{NCB''}{r_1} - \dfrac{NCB'}{r_1} + X' = \dfrac{NCB''}{r_1} - NCB'(\dfrac{1}{r_1} - \dfrac{1}{r_o}) = \dfrac{NCB''}{r_1} + NCB'.$

Substituting for NCB' and NCB" from equations (4) and (5) **gives**:

(10) $X'' = \dfrac{TCH}{\rho r_1} + \max \{MTB, \dfrac{(1 - \alpha)TCH}{\rho}\}$.

The Height of the Jumps

        Of course the effective cost of loans depends on the nominal interest rate i and decreases as i increases. Let the size of the jump at X' and X" be denoted by h' and h" respectively. Then:

(11) $h' = r_1(i - \rho)$, and

(12) $h'' = r_1\rho$.

The sum of the two jumps is given by:

(13) $h' + h'' = ir_1.$

The jump at X' decreases linearly with ρ and the jump at X" increases linearly with ρ; however, the total jump is independent of ρ. Both the total jump and each individual jump increase linearly with r_1. Only the first jump and total increase with i; the jump at X" is independent of i.

        The relative size of the jumps at X' and X" depends on the size of i relative to ρ. If i > $\rho/2$, the jump at X' is greater; if i = $\rho/2$, then h' = h"; if i < $\rho/2$, then the jump at X' is smaller. To assess the relative size of the jumps, we can use typical values of r_o, i, and ρ. If r_o is 20 percent, i is 6 percent and ρ is 3 percent, then the total jump is 1.5 percent and each individual jump is 0.75 percent. These costs are considerably greater than the usual variation in interest rates quoted by different banks to the same firm at a given time.

V. Implications

Cost of Bank Borrowing

        We have established that the marginal cost of bank debt is a step function at a given bank. The height of the steps depends on i, r_1, and ρ; their location depends on both the firm's tangible bank activity and the cost and constraint

parameters at any given bank. Such a cost of loans curve can be constructed for
each bank with which a multibank firm deals.

Let subscripts on variables denote banks, e.g., i_k is the nominal interest
rate at bank #k. To derive the cost of total bank borrowing, we must be able to
specify how a firm that acts optimally allocates its borrowing among its banks
as the total size of its bank borrowing is increased. Assuming that the variation in effective interest among banks is less than the size of the jumps in the
cost of loans at a given bank, a firm allocates its borrowing among banks by:
(1) first taking loans at its banks from the first step of the curve on the basis
of $\min_k \{i_k\}$ in an amount up to X_k' until all candidate banks have the first step
of the curve exhausted; (2) then taking loans from the second step of the
curve on the basis of $\min_k \{i_k + r_{1k}(i_k - \rho_k)\}$ in amounts up to $X_k'' - X_k'$ until all
candidate banks have exhausted borrowing on the second step; (3) borrowing all
additional funds at the bank with the minimum value of $i_k(1 + r_{1k})$.

It is the author's observation that corporate treasurers in large companies
generally carry out the above procedure for a subset of their banks. This cost
structure is one explanation for the conventional rule of thumb among corporate
treasurers that tangible bank activity and borrowing should be concentrated at
the same bank.

If i_k, r_{1k}, or ρ_k vary from bank to bank, then the firm following the
allocation procedure described above has a marginal effective cost of bank
loans curve that consists of three major steps with many small steps within the
first two steps. In the unlikely event that the variation in effective rates
exceeds the height of the jumps (i.e., that $i_k + r_{1k}(i_k - \rho_k) < i_j$ for some banks
k and j), then there are not three clearly distinct major steps with substeps
on the first two steps but rather just a large number of steps between $\min_k \{i_k\}$
and $\min_k \{i_k(1 + r_{1k})\}$. In any case it is clear that: (1) the marginal effective
loan cost curve is a step function with (generally) many steps for a firm with
many banks; (2) the marginal effective loan cost is monotone increasing.

For a firm with bank borrowing as a source of capital, both the marginal
cost of debt curve and the marginal cost of capital curve have discontinuities
due to the steps in the cost of bank loans. The existence of discontinuities
contrasts with the "smooth" cost of debt and cost of capital curves that have
generally been assumed in the literature.

This monotone increasing cost of bank debt curve has been developed with
the assumption that nominal interest rates and other parameters are fixed. The
more conventional treatment assumes that the interest rate increases as loan
size increases because of increasing default risk. If this assumption is
relaxed and the nominal rate is assumed to be a strictly monotone increasing
function of useful loan size, then the preceding analysis carries through in the
sense that one can substitute i(X) for i in equation (10) for the marginal

effective loan cost. However, although the curve has jumps at X' and X", it is no longer a step function but rises continuously between the jumps.

Uses by Firm and Bank Decision Makers

If the firm can establish the effective cost of bank loans in the presence of compensating balance requirements for each of the firm's banks (or potential banks), then it can use the information for: (1) a comparison of the actual cost of borrowing at alternative banks when there are different schedules of interest rates and compensating balance requirements; (2) a comparison of the cost of bank borrowing with the cost of alternative sources of financing; (3) a basis for a heuristic for the allocation of debt.

Banks are currently concerned about account profitability analysis and the need to change both the way they charge for their services and quote prices.[6] Information on the cost function of their clients and on how a firm reacts to prices is fundamental for: (1) the analysis of pricing decisions and forecasts of the effect of price changes on various classes of clients, and (2) models for determining bank strategies and policies for specifying constraints and constraint parameters.

Successful use by either a firm or a bank may require more detail in the model (e.g., inclusion of lines of credit, compensation for intangible services, differentiation between balances as demand deposits and low (or zero) interest certificates of deposit, etc.). However, the foregoing has established the basic structure of the problem; generalization to more complex situations should not be difficult.

REFERENCES

[1] Baxter, N.D., and H.T. Shapiro. "Compensating Balance Requirements: The Results of a Survey." *Journal of Finance,* vol. 19 (September 1964), pp. 483-496.

[2] Calman, Robert E. *Linear Programming and Cash Management - Cash Alpha.* Cambridge, Mass.: M.I.T. Press, 1968.

[3] Emmer, R.E. "Compensating Balances and the Cost of Loanable Funds." *Journal of Business,* vol. 30 (October 1957), pp. 268-275.

[4] Furniss, James P., and Paul S. Nadler. "Should Banks Reprice Corporate Services." *Harvard Business Review,* June-July 1966, pp. 95-105.

[5] Johnson, Robert W. *Financial Management,* 3rd ed. Boston, Mass.: Allyn and Bacon, Inc., 1966, chapter 13.

[6] Pogue, Gerald A.; Russell B. Faucett; and Ralph N. Bussard. "Cash Management: A Systems Approach." *Industrial Management Review,* Winter 1970.

[7] Robichek, A.A., and Stewart C. Myers. *Optimal Financing Decisions.* Englewood Cliffs, N.J.: Prentice Hall, Inc., 1965.

---

[6]See Furniss and Nadler [4] for a discussion of the repricing issue along with an historical explanation of the present pricing dilemma faced by banks.

Part VII

OPERATIONS AND CORPORATE SERVICES

THE management of bank operations is undergoing a transformation; from a position of relative neglect, it is being recognized as a major element in the overall management of commercial banks. Until recently, bank operations were clearly delegated a backseat position in terms of managements' attention. Most banking textbooks, while devoting several chapters to various aspects of bank lending, often neglect operations completely. As a result, banks lagged behind industry in applying innovative operations management techniques, leading to a relatively low quality of services.

Today few banks can afford to neglect operations management, and many have become aggressive in the management of their operations divisions. Several factors seem to be responsible for this. First is the increased competitiveness of banks in general. This higher level of competition necessitates tighter pricing of services, resulting in more careful cost controls. Competition has also generated additional services, particularly in the cash management area. A second reason for the increasing interest in efficient operations management is the rise in available electronics which can provide faster and often more cost effective services. Electronics have also led to the development of several innovative cash management services which are currently being marketed to corporations, in some cases by the operations divisions of major banks. The third contributing factor to the rising importance of bank operations is inflation. The high personnel and computer costs of today's operations represent a huge capital investment, which must return a profit if the bank is to be successful. Together these factors have generated a renewed examination of traditional methods of managing the operations function at commercial banks. Manage-

361

ment science, like banks, had long neglected bank operations as a source of increased profitability and an area for improving management capabilities. There are significant indications that this neglect is ending, and it is likely that management science research in bank operations will increase in response to bank management's renewed interest.

Parts VII and IX examine certain areas that have received attention in bank management science literature. Methodologies have been suggested for solving several types of operations problems. The discussions presented in Part VII deal with various aspects of bank operations management, while Part IX concentrates entirely on electronic funds transfer systems.

In Chapter 29, "Helping to Plan a Bank's Manpower Resources," bank personnel management is examined by R.C. Jones, S.R. Morrison, and R.P. Whiteman. The application of an operations research technique to the manpower planning problem at a large British commercial bank is discussed in general terms. While the model is not described in detail in the article, the problems inherent in applying a management science model to a task of this size are addressed. The behavioral and training aspects of implementing such a model are often more critical to success than technical considerations. Jones, Morrison, and Whiteman were involved in the implementation of this model and characterize it as "extremely valuable." The success of manpower models such as this points to the potential for further applications of management science techniques in bank personnel management.

One specific application in the bank personnel area is suggested by Mark G. Simkin and Ralph H. Sprague, Jr. in Chapter 30, "Staffing for Bank Telephone Inquiry Systems: A Decision Analysis." Using "decision analysis," Simkin and Sprague attempt to reduce costs and maintain services in staffing a telephone inquiry unit which answers calls from charge card holders. The methodology discussed could easily be adapted to other similar situations. The staffing decision revolves around forecasting activity levels (calls), determining patterns based on days of week or time of day, designing a telephone configuration, and evaluating the sensitivity of the plan to minor changes in decision variables. Data for the model are fairly simple to compile. The model could be applied periodically to revalidate the staffing configuration. Although it is relatively simple, this model could provide significant cost savings in several problem situations.

A more sophisticated approach to manpower planning is outlined by Shyam L. Moondra in Chapter 31, "An L.P. Model for Work Force Scheduling for Banks." Moondra discusses the basis for formulating a linear programming model. While LP models are appropriate in many circumstances, difficulties can arise in their use, as discussed in Part IV. Simpler models that may be nearly as effective for problem solving should generally be explored before choosing to implement a model based on techniques as sophisticated as linear programming. This is especially true when line managers who are likely to be unfamiliar with linear programming are involved.

In Chapters 32 and 33, the lock box location problem is discussed by Steven F. Maier and James H. Vander Weide. The lock box came into use as early as the 1940s when it was recognized that significant float time was being lost as payments of bills to corporations passed through the mail system. Earlier collection of these amounts makes more funds available for short-term investment by the corporation, or allows the firm to reduce its liquidity holdings which return little or no interest. The speeding of collections was handled by establishing post office boxes at regional points based on mail time. The corporation's regional banks assumed responsibility for emptying these collection lock boxes several times daily. Placing lock boxes in an optimal configuration increased the availability of funds significantly. This location problem is the subject of Chapter 32, "The Lock-Box Location Problem: A Practical Reformulation," by Maier and Vander Weide. Today, numerous corporations utilize the lock box technique to reduce mail float time and increase the availability of funds. As a result, banks involved in providing such services are interested in innovations in determining lock box locations.

In addition to lock boxes, there are two other major ways in which a business firm can improve its cash management system. First, recognizing that the other side of the coin of speeding collections is slowing disbursements, a firm can increase its disbursement float through judicious selection of the banks and branch offices from which it writes checks. Second, by maintaining optimal levels of bank deposit balances, a firm can reduce the costs of banking services. In Chapter 33, "A Unified Location Model for Cash Disbursements and Lock-Box Collections," Maier and Vander Weide briefly review the currently available models for lock box location, disbursement analysis, and deposit balance determination. They then present their own unified model for an optimally integrated cash management system. The models developed by Maier and Vander Weide in both Chapters 32 and 33 have been successfully implemented in several commercial banks, where they are being used to provide cash management services to corporate customers.

Part VII provides an examination of attempts to apply management science techniques to bank operations management problems. Much more research is needed into numerous potential applications of management science to diverse problems encountered in the operations area. Increased interest in operations cost efficiency may generate new applications of scientific approaches to bank operations management problems.

Chapter 29

HELPING TO PLAN A BANK'S MANPOWER RESOURCES*

By R. C. Jones, S. R. Morrison, and R. P. Whiteman

*This article is reprinted, with permission, from *Operational Research Quarterly*, Vol. 24, No. 3 (September, 1973), pp. 365-374.

A general description is given of how OR methods have been applied to manpower planning in a large British bank, with particular reference to management succession. The importance of close co-operation with senior management to ensure the success of the work is emphasised. Detailed mathematical formulations of the problems and their solutions are not discussed.

OUTLINE OF THE PROBLEM

NATIONAL WESTMINSTER BANK employs a total of approximately 50,000 people. The qualifications of this large group are very varied, ranging from the 16-year-old girl starting her first job at one of the Bank's 3500 branches to senior managers with a lifetime of experience behind them. As the Bank traditionally pursues a policy of training its own staff, its personnel policy has two important objectives. These are:

(i) To ensure that staff of the right quality are present in sufficient numbers to do all today's jobs.

(ii) To ensure that there will be sufficient staff of the right quality at all levels of seniority in the future. This implies that there must, at present, be the right numbers of able people at each level being trained for promotion to higher levels of responsibility.

Obvious problems would arise if there were a shortage of total staff numbers. A surplus would also be an embarrassment and lead to excessive costs. A shortage of staff appropriately trained and ready for promotion to a particular level might lead to staff being given responsibilities greater than their ability. A surplus of able, fully trained staff might lead to frustration with consequent lowering of morale and performance.

One effect of the Bank's tradition of training its own managerial staff, and of offering lifetime careers, is that it cannot deal with a shortage or surplus of managers by short-term hiring or firing. The Bank proceeds on a much longer time scale. The present manpower situation results from changes in the banking environment which have occurred over many years, and the personnel policies (relating, for instance, to recruitment and retirement) which have been pursued to take account of these changes. Similarly, decisions taken now to cope with present trends will affect the manpower situation many years into the future.

Because of this long time scale, combined with the large numbers of staff involved and the great value the Bank puts on its personnel, decisions on manpower policies merit, and are given, a great amount of thought and time by senior management.

This brief outline of some important aspects of National Westminster Bank's manpower situation should be sufficient to show that it would be inadequate to leave its development to chance. It is essential to forecast what the demands for staff will be in the future, and to plan a course of action so that those demands can be met. It is in this area that the Bank has found a fruitful application for operational research.

FIVE KEY FACTORS

The aim of the OR effort is to assist in forecasting the future development of the manpower situation, and in identifying policies which could be implemented to improve this development.

Initial consideration showed that there would be five major factors whose combined effects would determine the development of the manpower situation. These were:

Demand

Each year the Bank requires a particular total number of employees. This total number can be subdivided according to levels of seniority.

Retirement

Each year a number of staff reach retiring age and leave the Bank. The number of people reaching retirement age each year is determined by past patterns of recruitment and wastage and the Bank's policy on retirement age.

Wastage

Each year a number of staff leave the Bank for reasons other than retirement (i.e. dismissal, resignation, death, etc.). Wastage rates are different for different groups of people (e.g. wastage rates for women are higher than for men).

Promotion

Each year it is necessary to promote staff to fill the vacancies created at higher levels by retirement, wastage and expansion.

Recruitment

Each year it is necessary to recruit staff to replenish the numbers who have retired or wasted. Recruitment is normally only to the most junior levels. Recruits will inevitably have a mixture of abilities and ages and it is important to ensure that this mixture is appropriate for the Bank's staffing and promotion requirements.

Some of these factors are clearly more amenable to control by the Bank than others. The level of demand for staff is determined largely by the Bank's growth rate, which in turn depends on the national level of economic activity, and social trends concerning the use of banking facilities, as well as the impact of factors such as automation and rationalization. Retirement ages can be controlled by the Bank; however, the number of people reaching retirement age is less directly under the Bank's control, since it depends simply on the number of people who have stayed in the Bank sufficiently long to reach retirement age. Some measure of control can be exercised over wastage rates by changing working conditions, salaries, promotion prospects and so on, but other social and economic factors outside the Bank's control will also be influential. The Bank has considerable control over promotion and recruitment, although external factors may play a part in determining the type of people who apply to join the Bank.

PROJECTING THE MANPOWER SITUATION INTO THE FUTURE

A coherent personnel policy must take account of the interplay between these five factors. The factors which are under the Bank's control must be manipulated in such a way that the manpower situation develops as favourably as possible. Calculation of the most appropriate policies is a complicated process, partly because of the large range of variation which could occur in any of the five factors listed above, and partly because of the large numbers of staff involved. It was because of the size and complexity of the problem that it was decided to apply OR methods.

The basic approach

The basic approach which has been adopted centres around a computer program which relates all the different factors affecting the manpower situation in numerical terms. The easiest way to understand this program is to study how it is used.

First, assumptions are made about the future values of the five major factors affecting the manpower situation in the light of anticipated personnel policies. Thus, for instance, the number of jobs at each level of seniority in each year up to the planning horizon is specified; also the expected wastage rates for each type of staff are estimated. These values are fed into the program. The program then calculates how the manpower situation will develop from year to year into the future based on these assumptions starting from the present position. The results of the calculations are printed out in tabular form.

How does this program help management to carry out manpower planning? It helps chiefly by allowing management to experiment with different assumptions about the future, either proposed policies or possible developments that will affect the Bank, and to study how these assumptions affect the future manpower situation. By a process of trial and error the planner can develop a fuller understanding of how various factors will impinge on the staffing of the Bank. For instance, he can study what will happen as a result of a number of possible recruitment policies, and so be in a position to select the most desirable. He can go further and study what the effect will be on his chosen policy of an unexpected increase in wastage rates.

This central idea of calculating the likely future development, given a set of assumptions about basic factors, is referred to as "simulation", i.e. the future is simulated. A computer program which carries out calculations in this way is referred to as a "computer model", because it is, so to speak, a model of the real life situation on which experiments can be carried out. Thus we have a computer model which enables us to simulate the future.

It is important to emphasize that what comes out of the computer model depends critically on what assumptions are put in. Thus it is essential that management understand what assumptions are contained in the model, and this necessitates close co-operation between management and the project team. The model developed in the Bank is the result of very close collaboration between the OR Group and the Personnel Division. This, plus the high priority given to manpower planning, has greatly assisted the development of the model, the correct identification of problem areas and the communication of results.

Developing the model

Setting up the computer model involved about 12 man-months of effort. In addition to writing the main computer program for the model it was also necessary to determine what the existing manpower situation was, this of course being the starting point from which all projections would be made. To obtain the existing manpower situation involved collecting and checking a large number of items of information about every employee. Most of these items were already stored on computer files, and were therefore readily accessible, but the checking procedures brought to light a number of discrepancies. Being able to correct these discrepancies was, in itself, a valuable "spin-off" from the main work.

Once all of this information had been collected it was then classified into groups. Since the purpose of this classification was to construct a data base which represented the manpower situation in the Bank at the start of the exercise, it was not concerned with personal details, such as name and address. The object was to establish how many people there were in each category, categories being defined by combinations of sex, age, time in present job, ability, etc. Having determined how many people fell into each category, this formed the base from which projections could be made.

Outline of operation

The computer model is very simple in concept, although in practice there were a number of difficulties that had to be overcome. The model operates on an annual cycle, taking the starting point in each cycle as the manpower situation at the end of the last year. The manpower situation at the end of the current year is obtained by removing from last year's position—

(i) All people due to retire in the current year.

(ii) An allowance for estimated wastage.

This determines the number of promotions needed to fill vacancies at each level of seniority after allowing for any expansion or contraction of the Bank. These promotions are then carried out according to certain specified criteria. This leaves certain vacancies in the lower staff levels, so these are filled according to the specified recruitment policy. By repeating this cycle of activities for each year the computer model develops the manpower situation year by year into the future, under the specified assumptions.

This description of the calculation process is necessarily brief, but it should be adequate to demonstrate the basic simplicity of the approach. At every stage realism, rather than mathematical elegance, has been emphasized, which has meant that it has been necessary to use only the most rudimentary statistical concepts.

MAKING USE OF THE SIMULATION APPROACH

The problems studied

The two major problems that have been examined using the simulation model are the problem of providing managerial succession and the problem of specifying a recruitment policy. These two problems are related in that it is from the people brought into the Bank by the recruitment policy that managerial succession must be provided. However, in practice, it is possible to separate the two questions. The recruitment problem deals in the main with the younger, high wastage rate personnel in the Bank. The managerial succession problem, the problem of ensuring a steady flow of managers of the right calibre, deals with the older age ranges, and with retirement policies. In this paper, for the purpose of illustration, we shall focus on the model that was built to study the management succession problem.

Building the model

As mentioned before, setting up the data base to represent the starting position from which projections could be made was a large-scale exercise. However, although it was this exercise which posed by far the greatest practical problem, there were also conceptual difficulties to be overcome.

One example of such a difficulty was how to deal with geographical regions. Different parts of the country have different wastage rates, different calibres of staff are available for recruitment and there may be difficulties in transferring staff from one region to another. The conceptual problem centred around the extent to which it was necessary to include such detail in the model.

Another difficulty was that of deciding who should be included in the model. The majority of the Bank's staff come within the Domestic Banking Division, the division that provides the branch banking network in the U.K., and with the exception of certain people who are not in the main promotion stream, such as typists and part-timers, all its members clearly had to be in the model. However, once consideration extends to specialist departments and subsidiary companies it requires much more investigation and judgement to decide who can be treated as being a pure specialist, and hence outside the managerial line of succession, and who cannot. With all the various conceptual problems encountered, agreement on the approach adopted was obtained through discussion with senior management of the Bank, particularly that of Personnel Division.

Specifying assumptions and policies to be examined

One of the most valuable pay-offs from the manpower planning project has been the clarification of thought and understanding that has come about as a result of discussing the various problems that have arisen in specifying the models, and using them. This applies particularly to the five major factors mentioned earlier (retirement, promotion, recruitment, demand for jobs and wastage) about which assumptions must be made in order to make projections into the future.

With retirements, for instance, the need to specify future retirement policy initiated an exercise to determine what the future retirement pattern would be, given that a "no change" policy was adopted. This was not a simple exercise because of the large number of different retirement rules that exist in the Bank, due to it being a result of merging a number of previously separate organizations that had different policies towards retirement age. Men and women have different retirement rules, which also complicates the matter. However, the result of the exercise was to show that the retirement pattern for the next few years would be far from stable (see Figure 1).

This unstable pattern of retirements is, to a large degree, attributable to the unsteady level of recruitment, and the age distribution of recruits, during the years of depression in the 1930's, and during the Second World War.

Planning a steady flow of staff through the management stream would be considerably easier if such a fluctuating retirement pattern were not present.

Determining the promotion rules was also enlightening. The Bank does not have a series of rules which define precisely when each individual shall be promoted, as, needless to say, each individual and each job have special characteristics which need to be considered. However, it has been possible to set down broad guide lines, governing how quickly people of different potential move through the hierarchy, and thus to make the model realistic enough to give meaningful results.

Specifying the likely number of jobs in the Bank at each level of responsibility in the future was a demanding exercise as it required a long-term view to be taken of the future of the organization. It was necessary not only to discuss the branch rationalization programme, but also to talk to the Corporate Planning team about other possible areas of growth or change within the National Westminster Group, and relevant social factors.

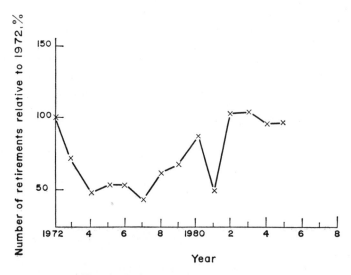

FIG. 1. *Forecast number of retirements.*

The discussions on future recruitment policy highlighted a number of interesting problems. What type of educational qualifications should the Bank be looking for? How many graduates does the Bank need? What will be the effect of raising the school leaving age? At what age is it reasonable to start defining a person's potential? What will be the role of women in the Bank in the future? The discussions of recruitment also emphasized the importance of wastage rates so that a subsidiary study was carried out to determine what were realistic wastage rates to include in the model. In the management succession model the recruitment aspect was included in a comparatively crude way. The model that was subsequently built to look specifically at recruitment was far more sophisticated.

Measuring the health of the manpower situation

Having built the manpower model, and having clarified the five major factors to the point where it was possible to start experimenting with different assumptions, there still remained the problem of how to measure the health of the manpower situation at any point in time. There is no single figure that can be extracted which indicates whether the state of things is good, indifferent or bad. It is necessary to calculate a number of different statistics and to interpret these intelligently. Some important indicators in any year are:

(i) Number of promotions.

(ii) Number of retirements.

(iii) Ages of promotions to particular levels of responsibility.

(iv) Level of seniority reached before retirement.

(v) Number of years spent in a particular job.

Another approach which has also proved valuable is to construct an ideal manpower situation for the Bank where there are just the right numbers of people of the right calibre moving smoothly through the various levels of seniority. The actual manpower structure in the Bank can then be compared with this ideal and the differences identified. The fact that there are differences is not necessarily a bad thing. The object of the comparison is to increase the understanding of the situation as it is.

Using sensitivity analysis

Numerous different simulations have been carried out, each experiment based on different assumptions and policies concerning the five major factors. After each series of simulations the results are discussed with management so that the directions of further experimentation can be defined. This process of jointly developing ideas for further work is of fundamental importance. In this sort of exercise there is little point in asking a project team to go away and study a problem and then to report back with the answer in 6 months.

Two different ways of obtaining useful sets of answers from the model have been used. The first way is to carry out three runs, one "optimistic", one "most likely" and one "pessimistic". As the names suggest, these runs are based on assumptions about the five major factors that are respectively as favourable as can be envisaged, the most likely, and as unfavourable as reasonably can be expected. This sort of approach is valuable in indicating the range of possibilities.

The second way of obtaining useful sets of answers is to select one of the assumptions and carry out runs for a series of different values for this assumption. For example, with demand for jobs, the number of jobs could be changed 10 per cent either way from the most likely value and the results obtained for these two cases. Studying the effect on the results of varying the selected assumption reveals how sensitive the situation is to the assumption. This process can be repeated for each assumption, and provided the choice of values to be tried for each assumption covers the likely possible range of values for that assumption, a much clearer picture of the relative significance of the various factors can be obtained.

These two approaches can be broadly classified as "sensitivity analysis". Both increase the understanding of the problem and point the way to the need for further experimentation or the need for further research into one of the factors. For example, it was the use of sensitivity analysis which clarified the necessity for more research to be carried out into wastage rates.

Is the approach worth while?

In order to assess whether or not the approach is worth while it is necessary to look at the costs and the benefits.

Costs. The major cost of the approach has been the cost of building the model. There are also computer running costs. The model requires large amounts of computer time and storage. However, since spare computer capacity is used, the cost of this is low.

In addition the approach requires that management are prepared to devote time to aid the building of the model, but more especially to discussing the assumptions and results. Without the involvement of the senior men who actually have to take the decisions the project would not have succeeded.

Benefits. The major benefit of the model is that it makes it possible to experiment with different assumptions and policies. This clarifies the problems and brings deeper understanding of the likely implications of various actions.

For example, it has been possible to forecast the numbers of promotions which will occur in future years (see Figure 2).

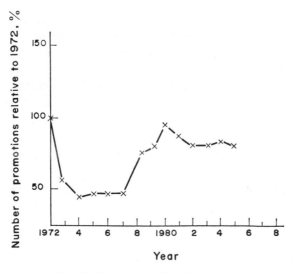

Fig. 2. *Forecast number of promotions.*

As mentioned earlier, the number of promotions occurring in a particular year is only one of a number of possible measures of the health of the manpower situation. However, it is a broad indicator of whether staff are being promoted sufficiently rapidly to satisfy their career aspirations, or whether they are being promoted too rapidly to receive adequate training. Figure 2 shows quite clearly that the level of promotions in the next few years will not be steady, and that it will, in the absence of appropriate corrective action, vary in response to the variation in the number of retirements shown in Figure 1.

Although the arithmetic calculations are simple in concept, they are very numerous. The ability of the computer to execute these many calculations with great rapidity leaves the mind free to take a broad, overall view of the situation, or to examine points of detail, as required.

The necessity for precisely specifying both the structure of the model and the values of the five major factors also contributes to clarification and understanding.

The facility for carrying out sensitivity analysis is an extension of the basic facility for experimentation. The idea of sensitivity analysis is, however, extremely powerful and adds significantly to bringing problems into sharper focus.

It must be emphasized that the problems which have been investigated are not neatly and easily defined, nor are proposed solutions absolutely clear cut. At both the problem-definition stage and the solution stage much discussion is required in order to agree on the significance and extent of problems, and the validity of solutions. However, the computer model provides a focus for such discussion, and encourages managers to think directly, and in numerate terms, about the consequences of their policies. This is a long-term process, and although manpower planning in the Bank has been in operation for about 3 years, proposed solutions are not yet fully implemented.

On balance it is our belief that this exercise has been, and continues to be, extremely valuable.

This view is given weight by the fact that the OR approach to manpower planning continues to enjoy the full support of those ultimately responsible for taking far-reaching decisions affecting the careers of 50,000 people in National Westminster Bank.

BIBLIOGRAPHY

1. Statistics and Manpower Planning in the Firm (1971) Special edition of *J. Inst. Statist.* **XX**, No. 1, March.
2. D. J. BARTHOLOMEW and B. R. MORRIS (1971) *Aspects of Manpower Planning.* EUP, London.
3. H. HOYLE and R. J. STUBBS (1970) Management stocktaking: an approach to manpower planning in banking. *Long Range Planning* **2**, 18.
4. J. J. LYNCH (1968) *Making Manpower Effective.* Pan, London.

Chapter 30

STAFFING FOR BANK TELEPHONE INQUIRY SYSTEMS: A DECISION ANALYSIS*

By Mark G. Simkin and Ralph H. Sprague, Jr.

*This article is reprinted, with permission, from *Journal of Bank Research*, Vol. 7, No. 1 (Spring, 1976), pp. 49-55.

The increasingly competitive banking environment has generated many efforts to increase productivity or reduce costs, while simultaneously increasing levels of customer service. These efforts have been characterized by increased use of information processing techniques and, to a lesser extent, by the use of decision support models and analyses.

One critical area in which both cost reduction and customer service are at stake is the staffing of telephone inquiry facilities for a charge card service. The problem of minimizing costs while maintaining appropriate levels of service for charge cardholders' inquiries and merchants' authorization calls is a particularly fruitful area for the application of modern information technology and decision analysis.

This paper describes a decision analysis for managing such a charge card telephone inquiry facility. The study was done on a manual system prior to the installation of on-line capability for servicing the inquiries. The methodology, approach and decision models are equally appropriate for a fully computerized system with changes only in the values of some parameters. Hence, this approach can be used to reduce costs or improve productivity while maintaining customer service in a wide variety of similar situations.

The Problem

A large bank maintains a staff of operators to handle three types of telephone inquiries related to the bank's very active charge card service. Charge authorization (type A) transactions are primarily calls from merchants checking on the credit status of customers making purchases. Billing inquiries (type B) are made by customers interested in the status or processing of their accounts. Credit references (type C) are credit checks initiated by other institutions. Each type of call represents a different type of customer requiring slightly different services. Because of these differences, the three types of inquiries are serviced by different telephone numbers with separate operators specifically trained to handle each type of call. Each telephone number connects to a rotary serving several lines (see Model I in Figure 1).

Because of the management difficulties in maintaining three separate staffs of specially trained operators, and because the three types of calls seemed to have different peak and slack periods, another alternative structure for the system is shown as Model II in Figure 1. This configuration uses a single telephone number for all three types of customers. The servicing staff is trained to process any type of customer, and all answering

Figure 1. Three Alternative Telephone Configurations

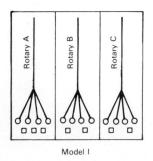

Model I

Three Trunks-Partitioned
Staff

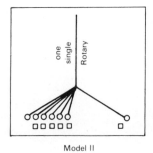

Model II

One Trunk-Pooled Staff

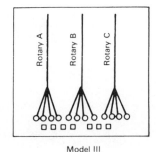

Model III

Three Trunks-Pooled Staff

personnel are combined in a common answering pool. There are two potential disadvantages to this second configuration: The same telephone number must be distributed to all three types of customers, and the operators must spend some time ascertaining the type of customer for each call.

As a compromise between the two systems, a third alternative configuration is illustrated as Model III in Figure 1. Under this system, the three different telephone numbers (rotaries) are retained, but as in the second model, the staff is trained to handle any type of call and thus is placed in a common answering pool.

The Decision

In general terms, the decision involves the development of a staffing plan that provides the optimum number of operators and lines, utilizing the best telephone configuration at the least cost, while maintaining or improving customer service. Such a multi-faceted decision requires answers to several questions.

1) What is the current and forecast activity level, in number of calls per hour, by type of call?

2) Does the activity pattern vary significantly during the day and on various days of the week?

3) What is the "best" telephone configuration?

4) What is the "optimal" number of operators for the "best" telephone configuration and given activity level?

5) How sensitive are cost and performance measures to changes in staffing levels, activity levels and system configuration?

The determination of performance measures and decision criteria for answering questions 3 and 4 is the crux of the matter. The increasingly competitive banking environment mentioned earlier makes performance measures exceedingly important. In the present study, the bank had received a growing number of complaints from merchants on the length of time required to obtain authorization. There were even reports of merchants encouraging customers to use a competing charge card because the authorization calls were much shorter. Possible performance measures are: 1) Average time required to service a call (service time); 2) average number of calls that must wait for an operator; 3) average hold time for calls that must wait; and 4) average number of calls lost (busy signal). Note that only measures 2, 3 and 4 are susceptible to changes in the staffing levels or the telephone configuration. Measure 1 depends on the efficiency of the

operators and the inherent physical processes of servicing inquiries. The next sections summarize the data gathering, and the development, validation and utilization of a decision model for this problem.

The Data

Data on incoming calls were gathered with the use of a continuous pen recorder installed by the telephone company on the switchboard in the bank. The pen recorder marked the beginning and end of each call on each telephone line. The total data gathered for the study included approximately one week's calls (1500) with call length measured to within two seconds accuracy, and approximately one month's calls (6000) accurate to within 15 seconds. These data were then used to derive patterns of activity during the day, patterns of activity across the days of the week and frequency distributions for the length of call and arrival rate.

The frequency distribution for the arrival rate was computed using the time between the arrivals of two successive incoming calls. Similar distributions were developed for service times (length of call) by day, and by two-hour time block within day.

An analysis of the activity patterns revealed wide variations in arrival rates throughout the day. Day of the week also made some difference, but not substantially. By dividing the day into two-hour time blocks, however, it was possible to classify the activity rates into "low," "medium" and "high" levels. The subsequent analysis uses these three sets of figures to develop optimal staffing levels for light, moderate and heavy periods of activity during a typical day.

The Model

Queueing problems are frequently attacked with simulation methods because the sequential event structure of simulation corresponds well with the queueing process. However, simulation models must be built, validated and run repeatedly to develop reliable results. Before going to this trouble and expense, therefore, it is wise to investigate available theoretical models. With some variations, the three telephone configurations all represent queueing systems with limited waiting lines for which some theory already exists. For example, Model I can be viewed as three separate subsystems, each with its own arrival rate and service length parameter. When both the inter-arrival rate and service length are exponentially distributed, it is possible to calculate the expected queue length (Lq) from the expression (see [Hillier and Lieberman, 1974]):

$$Lq = \frac{P_o\rho^{s+1}}{s!(1-\rho)^2}\left[1-\rho^{M-S}-(M-S)\rho^{M-S}(1-\rho)\right]$$

where: $\rho = \dfrac{\lambda}{\mu} = \dfrac{\text{arrival rate (customers per hour)}}{\text{service rate (customers per hour)}}$

M = maximum number of customers in the system (i.e., number of telephone lines)

s = number of service agents

P_o = the probability that the system is empty (i.e., no active calls)

Similar expressions for expected number in the system, expected waiting time and expected rejection rate can be derived. However, these computations apply only when the underlying prerequisite probability distributions are in evidence.

To test for the critical assumption of exponential distribution for service and interarrival times, a chi-square goodness-of-fit test was performed on the empirical frequency distributions. The first two columns of Figure 2 represent the test for interarrival time. Each of the three types of calls was found to have an exponential distribution with mean values as shown. The latter columns of Figure 2 represent a similar test upon the service time data. The exponential service distribution proved inapplicable for two out of the three types of calls.

Further analysis revealed that the service time distribution could be considered Erlangian, for which a different, more complicated theoretical model is available [see Page, 1972]. However, the special structure of Models II and III introduced further complications that eliminated the feasibil-

ity of a purely analytic approach. Model II requires the intermixing of different types of customers, each with a different service rate parameter, on a common incoming line. A theoretical model for such a structure would require the solution of a large number of simultaneous equations to accommodate all combinations of customer types in the system. Model III maintains partitioned lines for each customer type, but the number of operators is allowed to vary during the operation of the system—a condition for which there are also no applicable models. In light of these considerations, a computer simulation approach to the solution of the problem was developed. The analytic models mentioned above were useful, however, for validating components of the simulation model.

Simulation Analysis

The simulation model was developed using GPSS,[1] a simulation language particularly suited for building queueing models. The GPSS program was built to compare the performance of the three model structures by simulating their operation with the same arrival and service rates over the same length of simulated time. Initial testing utilized run lengths of two simulated hours. The adequacy of this run length was validated by several test runs of 24 hours of simulated time. Since the mean performance values were the same for the two-hour and 24-hour runs (at .01 level of significance), two-hour runs were used throughout the rest of the study.

During the data analysis stage, the interarrival rates were classified into low, medium and high

[1] For an excellent text on GPSS, see [Shriber, 1974].

Figure 2. Chi-Square Tests for Exponential Inter-Arrival and Service Distributions: Rotaries A, B and C

Rotary	Arrival Pattern		Service Pattern	
	Mean Interarrival Time (Min. per call)	Computed Chi-Square Statistic[1]	Mean Service Time (Min. per call)	Computed Chi-Square Statistic
A	1.80	14.0[1]	2.64	144.6[2]
B	1.74	10.9[1]	2.50	6.2[1]
C	2.32	3.7[1]	2.41	95.4[2]

[1] Accept exponential distribution at .05 level of significance.
[2] Reject exponential distribution at .05 level of significance.

levels. The service times (mean length of call) varied with the type of incoming call, but proved to be unrelated to the activity levels during the day or on different days of the week. The mean service times for charge authorization calls (A), for customer inquiry (B) and for credit calls (C) are included in Figure 2.

A separate set of simulation runs was performed for each of the three activity levels. Notice that it was neither necessary nor feasible to run a simulation for a "typical" day. The days of the week varied considerably in activity patterns so that several patterns for an eight-hour time period would be relevant. The large variety of staffing plans for allocating operators throughout the day would then result in an unmanageable number of possible configurations to be tested. The alternative approach generates a separate optimum number of operators for light, moderate and heavy periods. The staffing supervisors can then plan to vary the staff assignments throughout the day in two-hour time blocks based on expected activity levels.

Test Results

Three measures were used to portray the performance of the systems for different activity levels and staffing levels. Since customer satisfaction was the primary focus, the three measures were:

1) Calls rejected—the percentage of incoming calls that received a busy signal.

2) Calls held—the percentage of incoming calls that were placed on hold.

3) Hold time—the average waiting time, for calls placed on hold, before service begins. (The average total call length for calls placed on hold is the mean waiting time plus the mean service time.)

Figures 3, 4 and 5 show these performance measures for the three model configurations, over the full range of available staff, at a medium level of telephone activity. For Model I, one operator was assigned to each partition for a minimum staff of three. Additional staff were assigned one at a time, first to rotary A, then B, then C, etc. (The plotted measures are the weighted average of the means for the three rotaries.)

In terms of average hold times, Model I appeared to have a slight advantage over Models II and III, but this advantage is somewhat illusory since the lower averages in this most constrained configuration are attained at the expense of a much higher rejection rate (Figure 3) and a much higher percentage of calls held (Figure 5). In

Figure 3. Number of Calls Rejected as Per Cent of Total Incoming Calls (Medium Activity Levels)

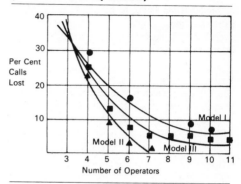

Figure 4. Average Hold Time in Minutes for Calls Held (Medium Activity Levels)

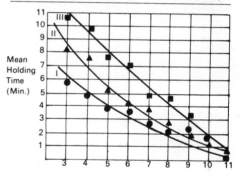

Figure 5. Number of Calls Which Must Hold as Per Cent of Total Incoming Calls (Medium Activity Levels)

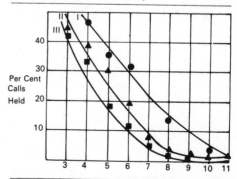

terms of lost calls, Model II was clearly the best configuration for any given staffing level as might be expected. A surprising result was the superiority of Model III in terms of queueing (per cent of calls which must wait). Compromising Model III's overall choice, however, was its notably higher rejection rate as compared with Model II.

Decision Analysis

The ultimate choice of model configuration and staffing level must also consider cost. The three basic types of cost considered in this system were as follows:

>The cost of the telephone equipment, lines and other physical facilities—basically a fixed cost once the telephone configuration is chosen.

>The labor costs of operators to staff the system—a variable cost (within limits) based on the number of operators assigned.

>Customer dissatisfaction costs—an intangible cost that varies with the performance of the system.

Conceptually, it should be possible to develop a total cost function that could be minimized by the proper choice of telephone network configuration and staffing levels for expected activity levels. A serious complication to this approach results from the difficulty of measuring customer dissatisfaction costs. This difficulty is further magnified by the multiple performance measures, each of which may have a different cost coefficient. A customer may be more displeased if his call is placed on hold, for example, than if he encounters a busy signal.

As an alternative to the measurement of dissatisfaction costs, however, it is possible for management to establish minimum levels of performance for each operating characteristic of the system. For example, management may establish the following minimal performance requirements: 1) Customers should complete their calls at least 90% of the time (rejection rate of 10% or less), 2) no more than 15% of incoming calls should need to hold and 3) for those that must hold, average holding time should not exceed two minutes.

It is now only necessary to identify which system configuration and staffing level incurs the least cost under light, moderate and heavy activity levels and satisfies the three criteria specified above. These data are presented in Figure 6. For example, the table indicates that for Model I, seven agents would be required to satisfy the performance criteria discussed above at a low level of telephone activity, eight agents would be required for a medium level of telephone activity,

etc. The associated operating costs for these staffing requirements are indicated in Figure 7. The monthly cost figures include fixed monthly cost of the telephone equipment and personnel expenses assumed at $5.35 per hour per operator. Other "overhead" costs are assumed constant for all three model types, and are therefore omitted from the analysis.

Figure 6. Minimal Agent Configurations Meeting Three Required Performance Criteria*

	Model Type		
Telephone Activity Level	Model I	Model II	Model III
Low	I-7	II-6	III-6
Medium	I-8	II-10	III-6
High	I-10	II-12	III-11

* Derived from performance curves of Figures 3, 4 and 5.

Figure 7. Minimal and Expected Average Monthly Costs for Three Telephone Configurations, Assuming Flexible Agent Schedules

		Model Type		
Telephone Activity Level	Weight	I	II	III
Low	.20	$7,042	$ 6,245	$ 6,229
Medium	.50	7,992	10,045	9,079
High	.30	9,892	11,945	10,979
Expected Costs		$8,372	$ 9,855	$ 9,079

Although the staffing level can be varied during each day based on expected activity levels, the structure of the telephone system (model type) must be selected for a longer period of time. If only one of the systems has the ability to handle the forecast peak load, the decision is obvious. If all three configurations will handle peak loading, the choice can be made by minimizing the weighted average cost. If, for example, the activity levels are expected to be high 30% of the time, average 50% of the time and low 20% of the time, the weighted average cost of each system can be used to indicate the optimal choice. Figure 7 shows these calculations, revealing model structure I as the best overall choice for the given weights. Staffing plans during each day can be designed to handle the expected activity level of scheduling, for example, 10 operators for heavy periods, eight operators for moderate periods and seven operators for light periods.

Generality of Decision Analysis Approach

The strength of this decision analysis lies not in the generation of an optimal decision for this particular situation, but in the generality of the approach. The steps used in the analysis can, and should, be repeated periodically to insure the continued appropriateness of the decision in the light of possible changes in the system. For example, periodic data-gathering on the number of calls and the call length aids in forecasting future load levels, and revalidates the decision rules. These data might be relatively small samples rather than the extensive data gathered for the initial study. When changes are detected in the number of calls per hour or the call length, new parameters can be submitted to the simulation model for reevaluation.

The analysis steps can also be reiterated to test a new alternative for the system structure. For example, an on-line inquiry system might be proposed to shorten the length of time required to service a call. The decision analysis described above could be used to answer the following questions:

>What will be the effect on the performance measures of the proposed system—mean length of calls, percentage calls lost, percentage calls that must hold?

>How many telephone lines and terminals will be required?

>How many operators will be needed for heavy, moderate and light periods of activity?

Summary

In summary, this paper has described a decision analysis to optimize the structure and management of a telephone inquiry system. Optimization is important in situations such as this because of the need to reduce costs, to improve productivity and to increase customer service levels simultaneously. The modeling and analysis approach can be used to periodically revalidate the initial decision, as well as to support decisions in modified or upgraded systems of similar structure. ☐

REFERENCES

Hillier, Frederick S. and Gerald L. Lieberman, *Operations Research*. (San Francisco: Holden Day, Inc.) 1974, p. 404.

Page, E., *Queueing Theory in O.R.* (New York: Crane, Russak & Co., Inc.) 1972, p. 81.

Shriber, Thomas, *Simulation Using GPSS*, John Wiley & Sons, Inc., c. 1973, p. 576.

Chapter 31

AN L.P. MODEL FOR WORK FORCE SCHEDULING FOR BANKS*

By Shyam L. Moondra

*This article is reprinted, with permission, from *Journal of Bank Research,* Vol. 6, No. 4 (Winter, 1976), pp. 299-301.

Formulation of Problem

The workload in many areas of bank operations has the characteristics of a non-uniform distribution with respect to time of day. For example, at Chase Manhattan Bank, the number of domestic money transfer requests received from customers, if plotted against time of day, would appear to have the shape of an inverted-U curve with the peak reached around 1 p.m. For efficient use of the resources, the manpower available, should, therefore, also vary correspondingly. Figure 1 shows a typical workload curve and the corresponding manpower requirement at different hours of the day.

A variable capacity can effectively be achieved by employing part-time personnel. Since part-timers are not entitled to all the fringe benefits, they are often more economical than full-time employees. However, other considerations may limit the extent to which part-time people can be hired in a given operating department. The problem is to find an optimum work-force schedule that would meet manpower requirements at any given time and also be economical.

The L.P. Model

We will make the following assumptions partly to simulate the real situation and partly to simplify the problem. It

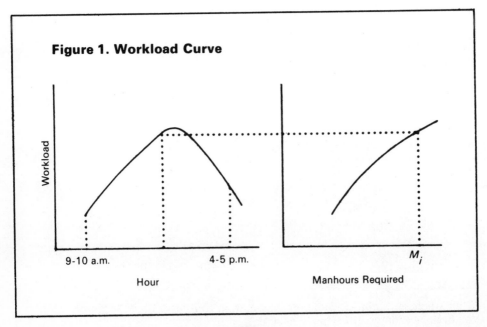

Figure 1. Workload Curve

should be emphasized that these assumptions are not required in their strictest sense, and can very easily be modified as needed. For simplicity's sake all the parameters are assumed to be deterministic.

1) By corporate policy, part-time man-hours are limited to a maximum of $a\%$ of the day's total requirement.

2) Full-time employees work for eight hours (one hour for lunch included) per day. Thus a full-timer's productive time is 35 hours per week.

3) Part-timers work for at least four hours but less than eight hours and are not allowed any lunch break.

4) 50% of the full-timers go out to lunch between 11 a.m. and 12 noon and the remaining 50% between 12 noon and 1 p.m. The model can be modified very easily for any other situation.

5) The shift starts at 9 a.m. and ends at 7 p.m. (i.e., overtime limited to two hours). For a given situation, if this assumption does not hold, two alternatives are: 1) The work left over at 7 p.m. should be considered as holdover for the next day, or 2) the model should be extended for the time periods beyond 7 p.m. (This will necessitate the introduction of additional variables).

6) A full-time employee is not allowed to work more than five hours overtime per week (so he is paid at the normal rate for overtime hours and not at one-and-a-half times the normal rate applicable to hours in excess of 40 per week). The fringe benefits are not applied to the overtime hours.

Notations: The following notations are used.

x = Average cost per full-time man-hours (fringe benefits included).

y = Average cost per overtime man-hour for full-timers (straight rate excluding fringe benefits, cf. assumption 6)

r = Average cost per part-time man-hour

M_i = Man-hours required for the ith hour
$i = 1, 2, \ldots\ldots\ldots\ldots\ldots, 9, 10$
(9 a.m. to 7 p.m.)

F_1 = Number of full-time employees

F_2 = Number of full-time employees working overtime between 5 p.m. and 6 p.m.

F_3 = Number of full-time employees working overtime between 6 p.m. and 7 p.m.

P_i = Number of part-time employees starting at the beginning of the ith hour ($i = 1, \ldots\ldots\ldots, 7$, since no part-timer can start after 3 p.m., cf. assumption 3)

Q_i = Number of part-time employees leaving at the end of the ith hour ($i = 4, \ldots\ldots\ldots\ldots, 10$, cf. assumption 3)

Objective Function: We want to minimize the total manpower cost given by

(1) $Z = 7 \times F_1 + y(F_2 + F_3) + r(10P_1 + 9P_2 + 8P_3 + 7P_4 + 6P_5 + 5P_6 + 4P_7 - 6Q_4 - 5Q_5 - 4Q_6 - 3Q_7 - 2Q_8 - Q_9)$

Example

The use of the above L.P. model is illustrated in the following example.

Input:
x = \$5.053
y = \$4.04
r = \$3.912
a = 40%
M_i = 14,25,26,38,55,60,51,29,14,9
for $i = 1,2,\ldots,10$

Output:
Using the two phase method as described in Hadley, the following results are obtained.

Constraints: For a given hour, the available man-hours should be at least equal to the required man-hours. Therefore, we have:

$$(2) \quad F_1+ \qquad\quad P_1 \qquad\qquad\qquad\qquad\qquad\qquad\qquad\qquad\qquad \geqslant M_1$$
$$(3) \quad F_1+ \qquad\quad P_1+P_2 \qquad\qquad\qquad\qquad\qquad\qquad\qquad\qquad \geqslant M_2$$
$$(4) \tfrac{1}{2}F_1^*+ \qquad P_1+P_2+P_3 \qquad\qquad\qquad\qquad\qquad\qquad\qquad \geqslant M_3$$
$$(5) \tfrac{1}{2}F_1^*+ \qquad P_1+P_2+P_3+P_4 \qquad\qquad\qquad\qquad\qquad\qquad \geqslant M_4$$
$$(6) \quad F_1+ \qquad\quad P_1+P_2+P_3+P_4+P_5 \qquad -Q_4 \qquad\qquad\qquad \geqslant M_5$$
$$(7) \quad F_1+ \qquad\quad P_1+P_2+P_3+P_4+P_5+P_6 \quad -Q_4-Q_5 \qquad\qquad \geqslant M_6$$
$$(8) \quad F_1+ \qquad\quad P_1+P_2+P_3+P_4+P_5+P_6+P_7-Q_4-Q_5-Q_6 \qquad \geqslant M_7$$
$$(9) \quad F_1+ \qquad\quad P_1+P_2+P_3+P_4+P_5+P_6+P_7-Q_4-Q_5-Q_6-Q_7 \quad \geqslant M_8$$
$$(10) \qquad F_2+ \quad P_1+P_2+P_3+P_4+P_5+P_6+P_7-Q_4-Q_5-Q_6-Q_7-Q_8 \geqslant M_9$$
$$(11) \qquad\quad F_3+P_1+P_2+P_3+P_4+P_5+P_6+P_7-Q_4-Q_5-Q_6-Q_7-Q_8-Q_9 \geqslant M_{10}$$

* cf. assumption 4

The part-timers work for at least four hours (cf. assumption 3). Therefore we have:

$$(12) \quad Q_4 \qquad P_1$$
$$(13) \quad Q_5 \qquad P_1+P_2-Q_4$$
$$(14) \quad Q_6 \qquad P_1+P_2+P_3-Q_4-Q_5$$
$$(15) \quad Q_7 \qquad P_1+P_2+P_3+P_4-Q_4-Q_5-Q_6$$
$$(16) \quad Q_8 \qquad P_1+P_2+P_3+P_4+P_5-Q_4-Q_5-Q_6-Q_7$$
$$(17) \quad Q_9 \qquad P_1+P_2+P_3+P_4+P_5+P_6-Q_4-Q_5-Q_6-Q_7-Q_8$$

Since part-timers work for less than eight hours (cf. assumption 3), we have:

$$(18) \quad Q_4+Q_5+Q_6+Q_7 \geqslant P_1$$
$$(19) \quad Q_4+Q_5+Q_6+Q_7+Q_8 \geqslant P_1+P_2$$
$$(20) \quad Q_4+Q_5+Q_6+Q_6+Q_7+Q_8+Q_9 \geqslant P_1+P_2+P_3$$

Total part-time man-hours cannot exceed the given limit (cf. assumption 1), therefore we have:

$$(21) \quad 10P_1+9P_2+8P_3+7P_4+6P_5+5P_6+4P_7-6Q_4-5Q_5-4Q_6-3Q_7-2Q_8-Q_9$$
$$a(\Sigma M_i)/100$$

We can now formally state our problem as:

Minimize Z given by (1), subject to (2) through (21) and
$F_1,F_2,F_3,P_1,P_2,P_3,P_4,P_5,P_6,P_7,Q_4,Q_5,Q_6,Q_7,Q_8,Q_9 \geqslant 0$

Summary

Since the number of employees cannot be fractional, the use of linear programming is only an approximation. For truly optimum results, this problem should be formulated as an integer programming problem.

The man-hours required for each hour of the day were assumed to be de-terministic. In a real situation, it would be found that there is a wide fluctuation in these man-hours from day to day. To account for this variability, one should revert to stochastic linear programming.

The results of the example given in Figure 2 show that the optimum work-force schedule allows for an idle time of 26 man-hours in the entire day. Part of

Figure 2. Work-Force Schedule

Time Period	Number of Persons Required	Number of Persons Available		
		Full-time	Part-time	Total
9-10 a.m.	14	29	—	29
10-11	25	29	—	29
11-12	26	15	11	26
12-1	38	14	26	40
1-2	55	29	26	55
2-3	60	29	31	60
3-4	51	29	22	51
4-5	29	29	5	34
5-6	14	9	5	14
6-7 p.m.	9	9	0	9

Figure 3. Time Schedules

FULL-TIME EMPLOYEES

Number of Employees	Starting Time	Number of Employees	Lunch Period	Number of Employees	Leaving Time
29	9 a.m.	14	11-12	20	5 p.m.
		15	12-1	9	7 p.m.

PART-TIME EMPLOYEES

Number of Employees	Starting Time	Number of Employees	Leaving Time
11	11 a.m.	9	3 p.m.
		2	4 p.m.
15	12 Noon	15	4 p.m.
5	2 p.m.	5	6 p.m.

this idle time in the optimum solution is due to the restriction that an employee can start only at the beginning of an hour (or leave at the end of an hour). If we reduce our time period from one hour to half-an-hour (or even better to 15 minutes), the optimum results would show a markedly improved schedule with lesser idle time. This would, however, increase the number of variables and, therefore, the cost of computation. □

REFERENCE
Hadley, G., "Linear Programming," Addison-Wesley, Reading, Massachusetts, 1962.

Chapter 32

THE LOCK-BOX LOCATION PROBLEM: A PRACTICAL REFORMULATION*

By Steven F. Maier and James H. Vander Weide

*This article is reprinted, with permission, from *Journal of Bank Research,* Vol. 5, No. 2 (Summer, 1974), pp. 92-95.

Corporate treasurers have long known that they can often significantly increase the amount of funds available for investment by locating check collection points, commonly called lock-boxes, in their customer distribution areas. Several years ago, Kraus, Janssen and McAdams [1970] (hereafter referred to as KJM) demonstrated how the problem of locating lock-boxes so as to maximize the return on these newly available funds minus the fixed and variable costs of the lock-box system can be formulated as a special case of a general class of fixed charge location-allocation problems.[1] Since then, other scholars have discovered several special algorithms that can be used to solve reasonably large scale lock-box problems in a matter of seconds. (See, especially, [Bent, 1972], [Bulfin and Unger, 1973], [Ciochetto, et.al., 1972] and [Khumawala, 1972].) Despite these academic successes, however, the bankers who solve lock-box problems for their corporate customers have generally been less than enthusiastic about the possibility of implementing the KJM approach. In this paper, we briefly discuss why the KJM approach is difficult to implement, and then present a different approach to this problem that should have considerable appeal to the corporate banker.

Data Requirements of KJM Approach

The KJM approach to the lock-box problem can be described mathematically by Problem I:

Problem I

$$(1) \quad max \ G = \sum_{i=1}^{m} \sum_{j=1}^{n} A_{ij}x_{ij} - \sum_{j=1}^{n} F_j z_j$$

[1] Kraus, Janssen and McAdams actually thought that they had formulated the lock-box problem as a special case of the fixed charge transportation problem. In the fixed charge transportation problem, however, the fixed charges are associated with the arcs rather than the nodes. It is possible to reformulate the KJM model as a fixed charge transportation problem, but since this significantly increases the number of variables [from $(m) \times (n)$ to $(mn + m) \times (m + n + 1)$], this reformulation would not be tractable from a computational standpoint. For a complete discussion of the relations between the various fixed charge location-allocation problems, see [Ellwein, 1970], Appendix A.

$$(2) \ s.t. \quad \sum_{j=1}^{n} x_{ij} = 1$$
$$\text{for } i = 1,2,\ldots,m$$

$$(3) \qquad x_{ij} \leq z_j$$
$$\text{for } i = 1,2,\ldots,m; j = 1,2,\ldots,n$$

$$(4) \qquad x_{ij} \geq 0$$
$$\text{for } i = 1,2,\ldots,m; j = 1,2,\ldots,n$$

$$(5) \qquad z_j = 0 \text{ or } 1$$
$$\text{for } j = 1,2,\ldots,n$$

where

$A_{ij} = \alpha(T_i^* - T_{ij}) \ D_i - C_{ij}$ = the variable net benefits stated in dollars per day obtained from clearing group i's check through lock-box j,

α = the firm's daily opportunity cost of capital,

T_{ij} = average mail time in days from group i to lock-box j + average clearing time in days from lock-box j to group i's bank,

T_i^* = average time in days from group i to the firm's main office + average clearing time in days from the main office to group i's bank,

D_i = total incoming funds from group i,

C_{ij} = differential cost of clearing group i's checks through bank j instead of the main office,

x_{ij} = one if group i's checks are sent to lock-box j, zero otherwise,

F_j = the fixed charge per period for maintaining lock-box j,

z_j = one if lock-box j is being used, zero otherwise.

As noted earlier, the objective of the KJM approach is to locate lock-boxes so as to maximize the return on the newly available funds minus the fixed and variable costs of the lock-box system. Constraint set (2) is used in this formulation to insure that all of the checks are assigned to a lock-box, while constraint set (3), along with (5), is needed to insure that no check is sent to a "closed" lock-box.

To implement the KJM approach, one must obviously know or estimate 1) the mail and clearing times relating group i and lock-box j as well as the times for the current system using only the main office, 2) the total amount of incoming funds from each group i, 3) the variable and fixed costs associated with the firm's present system, 4) the firm's opportunity cost of capital, and 5) the variable and fixed charges for processing group i's checks through lock-box j. Unfortunately, while reliable estimates of data requirements 1) through 4) can often be obtained at only a modest cost, reliable estimates of data requirement 5) are usually both costly and difficult to obtain.

The cost of obtaining estimates of variable and fixed lock-box charges is clearly a function of the number of such charges which have to be determined. In most practical studies this number will be quite large. Suppose, for instance, that the bank has a list of 50 possible lock-box sites and that there are, on average, four banks offering lock-box services at each site. The bank doing the study would then have to request price information from 200 different banks. If, in addition, the variable and fixed lock-box charges of these 200 banks changes quite rapidly over time, the acquisition cost of this information can be very high indeed.

Even more frustrating, however, is the fact that many banks are unwilling to quote lock-box prices that are independent of the other bank services that the particular firm is currently buying. It is common practice, for instance, for banks to give credit toward lock-box services for deposit balances required as part of a short-term credit agree- ment. This practice clearly makes it difficult for the bank performing the lock-box study to determine the firm's true costs of lock-box services.

In view of the above difficulties, it is suggested in the next section that the data collection be divided into two phases, in which the bank gathers data requirements 1) through 4) and the firm data requirement 5). By first optimizing the potential float savings by geographical location, the amount of effort required to obtain the variable and fixed bank charges is greatly reduced.

A Practical Reformulation

Most of the difficult informational requirements of the KJM approach can be avoided by using a simple three-stage solution procedure. In the first stage, the bank attempts to determine a functional relationship between the maximum float reduction benefits from the customer's lock-box system and the number of lock-boxes in the system. This can be accomplished by solving the following location-allocation problem for all values of the parameter r from one to the total number of lock-boxes in the pool of potential lock-box sites:

Problem II

(6) $\quad max \ G' = \sum_i \sum_j A_{ij} x_{ij}$

(7) $\quad s.t. \quad \sum_j x_{ij} = 1$

$\qquad\qquad\qquad$ for $i = 1,2,\ldots,m$

(8) $\qquad\qquad \sum_i x_{ij} \leq m z_j$

$\qquad\qquad\qquad$ for $j = 1,2,\ldots,n$

Figure 1*

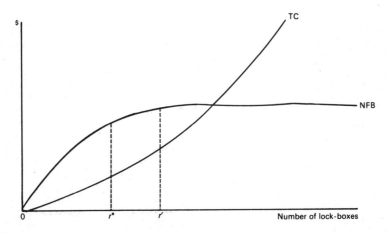

* Although the NFB and TC curves are really only defined for integer values of r, we have drawn them as continuous curves for the sake of the exposition.

(9) $\sum_j z_j = r$

(10) $x_{ij} \geq 0$

           for $i = 1,2,\ldots,m; j = 1,2,\ldots,n$

(11) $z_j = 0$ or 1

           for $j = 1,2,\ldots,n$.

where

$A'_{ij} = \alpha(T_i^* - T_{ij}) \, D_i$ = the benefits stated in dollars per day obtained from clearing group i's checks through lock-box j,

r = the number of lock-boxes currently being considered from the pool of potential lock-box sites.

In contrast to the KJM formulation, the objective in problem II is simply to maximize the return on the funds made available by the float reduction. Since the costs of the lock-box system are not included in this objective function, or in the constraints (7) through (11), the optimal solution to problem II, were it not for constraint (9), would be to locate a lock-box at every available site and then assign checks to the nearest lock-box. When the constraint (9) is included, however, and problem II is solved for all values of r, the banker obtains the desired relationship between the maximum float benefits and the number of lock-boxes in the customer's lock-box system. Although the solution to this problem is not trivial, algorithms do exist that can solve fairly large-scale problems in a small amount of time. (See, [Ellwein and Gray 1971] and [Spielberg, 1969].) The result of this stage of the solution procedure would then be a curve that may resemble curve NFB in Figure 1.

The second stage of the solution procedure should probably be performed by the bank's customer himself. With the best lock-box regions for each value of r in hand, the bank's customer attempts to determine a functional relationship between the total costs of his lock-box system and the number of boxes in the system. He does this by negotiating for himself the "best" lock-box deal he can obtain from a bank in the relevant regions, and then adding to this price figure his search, negotiation and administration costs for each value of r. The result of this second stage of the procedure would perhaps be a curve shaped like the TC curve in Figure 1.

The final stage of the solution procedure now obviously involves making a comparison of the benefits and costs of the firm's lock-box system. If the curves are shaped like those in Figure 1, the optimal number of lock-boxes is determined by that point, r^*, on the abscissa where the vertical distance between the NFB and TC curves is great-

est. The optimal distribution of lock-boxes is then given by the solution to problem II for $r = r^*$.

The three-stage solution procedure just described has several advantages over the KJM approach. First, there is likely to be a large reduction in the number of lock-box prices that must be determined in order to solve a particular lock-box problem. Recall that in our approach lock-box prices need not be determined at all until after the NFB curve is known. If this curve becomes nearly horizontal for optimal lock-box combinations beyond some number r', then the TC curve, which is almost certainly monotonically increasing in r, need not be computed beyond r'. A considerable savings could result when r' is relatively small. Second, when computing the total cost curve, TC, the firm can include search, negotiation and administration costs not included in the KJM model. In addition, the firm can more easily account for the dependence of lock-box charges on the other bank services it is purchasing. The true costs of the firm's lock-box system are thus more closely approximated when our approach is used. Finally, when lock-box prices change, as they frequently do, the solution does not have to be recomputed from scratch, as it would in the KJM approach. Instead, only the relatively inexpensive steps two and three need to be reconsidered. This last advantage could represent a considerable savings in both time and money.

Concluding Remarks

In this paper, we presented an approach to the lock-box problem which, from the banks' point of view, has several advantages over previously considered approaches. Nevertheless, it may be argued that, because float savings and system costs are not considered simultaneously, the suggested three-stage approach does not yield a global optimum solution. This is indeed true, but is of little consequence if the "best deal" the firm can negotiate for lock-box services does not vary significantly between Federal Reserve cities. (Federal Reserve cities are a natural choice for lock-box sites, since they permit rapid deposit with the Federal Reserve and, because of their size, give excellent mail times.) In any case, however, the authors believe this approach yields a more reasonable and accurate model of the problem when the cost and difficulty of data collection is considered.   □

REFERENCES

Bent, D. H., "Branch-and-Bound for Facility Location," *Infor*, Vol. 10, No. 1., February, 1972, pp. 1-7.

Bulfin, R. L. and V. E. Unger, "Computational Experience with an Algorithm for the Lock-Box Problem," Proceedings of the 28th ACM National Conference, Atlanta, August, 1973.

Calman, R. F., Linear Programming and Cash Management/Cash Alpha, The M.I.T. Press, Cambridge, Massachusetts, 1968.

Ciochetto, F. F., H. S. Swanson, J. R. Lee and R.E.D. Woolsey, "The Lock-Box Problem and Some Startling But True Computational Results for Large Scale Systems," Paper presented at the 41st National Meeting of ORSA held in New Orleans on April 26-28, 1972.

Ellwein, L. B., "Fixed Charge Location — Allocation Problems with Capacity and Configuration Constraints," *Technical Report* No. 70-2, Department of Industrial Engineering, Stanford University, August, 1970.

Ellwein, L. B. and P. Gray, "Solving Fixed Charge Location —Allocation Problems with Capacity and Configuration Constraints," *AIIE Transactions*, Vol. 3, No. 4, December, 1971, pp. 290-98.

Khumawala, B. M., "An Efficient Branch and Bound Algorithm for the Warehouse Location Problem," *Management Science*, Vol. 18, No. 12, August, 1972, pp. 718-31.

Kraus, A., C. Janssen and A. McAdams, "The Lock-box Location Problem, A Class of Fixed Charge Transportation Problems," *Journal of Bank Research*, Autumn, 1970, pp. 51-58.

Pogue, G. A., R. B. Faucett and R. N. Bussard, "Cash Management: A Systems Approach," *Industrial Management Review*, Winter, 1970, pp. 55-73.

Spielberg, K. "An Algorithm for the Simple Plant Location Problem with Some Side Conditions," *Operations Research*, Vol. 17, No. 1, January-February, 1969, pp. 85-111.

Chapter 33

A UNIFIED LOCATION MODEL FOR CASH DISBURSEMENTS AND LOCK-BOX COLLECTIONS*

By Steven F. Maier and James H. Vander Weide

*This article is reprinted, with permission, from *Journal of Bank Research*, Vol. 7, No. 2 (Summer, 1976), pp. 166-172.

The benefits from an improved corporate cash management system generally stem from three sources. First, the firm can often achieve a considerable reduction in its collection float by locating lock-boxes in strategic customer areas and utilizing devices such as wire transfers to shorten the time between customer mailing and fund availability. Second, the firm can usually increase its disbursement float by choosing wisely the offices and banks from which it disburses. Finally, the firm can reduce the costs of banking services it receives by carefully setting the levels of its bank deposit balances. In this paper, we provide a brief review of the models that are currently available to analyze each of these areas, and then present a unified model which can be used to optimally design an entire cash management system.

The Lock-Box Location Problem

It is well-known that corporate treasurers can sometimes significantly increase the amount of funds available for investment by locating check collection points, commonly called "lock-boxes," in one or more of the firm's major customer areas. The problem of locating those check collection points which minimize the value of uncollected funds can be formulated mathematically as follows:

(1) MINIMIZE
$$W = \Sigma_k \Sigma_m [\rho(q_{mk} + r_{mk}) + e_{mk}] \cdot Y_{mk} + \Sigma_k f_k^C \cdot Z_k^C$$
(2) s.t. $\quad \Sigma_k Y_{mk} = b_m \qquad \forall \ m$
(3) $\qquad \Sigma_m Y_{mk} \leq (\ \Sigma_m b_m) Z_k^C \qquad \forall \ k$
(4) $\qquad Y_{mk} \geq 0, \ Z_k^C = 0 \ or \ 1 \qquad \forall \ k,m$

where Y_{mk} = the number of deposit items from customer group m processed by bank k

b_m = the total number of checks to be processed from customer group m

q_{mk} = the dollar value of the mail float carried as accounts receivable balances that is generated when one check is mailed by customer group m to bank k

r_{mk} = the dollar value of the collection float that is generated when one check of customer group m is cleared through bank k

e_{mk} = the variable bank costs of processing one check from customer group m through a lock-box operated by bank k (if this cost does not differ for customer groups, then use e_k)

ρ = the opportunity cost of ledger balances

f_k^C = a fixed charge for using bank k as a collection point

Z_k^C = one if bank k is used as a lock-box site, zero otherwise

The constraint sets (2) and (4) together insure that all the checks will be allocated, while constraint set (3) insures that no checks will be sent to a "closed" lock-box.

In this model, a homogeneous customer group is defined as a collection of customers whose combined mailing and clearing time to each potential lock-box site is the same. Although this does not require that customers be geographically contiguous, in practice customers are grouped by the first two or three digits of their ZIP codes.

The lock-box problem is equivalent to the simple warehouse location problem. Both problems have received extensive coverage in the O.R. literature (see, for example, [Drysdale and Sandiford, 1969], [Feldman, et. al., 1966], [Kraus, et. al., 1970], [Kuehn and Hamburger, 1963], [Shanker and Zoltners, 1972] and [Spielberg, 1969].) In fact, both of these formulations are part of a class of models referred to as the fixed charge location allocation problem by Ellwein [1970] and Ellwein and Gray [1971]. The name stems from the fact that the problem may be approached in two stages. First, one selects a subset of the possible bank location sites and second, one allocates the customers among those selected sites in a manner which minimizes the mail and collection float.

The first stage of the problem is combinatorial in nature, since the number of possible subsets of the location sites is $2^K - 1$ where K is the number of banks under consideration. The second stage of the problem can be solved in general as a transportation problem; however, for the lock-box problem this simplifies further because the bank collection activities are uncapacitated. This simplification permits a solution to be obtained for the second stage of the problem by assigning each customer group to the bank location that gives the minimum float. Because of the simple nature of the second stage, the algorithms that have been proposed are primarily concerned with finding an efficient method for searching the feasible subsets of location sites. Both branch and bound and implicit enumeration have been shown to be efficient and capable of finding the optimal solution to reasonably sized versions of this problem in a matter of seconds. (See, [Bent, 1972], [Bulfin and Unger, 1973], [Ciochetto, et. al., 1972], [Davis and Ray, 1969], [Effroymson and Ray, 1966], [Khumawala, 1971 and 1972] and [Pogue, et. al., 1970].)

In this paper we will not be further concerned with the computational aspects of the lock-box problem. Instead, we will examine whether this model, which focuses only on the collection side of the cash management function, is in fact a useful planning tool. In a previous paper [1974], we focused our attention on the difficulties inherent in implementing this model because of the high cost of obtaining bank service price information. Now we will ask the more fundamental question: Can the cost of operating a lock-box system be considered independently of the other cash management costs? With that as our goal, we proceed to review the models for the disbursement activity.

The Corporate Payment Problem

Corporate cash managers can also often generate significant cash savings from a more efficient use of their disbursement system. This savings is achieved by locating the check disbursement activity at offices and banks with "slow" mail and clearing times, respectively. The problem of locating those disbursement activities which maximize the net benefits from the increased disbursement float was first discussed by Shanker and Zoltner [1972, Spring]. The formulation that follows is an extension of Shanker and Zoltner's work:

(5) MAX $W = \sum_i \sum_j \sum_k (\rho \cdot p_{ijk} - d_{jk}) X_{ijk}$
$\qquad - \sum_k f_k^D \cdot Z_k^D - \sum_i f_i^R \cdot Z_i^R$
$\qquad - \sum_i \sum_k f_{ik}^{DR} \cdot Z_{ik}^{DR}$

(6) s.t. $\sum_i \sum_k X_{ijk} = a_j \qquad \forall j$

(7) $\qquad \sum_i \sum_j X_{ijk} \leq (\sum_j a_j) Z_k^D \qquad \forall k$

(8) $\qquad \sum_j \sum_k X_{ijk} \leq (\sum_j a_j) Z_i^R \qquad \forall i$

(9) $\qquad \sum_j X_{ijk} \leq (\sum_j a_j) Z_{ik}^{DR} \qquad \forall i,k$

(10) $\qquad X_{ijk} \geq 0;\ Z_k^D,\ Z_i^R,\ Z_{ik}^{DR} = 0$ or 1 $\qquad \forall i,j,k$

where X_{ijk} = the number of checks to be issued by regional office i to creditor group j on bank k

a_j = the total number of checks to be issued to creditor group j

p_{ijk} = the dollar value of the float generated by disbursing one check from regional office i to creditor group j on bank k

d_{jk} = the per item bank cost of processing one check for creditor group j through bank k (if this cost does not differ for creditor groups, then use d_k)

ρ = the opportunity cost of ledger balances

f_k^D = a fixed charge for disbursing at bank k

Z_k^D = one if bank k is used for disbursements, zero otherwise

f_i^R = a fixed cost to the firm for locating and maintaining a disbursement activity at regional office i

Z_i^R = one if a disbursement activity is located at regional office i, zero otherwise

f_{ik}^{DR} = a fixed cost to the firm for maintaining a relationship between regional office i and bank k

Z_{ik}^{DR} = one if a relationship is established between regional office i and bank k, zero otherwise

Here, the constraint set (6) is needed to insure that all of the checks that are owed to creditor group j are processed while the constraint sets (7), (8) and (9) are needed to insure that all activities occur through "open" offices and banks.

On first inspection, it may appear that this model is considerably more difficult to solve than that of the lock-box location problem. This is in fact not the case. The two-stage approach described in the previous section can still be applied to this model with no serious increase in complexity. However, it would generally be true that the number of integer 0-1 variables would be considerably greater here than in the lock-box problem. Again, we must caution against overenthusiastic acceptance of the solution of this model, since it makes the very strong implicit assumption that the cost of operating the disbursement system is independent of other cash management costs.

A Systems Approach to Cash Management

The two preceding models described in this paper are characterized by their failure to view the collection and disbursement activities in a framework which properly considers the interrelationships between them. Calman [1968] first proposed a comprehensive model of the firm's entire banking system. This model, which was later revised by Pogue et. al. [1970], provides a means of determining the true costs of the various components of the system. A limitation of their model is that it only determines activity levels within the firm's current banking system. As the two previous models indicate, firms often want to consider possible changes in the current banking structure. Therefore, in the next section we present a cash management model which unifies the two previous location models along the lines suggested by Calman and Pogue into a model capable of locating banking activities as well as determining their optimal levels.

A Unified Location Model

The key to a unified cash management model is the explicit determination of the optimal level of total bank compensation. In order to appreciate why this is so, one must understand the service pricing policy of commercial banks. Generally, commercial banks offer their services in a package for which they are partially compensated by a minimum balance requirement on a line of credit. When a compensating balance is required, the bank will often allow a service charge credit to be earned on the balance, which may be used to offset charges for other bank services. This policy often permits the firm to obtain double use of such funds. If a firm has already established its lines of credit, it may have a sizable pool of service charge credit that it can use to offset lock-box and disbursement charges. Therefore, unless all of the firm's banking activities are considered simultaneously, it is impossible to establish a basis for a cost analysis. It is this conclusion that makes the cost information required by the first two models impossible to obtain and leads us to the consideration of a unified approach.

In this model we will consider three separate ways of compensating a bank for its services. First, the bank can be paid in the form of cash fees FEE_k. Second, the bank can give a service charge credit c_k^N for each dollar of average net collected balances NCB_k on deposit. (The net collected balance is the

true bank balance.) Finally, the bank can give a credit c_k^T for each dollar of tax payments TP_k the firm makes through the bank. (The reason the bank will allow credit is that there is often a substantial delay between the time the firm is required to pay its taxes and the time the U.S. Treasury actually withdraws funds.) We assume that the bank must be compensated for its total cost of processing disbursements TCD_k, its total cost of processing lock-box collections TCC_k and the value of any other tangible or intangible services V_k it performs for the firm. With these assumptions, we can write the bank compensation constraint as:

$$(11) \quad FEE_k + c_k^T \cdot TP_k + c_k^N \cdot NCB_k \geq TCD_k + TCC_k + V_k$$

which must hold for each bank k under consideration in the system. Each of the variables in this equation is subject to additional constraints, which we now explore in some detail.

The tax payments the firm makes thru its banks is constrained by its total tax liability TPP. We express this as:

$$(12) \quad \Sigma_{k=1}^{K} TP_k \leq TTP$$

Because of its existing lines of credit, the firm must maintain a minimum level of net collected balances in each bank. Thus,

$$(13) \quad NCB \geq g_k,$$

where g_k is the required minimum balance.

Since an assumption of our model is that all parameters are known with certainty, the firm will generally find it optimal to allocate its cash balances to banks in such a way that equation (13) holds with equality. In practice, firms may desire to keep net collected balances above those required by its credit agreements because of the uncertainties associated with the timing of collections and disbursements and because of the desire to maintain access to bank loans in the event of an unforeseen credit need. These uncertainties can easily be incorporated into the model at this point through the introduction of chance constraints. Since an excellent discussion of these constraints is contained in Pogue, Faucett and Bussard [1970], however, we will proceed under our initial assumption.

In order to evaluate the benefits from a redesigned cash management system, we must find a relationship between the firm's average ledger cash balance and the net collected balance on which the bank bases its computations. These two figures differ because of delays in the payment of checks written by the firm and the collection of checks received by the firm.

The delay in payments (positive float) is due

to two factors: the mail delay between the firm's regional office i that issued the check and the location j of the vendor's receiving address; and the clearing time from the vendor's bank back to the firm's bank k upon which the check was drawn. (In addition to the mail and clearing float, there are generally various small delays such as the time the customer needs to process the check. For the purposes of this model, we assume these delays are independent of the issuing location and the bank on which the check was drawn.) If we let X_{ijk} denote the number of checks to be issued by regional office i to creditor group j on bank k, and let p_{ijk} denote the average dollar value of the float generated by disbursing one check for group j from regional office i through bank k, then $\Sigma_i\Sigma_j p_{ijk} X_{ijk}$ will represent the total amount of positive float associated with bank k.

Similarly, the delay in collections (negative float) has two contributions: The mail time from customer group m's location to a lock-box located at bank k; and the clearing time from bank k back to the customer's bank. The mail time, however, does not affect the relationship between the firm's average ledger cash balance and its net collected balances because both balances are computed after the mail time has elapsed. Using our previous definition of Y_{mk} as the number of deposit items processed from customer group m by bank k, and letting r_{mk} be the average dollar value of the collection float generated when one check of customer group m is cleared through bank k, we can formulate the negative float associated with bank k as $\Sigma_m r_{mk} \cdot Y_{mk}$.

The relationship between NCB_k, the net collected balance, and BAL_k, the ledger balance, can now be expressed as:

$$(14)\quad NCB_k = BAL_k + \Sigma_{i=1}^{I}\Sigma_{j=1}^{J} p_{ijk}\cdot X_{ijk} - \Sigma_{m=1}^{M} r_{mk}\cdot Y_{mk}$$

which holds for all banks k under consideration.

Additional constraints are required to guarantee the assignment of all checks to one of the lock-box or disbursement account locations. These constraints were used in the previous models and are simply rewritten here as:

$$(6)\quad \Sigma_{i=1}^{I}\Sigma_{k=1}^{K} X_{ijk} = a_j \text{ for all creditor groups } j.$$

$$(2)\quad \Sigma_{k=1}^{K} Y_{mk} = b_m \text{ for all customer groups } m.$$

Returning now to the right hand side of the bank compensation constraint (11), we derive a formula that relates the disbursement activity levels X_{ijk} to the bank's total cost for operating the disbursement system TCD_k. We assume that the costs of operating the disbursement system can be divided into fixed and variable portions. If we let d_{jk} be the cost of process-

ing one check from creditor group j through bank k, then the variable portion can be expressed as: $\Sigma_i\Sigma_j d_{jk}\cdot X_{ijk}$. The fixed costs, those costs that do not depend on the level of various activities, can be either attributed to the individual regional offices that use the account or to the bank's maintenance of that account. Therefore, in this model the treatment of the fixed charges f_{ik}^C, f_k^D and f_{ik}^{DR} differs from that of the previous models. We have divided the fixed charges into the portion the bank incurs $\hat{f}_{ik}^C$, $\hat{f}_k^D$ and $\hat{f}_{ik}^{DR}$ and therefore must receive compensation for, and the portion that the firm incurs f_{ik}^C, f_k^D, f_i^R, f_{ik}^{DR} and must therefore be accounted for, but for which it does not have to compensate its banks.

With these assumptions, we can express TCD_k as:

$$(15)\quad TCD_k = \Sigma_{i=1}^{I}\Sigma_{j=1}^{J} d_{jk}\cdot X_{ijk} + \Sigma_{i=1}^{I}\hat{f}_{ik}^{DR}\cdot Z_{ik}^{DR} + \hat{f}_k^{D}\cdot Z_k^{D}$$

which holds for each bank k. The variables Z_{ik}^{DR} and Z_k^{D} are integer 0-1 variables that indicate the existence of a disbursement account at bank k (Z_k^{D}) or the existence of regional office-bank relationship (Z_{ik}^{DR}).

The analysis of the total cost of processing lock-box collections is similar. Letting e_{mk} be the cost of processing one customer check from customer group m at the lock-box located at bank k, we have as the variable portion of TCC_k: $\Sigma_m e_{mk}\cdot Y_{mk}$. If we let $\hat{f}_k^C$ be the fixed charge assessed by bank k for servicing the lock-box, then the total cost of collections can be written as:

$$(16)\quad TCC_k = \Sigma_{m=1}^{M} e_{mk}\cdot Y_{mk} + \hat{f}_k^{C}\cdot Z_k^{C} \text{ for each bank } k.$$

where Z_k^C is an integer 0-1 variable that indicates the existence of the lock-box at bank k.

A final set of constraints are needed to control the values of the integer variables Z_k^D, Z_k^C, Z_i^R and Z_{ik}^{DR}. They are constraints (3), (7), (8) and (9) from the previous models:

$$(3)\quad \Sigma_{m=1}^{M} Y_{mk} \le (\Sigma_{m=1}^{M} b_m)\cdot Z_k^{C} \text{ for all banks } k.$$

$$(7)\quad \Sigma_{i=1}^{I}\Sigma_{k=1}^{K} X_{ijk} \le (\Sigma_{j=1}^{J} a_j)\cdot Z_k^{D} \text{ for all banks } k.$$

$$(8)\quad \Sigma_{j=1}^{J}\Sigma_{k=1}^{K} X_{ijk} \le (\Sigma_{j=1}^{J} a_j)\cdot Z_i^{R} \text{ for all regional offices } i.$$

$$(9)\quad \Sigma_{j=1}^{J} X_{ijk} \le (\Sigma_{j=1}^{J} a_j)\cdot Z_{ik}^{DR} \text{ for all regional office } i \text{ and bank } k \text{ combinations.}$$

The last part of the model to be specified is the objective function. We assume that the firm wishes to minimize the cost of its banking system. The cost of the system can be viewed as consisting of two portions. First, there is the direct out of pocket costs. These include the fees paid to the bank and the fixed costs of the various banking relationships:

$$\Sigma_{k=1}^{K} FEE_k + \Sigma_{k=1}^{K} [\bar{f}_k^C \cdot Z_k^C + \bar{f}_k^D$$
$$\cdot Z_k^D + \Sigma_{i=1}^{I} \bar{f}_{ik}^{DR} \cdot Z_{ik}^{DR}] + \Sigma_{i=1}^{I} \bar{f}_i^R \cdot Z_i^R$$

where $\bar{f}_k^C$, $\bar{f}_k^D$ and $\bar{f}_{ik}^{DR}$ represents the fixed cost to the firm respectively of its collection, disbursement and regional office relationships. The cost $\bar{f}_i^R$ represents the fixed cost for locating and maintaining a disbursement activity at regional office i.

The second portion of the objective function evaluates the savings from decreased collection and increased disbursement times in the form of lower cash requirements to operate the banking system. More explicitly, we measure the change in the firm's ledger balance $\Sigma_k BAL_k$ and the reduction in receivables due to reduced mail collection times $\Sigma_m \Sigma_k q_{mk} \cdot Y_{mk}$. We evaluate these savings by using the opportunity cost ρ of the ledger balances. Combining these savings terms with the previous costs we have as our objective function the following:

(17) MINIMIZE $W = \rho \, (\Sigma_{k=1}^{K} BAL_k +$
$$\Sigma_{m=1}^{M} \Sigma_{k=1}^{K} q_{mk} \cdot Y_{mk}) + \Sigma_{k=1}^{K} FEE_k +$$
$$\Sigma_{k=1}^{K} [\bar{f}_k^C \cdot Z_k^C + \bar{f}_k^D \cdot Z_k^D +$$
$$\Sigma_{i=1}^{I} \bar{f}_{ik}^{DR} \cdot Z_{ik}^{DR}] + \Sigma_{i=1}^{I} \bar{f}_i^R \cdot Z_i^R$$

Computational Considerations

The unified location model fits into the framework of the fixed charge location allocation formulation, and may therefore be solved by the two-stage procedure previously described. Two major considerations in the use of branch and bound or implicit enumeration as a solution technique should be mentioned. First, the second stage of the solution process can no longer be solved by a simple assignment of customers to the nearest bank location and vendors to the furthest bank location; rather one must solve a linear program to find the optimal choice of these assignments. Second, the number of integer 0-1 variables is potentially greater in this model than in either of the previous ones. Because of the sensitivity of integer programs to the number of integer variables involved, the user must be cautious when defining his set of bank and regional office locations. He should be especially cautious about the number of regional office-

bank relationships he wishes to consider, since the number of integer variables is given by $I + 2K + IK$ where I is the number of regional offices and K is the number of banks. After careful consideration of reported computational experience, the authors believe that a problem containing 25 potential bank sites and three potential regional offices is within the range of available integer programming codes. (See specifically [Ciochetto, et. al., 1972], [Davis and Ray, 1969], [Ellwein, 1970], [Khumawala, 1971 and 1972] and [Spielberg, 1969].)

Post Optimal Analysis

A solution to the dual problem of the proposed unified location model can provide additional information about the sensitivity of the model to changes in some of its parameters. For instance, the shadow price associated with constraint (13) can be used to measure the cost of an increase in a required compensating balance level. In addition, the shadow prices on constraints (2) and (6) can measure the impact of a shift in creditor or customer geographic distribution. Unfortunately, the integer nature of the model precludes using simple shadow price information to measure the cost of different office and banking relationships. However, this information could be obtained as a byproduct of the branch and bound or implicit enumeration algorithm chosen as a solution procedure.

Concluding Remarks

In this paper we were concerned with the question of whether the lock-box and disbursement portions of the cash management problem could be unified in one model. The need for this unification arises from the interrelationship between the costs of these two activities. Following Calman and Pogue, we found that the key to such a unification was the explicit consideration of the total level of bank compensation. The proposed model is designed to locate bank activities as well as to determine the optimal levels of these activities.   □

APPENDIX A
Summary of the Model

Objective Function

(18) MINIMIZE $W = \rho(\Sigma_{k=1}^{K} BAL_k + \Sigma_{m=1}^{M} \Sigma_{k=1}^{K}$
$$q_{mk} \cdot Y_{mk}) + \Sigma_{k=1}^{K} FEE_k + \Sigma_{k=1}^{K} [\bar{f}_k^C \cdot Z_k^C$$
$$+ \bar{f}_k^D \cdot Z_k^C + \Sigma_{i=1}^{I} \bar{f}_{ik}^{DR} \cdot Z_{ik}^{DR}] + \Sigma_{i=1}^{I} \bar{f}_i^R \cdot Z_i^R$$

Constraints

All creditor checks must be processed:

(6) $\Sigma_{i=1}^{I} \Sigma_{k=1}^{K} X_{ijk} = a_j$ $\forall_j$

All customer deposits must be processed:

(2) $\Sigma_{k=1}^{K} Y_{mk} = b_m$ $\forall_m$

Definition of net collected balances:

(14) $NCB_k = BAL_k + \Sigma_{i=1}^{I} \Sigma_{j=1}^{J} p_{ijk} \cdot X_{ijk}$
$$- \Sigma_{m=1}^{M} r_{mk} \cdot Y_{mk}$$ $\forall_k$

Net collected balances can support either compensating balances or supporting balances:

(13) $NCB_k \geq g_k$ $\quad \Psi_k$

Definition of TCD_k:

(15) $TCD_k = \Sigma_{i=1}^I \, \Sigma_{j=1}^J \, d_{jk} \cdot X_{ijk} + \hat{f}_k^D$
$\cdot Z_k^D + \Sigma_{i=1}^I \hat{f}_{ik}^{DR} \cdot Z_{ik}^{DR}$ $\quad \Psi_k$

Definition of TCC_k:

(16) $TCC_k = \Sigma_{m=1}^M \, e_{mk} \cdot Y_{mk} + \hat{f}_k^C \cdot Z_k^C$ $\quad \Psi_k$

Bank compensation constraint:

(11) $FEE_k + c_k^T \cdot TP_k + c_k^N \cdot NCB_k \geq TCD_k$
$+ TCC_k + V_k$ $\quad \Psi_k$

Constraints for integer variables Z_k^C:

(3) $\Sigma_{m=1}^M \, Y_{mk} \leq (\Sigma_{m=1}^M \, b_m) \cdot Z_k^C$ $\quad \Psi_k$

Constraints for integer variable Z_k^D:

(7) $\Sigma_{i=1}^I \, \Sigma_{j=1}^J \, X_{ijk} \leq (\Sigma_{j=1}^J \, a_j) \cdot Z_k^D$ $\quad \Psi_k$

Constraints for integer variable Z_i^R:

(8) $\Sigma_{j=1}^J \, \Sigma_{k=1}^K \, X_{ijk} \leq (\Sigma_{j=1}^J \, a_j) \cdot Z_i^R$ $\quad \Psi_i$

Constraint for integer variable Z_{ik}^{DR}:

(9) $\Sigma_{j=1}^J \, X_{ijk} \leq (\Sigma_{j=1}^J \, a_j) \cdot Z_{ik}^{DR}$ $\quad \Psi_{i,k}$

Constraint on available tax payments:

(12) $\Sigma_{k=1}^K \, TP_k \leq TTP$

We assume the continuous variables FEE_k, X_{ijk}, Y_{mk}, NCB_k, and TP_k are non-negative and BAL_k is unrestricted in sign. The integer variables Z_k^D, Z_k^C, Z_i^R, and Z_{ik}^{DR} are all restricted to be either 0 or 1.

REFERENCES

Balas, Egon, "An Additive Algorithm for Solving Linear Programs with Zero-One Variables," Operations Research, Vol. 13, 1965, pp. 517-546.

Bent, D. H., "Branch-and-Bound for Facility Location," Inform, Vol. 10, No. 1, February, 1972, pp. 1-7.

Bulfin, R. L., and V. E. Unger, "Computational Experience with an Algorithm for the Lock Box Problem," Proceedings of the 28th ACM National Conference, Atlanta, August, 1973.

Calman, R. F., Linear Programming and Cash Management/Cash Alpha, The M.I.T. Press, Cambridge, MA, 1968.

Ciochetto, F. F., H. S. Swanson, J. R. Lee, and R. E. D. Woolsey, "The Lock Box Problem and Some Startling But True Computational Results for Large Scale Systems," presented at the 41st National Meeting of ORSA held in New Orleans on April 26-28, 1972.

Davis, P. S. and T. L. Ray, "A Branch-Bound Algorithm for the Capacitated Facilities Location Problem," Naval Research Logistics Quarterly, Vol. 16, No. 3, Sept., 1969, pp. 331-344.

Drysdale, J. K. and P. J. Sandiford, "Heuristic Warehouse Location—A Case History Using a New Method," Canadian Operational Research Society Journal, Vol. 7, No. 1, March, 1969, pp. 45-61.

Effroymson, M. A. and T. L. Ray, "A Branch-Bound Algorithm for Plant Location," Operations Research, Vol. 14, No. 3, May-June, 1966, pp. 361-368.

Ellwein, L. B., "Fixed Charge Location—Allocation Problems with Capacity and Configuration Constraints," Technical Report No. 70-2, Department of Industrial Engineering, Stanford University, August, 1970.

Ellwein, L. B. and P. Gray, "Solving Fixed Charge Location-Allocation Problems with Capacity and Configuration Constraints," AIIE Transactions, Vol. 3, No. 4, December, 1971, pp. 290-297.

Feldman, E., F. A. Lehrer, and T. L. Ray, "Warehouse Location Under Continuous Economics of Scale," Management Science, Vol. 12, No. 9, May, 1966, pp. 670-684.

Khumawala, B. M., "An Efficient Heuristic Algorithm for the Warehouse Location Problem," Krannert School of Industrial Administration Paper Series, No. 311, Purdue University, May, 1971.

Khumawala, B. M., "An Efficient Branch and Bound Algorithm for the Warehouse Location Problem," Management Science, Vol. 18, No. 12, Aug., 1972, pp. 718-31.

Kraus, A., C. Janssen, and A. McAdams, "The Lock-Box Location Problem, A Class of Fixed Charge Transportation Problems," Vol. 1, No. 3, Journal of Bank Research, Autumn, 1970, pp. 51-58.

Kuehn, A. and M. Hamburger, "A Heuristic Program for Locating Warehouses," Management Science, Vol. 9, No. 4, July, 1963, pp. 643-666.

Land, A. H. and A. G. Doig, "An Automatic Method of Solving Discrete Problems," Econometrica, Vol. 28, 1960, pp. 497-520.

Levy, F. K., "An Application of Heuristic Problem Solving to Accounts Receivable Management," Management Science, Vol. 12, No. 6, February, 1966, p. 62.

Maier, S. F. and J. H. Vander Weide, "The Lock-Box Location Problem: A Practical Reformulation," Journal of Bank Research, Vol. 5, No. 2, Summer, 1974, pp. 92-95.

Pogue, G. A., R. B. Faucett, and R. N. Bussard, "Cash Management: A Systems Approach," Industrial Management Review, Winter, 1970, pp. 55-73.

Sa, Graciano, "Branch-and-Bound and Approximate Solutions to the Capacitated Plant-Location Problem," Operations Research, Vol. 17, No. 6, Nov.-Dec., 1969, pp. 1005-1016.

Shanker, R. P. and A. A. Zoltners, "An Extension of the Lock-Box Location Problem," Journal of Bank Research, Vol. 2, No. 4, Winter, 1972, pp. 236-244.

Shanker, R. J. and A. A. Zoltners, "The Corporate Payment Problem," Journal of Bank Research, Vol. 2, No. 1, Spring, 1972, pp. 47-53.

Spielberg, K., "An Algorithm for the Simple Plant Location Problem with Some Side Conditions," Operations Research, Vol. 17, No. 1, Jan.-Feb., 1969, pp. 85-111.

Part VIII

THE TRUST PORTFOLIO

N EARLY 3,800 banks in the United States today offer substantial trust services to both individual and corporate clients. The extent of services varies. Because trust services usually involve high operating costs, the concentration of banks offering the full range of trust services is in the larger population and industrial centers where demand is sufficient to support the services. An additional reason for this concentration may be the "economies of scale" that result as volume rises. However, while some research has indicated that such economies exist, they probably diminish beyond a certain point, and several moderate size banks have been successful in establishing extensive trust services.

One of the primary functions of the trust department is to invest funds on a profitable basis. The sources of trust funds are varied; among them are pension funds, endowments, and private trusts. Pension funds constitute the most important source of investment trust funds.

Trust investment involves the successful trade-off between risk and a high rate of return. In most cases, investment instruments that offer the highest return also involve the highest levels of risk. The trust manager must determine acceptable levels of risk and then maximize return within this constraint. Investments in stock are a major emphasis of most bank trust departments, and management of stock portfolios is the focus of Part VIII.

Selection of a high return, low risk stock portfolio is not simple. Tremendous amounts of research have been devoted to explaining the movements of the stock market and individual stocks. The development of the efficient market hypothesis has intensified this debate in recent years. Understanding the movements of stocks and the market as a whole is, of course, fundamental to the task of the trust manager. W. H. Wagner and S. R. Quay examine a useful investment framework in light of recent evidence in Chapter 34, "New Concepts in Portfolio Management." Because Wagner and Quay have been personally involved in the trust portfolio selection process, their explanations are based on practical experience with selection criteria. The authors not only provide a conceptual view of recent developments in portfolio selection theory, but also interpret the implications for managing portfolios in practice.

In addition to selecting low risk, high return investments, the trust manager must evaluate the timing of transactions to maximize overall portfolio performance. The decision of long-term holding strategies versus short-term active trading strategies constantly faces the portfolio manager. Many trust managers invest a great deal of time and resources in attempting to predict major swings in the market which can be exploited through active trading. Other portfolio managers feel that transaction costs and other factors offset the value of attempting to exploit short-run shifts. Numerous attempts have been made to apply management science models to the complex tasks of formulating a trust portfolio strategy. Implementation and management acceptance of such models are often a formidable hurdle in their successful application.

The broad scope of the trust management problem is made evident in Chapter 35, "An Investment Decision Making System," by David M. Ahlers. The model described by Ahlers has been successfully implemented, and it points to the need to consider behavioral factors in the design of management science models. Ahlers incorporates the decision making process in his model for improving trust department performance. More important than the model itself, however, may be his insight into the implementation of a management science model. Ahlers provides a useful framework for evaluating the proposed investment model in practical terms.

Chapter 36, "Constructing a Model for Managing Portfolio Revisions," by Bernell K. Stone and Robert Reback, focuses on the need to continually evaluate security holdings. There is a distinct trade-off between meeting the goals of a portfolio strategy and incurring transaction costs. Stone and Reback suggest a unique approach to this trade-off. Through the application of a linear programming formulation, they provide a model for improving portfolio revisions and examine the computational feasibility of related problems. Stone and Reback also suggest the possible use of goal programming techniques if more sophistication is desired. While this technique might be superior to the LP approach, it also involves more computation, and a trade-off must be made between computational simplicity and model sophistication. This trade-off can be crucial if it involves incurring additional cost. The linear programming model appears extremely promising as a practical management model which could aid the portfolio manager.

Part VIII focuses on the various decisions facing the manager of a commercial bank trust department. The recent development of "index funds" based on the efficient capital market theory has clouded the nature of trust portfolio selection. Continuing research on market forces may reshape the future of trust management, and trust managers must be continually abreast of developments in this area. While setting portfolio selection criteria based on the most up-to-date knowledge of investment theory is of central importance, trust management efficiency can be significantly improved through analysis of such factors as transaction costs, tax considerations, and leverage analysis. The trust manager must deal with the total trust function to provide the highest levels of service at the lowest cost to the bank. The development of trust management models that include all aspects of the trust function can aid the trust manager in this complex task.

Chapter 34

NEW CONCEPTS IN PORTFOLIO MANAGEMENT*

By W. H. Wagner and S. R. Quay

*This article is reprinted, with permission, from *Journal of Bank Research,* Vol. 3, No. 2 (Summer, 1972), pp. 102-110.

The intent of this paper is to contextualize for the investor the results of recent studies of the securities markets and their implications for investment methods. These studies have led to the development of new techniques which should significantly refine the contemporary practice of portfolio management. The embodiment of these techniques emphasizes the specification of risk in determining an investment policy, the elimination of uncompensated risk, and the reduction of operating costs. This approach allows the investor to explicitly state his portfolio objectives as well as accurately evaluate the subsequent performance of the portfolio manager. To further the understanding of this new approach, an actual application of its principles is briefly described. This application—by Wells Fargo Bank—involves the management of a substantial portion of the Pension Fund of the Samsonite Corporation. The concepts contained in this paper should thus enable an investor to improve his ability to evaluate current portfolio management alternatives in light of these new concepts.

Information can move share prices. Therefore, investors and their advisors eagerly assess new information with regard to the prospects of each stock. Since a common stock represents a claim on future returns, any information that indicates a possible change in these expected returns (or the uncertainty about these returns) will cause a change in the price investors are willing to pay for a particular security. Since new information has potential value, it is not surprising that the search for it is highly competitive.

Each investor, therefore, pits his resources and knowledge against all other similarly motivated investors. However, unless an investor, or his advisor, has privileged knowledge, superior insight or unusual speed, it would seem difficult to consistently outperform all other investors. If an investor does show superior performance, others will be attracted to his methods, thereby subverting his advantage. Numerous studies of the ability

of financial managers to predict market turns,[1] the ability of security analysts to select underpriced stocks[2] and the performance of mutual funds[3] have confirmed the difficulty of attaining consistently superior performance.

Yet it is obvious that all investors do not obtain equal rates of return, particularly over short intervals. This, however, does not necessarily imply that superior performance is attained solely, or even for the most part, as a result of skill. All players of slot machines do not lose at equal rates; but as a direct consequence of the design of the machine, all players certainly have the same expected rate of return. Thus, the effects of chance should not be inadvertently misspecified as being those of skill. The securities market needs no artificial source of uncertainty; there is a whole range of economic forces which contribute to the rapid fluctuations in the assessed values of stocks. This high volatility generates well publicized success stories, but it also generates obliviscent failures. Although the financial manager in the midst of receiving accolades for last year's brilliant performance may be distinctly unimpressed by the argument that his success was due more to luck than skill, investors should be aware that there is little factual evidence that successful past performances are of much value in predicting future superiority.[4]

The search for new information continues. It is both extensive and expensive. However, an increasing amount of empirical evidence [Fama, 1970] has not only shown that information is nonsystematic in its frequency, direction and magnitude, but also that the corresponding effects of this information upon a stock's price are nonsystematic. This, in essence, is what the frequently

---

[1] Consistency of mutual fund managers to outperform market returns was studied in [Treynor and Mazuy, 1966, pp. 131-136]. Consistency of ability to outperform the market was studied by [O'Brien, 1970, pp. 91-103].

[2] Brokerage recommendations were studied by [Malkiel and Cragg, 1970, pp. 601-617]. Also, see [Ramsey and Behrens, 1969].

[3] See [Friend, Blume and Crockett, 1970]. A paper which concentrates on evaluating performance in efficient markets is [Jensen, 1968, pp. 389-416].

[4] This topic is covered in a highly readable article by [Black, 1971].

misunderstood "Random Walk" concept has asserted by stating that successive observations of stock returns are not systematically related[5] and that stock prices reflect the random pattern of the arrival of information. Obviously, the idea that new information has potential value remains unaltered. However, the mounting evidence of the validity of Random Walk provides less and less rationale for the continuance of expensive research.

Market Efficiency

The Random Walk evidence of market efficiency as well as other, more apparent, characteristics, such as large numbers of buyers and sellers, easy access and small transaction costs have led economic theoreticians to investigate the matter of efficiency in the market place. The studies they have conducted have examined the behavior of models of perfect markets. These results have then been compared to the behavior of actual markets. In general, the conclusions they have derived have verified many commonly held premises concerning economics and finance.[6] Even though the "Theory of Efficient Markets"[7] (as it will be termed for the purposes of this paper) is still in its adolescence, practical applications have already been developed for the financial community. These applications have resolved, at least partially, some heretofore puzzling and hotly debated issues.

For example, the issue concerning the speed at which new information becomes imbedded in the market price of securities is an undeniably important one. In a market which is perfectly efficient, the dissemination of information is instantaneous, but much of the research and analysis currently done would seem to imply that this information may take weeks, or even months, to become fully reflected in the prices of securities. However, the evidence that supports the Random Walk suggests that information is taken into account quite rapidly—in fact, much quicker than most investors are able to act. Thus, the Theory of Efficient Markets and the essential validity of the Random Walk attest to the existing efficiency of the financial community as it successfully evaluates, communicates and acts on information affecting stock prices.

The question remains whether the same results could be achieved at less cost. To what extent does "research" and "analysis" consist of rehashing information already reflected in the price of the stock, and thus does not lead to returns which offset the cost of that research and/or analysis? As Henry C. Wallich states:

> "Once the best available judgment has put prices where they belong, there is no social benefit in duplicating the work. Furthermore, since enough investors will be analyzing securities in their own self-interest, it is hard to see why the marginal investor, and therefore any investor, should pay for securities analysis. Correct pricing of securities, like television and radio, is a public good available free to all even though it costs money to produce. Anybody can get the benefit of the combined best judgment by simply accepting the prices set by the markets." [Wallich, 1970]

Undoubtedly, directors and employees of firms, as well as suppliers and customers, are exposed to special information, but it appears to be rare, small, fleeting and difficult to detect. As the Random Walk evidence shows, this information is imbedded in market prices in a matter of days, or even hours. Whether enough potential information remains to require the services of an army of security analysts is very much open to doubt.

In conclusion, investors and their advisors operate in a competitive market where available information is rapidly discounted, and where consistently superior performance is difficult to achieve. To ignore this is to attribute to skill that which can be explained by luck, and thus to pursue a futile search for skill. It seems clear that the market would be just as efficient, and investors would do no worse, individually or on the average, with considerably less emphasis on "picking winners" than one currently finds.

Risk and the Rate of Return

The cartoon of a man selecting his portfolio by throwing darts at the exchange listing in the *Wall Street Journal* contains much of the essence of the Theory of Efficient Markets. However, it ignores a source of true differentiability between stocks which can lead investors to make more rational choices in their portfolio composition. This key factor is the counterplay of uncertain outcomes and expected rewards. Investors assuredly prefer less uncertainty about future wealth than more uncertainty. If this were not true, stocks would

[5] The doctoral dissertation by Fama at the University of Chicago is the most comprehensive work available on the Random Walk Hypothesis. See [Fama, 1965, pp. 34-105].
[6] It should be noted that the assumptions used in the models need only capture the essence of price formation in actual markets; assumptions of perfect market efficiency are not required. Even when differences have occurred between models of efficient and actual markets, these differences are generally inconsequential since they do not cause substantial departures from the behavior predicted by the economists' efficient market assumptions.
[7] The most comprehensive and rigorous statement of the theory to date is provided by [Fama, 1965].

not yield greater returns over the long run than such fixed obligations as bonds.

The fact that a common stock cannot be separated from its inherent uncertainty causes investors to place their funds at some risk whenever they purchase any common stock. Since all investors are averse, at least to some degree, to this risk, they apparently insist upon compensation for bearing this unwanted, but unavoidable, quantity. The compensation for accepting the possibility of greater fluctuations in the value of their assets takes the form of higher expected returns and, as such, is similar to the behavior of a loan company which charges higher interest rates to those clients with lower credit ratings.

Studies [Friend, et al., 1970] of mutual funds have shown that over the long run higher risk "growth" funds have outperformed lower risk "balanced" funds, but that investors in the higher risk funds have paid the penalty of having greater fluctuation in the value of their assets. Of course there are, and will continue to be, times when the high risk funds decline rapidly, and investors who are forced to ' cash in during these times can expect to incur a loss. However, in the long term, the average investor in high risk funds will outperform more conservative investors due to the systematic acceptance of higher risk.

Obviously, the quantification of present risk would be advantageous. The Theory of Efficient Markets suggests that the volatility of an individual security can be calculated to reflect the responsiveness of that security to changes in a market index. Thus, a high risk stock would be one that was highly responsive to the market; changes in the price of the stock would be larger than the corresponding changes in the market index. A low risk stock, on the other hand, would exhibit proportionally smaller changes than the market index.[8]

Detractors of the Theory of Efficient Markets often challenge the use of the volatility measure, commonly called beta, as a predictor of uncertainty. They argue that an investor's probability of incurring a loss from an investment cannot be quantified. Furthermore, they state that measures from past periods are meaningless since no risk exists after the fact. Either the hazards occurred or they did not, and as a consequence, the investor was left either richer or poorer. Strangely enough, and ironically, they are joined in this

[8] An excellent introduction to efficient markets is [Brealey, 1969]. Chapter 6 discusses the effect of market influence on prices.

[9] Strangely, because many of these critics were the same ones who initially resisted the Random Walk concept when it was first introduced, and ironically, because just as the essential validity of Random Walk is finally achieving grudging acceptance, the evidence of beta's usefulness is steadily increasing.

argument by the Random Walk idea that past prices have no predictive value.[9]

Proponents of the Theory of Efficient Markets, however, do not assert that future uncertainty can be measured with the precision of a micrometer. Instead, they simply state that useful estimates of risk can be gauged from measures of past volatility. Thus, even though these measures contain considerable error for individual securities, the portfolio manager can use these estimates when constructing portfolios because the individual errors tend to cancel one another. Moreover, measures of portfolio volatility have been shown to be reasonably stable over time. Therefore, past measures of portfolio volatility can be used to estimate future levels of volatility.

Risk and the Effects of Diversification

By combining individual securities into a diversified portfolio, investors can effectively reduce the risk of their portfolio. This effect was well illustrated in a study done by Professors James Lorie and Lawrence Fisher [Lorie and Fisher, 1970]. This study showed that the volatility of a diversified, 32 stock portfolio was one third less than that of the average single stock portfolio. Since diversification is not only a common practice, but also easy, even trivial, to obtain, investors should not compensate for those risks which can easily be eliminated through diversification. Thus, an investor who holds an undiversified portfolio may be viewed as behaving in an injudicious manner, and other investors should not be expected to compensate him for the additional risk he willingly incurs by his indiscretion.

However, risk in common stocks can never be completely removed by diversification. Certain events affect large numbers of securities; some events affect all. Because of these causal events, the fluctuations in return on any one issue are to some extent related to the fluctuations of all other issues. Thus, through the simple device of holding diversified portfolios, risk can be reduced, although never eliminated entirely. Moreover, while one cannot accurately estimate future rates of return based on the volatility measures, one can be confident that, over the long run, future rates of return will be proportional to the level of volatility assumed; in other words, more volatile portfolios will generate higher long term rates of return.

Implications for Portfolio Managers

The implications of the Theory of Efficient Markets about various investment management activities should cause investment managers and their clients to reassess the relative emphasis and importance of these activities. In light of the evidence already at hand, a reassessment would strongly suggest a de-emphasis in activities relating to the selection of particular stocks and a subsequent increase in the relative importance attached to managing the portfolio as a whole in relation to the client's needs. This stresses the identification and satisfaction of the client's desires rather than the purchase and sale of particular securities. Furthermore, it supports an increased emphasis on manager/client interaction by segregating those items that are under the portfolio manager's control from those that are not. The client's goals may then be more accurately specified, and the portfolio manager may subsequently be evaluated with respect to those factors over which he has some active control.

Previous attempts of managers and clients to discuss objectives in terms of desired rates of return have often been understandably vague because the portfolio manager simply cannot control the rate of return on a portfolio whose assets are not risk-free. The level of risk, however, can be effectively controlled by the portfolio manager, and the Theory of Efficient Markets provides the means of measuring this risk. Therefore, it is no longer necessary to discuss the desired risk level in such well intentioned, but vacuous expressions as "conservative" or "businessman's risk." Uncertainty can now be meaningfully estimated in terms of the volatility of rates of return over time, and the objectives of clients can be constructed in terms of these measurements.

Furthermore, utilizing these risk measures, the manager can construct a portfolio to achieve any specified risk exposure. By diversifying, he can minimize those risks which carry no compensating return. With total risk and diversification under control, the manager can then predict the long run return on the portfolio relative to the return on the market. Changes in risk level (timing) and concentration in particular issues (selectivity) are practiced only as supplements to this basic portfolio efficiency control.

By being able to measure the degree of uncertainty present in the investor's current portfolio, the manager is able to discuss its acceptability to the investor. Moreover, the portfolio manager can construct examples which illustrate the effects of choosing different risk levels and thereby assist the client in matching possible wealth levels against expected expenditure patterns. Of course, the final decision of acceptable risk level remains the choice of the client and not his alter-ego in the person of the manager.

Henceforth, the portfolio manager is evaluated on his ability to deliver the return commensurate with the specified risk objectives. The contributions of any attempted timing and selectivity strategies, as well as their costs, can be evaluated in contrast to the efficient portfolio standard. The manager's performance can also be judged on the basis of his avoidance of uncompensated risk, his compliance with other constraints imposed by the client and the minimization of expenses incurred in managing the portfolio. All of these can be quantified and then viewed objectively.

It should be pointed out that the client should not evaluate the portfolio manager on the basis of investment return over short time horizons, since this is likely to lead to erroneous decisions based on insufficient information. It takes time for the systematic effects in stock prices to compound to the point where they are greater than the effects of random variation. To evaluate a manager before the systematic effects are established is to judge him on a confluence of random occurrences, i.e. luck. Five to seven years appears to be a reasonable horizon over which to judge investment performance.

Further Application

In their study of mutual funds [Friend, et al., 1970], Prof. Irwin Friend and his associates at the Wharton School of Economics suggested that a new fund could be constructed that offered investors both high diversification and controlled risk at a low cost. Such a fund would be in the spirit of the Theory of Efficient Markets and would be expected to generate average returns equal to those available from conventional management at the same risk, but at significantly lower cost.

The portfolio of this fund would consist of small positions in 100 to 500 securities, carefully selected to meet the risk objectives of the investors. The high diversification would maximize the systematic return for bearing risk, while insulating the portfolio from the possibility that large changes in the value of any one stock would unbalance the control of this risk.

Positions in particular issues would be altered only to maintain risk levels and diversification. Thus, turnover would be quite low. When a transaction is required, the portfolio manager would retain considerable freedom to select alternative securities of similar characteristics. He could, for example, trade only those securities which netted the maximum tax advantage to the client. Furthermore, he could take advantage of the availability of securities through markets other than the organized exchanges. He would minimize supply and demand problems by not attempting to buy or sell large amounts of a particular security at a particular time [Cuneo and Wagner, 1972].

Figure 1. Samsonite Corp. Weekly Performance Monitor.

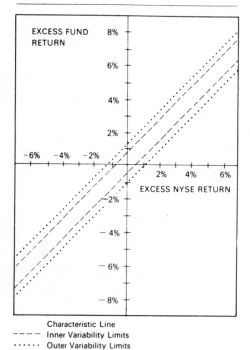

- —— Characteristic Line
- – – – Inner Variability Limits
- · · · · · Outer Variability Limits
- —— 1.00 Beta

Transaction costs,[10] therefore, could be substantially reduced. This reduction of transaction costs and the low turnover rate would thus enhance the portfolio return.

Controlled risk exposure, efficient diversification and low transaction costs would compete effectively with conventionally managed portfolios in terms of net rate of return to the clients. Thus, the contribution of the Theory of Efficient Markets can be summarized as the deletion of those investment management activities that do not yield compensating return in favor of increased emphasis on activities that can be shown to be valuable. Many activities which appeared necessary or profitable before the Theory of Efficient Markets are now found to be unjustifiable, in the sense that the cost of providing those services

[10] Round trip transaction costs as high as 10% were estimated by [Ellis, 1971].

probably exceeds the benefit. Improved services extended at a lower net cost yield a tangible benefit to investors.

Current Application

Wells Fargo Bank has developed applications of the efficient market concepts for a variety of actual investment situations. One of the most interesting of these applications involves the management of a substantial portion of the pension fund of Samsonite Corp. In a letter of agreement, the investment objectives of this fund are stated as follows:

> The Samsonite funds are to be managed to the best of Wells Fargo Bank's ability to the following quantitative specifications:
>
> | | |
> |---|---|
> | Total Relative Risk | 1.0 |
> | Portfolio Beta | .98 |
> | Control Limits on Portfolio Beta | ± .08 |
> | Minimum Correlation Coefficient | .95 |
> | Maximum Annual Turnover Rate | 15% |

The investment strategy implemented to meet these criteria keeps the Samsonite pension funds fully invested in a widely diversified portfolio of securities (currently 115) listed on the New York Stock Exchange. The purchase candidate list is screened to remove any securities which are regarded as obvious problems. The remaining issues are then assigned an industry classification, and this categorization is used as an additional control of diversification. In an effort to reduce trading costs, the investment strategy also encompasses the willingness to accept for purchase any one of a number of roughly similar securities. Thus, the constituent issues are selected on the basis of the attractiveness of their price as well as their contribution to the specifications of the portfolio. Furthermore, since market timing and security selection are not emphasized in this strategy, operation costs are greatly reduced.

The client is provided with periodic performance reports which permit him to assess the achieved performance against the prespecified objectives and to evaluate those objectives in light of actuarial requirements. Since the essential goal of the portfolio is to replicate the market, the expected return on the portfolio should essentially equal that of the market. Of course, some variation will occur in the actual results, but if this variation is within statistical limits, called confidence bands, then the performance of the portfolio can be said to be achieving its desired objectives. In this regard, see the graph of the performance of the portfolio with respect to the market since it became fully invested on September 1, 1971.

This display does not provide proof, of course, of the viability of the investment strategy used to manage these funds. Thus far, the graph does indicate that it is possible to successfully manage a portfolio according to pre-specified risk objectives, but this limited evidence cannot, as yet, demonstrate the attainment of the expected commensurate systematic returns. As stated earlier, a period of five to seven years appears necessary before a proper assessment of the investment performance can be made. However, the performance reports presented to the Samsonite Corp. so far substantiate the application of these new concepts in portfolio management.

Future Implications

The implications of Efficient Market Theory are clear. As summarized by Prof. James Lorie [Lorie, 1971], "the most important nonroutine function of . . . investment counselors is choosing an investment policy for each account and specifying that policy so precisely that portfolio managers can be controlled and evaluated. Because of the efficiency of markets, the overwhelmingly most important influence on the returns of portfolios is their riskiness. Investment policy should, therefore, be expressed in terms of risk."

Services are now being offered which embody these principles. These services represent a significant advance of positive value to investors. Nonetheless, the Theory of Efficient Markets is still growing vigorously. The full implications of efficient markets may likely antiquate the ideas expressed here. To the investor aware of new developments, continuing improvements in portfolio management methods will be forthcoming. ∎

REFERENCES

Black, Fischer, "Implications of the Random Walk Hypothesis for Portfolio Management," *Financial Analysts Journal*, March-April 1971.

Brealey, Richard A., *An Introduction to Risk and Return in Common Stocks*, Cambridge: MIT Press, 1969.

Cuneo, Larry J. and Wayne H. Wagner, "Reducing the Cost of Stock Trading," *Proceedings of SASP*, May 1972.

Ellis, Charles O., "Portfolio Operations," *Financial Analysts Journal*, September-October 1971.

Fama, E. F., "The Behavior of Stock Market Prices," *Journal of Business*, January 1965.

Fama, E. F., "Efficient Capital Markets: A Review of Theory and Empirical Work," *Journal of Finance*, May 1970.

Friend, Irwin, Marshall Blume and Jean Crockett, *Mutual Funds and Other Institutional Investors: A New Perspective*, New York: McGraw-Hill, 1970.

Jensen, Michael C., "The Performance of Mutual Funds in the Period 1945-64," *Journal of Finance*, May 1968.

Lorie, James H., "Four Cornerstones of a New Investment Policy," *Institutional Investor*, November 1971.

Lorie, James H. and Lawrence Fisher, "Some Studies of Variability of Returns on Investments in Common Stocks," *Journal of Business*, April 1970.

Malkiel, Burton G. and John G. Cragg, "Expectations and the Structure of Share Prices," *American Economic Review*, September 1970.

O'Brien, John W., "How Market Theory Can Help Investors Set Goals, Select Investment Managers and Appraise Investment Performance," *Financial Analysts Journal*, July-August 1970.

Ramsey, Carl M. and Charles Behrens, "Analyzing the Performance of Security Analysis," presented at the Seminar for Analysis of Security Prices, Chicago, November 1969.

Treynor, Jack L. and Kay K. Mazuy, "Can Mutual Funds Outguess the Market?", *Harvard Business Review*, July-August 1966.

Wallich, Henry C., "What Does the Random Walk Hypothesis Mean to Security Analysts?", *Financial Analysts Journal*, May 1970.

Chapter 35

AN INVESTMENT
DECISION MAKING SYSTEM*

By David M. Ahlers

*This article is reprinted, with permission, from *Interfaces: Practice of Management Science,* Vol. 5, No. 2, Pt. 2 (February, 1975), pp. 72-90.

ABSTRACT. This paper describes the design, implementation and evaluation of a system for the management of pension funds by a large institutional investor. As a direct result of this management science based system, which had been in operation for over three years prior to this study, the jobs of security analysts, portfolio managers and the management of the investment function were significantly changed. The institution publicly acknowledged the success of this system in its annual reports and internally acknowledged the additional business revenues generated by this new approach to money management.

   Three major aspects of this research which spanned a period of over six years are discussed. Initially the behavioral science analysis which helped to determine why classic portfolio selection or equity valuation models had not been accepted by the organization is reviewed. This phase also contains an analysis of the necessary changes to information flows and job responsibilities before the organization could reasonably be expected to accept any normative portfolio management tools.

   The focus is then directed toward the key management science concepts incorporated in the Management Information System which was designed to remove the behavioral barriers to change. The major tools and concepts employed and presented in this phase are the use of the triangular distributions to collect conditional, subjective forecasts and to provide subjective distribution feedback, loss functions which are based on the impact of outcomes to the institution and not on squared error variability and the construction of feedback measures which are consistent with the organizational responsibilities of the individual.

   The third phase of this study is an evaluation of whether investment performance was actually improved by the new system. Testing this and related hypotheses is complicated by the fact that it was difficult enough to convince management to install one new money management system, let alone several systems simultaneously to permit controlled tests. Some aspects of this are discussed in the final section.

Introduction

   The ultimate focus of this research is on organizational change. Leavitt [5] pictured the major components of organizational change as consisting of the structure, task, technology (tools) and people (actors) with each   one interrelated to the other three.

   Thus, tests of alternative organization structures cannot be conducted properly without explicit consideration of the remaining three components. An estimation of the economic value of portfolio management algorithms, for example, without consideration of institutional practices, the incentives for the portfolio manager to use this new tool or his ability to use it would be incomplete. It is in this context that the organizational alternatives examined in this research will be evaluated.

The Pension Fund Management Environment
Size and Concentration

Pension trusts were the most rapidly growing segment of fiduciary assets from 1963 to 1971. During this time, pension funds managed by banks increased from approximately 43 to 110.6 billion dollars, an annual compound growth rate of 12.5%. The management of these funds is highly concentrated. In 1970, over 75% of pension fund assets were managed by only 22 banks. The concentration is even more acute when one considers that the top two banks manage about 25% of the total. Also, approximately 90% of all pension funds over 50 million are managed by banks. In terms of this study, the three firms which permitted the author to review their pension management processes in depth represented 20% of the total market in 1970.

In addition to size as a measure of market impact, in 1971 institutions accounted for over 62% of all shares traded on the NYSE and turned their portfolios over 50% more frequently than the average for the market as a whole.

In these institutions the most active accounts have consistently been pension funds.

The result of the size, concentration and activity level characteristics of pension funds is that the future value of pension benefits for millions of people are strongly affected by the decisions made by a relatively small number of corporate treasurers. The focus of the study presented here is on pension funds managed by banks.

Investment Policy

Whatever return goals may be set for a pension fund, the decisions made by portfolio managers are tightly constrained by the "Prudent Man Principle." Farnum, [4] who at the time was in charge of the largest pension fund management department in the United States, stated the Prudent Man Principle as:

> "The time tested standard is that a trustee is required to employ such diligence and such prudence in the care and management of trust property as in general prudent men of discretion and intelligence employ in their own affairs. A bank trustee may in some important respects be held to an even higher degree of care since it holds itself out to be an expert and because it is better equipped than the ordinary man."

In his section on Investments, he made additional comments on prudent investments and outlined some of the risks in not investing prudently.

> "Pension and profit sharing trusts make no distinction between principle and income. . . . .
> State laws protect the trust beneficiary. For instance, in New York State, section 100-b of the banking law provides that all investments by a bank shall be at its sole risk, and the capital stock, property and effects of the bank shall be liable for losses, unless the investments are proper and permitted in the trust instrument."

The notion that the bank is directly liable for all breaches in prudent policy has been institutionalized for all members of the Federal Reserve system.

Member banks are expected to have capital, in addition to all other capital requirements, sufficient to cover claims under the prudent man principle up to 200% of gross trust department earnings.

The recent trend indicates that safety may have become the prime consideration of portfolio managers, because of the growing number of law suites which seek to hold portfolio managers responsible for losses on individual stocks regardless of overall portfolio performance. This, ccoupled with the prudent man principle, is at least one of the reasons pension fund managers have made little use of mean-variance portfolio tools in that they may lead to investment decisions which could result in successful malfeasance suits against the managers or their organizations.

Functional Organization

Figure 1 is a behavioral flow chart of one of the two major forms of pension fund management used by institutions in this study. Diamonds are intended to point out areas which are more decision making than processing oriented. Rectangles illustrate the latter. Dashed lines indicate feedback flows. Each of the four basic components of the decision-making process is stated at the bottom of the figure. The process depicted, however, is tactical and excludes any strategic planning activities. Figure 1 is also an historic document in terms of this research. It is a copy of a slide made in 1968 for an executive meeting with the head of a major trust department. The issues raised by an analysis of this slide subsequently lead to fundamental changes in the functional organization of this department and, as a by-product, generated the date for this research. Although some steps in Figure 1 were unique at the time to one institution, most were found in all the institutions examined. The common functional steps in the pension fund management processes are outlined below.

P/E and Earnings per Share Forecasting

Future prices were most commonly forecasted by combining separately estimated price earnings ratios and earnings figures.

$$(1) \quad \hat{P}_t = (\widehat{P/E})_t \hat{E}_t,$$

where $\quad t \quad$ = forecast horizon, usually between 6 and 18 months,

$\hat{P}_t \quad$ = estimated price in t periods,

$(\widehat{P/E})_t$ = estimated P/E in t periods[2],

$\hat{E}_t \quad$ = estimated earnings per share in t periods.

This two-component, one stock at a time method of forecasting is shown in the analysis portion of Figure 1. The IR Policy diamond indicates that a policy committee comprised of the management of the Investment Research Department was responsible for supplying the *P/E* estimate.

At this point, it is important to bear in mind that regardless of the economic or statistical merits of (1), the unanimity of this approach among pension fund managers makes it a significant factor in the market and in the analysis of pension management systems.

FIGURE 1

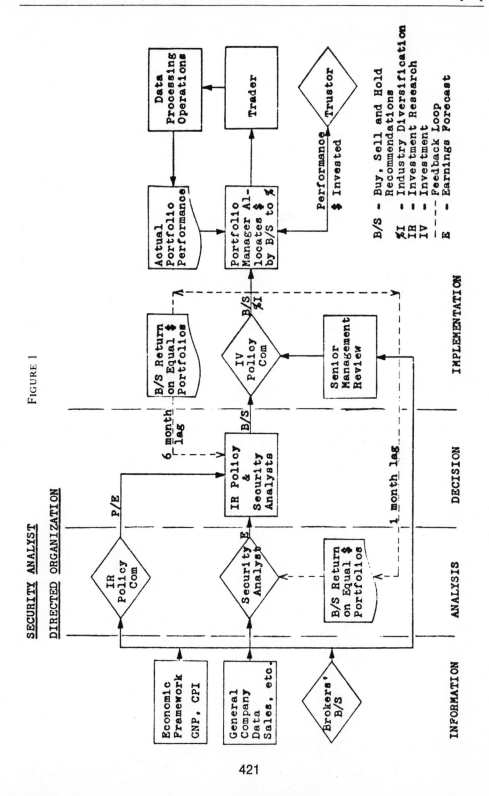

Qualitative Recommendations

Using $\hat{P}_t$ from (1) future returns were estimated by

$$(2) \quad \hat{R}_t = \left(\frac{\hat{P}_t - P_0}{tP_0}\right) n + \hat{d}_t,$$

where $\hat{R}_t$ = estimated annual return over next t periods,
    P_0 = current price,

   n = number of periods per year, e.g., if t were in terms of months, $n = 12$,
   $\hat{d}_t$ = estimated annual dividend return, usually just the current annual dividend divided by P.

Then depending on the magnitude of $\hat{R}_t$ and its algebraic sign combined with an assessment of the reliability of $\hat{P}_t$, a qualitative Buy, Sell or Hold decision was made. This was usually done by a committee which met once or twice a week to consider a formal agenda of five to ten stocks with others treated on a much more cursory basis as necessary.

Industry Diversification & Management Review

All institutions in this study sought to achieve diversification by setting policies which would limit the maximum percentage of a fund which could be invested in the same industry. Similar diversification is legally required for Common Trust Funds, e.g., funds in which multiple pension funds might hold shares or units, by the controller of the Currency. Diversification limits were set by the Investment Policy Committee represented by **IV POLICY** in Figure 1.

The Investment Policy Committee also fulfills a regulatory requirement by reviewing all qualitative recommendations and either accepting or changing them. The Board of Directors then reviews investment policy committee actions and also makes allocation of capital to cover potential losses. This is consistent with Federal Reserve regulatory policies.

Portfolio Allocation

Pension fund managers in large institutions may be responsible for fifty or more accounts. Many managers argue that to be fair to all accounts, good buys should be prorated over each of them. Consequently, after buys and sells have been selected, managers frequently find, given industry constraints, that the actual portfolio management task has become an arithmetic allocation problem. Indeed, many institutions employ clerical support personnel to do this job. The portfolio manager, therefore, is represented by a rectangle in Figure 1 in keeping with the convention of using this form to indicate essentially processing operations.

---

[2]This estimate was frequently made conditional upon the forecasted P/E for one of the market indexes, for example the DOW. In this event, (1) becomes

$$(3) \quad \hat{P}_t = (\widehat{P/E}|\widehat{P/E_x})_t \hat{E}_t$$

Analysts refer to this as a market relative.

Performance Reports

There was a wide range of performance reports in the institutions covered. However, all had at least some form of equal dollar analysis. In this type of feedback report, the percent returns, ignoring transaction costs, management fees and operating expenses, are averaged for each qualitative grouping. The return computed is equivalent to having invested an equal dollar amount in each security in each group. The numbers on the dashed lines give the number of months between when a recommendation was made and when an analysis of the actual performance was received. The portfolio performance reports received by the portfolio manager and the trustor had a number of different statistics such as capital appreciation, income yield, etc., but all included the Bank Administration Institute (BAI) time weighed return or an approximation, for example the Financial Executives Measure. In addition to these measures, performance reports prepared by A. G. Becker contained variants of the Sharpe, Treynor and Jensen risk-adjusted performance measures. There is, of course, much more to the functional pension fund management process than this brief overview contains. Not presented, for example, is the structure of meetings in which security analysts attempted to sell their ideas to critical portfolio managers and policy committees. Allocation of commission dollars to obtain recommendations from brokers is shown in Figure 1, but not treated in detail. Figure 1 does, nevertheless, provide sufficient functional structure to address the central management problems and alternatives.

Behavioral Analysis

The framework proposed by Leavitt shows organization structure as one component of organizational change, but it does not elaborate on the way organization structure facilities organizational change. Cyert and March [3] have tackled this problem and used a basic feedback-control system approach to deal with it. They have summarized the primary components and interrelationships of their descriptive theory of organization change in the form of a flow chart which can be used to judge whether or not the pension fund management process is conductive to change. Their structure also generates a ready check-off list for an analysis of a functional organization chart:

1. Are all feedback loops closed? This requirement is a variant of the concept that managers should have the authority to make decisions for which they are held responsible.
2. Does the organization have adaptive or learning capabilities? In order for this to be possible:
   a) Goals must be measurable,
   b) Feedback must be in goal and decision dimensions and be received in time to effect subsequent decisions.
3. Is the system dynamically stable? That is, are there procedures to dampen shocks to the system? In Cyert and March's framework, negotiation with the environment to reduce uncertainty and thereby the potential for shocks along with search for new decision rules supply dampening forces.

As the first step in a behavioral analysis this check-off list is applied to Figure 1.

Beginning with item 1, closed feedback loops, we can find several which are not closed. Open loops, for example, existed for Senior Management, the Investment Policy Committee, Economics Department, Traders, Brokers and the Trustor himself. In all these centers of decision making authority, measurable feedback on performance impact is missing. Thus, any search for new decision making rules, in spite of pressures to do so, would appear to be unlikely.

These areas might have, however, implicitly perceived their goals to be other than performance related. Senior management, for example, might have informally established its goals in terms of participation. Negative external feedback would have then very possible resulted in an increase in the frequency and length of senior management reviews but would not have changed the functional decision processes. The point to be made is that even though the pension fund management process shown in Figure 1 might have had closed feedback loops for Senior Management, etc., these loops would not have been performance oriented and changes made by the organization in response to negative feedback through such loops would have resulted in improved performance only by chance.

With respect to check-list item 2, it is clear that the organization described in Figure 1 would have great difficulty in adapting to new circumstances. Goals, for example, were frequently expressed in non-measurable terms. This can be seen by referring back to Farnum's prudent man principle which sets a qualitative guideline.

On the other hand, in several institutions goals were expressed in terms such as "X percent more than the DOW." While this is certainly measurable and in the right direction to support an adaptive organization approach, the pure return dimensions of this goal fail to take into account several organizational factors. Decisions were made by portfolio managers in terms of buy and sell recommendations, not in terms of expected return relative to the DOW. Thus the match up of feedback and goal dimensions required by item 2b was not met. Goals were not the only problem. The security ananysit's job in Figure 1 was to forecast earnings and yet his feedback and evaluation were in terms of equal dollar performance reports. Similarly, both the Investment Research and Investment Policy Committees were in a similar position to effect decisions and yet avoid substantive evaluation.

The portfolio manager, on the other hand, received unambiguous, if not risk-adjusted, performance results on a quarterly schedule. As Figure 1 illustrates, the trustor also received these results and used them to allocate funds among different institutions. It was and still is common for large funds to have six or more trustees. If the results were inadequate the portfolio manager could have legitimately blamed the process generating the buy-sell decisions, since his influence on the portfolio composition had been minimal. For these reasons, Figure 1 has been labeled a "Security Analyst Directed Organization."

Item 3 on the check list deals with stability of the system. Until the advent of external performance measurement pressures the pension fund management process was extremely stable and immune to change. The organizational problems raised in the analysis of check-list items 1 and 2 all point to the great difficulty the process would have had in generating internal forces for change. In addition, the uncertainty avoidance involved in arriving at a single best guess earnings estimate to summarize a complex corporate analysis is consistent with similar stabilizing behavior observed by Cyert and March in many other corporations.

The formal organizations structures, reasonable on the surface in grouping similar activities, reinforced the behavioral inertia to change. Informal feedback among security analysts, portfolio managers and traders was discouraged by having them in different departments reporting to different managers and frequently in different physical locations as well.

Contrasted against these internal structures which made change difficult, developments in performance measurement took a form which made change inevitable. The thrust on the part of the performance measures was not to negotiate away uncertainty, but to make it explicit and measurable. Goals in measurable form if not initiated by pension fund managers, were supplied to them by their customers. In short, during the late 1960's the pension fund industry was caught between strong external pressures for change and an internal structure unable to 'change. It should now be clear that growth in itself was not the problem, but only one of the factors which combined to disclose the real organization problems.

Off-The-Shelf Management Science

The fourth component of Leavitt's organizational change is technology or tools. By 1968, a substantial body of management science literature had developed on mathematical approaches to stock price forecasting and portfolio management. Could these tools have been used to breach some of the organizational barriers to change? Although a comprehensive review of this research is beyond the scope of this study, the two following examples should provide an answer to this question.

Portfolio Selection

Markowitz's 1952 landmark paper [6] needs no introduction. It was designed to select securities which would maximize portfolio return over the next period subject to a given level of risk measured by the expected variance of this return. Markowitz recognized that the variance of return for a common stock portfolio would be less than a sum of the individual variances unless all the stocks in the portfolio were perfectly correlated, a virtually impossible case. Thus, his algorithm provided a mathematically rigorous method to combine quantitative estimates of future returns and covariances between these returns to determine just the right diversification mix for each optimal risk return combination. During 1970, the author made an informal survey of seven large institutions which accounted for over 50% of all pension funds. Not one was using the Markowitz algorithm or Sharpe's Beta model simplification to manage pension funds nor were they aware of any institutions which were. Why was this important new tool not used by pension fund managers? The answer to this question can be found in Figure 1.

FIGURE 2

RISK VS VARIANCE: PAYOFFS TO THE MANAGER

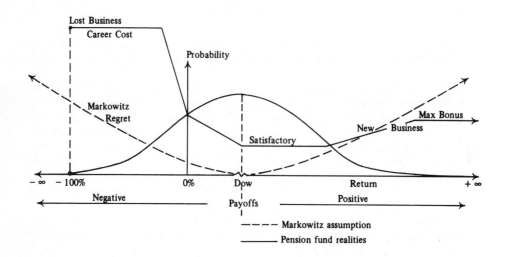

FIGURE 3

RISK VS VARIANCE: LOCATION

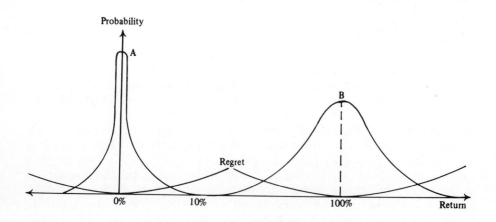

Qualitative Inputs

To the portfolio manager, the use of Markowitz algorithm presented many problems. In Figure 1 the manager's input data was expressed in qualitative buy-sell terms. The Markowitz algorithm, however, requires quantitative estimates of returns and covariances. Hence, in this organization form the necessary data to derive the algorithm is absent. In addition, there is a great difference between the risks faced by pension fund managers and the form of risks assumed by Markowitz.

Markowitz's definition of risk is pictured in Figure 2. "Regret" by the investor in Markowitz's framework is assumed to be zero if the actual return should happen to be R and grows quadratically as actual return differs in direction from R. Risk is computed via the calculus by summing all values of Regret between + and - infinity times the probability of each value. Markowitz was aware that investors do not usually regret doing better than average. He was quick to point out the normal probability curve he had assumed for expected returns was symmetric. Thus, the risk above R would equal the risk below R. The disadvantage of using risk can be seen by referring to Figure 3. Even though it is almost certain, assuming normal probability distributions, that portfolio B will have a higher return than A, Markowitz's risk measure would classify B as much riskier than A. This anomaly was noted by Baumol in 1963 [2], and prompted him to consider a minimum return criteria to incorporate risk. The point to be made here, however, is that if a pension fund manager had a forecast of say 10% return for the Market, A, not B as indicated by Markowitz, would be perceived as the risky portfolio. This conflict with the pension fund manager's operating definition of risk would make acceptance of portfolios generated by Markowitz's algorithm highly unlikely. Finally, Markowitz's use of variance to measure investment risk in general should be examined in the specific context of fiduciary investment.

First of all, the assumption of normality and therefore symmetrically distributed returns can not be valid since losses on securities purchased by pension funds are limited to the purchase price of these securities, e.g., —100% and not —∞%. Thus, variance computed as though returns were normally distributed would tend to overstate downside risk.

Secondly, the assumption of a quadratic regret function centered about expected return does not describe accurately the actual regret and reward functions facing the pension fund manager. There is, from a personal point of view, great reluctance on the part of a pension fund manager to take risks which might result in below market or, in particular, negative returns. On the other hand, it is hard to establish how far above the market a portfolio manager must attain consistently to attract significant new business. Thus, the portfolio manager has tangible evidence on the costs to him of assuming too much downside risk and limited information on the benefits associated with higher opportunity risks. Figure 2 highlights this conflict, even when the location problem shown in Figure 3 is not a factor, between Markowitz's assumptions and the realities of pension fund management.

In addition, there are further problems with Markowitz algorithm. These have to do with single period solution and beta variability, to men-

FIGURE 4

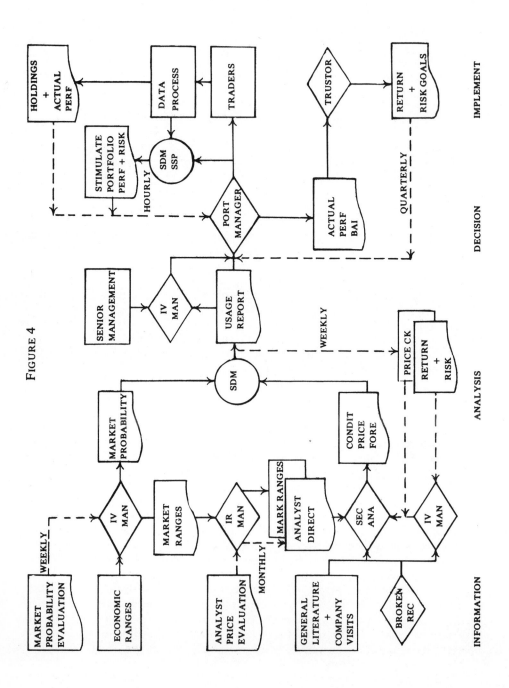

tion a few. These go a long way to explain why this algorithm hasn't been used by pension fund management.

Security Evaluation Models

The second major area of research has been in the development of stock price forecasting models[3]. Even though some of the models were constructed within money management firms and demonstrated competitive performance when compared to security analysts, their actual use was very limited. None appear to have been in use for the last three years and the author has not been able to find any pension management firms which actively use such models in stock selection.

It is difficult to explain the failure of this new tool on the basis that it does not correspond to the problem perceived by the security analyst or portfolio manager. There is, however, at least one plausible explanation. The absence of effective feedback loops in Figure 1 as discussed earlier, prevents management from making a substantive comparison of model vs. analyst forecasts as well as the analyst vs. himself or other analysts. Given the strong safety first philosophy necessary under Prudent Man regulations, it would be an unwise management decision to accept the recommendations of a computer model over those of an experienced analyst unless justified by rigorous statistical tests over a number of market cycles. The reason for this negative judgment can be tracted to a basic conflict between assumptions underlying these tools and pension fund management realities plus an inherent organizational barrier to new technology due to the absence of structured and effective feedback systems. In the next section, the steps which were taken at one major institution to structure its pension fund decision making procedures are described. As a result of this effort, the institution was able to construct effective feedback loops and to generate the data necessary to evaluate the likely benefits of alternative approaches to pension fund management.

Structured Decision Making

Structured Decision Making or SDM was a project initiated by the author to remove the organizational barriers to change.

The SDM system concept is a critical bridge between pension management systems of the past and those of the future. Its structure provides tools to breach the barriers of organizational change and its operation over a period of years provided the data to examine the benefits and costs of alternative approaches to pension fund management.

Figure 4 illustrates the SDM system. Comparison with Figure 1 will show that SDM was an evolutionary step. All external information inputs were the same and the management system was still composed of the same organization groups. In fact, the formal organization chart remained unaltered after SDM was installed. Important changes were made, however, to the functional or internal decision making structure. These changes in terms of new tools, reports and responsibilities are discussed in the following sections.

---

[3]A full reference to the literature in this field can be found in the author's Ph.D. thesis [1].

FIGURE 5

CONFIDENTIAL DATE

FORECASTED PRICES

COMPANY NAME	CURRENT PRICE	LOW MARKET LOW	LOW MARKET MOST LIKELY	LOW MARKET HIGH	MIDDLE MARKET LOW	MIDDLE MARKET MOST LIKELY	MIDDLE MARKET HIGH	HIGH MARKET LOW	HIGH MARKET MOST LIKELY	HIGH MARKET HIGH	DIV
AEROSPACE											
BOEING ¼	25.	12.	15.	17.	16.	20.	25.	18.	20.	30.	0.40
GEN DYNAMICS	29.	15.	20.	25.	18.	25.	30.	20.	30.	35.	0.0
GRUMMAN	20.	11.	14.	16.	13.	17.	18.	15.	19.	25.	1.00

FIGURE 6

CONFIDENTIAL DATE

RETURN FORECASTS

COMPANY NAME	MARKET 1: LOW EXP % RETRUN	MARKET 1: LOW 50–50 RANGE	MARKET 1: LOW MKT LOSS PROB	MARKET 2: MIDDLE EXP % RETURN	MARKET 2: MIDDLE 50–50 RANGE	MARKET 2: MIDDLE MKT LOSS PROB	MARKET 3: HIGH EXP % RETURN	MARKET 3: HIGH 50–50 RANGE	MARKET 3: HIGH MKT LOSS PROB	OVERALL RANGE
AEROSPACE										
BOEING	− 39	− 42 − 36	100	− 16	− 21 − 11	100	− 6	− 15 1	100	− 50 24
GEN DYNAMICS	− 30	− 36 − 25	100	− 15	− 22 − 9	100	− 1	− 9 7	100	− 48 22
GRUMMAN	− 25	− 29 − 21	100	− 13	− 17 − 9	100	5	− 2 13	99	− 39 33
MARTIN MARIETTA	− 2	− 9 4	39	11	5 18	57	32	23 41	50	− 26 53
MC DONNELL DOUGLAS	− 21	− 25 − 18	99	− 6	− 12 1	96	26	14 38	67	− 34 69
NORTH AMER ROCKWELL	− 33	− 36 − 30	100	− 7	− 12 − 2	100	5	− 3 14	99	− 44 33
UNITED AIRCRAFT	− 16	− 26 − 7	78	22	14 32	27	41	31 52	30	− 39 74

Information

There are three new reports in this phase of the system. Two of these are feedback reports, as indicated by the dashed lines, and will be reviewed later after the reports for which they provide feedback are introduced. This exposition difficulty is actually a good sign, since it is indicative of the closed loop nature of the new system.

The third new input is entitled "Economic Ranges" and is an expanded version of the "Economic Framework" in Figure 1. Its purpose is to enable the economists who support the pension management effort to elaborate in written form on the full range of possible economic environments over the next year. This is in contrast to the verbal best guess scenario they had provided under the old system. Economic alternatives are defined in terms such as GNP, Industrial Production, Consumer Prices, etc. and are assigned probabilities.

Analysis

Investment Management, the Investment Policy Committee in Figure 1 translates the Economic Range inputs into three mutually exclusive environments for the equity markets characterized by ranges and associated probabilities for the Dow Jones Industrial Index.

The Investment Research Policy Committee in Figure 1 discusses with the security analysts the implications of each market range and the corresponding economic conditions for their industries and companies. The Analyst Direction report is based on a statistical analysis of past forecasting errors made by each analyst for every company he follows.

The security analyst, having researched each of his companies and having received the market and feedback information from his management, is now in a position to make his forecasts. The form of these forecasts, however, is very different from the qualitative recommendations he used to make and is the key to the SDM system. The analyst forecasts conditional on each market range a low, most likely and high price for each of his companies twelve months in the future. He also forecasts the average dividend he expects to prevail over the next twelve months. These forecasts are updated on a weekly basis and provide the data for the Conditional Price report. A copy of a page from this report is shown in Figure 5. The initial reports from the SDM system are feedback reports to the analysts and management. Figure 6 is the Return and Risk feedback report corresponding to the conditional price forecasts in Figure 5. Prior to discussing this report, it is important to clarify the assumptions behind it. The low, most likely and high estimates are assumed to define a triangular probability distribution. The distribution defined by the estimates for Boeing in Figure 5 are given in Figure 7. It is appparent that unlike the normal distribution assumed by Markowitz, the triangular distribution need not be symmetric nor need it extend to plus and minus infinity. This flexibility, for example, permitted the Boeing analyst to reflect his increasing optimism as the market scenario improved without letting his best guess or most likely estimates go above $20. It is useful at this point to note that the expected value of this distribution can be found by simply averaging the three parameters. The expected percent return can be computed by adding the expected dividend to the expected price then sub-

FIGURE 7

CONDITIONAL PRICE FORECASTS FOR BOEING AIRCRAFT

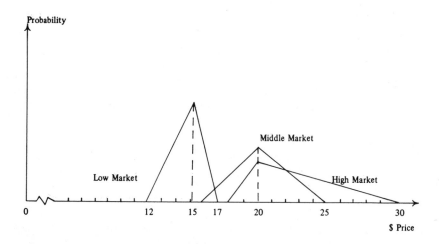

FIGURE 8

CONDITIONAL RETURN FORECASTS

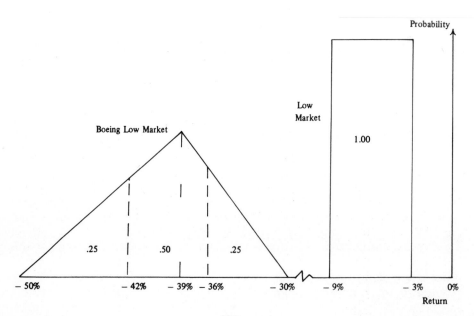

tracting and dividing by the current price. This is called the EXP% RETURN in the report shown in Figure 6 and is calculated for each market. The 50-50 RANGE of -42% to -36% states that, given the triangular distribution formed from the analysts' estimates for the low market, there is a 25% chance returns will be below -42%, a 25% chance it will be above -36% and a 50% chance it will fall in between. The assumption of the triangular distribution enables one to calculate the minimum and maximum to be -50% and -30% respectively. A further simplifying assumption is made in SDM of the independence within a market environment between market and stock returns. Thus, if the market turned out to be at its lowest possible anticipated return this would provide no information on what value between -50% and -30% Boeing might have returned. However, this assumption is not needed to compute the probability that Boeing returns will be below market returns. From Figure 8 this probability is clearly 100% for the low market. Again, this result is also given in Figure 6 for Boeing. The purpose of the expected return, 50-50 range and market loss probabilities is to generate feedback to the analyst on the implications of his forecasts and to supply this information in dimensions different from his original low, most likely and high estimates. The feedback approach in SDM is designed to minimize any compatibility biases.

If, for example, the -39% seemed "too low" or if the analyst felt he needed better odds than 50-50 to bet that return would, given a low market, fall between -42% and -36%, he might revise his original price estimates upward and spread them out a little more as well. This revision process would continue until the analyst was satisfied with both his price estimates and their implications, SDM, in this way, facilitates a repeated convergent and unbiased sampling of the analysts' subjective beliefs concerning future price performance conditional on a particular market environment. The Price Check Report is an analysis of the overlap in price ranges between adjacent markets. If the Boeing analyst had forecasted a high of $15.00 for the low market, then according to the probability assumptions, it would have been impossible for Boeing to sell for $15.50. This feedback report identifies such unlikely gaps. While the analysts are translating their research into conditional price estimates, the management of the Investment Department translates its valuation of the macro economic situations into probabilities for the three mutually exclusive market environments.

When the analysts' feedback cycle is complete, the SDM system produces the Usage Report. This report is shown in Figure 9. This report combines the expected returns in each market with the market probabilities at the top of the report into an overall expected return. The overall expected return for Boeing is computed by

$$.2 (-39\%) + .7(-16\%) + .1 (-6\%) = -19\%$$

This report also introduces the concept of expected gain or loss.

The Loss line, which measures how far each possible return is below the market return, when multiplied times the probability of each possible return gives a more representative measure - the expected loss. Both Boeing and General Dynamics, for example, have in Figure 6 a 100% chance of falling

FIGURE 9

STOCK INVESTMENT REPORT (USAGE REPORT)

MKT WEIGHTS = 20% 70% 10%

	COMPANY NAME	----OVER ALL MKTS---- EXP % RET	EXP LOSS	CUR PRICE	------- EXP % RET------- MKT 1	MKT 2	MKT 3
361	MAYTAG	− 9	21.2	43	− 17	− 8	0
362	HERCULES	− 9	21.2	56	− 23	− 8	11
363	AMP	− 9	21.2	75	− 19	− 8	4
364	JOY MFG	− 10	21.6	71	− 20	− 8	0
388	BOEING	− 19	31.4	25	− 39	− 16	− 6
385	GEN DYNAMICS	− 17	28.9	29	− 30	− 15	− 1
377	GRUMMAN	−14	25.8	20	− 25	− 13	· 5

		-------------------- RELATIVE TO MARKET--------------					
		--------EXP LOSS--------- MKT 1	MKT 2	MKT 3	--------EXP GAIN-------- MKT 1	MKT 2	MKT 3
361	MAYTAG	12	22	33	0	0	0
362	HERCULES	17	22	22	0	0	0
363	AMP	14	22	29	0	0	0
364	JOY MFG	14	22	33	0	0	0
388	BOEING	33	30	39	0	0	0
385	GEN DYNAMICS	25	29	35	0	0	0
377	GRUMMAN	20	27	28	0	0	0

below the market. Boeing, however, is generally lower in all markets. This is reflected in the overall expected loss figures of 31.4% for Boeing vs. 28.9% for General Dynamics. The concept of expected gain is the mirror image of expected loss and represents the opportunity to outperform the market. Senior and Investment Management play a similar review and responsibility role, but they now have access to the assumptions and forecasts of the security analysts prior to any effort to classify stocks as buy, sell or hold.

Decision

In SDM the working document for the portfolio manager is the Usage Report. He is now responsible, given the needs of each Trustor, for determining which stocks should be bought and sold. The Usage Report supplies him with his downside risk in expected loss terms if he buys or holds a security and with his opportunity risk if he sells or fails to buy. It also provides him with the overall or unconditional expected return to weigh against his relative values for loss and gain risk. Although the Usage Report can be very valuable to a portfolio manager on one stock at a time basis, and, therefore, an aid in following the Prudent Man philosophy, it could easily mislead him when considering the portfolio as a whole. If A and B are two securities with the same triangular distribution and are not correlated then a portfolio composed of ½A and ½B will have the same expected return but lower expected gain and loss than either A or B singly.

In short, while the return for a portfolio is equal to a weighted average of the component stock returns, a similar weighted average of the risks for each security would overstate the risks for the portfolio. The SDM system tackles

434

this problem by including an on-line computer terminal facility which permits the portfolio manager to evaluate the effect on expected portfolio return, loss and gain due to changes in portfolio composition. In Figure 4 this part of the system is shown by SSP which represents Simulated Stock Performance.

Information — Feedback Reports

SDM had been in operation for approximately two years before the internal performance evaluation reports shown in the Information component were introduced. The initial year was simply the delay between making the forecasts and their realization. The second year was used to begin developing statistics on forecasting performance.

The function of the Market Probability Evaluation Report is to give Investment Management feedback on their ability to pick markets by assigning probabilities to market ranges. If, for example, given the management forecasts at the top of Figure 9 the middle market did occur twelve months later, the management score according to SDM would be 78% based on maximum likelihood approach out of 100% maximum. On the other hand, if the high market had occurred, their score would havev been only 13%. The central feature of the Analyst Price Evaluation Report is that the analyst is only evaluated in the market which actually occurred. His conditional expected return for the market range is compared with the actual return and statistics which give the sign and magnitude as well as the likely variation in the analyst forecasting errors as generated by SDM.

SDM And Organizational Change

Did the SDM effort remove any organizational barriers to change? Since the organization adopted the SDM approach and thereby made fundamental changes in its management style the answer must be, "Yes". In fact, the Trust Department conducted a national advertising campaign featuring the SDM concepts and the institution included a copy of this advertisement in its 1972 annual report. On a more fundamental level, and in the context of the Cyert and March framework, the primary barriers to organizational change removed by SDM are outlined below.

Closed Feedback Loops

Security analysts are held responsible and evaluated on their price forecasting ability in the market which occurs. They are not responsible for predicting market levels nor are they able to make implicit risk return tradeoffs in determining buys and sells. Portfolio managers receive forecasts and risk measures which permit them to tailor risk-run tradeoffs to specific Trustor needs. Management determines the degree to which the institution will bet on any market level and is accordingly evaluated in their ability to make this judgment.

Organizational Learning Capabilities

Organizational learning is greatly enhanced by having measurable return goals and risk constraints and by matching the dimensions in which decisions are made with the feedback on these decisions. Organizational learning also took place in a more liberal sense. Security analysts and portfolio managers learned about concepts in statistics and decision theory and had the oppor-tunity to use them daily.

Organizational Stability

As the incidence of uncertainty absorption is reduced and as feedback loops are closed the organization will become more dynamic and, therefore, less stable. No longer does the institution have to offer one investment image to facilitate internal control. As the price evaluation evidence builds up, analysts are unlikely to retain a consistent under or over estimation bias, but will alter their forecasts appropriately.

Evaluation of SDM Performance

During the installation of the SDM system the management of the Trust Department of the Bank, my staff and even our customers had faith that better ways of making decisions would necessarily generate better investment results. More sophistocated tools or expanded information flows need not necessarily improve the quality of decisions. However, it is evident in the context of Leavitt's components of organizational change, that SDM did in fact effect change. It is also important to note that Leavitt's framework does not consider whether or not the performance of the organization was im-proved by this change. The basic research approach of this evaluation study was to simulate alternative systems using the forecasts, structured in terms of both quantitative detail and controlled subjective sampling, gathered in SDM. If we accept that once forecasts are supplied by the analysts and goals of the trustor are established the remaining task facing the portfolio manager can be reduced to a mathematical problem, then a mathematical model could be used to simulate this facet or portfolio management. The appropriateness of the model would not depend on whether it produced optimal results, but on whether its results were at least as good as those which would have been produced by a portfolio manager working with the same data. If the model is constructed in a manner which does not incur the problems encountered by the off-the-shelf portfolio models, then this model could also be used to draw inferences about the performance of systems in which pension fund managers employed the model as a decision-making aid. In addition to these simulation requirements, the model must be general enough to represent all the alternative systems under examination if controlled, statistical evaluations are to be made. An algorithm was constructed (See [1] for full details) and used to simulate various management system configurations over the data collected through the SDM system. The simulation was conducted from Jan-uary 1970 to November 1971 since both the stock market and the economy went through reasonably complete cycles during this period.

Again, the scope of this paper does not permit a complete review of all the findings. However, the results relevant to the management issues raised else-where in this paper are summarized below.

1. Does market efficiency dominate any potential benefits from a port-folio management system beyond risk-return balancing?

The answer, contrary to the opinions held by many economists, appears to be "No". When randomly selected portfolios were compared against those selected from the same universe by an SDM type system, there was less than a 1 in 5,000 chance that SDM portfolios were not in fact outperforming the random portfolios.

2. Do portfolios constructed according to classic portfolio theory significantly outperform risk-adjusted single stock selection systems?

> Contrary to traditional financial theory, the answer is again, "No". There was a 78% chance, given the simulation results, that the hypothesis above was indeed false. Apparently, the assumptions and stability of parameters required by modern portfolio theory are not met and the robustness of more simplistic, one stock at a time systems still provides a superior management approach.

3. How much performance, if any, does an institution give up by using qualitative vs. quantitative systems?

> According to the analysis, institutions which are using buy-sell-hold recommendations are giving up a significant amount of return by not going to SDM type systems.

4. Do numerical feedback systems to security analysts and managers necessarily improve portfolio performance?

> Feedback correction to analysts' forecasts beyond the informal feedback obtained from managers and peers does not improve performance. In addition, the instability in the correction estimates can significantly degrade performance.

In addition to points 2 and 4, many other results turned out to be contrary to current theories of normative investment behavior. This would strongly suggest that it is necessary to test the value of new management science tools in their organizational context before labeling any successful implementation as an overall success for the corporation.

Conclusion

The portion of the research study presented in this paper strongly supports the need to do a behavioral analysis of a decision process prior to attempting any changes through the introduction of management science concepts or tools. It also supports the notion that much of the benefit derived from a management science approach is obtained from the early structuring phases of the analysis and not from the introduction later of sophisticated models. And finally, the simulation results emphasis the difference between the implementation of management science systems and the ultimate value of these systems to the corporation.

BIBLIOGRAPHY

1. D. H. Ahlers, *An Evaluation of Alternative Investment Decision-Making Systems,* unpublished Ph.D. Thesis, Carnegie-Mellon University, 1974.
2. W. J. Baumol, "An Expected Gain Confidence Limit Criterion for Portfolio Selection," *Management Science,* Vol. 10, No. 1 (Oct. 1963), pp. 174-182.
3. R. M. Cyert and J. G. March, *A Behavioral Theory of the Firm,* Prentice-Hall, Englewood Cliffs, 1963.
4. C. W. Farnum, "Corporate Fiduciaries of Employee Benefit Funds — An Outline of Responsibilities and Supervision," *Old Age Income Assurance, Part V,* Joint Economic Committee, Congress of the United States, U. S. Government Printing Office, Washington, D. C., 1968, pp. 257-263.
5. H. J. Leavitt, "Applied Organization Change In Industry: Structural, Technical, and Human Approaches," Chap. 4 in Cooper, W. W., et all (eds.), *New Perspectives In Organization Research,* Wiley, New York, 1964.
6. H. Markowitz, "Portfolio Selection," *Journal of Finance,* (March 1952), pp. 77-91.

Chapter 36

CONSTRUCTING A MODEL FOR MANAGING PORTFOLIO REVISIONS*

By Bernell K. Stone and Robert Reback

*This article is reprinted, with permission, from *Journal of Bank Research,* Vol. 6, No. 1 (Spring, 1975), pp. 48-60.

This paper formulates the task of revising an existing portfolio in the presence of transaction costs as a linear program (LP). The LP formulation is developed for both single- and multi-period revisions. Linear goal programming techniques are incorporated within the models to provide a vehicle for attaining an appropriate trade-off between portfolio goals and the transaction costs associated with goal attainment. Finally the paper shows that the solutions obtained from the linear programs are highly congruent with maximization of expected utility. Moreover, the solutions are also very close to those obtained from the usual quadratic programs but are computationally far simpler so that they provide a much more viable basis for implementing computer-assisted portfolio management systems.

PROBLEM BACKGROUND

Markowitz [1952] formulated the portfolio selection problem as a parametric quadratic programming problem. During the past two decades, both the academic and investment communities have expended considerable effort to convert the basic Markowitz model into an operational portfolio management system. Three major areas of effort have been: First, conversion of portfolio selection models into portfolio revision models; second, the use of index models of security return to simplify both the informational and computational requirements of the basic Markowitz model; and third, the development of approximation techniques to reduce the quadratic programming problem to a linear programming problem.

Transaction Costs and Portfolio Revision

Transaction costs are all costs incurred in executing security transactions, including the direct trading costs of brokerage commissions, transfer taxes and large block trading costs.[1] The income

tax consequences of trading can also be regarded as transaction costs; however we shall restrict our treatment of transaction costs to direct trading costs incurred at the time of the transaction.

Portfolio selection involves choosing a collection of securities from the universe of candidate securities. Portfolio revision involves selling some current holdings and purchasing new securities. The decision variables in portfolio selection are the amount of each security held. The decision variables in portfolio revision are the amounts sold and purchased.

If there were no transaction costs, solving the portfolio selection problem would be equivalent to solving the portfolio revision problem since portfolio revision could be regarded as altering the current portfolio to obtain the selected portfolio. Transaction costs necessitate consideration of current holdings. A trade is justified only if the risk-adjusted expected gain from trading exceeds the associated transaction costs. In the presence of transaction costs, solutions to the portfolio selection problem are generally poor proxies for the portfolio revision problem since they typ lly involve many trades that are only marginally b r than current holdings.

A single-stage portfolio revision model is one that considers current expectations, current holdings and transaction costs and obtains a schedule of purchases and sales. The new portfolio is then held without further change until the next revision point when the model is presumably used again to generate a new schedule of purchases and sales. A multi-stage portfolio revision model is one that develops a series of planned portfolio revisions rather than a single revision at a point in time. A multi-stage model allows the portfolio manager to develop intertemporal trading plans that use information about the expected time path of future security prices and the expected cash flows into or out of the portfolio while also including the effect of trading costs associated with the intertemporal plan. Even though only the current revision is implemented in a multi-stage model, the consideration of planned future revisions and their associated transaction costs reduces the danger of implement-

[1]Pogue [1970b, pp. 19-20] identifies the major transaction types as ordinary auction market sales, exchange distributions, specialist block purchases, special offerings and secondary distributions.

ing revisions that are attractive on a short-term basis but suboptimal because they necessitate extensive trading at the next revision point. We comment further on the relative importance of single and multi-stage models in the final section.

As Pogue [1970b, p. 19ff] cogently argues, the development of operational portfolio management models requires explicit treatment of transaction costs. Pogue [1967, 1970a,b] has developed portfolio revision models in a quadratic programming (QP) framework. In [1970a], Pogue formulates a single-stage model that takes account of margin requirements and short sales as well as transaction costs. In [1970b], he presents a multi-stage model for treating intertemporal strategies.[2]

Because of the dependence of Pogue's models on quadratic programming, the computational effort required to find the best revised portfolio is substantial, especially for an intertemporal model. For instance, Pogue [1970b, p. 33] reports 10 minutes of IBM 360-65 time for a ten period example with only a 30 stock universe. Since computation and computer memory requirements both grow explosively with the number of securities considered in a QP model, computational limitations severely restrict the number of securities that can be realistically considered for investment. While the LP models developed in subsequent sections are in the spirit of Pogue's treatment of transaction costs, the LP formulations greatly simplify the computational task while providing essentially comparable solutions.

Index Models of Security Returns

An index model relates return on a security to return on an investment in the securities comprising an index. Such models have been formulated by Sharpe [1963] and Cohen and Pogue [1967]. The Sharpe model relates security return to return on a market index; Cohen and Pogue extend the basic model to include an industry index.

In the basic market-index model, return on a security is given by[3]

$$(1) \qquad \tilde{R}_j = \alpha_j + \beta_j \tilde{R}_M + \tilde{\varepsilon}_j$$

where $\tilde{R}_j$ and $\tilde{R}_M$ are respectively the return on security j and the return on an investment in a representative market-index, where α_j and β_j are constants characteristic of security j and where $\tilde{\varepsilon}_j$ is the fluctuation of the company-specific component of return about its expected value. The β_j measures the sensitivity of a security's return to return on the market index. It is variously called market responsiveness, volatility and simply "beta."[4]

The benefits of an index model are reduced informational and computational requirements. For a universe of N securities, the number of data items required to specify portfolio variance is reduced from $N(N-1)/2$ to $2N + 1$. For $N=400$, (roughly the size of a typical approved list for a trust department), this difference is 79,800 data items versus 801 data items. (See Sharpe [1970, pp. 117-118] for further details.) In addition to the informational simplification, the use of the index model of (1) reduces the quadratic program of the Markowitz formulation to a special class of quadratic programming problem called a "diagonal quadratic" that is computationally much simpler than the general model.[5]

LP Portfolio Selection Models

In considering the limited extent to which the QP based models have led to operational portfolio management systems, Sharpe [1971, p. 1264] observed that: "If the essence of the portfolio analysis problem could be adequately captured in a form suitable for linear programming methods, the prospects for practical application would be greatly enhanced."

Sharpe [1967] observes that for a well-diversified portfolio, the portfolio standard deviation σ_p is approximately $\beta_p \sigma_M$ where β_p is portfolio volatility and σ_M is standard deviation of return on the market index. Let λ be the rate at which expected portfolio return must be increased per unit of standard deviation. Then the risk-adjusted expected portfolio return, $\bar{R}_p - \lambda \sigma_p$, can be approximated by $\bar{R}_p - \theta \beta_p$ where $\theta \equiv \lambda \sigma_M$ is the rate at which expected return must be increased per unit of volatility. Let X_i denote the relative investment in

---

[2]The problem of multi-period portfolio selection has been approached by Tobin [1958], Mossin [1968] and Crane [1971]. Tobin and Mossin extended the basic Markowitz framework for security selection, while Crane developed a stochastic programming model for bond portfolio management. However, these multi-period portfolio selection approaches do not consider transactions costs. The incorporation of transaction costs into the multi-period problem was first considered by Smith [1967]. However, as Chen, Jen and Zionts [1971] noted, Smith's procedure of making pair-wise switches with securities to approach a "target portfolio" does not either guarantee optimality nor consider future portfolio changes. Chen, Jen and Zionts proposed a multi-period dynamic programming model that directly considers transfer costs. However, as the authors point out, their formulation has the disadvantage of computational enormity. Bradley and Crane [1972,1973] explicitly treat transaction costs in a multi-period model for bond portfolio management by use of a decomposition algorithm; however, their model seems to be limited to bonds and not applicable to stock portfolios. Thus, Pogue's work seems to be the most relevant existing model for treating transaction costs in both a single- and multi-period framework. Therefore, in considering alternatives to our model, we shall primarily restrict ourselves to a comparison with Pogue's model.

[3]There is an extensive literature on index models and tests of their validity. For surveys, see for instance Sharpe [1970, Chs. 7 and 8] and Jensen [1973]. For a description of their use in portfolio management, see Wagner and Quay [1972].
[4]There are numerous services that provide estimates of beta including Merrill Lynch, Oliphant, Butcher and Sherrerd, and Value Line.
[5]See Sharpe [1963] for details.

security i. Then risk-adjusted expected return can be expressed as a linear function of the X_i's, i.e.

$$(2) \quad \bar{R}_p - \theta \beta_p = \sum_{i=1}^{N} X_i \bar{R}_i - \theta \sum_{i=1}^{N} X_i \beta_i$$

$$= \sum_{i=1}^{N} X_i(\bar{R}_i - \theta \beta_i) = \sum_{i=1}^{N} X_i CE_i$$

where the certainty equivalent for security i has been defined as $CE_i = \bar{R}_i - \theta \beta_i$. Thus, the approximation of σ_p by $\beta_p \sigma_M$ has resulted in the replacement of the quadratic objective function by a linear one.

Stone [1973] extends Sharpe's certainty-equivalent formulation by adding to Sharpe's expression for the certainty equivalent an approximation for each security's contribution to independent variance so that the certainty equivalent becomes

$$(3) \quad CE_i = R_i - \theta \beta_i - \theta' F_i \sigma_i^2$$

where θ' is the rate of substitution of expected return for the independent component of variance, F_i is the upper limit on investment in security i, and σ_i^2 is the variance of $\tilde{\varepsilon}_i$, the independent component of return. The actual contribution of security i to independent portfolio variance is $X_i^2 \sigma_i^2$, while the linear estimate is $X_i F_i \sigma_i^2$. However, if $X_i = 0$ or $X_i = F_i$, there is no error in the linear approximation.

The success of this simple linear approximation is due to the fact that both the LP and QP models tend to select most securities at the level of either zero or the upper bound.[6][7]

Stone [1973] also shows how skewness can be included in an LP portfolio selection model by first formulating the cubic program required to treat skewness exactly and then showing that, within the framework of an index model, one can develop a certainty equivalent generalization of (3) that treats market skewness exactly and approximates the less important independent component of skewness quite accurately.

The key attribute of all of these LP models is that the portfolio certainty equivalent is representable as a linear average of certainty equivalents for the individual securities, i.e. $CE = \sum_{i=1}^{N} X_i CE_i$.

[6]Experimentation with QP models has shown that without upper bound constraints, the solutions tend to concentrate holdings in a very limited number of securities. When diversification is forced by adding upper bound constraints, then the QP solutions have most securities at the level of O and F_i with only a few securities held at intermediate levels. For further discussion on this point, see Cohen and Hammer [1966, p. 298].

[7]With this approximation, the difference between the linear and mean-variance certainty equivalents shifts from about $(1/n)\%$ to $(1/n^2)\%$. In addition, a piece-wise linear rather than simple linear approximation allows one to approximate the quadratic solution with any selected degree of accuracy. See Stone [1973] for details.

However, while the models based on certainty equivalents for individual securities are computationally simple linear programs that exploit the informational simplicity of index models, their use in operational portfolio management systems requires their conversion from portfolio selection models into portfolio revision models in a fashion analogous to Pogue's conversion of the QP model of portfolio selection into a QP model of portfolio revision.

The next three sections of this paper carry out the development of some LP models for portfolio revision. For expositional simplicity, we first formulate a basic model for a single-stage revision, then introduce goal programming techniques, and finally extend this formulation to a multi-stage model.

THE BASIC MODEL—
A SINGLE-STAGE REVISION

Let Q_i° and Q_i be the dollar amount of security i in the portfolio before and after revision respectively. Let P_i and S_i be respectively the dollar amounts of security i purchased and sold in revising the portfolio. These variables are related by

$$(4) \quad Q_i = Q_i^\circ + P_i - S_i.$$

Let $V^\circ = \sum_{i=1}^{N} Q_i^\circ$ and $V = \sum_{i=1}^{N} Q_i$ denote the current market value of the portfolio before and after revision. The market values before and after revision differ by the total transaction costs incurred in revising the portfolio, i.e.,

$$(5) \quad V^\circ = V + TTC$$

where TTC denotes the total transaction costs. The total transaction costs are related to the decision variables P_i and S_i by the formula

$$(6) \quad TTC = \sum_{i=1}^{N} P_i \cdot CP_i + \sum_{i=1}^{N} S_i \cdot CS_i$$

where CP_i and CS_i are the transaction cost per dollar in purchasing and selling securities, respectively.

The reduction in current market value from transaction costs is justified only if the risk-adjusted return on the new portfolio exceeds the risk-adjusted expected return on the current portfolio by an amount sufficient to justify the foregone transaction costs. Let CE° and CE be risk-adjusted expected return on the original and revised portfolio, respectively. Then, the risk-adjusted expected future value of the current and revised portfolio are given by $V^\circ(1 + CE^\circ)$ and $V(1 + CE)$ respectively. The improvement in the revised portfolio justifies the foregone transaction costs only if $V(1+CE)$ is greater than $V^\circ(1+CE^\circ)$, i.e., only if

(7) $\quad V(1+CE) - V^\circ(1+CE^\circ) > 0.$

In revising the portfolio, the objective is not simply to find a set of acceptable trades that satisfy Condition (7), but to find that particular set of trades that gives the largest value of $V(1+CE)$. Thus, the objective function is to maximize OBJ given by[8]

(8) $\quad OBJ = V(1+CE) - V^\circ(1+CE^\circ).$

In order to express the objective function in terms of our decision variables, we rewrite it as

(9) $\quad OBJ = V \cdot CE - V^\circ \cdot CE^\circ + V - V^\circ$
$\qquad\qquad = V \cdot CE - V^\circ \cdot CE^\circ - TTC.$

The quantities $V \cdot CE$ and $V^\circ \cdot CE^\circ$ are given by

$\sum_{i=1}^{N} Q_i CE_i$ and $\sum_{i=1}^{N} Q_i^\circ CE_i$, respectively.

Therefore,

(10) $\quad V \cdot CE - V^\circ \cdot CE^\circ = \sum_{i=1}^{N} (Q_i - Q_i^\circ)CE$

$\qquad\qquad\qquad\qquad = \sum_{i=1}^{N} (P_i - S_i)CE_i.$

Thus the objective function can be written as

(11) $\quad OBJ = \sum_{i=1}^{N} (P_i - S_i)CE_i - \sum_{i=1}^{N} P_i \cdot CP_i$

$\qquad\qquad\qquad - \sum_{i=1}^{N} S_i \cdot CS_i.$

Constraint Formulation

There are four major classes of constraints: 1) Nonnegativity, 2) cash conservation, 3) prohibition of short sales and 4) diversification. We now specify these constraints in terms of the decision variables. *Nonnegativity.* The nonnegativity constraints simply require that decision variables P_i and S_i not be negative, i.e.,

(C1) $\quad P_i \geq 0; S_i \geq 0 \qquad\qquad i = 1,...,N.$

Cash conservation. The cash conservation constraint requires that the dollar purchases equal the dollar sales less funds required for transaction costs, i.e.

(12) $\quad \sum_{i=1}^{N} P_i = \sum_{i=1}^{N} S_i - TTC.$

[8]This objective function is equivalent to maximizing $V(1 + CE)$ since the term $V^\circ(1 + CE^\circ)$ is a constant characteristic of the current portfolio.

Substitution for TTC from (6) and grouping terms with common values of P_i and S_i gives

(C2) $\quad \sum_{i=1}^{N} P_i(1 + CP_i) - \sum_{i=1}^{N} S_i(1 - CS_i) = 0.$

Implicit in the formulation of (C2) is the assumption that all transaction costs involve immediate cash outflows from the portfolio. Other components, such as tax payments, must be handled as future cash outflows.

There is another complexity associated with transaction costs. In both the objective function and constraint (C2), the transaction costs per dollar have been treated as constants. In fact, both brokerage and block trading costs depend on the size of the trade. While this dependence on trade size destroys the exact linearity of the model, the use of a linear programming framework can be retained by using a piece-wise linear approximation to the actual transaction costs.[9]

Short-Sale Prohibition. The prohibition on short-sales says that the net dollar position in security i cannot be negative, i.e., $Q_i^\circ + P_i - S_i \geq 0$. Rewriting this gives

(C3) $\quad S_i - P_i \leq Q_i^\circ \qquad\qquad i = 1,...,N.$

Because of the presence of transaction costs in the objective function, the model will never make both purchases and sales of the same security. When P_i equals 0, (C3) becomes $S_i \leq Q_i^\circ$, which says that total cannot exceed initial holdings. Thus (C3) precludes short sales.

Diversification. The key to the certainty-equivalent portfolio selection models is forcing diversification by limiting the fraction that can be invested in any one security to some prespecified amount F_i.

Expressing the dollar holdings of security i as a fraction of the initial portfolio value means that the diversification requirement is $Q_i/V^\circ \leq F_i$.[10] Multiplying through by V°, replacing Q_i by $Q_i^\circ + P_i - S_i$, and rewriting gives

(C4) $\quad P_i - S_i \leq F_i V^\circ - Q_i^\circ \qquad\qquad i = 1,...,N.$

As written, (C4) automatically ensures rebalancing of the portfolio by forcing the sale of security i whenever its proportion of the current value revision exceeds F_i. However, the rebalancing decision can be placed under control of the portfolio manager by allowing him to replace the prespecified

[9]See Pogue [1970a,b] for details on piece-wise linear approximations for transaction costs; see Dantzig [1955] for details on the basic technique of piece-wise linear approximations.
[10]An alternative to expressing the fraction in terms of initial market value is to use the value after revision. Then the diversification requirement is

$\qquad\qquad Q_i/V \leq F_i$ and the analogue to (C4) is

(C4a) $\qquad P_i - S_i + F_i TTC < F_i V^\circ - Q_i^\circ.$

fraction F_i by the current proportion in the portfolio when this proportion exceeds F_i and rebalancing is not desired.

Summary of the Basic Problem

Gathering together the objective function and the basic constraints gives:

$$\text{Max } OBJ = \sum_{i=1}^{N} (P_i - S_i)CE_i$$

$$- \sum_{i=1}^{N} P_i \cdot CP_i - \sum_{i=1}^{N} S_i \cdot CS_i$$

(C1) $P_i \geq 0; S_i \geq 0$ $i = 1,..., N$

(C2) $\sum_{i=1}^{N} P_i(1 + CP_i) - \sum_{i=1}^{N} S_i(1 - CS_i) = 0$

(C3) $S_i - P_i \leq Q_i^{\circ}$ $i = 1,..., N$

(C4) $P_i - S_i \leq F_i \cdot V^{\circ} - Q_i^{\circ}$ $i = 1,..., N.$

The Relative Variable Formulation

The preceding has structured the problem in terms of the decision variables $\{P_i, S_i | i = 1,..., N\}$ which measure the dollar amount bought and sold for each security. While dollar variables facilitate structuring of the objective function and constraints, it is usual in portfolio theory to express decision variables in terms of fractions of total portfolio value. In order to restructure the problem in terms of relative values, we define the variable X_i°, X_i, Y_i and Z_i as:

$X_i^{\circ} = Q_i^{\circ}/V^{\circ}$ = fraction of security i held in the original portfolio

$X_i = Q_i/V$ = fraction of security i held in the revised portfolio

$Y_i = P_i/V^{\circ}$ = fraction of security i purchased

$Z_i = S_i/V^{\circ}$ = fraction of security i sold.

Note that Y_i and Z_i are expressed as fractions of the original and not the revised portfolio. The decision variables in a relative value formulation are Y_i and Z_i.

Since $Q_i = Q_i^{\circ} + P_i - S_i$, the relative variables are related by

(13) $X_i = (X_i^{\circ} + Y_i - Z_i)(V^{\circ}/V).$

The factor (V°/V) reflects the change in portfolio value used to compute the fractional investment before and after revision.[11]

To express the objective function in terms of relative variables, divide both sides by the constant V° giving a new objective function OBJ_1 of

(14) $OBJ_1 = OBJ/V^{\circ} = \sum_{i=1}^{N} (Y_i - Z_i)CE_i$

$$- \sum_{i=1}^{N} Y_i \cdot CP_i - \sum_{i=1}^{N} Z_i \cdot CS_i.$$

Maximizing OBJ_1 is equivalent to maximizing the previous objective function since maximizing a constant times any quantity is equivalent to maximizing the quantity itself. When expressed in relative variables, this statement of the objective function says to "maximize the increase in risk-adjusted expected return less the transaction costs per dollar incurred in obtaining the improvement in expected return."

In a similar fashion, we can respecify the constraints by dividing both sides of each constraint by V°. This gives

(C1') $Y_i \geq 0; Z_i \geq 0$ $i = 1,..., N$

(C2') $\sum_{i=1}^{N} Y_i(1 + CP_i) - \sum_{i=1}^{N} Z_i(1 - CS_i) = 0$

(C3') $Z_i - Y_i \leq X_i^{\circ}$ $i = 1,..., N$

(C4') $Y_i - Z_i \leq F_i - X_i^{\circ}$ $i = 1,..., N.$

Risk-Return Trade-offs in the Context of the Basic Sharpe Model

In Sharpe [1967], the certainty equivalent is given by $CE_i = E_i - \theta\beta_i$. Thus the parametric objective function for the portfolio revision model is

$$OBJ_1 = \sum_{i=1}^{N} (Y_i - Z_i)E_i - \theta \sum_{i=1}^{N} (Y_i - Z_i)\beta_i$$
$$- TC = E_p - \theta\beta_p - TC$$

where $TC = TTC/V^{\circ}$ is the transaction cost per dollar of portfolio value.

By varying the parameter θ, one generates a transaction-cost-adjusted efficient frontier that is the portfolio revision analogue of the piece-wise linear frontier of the portfolio selection problem. This frontier summarizes the efficient (E_p, β_p) combinations available in the presence of transaction costs given the initial holdings.

An alternative to generating the entire frontier is to choose an appropriate value of θ, find the best solution and then use sensitivity analysis to see if other values of θ should be considered. This approach is computationally easier than generating the entire frontier, especially if the model is available on a time-shared computer.

---

[11]If there were no transaction costs, then $V^{\circ} = V$ and (29) becomes $X_i = X_i^{\circ} + Y_i - Z_i$, which says that the new fraction equals the old fraction plus the net fraction purchased. The presence of transaction costs destroys this identity. Even if $Y_i = Z_i = 0$, we have $X_i = X_i^{\circ}$ (V°/V) because of other trades that reduce the market value.

MAINTAINING TARGET RISK LEVELS IN A SINGLE-STAGE REVISION

Portfolio managers typically attempt to maintain target risk levels for their portfolios. For simplicity of exposition, let us assume that these target risk levels are characterized by target levels of portfolio beta. The next two subsections present alternative methods for maintaining a target beta; then the last subsection evaluates the two methods and briefly considers other portfolio goals for which the techniques are applicable.

A Target Volatility Constraint

Let β_p° and β_p denote the beta of the portfolio before and after revision, respectively. They are given by

$$(15) \quad \beta_p^\circ = \sum_{i=1}^{N} X_i^\circ \beta_i$$

$$(16) \quad \beta_p = \sum_{i=1}^{N} X_i \beta_i$$

$$= (V^\circ / V) \left[\beta_p^\circ + \sum_{i=1}^{N} (Y_i - Z_i)\beta_i \right].$$

The current volatility β_p° is a parameter that depends only on current holdings; however, β_p is a decision variable whose value depends on the amounts purchased and sold of various securities.

Let β_p^* denote the target level of volatility. To force the volatility of the revised portfolio to equal β_p^*, we can add to the model the constraint that[12]

$$(17) \quad \beta_p = \beta_p^*$$

Adding this linear constraint to the problem will force the revised portfolio to have a beta of β_p^*. Such a constraint may be an overly stringent restriction. Typically volatility targets are "fuzzy" in the sense of representing an approximate level regarded as desirable by the portfolio manager. However, the portfolio manager is typically not willing to incur otherwise unnecessary transaction costs to adjust volatility by a small amount. Moreover, for a sufficiently great return, the target volatility level may be compromised. To treat the fact that (17) may be an overly stringent constraint, we introduce goal programming techniques.

The Goal Programming Approach to Target Volatility

An alternative to forcing the model to select a portfolio with a particular level of volatility β_p^* is

to allow the portfolio manager to specify the target volatility along with the cost of deviating from the target level; cost must be specified in terms of the additional risk-adjusted return that must be obtained as compensation for each unit of deviation from the target level.

Let deviations from the target volatility be defined as:

$$(18) \quad d_1 \equiv \max\{\beta_p^* - \beta_p, 0\} = \text{amount below target if below}$$

$$(19) \quad d_2 \equiv \max\{\beta_p - \beta_p^*, 0\} = \text{amount above target if above.}$$

The deviation of the actual volatility from the target can be expressed in terms of decision variables by using (16). This gives

$$(20) \quad \beta_p^* - \beta_p = \beta_p^* - \frac{V^\circ}{V} \left[\beta_p^\circ + \sum_{i=1}^{N} (Y_i - Z_i)\beta_i \right].$$

Multiplying this deviation by V gives

$$(21) \quad V(\beta_p^* - \beta_p) = V\beta_p^* - V^\circ \beta_p^\circ$$

$$- \sum_{i=1}^{N} (V^\circ Y_i - V^\circ Z_i)\,\beta_i$$

$$= V^\circ(\beta_p^* - \beta_p^\circ) - \beta_p^*(TTC)$$

$$- \sum_{i=1}^{N} (P_i - S_i)\beta_i.$$

Let D_1 and D_2 be two new decision variables defined by

$$(22) \quad D_1 \equiv V d_1 = V \max\{\beta_p^* - \beta_p, 0\}$$

$$(23) \quad D_2 \equiv V d_2 = V \max\{\beta_p - \beta_p^*, 0\}.$$

The variables D_1 and D_2 are the deviations from target volatility times the market value of the portfolio.[13]

Let π_1 be the rate at which the portfolio manager is willing to substitute risk-adjusted future portfolio value per unit deviation below the target volatility level and let π_2 be the rate at which the portfolio manager is willing to substitute risk-adjusted future portfolio value per unit deviation above the target volatility level. The parameters π_1 and π_2 are called penalty costs.[14] Let us define a penalty function PF

---

[12] When expressed in terms of decision variables, (17) becomes

$$\sum_{i=1}^{N} P_i(\beta_i + \beta_p^* \cdot CP_i) - \sum_{i=1}^{N} S_i(\beta_i - \beta_p^* \cdot CS_i) = V^\circ(\beta_p^* - \beta_p^\circ).$$

[13] The quantity $V\beta_p$ is the sensitivity of future portfolio value to return on the market. To see this, let $W = V(1 + R_p)$ be the future portfolio value. Differentiating W with respect to return on the market index gives

$$dW/dR_{\text{U}} = d[V(1 + R_p)]/dR_{\text{U}} = V(dR_p/dR_{\text{U}})VB_p$$

since $dR_p/dR_{\text{U}} = \beta_p$.

[14] In most problems, π_1 and π_2 are not constants. Rather, they increase with the size of the deviation from the target volatility. As in the case of transaction costs, the increasing level of penalty costs can be treated by using a piece-wise linear approximation. Again, for simplicity of exposition, we shall treat the penalty costs as constants with the understanding that a more realistic piece-wise linear approximation can be used.

as the adjustment to the objective function that reflects the deviation of the actual volatility from the target level. The penalty function is

(24) $PF = \pi_1 D_1 + \pi_2 D_2$.

We obtain the extended portfolio revision model by substracting PF from the objective function and adding the following constraints:

(C5) $D_1 \geq V(\beta_p^* - \beta_p) = V^\circ(\beta_p^* - \beta_p^\circ) - \beta_p^* TTC$

$$- \sum_{i=1}^{N} (P_i - S_i)\beta_i$$

(C6) $D_2 \geq V(\beta_p - \beta_p^*) = V^\circ(\beta_p^\circ - \beta_p^*) + \beta_p^* TTC$

$$+ \sum_{i=1}^{N} (P_i - S_i)\beta_i$$

(C7) $D_1 \geq 0; D_2 \geq 0$.

Since D_1 and D_2 can never be negative and since they enter the objective function with negative coefficients, the optimization algorithm will make them as small as possible consistent with the objective function and the other constraints. Thus either D_1 or D_2 will always be zero and the constraint on the other one will hold as an equality. Constraints (C5), (C6) and (C7) force the values of D_1 and D_2 in the optimal solution to be consistent with the definitions given in (22) and (23).

The technique of using penalty functions based on deviations from target levels and adding constraints such as (C5), (C6), and (C7) is known as goal programming since it involves maximizing an objective function expressed in terms of conflicting goals.[15] In this case, the conflicting goals are risk-adjusted return and target volatility. The penalty costs π_1 and π_2 reflect the relative importance of those goals.

Since the parameter θ in the certainty equivalent $CE = E_p - \theta\beta_p$ already reflects the rate of substitution of return for volatility, the parameters π_1 and π_2 reflect higher order trade-offs not included by the linear trade-off measured by θ. They simply measure acceptable rates of substitution and can be specified as subjectively acceptable trade-offs in the same fashion as θ represents the trade-off between E_p and β_p.

Portfolio Goals—A Synthesis

We have illustrated the use of goal programming for attaining target volatility levels. It can be used equally well for other targets such as desired

dividend rates, target cash levels, price-earnings ratios, etc.

The use of goal programming techniques to attain target goals is superior to the use of constraints because: (1) In the presence of transaction costs, it avoids forcing trades to hit targets exactly since trades are made only if the value of goal attainment exceeds the associated transaction costs; (2) it incorporates the trade-off between alternative goals. An additional benefit of goal programming occurs when there are multiple conflicting goals that cannot all be simultaneously met. Then, goal programming leads to the best feasible solution that automatically trades off goal conflicts in terms of the relative importance of each.

THE MULTI-STAGE FORMULATION

In the single-stage revision, we assumed that the portfolio manager had estimates of expected return over some time horizon of unspecified length. The model chose the best revised portfolio for that time horizon. An intertemporal model is required to use information about the time path of future prices and to take account of revisions necessitated by cash inflows and outflows. This section develops a multi-stage extension of the single-stage model designed to treat intertemporal issues.

Notation

We shall continue to use a superscript naught (°) to denote a value before revision and we shall add a subscript t to denote the stage of the revision. Thus, we have:

Q_{it}° = dollars invested in security i before revision at stage t

Q_{it} = dollars invested in security i after revision at stage t

P_{it} = dollar purchase of security i at stage t

S_{it} = dollar sale of security i at stage t

V_t° = $\sum_{i=1}^{N} Q_{it}^\circ$

= portfolio value before revision at stage t

V_t = $\sum_{i=1}^{N} Q_{it}$

= portfolio value after revision at stage t

TTC_t = transaction costs incurred in revision at stage t.

The first revision is number 1; the final revision is number T. Thus there are a total of T stages in the intertemporal model. While the model develops a series of planned revisions, only the current (stage one) revision is actually implemented. The subsequent revisions represent the best future plan given current holdings, current information, risk prefer-

---

[15]For further details on goal programming, see such works as Charnes and Cooper [1967], Ijuri [1965] or Lee [1972]. In Chapters 5 and 6, Lee describes algorithms for implementing goal programming. In Chapter 9, Lee considers the use of goal programming in portfolio selection but not revision in a formulation that complements the one presented in this paper.

ences and transaction costs. The reason for developing an intertemporal model is to include within the model the costs of planned future revisions and avoid thereby suboptimization from implementing attractive short-term strategies that involve excessive transaction costs beyond the first stage.

The Intertemporal Objective Function

The single-stage objective function was to maximize the increase in risk-adjusted future value. The multi-stage extension is to maximize a weighted sum of increases in risk-adjusted future value, i.e.,

$$(25) \quad OBJ = \sum_{i=1}^{T} w_t \cdot \Delta RAFV_t$$

where $\Delta RAFV_t$ is the change in risk-adjusted expected future value at stage t and w_t is the relative importance of the values at each stage. The quantity $\Delta RAFV_1$ is the objective function of the single-stage revision, i.e.,

$$\Delta RAFV_1 = V_1(1 + CE_1) - V^{\circ}(1 + CE_1^{\circ})$$
$$= \sum_{i=1}^{N} (P_{i1} - S_{i1})CE_{i1} - TTC_1.$$

In a similar fashion for $t \geq 2$,

$$\Delta RAFV_t = V_t(1 + CE_t) - V_t^{\circ}(1 + CE_t^{\circ})$$
$$= \sum_{i=1}^{N} (P_{it} - S_{it})CE_{it} - TTC_t.$$

By substituting the expressions back into (25) and rearranging terms, the intertemporal objective function for a T-period horizon can be expressed in terms of the decision variables P_{it} and S_{it} as

$$(26) \quad OBJ = \sum_{t=1}^{T} \sum_{i=1}^{N} P_{it}[w_t(CE_{it} - CP_i)]$$
$$- \sum_{t=1}^{T} \sum_{i=1}^{N} S_{it}[w_t(CE_{it} + CS_i)].$$

The coefficients of the decision variables involve only certainty equivalents, transaction costs and weights. There are no stochastic variables in the objective function.

To extend the objective function to include target value of portfolio volatility and to allow for changes in the target from period to period, define β_{pt}^* to be the target volatility in period t. In analogy to the single-stage penalty function as a weighted sum of penalty functions for each stage, i.e.,

$$PF = \sum_{t=1}^{T} w_t(\pi_1 D_{1t} + \pi_2 D_{2t})$$

where D's are stage t analogues of the previously defined deviations from target levels.

The Stochastic Nature of Future Stage Revisions

In the single-stage model, there are no random variables in the problem. All parameters in the constraints are known with certainty. However, in going to the multi-stage formulation, the values of parameters characterizing portfolios at future revision times are uncertain since they depend on realized returns. For instance, the quantities Q_{i1}° and V_1° depend on current holdings and are known with certainty while Q_{it}° and V_t° for $t \geq 2$ depend on realized returns as well as previous portfolio decisions. Let $A_i(t+1,t)$ denote total appreciation of security i over the time interval from stage t to $t + 1$ and let $NCF(t+1,t)$ denote cash inflow from stage t to stage $t + 1$. Then $Q_{i,t+1}^{\circ}$ and V_{t+1}° are given by

$$(50) \quad Q_{i,t+1}^{\circ} = Q_{it}^{\circ}[1 + A_i(t+1,t)]$$

$$(51) \quad V_{t+1}^{\circ} = \sum_{i=1}^{N} Q_{i,t+1}^{\circ} + NCF(t+1,t).$$

Given the state of stochastic programming and given our objective of formulating computationally feasible portfolio revision models, we shall use expected values of future portfolio parameters in our constraint formulation for the multi-stage model. Thus, the output of the model will be the best intertemporal strategy if expectations are realized. Since uncertainty about future returns has already been accounted for via the risk-adjustment in the objective function and since the primary purpose of a multi-stage model is to reflect future transaction costs, the use of expected values amounts to the development of intertemporal strategies on the basis of expected transaction costs. While this approach is not optimal in the sense of stochastic optimization before consideration of computation and information costs, its justification is a compromise between the amount of information used in assessing potential future transaction costs and computational expediency. The approach will tend to prevent high concentrations in securities that promise high short-term returns if such concentrations are contrary to the long-term investment policies.

Constraint Formulation

The first stage constraints for non-negativity, cash conservation, stock-sale prohibition, diversification and target volatility are identical to the single-stage model. For subsequent stages, the same form of the constraints can be preserved by using expected values for Q_{it}° and V_t°. Letting bars denote expected values, we have:[16]

(C1*) $P_{it} \geq 0; S_{it} \geq 0$

(C2*) $\sum_{i=1}^{N} P_{it}(1 + CP_i) - \sum_{i=1}^{N} S_{it}(1 - CS_i) = 0$

(C3*) $S_{it} - P_{it} \leq \bar{Q}_{it}^\circ$

(C4*) $P_{it} - S_{it} \leq F_{it} \bar{V}_t^\circ - \bar{Q}_{it}^\circ$

(C5*) $D_{1t} \geq \bar{V}_t^\circ \beta_{pt}^* - \sum_{i=1}^{N} \bar{Q}_{it}^\circ \beta_i - \beta_{pt}^* \cdot TTC_t$

$\qquad\qquad - \sum_{i=1}^{N} (P_{it} - S_{it})\beta_i$

(C6*) $D_{2t} \geq \sum_{i=1}^{N} \bar{Q}_{it}^\circ \beta_i - \bar{V}_t^\circ \beta_{pt}^* + \beta_{pt}^* \cdot T\bar{T}C_t$

$\qquad\qquad + \sum_{i=1}^{N} (P_{it} - S_{it})\beta_i.$

(C7*) $D_{1t} \geq 0; D_{2t} \geq 0.$

In addition to writing analogues to the single-stage constraints, we must add definitional constraints for $\bar{Q}_{it}^\circ$ and $\bar{V}_t^\circ$ and take account of dividends and other cash inflows. Let asset N be cash and let $D_i(t+1, t)$ be the expected dividend yield from security i between stages t and $t+1$. Then the additional constraints required to complete the intertemporal model are:

(C8*) $\bar{Q}_{it} = \bar{Q}_{it}^\circ + P_{it} - S_{it}$

(C9*) $\bar{Q}_{i,t+1}^\circ = \bar{Q}_{it}[1 + A_i(t+1,t)]$ $t > 1, i \neq N$

(C10*) $\bar{Q}_{N, t+1}^\circ = \bar{Q}_{Nt} + \sum_{i=1}^{N} \bar{Q}_{it} D_i(t+1,t)$

$\qquad\qquad + \overline{NCF}(t+1,t)$ $t > 1$

(C11*) $\bar{V}_{t+1}^\circ = \sum_{i=1}^{N} \bar{Q}_{i,t+1}^\circ.$

In (C10*), letting the summation include N allows for the cash to be invested in short-term notes between revisions, where $D_N(t+1, t)$ is the expected yield on short-term notes. If cash is not invested in short-term notes, then $D_N(t+1, t) = 0$.

This formulation of the multi-stage revision is not only an LP, but is amenable to decomposition.[17] Moreover, the subproblems are solvable by a variant of the knapsack problem that can be solved very efficiently without the inversion of any matrices. Thus, this formulation not only provides the computational feasibility associated with linear programming but is so structured that special purpose linear algorithms make even greater computational efficiency possible.

THE VALIDITY OF THE LP OBJECTIVE FUNCTION

This subsection shows that maximizing the LP objective function in the absence of penalty costs is, to first-order, equivalent to maximizing the increase in expected utility of future wealth in the presence of transaction costs.

Let W^* denote the certainty equivalent level of future wealth. By definition of certainty equivalent, expected utility $\bar{U}$ is related to the certainty equivalent W^* by $\bar{U} = U(W^*)$. Therefore, the first-order change in expected utility from a revision of the portfolio is given by $\triangle \bar{U} = [dU(W^*)/dW^*] \triangle W^*$. Since the certainty equivalent value of the portfolio before and after revision is $V^\circ(1+CE^\circ)$ and $V(1+CE)$, the change in W^* is given by $\triangle W^* = V(1+CE) - V^\circ(1+CE^\circ)$. When the certainty equivalent rate CE can be written as a linear sum of the certainty equivalents for individual securities, then substitution from (10) gives

$$\triangle W^* = \sum_{i=1}^{N} (P_i - S_i)CE_i - TTC.$$

Hence, the first-order change in expected utility is related to the objective function by

$$\triangle \bar{U} = (dU/dW^*)\left[\sum_{i=1}^{N} (P_i - S_i)CE_i - TTC \right].$$

The expression within brackets is the single-stage LP objective function without the penalty function adjustment. The quantity dU/dW^* is the rate of increase of utility with wealth evaluated at the certainty equivalent of the current portfolio. To first order, it is a constant characteristic of a particular utility function. Therefore, the maximization of the basic single-stage LP objective function is the first-order equivalent of maximizing the increase in utility subject to the conditions that: 1) There exists an appropriate expression for the certainty-equivalent rate CE such that $W^* = V(1+CE)$; 2) the expression for CE is expressable as

---

[16]In writing Constraints (C5*) and (C6*), the term $V_t^\circ \beta_p^-$ in the single-stage constraints of (C5) and (C6) has been replaced by the expression $\sum_{i=1}^{N} \bar{Q}_{it}^\circ \beta_i$. To see the reason for this change, note that

$$V_t^\circ \beta_{pt}^\circ = V_t^\circ \sum_{i=1}^{N} (Q_{it}^\circ / V_t^\circ)\beta_i = \sum_{i=1}^{N} Q_{it}^\circ \beta_i.$$

For $t > 1$, the expected value of $V_t^\circ \beta_{pt}^\circ$ is given by $\sum_{i=1}^{N} \bar{Q}_{it}^\circ \beta_i$; for $t = 1$, no expected value is required since these terms are parameters defined by current holdings.

[17]The reduction of the intertemporal bond portfolio revision problem to one solvable by decomposition is the technique used by Bradley and Crane [1972] to obtain a computationally feasible problem.

448

a linear sum of the certainty equivalents associated with each security.

The preceding analysis has established that whenever the utility function and the return distribution are such that mean-variance or mean-variance-skewness representations are valid, then linear approximations for the certainty equivalents are obtainable within the framework of the market-index model. Since the key to the validity of the linear (or piece-wise linear) approximations is the rapid decrease in the size of the independent moments with increasing portfolio size[18] and since β_p effectively summarizes the effect of all moments of the systematic component of return, it is reasonable to argue that the formulation is also amenable to multi-moment representations of expected utility that go beyond variance and skewness where the generality of the result is limited only by the validity of a market-index model.[19] Thus, with properly defined certainty equivalents, these LP models are of potentially more general validity than mean-variance based QP models.

SUMMARY AND CONCLUSION

In this article, we have structured the problem of revising a portfolio in the presence of transaction costs as a linear program. We have presented three models—a basic single-stage revision, a single-stage revision with goal programming to account for target portfolio goals and a multi-stage model to treat intertemporal effects. There are two major contributions: The reduction of portfolio revision to an LP and the introduction of goal programming techniques. We now evaluate these contributions.

Since Pogue's QP-based models are the primary alternative to LP-based portfolio revision, a comparison of the LP and QP models is an appropriate evaluation framework. Within the framework of the market-index representation of security returns, the LP solution is, as indicated previously, an extremely good approximation to the QP solution. Within that framework, the LP affords dramatic improvement in computational feasibility and the concomitant ability to consider large security universes with negligible cost in accuracy. All models are amenable to solution within a time-shared computing environment. The major limitation of the LP formulation is that it is clearly limited to a single market-index environment while the QP model is not. In practical terms, the major limitation seems to be the preclusion of industry effects via the addition of an industry term to the market-index model as done by Cohen and Pogue [1967].

The use of goal programming techniques is not limited to an LP model. They can for instance be incorporated within the Pogue model. The benefits of goal programming are: 1) Automatic treatment of trade-off between transaction costs incurred in attaining goals and the benefit of goal realization; 2) increased user control over model results; 3) the avoidance of infeasibility from incompatible goals; and 4) more efficient sensitivity analysis since goals shifts are evaluated automatically within the basic solution. The costs of goal programming are increased computation. Within the framework of the simplex algorithm, these costs are negligible.[20] However, like the use of target level constraints, goal programming techniques destroy the knapsack like structure of the basic single-stage model and thus make hand solutions impractical.

In going from a single-stage to multi-stage model, both the computational and informational size of the model increases. Thus, the trade-off here is between completeness and simplicity. Preference for a single-stage over a multi-stage model depends to a great extent on the organizational context in which the model is to be used. At present, portfolio managers revise portfolio by reducing the universe to attractive candidates, considering possible trade contributions and judgementally evaluating the attractiveness of the new versus the old portfolio. The single-stage model can operate as an efficient vehicle to search a data base of stocks and generate a suggested trade program that is then judgementally evaluated. Viewed as a systematic search procedure, the single-stage model can be an intermediate step in developing multi-stage computer-assisted portfolio management.

To summarize, the family of LP portfolio revision models presented herein are limited by their dependence on a single-index market model. However, within this framework, they are extremely efficient portfolio revision techniques that provide answers highly congruent with existing nonlinear models. Because of their efficiency and because most current security evaluation techniques are structured in terms of a market-index model, these LP models seem to provide a viable basis for implementing computer-assisted portfolio management systems.   □

---

[18]If n is the number of securities in the portfolio, then no correlation between the non-market-related returns of securities means that the kth moment of the independent component should decline as $1/n^k$ for even moments and even faster for odd moments. Reback [1972, Appendix 4-2] investigates this empirically for random samples of NYSE stocks and, while finding that the actual decline is slower than the $1/n^k$ rate (due presumably to omitted factors such as industry effects), the decline is rapid and faster for higher moments as expected.

[19]For a more detailed treatment of volatility as a general measure of market risk, see Reback [1972, esp. Ch. 4, Part III] and Stone [1973].

[20]Each goal involves the addition of two decision variables and one additional constraint in comparison to constraining the solution to hit a particular target.

REFERENCES

Ahlers, David M., *An Evaluation of Investment Decision Making Systems*, Doctoral Dissertation, unpublished, Carnegie-Mellon University (1974).

Bradley, Stephen P. and Dwight B. Crane, "A Dynamic Model for Bond Portfolio Management," *Management Science*, Vol. 4, No. 2, (October 1972), pp. 139-51.

——————————————., "Management of Commercial Bank Government Security Portfolios: An Optimization Approach Under Uncertainty," *Journal of Bank Research*, Vol. 4, No. 1, (Spring 1973), pp. 18-30.

Charnes, A. and W. W. Cooper, "Appendix B–Basic Existence Theorems and Goal Programming" in Management Models and Industrial Applications of Linear Programming, Vol. I, New York: John Wiley and Sons, Inc., (1967).

Chen, Andrew H. Y., Frank C. Jen and Stanley Zionts, "The Optimal Portfolio Revision Policy," Journal of Business, Vol. 44, No. 1, (January 1971), pp. 51-61.

Cohen, Kalman J. and Frederick S. Hammer, "Editorial Comment on 'A Simplified Model for Portfolio Analysis'," in *Analytical Methods in Banking*, Homewood, Illinois: Richard D. Irwin (1966), pp. 296-299.

Cohen, Kalman J. and G. A. Pogue, "An Empirical Evaluation of Alternative Portfolio Selection Models," Journal of Business, Vol. 40, No. 2, (April 1967), pp. 166-93.

Crane, Dwight B., "A Stochastic Programming Model for Commercial Bank Bond Portfolio Management," Journal of Financial and Quantitative Analysis, Vol. 6, No. 3, (June 1971), pp. 955-976.

Dantzig, G. B., "Upper Bounds, Block Triangularity, and Secondary Constraints," Econometrica, Vol. 23, No. 1, (January 1955), pp. 174-183.

Ijuri, Y., *Management Goals and Accounting for Control*, Chicago: Rand McNally (1965).

Jensen, M. C., "Capital Markets: Theory and Evidence," *The Bell Journal of Economics and Management Science*, Vol. 3, No. 2, (Autumn 1972), pp. 357-98.

Lee, Sang M., *Goal Programming for Decision Analysis*, Philadelphia: Auerbach (1972).

Markowitz, Harry M., "Portfolio Selection," *The Journal of Finance*, Vol. 7, No. 1, (March 1952), pp. 77-91.

Mossin, Jan, "Optimal Multi-Period Portfolio Policies," *Journal of Business*, Vol. 41, No. 2, (April 1968), pp. 215-229.

Pogue, Gerald A., *An Adaptive Model for Investment Management*, Unpublished Doctoral Dissertation, Carnegie-Mellon University, (1967), Chapters 5 and 6.

——————————————., "An Extension of the Markowitz Portfolio Selection to Include Variable Transaction Costs, Short Sales, Leverage Policies, and Taxes," *Journal of Finance*, Vol. 25, No. 5, (December 1970), pp. 1005-1028.

——————————————., "An Intertemporal Model for Investment Management," *Journal of Bank Research*, Vol. 1, No. 1, (Spring 1970), pp. 17-33.

Reback, Robert, Market Volatility and the Portfolio Revision Process, unpublished Doctoral Dissertation, Cornell University (1972).

Sharpe, William F., "A Simplified Model for Portfolio Analysis," *Management Science*, Vol. 9, No. 2, (January 1963), pp. 277-293.

——————————————., "A Linear Programming Algorithm for Mutual Fund Portfolio Selection," *Management Science*, Vol. 13, No. 7, (March 1967), pp. 499-510.

——————————————., *Portfolio Theory and Capital Markets*, New York: McGraw Hill, (1970).

——————————————., "A Linear Programming Approximation for the General Portfolio Analysis Problem," *Journal of Financial and Quantitative Analysis*, Vol. 6, No. 5, (December 1971), pp. 1263-76.

Smith, Keith V., "A Transition Model for Portfolio Revision," *Journal of Finance*, Vol. 22, No. 4, (September 1967), pp. 425-439.

Stone, Bernell K., "A Model for Bond Portfolio Management," *AIDS Proceedings*, (1972), pp. 357-365.

——————————————., "A Linear Programming Formulation of the General Portfolio Selection Problem," *Journal of Financial and Quantitative Analysis*, Vol. 7, No. 4, (September 1973), pp. 621-636.

Tobin, James, "Liquidity Preferences as Behavior Towards Risk," *Review of Economic Studies*, Vol. 25 (February 1958), pp. 65-86.

Wagner, W. H. and S. R. Quay, "New Concepts in Portfolio Management," *Journal of Bank Research*, Vol. 3, No. 2, (Summer 1972), pp. 102-110.

Part IX

ELECTRONIC FUNDS TRANSFER SYSTEMS

M UCH of the new interest in management of bank operations centers on the electronic aspects of funds transfer. Annual check volume in the United States was about 24.3 billion in 1974, and was growing at an average rate of 7.3% a year during the early 1970s. Estimates of annual nationwide check processing costs place the figure at nearly $7 billion. The soaring volume of checks handled and the rising processing costs are the basis of a major processing problem facing the U.S. payments system. The principal reason for the problem is the use of the paper check. The processing devoted to check clearing activities represents a major drain on both the monetary and manpower resources of a commercial bank.

One widely discussed solution to these problems in the nation's payments mechanism is the development of an Electronic Funds Transfer System (EFTS). This system would be based on modern electronic technology and would greatly reduce the transaction time involved in payments and collections. A total system would initially revolve around the bank card which is already widely used. With such a card, a firm or an individual could negotiate a purchase, collection, or other transaction involving funds transfer without the use of checks. Purchases could occur with transfer of funds completed at the point of sale. A total system might include automated teller machines (ATMs), automatic payroll deposit, automated bill payment, and a teller terminal that would provide instantaneous information on an account's current status. With a nationwide EFTS, a nearly "checkless" society would become a real possibility.

Despite the advantages that EFTS offers, it has not come on line as quickly as many, including the Federal Reserve, predicted.

Results of EFTS applications have been mixed, and while some banks have enjoyed positive results, others have experienced significant losses. Articles in both *Fortune* (May and June, 1977) and *Business Week* (April 18, 1977) have focused on the problems that have delayed the development of EFTS. Theses problems include:

(1) The exact impact of EFTS on float time is yet to be resolved. This question could weigh heavily in profitability questions.

(2) Acceptance levels among the consuming public are still unclear, although there are some positive indications.

(3) High initial investments represent a relatively high risk prospect for most banks. As manufacture of EFTS components increases, cost *may* fall, but this is uncertain.

(4) Significant regulatory and public policy issues remain unanswered. This is particularly true in states that do not allow branch banks.

(5) Concern has been expressed in economic circles over the speeding up of the M1 (demand deposits, currency, and coins) component of the money supply. There could be serious changes in the Federal Reserve's ability to control monetary expansion.

The future of EFTS is still in doubt, and opinions vary widely among banks and bankers. Some form of EFTS is likely in the future because of the benefits that the system offers. However, the move toward a total system may continue at a very slow pace.

The questions surrounding EFTS often center around the system's impact on float time. Michael J. Hosemann has been involved in float research as part of the Atlanta Payments Project, an EFTS system. Hosemann discusses his research and the framework for cost-benefit analysis of an EFTS in Chapter 37, "Measuring the Impact of Electronic Funds Transfer Systems on Float." The Atlanta system included automated bill payment, direct deposit of payrolls, and point of sale funds transfer. The results of the Atlanta study indicate that some banks will, on balance, lose float time on transactions under EFTS, but that most of the loss will be offset by savings made possible by the system. The article by Hosemann provides an example of how management science analysis will be involved in the development of EFTS.

Another key issue in committing a bank to the high initial investment in EFTS is customer acceptance at the retail level. Customer acceptance will play a vital role in determining the profitability of EFTS for banks which compete heavily in the retail sector. On the one hand, banks do not want to invest large amounts in uncertain projects. On the other hand, however, they must provide innovative customer services to compete effectively in the retail market. Careful analysis must underlie the major strategic decisions involved in moving towards EFTS.

Chapter 38, "The Public Policy Implications of EFTS," by James F.

Dingle, provides an interesting look at the more general issues involved in the movement towards EFTS. This chapter describes a Canadian study examining broad public policy issues and the impact of EFTS on various elements of transactions. An interesting aspect of Dingle's conclusions is his belief that EFTS will lead to the development of more computer-based decision models due to the need for faster response time. If this conclusion is correct, management science will receive a significant stimulus from the development of Electronic Funds Transfer. Dingle's article offers a useful examination of important broad issues and implications of EFTS.

Chapter 39, "Consumer Choice and Use of Bank Credit Cards: A Model and Cross-Section Results," by Kenneth J. White, provides an approach for more detailed examination of consumer acceptance levels. The article specifically considers the choice between checks and credit cards and examines a model for determining transaction costs. White presents a methodology for analyzing various factors that influence the overall cost effectiveness of electronic systems. He concludes that significant savings will be realized once merchants establish on-line point of sale terminals. The task will then be educating the public on cost savings.

The purpose of Part IX is to familiarize readers with some current issues in electronic aspects of bank operations and the use of management science techniques in evaluating opportunities in this area. While increased use of computers resulting from a move towards EFTS would probably lead to greater use of computer-based decision models, management science techniques should also be applied to evaluate the benefits of developing various aspects of EFTS. Cost analysis, in particular, should be carefully pursued by banks planning investments in this area. Despite the problems involved in EFTS and its high initial cost, some form of the system is likely to be developed in the future. The speed with which it will proceed, however, is uncertain.

Chapter 37

MEASURING THE IMPACT OF ELECTRONIC FUNDS TRANSFER SYSTEMS ON FLOAT*

By Michael J. Hosemann

*This article is reprinted, with permission, from *Journal of Bank Research*, Vol. 3, No. 3 (Autumn, 1972), pp. 136-154.

This paper reports the findings of an analysis of the costs of float eliminated by three proposed Electronic Funds Transfer Systems (EFTS) currently being implemented by the Atlanta Payments Project.* The paper also describes a model which permits bankers engaged in EFTS design to quantify the gains (or losses) of float displaced by specific EFT systems alternatives.

A common objective of all electronic funds transfer systems is to increase the efficiency and productivity of the payment system by eliminating paper from payment transactions. Automating payment transactions, however, permits them to be carried out at much greater speeds than presently. Shortening the time frame for deposit and collection of items has many implications, not the least of which is the effect of accelerated payment on bank deposit size and volatility. Responsible EFT systems designers must, therefore, answer the question: What are the costs and benefits to banks from accelerated payment brought on by various EFT system alternatives?

This study seeks to answer this question for the Atlanta banking community relative to three EFT systems proposed by the Atlanta Payment Project. These alternatives are the Bill-Check, Direct Deposit of Payroll and Point of Sale funds transfer systems.

> The Bill-Check system is the Atlanta Payment Project's method of automating regular bill payments prior to their entry into the banking system. Under this system a merchant sends a bill-check to a customer. When the customer is ready to pay, he signs the remittance portion of the bill and forwards it to the merchant. This signed bill-check is a one-time payment authorization to the merchant. The firm produces a magnetic tape containing such authorizations and delivers this tape to its bank which forwards the entries through an automated clearing house to the consumer's bank. The bill-check system permits the consumer to retain control over the timing and amount of his regular payments. The system requires only minor modifications in merchant billing and remittance processing systems.

> The Direct Deposit of Payroll (DDP) is a system which automates actual paychecks. Under the plan an employer will generate magnetic tape records containing employee payroll amounts, employee bank ABA numbers and employee bank account numbers. This tape is routed through an automated clearing house from the employer's bank to the employee's bank for credit to the employee's account on a designated payday. The system offers the employee heightened convenience and more timely crediting of his payroll amount, and it offers the banking system substantial per item savings.

> The Point of Sale (POS) funds transfer system is a system designed to automate payments at their source, the retail point of sale. This system is perhaps the most important of the systems recommended. It offers a large ultimate payoff to the banks not only by reducing unit costs but also by generating new sources of revenue. In the fully developed system, the customer will utilize a plastic card in an electronic terminal, and pay for a purchase either by direct transfer from his DDA account, by credit from his bank charge account or by conventional check. The system permits the merchant to positively verify each purchase at the time of transaction. It promises merchants significant savings on losses from bad checks as well as from fraud and credit abuse. The system offers the consumer a convenient means of payment as well as protection through the use of a customer keyed secret code as a trigger for transactions.

Thrust of the Present Study

While other studies of the costs of float have approximated the impact of EFTS on bank float, the present study sought to measure actual float change with specific EFTS alternatives. The experimental findings published in this article are thus unique in this respect.

Any discussion about the speed at which items are paid sooner or later embraces the topic of float. Float is a label which is used loosely to describe a variety of financial situations.

456

For example, bankers generally agree that:

1) Float arises from the item collection process.

2) Banks lose float on payable through drafts.

3) Wire transfers reduce float for banks.

4) Zero balance corporate cash management policies erode bank float and bank balances.

5) Lock box arrangements attack the remittance float of corporations.

In fact, Thomas R. Atkinson [1] identifies seven distinct float concepts prevalent in banking circles. Since float has not been accurately quantified, bankers are uncertain about the impact of EFT systems on float, although they suspect float is important to their earning power. Atkinson recognizes this in his study:

"Particularly in the larger banks, however, there is a suspicion that a considerable portion of the volume of bank funds and therefore, the profitability of the bank is derived from float." [2]

A Definition of Float

In attempting to build a definition of float, three assertions may be made.

1) The term "float" is applied chiefly to transactions involving the transfer of assets from the account of one party to that of another, or payment transactions.

2) The term is used predominantly to describe assets which are held for a prolonged time in the hands of one party as earning assets, (or which are held for an abbreviated time by another party), because of a delay between an authorization to pay, (e.g. the issue of a check), and the actual settlement of that payment, (i.e. the payment of that check).

3) Reactions to float are twofold depending on viewpoint. Float is good if it is favorable; that is, if it prolongs earning assets. Conversely, float is bad if it is unfavorable; that is, if it foreshortens the time assets are held.

Commercial bankers are familiar with the most common type of float, called "commercial bank float" or "collection time float." Essentially this type of float describes funds which are prolonged in the coffers of drawee banks by delays in the item collection process. Bankers label the daily *Items in Process of Collection* figure on the balance sheet as the "float figure." This figure is the object of many float reduction programs, all of which seek to reduce the average collection time of deposited items. These programs are based on the simple logic that the faster funds are collected the faster they become earning assets. However, because bankers are justifiably preoccupied with this float, they develop a bias against comprehending float in other contexts.

In this paper, the reader is implored to expand his view of float beyond the confines of strict collection time, and to consider float in a much expanded context. The reason is that for the first time electronic funds transfer systems permit banks to create a payment system in which funds flow from debtor account to creditor account almost instantaneously. Such a rapid flow will reduce to zero not only "collection time" on items but also "deposit time." In effect, items will be deposited in the banking system and collected instantaneously. Such systems change not only conventional collection time float but also deposit time float. This means that some EFT systems permit banks to alter float costs beyond the point where items traditionally enter the banking system. With this point in mind, let us now discuss the roots of the float phenomenon.

The Roots of the Float Phenomenon

If one examines the majority of usages of the term float, as applied to check payments, one may readily discern a common thread linking them all: Inefficiency caused by structural complexity. The current check payment system is structurally complex. To settle an obligation by check requires many parties and many handlings. The simplest bill payment often requires handling by the payor, the postal service, the payee, the payee's bank, the payor's bank, perhaps an intermediate correspondent bank, check couriers, mail sorting clerks and route men and perhaps even airline personnel. Add to this structural complexity, the great volume of daily check payments passing through the 14,000 banks in the nation, and the outcome is predictable. The volume and the structural complexity make the paper check payments system relatively inefficient.

Fenner and Long [3] have noted that, "the average item remains in the bank distribution and processing system for about 2.6 business days." Delays of this magnitude are indeed significant when one multiplies them by the average value of items in the collection process for all banks in the system. Because of such delays, funds lie as earning assets in drawee bank demand deposit

---

[1] Atkinson, Thomas R. (of Carter H. Golembe Associates), *Bank Float in a New Payments System*, American Bankers Association, 1971, p. 11.

[2] Atkinson, ibid.

[3] Fenner, Linda and Long, Robert, *The Check Collection System, A Quantitative Description*, Bank Administration Institute, 1970, p. 18.

accounts for significant time spans, (i.e. 2.6 days on the average). While small individual customers are not alert to the earning power of such "prolonged" assets, bankers and corporate treasurers, who are in the business of optimizing earning assets, are quite aware of the profit potential. Since electronic funds transfer systems threaten to remove the "inefficiency," or float, from payment settlements, they are of vital interest to bankers.

Float has been defined above as the term used by bankers to describe deposits which are prolonged in drawee accounts because of delays between authorizations to pay and actual settlement. Wherever there is a delay in settlement, the payee is denied earning assets for the time of settlement and the payor enjoys earning assets in the amount of the transaction for the same period.

Because of inefficiencies in the present system the drawee bank in a payment transaction is the beneficiary of favorable float and the bank of first deposit (or payee's bank) is the recipient of unfavorable float. That is, the payee's bank must await settlement before it enjoys a real increase in investible assets. The greater the inefficiency, or the longer the duration from check issue to payment, the greater is the return to the drawee bank. At the same time, delays in settlement cost the payee bank a loss of investment opportunity.

The reader should realize one additional fact about the alleged multiple varieties of float. Float generated from items in process of collection is not generically different from lock box float, payable through draft float, zero balance cash management float of corporations, float created by credit card purchases or float in securities transactions. All forms of float are caused by delays in settlement. In each float transaction there is a beneficiary and a benefactor. The two roles may be held by banks, corporations or individuals in a variety of combinations. Float control programs by banks seek to reduce delays or inefficiencies, in collections from other banks. Float control programs by corporations seek to accomplish the same end for corporations.

Thus, the speed (or lack thereof) at which settlement is achieved magnifies the earning assets of a float beneficiary and diminishes the earning power of the benefactor. Since EFT systems will quicken the pace of settlement, these gains and losses will significantly diminish. Indeed, when EFT development reaches the state where an authorization to pay and settlement occur simultaneously, float will cease to exist.

The problem facing the float analysis team of the Atlanta Payments Project was to measure the magnitude of float changes for the Bill- Check system, Direct Deposit of Payroll and the retail Point of Sale transfer system. To measure float change the team sampled actual payroll checks, bill payment items and retail and grocery items in the Atlanta community. They subjected the data to the rigors of a float analysis model which identified the float gains and losses for each bank represented as a drawee or first deposit bank in the samples. The outcome of the analysis was a statement of the monthly interest gains or losses that each Atlanta bank could expect from a particular EFT system.

The Present Payment System

In order to gain a clear idea of float under the present check-based payment system, it is valuable to review the timing of the activities in the life cycle of an item (Figure 1). In a typical check payment transaction a check issuer provides an item to his creditor in payment for goods or services. The latter party presents this item to a bank of first deposit for credit to his account. This bank forwards the item through the collection process to the drawee bank for payment. The item may pass through an intermediate bank (i.e. correspondent bank or Federal Reserve) on its way to payment. The intermediate bank credits the bank of first deposit when it receives credit for the item. When the drawee bank receives the item, it credits the presenting bank and debits the issuer's account.

Three important points emerge from this narrative.

> A considerable time delay occurs between the issue of an item and its payment by the drawee bank. This time may be divided into two convenient segments: Deposit time and collection time.

Deposit Time (D)—the time in days from the issue of a check to its first deposit in a bank.

Collection Time (C)—the time in days from first deposit of an item to payment of that item by the drawee bank.

> The drawee bank has the use of the face value of the item for $(D + C)$ days because of the delay between issue and payment.

> The bank of first deposit waits for C days in order to obtain an increase in deposits from the item.

For simplicity, this study will specify two types of float: 1) Deposit time float is float generated by delays in depositing items. 2) Collection time float is float generated by item collection delays.

Each bank plays two roles in the collection process: It is a drawee bank on some items and a

Figure 1. The Participants in the Life Cycle of an Item.

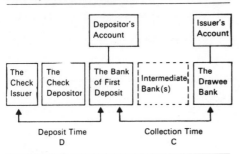

Deposit Time
D

Collection Time
C

Figure 2. Float

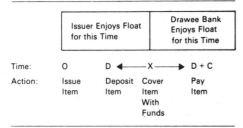

first deposit bank on others. As a drawee bank, it benefits from collection time float and deposit time float. As a bank of first deposit it suffers from collection time float. An example, illustrates this. Suppose a $300 item requires two days for deposit and three days for collection. Bank F is the bank of first deposit. Bank D is the drawee bank. Because Bank F awaits collection, it loses the investment potential of $300 for 3 days, (or 900 dollar days). Bank F suffers a collection time float disadvantage as a bank of first deposit. Bank D enjoys the earnings on $300 for 5 days (or 1500 dollar days), because of deposit and collection delays. As a drawee bank, it enjoys collection time and deposit time float advantages. Drawee banks and banks of first deposit are the parties which are most deeply affected by float in the payments system.

Intermediate banks (i.e., correspondent banks,) experience no significant float effect presently because they defer credit until collection. If float becomes apparent, these banks change their crediting schedules to conform to their collection experience. Check depositors share the float effects of the first deposit bank. Individuals are generally not concerned with the short-term investment aspects of their float "losses," but corporate depositors are quite concerned. All depositors cause float to increase for drawee banks by

delaying their check deposits. Check issuers fall into two float classes: Those who do not avail themselves of float as drawees and those who take advantage of float.

Large corporations have a financial size that justifies the investment of their idle DDA funds in the short-term securities market. The average check issuer lacks this size. Large corporations use float by covering the checks they issue at a point in time after their issuance. In effect, these corporations take for themselves part of the float that normally accrues to their drawee bank. The drawee bank and the issuer are treated together for the purposes of this analysis. Consider Figure 2 and the accompanying rationale.

For a particular payment transaction, there is a fixed amount of float available for a given item. It is clear that the drawee bank enjoys all the float if the issuer covers his item at the time of issue. On the other hand, the issuer enjoys all the float if he waits until payment to cover his items. (Such is the case with payable-through drafts.) Because of these facts this analysis considers the drawee bank and the issuer as a unit.

Float Under EFT Systems

When deposit and collection times change with electronic payment, float changes also. Consider the timing changes with the EFT system proposed by the Atlanta Payments Project. Under both the direct deposit of payroll system and the point of sale funds transfer system, deposit and collection will be effected in one day or less, i.e.

$$D + C < 1 \text{ day}$$

The Bill-Check system will not change deposit or collection time. In light of these facts the project assumed that the DDP and POS systems may be considered instantaneous systems. This hypothesis implies that since deposit and collection times have a value of zero, float also has a value of zero. If float vanishes under EFT, then a measure of present float becomes a measure of float change under EFT. For the project team, the task of measuring float change with EFT was simply the task of measuring present float for specific payments.

What does the assumption mean for banks in their dual roles as drawee and first deposit banks? Simply, if a bank in its role as drawee presently enjoys a float gain, it will lose this gain with EFT; if a bank in its role as bank of first deposit presently suffers a float loss, it will gain under EFT by having its loss removed.

Figure 3 summarizes float changes with EFT for a hypothetical item with a face value of z

Figure 3. The Conceptual Float Analysis Model

		Depositor's Account		Issuer's Account
		Deposit Time – D	Collection Time – C	
The Check Issuer*	The Check Depositor	The Bank of First Deposit	Interme-diate Bank(s)	The Drawee Bank*
Float Effect of Present System	* For simplicity the float effect for the check issuer is discussed with that of the Drawee Bank	Shares Float Effect of his bank	Waits C Days for a Real Deposit Increase of $Z	No Float Effect	Real Deposits are Inflated by $Z for D + C days
Float Effect with EFT			Obtains Real Deposit Increase at Time 0		Real Deposits are Reduced at Time 0
Net Change in Float			*Gains* Real Deposit Increase of $Z in D + C Days	No significant Change	*Loses* $Z for D + C days

dollars. D equals deposit time and C is collection time.

Note that because EFT systems cause both deposit and collection times to approach a value of zero, first deposit banks will actually gain an investment opportunity of the amount of the transaction, (e.g. $z), for $D + C$ days. EFT items will be deposited in the banking system more quickly and thus displace deposit time float as well as collection time float. In effect EFT systems permit banks which are presently experiencing a float loss on a particular type of payment to gain by removing the loss. Thus EFT systems of this nature permit banks to impact float costs that are presently caused outside the banking system.

The conceptual float model described above forms the basis for a mathematical float model to be explained below. The real value of the conceptual model is that it provides a way to approximate float change with EFT from measurements of present deposit time and collection time float.

The Float Measurement Process

Figure 4 describes the steps used by the team to reach their objective.

Step 1: Capture Payment Samples

During Spring and Summer of 1971 the team collected data in the following format from 18,-850 cancelled payroll checks at eleven businesses in Atlanta.

They sampled 58,000 utility payment items (i.e., natural gas, telephone, water, sewer, mortgage, rent and insurance premiums,) and 10,000 grocery and retail store checks from the deposits of seventeen firms at their Atlanta banks. The data format for these samples appears below.

Item Amount	Depositing Firm	Deposit Bank	Drawee Bank	Collection Time in Days

These data constitute payroll, electronic bill payment and point of sale check transactions. The team weighted each data file so that the expanded

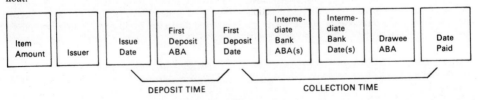

Item Amount	Issuer	Issue Date	First Deposit ABA	First Deposit Date	Interme-diate Bank ABA(s)	Interme-diate Bank Date(s)	Drawee ABA	Date Paid

DEPOSIT TIME   COLLECTION TIME

Figure 4. The Float Measurement Process

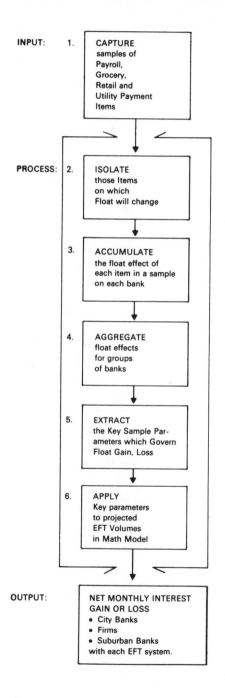

INPUT: 1. CAPTURE samples of Payroll, Grocery, Retail and Utility Payment Items

PROCESS: 2. ISOLATE those Items on which Float will change

3. ACCUMULATE the float effect of each item in a sample on each bank

4. AGGREGATE float effects for groups of banks

5. EXTRACT the Key Sample Parameters which Govern Float Gain, Loss

6. APPLY Key parameters to projected EFT Volumes in Math Model

OUTPUT: NET MONTHLY INTEREST GAIN OR LOSS
• City Banks
• Firms
• Suburban Banks
with each EFT system.

file represented a monthly profile for each payment type.

Step 2. Isolate Payments on Which Float Will Change

Float will not change on certain EFT items. For example, on DDP items first deposited at the drawee bank, there is no bank float. However, firms which manage float may experience a change. (It should be noted that the team applied the same analysis technique to each payment sample. Since the greatest float change occurred for payroll items, this exposition will highlight the DDP float analysis.)

The team subjected the payroll float data file to analysis. One purpose of this analysis was to accumulate the effects of those items which contribute to the float advantage and disadvantage of each bank represented in the sample.

For a given payroll drawn on a city bank one expects checks to be deposited at one of the following: The drawee bank, other city banks, surburban banks in the metropolitan area or banks outside metropolitan boundaries. The important features of this pattern are: 1) Checks deposited at the drawee bank do not create float because their payment involves an intra-bank transfer of funds. 2) Float on checks deposited at banks outside the metropolitan area will only be changed as a DDP system is expanded. 3) A DDP system will reduce deposit and collection time only on payroll checks deposited in city banks (other than the drawee bank) and on payroll items deposited in suburban banks. The team, therefore, deleted those items from the sample which did not change float with EFT. Figure 5 illustrates the checks which experience a change in float.

In order to build an intuitive notion about payroll float change it is helpful to note the following facts about Figure 5. From the collective viewpoint of Atlanta's city banks.

1) Present Payroll Float Gain checks (dotted portion of Figure 5) outnumber Float Loss Checks (cross-hatched portion).

2) Present Float Gain checks have longer average "floating" times (3.01 days) than present float loss items (2.35 days).

Present gain checks outnumber loss checks because large Atlanta firms draw their payroll on large Atlanta banks and these banks individually control large shares of the consumer DDA market. The present gain items float longer because they include items deposited in suburban banks, and these items experience longer average collection times because suburban banks deliver their deposits to their large city bank correspondents for DDA processing. The delivery process prolongs collection time on payroll items.

Since present gain items for Atlanta city banks outnumber loss items and "float" longer, the city banks presently experience a float gain on payroll items. In view of the fact that a direct deposit of payroll system will shrink deposit and collection time, the city banks will lose their float advantage under such a system. The objective of the three remaining processing steps is to quantify this loss.

Step 3. Accumulate Float for each Bank

The project team processed each payment file with computer programs which also measured deposit time float and collection time float for each item. The programs accumulated the float gain and loss contributions of each item to a pair of banks. As an illustration, assume one wished to accumulate the float contributions of two payroll items to the banking system. Suppose one knew the following data about each item:

	Item #1	Item #2
Item Amount	$300	$700
Deposit Time	2 days	4 days
Collection Time	3 days	2 days
First Deposit Bank	Bank A	Bank C
Drawee Bank	Bank B	Bank A

The product: (Amount) (Float Time) measures the float contribution of a given item. For the drawee bank this product is positive. For the first deposit bank it is negative. The present net float contribution of the two items given above for each bank is shown in Figure 6. That diagram indicates the float contributions of two items to the three banks. Banks A and B are net float gainers while Bank C is a float loser. The project team employed a computer analysis of this type on a large scale to assess the present net float posture of each bank in the DDP sample.

Step 4. Aggregate Float for Groups of Banks

The team grouped the float gains and losses of Atlanta city banks together to make computations manageable. Suburban bank float effects were likewise grouped. Output from this stage enabled the team to define and calculate the key sample

Figure 5. Payroll Checks on Which Float Will Change

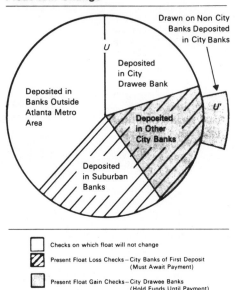

☐ Checks on which float will not change

▨ Present Float Loss Checks – City Banks of First Deposit
    (Must Await Payment)

☐ Present Float Gain Checks – City Drawee Banks
    (Hold Funds Until Payment)

U – Payroll Checks Drawn on City Banks
U' – Payroll Checks Drawn on Non-City Local Banks

characteristics that affected net float gain or loss to these groups of banks.

Step 5. Extract Key Sample Parameters

What factors determine whether a bank gains or loses float? The team found that two critical variables govern the net float position for a particular bank. These were: 1) The relative number of present float gain checks to present float loss checks. 2) Floating time; in particular, the floating time for gain checks and the floating time for loss checks.

Checks which are presently drawn on other local banks and first deposited in Bank A are float gain checks for this bank under EFT. On the other hand, items drawn on Bank A and first deposited in other local banks are float loss checks for this bank under EFT. The ratio of the number of float gain checks to the number of float loss checks differs from bank to bank.

The size of the ratio is itself a function of another important variable—payment type. Certain types of payments generate more float loss checks for large banks than others. For example, payroll items are likely to offer large city banks a float loss under EFT because the majority of payroll items are drawn on large banks. (Large firms tend to do business with large banks.)

Checks automated at the point of sale are likely to offer city banks a preponderance of float gain checks. Large ·merchants also conduct their finance at large banks. The number of items deposited by merchants at city banks exceeds the number of those items drawn on these same banks. Because of this, POS items offer a float gain to city banks under EFT.

Figure 6. The Float Contributions of Two Items

(Values in Dollar-Days)

	Bank A	Bank B	Bank C
Item #1	−1,500	+1,500	
Item #2	+4,200		−4,200
Net Float Contribution of these items	+2,700	+1,500	−4,200

The magnitude of float gains or losses is also contingent on the duration of floating times. If float loss checks under EFT outnumber float gain checks and float loss checks have longer floating times for particular banks, then those banks will suffer net float losses with EFT. Such is the case with the direct deposit of payroll system for the Atlanta city banks.

The float analysis required the project team to compute average floating time for both float gain and float loss items. The derivation of R', average floating time for float loss items, is presented in Figure 7 so that the reader may understand the computation process. A series of computer programs accumulated the amounts of city bank payroll float loss items cleared for six clearing time values. Their values were: 0 days, 1 day, 2 days, 3 days, 4 or 5 days, and 6 days or more. One recalls from Figure 5 that city bank float loss items fall into two groups: Items drawn on a city bank, deposited in other city banks; and items drawn on a city bank, deposited in suburban banks.

The computer program accumulated the amounts and clearing time for each of these groups separately. This output appears in Figure 7.

Line 1 in Figure 7 shows that $768,000 in payroll float loss items deposited in city banks cleared immediately (in 0 days) while $2,459,000 in payroll loss items cleared in 1 day, $789,000 cleared in two days and so on. Line 2 relates that $116,000 in payroll float loss checks deposited in suburban banks cleared immediately while $1,040,000 in items cleared in 1 day and $1,889,000 in payroll items required two days to clear. Line 3 (the sum of lines 1 and 2) shows total deposit amounts for all float loss items for the specified clearing times. Line 4 indicates the float values of corresponding deposit amounts on line 3. (For example, $2,678,000 clearing in 2 days has a float value of 5,356,000 dollar days.)

Figure 7. Deposit Amounts for Specified Clearing Times for DDP Float Loss Checks

(Values in $000's)

Clearing Times in days	0	1	2	3	4.5	6+	TOTAL
Deposit Amounts for the Clearing Times (in days) for Float Loss Items Deposited in City Banks	768	2,459	789	986	1,267	482	6,751
Deposit Amounts for the Clearing Times (in days) for Float Loss Items Deposited in Suburban Banks	116	1,040	1,889	2,514	2,690	1,700	9,949
TOTAL Deposit Amounts for the Clearing Times for all Float Loss Checks	884	3,499	2,678	3,500	3,957	2,182	16,700
Float Value of These Deposits in Dollar-Days	0	3,499	5,356	10,502	17,808	13,096	50,261

One may compute the average clearing time for all float loss checks by dividing their total float value by the total deposit value. These values are found at the bottom right of Figure 7. This computation is shown below:

R′ or Average
Clearing Time
for Float Loss
Checks to
City Banks

$$R' = \frac{\text{TOTAL FLOAT VALUE}}{\text{TOTAL DEPOSIT VALUE}} \quad \begin{array}{l}\text{Of these checks}\\ \hline \text{Of these checks}\end{array}$$

$$R' = \frac{50{,}261{,}000 \text{ dollar days}}{16{,}700{,}000 \text{ dollars}}$$

$$R' = 3.01 \text{ days}$$

The other important floating time value (for float gain checks), $D + C = 2.35$ days, was produced in a similar fashion.

Step 6. Calculate Net Interest

The team calculated net monthly interest gains or losses to each sample bank by applying the values of the two key float variables mentioned above to monthly payment volumes. The vehicle for this application was a mathematical float model. This model is based on the formula for computing simple interest,

$I = PRT$, where
$I =$ Interest
$P =$ Principal
$R =$ Rate
$T =$ Time

The project chose this vehicle because the float change with EFT systems is dependent on the dollar volume of payments automated (P), the interest rate (R) and floating time (T) for automated payments. These facts make the simple interest structure a natural choice for the model. The model is as follows:

$$I_{NET} = VR\left[F_{GAIN} - F_{LOSS}\right]$$

$I_{NET} =$ Net monthly interest gained or lost by this bank with the EFT system.

$V =$ Monthly value of automated check payments drawn on this bank or principal.

$R =$ Annual interest rate.

$F_{GAIN} =$ The positive contribution of float gain checks to a bank as a bank of first deposit.

$F_{LOSS} =$ The negative contribution of float loss checks to a bank as a drawee bank.

The model offers several important advantages to the user.

> It permits the banker to determine float change with the adoption of any EFT system without an extensive data collection effort. The important base variable, V, (the monthly value of automated check payments drawn on this bank) is easily calculable by the banker.

> It permits the banker to perform quick sensitivity analyses on the important float variables. One may vary any one of the independent variables and quickly determine the impact of the change on float for his bank.

> It permits the user to calculate EFT float changes for any interest rate. It does not limit him to a specific rate.

> It is applicable to an EFT float analysis for any bank, and is not limited to Metropolitan Atlanta alone.

The Expanded Model

Below is presented the expanded mathematical model.

The Simplified Model:

$$I_{NET} = VR\left[F_{GAIN} - F_{LOSS}\right]$$

The Expanded Model:

$$I_{NET} = VR\left[\left(\frac{D}{N}\right)\frac{(.825)}{365}\left(D+C\right) - \left(P\right)\frac{(.825)}{365}R'\right]$$

In the expanded model:

where

$I_{NET} =$ The net monthly interest gained or lost by a bank for EFT payments of a given type (e.g., direct deposit of payroll items).

$V =$ The monthly value of automated check payments of this type drawn on this bank.

$R =$ The annual interest rate. (The project chose 7.3% per annum as a rule of thumb because it is convenient. At this rate the interest on $1,000,000 for 1 day is $200.)

$\dfrac{D}{N} =$ The ratio of the number of items giving this bank a float gain with an EFT system to the number of items giving a float loss with that EFT system. (A more precise definition is: The number of EFT items drawn on other banks, deposited in this bank, divided by the number of EFT items deposited in other banks, drawn on this bank.)

(.825) = The reserve requirement reduction of 17.5%; that is (.825) = (1.000 − .175).

365 = A factor to convert annual interest rate to daily interest rate.

$D =$ The average value of deposit time for float gain checks.

$C =$ The average value of collection time for float gain checks.

$D + C =$ The average clearing time for float gain checks. (Note: D and C measure floating time for check candidates for EFT that are presently first deposited at the named bank.)

$R' =$ The average clearing time, (i.e. deposit time plus collection time), for float loss checks. R' measures floating time for check candidates for EFT that are presently drawn on the named bank but deposited elsewhere.)

$P =$ A reduction factor to account for float enjoyed by the check issuer instead of by the drawee bank. (For example, if 30% of the float on payrolls drawn on a bank are enjoyed by its check issuers, then that bank enjoys only 70% of the total float available. In this case P has a value of .70).

This model permits a banker to compute the float impact of a specific EFT system on his bank quickly and easily. The only variable that requires research is V. It can be approximated by using the following relationship:

$$V = N \quad A$$

where

$V =$ The monthly value of automated check payments of this type drawn on this bank monthly.

$N =$ The number of EFT check candidates drawn on this bank monthly.

$A =$ The average value of an EFT check candidate from Atlanta Payments Project data.

The banker has the option to use Atlanta Payments Project values for the remaining variables, or to create his own values for these variables, that is, for $\dfrac{D}{N}$, D, C, R' and P. These values may be found in the Parameter Table below.

To simplify use of the model for bankers, a nomograph was created. The nomograph is a graph that enables one with the aid of a straight edge to read the value of the dependent variables, F_{GAIN} and F_{LOSS}, when the values of the independent variables D, C, R' and $\dfrac{D}{N}$ are known. (Recall that F_{GAIN} expresses the positive contribution of float loss checks to a bank in the drawee role.) In effect the nomograph permits the user to apply the simplified model rather than the expanded one to his EFT float situation.

The float nomograph plots floating time values along the horizontal axis against float contribution values (i.e. the values of F_{GAIN} and F_{LOSS}) along the vertical axis. (See the Float Nomograph, Figure 8.) There are 18 radials eminating from the origin of the axes. These radials are labeled with values for the ratio, $\dfrac{D}{N}$. A given radial describes the float contributions of checks for a given $\dfrac{D}{N}$ value for the floating time specified on the horizontal axis. The project team constructed a Float Nomograph Worksheet to aid the reader in using the Nomograph. This worksheet also follows below as Figure 9.

Float Change for the Atlanta Banks

The Atlanta Payments Project measured float changes for three EFT Systems: 1) The direct deposit of payroll system, 2) the electronic bill payment system and 3) a funds transfer system at the point of sale.

Float Change with Direct Deposit of Payroll

The following assumptions underlie the DDP analysis.

1) The DDP analysis assumes that all the payroll checks in a metropolitan DDP system are drawn on four large Atlanta banks. The payroll sample had this characteristic. The bulk of payroll checks are issued by large employers who are customers of the large banks.

Figure 8. The Float Nomograph

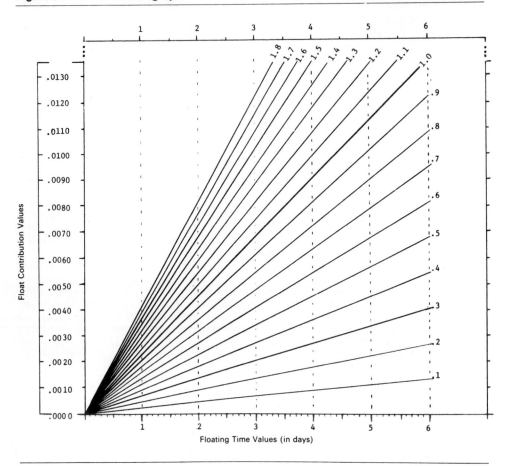

2) The DDP analysis assumes that 30% of payroll float is enjoyed by check issuers rather than by their drawee banks. A DDP survey of 100 area firms produced this finding.

3) The DDP analysis employs a float gain to float loss ratio; $\frac{D}{N}$ of .503. The average Atlanta bank has roughly two paychecks deposited in other local banks and drawn on itself for every one paycheck deposited in itself and drawn on other local banks.

4) The DDP analysis aggregated float for the four city banks in order to keep calculations manageable. Individual bank float losses are easily derived from the aggregate.

5) All the analyses employ an interest rate of 7.3%. This rate was chosen for convenience. The interest on $1,000,000 for 1 day is $200 at this rate. A 50% reduction in this rate reduces float interest losses by 50%.

6) The DDP analysis employed the following floating time values, which were found to be sample characteristics: The average clearing time for the float gain checks was 2.35 days; the average clearing time for float loss checks was 3.01 days. These two figures differ because float loss checks include checks deposited in suburban banks and these checks take longer to clear.

7) The authors derived estimates of DDP volume from data about automated payroll checks drawn in metropolitan Atlanta from an earlier study. These DDP volume estimates were introduced into the mathematical model. The output of the model describes the monthly interest losses on float for four large Atlanta banks with a DDP

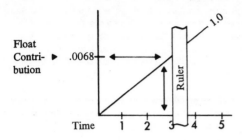

Float
Contri- ▶ .0068
bution

Time   1   2   3   4   5

Worksheet Instruction:

(c) Read upward along the left edge of the ruler to the point where it intersects the prime radial, labeled 1.0 on the Nomograph. Read horizontally from this point to find the float loss contribution value of the loss checks, i.e., F_{LOSS}. The value of F_{LOSS} is .0068.

(d) A percentage of float loss checks may not represent a float loss to the bank but rather to one or more customers. If this is so, reduce the factor, F_{LOSS}, by this percentage.

Comment:

Float on 20% of Bank A's payroll checks is enjoyed by commercial customers. Thus Bank A loses float on 80% of total float loss checks. As a result, $.80 \times F_{LOSS} = .0054$.

(e) Enter this modified value of F_{LOSS} in the appropriate box. The workspace now reads:

$$\begin{array}{cccc} & V & R & [F_{GAIN} - F_{LOSS}] \\ I_{NET} = & \$56,469,000 & .043 & [.0042 - .0054] \end{array}$$

5. Calculate $F_{GAIN} - F_{LOSS}$.

6. Multiply this sum by the product, $(V \bullet R)$.

7. This new product indicates the monthly change in earnings on float for the bank with the specified EFT system. (A positive sign indicates an interest gain. A negative sign indicates an interest loss.) In this example:

$$I_{NET} = -\$2,913.80$$

This indicates that Bank A will lose monthly earnings approaching $3,000 on float with its direct deposit of payroll system.

---

system. The team converted these interest losses into monthly interest losses per DDP item to simplify the findings.

The project team analyzed the payroll payments in the manner described earlier. That is, they extracted the values of the key sample variables and computed the value of $(F_{GAIN} - F_{LOSS})$ for the Atlanta city banks, Atlanta suburban (non-city) banks and for firms. They applied the mathematical model to the result and computed the monthly interest gains and losses to the respective economic units with a DDP system. These results are:

> The Atlanta city banks will lose 2.9¢ per month in float earnings (interest) for each payroll check automated in a direct deposit of payroll system.

> Atlanta firms will lose a comparable 2.8¢ per DDP item.

> Suburban Atlanta banks will gain 5.8¢ per month for each check captured by a DDP system.

Some Atlanta firms make a practice of covering payroll items with good DDA funds after the checks are issued to their employees. This practice is based on the knowledge that the check clearing process is relatively slow. These firms thus share the present float gains of the Atlanta

city banks and will see this gain removed by an automated system. This phenomenon helps reduce the magnitude of the float loss for the Atlanta city banks under such a system.

A 2.9¢ per DDP item per month interest loss due to float removed is by no means insignificant to city banks. However, the net savings of a direct deposit of payroll system projected by the Atlanta Payments Project is on the order of 10¢ per item. Savings of this magnitude are achievable because the DDP system impacts the very volatile receiving costs associated with processing payroll items on peak days. While the absolute cost of the float loss on payroll items is large indeed, the relative cost is small because of this huge projected savings. Thus, float losses from a DDP system do not present a grave cost barrier to implementation of this system in Atlanta.

Float Change with Electronic Bill Payment

Long before the Bill-Check system was created, the project team had captured and performed an analysis of float for bill payment samples. The payments sampled by the team included:

1) Telephone payments
2) Natural gas payments
3) Water utility payments

4) Sanitation payments
5) Mortgage payments
6) Rental payments
7) Insurance premium payments

Data from these payments was destined for float analyses of various EFT preauthorization systems. When the Bill-Check system emerged as the bill payment system solution for the Atlanta Payment Project, the project team diverted its efforts from a float analysis of preauthorized payments. However, the critical parameters discovered by the project team have been generated for the use of other payment groups. These properties are found in the Float Parameter Table, Figure 10. The Bill-Check system will simply not change float. It does not shorten deposit time nor does it reduce collection time on bill payment items.

Float Change with the POS System

While Atlanta city banks stand to gain float interest on grocery and retail items automated by a POS system, the project team found the actual gain slight. Two facts explain this finding: 1) Floating times for the items are short. 2) Float gain checks only slightly outnumber float loss checks.

Floating times are short because merchants tend to deposit items they receive quickly. Secondly, the majority of items are drawn on city banks. As such, collection times are short.

Figure 10. Float Parameter Table

| Type of Payment | Average Value per Item | Average Delay in Clearing (days) | | Float Gain to Loss Ratio Value |
		EFT Gain Items $T_D + T_C$	EFT Loss Items (T_R)	$\frac{D}{N}$
Payroll*	$188.23	2.35*	3.01*	.501
Telephone	20.55	1.68	1.00	3.869
Natural Gas	9.23	1.64	1.00	9.788
Water	11.90	1.50	1.00	2.152
Sanitation	15.18	1.44	1.00	1.906
Mortgage	174.73	1.36	1.00	2.152
Rent	155.54	1.31	999	1.736
Insurance	33.91	1.61	.967	3.705
Grocery	41.06	2.09	2.00	1.194
Retail	30.12	2.27	2.00	1.528

*Times listed in the table describe actual average deposit and collection times for both gain and loss items. The authors *estimated* deposit times for regular bill payment and point of sale item candidates in determining average delay in clearing values.

Float gain checks hold a slight majority compared to float loss checks. The ratio of EFT float gain to float loss checks exceeds the value of 1 slightly for both retail and grocery checks. (For grocery items $D/N = 1.19$ and for retail items $D/N = 1.53$). This characteristic reflects the heavy market penetration of large city banks in the retail market. Over 75% of grocery and retail items sampled were drawn on the large city banks. Items drawn on other banks, deposited in a particular city bank, only slightly exceeded items drawn on this bank, deposited elsewhere. Because of this, the Atlanta city banks do not reap outstanding float benefits from a POS system. Consider the following findings.

> A point of sale funds transfer system will generate a net interest gain due to float change of slightly over a half cent per POS item per month for Atlanta city banks.

> This system will cause Atlanta suburban banks to lose interest of approximately four tenths of one cent per POS item per month, because of float change.

These results mean, for example, that when 1,000,000 items are flowing monthly through the POS system, Atlanta city banks will share a gain totaling $5,500 per month in earnings because of a favorable change in float.

Summary and Conclusions

This project set about answering the question: What are the float costs and benefits to banks from accelerated payment through EFT systems? The following summarizes the major findings of their research.

> Substantial sums of demand deposits are involved in float.

> Float describes deposits which are prolonged in drawee bank accounts because of settlement delays in payment transactions.

> Float is caused by delays in settlement which in turn are caused by the structural complexity of the check payment system.

> Delays in settlement magnify the earning assets of float beneficiaries (drawee banks) and diminish the earnings of float benefactors (first deposit banks). The latter must await settlement in order to gain real deposit increases.

> For a given payment type a given bank is both a beneficiary and a benefactor of float. Namely, that bank gains float on payments drawn on it deposited elsewhere while it loses float on payments drawn on banks elsewhere, but deposited in that institution.

> EFT systems will change float for banks by removing (or reducing) delays in settlement.

> If a bank is a present net float beneficiary for a specific type of payment, then under instantaneous payment its present net gain will be removed. (For example, suppose Bank A gains $5 million in deposits over a month as a beneficiary while it loses $4 million as a benefactor. Its net float gain is $1 million. Suppose an EFT system reduces both deposit time and collection time for these payments to zero. Under EFT the bank will have its net float gain of $1 million removed.)

> Present net float gains (or losses) are more important for particular banks than are gross float gains or gross float losses because it is the net float that will be removed with EFT systems.

> This study found that the large Atlanta city banks, who will finance a direct deposit of payroll system, are presently net float gainers on payroll items. They stand to lose float earnings (i.e. interest) of 2.9¢ per DDP item per month. This float loss is rendered less significant by a large per item net savings with such a system. The Atlanta city banks are net float beneficiaries on payroll payments because they dominate the commercial account market in Atlanta and are therefore drawee banks for the great bulk of payroll items. As such, roughly two payroll checks benefit a city bank for every one item that works in its disfavor.

> The study learned that Atlanta firms as payroll drawees are present float gainers at a rate of 2.8¢ per item per month by virtue of the fact that certain firms transfer funds to their bank to cover payrolls after the payroll checks have been issued to employees. A DDP system will remove this present net gain.

> Atlanta suburban banks are present float benefactors for payroll items in the area. That is, they are first deposit banks for items largely not drawn on themselves. These suburban banks suffer a present loss approximating 5.8¢ per item per month. Under DDP this loss will be removed.

> The Bill Check system, being designed to retain consumer control over the timing of his regular bill payments, will not appreciably reduce deposit time or collection time on regular bill payments in Atlanta. Thus, float will not change on such payments. On the other hand radical changes in deposit time float are posed by regular bill payment plans involving preauthorization. However, with regard to regular bill payment, there is a natural impetus on the part of the customer to defer payment while he reviews the reasonableness of charges assessed him. In addition to this natural delay, mail delays further

lengthen deposit times of regular bill payment items. Regular bill payment preauthorization plans would cause large changes in deposit time float by limiting the time delays described above. However, the success of such plans is presently thwarted by low levels of consumer acceptance. Barring further enhancements of preauthorization systems with incentives like discounts, it appears that preauthorization plans will not get widespread consumer acceptance. The Bill Check has the potential for widespread acceptance because it permits the consumer to retain control over his payment habits.

> The Point of Sale funds transfer system (POS) will, surprisingly, have little effect on float for any economic units in Atlanta. Present float losses of Atlanta city banks roughly equal present float gains for retail and grocery payments. (These payments are prime candidates for POS automation.) The reason for the trade-off is simply that the Atlanta city banks dominate not only the commercial account market (i.e. retail and grocery store account market), but they also tower over other banks in capturing the retail market (i.e. the people who write grocery and retail checks). Thus for a particular city bank, each loss check (i.e. an item drawn on another bank, deposited in this bank) is matched by a gain check (i.e. an item drawn on itself, deposited in another bank). The typical city bank is a slight net float loser presently. A POS system will remove this loss. Atlanta suburban banks will sustain a corresponding slight net float loss under a POS system.

Thus, because the Atlanta city banks have roughly balanced positions as beneficiaries—benefactors in retail and grocery payment float, the float change with faster settlement will be slight.

> How applicable are these findings to banks in other metropolitan areas contemplating EFT system implementations? This study defines the important variables that control net float gain or loss for parties. It has related these variables in mathematical and graphical models which bankers in other locales may use to define the float costs or benefits that flow from automating specific payments. The research team provides experimental values for the critical variables that were found to be characteristic of float in Atlanta. Whether or not these same values apply to other metropolitan areas depends on how closely those areas compare to the Atlanta banking community. The Atlanta environment can be characterized generally as one in which a handful of large city banks dominate both the wholesale and retail banking markets. They are able to reach wide

retail market penetration by virtue of extensive branching. A clever use of the experimental values provided by this study in which the user adapts particular variables to fit local conditions will reward the user with results that are far more meaningful than heuristic guesses—the only tools available to date. Thus while this project has not answered the question of applicability to other areas, it has created the tools that may provide the answer.

> The suspicions of some bankers that float constitutes a large part of bank earning power are justified in some measure by the present study. What is apparent is that payment type, bank market penetration in the commercial and retail markets, and length of floating time are the three crucial variables that determine the net float posture for a given bank. ■

How to Use the Float Nomograph and the Worksheet

Suppose a vice president of Bank A wishes to assess the float impact of a Direct Deposit of Payroll system on his institution. He should pursue the six step procedure outlined on the WORKSHEET.
Note: The authors will "walk" the reader through the WORKSHEET instructions and provide suitable comments along the way.)

Float Nomograph Worksheet

1. Enter the monthly value of payments by checks to be automated by the EFT system in the box labeled V.

Comment:

Bank A will automate 300,000 payroll items monthly with its DDP system. The monthly value of these items may be computed as follows:

$$V = N \bullet A$$

$$V = (300,000) \ (\$188.23)$$
$$\overline{\text{pay check}}$$
(See Atlanta Payments Project Vol. 5, p. 166)

$$V = \$56,469,000$$

$$\begin{array}{cccc} & V & \bullet & [R & F_{\text{GAIN}} - F_{\text{LOSS}}] \\ I_{\text{NET}} = & \$56,469,000 & \bullet & [& - &] \end{array}$$

2. Enter the interest rate the bank earns on float in the box labeled R.

Comment:

Bank A currently earns 4.3% in the government securities market.

$$\begin{array}{cccc} & V & \bullet & R & [F_{\text{GAIN}} - F_{\text{LOSS}}] \\ I_{\text{NET}} = & \$56,469,000 & \bullet & .043 & [\ - \ ] \end{array}$$

3. Find the Value of F_{GAIN} as follows:

(a) Add deposit and collection time for float gain items, (i.e., $D + C$).

Comment:

Bank A's float gain payroll checks (items drawn on others deposited in this bank), require an average of 1.2 days from issue to deposit and 1.1 days for collection. Thus $D + C = 2.3$ days.

(b) Select a value for the ratio $\dfrac{D}{N}$ that describes the float gain items for the bank, (or use Atlanta Payment Project values from the Parameter Table.) Locate the ratio radial with this value on the nomograph.

Comment:

The number of payroll checks drawn on Bank A by its customers totals 500,000 monthly. Because of its location near a factory district, Bank A receives a large number of payroll checks for first deposit that are drawn on other banks. These are EFT float gain checks. They number 400,000.

Thus, the value of $\dfrac{D}{N} = \dfrac{400,000}{500,000} = .8$

(c) Place the left edge of a ruler parallel to the vertical axis of the Nomograph at the $D + C$ value on the Time axis (2.3 days).

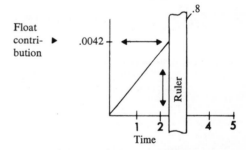

(d) Read upward along the left edge of the ruler to the point where it intersects the ratio radial selected in (b) above. Read horizontally from this point to find the float gain contribution value of the gain checks. The value of F_{GAIN} is .0042.

(e) Enter this value in box F_{GAIN}.

4. Find the value of F_{LOSS} as follows:

(a) Decide on an average clearing time, R', for float loss checks for the bank, (or use Atlanta Payment Project values from the Parameter Table.) In this example, Bank A will use the Atlanta Payments Project value of 3.0 days for R'.

(b) Place the left edge of the ruler parallel to the vertical axis of the nomograph at the R' value on the Time axis (3.0 days).

Figure 9. Float Nomograph Worksheet

1. **ENTER** the monthly value of payments by checks to be automated by the EFT system in the box labeled V in the workspace.

2. **ENTER** the interest rate your bank earns on float in the box labeled R in the workspace.

3. **FIND** the value of F_{GAIN} as follows:

    (a) Add deposit and collection time for float (i.e., D + C).

    (b) Select a value for the ratio $\frac{D}{N}$ that describes the float gain items for your bank, (or use Atlanta Payment Project values from the attached Parameter Table.) Locate the ratio radial with this value on the nomograph.

    (c) Place the left edge of a ruler parallel to the vertical axis of the NOMOGRAPH at the D + C value on the Time axis.

    (d) Read upward along the left edge of the ruler to the point where it intersects the ratio radial selected in 3 (b) above. Then read horizontally from this point to find the <u>float **gain** contribution</u> value of the gain checks.

    (e) **ENTER** this value in the box labeled F_{GAIN} in the WORKSPACE.

4. **FIND** the value of F_{LOSS} as follows:

    (a) Decide on an average clearing time R' for float loss checks, for your bank, (or use Atlanta Payment Project values from the attached Parameter Table.)

    (b) Place the left edge of the ruler parallel to the vertical axis of the nomograph at the R' value on the Time axis.

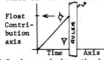

    (c) Read upward along the left edge of the ruler to the point where it intersects the prime radial, labeled 1.0 on the NOMOGRAPH. Then read horizontally from this point to find the <u>float loss contribution value</u> of the loss checks, i.e., F_{LOSS}

    (d) A percentage of float loss checks may not represent a float loss to your bank but rather to one or more of your customers. If this is so, REDUCE the factor, F_{LOSS}, by this percentage.

    (e) Enter this modified value of F_{LOSS} in the appropriate box in the WORKSPACE.

5. **CALCULATE** the algebraic sum $\left[F_{GAIN} - F_{LOSS}\right]$ in the workspace. Be careful of the Algebraic sign of the result!

6. **MULTIPLY** this sum by the product, (V · R) in the workspace.

7. This new product (with the proper sign) indicates the Monthly change in earnings on float for your bank with the specified EFT system. (A positive sign indicates an interest gain. A negative sign indicates an interest loss.)

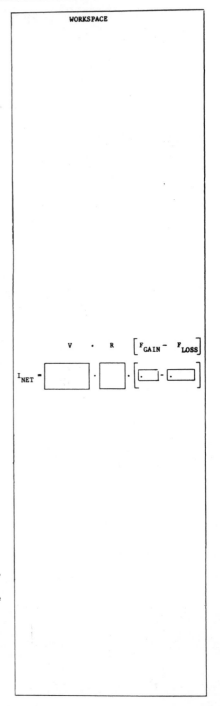

WORKSPACE

$$I_{NET} = \boxed{} \cdot \boxed{} \cdot \left[\boxed{} - \boxed{}\right]$$

$$\phantom{I_{NET} =}\ \ V\ \ \cdot\ \ R\ \ \left[F_{GAIN} - F_{LOSS}\right]$$

Chapter 38

THE PUBLIC POLICY IMPLICATIONS OF EFTS*

By James F. Dingle

*This article is reprinted, with permission, from *Journal of Bank Research,* Vol. 7, No. 1 (Spring, 1976), pp. 30-36.

The Public Policy Implications of EFTS

There is a growing understanding of the extent to which electronic systems for financial transactions (commonly but imprecisely known as EFTS) will restructure many aspects of financial markets during the next few decades. This article is intended to serve as a guide showing probable developments based on the gradual extension of the use of electronic systems in various financial contexts. It points out the ways in which public policy, particularly monetary policy, is most likely to evolve as a result of this trend.

The method used in the paper entails two steps. A probable future scenario is prepared for four sectors of the economy—private individuals, nonfinancial corporations, financial intermediaries and the government. These scenarios take into account the currently available technology of computers and communication devices as well as the ways in which financial institutions plan to apply this technology. Special attention is given to the extent and speed with which customers in these four sectors will react to such flow of market information as prices, interest rates and exchange rates. The second step is a consideration of how stabilization policy might be conducted, given the outlined scenario. In order to identify potential problems, the logic of policy formation is traced—from its objectives, through the various policy instruments to their lagged impact on the economy. Summary tables of the analyses are also included.

In very broad terms, the results suggest a strong need for the financial community to react much more rapidly to short-run market trends occurring in all countries. In response, public policy will have to rely increasingly on computerized information systems and preprogrammed control routines. The technology is consequently biased toward dirigisme.

A Probable Scenario

Private Individuals. Money cards used in a similar way as credit cards by individuals shopping in retail stores will cause bank deposits to be trans-ferred electronically and with very little delay to the accounts of the vendors. The demand for bank notes and coin will thus gradually decline. The computer terminals located in the retail outlets will also be able to provide the individual with instant bank credit in accordance with prearranged credit lines. Consequently instead of "bounced" checks there will be immediate overdraft loans. Consumer expenditure will thus be determined to a certain extent by the size of these credit lines. Private individuals will authorize regular electronic transfer of their wages or salaries directly from their employers to personal bank accounts and pre-authorize such regular payments as mortgage interest and insurance premiums to third parties. The distinction between such credit transfers and payments for retail purchases will not be significant due to a shortened clearing lag. Counterfeiting will give way to card theft and wiretapping. Large currency payments will become increasingly rare and therefore suspect. Moreover, payments made nationally and internationally for illegal activities could become relatively less anonymous due to the ease with which electronic transactions can be audited.

Nonfinancial Corporations. The typical corporate treasurer will utilize a computer terminal rather than checks or drafts for an increasing proportion of company payments. The direct depositing of employees' wages mentioned earlier provides an example. The same terminal will provide reports on the cash balances of the corporation at the completion of each clearing period, which may be shortened from the current one day to one-half or one-quarter day. As a result, the management of the corporation's cash position will become increasingly sensitive to changing money market conditions and exchange rates. The ability to borrow by overdraft loans with negligible lag and at market rates will compensate for the fact that float—the payment items in the process of settlement—will be drastically reduced. Semilegal transactions, such as "check kiting" and the duplication of financial investments in two countries over the weekend, will therefore become

Figure 1. Changes in Behavior Likely to be Caused by Electronic Systems for Financial Transactions

Sector:	Regular Payments	Borrowing	Lending	Foreign Exchange	Nonlegal
Private Individuals	Money cards partially displace bank notes and coin. Expenditure constrained by credit lines, not by budgets. Preauthorization of mortgage, insurance items.	Instant credit. Automated credit authorization systems, eventually linked internationally.	Wages automatically deposited with, also invested by banks. Access to financial intermediaries by telephone and by retail store terminals.	By banks, with exchange rates set more frequently.	Counterfeiting becomes card theft, wire tapping. "Bounced" checks become automatic overdraft loans.
Nonfinancial Corporations	Wages deposited directly in banks. Terminals used instead of checks for cash management.	Money markets used for one-hour loans. All countries become sources of immediate funds. Overdraft loans replace float.	Minimized cash balances. One-hour term deposits. Delegation by small firms of cash management to banks.	By banks, SWIFT. Exchange rate developments influence hourly cash management.	Check "kiting" eliminated by a zero settlement lag. Weekend investment duplications will grow until a universal settlement lag is established. Instant "payoffs"
Financial Intermediaries	Automated settlements and deposit accounting by banks. Service charges pro rata. Nonbanks negotiate access to automated clearings. Provision of accounting, portfolio services.	Demand deposits bear interest or decline radically. Time deposits defined with hourly maturities. Savings instruments designed for automatic wage deposit flows.	By money cards and preestablished credit lines. Prime lending rate sensitive to world money market rate. Overdraft loans large if settlement lag zero.	Correspondent balances decline radically. Hourly management of the net foreign assets. Westward cash flow at the close of day's business.	The derivation of information from clients' settlements.
Government	Social Security and interest transfers deposited directly. Tax revenues withheld automatically. Income tax return calculations centralized, using computer data banks.	A paperless personal savings instrument evolves. Special short-term debt issues for nonresidents. Government bonds reside in automated securities depositories; development of purely book-entry debt.	Lender-of-last-resort function will be performed in a zero-lag money market. Continuous adjustment of bank reserves, as open market purchases clear immediately.	Speed and scope of exchange market intervention greatly enlarged.	Legality of electronic payments may be long in question. Probable invasions of privacy by misuse of data banks.

increasingly difficult. In short, the demand-for-money function of corporations will probably decline, and simultaneously become more responsive to short-term yields around the world.

Financial Intermediaries. Banks will continue to computerize the settlement of payment orders as well as the related deposit accounting operations. Banks will gradually extend the use of banking terminals located in retail stores. One result of this development will be a further reduction of float, because the accounts of both payers and payees will be adjusted at the same time. A widening range of services will be offered to clients, in-

cluding cash and financial portfolio management. The charges for these services and for normal payments processing may tend to be closely related to the costs involved. Conversely, banks might restrict the access of near-banks to electronic systems or charge them exorbitant rates for services as a means of limiting the competition from such financial intermediaries. Moreover, banks could utilize the computers of clearing systems to derive useful information concerning the transactions of private individuals and corporations. Internationally, the correspondent balances of banks will be increasingly tightly managed as the facilities provided by SWIFT expand.[1] The reduced lags in the settlement processes within and between nations may be sufficient to permit working balances to be passed on to time zones farther west as business closing hours lengthen correspondingly. At the very least a world short-term money market interest rate will evolve analogous to the deposit and loan rates prevailing in the Euro-dollar market. An increasingly large portion of domestic banking operations will become sensitive to this international rate.

To remain competitive with banks, the near-banks or nonbank intermediaries will either share directly in the establishment of the automated payments system or negotiate access to it. In addition, they will extend the range of financial services that they provide to the public. Consequently, the distinction between near-banks and banks may fade, subject to legal constraints. In financial markets such as those for stocks and bonds the gradual development of depositories using computers to record the changing ownership of securities will be observed. Market trends will be influenced by the widening use of rapid information services carrying the current price developments, as well as by purchases and sales made on the advice of computer-assisted portfolio management counselors.

Government. Social Security benefits, interest payments, pensions and government salaries will be deposited directly in the bank accounts of recipients by electronic transfers. The withholding of income taxes and the collection of sales taxes are likely to be integrated with the payments system. Even the yearly calculation of individual tax returns may be done automatically by governments, since increasing proportions of the relevant information will be held in public-sector data storage devices. The management of the public debt will probably entail the development of a paperless personal savings instrument based on the automatic withholding of an agreed proportion of regular income payments. The payments associated with central bank intervention in the securities and exchange markets will be effected by computer terminals.

Public Policy Issues

While the objectives of public policy are unlikely to change significantly over the next few decades, the evolving financial structure of the economy

will necessitate certain governmental responses. A primary issue concerns the information upon which policy is based. The flow of regularly reported information from which policy agencies derive current measurements of the state of the economy is now of such scale and such urgency that the operations of collation, summarization and analysis can only be performed by computer. Yet ironically, automating the generation of these reports by many respondents has rendered the flow of information significantly less reliable in the short run. Worst still, the ability to alter quickly the detail contained in the reports to understand a particular current economic problem has often been reduced rather than increased by the use of computers. Nevertheless, these losses can be compensated for by the opportunity to derive fully up-to-date and highly detailed data on the current economic scene from a new and computerized payments system, and to plan for the swift processing of this flow of information in a manner that facilitates policy decision-making. A second and equally important issue for public policy is the need to revise the various control instruments in the light of the changed relationships and response speeds within the financial world. These two issues are examined here, sector by sector.

Private Individuals. The objectives of governmental policy are full employment, price stability and an equitable distribution of income. The instruments used to achieve these objectives include changes in tax rates and tax structure, combined with changes in the cost and the availability of credit. The basic character of these instruments, nevertheless, may change only slightly over time. Automated payments and instant credit will, however, greatly increase the importance of consumer credit lines and automated credit authorization devices. The control over the availability of credit to individuals could be tightened if it were possible to vary the credit lines in a countercyclical manner. Such a new policy instrument might indeed prove necessary to offset the destabilizing effects of the much shorter lags in consumer reactions. In a period of hyperinflation, for example, the instant availability of all personal deposits would greatly facilitate the hoarding of goods. In more usual periods, the pre-authorized depositing of wages and salaries with financial intermediaries will imply a new character for the choice as to how personal savings are allocated, because it tends to place these decisions in the hands of portfolio guidance services of financial intermediaries. Depending on the similarity of the computer programs used in this regard, savings behavior could become significantly more homoge-

[1] See William Hall, "SWIFT, the Revolution Around the Corner" in *The Banker*, June 1973 pp. 633-39, for a description of the Society for Worldwide Interbank Financial Telecommunications.

neous. Finally, the flow of information concerning households that is used in policy formation could be broadened and accelerated by the use of automated payments data to generate the consumption statistics for the National Accounts.

Nonfinancial Corporations. The objectives of public policy in this case include those stated in the preceding section, since the inflationary aspects of price and wage formation are to be minimized while maintaining the level of employment. In addition, a desire often exists to control the degree of concentration within various industrial sectors, e.g., foreign ownership and the performance of corporations with respect to broader social objectives such as reducing pollution and easing congestion. The instruments of policy are and will continue to be variations in taxes, tariffs and credit conditions, the last being controlled principally by influencing the growth of commercial banking operations. As corporate financial behavior evolves in terms of internationally and closely managed cash positions, the fundamental relationships between national income, interest rates and monetary aggregates will gradually shift. It will thus be essential to extend the range of information reported on these items to follow the evolution. For example, the foreign cash holdings of domestic corporations are of major importance. Conceivably small and medium-sized corporations will allow their banks to manage their cash positions on a regular basis. Such a tendency could lead to a significant increase in the homogeneity of financial behavior, which implies de facto concentration. The degree of homogeneity will also rise as a result of shorter reaction lags. Not only will the information on interest levels and exchange rates move through the markets more swiftly in the future, but the use of computers to aid in financial decision-making, combined with the swifter settlement of transactions, will tend to increase the pace and the scale of daily financial market developments. In response, the policy agencies will, of necessity, speed up the incoming flow of information and very likely increase the degree of detail to develop more sensitive indicators of corporate behavior. Agencies will rely increasingly on the computer as an aid in setting the levels of the various policy instruments. Central banks in several industrial countries including the U.S. are already quite advanced in the techniques of control econometrics, although applications are just beginning to be reported.

Banks. Policy objectives within this context include ensuring the security of the institutions against financial collapse, and controlling the degree of concentration in banking (or the degree of discrimination against near-banks) and the degree of foreign control. Bank deposits must be a generally acceptable means of payment: Easy and inexpensive to use and secure against fraud. The instruments of policy vary widely from country to country, combining deposit reserve requirements, the management of the supply of reserves, open-market operations in securities and foreign exchange control or market intervention. In the next decade, the central banks must ensure that money transferred by electronic means continues to be a reliable, convenient, secure and legal aspect of society. The regularly used techniques of monetary policy for stabilization purposes must evolve in step with their financial contexts. For example, the continuous control of the supply of bank reserves during the day may become necessary. In such a case, a computer terminal linking the central bank to the automated payments system would be needed for the settlements arising from securities and exchange market intervention. The central banks must also monitor the process of computerizing the payments system to prevent this extremely costly mechanism from being used to heighten barriers to entry into banking or into financial intermediation in general. National contexts in which a concentrated private banking sector has by law the control over the payments system demand particularly subtle policies. Regarding on-going stabilization policy, the monitoring of electronic transactions could be used to develop refined measures of monetary velocity as well as greater detail in the National Accounts, to be available after a brief processing lag. Without the assistance of computers, however, this new information would quickly saturate the policy-makers and have an adverse effect on the quality of the decisions made. The inclination to use control-theoretic models of the economy will gradually mount. Consequently the political and social implications of model usage should be considered.

Nonbank Financial Intermediaries. Within this context the objectives of public policy include ensuring the security against institutional collapse and influencing the degree of concentration, the extent of foreign control and the responsiveness to monetary policy. The instruments of policy are relatively few in number, reliance being placed on adjustments in commercial bank activity that are passed along to near-banks by the normal stimulus of financial market conditions. The ability of individuals and corporations to move their cash balances swiftly to near-banks in response to interest rate changes will increase monetary velocity, heighten competition between banks and near-banks and accentuate the interest cost as opposed

Figure 2. Public Policy Responses to Changed Financial Behavior

Sector:	Policy Aspect:					
	Objectives	Economic Structure	Response Lags	Instruments	Information Base	Constraints
Private Individuals	Full employment. Price stability. Distribution of income.	Consumption function includes credit lines. Declining demand for currency. Savings allocation choices made by banks, homogeneously.	Shorter lags due to instant cash and credit.	Variable credit lines. Income tax withholding at more easily varied rates.	Monitor outstanding credit and unused lines. Monitor payments to generate National Accounts consumption flows.	Privacy questions posed by centralized and international credit authorization systems. Effects on bank profits. Appearance of directly controlling consumption.
Nonfinancial Corporations	Price and wage formation. Degree of concentration. Degree of foreign control. Quality of life.	Continuous and internationally managed cash positions. Demand for cash falls and becomes highly interest sensitive. Delegation of cash management to banks.	Responses to rate changes occur in a few minutes within countries. Somewhat longer lags internationally due to working hours and time zones.	Cost and availability of bank credit. Continuous influence by money market and exchange rates. Choice of the optimal settlement lag.	Monitor stocks and flows of corporate bank balances. Monitor inventory investment for National Accounts.	Political acceptability. Legal structures.
Banks	General acceptability of money. Security against bank collapse. Control of monetary aggregates. Degree of concentration. Degree of foreign control.	Demand for excess bank reserves drops to zero. Interbank reserve markets evolve. Greater use of a world short-term rate. Discrimination in automated settlements.	Transactions clear immediately. Lags virtually zero for the sum of managed accounts. Credits extended immediately under automated systems.	Continuous control of the reserve supply. Open-market purchases by terminal, with immediate effect. Possible directives in terms of industries' or regions' credit.	Refined monetary aggregates. New definitions to match new types of deposits. Greater sectoral detail. Better velocity measures.	Saturation point reached on financial information. Computerized monetary policy poses political problems.
Nonbank Financial Intermediaries and Markets	Security against collapse. Degree of concentration. Degree of foreign control. Market stability.	Spread of bank-like services. Velocity rises. Control by banks in the form of shared service routines such as those for portfolio management. Homogeneity and "rationality" rise.	Lags virtually zero for the items under computer control. Transactions clear immediately.	Extension of reserve requirements to near-banks.	Monitor near-banks in a manner consistent with bank reporting.	Differing legislation for various types of near-bank.
Nonresidents	Balance of payments. Speed of exchange rate movements. Control of excessive speculation.	Short-term capital movements respond immediately to news. High degrees of market integration across borders.	Lags very short, though constrained by working hours and time zones.	Exchange market intervention capacity and speed increase. Possible use of computers to scale and time the interventions.	Exchange market monitors by automated settlements. Detailed data on nonresident transactions.	The requirements to finance and to neutralize the effects of exchange intervention.

to the credit availability impact of monetary policy. Extending uniform reserve requirements to the deposits of near-banks could thus be justified on the grounds of both efficiency and equity. Information reported by near-banks could be standardized and made consistent with bank reporting. The extension of the information base would be constrained in the short run, however, by differing legislation covering the various types of financial intermediary.

Nonresidents. The maintenance of a viable balance of payments, which may be seen as an objective of policy, frequently amounts to the control or neutralization of destabilizing short-term capital movements. The instruments of policy include the use of bank reserve management and open-market operations to influence relative interest rates, direct intervention to guide the price of the domestic currency on the exchange markets, directives concerning banking-sector foreign positions and the administrative control of certain transactions with nonresidents. In the future, as the speed and scale of short-run capital movements grow under the influence of world-wide cash management and electronic systems for international payments, exchange market intervention by central banks may eventually be backed up by high-speed information systems based on the flow of automated payments, combined with computer routines that translate the strategies of the monetary authorities into the volume, pricing and timing tactics of market intervention. The constraints to finance or neutralize these intervention payments in the domestic context may lead to the development of special short-term government debt instruments designed specifically for nonresidents.

The Overall Impression

The combined impact of swifter reaction speeds and more homogeneous behavior in the context of electronic systems for many transactions may well render the financial system less stable because the dampening effect of slow and varying reactions in different institutions and countries will gradually be lost. The response of public policy seems likely to involve a greater reliance on mechanized high-speed information systems generating economic indicators and on computer aids to decision-making. The latter aspect will force the quantification of the various policy objectives mentioned above. The choice of specific targets for the rates of inflation and employment, for example, is rightly considered a political decision due to the implications of the two numbers for the distribution of income between sectors of the economy. But politicians will be noticeably reluctant to make such precise choices because of possible adverse reactions by their constituents. Consequently technicians within policy-making groups will be tempted to specify the goals of policy themselves and to set the instruments of policy accordingly. Such a development appears undesirable.

Finally, the new technology of electronic transactions would appear to be biased towards dirigisme. This results from the gradual diminution of the human element in the decisions being taken in all sectors of the economy. Markets exist only when people trade. But portfolio yield-maximizing computer routines interacting electronically no more form a market than do the state planners who allocate resources in a fully controlled economy. Consequently care must be taken to ensure that the long-run impact of the new financial technology corresponds broadly to the national philosophy. ☐

Chapter 39

CONSUMER CHOICE AND USE OF BANK CREDIT CARDS: A MODEL AND CROSS-SECTION RESULTS*

By Kenneth J. White

*This article is reprinted, with permission, from *The Journal of Consumer Research.* Vol. 2, No. 1 (June, 1975), pp. 10-18.

"If futurists are holding their breath for a cash-less society, surely they will be breathless long before they are cashless."[1]

Since 1960 bank credit cards have seen phenomenal growth as a means of payment replacing both cash and checks for many types of transactions. Although the advantages of these cards seem to dominate those of checks and cash for many transactions the usage of bank credit cards has not become as widespread as was expected. Many consumers, for one reason or another, have been reluctant to use their cards to their maximum potential. If consumers do not use credit cards, is their behavior irrational or is it actually an outcome of utility maximization? This study analyzes the use of credit cards in the payments mechanism. If it is assumed that consumers wish to minimize the "costs" of making transactions one might hypothesize that the credit card will only be used by those consumers who perceive lower costs in using credit cards than other transactions vehicles. A cross-section study of households was used to identify some of the factors influencing the decision to use alternative means of payment.

PAYMENTS SYSTEMS AND THE COSTS OF TRANSACTIONS

In a competitive economy new innovations of the payments mechanism are not easily forced upon the public. Innovations have rationally been accepted by the public only when they have reduced the costs of making transactions. Coins replaced barter because they eliminated the double coincidence of wants problem and the difficulties of a non-standardized unit of account. Paper currency replaced coins because it was less cumbersome to carry and store. The check replaced currency because it reduced the need to carry large amounts of cash and provided a relatively efficient means for individuals to transfer large sums of money. Credit cards further reduced the costs of transactions since they allowed the consumer to buy goods without having funds available at the time of purchase. Credit cards also help to link together purchasing and financing decisions. It must be recognized that the introduction of each of these developments did not completely eliminate the older methods. All five means of payment are currently in use because each method is preferred for a subset of transactions. Coins are preferred for bus rides where the amount of the transaction is low and the associated costs must be kept at a minimum. Checks are preferred for paying telephone bills since

payment is usually sent through the mail. Credit cards are preferred when traveling since out-of-town checks are not readily accepted and it is undesirable to carry large amounts of cash. Barter is still used for some transactions; many people trade their old cars in for new cars. Presumably, an individual will use the least cost means of payment for each of his transactions.

Fixed Transactions Costs

It is possible to enumerate some of the costs associated with each transactions vehicle. First, every transaction has a fixed cost component independent of the size or type of transaction. The fixed cost of a cash transaction is usually minimal. In most cases one needs only to take the cash out of his pocket. A check transaction requires one to carry a check and write it out to the payee. The fixed check cost also includes bank service charges that must be paid for clearing the check. The fixed cost of a credit card transaction is that associated with the need to carry the card and the waiting time required for all the necessary paper work. In addition, there is a cost involved in writing a check to make a payment when the credit card bill arrives. However, this cost is only incurred once for each month the card is used.

These fixed costs vary across individuals and help explain why different people will use different methods to carry out the same transaction. Among the factors that might explain variations in these costs are the demographic characteristics of the individual making the transaction. For example, one might expect some older persons to resist innovations. Those who have grown up in a computerized society may be less resistant to such banking innovations as credit cards. Some foreigners may be unaccustomed to the subtleties of modern American banking and may even be reluctant to accept the check as an appropriate transactions vehicle. The transactor's sex may also be a factor influencing the relative fixed costs of different transactions vehicles; however, the influence of one's sex on transactions costs is difficult to predict a priori. One hypothesis is that the inconvenience of carrying a checkbook is small for females who carry purses; therefore, the fixed cost of a check transaction is expected to be lower for females than for males. Undoubtedly, there are other factors at work. Purchasing habits may differ among males and females. An individual's race may also affect the relative fixed transactions costs associated with different means of payment. Nonwhite persons may find it difficult to get merchants to accept their checks. Since credit payments are guaranteed by the bank, the merchant who fears bad checks may encourage the use of credit cards. Hence, nonwhites may

[1] "What Ever Happened to the Cashless Society?," *Morgan Guaranty Survey* (February 1972) p. 13.

find that check transactions are relatively more "costly" for themselves than for white persons. Education may also affect the relative costs to an individual of using different transactions vehicles. We would expect more educated persons to accept new banking developments faster than those who have been poorly educated. In short, the demographic characteristics of an individual may reveal information about his background which may affect the relative perceived fixed costs associated with the use of different means of payment.

Although the demographic characteristics of the consumer yield some information about the relative fixed costs of making transactions, other variables may also be determining factors. Upon being introduced to a new means of performing transactions the consumer must go through a stage where he learns to accept the new device as an integral part of his financial behavior. After this "learning-by-doing" stage is completed some of the psychic fixed transactions costs may be reduced. For example, an individual who has used a credit card for many years probably feels no anxiety when he pulls it out of his wallet. However, an individual who has just received the card and is not comfortable using it may feel that paying by credit card is still a complicated process and not worth the trouble. Therefore, the fixed costs of a credit card transaction relative to other types of transactions are expected to be a decreasing function of the length of time an individual has been using the card. Although this time interval is one factor reducing costs it does not reveal very much about past usage. There are some people who have held credit cards for years without using them. An additional factor influencing the "learning-by-doing" effect is that those individuals who have charged high amounts on their cards in the past probably have accepted the card as a useful transactions vehicle that can be used at low cost. One might hypothesize, therefore, that individuals with high outstanding card balances in the past will view the fixed cost of a credit card transaction to be low.

Variable Transactions Costs

The fixed costs associated with each transactions vehicle will differ among individuals but remain independent of the transaction size. However, some transactions costs are variable and are determined by the dollar value of the transaction. Large currency transactions are costly due to the possibility of theft before the cash is spent. Thus, the cost of a cash transaction ought to rise with the size of transaction while the cost of a check transaction is expected to be invariant with respect to size. In contrast, credit card transactions have a U-shaped variable cost structure. In effect, every credit card transaction implies an interest free loan for at least thirty days. Therefore, total transactions costs ought to decrease as the size of the transaction increases. However, consumers may find merchants reluctant to accept bank credit cards for large purchases because the bank takes a percentage of the sale as its fee. If the transaction is very large the merchant might prefer to do his own billing or he might encourage a check transaction and accept the risk. Currently, some merchants discourage large credit card transactions by giving "discounts for cash." In this case the relative cost of the credit card transaction would increase with the size of the transaction. The net result of these opposing

effects is the U-shaped cost curve for credit card transactions. The rising portion of the cost curve may also reflect the fact that the consumer feels he is "going into debt." Figure 1 shows a set of hypothetical average total cost curves for single transactions of different sizes.

So far, this discussion of transactions cost has ignored current holdings of cash, demand deposits, and available credit. We might expect a $10 cash transaction to be more "costly" for an individual with $10.50 in his pocket than for one with $100.00. Because cer-

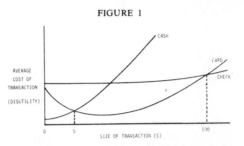

tain precautionary balances are often desired for each transactions vehicle we would predict that transactions which substantially reduce these balances are relatively costly and that a consumer would prefer to use an alternate means of payment. Hence, in addition to the cost relationship shown in Figure 1 there is a cost component which is a function of the transaction size relative to the current balance of each asset. The balance in the credit card case will be the amount of available credit.

Qualitative Transactions Costs

The above discussion was concerned with fixed transactions costs which varied among individuals and variable costs which varied with the size of transaction. A third type of cost is present which is determined by the type of transaction. Some goods cannot be purchased by credit card or check without extremely high costs resulting to either the merchant, the consumer, or both. One such example is bus rides. Cash is the only acceptable means of payment. Other types of transactions are relatively more costly for cash customers than for credit card customers. Car rentals are a good example since a cash customer may be forced to leave a deposit. In short, the type of transaction may largely determine the means of payment and may override the fixed and variable cost considerations. Unfortunately, in this empirical study where transactions are not clearly identified, it is impossible to introduce the qualitative costs associated with the type of transaction.

A FORMAL SPECIFICATION OF THE TRANSACTIONS COST STRUCTURE

A more formal specification of the cost structure can be developed. Total transactions costs are composed of fixed costs dependent on the characteristics of the consumer, variable costs related to the size of transaction, and qualitative costs which are determined by the nature of the good. Fixed costs for a single individual are expressed by:

$$FC_{ij} = f_i(DEMOS, EXP_i, HICRD, SC) \quad (1)$$

where FC_{ij} is the fixed cost of the jth transaction using the ith transaction vehicle ($i =$ cash, checks, credit cards); $DEMOS$ is a vector of variables describing an individual's demographic characteristics; EXP_i is the months of experience that the individual has had using the ith vehicle; $HICRD$ is the highest outstanding credit card debt; and SC is a binary variable with a value of one for those paying service charges on their checking accounts and zero otherwise.

Variable transactions costs can be written as:

$$VC_{ij} = g_i(SIZE_j, BAL_i) \quad (2)$$

where VC_{ij} is the variable cost of the consumer's jth transaction using the ith vehicle, $SIZE_j$ is the size of the jth transaction in dollars, and BAL_i is the balance of the ith vehicle before the transaction is made.

The third component of total cost is the qualitative cost. This component may be written as:

$$QC_{ij} = h_i(TYPE_j) \quad (3)$$

where QC_{ij} is the qualitative cost of the jth transaction using the ith transactions vehicle, and $TYPE_j$ is a qualitative variable indicative of the type of good purchased in the jth transaction.

Combining equations (1), (2), and (3) gives a formal specification of the total transaction cost:

$$\begin{aligned} TC_{ij} &= FC_{ij} + VC_{ij} + QC_{ij} \\ &= f_i(DEMOS, EXP_i, HICRD, SC) \\ &\quad + g_i(SIZE_j, BAL_i) \\ &\quad + h_i(TYPE_j) \end{aligned} \quad (4)$$

If consumers know the specification of equation (4), they could compute the transactions cost associated with each transactions vehicle before making a purchase. After doing these calculations the rational consumer would use the means with the lowest expected cost. However, few consumers are capable of mentally performing these computations so rules of thumb are often used as the decision mechanism. A common rule of thumb might be that cash should be used for any transaction less than five dollars. The hypothetical cost curves shown in Figure 1 indicate that this rule of thumb may be indicative of cost minimizing behavior. After a period of adjustment, it is reasonable to expect consumers to recognize the pecuniary and psychic costs associated with the different transactions vehicles and the rules of thumb will approximate a cost minimization process. Baumol and Quandt [1964] have shown that such rules of thumb can lead to optimal decision making.

Although a cost minimizing decision rule is implicitly used in choosing the appropriate means of payment it is impossible to compute the level of these costs directly. After the fact it can be argued that the choice of a particular transactions vehicle by a consumer implies that he believes this to be a least cost means of payment. With some additional assumptions about an individual's perceptions of costs it is also possible to draw conclusions about the relative costs of using different methods. If a large sample of transactions is available these costs can be computed indirectly, as is discussed in the next section.

TRANSACTIONS COSTS AND THE DISTRIBUTION OF TRANSACTIONS

Consider a hypothetical consumer who viewed his transactions costs as shown in Figure 1. Using rules of thumb to compute the relative transactions costs before making each purchase the consumer distributes his transactions over the three possible means of payment so as to minimize total costs. The relative frequency distribution of these transactions can be plotted as shown in Figure 2. The distribution will be closely tied to the consumer's perception of the relative costs. If the costs were perceived to differ by a great deal then the relative frequencies would also be quite different. The relative frequencies for a given transactions vehicle can be interpreted as the probability that the consumer will use that vehicle given the size of the transaction. Considering only transactions performed by cash, checks, and credit cards these probabilities must sum to one for any given transaction size. Therefore, from Figure 1 and Figure 2, the probability of using any particular means of payment for a given transaction should increase as its relative transactions cost decreases.

Although the size of transaction may be an important determinant of the distribution of transactions, Figure 2 does not portray all the factors determining this distribution. Earlier, we discussed other variables that affect transactions costs. Since there is a simple correspondence between these costs and the frequency distribution of transactions, Figure 2 can be generalized to several dimensions so that all the variables of equation (4) are included as determinants of the distribution. In theory it is possible to estimate the probability of using any given transactions vehicle with explanatory

FIGURE 2

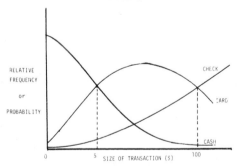

variables shown in equation (4). Consequently, the impact of each of these variables on the cost of transactions could be determined. Knowledge of these individual cost components would yield a great deal of information about the payments mechanism and the behavior of consumers in response to the introduction of bank credit cards.

Our analysis suggests that a rational consumer could be expected to minimize the costs of making transactions by choosing the appropriate transactions vehicle. The greater the perceived cost saving of using one particular means of payment over the others the larger the probability that the least-cost method would be used. Our objective is to find the determinants of the costs associated with different transactions vehicles.

Equation (4) cannot be estimated directly. A quantitative measurement of the costs is not possible. However, a qualitative measurement is possible by estimating the corresponding probability function. To measure the cost components indirectly it is necessary to derive equations predicting the probability of a consumer choosing each vehicle for payment. These probabilities are unknown. We observe only whether the vehicle was or was not used. The direct objective is to predict the value of this dichotomous variable from the given set of explanatory variable values. The estimated parameters of the probability function will yield results indicating the relative importance of the variables in equation (4) in determining the transactions cost structure.

THE SAMPLE DATA FILE

The previous discussion examined cash, checks, and credit cards as the means of payment most commonly used by households. A complete analysis of all three types is not possible at this time since data on the cash transactions of households are unavailable. However, an excellent compilation of transactions data on a sample of household credit card and check transactions was obtained from a cooperating bank. The available data allowed a partial analysis of the relative costs of check and credit card transactions.

An initial cross-section sample of 649 households in a large metropolitan area was chosen from the files of the bank. All households had both a check account and a bank credit card account at the bank. Demographic data on each household was obtained from the credit card application and other bank records. The available information included Age, Race, Sex, and Marital Status of the household head. Unfortunately, this information was missing for many households and almost half the sample had to be eliminated. In addition to the demographic variables, a complete listing of all credit card and check transactions was obtained from the respective monthly statements for the period February-June 1972. The checking account statement showed the amounts and number of debits and credits cleared on each day during a month. The credit card statement showed the amount of each transaction and the date the transaction was recorded on the bank's books. A total of 27,900 separate transactions were available for analysis.

Although the amount of data available was considerable, it did not include all transactions of the household. Many individuals had additional accounts at other banks which were not being monitored. Hence, some transactions are unavoidably not recorded. Furthermore, no information was available about a household's ownership and utilization of other credit cards. Nevertheless, the card issued by the cooperating bank was the most widely used one in the geographical area.

The vector of demographic variables used as determinants of the fixed transactions costs in the theoretical model is defined and coded below.

Variable	Definition
AGE	Age in years of head of household
RACE	1 = head of household is nonwhite
	0 = head of household is white
SINGLE MALE	1 = Account belongs to single male
	0 = Otherwise

SINGLE FEMALE   1 = Account belongs to single female

                                  0 = Otherwise

The head of household for married couples is assumed to be the husband.

The most serious problem in estimating the theoretical model is that the variable *TYPE,* used to indicate the nature of the transaction, is unknown and must be omitted from the equation. Hence, there is no indication of the importance of qualitative transactions costs in the decision process. Furthermore, the omission of this variable may bias the estimated coefficients of the included independent variables. Until sufficient data are available on all transactions the specification of the estimated equation must remain incomplete.

SPECIFICATION OF THE PROBABILITY FUNCTION

Since this analysis is restricted to credit card and check transactions the respective probabilities of usage must sum to one for any given transaction. Only one equation need be estimated for the model to be identified. The variables of equation (4) as modified above are recast into a probability function to be estimated using probit analysis.

In the probit model $F(z)$ denotes the value of the standard normal cumulative distribution at z. Next an index I is defined implicitly by $F(I) = P$ where P is the probability of the event occurring and lies between 0 and 1. The index I is linear in X; i.e.: $I = X'\beta$ where X is the vector of independent variables. The probit specification is:

$$P(X) = F(I) = F(X'\beta) = \int_{-\infty}^{X'\beta} (2\Pi)^{-\frac{1}{2}} e^{-\frac{t^2}{2}} dt \quad (5)$$

or

$$F^{-1}(P(X)) = I = X'\beta = \beta_0 + B_1 X_1 + \ldots + \beta_k X_k \quad (6)$$

where $P(X)$ is the conditional probability of the event occurring given the values of the X's. The parameters $\beta_0, \ldots, \beta_k$ are estimated by maximum likelihood methods.[2]

Equation (7) describes the probability that the credit card will be used for an individual's jth transaction.

$$P_{c,j} = F(I)$$

$$I = B_0 + B_1 AGE + B_2 SINGLE\ MALE$$
$$+ B_3 SINGLE\ FEMALE + B_4 RACE + B_5 EXP_c$$
$$+ B_6 HICRD + B_7 SC + B_8 SIZE_j + B_9 BAL_c$$
$$+ B_{10} BAL_d + e_j$$

The subscripts c and d represent the credit card and demand deposit accounts respectively and e_j is an error term. The estimated coefficients of equation (7) indicate the influence of each independent variable on the index I which is transformed into the probability of credit card usage by using the cumulative normal distribution. Knowledge of these estimates should reveal the important determinants of the costs of using the credit card as a means of payment. The empirical results are presented and interpreted in the next section.

[2] A more detailed explanation of the probit model can be found in Goldberger [1964] or Theil [1971].

RESULTS

Table 1 gives the estimated regression coefficients for equation (7) using probit analysis. Means, standard deviations and correlation coefficients of the variables are given in Table 2. Most of the coefficients are statistically significant at the .01 level and the results support most of the prior hypotheses.[3] However, the learning-by-doing hypothesis is rejected. The EXP_c and $HICRD$ variables both had negative coefficients. Although the coefficients on these variables differ from the expected sign and were significantly different from zero at the .01 level they were among the least significant of all variables in the model. The coefficient on the binary variable for single females was negative as

TABLE 1

PROBABILITY OF CREDIT CARD USAGE PROBIT ANALYSIS

Variable	Coefficient	Standard Error	Coefficient / Std. Error
AGE	−.0073	.00096	− 7.6
SINGLE MALE	.1039	.0315	3.3
SINGLE FEMALE	−.0288	.0404	− 0.7
RACE	.3503	.0408	8.6
EXP_c	−.0010	.00044	− 2.3
HICRD	−.000064	.000023	− 2.7
SC	.0643	.0235	2.7
SIZE ($)	−.0066	.00032	−20.7
BAL_c ($)	.00021	.000020	9.8
BAL_d ($)	−.0000068	.0000051	− 1.3
INTERCEPT	−.8203	.0370	−22.2

n = 27,900 transactions.

predicted but was not significantly different from zero. The coefficient on the demand deposit balance variable (BAL_d) was of the expected sign but also not significantly different from zero. The coefficients on all the remaining variables were significant at the .01 level and supported the hypotheses generated from the theoretical model. A likelihood-ratio test clearly rejected the null hypothesis that there was no relationship between the dependent variable and the set of all explanatory variables.

Although these results support the cost minimization model, a closer look at the estimates is warranted. First, with a sample size of 27,900 transactions high significance levels are to be expected, so the results are hardly surprising. Second, an examination of the coefficients in the regression reveals that large changes in the independent variables are required to raise the probability of credit card usage very much. Our results

[3] Hypothesis testing of coefficients in the probit model can be done by a likelihood ratio test. However, an easier method of testing individual coefficients uses the fact that the maximum likelihood estimates of the coefficients in large samples are approximately normally distributed. Thus, hypotheses can be tested by examining the ratio of the estimated coefficient to its standard error. For large samples this ratio is approximately distributed as a standard normal random variable.

indicate that the most important variables in the analysis in terms of their effect and significance are *SIZE, BAL_c, RACE,* and *AGE.* Surprisingly, *RACE* has one of the strongest effects. The model indicates that the probit index will be .35 greater for a nonwhite individual than for a white one. As explained below, this could raise the probability of credit card usage by as much as .13.

The probit coefficients indicate the effect of a unit change in one of the independent variables on the probit index $I;$ this relationship is linear. However, the probabilities themselves are nonlinear in the index. A given change in the index will have its greatest effect when the probability is 0.5, the point where the index is 0.0. This characteristic follows directly from the fact that the index comes from the cumulative normal distribution. The nonlinear relationship somewhat complicates the interpretation of the coefficients. For exposition, it is convenient to examine a small number of hypothetical cases.

Consider Table 3 and its corresponding Figure 3, which show how the probability of credit card usage varies with the size of transaction. Four separate cases are presented. Each is that of a married couple with assumed mean values of the variables EXP_c, $HICRD$, BAL_c, and BAL_d. It is also assumed that no service charges are paid on the checking account. In each case I is the predicted index from the regression equation and the $\hat{P}_c$ were obtained from a table of the cumulative normal distribution. The four cases show the effect of age and race on the probabilities. These variables have their greatest impact when the transactions size is relatively low. As expected the probability declines as the transaction size increases. However, the probability is continuously lower than the corresponding probability of check usage at each transaction size. Since credit cards can only be used for a small subset of all of the consumer's transactions it is not surprising to find this result.

The results indicate that race has a substantial effect on the probability of credit card usage. This supports the hypothesis stated earlier suggesting that nonwhites may find it more difficult to get merchants to accept their checks so they use their cards instead. An alternative supporting hypothesis is that nonwhites may tend to borrow more and use the credit card as a means of financing purchases. It is also conceivable that the nonwhites in the sample are atypical of the class of cardholders and have other distinguishing characteristics which have not been quantified here. The impact of age is as expected; older persons tend to use their cards less. However, the age effect is not quite as strong as the race effect.

Our original objective was to identify the cost components of using various transactions vehicles. The individual's perception of the cost differential of using one means of payment over another increases as the respective probability of usage increases. Hence, the magnitude of the coefficients in the probit equation provide some information on these perceived cost differentials. The analysis suggests that nonwhite persons

TABLE 2
SUMMARY STATISTICS OF VARIABLES IN EQUATION (3-8)

Variable	Mean	St. Dev.	Correlation Matrix									
			AGE	S. MALE	S. FEM.	RACE	EXP$_c$	HICRD	SC	SIZE	BAL$_c$	BAL$_d$
AGE	37.65	12.14	1.0000									
S. MALE	.11	.31	— .1248	1.0000								
S. FEMALE	.07	.26	— .0155	— .0982	1.0000							
RACE	.05	.22	— .0225	.0992	.0436	1.0000						
EXP$_c$	28.73	26.11	.4141	— .0392	— .0398	— .0438	1.0000					
HICRD	553.50	487.50	.1273	— .0657	— .1551	— .0576	.2246	1.0000				
SC	.25	.43	— .1141	— .0029	— .1101	.0555	— .0105	.1608	1.0000			
SIZE	41.06	183.70	.0213	.0047	— .0067	— .0093	.0149	— .0069	— .0246	1.0000		
BAL$_c$	472.10	498.00	.1607	— .0762	— .0785	— .0962	— .0764	— .1312	— .1514	.0227	1.0000	
BAL$_d$	538.50	1872.00	.0952	— .0089	— .0177	— .0272	— .0158	— .0312	— .0964	.0840	.2785	1.0000
P$_c$	.12	.32	— .0648	.0252	— .0068	.0532	— .0537	— .0298	.0195	— .0484	.0404	— .0044

perceive lower costs in using credit cards than do whites. The results also indicate that older persons perceive higher costs in using their credit cards than do younger persons. The coefficients on the variables BAL_c and BAL_d suggest that a reduction in the amount of available credit card credit or an increase in the current demand deposit balance will tend to increase the perceived costs of a credit card transaction. In contrast, the imposition of service charges on checks written will decrease the relative cost of a credit card transaction. The evidence also suggests that males probably find credit cards relatively more convenient to use than do females, possibly for the reasons cited earlier or because they purchase different types of

TABLE 3

PROBIT ANALYSIS PREDICTIONS

Transaction Size (dollars)	White 25 yr. old		White 60 yr. old		Non-white 25 yr. old		Non-white 60 yr. old	
	$\hat{I}$	$\hat{P}_C$	$\hat{I}$	$\hat{P}_C$	$\hat{I}$	$\hat{P}_C$	$\hat{I}$	$\hat{P}_C$
0.00	− .96	.17	−1.22	.11	− .61	.27	− .87	.19
5.00	− .99	.16	−1.25	.10	− .64	.26	− .90	.18
10.00	−1.03	.15	−1.28	.10	− .68	.25	− .93	.17
15.00	−1.06	.14	−1.32	.093	− .71	.24	− .97	.16
20.00	−1.09	.14	−1.35	.088	− .74	.23	−1.00	.16
25.00	−1.13	.13	−1.38	.084	− .78	.22	−1.03	.15
35.00	−1.19	.12	−1.45	.074	− .84	.20	−1.10	.14
50.00	−1.29	.10	−1.52	.064	− .94	.17	−1.20	.11
75.00	−1.45	.074	−1.71	.044	−1.11	.13	−1.36	.087
100.00	−1.62	.053	−1.88	.030	−1.27	.10	−1.53	.063
150.00	−1.95	.025	−2.21	.014	−1.60	.055	−1.86	.031
200.00	−2.29	.011	−2.54	.005	−1.93	.027	−2.19	.014

FIGURE 3

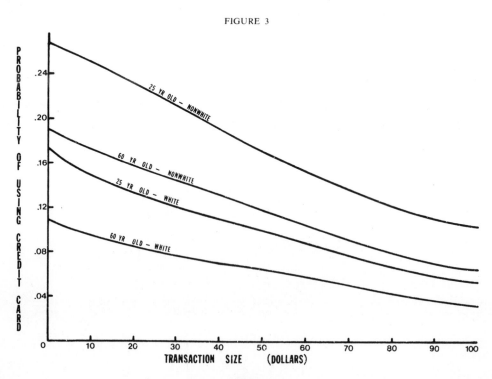

488

goods. In general, we have evidence here that different individuals do perceive different costs associated with transactions by check and by credit card. These costs depend on an individual's current financial standing as well as his demographic background. The hypothesis that individuals consciously or subconsciously minimize the costs of making transactions by choosing the appropriate means of payment seems to be supported by the results.

One note of caution is required in interpreting the above results. Since no variables indicative of the nature of the transaction were included in the estimated equation, there is no measure of the qualitative transactions costs discussed earlier. If an individual's transactions are correlated with the included explanatory variables then the estimated coefficients may be biased. For example, the results indicate that younger persons are more likely to use their cards than older persons. If young people are more likely to purchase the types of goods that can be paid for with credit cards, then part of the qualitative transactions costs have been included in the age effect. Without adequate information on the nature of each transaction these effects cannot be separated.

CONCLUSION

This analysis attempted to identify some of the factors influencing the costs associated with the use of different transactions vehicles. The analysis has been successful with the qualifications noted above. However, only limited policy conclusions can be formed from the results. If it is desired to increase the use of credit cards for transactions as an intermediate step toward an electronic funds-transfer system, then one major requirement is an increase in the perceived cost saving of using the credit card. A first step requires the cost of credit card operations to be brought below that of checks so that banks have an incentive to pass cost savings on to the customer. This will not be done until electronic on-line terminals are used by merchants to eliminate all the paper work currently required to process credit-card transactions. The technology is currently available. After it is fully utilized the major problem will be educating the public so that they recognize their own cost savings.

REFERENCES

Baumol, W. J. and R. E. Quandt. "Rules of Thumb and Optimally Imperfect Decisions," *American Economic Review*, 54 (March 1964), 23-46.

Goldberger, A. S. *Econometric Theory*. New York: John Wiley & Sons, 1964

Theil, H. *Principles of Econometrics*. New York: John Wiley & Sons, 1971.

"What Ever Happened to the Cashless Society?," *Morgan Guaranty Survey* (February 1972), p. 13.

Part X

HOLDING COMPANIES AND CAPITAL STRUCTURE

THE bank holding company evolved from an effort by banks to circumvent regulations governing branching and other aspects of bank expansion. The 1960s saw tremendous growth through acquisition and merger. While some bank holding companies comprise several relatively equal bank subsidiaries, the most significant holding companies involve one major bank. Often, this major bank is the only banking component in the structure of the holding company. In 1971 bank holding companies, which numbered more than 150, controlled nearly 40% of the total assets of banks nationwide. By 1972 they controlled nearly 63% of deposits nationwide, although growth through acquisition had begun to slow significantly.

Other principal reasons for the bank holding company include a desire to increase retail volume, to improve service to a particular area or industry, and to expand earning capacity. The focus of Part X is the management of bank capital structure and holding companies. This examination will forego discussions of the extensive regulatory questions raised by holding company expansion, and will deal instead with management science techniques that can aid in planning and managing bank capital structure and holding companies.

The long-term goal of bank management is to maximize the profits of its shareholders. The prime element of this goal is the bank's stock price. Although short-run market forces must be allowed for, the long-run growth in share price is one significant measure of management's success in the eyes of its investors.

In Chapter 40, "Bank Equities and Investor Risk Perceptions: Some Entailments for Capital Adequacy Regulation," H. Prescott Beighley, John H. Boyd, and Donald P. Jacobs have employed regression analysis to isolate the variables that impact on investors' perceptions of a bank's stock. Although their work focuses on regulatory implications of these variables, the article provides valuable insights into the factors that influence management's decisions regarding capital structure. Capital adequacy and risk perceptions are important considerations in management's long-term planning.

Earnings are, of course, a prime determinant of share price. However, the price-earnings (PE) ratios of banks can vary considerably. Given a certain level of earnings, banks would also like to utilize other factors to increase stock price. Richard A. Shick and James A. Verbrugge have examined these factors in Chapter 41, "An Analysis of Bank Price-Earnings Ratios." Shick and Verbrugge develop an approach that isolates the characteristics of high PE ratio banks. The chapter begins with a summary of previous research in this area. Then, using multiple discriminant analysis, the authors isolate variables that determine a high PE bank and develop a model that can discriminate between high and low PE banks. Shick and Verbrugge provide useful insights into the factors that affect the price-earnings ratio of a bank. In its desire to maximize stock price, a bank must constantly maintain these factors in a positive direction.

Peter C. Eisemann looks at holding companies in Chapter 42, "Diversification and the Congeneric Bank Holding Company." He suggests the use of the Markowitz portfolio selection model for determining the optimal bank holding company structure. Eisemann provides evidence indicating that many holding companies operate suboptimally and do not efficiently diversify. There is a scarcity of research in the area of bank diversification planning, and the article by Eisemann provides a framework for examining diversification opportunities.

As a bank acquires subsidiaries and expands through mergers to become a holding company, its plannng and control problems increase rapidly. Yet, little attention has been given to the complex task of bank holding company planning, which require the planner to deal with numerous considerations simultaneously. Managers are not likely to be capable of simultaneously dealing with the numerous variables and constraints involved in even a rather simple, small one-bank holding company. As suggested in Part IV, linear programming is one means of considering numerous variables and constraints simultaneously.

The evolution of the bank holding company has contributed to the complexity of today's banking environment. Its management faces a critical problem of simplifying complex issues and planning in the face of widely varying circumstances. Management science techniques lend themselves to this sort of management dilemma, and they should prove extremely useful in the future development of bank holding company management.

Part X focuses on the capital structure of commercial banks and bank holding companies. Capital structure management requires executives to view the overall firm in a strategic manner. Although management science has been limited in this area by the paucity of information available from banks, research will hopefully continue. The potential for significant contributions to effective management would seem extensive, if the problems can be overcome.

The final chapter in Part X illustrates the difficulties that can be encountered in attempting to deal with capital structure issues. Limited information makes the use of traditional statistical tests extremely problematical. Shimon D. Magen's article in Chapter 43, "Cost of Capital and Dividend Policies in Commercial Banks," points out the difficulties management science researchers have encountered in the area of capital structure. The "cost of capital" issue addressed in Magen's article is extremely relevant and often misunderstood by management. Magen emphasizes the difficulty of analyzing the factors involved in bank cost of capital. To reiterate the obstacles to research in this management area, we have included in Chapter 43 a critical comment by Thomas R. Harter on Magen's article. Our intention is not to cast aspersions on the quality of Magen's analysis, but instead to point out the difficulty of research in this area, which centers on the basic lack of useful data for testing research models. The Magen article points to the need for further work in this area, since it is of extreme importance to the effective management of a commercial bank.

Chapter 40

BANK EQUITIES AND INVESTOR RISK PERCEPTIONS: SOME ENTAILMENTS FOR CAPITAL ADEQUACY REGULATION*

By H. Prescott Beighley, John H. Boyd, and Donald P. Jacobs

*This article is reprinted, with permission, from *Journal of Bank Research*, Vol. 6, No. 3 (Autumn, 1975), pp. 190-201.

I. INTRODUCTION*

The purpose of this paper is to rigorously explore the relationship between the financial structures of banking firms and the market values of their equity securities. For the most part, it is an extension of an earlier study done by the same authors under the sponsorship of the Association of Reserve City Bankers.[1] As discussed below, a different data base is used in the present study than in the previous study (hereafter referred to as the RCB study) and an additional time period is tested.

In the RCB study broad financial trends in the bank holding company industry were investigated and, where possible, implications for capital structure policy and practice were drawn. A major impetus for this research was the increased concern over capital adequacy that resulted from the rapid growth of bank holding companies subsequent to the passage of the 1970 amendments to the Bank Holding Company Act.

As noted in the RCB study, the holding company movement has greatly complicated the bank regulators' task in determining appropriate standards of capital adequacy and, more generally, in monitoring the capital position of banking firms. The holding company form of organization has allowed banking firms to adopt complicated financial structures, often employing double leverage with debt funding at both the parent and operating levels. Through holding companies, banking firms are now able to enter credit markets not generally available to commercial banks, viz. commercial paper; and, through their nonbank affiliates, to enter new lines of business in which bank regulators have had little prior experience in determining risk exposure or appropriate capitalization standards. Overall, the movement has resulted in a quantum expansion in the scope and complexity of capital regulation, a challenge to which the au-

thorities are still responding. To understand the scope of the regulatory dilemma, it must be understood that there is no generally accepted operational definition of adequate capital for a bank, let alone for a bank holding company which is, inherently, a more complex organization.

It was further argued in the RCB study that net social benefits might accrue if some of the responsibility for capital regulation could be transferred to the private sector. The argument runs that if market forces, rather than regulatory decree, are used to set capital adequacy standards, the social contributions of the banking industry will be enhanced, provided the standards set in the private marketplace are compatible with the overall regulatory goals of maintaining confidence in the banking system. In other words, in a free-market economy it is desirable, *ceteris paribus,* to have capital standards set by private market forces rather than by administrative edict.

If such a policy could be successfully employed, two types of social benefits would accrue. First, the regulators' burden in defining appropriate capital adequacy standards would be eased, thereby freeing scarce resources. Second, the competitive performance of the banking industry would be enhanced. For example, greater flexibility in determining financial structure would result in a more efficient allocation of resources since bankers would be able to be more responsive to their individual operating environments.

Whether this transfer of responsibility could be successfully undertaken depends on the joint behavior of bankers, bank creditors and bank equity investors. Do bank equity investors and creditors perceive different degrees of risk to be associated with different capital structures? If so, do managements react to stockholder and creditor preferences in making their financial structure decisions? And if management is in fact responsive to the preference of shareholders and creditors, are these preferences compatible with the preservation of a sound banking system? That is, in the absence of regulator-determined capital adequacy standards, would stockholders and creditors influence capital

*A statement of the problem and a summary of the study's major findings and conclusions appear in Sections I and II; a more technical treatment of theoretical and statistical methodology is presented in Sections III and IV.
   [1] Donald P. Jacobs, H. Prescott Beighley and John H. Boyd, *The Financial Structure of Bank Holding Companies,* Association of Reserve City Bankers, 1975.

structure decisions in such a way that society would be better off than it is under present capital adequacy policy?

Acceptable answers to these questions must be found before a change in the direction of de-regulating capital adequacy standards can be recommended. The primary concern of this study is with the first question: Are equity investors sensitive to perceived leverage risk? Investors must exhibit sensitivity in order for the transfer to the private sector of responsibility for capital adequacy standards to be successful.

The empirical tests carried out in connection with the RCB study indicated that bank holding company stock prices were insensitive to leverage in 1970 and 1971, but that the relationship became significant in 1972 and even more highly significant in 1973. In that year we estimated that, on average, a 10% increase in consolidated holding company leverage would, *ceteris paribus*, result in a 4.7% decrease in share price. Thus the evidence strongly suggested that bank holding company equity market participants are aware of and respond to leverage in their buying and selling decisions. The results for 1972 and 1973 were highly significant in a statistical sense, and we attributed the apparent increase in the importance of leverage to a "learning curve" phenomenon. That is, the bank holding company industry was in the process of significant change during the period, and the new hybrid firms were complex and difficult to analyze. We hypothesized that it had taken equity market participants time to learn how to appraise the potential risks and rewards in the industry—a learning process during which leverage was accorded increasing importance as a measure of risk.

These empirical results must be regarded as tentative and, to some extent, controversial. As discussed above, however, they have important public policy connotations, and additionally, should be of great interest to bank managers. Given the complexities of the problem and the difficulties of statistical inference, we stopped short of making recommendations for major regulatory change. However the evidence seemed overwhelming that the authorities should at least give added weight to market measures, such as stock prices, in reaching their decisions. Moreover, the evidence seemed equally great that given the importance of the subject and the limited amount of existing research, additional research was warranted. That is, in essence, the purpose of the present paper.

Our original results were obtained from a limited sample of about 90 bank holding companies,

obtained via questionnaire and covering the years 1970 through 1973. The empirical tests suggested that only consolidated measures of holding company leverage were significant in determining equity values. Consolidated leverage measures are, of course, available in published sources, which meant that data could be obtained more easily and the sample size increased. Also, it seemed important to expand the tests to include 1974, a period of major turmoil in the financial markets, and a watershed year for bank stock prices. Finally, we wished to go into greater detail with regard to measurement and definition of variables, sample characteristics, structural form of the regression equations and statistical methodology.

II. SUMMARY OF FINDINGS

The empirical findings of this study indicate that consolidated leverage[2] is a statistically significant determinant of share price. In particular, once the effects of other share price determinants—such as dividends, earnings growth, firm size and loan loss rate—are accounted for, an increase in leverage will lower share price. This result is consistent with the results reported in the RCB study and holds true for a number of different equation specifications, for different subsamples, and for the year 1974 which was not included in the earlier study.

Even though increased leverage will likely increase earnings per share, it also increases the degree of perceived investment risk. For low levels of leverage it is expected that the earnings effect will dominate the risk effect but, as leverage increases, the risk effect will become dominant. In any event, once the earnings effect, which tends to raise share price, is accounted for, the risk effect operates in such a way that investors require a higher rate of return to compensate for the extra risk they perceive. Accordingly, they are willing to pay less for the security and share price falls as leverage is increased.

As mentioned in the introduction, it was reported in the RCB study that consolidated leverage became increasingly important as a determinant of stock prices over the period 1970 through 1973. Results of the current study, however, are not consistent with interpreting this phenomenon as a "trend." In particular, the data suggest that leverage became less important as a determinant of equity values in 1974, although it remained highly significant in a statistical sense. This finding

---

[2] Consolidated leverage is defined as the ratio of deposits plus long-term debt plus short-term debt to the book value of common equity for the consolidated firm.

is somewhat paradoxical since 1974 was a disaster year for many bank stocks, and a period during which investors were obviously concerned about risk. Further examination of the data revealed, however, that the paradox is not as great as it might seem at first glance. When a measure of loan losses was introduced as an additional explanatory variable, it was insignificant in 1972, marginally significant in 1973 and very highly significant in 1974. What apparently occurred in 1974, therefore, is that bank equity investors shifted emphasis somewhat, away from leverage as a measure of perceived risk toward indicators of realized or potential portfolio loan losses. In this context, it is important to note that during 1974 securities analysts and the financial press stressed the losses of banking firms and the adequacy of loss reserves. Only time will tell whether this shift is temporary or permanent.

Several areas of uncertainty remain and these may represent fruitful topics for future research. There appear to be distinct differences in regression results when the sample is partitioned by size class. In particular, for the subsample of larger banking firms, leverage seems to become a larger and more significant determinant of stock price through time. For the subsample of smaller firms, however, its influence seems to decline, even though it remained highly statistically significant even in 1974. This observed result may be due to systematic differences in operating characteristics across size classes of banks, or to differences in the depth and breadth of the market for their equity securities. In any case, the results are clearly sample-sensitive and, until more time has passed and more tests are carried out, it would be premature to conclude that leverage is either increasing or decreasing in importance.

The combined evidence provided by the two studies, covering the period 1970 through 1974, is very strongly suggestive that the market for the equity securities of banking firms is sensitive to leverage. Therefore, the possibility of allowing the marketplace a greater role in the determination of capital adequacy remains viable. A move to less regulatory intervention may be rejected on other grounds, but it should not be rejected on the basis that the equity markets are myopic with regard to the capitalization of banking firms.

The question that must now be answered is whether the action of investors would effectively constrain leverage ratios so as not to impair confidence in the banking system. It can be argued that investors may be willing to accept more leverage risk than management since they reduce total risk by holding diversified portfolios in which only a fraction of their total wealth may be invested in bank equities. On the other hand, the losses incurred by bank management in the event of failure are likely to be greater, perhaps resulting in loss of jobs and reputation. Moreover, it may be argued that neither investors nor bank managers can be expected to correctly take account of the social costs of a failed bank. Thus, even though both are concerned about leverage risk and the chances of failure, they may allow capital ratios to fall to a point where the social costs of the increased risk outweigh the benefits to society from deregulating capital adequacy standards.

Thus, we do not, at this time, have sufficient empirical evidence to argue for a complete transfer of responsibility from the regulatory authorities to the marketplace in determining capital adequacy standards. However, since our results indicate that investors strongly perceive leverage and loan loss risks, we conclude that the regulators should make greater use of information provided by the financial marketplace in setting standards of capital adequacy.

Moreover, banking authorities should endeavor to improve the performance of bank equity markets by encouraging banking firms to disclose more relevant information. This is especially true for smaller banks whose equities are often traded in highly imperfect markets.

III. THE REGRESSION MODEL

The basic regression model used in this study is a fairly standard one, and thus it will be discussed only briefly.[3] It can be derived directly from the formula for the present value of an income stream, growing at a rate g and discounted at the rate k. Defining PV = present value, I = income in the current period, i = time period and t = total number of periods:

$$PV = \sum_{i=0}^{t} \frac{I(1+g)^i}{(1+k)^i}. \qquad (1)$$

It can be shown that if $k > g$ and as $t \to \infty$:

$$PV = \frac{I}{k-g}. \qquad (2)$$

In applying this present value formula to the specific case of a common stock, I is taken to

[3] See, for example, R. S. Bower and D. H. Bower, "Risk and the Valuation of Common Stock," *Journal of Political Economy*, 77, 3 (May-June 1969), pp. 349-63; M. J. Gruber, *The Determinants of Common Stock Prices*, Pennsylvania State University, 1971; and A. Ofer, "Investors Expectations of Earnings Growth, Their Accuracy and Effects on the Structure of Realized Rates of Return," *Journal of Finance* (forthcoming).

represent either dividends or earnings per share. In theory, I should probably represent dividends since the present value formula applies specifically to cash received by shareholders; however, the logic is identical in either case. The variable g is defined as the future rate of growth in dividends or earnings per share expected by holders of the stock, and k as the discount rate that market participants deem appropriate given the firm's risk class.[4]

Given these assumptions PV is the equilibrium price per share; i.e., the present value of the income stream generated by holding one share of stock. Only to the extent that different investors hold divergent beliefs about k and g will trading occur, and the equilibrium price will change only as events alter the market's perception of k and g.

The problem with this simple relationship is that, while P and I may be directly observable, g and k are not, thus proxy measures must be used for growth and risk expectations. If proxy measures must be used (say g' and k'), it cannot be expected that the specific functional form of (2) will be maintained. Most researchers have adopted a more general form:

$PV = PV(I, k', g')$, where

$$\frac{\partial PV}{\partial I} > 0, \quad \frac{\partial PV}{\partial g'} > 0, \quad \frac{\partial PV}{\partial k'} < 0, \qquad (3)$$

and, for purposes of convenience in empirical testing, have assumed that the relationship is linear or log-linear. The signs of the partial derivatives are those that are expected, based on equation (2) and assuming that k' and g' are good proxy measures.

This is the approach taken in the present study. Both linear and log-linear forms of the model are tested and several different proxy measures of I, g and k are employed. All variables used in empirical tests are defined in Figure 1.

In our empirical testing I is represented either by dividends per share (DIV) or net operating earnings per share (NOE). Historical growth in earnings (G) is used as a proxy measure for growth expectations.

Several different risk proxies are introduced including size of firm ($TASS$), consolidated leverage (LEV) and loan charge-offs ($LOSS$). $TASS$ is an indirect measure of the operating risk of the firm. It is widely believed that large firms can diversify more easily than small ones and that diversification, either by product line or market, can effec-

tively reduce risk. Increased leverage is believed to result in greater variability in earnings per share and an increased probability of bankruptcy at some future date. The loan loss variable is introduced to represent the probability of future defaults that may be expected to reduce earnings and dividends.

Each of these variables has been discussed extensively in the literature and should require no further defense here. Based on the above arguments, it is expected that:

$\partial P/\partial G > 0,\ \partial P/\partial TASS > 0,\ \partial P/\partial LEV < 0,$
$\partial P/\partial LOSS < 0,\ \partial P/\partial DIV > 0,$
and $\partial P/\partial NOE > 0,$

where P, per share market value, is the empirical counterpart of PV.

IV. DATA BASE AND REGRESSION RESULTS

All data used in the study were obtained from published sources. The primary source of financial data was the *Bank Stock Quarterly*, published by M. A. Schapiro & Co., Inc.; additional information was obtained from Moody's *Bank and Finance Manual*. Stock price data were obtained from the *American Banker*, the *Bank and Quotation Record* and the *Wall Street Journal*.

The first step in constructing the sample was to identify those firms for which complete information could be obtained for each of the three valuation years, 1972, 1973 and 1974. This preliminary sample was then modified by deleting organizations deemed inappropriate in accord with the following criteria: 1) Failure or forced reorganization of the institution prior to July 1975, 2) reported net operating losses in any year between 1969 and 1974 and 3) nonpayment of cash dividends in 1972, 1973 or 1974. A total of eight organizations were deleted on the basis of these criteria, resulting in a final sample of 113 banking organizations. Each of the eight deleted firms was for one reason or another highly atypical of large banking organizations in the United States.[5]

Nearly all of the 113 firms in the sample are holding company organizations, attesting to the popularity of this form of organization. And while the number of sample firms represents but a small fraction of the total number of banking firms in the nation, they account for over two-thirds of the assets held by all U.S. banks.

---

[4] It can be shown that this model is equally applicable if the investor intends to hold the stock for a specific, finite period.

[5] For example, in one of the deleted organizations the assets of the parent firm were larger than those of the bank affiliate, with the result that the bank was not the dominant element in the bank holding company. In a typical bank holding company, the bank affiliate accounts for approximately 95% of the banking holding company's total consolidated assets.

Data from the sample firms were used to construct the variables defined in Figure 1. These variables were then used in tests of the stock price valuation model discussed in Section III. Three years were studied: Year-end 1972, 1973 and 1974. Several alternative specifications of the model were tested in each of the years, and regres-

Figure 1. Empirical Variable Notations and Definitions

Variable	Definition
P	Price per share; an arithmetic average of three end-of-month bid common stock price quotations—the last month of the year being evaluated and the first two months of the following year.
NOE	Per share net operating earnings for the year being evaluated.
DIV	Per share cash dividends paid out in the year being evaluated.
TDIV	Total cash dividends paid out in the year being evaluated, in billions of dollars.
G	A four-year geometric average of annual NOE growth rates.* For evaluation in year t, $$G = \sqrt[4]{(1+g_t)(1+g_{t-1})(1+g_{t-2})(1+g_{t-3})} - 1$$ where $g_t = \dfrac{NOE_t - NOE_{t-1}}{NOE_{t-1}}$
TASS	Total consolidated assets at the end of the year being evaluated, in billions of dollars.
LEV	Ratio of total deposits and all other liabilities to the book value of common equity, at the end of the year being evaluated.
LOSS	Ratio of actual loan charge-offs, net of recoveries, during the year being evaluated to total loans at the end of the year being evaluated.
NOSH	Number of shares of common stock outstanding at the end of the year being evaluated.
DG	A (0,1) dummy variable. $DG = 1$ if net operating earnings did not decrease in the current year or in any of the three preceding years; otherwise, $DG = 0$.

*For 1972, G is calculated using three rather than four annual growth rates since NOE data were not reported for 1968. Also, to allow logarithms to be taken in cases where $G \le 0$, a transformation was made whereby earnings growth was redefined as log $(1 + G)$.

sion results are summarized in Figure 2 (1972), Figure 3 (1973) and Figure 4 (1974).

The specification of the valuation model used in Regression A is exactly the same as that used in the earlier RCB study. Coefficient estimates for the explanatory variables are quite similar to those reported in the RCB study for 1972 and 1973, the years common to both studies. As in the earlier study, variables NOE, G and TASS are all positive

and highly significant, while *LEV* is negatively and highly significantly related to share price.

When Regression A was tested in 1974, coefficient estimates for *NOE* and *TASS* continued to be positive and highly statistically significant (1% level), while the coefficient estimate for *LEV* continued to be negative and statistically significant (5% level). The coefficient estimate on *G*, however, was not statistically significant at the 10% level.

On the belief that the model was sensitive to the specification of earnings growth, an alternative measure was tested. The original variable *G* seemed to work well in periods when historical earnings grew fairly consistently from year to year, i.e. 1971-1973. Between 1973 and 1974, however, 38% of the sample firms showed declining earnings. To more precisely represent this phenomenon, a binary (0,1) variable (*DG*) was defined, having a value equal to +1 if *NOE* had never declined during the preceding four years, zero otherwise. When variable *G* in Regression 1974-A was replaced by *DG*, its coefficient estimate became positive and statistically significant at the 5% level. This suggests that the most appropriate growth measure may change through time and, in particular, indicates that investors were sensitive to the earnings declines in 1974. As will be reported, 1974 seems to be different than the other test periods in several important respects.

In Regression B, Figures 2, 3 and 4, dividends per share (*DIV*) are substituted for earnings per share. As explained in Section III, either variable can be used, although *DIV* may be theoretically preferable since it represents actual cash paid to investors. Regression results are mixed when this change is made. In 1972 and 1973 Regression B has lower coefficients of determination than Regression A, and *DIV* is less significant than *NOE*; in 1974, however, these results are reversed.

In every year the coefficients of *G* and *LEV* are larger in absolute value and more significant when *NOE* is replaced by *DIV*. This is particularly noticeable with the growth variable *G* in 1974; it is totally insignificant in Regression A yet highly significant in Regression B. This undoubtedly results from the fact that in 1974 *NOE* and *G* are quite highly correlated, reflecting the sharp change in earnings trends at many banking firms. Regression B, employing dividends per share, does not suffer from this multicollinearity problem and, therefore, is probably preferred.[6] In any case, results with leverage and loss measures are never importantly dependent upon the choice of *NOE*

[6] In 1974 the simple correlation between G and NOE is .51; between DIV and DIV, .013.

Figure 2. Summary of Regression Results for 1972

Regression Ident.	Dependent Variable	Constant	NOE	DIV	G	TASS	LEV	LOSS	I/NOSH	R^2 / F
A	log P	1.6330	0.5667*** (10.8969)		1.4789*** (4.7392)	0.0861*** (3.5276)	−0.3220*** (3.6496)			.6740 / 55.82
B	log P	1.9510		0.4561*** (7.9618)	2.3984*** (5.7830)	0.0989*** (3.4739)	−0.4230*** (4.2473)			.5687 / 35.60
C	log P	1.9678		0.4565*** (7.9229)	2.4057*** (5.7364)	0.1000*** (3.3954)	−0.4276*** (4.0957)	0.0043 (0.1522)		.5689 / 28.23
D	P	26.8122		14.3094*** (10.0149)	76.4558*** (5.0491)	0.4055*** (2.7541)	−0.8052*** (3.7621)	−78.7167 (0.1550)		.5739 / 28.82
E	$\log\left(\frac{P}{NOE}\right)$	1.2711			2.1985*** (5.6859)	−0.0003 (0.0102)	−0.1208 (1.0733)	0.0250 (0.8025)		.2349 / 8.29
F[a]	log P	3.4147		0.5474*** (10.3499)	2.5278*** (5.8820)		−0.3094*** (3.1989)	−0.0053 (0.1847)	0.4817*** (7.9465)	.5421 / 25.34

Notes: All explanatory variables are in common logarithms except those in Regression D.
In Regressions other than D, earnings growth has been measured as log(1+G) so that common logarithms could be taken in cases where $G \leq 0$.
t-statistics appear in parentheses below coefficient estimates.
* Denotes significance at the 10% level
** Denotes significance at the 5% level
*** Denotes significance at the 1% level
[a] The variable TDIV was used in place of DIV in this regression

versus *DIV* as an explanatory variable. In all three valuation years Regression B coefficient estimates for *DIV*, *G*, *TASS* and *LEV* are of the expected sign and statistically significant at the 1% level.

Leverage, Loan Losses and Share Price

In both Regressions A and B, the coefficient estimates on *LEV* decrease in absolute value over the sample period. For example, in Regression B the coefficients are −0.4230 in 1972, −0.3900 in 1973 and −0.2412 in 1974. This means that, while in 1972 a 10% increase in *LEV* would have lowered share price in the typical banking firm by about 4.2%, *ceteris paribus*, the same change in 1974 would have lowered prices by only about 2.4%. This result is unexpected in view of the increased degree of caution exhibited by investors in bank equities during 1974, especially after the failure of the Franklin National Bank. One would expect that *LEV*, as a measure of perceived risk,

would be regarded more importantly by investors in 1974 than in the earlier years. Moreover, the *LEV* coefficient estimates declined slightly between 1972 and 1973 while in the earlier RCB study they increased between these same two years, the only periods in which the two samples overlap. In fact, in the RCB study we observed a general increase in the impact of leverage over the four year period 1970-1973, and concluded that this might represent a "learning curve" phenomenon. Thus there seems to be a substantive difference between the two sets of tests, which must be further examined.

To shed more light on the issue, two procedures were applied. First, attempts were made to determine if differences between the *LEV* coefficient estimates in the present study and those in the earlier RCB study could be attributed to specific sample differences. Second, attempts were made to identify additional risk measures that might have

Figure 3. Summary of Regression Results for 1973

Regression Ident.	Dependent Variable	Constant	NOE	DIV	G	TASS	LEV	LOSS	I/NOSH	R^2 / F
A	log P	1.3497	0.6316*** (10.9485)		2.9083*** (6.6555)	0.1660*** (5.7516)	-0.2739*** (2.8504)			.7399 / 76.79
B	log P	1.7066		0.5249*** (8.0374)	4.2660*** (7.2481)	0.1819*** (5.4043)	-0.3900*** (3.6085)			.6565 / 51.61
C	log P	1.5247		0.5066*** (7.7334)	4.0551*** (6.8139)	0.1696*** (4.9767)	-0.3539*** (3.2476)	-0.0538* (1.7601)		.6662 / 42.71
D	P	12.2142		12.4862*** (8.7633)	125.040*** (7.0860)	0.4387*** (3.5633)	-0.3362* (1.8671)	-1124.00** (2.5668)		.5906 / 30.88
E	$\log\left(\dfrac{P}{NOE}\right)$	0.8129			3.6400*** (7.3702)	0.0667** (2.1455)	-0.0378 (0.3480)	-0.3032 (0.9791)		.3959 / 17.70
F[a]	log P	3.1615		0.6576*** (10.6644)	4.3841*** (6.9896)		-0.1452 (1.4747)	-0.0654** (2.0284)	0.5405*** (7.5733)	.6253 / 35.71

Notes: All explanatory variables are in common logarithms except those in Regression D.
In Regressions other than D, earnings growth has been measured as log(1+G) so that common logarithms could be taken in cases where $G \leq 0$.
t-statistics appear in parentheses below coefficient estimates.
   * Denotes significance at the 10% level
  ** Denotes significance at the 5% level
 *** Denotes significance at the 1% level
   [a] The variable TDIV was used in place of DIV in this regression

influenced investor behavior in 1974, but not in earlier years; i.e., risk measures that were adopted by investors in place of, or in addition to, leverage.

First, Regressions A and B were re-estimated using only those observations common to both the RCB sample and the *Bank Stock Quarterly* sample used in the present study. There were 75 observations common to both. The following coefficient estimates for LEV were obtained from the overlapping subsample:[7]

Year	Regression A	Regression B
1972	—0.1050	—0.2583
1973	—0.2246	—0.3682
1974	—0.3091	—0.4008

These estimates are somewhat smaller than those obtained when either of the two full samples is

---

[7] Since Regressions A and B were tested using logarithmic values of the variables, the resulting coefficient estimates represent elasticity coefficients of price with respect to the untransformed independent variables.

used. Note, however, that when the overlapping subsample is employed, the coefficient of *LEV* increases through time in absolute value, consistent with the earlier study. Thus the time trend in the leverage coefficient is clearly sample sensitive.

Mean firm size varies among the three samples: In 1973 mean values of *TASS* for the current sample, the RCB sample and the overlapping subsample are $4.76 billion, $5.06 billion and $6.39 billion respectively. Thus, it appears that the inclusion of additional (smaller) banking firms in the current sample may be affecting the coefficient estimates of *LEV*.

To test this hypothesis, the current sample was partitioned into two parts according to firm size, and the regressions were re-run using these subsamples. Coefficient estimates on *LEV* based on the subsample of larger firms increased between 1972 and 1973 for both Regressions A and B. For the subsample of smaller firms, however, these

Figure 4. Summary of Regression Results for 1974

Regression Ident.	Dependent Variable	Constant	NOE	DIV	G	TASS	LEV	LOSS	I/NOSH	R^2 / F
A	log P	1.1662	0.6567*** (14.3538)		−0.1454 (0.4663)	0.1698*** (5.6913)	−0.2273** (2.2926)			.8164 / 120.03
B	log P	1.3904		0.6664*** (15.5077)	2.2307*** (8.1024)	0.1511*** (5.2658)	−0.2412*** (2.5723)			.8345 / 138.16
C	log P	1.1884		0.6411*** (14.9781)	1.9782*** (6.9752)	0.1456*** (5.2116)	−0.2430*** (2.6668)	−0.0850*** (2.7082)		.8453 / 116.90
D	P	9.3584		9.3182*** (13.0394)	40.1057*** (5.3588)	0.2756*** (4.0664)	−0.1716 (1.4996)	−576.629** (2.4269)		.7605 / 67.94
E	$\log\left(\dfrac{P}{NOE}\right)$	0.7469			−1.1525*** (3.1157)	0.0806** (2.3381)	−0.0420 (0.3551)	−0.0330 (0.8092)		.1363 / 4.26
F[a]	log P	3.2503		0.7660*** (18.2125)	2.1206*** (7.3488)		−0.0858 (1.0924)	−0.0818** (2.5124)	0.6400*** (14.0313)	.8343 / 107.77

Notes: All explanatory variables are in common logarithms except those in Regression D.
In Regressions other than D, earnings growth has been measured as log(1+G) so that common logarithms could be taken in cases where $G \leq 0$.
t-statistics appear in parentheses below coefficient estimates.
 * Denotes significance at the 10% level
 ** Denotes significance at the 5% level
 *** Denotes significance at the 1% level
 [a] The variable TDIV was used in place of DIV in this regression

estimates decreased between the same years. It appears, therefore, that the increase between 1972 and 1973 in the importance of LEV, reported in the RCB study, holds true for larger firms. It does not hold true for the smaller banking firms that are included in the present study.[8]

It is impossible to compare results for 1974, since 1974 data for the RCB firms have not yet been collected. We feel fairly confident, however, that the importance of LEV decreased between 1973 and 1974. This statement is based on the results obtained from applying Regressions A and B to the full Bank Stock Quarterly (current) sample, to the subsample of Quarterly firms that overlap the RCB study and to the two subsamples obtained by partitioning the Quarterly sample. In every case, coefficient estimates for LEV are less in 1974 than in 1973, further supporting this unexpected result.

One possible explanation is that in 1974 many banking firms sought to slow their rates of expansion, thereby lowering the rates at which their financial leverage increased. In fact, some firms publicly announced that they were adopting "slower growth" policies. Accordingly, it may be that investors became less concerned about leverage risk as the expansion of financial leverage was curtailed.

In addition, many firms encountered a substantial increase in the rate of loan losses in 1974 as compared to previous years. Much public attention was focused on loan losses, and it is likely that investors in bank equities became more aware of losses as an indicator of investment risk.

To test this hypothesis, a measure of loan losses (LOSS), defined as the ratio of actual loan losses

8 Coefficient estimates for LEV for the two subsamples were:

	Larger Banks		Smaller Banks	
Year	Regression A	Regression B	Regression A	Regression B
1972	−0.1129	−0.3407	−0.4141	−0.4897
1973	−0.3119	−0.3934	−0.2143	−0.3875

(net of recoveries) to total loans, was introduced. These results are reported in Regression C of Figures 2-4.

In Regression C, coefficient estimates on *DIV*, *G*, *TASS* and *LEV* are all of the expected sign and statistically significant (1% level) in all three valuation years. Coefficient estimates on *LOSS* have the expected negative sign, and are statistically significant in 1973 and 1974. Moreover, they increase in absolute magnitude from 0.0043 in 1972 to −0.0538 in 1973 to −0.0850 in 1974. Their degree of statistical significance also increases, from insignificance at the 10% level (1972), to statistical significance at the 10% level (1973), to statistical significance at the 1% level (1974). Thus, it seems that investors have come to view loan losses as an important measure of risk and hence as an important determinant of share price.[9]

Alternative Structural Forms

For completeness, we tested several different regression models, in addition to the log-log form used in Regressions A-C. Regression results using untransformed variables appear as Regression D in each of the three years. Excepting 1972, coefficients of determination are lower in the linear model than in the nonlinear models reported in Regressions B and C, and coefficient estimates for *LEV* are not as highly significant.[10] Thus, although the log-log form seems to give a slightly better explanation of the data, the results using a linear form are generally consistent.

Semi-log specifications, in which *P* was not transformed but where logarithms of the explanatory variables were used, generally were not as good as the log-log specifications but somewhat better than the linear specifications. This evaluation is based upon a comparison of the coefficients of determination and degree of statistical significance observed in coefficient estimates.

Price/Earnings as the Dependent Variable

In Equation (2) *P* is linear-homogeneous in *I*. It is frequently assumed that this also holds true for Equation (3) in which case (3) may be rewritten:

$$P/I = \phi(k', g'). \tag{4}$$

In this form the dependent variable becomes price/earnings, which has certain advantages for empirical testing.[11] In particular, the transformation tends to scale the data, allowing direct comparison across firms of different size and reducing the statistical problems associated with heteroskedasticity.

Since the price/earnings ratio (*P/NOE*) has been used as the dependent variable in a number of valuation studies, we also experimented with this form. The results are presented as Regression E, Figures 2-4. In general, Regression E has all the symptoms of being badly misspecified; e.g., low explanatory power, and variables suggested by the theory entering insignificantly or with the wrong (unexpected) sign. This specification problem is particularly apparent when Regression E is compared with Regressions A through D. Although the regressions are not presented here, results were equally poor when price/dividends was used as the dependent term.

There are at least two not mutually exclusive explanations for these poor results. First, earnings per share tends to be correlated with the other explanatory variables, and when it is used to deflate the dependent term spurious multiple correlations may result. Second, and perhaps more important, this form of the equation implicitly assumes that the elasticity of price with respect to earnings is constant and equal to unity.[12] However, the data do not support this assumption. The elasticity of *P* with respect to *NOE* can be directly estimated from Regression A, and it is significantly less than one in all three valuation periods. Similarly, the elasticity of *P* with respect to *DIV* can be estimated from Regressions B, C and D, and again, it is always significantly less than unity.

It may be argued that we have not correctly measured current earnings per share, and that a measure of normalized or "permanent" earnings is needed. To overcome this problem some researchers have computed smoothed versions of earnings per share, where current *NOE* is represented by a weighted average over several periods. This tends to mitigate the effects of short-run fluctuations, which the market may not regard as "permanent." However, the weighting scheme is essentially arbitrary and there is no *a priori* basis for choosing one set of weights as superior to any other. In addition, there is no guarantee that the unitary elasticity assumption will be met. For all these reasons, we prefer to treat price per share as the dependent

---

[9] An alternative measure of loan losses was also tested. This variable was defined as the ratio of the provision for loan losses, included in operating expenses, to net operating income. The explanatory power of this loan loss variable was not as good as the variable *LOSS*, although its coefficient estimate was negative and statistically significant in 1974 at the 10% level.

[10] It is interesting to note that if variable *G* in Regression 1974-D is replaced by the binary growth variable *DG*, defined above, the coefficient estimate of *LEV* becomes statistically significant (1% level).

[11] Price/dividends is infrequently used because of the difficulty in treating firms with zero payout ratio.

[12] That is, $(\partial P/\partial NOE)(NOE/P) = 1$.

variable and allow the data to determine the elasticities, as is done in Regressions A through D.[13]

Stock Splits and Dividends

There is still one problem with regard to the specification of the model used in Regressions A-D. Over time, stock splits and dividends made by the sample firms have affected values of the per share variables P, NOE and DIV. That is, the particular values of these variables that were observed in each of the valuation years have been influenced by the history of stock splits and dividends experienced by the sample firms. If in Regression C, for example, a typical firm were to have a two-for-one stock split, theoretically both DIV and P should fall by 50%. This would not be the case, however, since a 50% fall in DIV would produce a fall in P much less than 50%, due to the fact that the coefficient estimate on DIV is substantially less than unity.

It is possible that this problem might bias the coefficient estimates and significance tests of DIV. However, it is highly implausible that it would effect the results for LEV or $LOSS$ unless somehow they were (spuriously) related to historical stock splits. Nonetheless, two separate methods were applied in an attempt to eliminate any possible bias from this source. First, DIV was replaced by two variables, $TDIV$ (total dividends) and $1/NOSH$ (the inverse of total number of common shares). The product of $TDIV$ and $1/NOSH$ equals DIV. By entering these terms separately, we allow for the possibility that each variable may influence share price, but differently. Theoretically, if $NOSH$ measures the number of units of equity ownership outstanding, and nothing more, the elasticity of P with respect to $1/NOSH$ will be unity.[14]

The results with this form of the model are shown in Regression F, Figures 2-4. The coefficient of $1/NOSH$ is positive and highly significant in all three years as expected, but it is also significantly different than one. This undoubtedly occurs because $1/NOSH$ is entering as a proxy measure for firm size. In fact, $TASS$ and $1/NOSH$ are so highly correlated that $TASS$ must be dropped as an explanatory variable. Even so, $TDIV$ and $1/NOSH$ are still highly collinear (simple correlation of approximately —.85 in all three years), so that results of Regression F must be interpreted cautiously.

In Regression F leverage is highly significant in one year only, 1972, but it has the expected negative sign and a t-value greater than one in all three years. $LOSS$ is insignificant in 1972 but negative and significant (5% level) in 1973 and 1974. Perhaps more important, the coefficient of $TDIV$ is always very similar to that of $1/NOSH$, and also to that of DIV in Regression C. This increases confidence in Regression C which is preferred to F since it is not troubled by extreme multicollinearity.

One additional test was performed to determine whether the historical occurrence of stock splits and dividends might have somehow biased the results with risk variables. Under the assumption that the number of shares after a split is greater than the number before, the effects of splits can be removed by multiplying current per share values by an appropriate adjustment factor greater than one. Rather than attempt to determine the correct adjustment factor for each firm, which depends on its entire past history, a set of adjustment factors was arbitrarily specified. These factors were 1.0 (no splits), 1.25 (five-for-four split), 1.5 (three-for-two split), 1.75 (seven-for-four split) and 2.0 (two-for-one split). A random number generator was then used to select a particular value for the adjustment factor; each factor was assigned the same probability in the selection process.

Regression 1974-C was then run 15 times, each time with a different distribution of P and DIV due to differences in the adjustment made to each firm in each run. The adjustment factor varied across firms in any one run as well as across different runs of the model. Coefficient estimates from the 15 regressions obtained in this manner were not as statistically significant as those obtained in Regression C, Figures 2-4, but in all cases the coefficient estimate of LEV was negative and significant at least at the 10% level. Coefficients of $LOSS$ were always of the expected (negative) sign and statistically significant at approximately the 5% level. This provides additional evidence that the effects of stock splits notwithstanding, LEV and $LOSS$ coefficients are relatively uniform in magnitude and statistically significant.[15]   □

---

[13] One potential advantage in using price/earnings is that it tends to scale the data, reducing the statistical problems associated with heteroskedasticity. However, tests indicated relatively homoskedastic error terms when log P was used as the dependent variable. This is undoubtedly due to the homogeneous nature of the sample—all large banking firms—and the scaling effect of the logarithmic transformation.

[14] If $NOSH$ measures only the number of outstanding units of equity ownership, the total market value of the firm, T, should be invariant with respect to $NOSH$. In other words, if the number of shares is doubled, each new share should be worth precisely half as much as one old share. It is clear that $P * NOSH = T$ which implies that $\partial P / \partial (1/NOSH) * (1/NOSH)/P = 1$.

[15] There are several reasons why the statistical significance of the explanatory variables may be expected to drop when the data are manipulated in this manner. First, it introduces a certain amount of random noise into the dependent variable. Second, both price per share P and dividends per share DIV are multiplied by the same adjustment factor. This assumes that the elasticity of price with respect to dividends is unity; but as explained previously, this is probably not the case.

Chapter 41

AN ANALYSIS OF BANK PRICE-EARNINGS RATIOS*

By Richard A. Shick and James A. Verbrugge

*This article is reprinted, with permission, from *Journal of Bank Research*, Vol. 6, No. 2 (Summer, 1975), pp. 140-149.

The determinants of price-earnings (PE) ratios have long been one of the central areas of financial research. Empirical studies such as those of Malkiel [1970] and Malkiel and Cragg [1970] have demonstrated that PE ratios for utility and industrial firms are related to factors such as dividends, growth and risk. Similar but more limited studies on bank stock prices have not established growth or risk as being significantly related to PE ratios; however, dividends and a regional dummy variable have been found to be significant. (See, for example, Durand [1957], Peltzman [1968] and Fredman and Wert [1970]).

Given the paucity of empirical results for banks, the purpose of this paper is to develop a model that identifies the characteristics separating banks with high price-earnings ratios from those with low price-earnings ratios.[1] Specifically, we hope to show 1) that bank PE ratios are systematically related to growth and risk variables and 2) that the use of a regional dummy varable is a simplified proxy for the characteristics of the firm's market area. The technique used for this study is multiple discriminant analysis (MDA) which has recently been applied to a variety of finance and banking problems.[2]

The paper will proceed along the following lines. A brief summary of previous studies is given in Part I, followed by a discussion of the multiple discriminant analysis technique in Part II. Part III describes the sample of banks and the variables used in the analysis. This is followed in Part IV by the four step procedure used to develop and test the model. In the first step of this procedure the original set of variables is submitted to the stepwise MDA procedure for each year 1967-1972. On the basis of these results several alternative models are formulated from the variables that appear repeatedly during the six years. These models are then estimated using the single-step MDA procedure. The final model is selected on the basis of its ability to discriminate over the six cross-sections and the requirement that the variables have a reasonable economic interpretation. In the last step, the validity of the model is tested on a holdout sample of banks for each year. Finally, Part V presents conclusions and implications.

I. Summary of Previous Studies

The number of published studies on bank stock prices is limited. One of the first and most extensive by Durand [1957] concluded, among other things, that "only two factors, dividends and earnings, seem to play a systematic and easily demonstrable role in determining ratios of bank stock prices to book value." Furthermore, he was unable to find a relationship between bank stock prices and obvious measures of growth such as the rate of increase in bank earnings. A more recent study by Peltzman [1968] experienced similar difficulties. While finding a significant relationship between prices and earnings and dividends, Peltzman was unable to find any relationship between prices and growth or variance in return. In their study of bank stocks, Fredman and Wert [1970] asserted: "We hold that risk is not an important consideration in the valuation of bank equities since their earnings are reasonably stable and somewhat predictable over time; although not so stable as utilities." They fail to mention, however, that risk variables have been found to be significant factors influencing prices of utility stocks [Malkiel, 1970]. Thus, the results of prior research efforts suggest that only current earnings

---

[1] In addition to being of general interest, the results of this study should be potentially useful from an applied viewpoint of bank managers. First, if managers follow the normative goal of financial management and maximize the wealth of their shareholders, financial decisions must be made in light of their impact on this wealth. Second, even if managers do not follow this goal, expansion via merger or acquisition and the marketing of new equity issues are facilitated by relatively high price-earnings ratios. Hence, it is important for decision-makers to know what set of factors is associated with firms whose shares have been consistently valued at premium prices.

[2] For example, MDA has been used in studies of the capital adequacy of banks (Dince and Fortson [1972]), commercial bank profitability (Haslem and Longbrake [1971]), prediction of bank failures (Meyer and Pifer [1970] and corporate bankruptcy (Altman [1968]). The technique has also been used to classify a sample of industrial firms by high and low price-earnings ratios (Walter [1959]), to analyze industrial bond ratings (Pinches and Mingo [1973]) and to study stock price variability (Klemkosky and Petty [1973]).

and dividends are significant factors influencing prices while risk and growth are unimportant.[3]

II. Description of Technique

MDA is a multi-variate statistical technique which classifies an observation into one of several groupings using a linear combination of explanatory variables. Within the context of the present study, a combination of independent variables is derived where each variable is a characteristic of the individual bank. The resulting discriminant function takes the general form:

$$Z_i = b_1 X_{1i} + b_2 X_{2i} + \ldots + b_p X_{pi}$$

where Z_i = the discriminant score for the ith bank

b_p = the discriminant coefficient for the variable p

X_{pi} = the ith bank's value for the pth independent variable

A Z-score is then calculated for each bank and the classification into the two groups is made as follows:

if $Z_i > Z^*$, classify the bank as belonging to group 1, i.e., high PE

if $Z_i < Z^*$, classify the bank as belonging to group 2, i.e., low PE

where Z^* is the critical value for the discriminant score.[4]

Two discriminant analysis programs are used. The stepwise program (BMD07M) is a procedure used to find a subset of explanatory variables that discriminates between the two groups. Explanatory variables are added at each step that reduce the unexplained variation of the dependent variable by the greatest amount, given the explanatory variables already included in the equation from prior steps. Following the selection of the variables, a discriminant function is calculated from the discriminant analysis for two groups program (BMD04M).

III. Selection of Sample Banks and Variables Used in the Analysis

The primary source of data for this study is the Bank Compustat tape complied by Investors Management Sciences which contains information for approximately 110 banks. Because of incomplete

information, not all banks could be included in the sample. The criteria for inclusion are complete information on the variables desired for a given year plus information for four previous years in order to compute growth rates for selected items. On the basis of these criteria, the years 1963-1972 contain complete data for approximately 80 banks. The banks are classified into high and low PE groups as follows. Using the closing price for the end of the year and earnings per share for the year, an average PE ratio and standard deviation are computed for the 80 banks for each year. Those banks with a PE ratio higher than the mean plus one-half standard deviation are considered as high PE while those banks with price-earnings ratio lower than the mean minus one-half standard deviation are classified into the low PE group. Fourteen banks falling within the range of plus or minus one-half standard deviation are considered as mid-group banks and not included in the sample. The remaining 66 banks are used: 40 in the estimation procedure and 26 in the holdout sample.

In the typical equity valuation model, share price is assumed to be the present value of an expected dividend stream discounted at the investors' required rate of return for that firm. Using this basic assumption, Malkiel and Cragg [1970] have shown that a firm's price-earnings ratio will be a function of its payout ratio, the expected dividend growth rate and the risk associated with the future returns. Accordingly, our approach is to define variables that fall into these three categories. In addition, to take account of the general feeling in banking circles that banks should be analyzed by traditional financial statement ratios, two additional classifications of variables are created—income-expense ratios and asset-liability ratios.

A set of 41 variables was defined and classified into the categories listed in Figure 1. As a means of testing for the influence of growth on PE ratios, we defined both long-term growth and short-term growth characteristics of the firm. The long-term growth variables, GL1-GL4, are the slopes of the log-linear trend lines fitted to total assets, operating income, dividends and net income available for common shareholders for a five year period ending with the cross-section year; i.e., 1963-67 for the 1967 cross-section, 1964-1968 for the 1968 cross-section, etc.[5] Variables GS1-GS8 rep-

---

[3] Similar conclusions were reached by Van Horne and Helwig [1966]. However, their study was limited to banks with deposits of less than $10 million.

[4] Z^* is calculated as an arithmetic average of the mean Z scores for the high and low PE groups. This procedure is valid (1) when the cost of misclassification are equal and the *a priori* probabilities of the two populations are equal or (2) when the product of the costs and probabilities are equal for the two groups. These assumptions were made in most of the MDA studies cited.

[5] The equation is
$$\log_e Y_t = a + bT + u_t$$
where
$\log_e Y_t$ = natural logarithm of the variable on which the growth is being estimated
T = Time variable
u_t = Random error term

Figure 1. Variable Definitions

1. Growth Variables: Long-term (GL)

GL1. Five year average annual growth of total assets.

GL2. Five year average annual growth of operating income.

GL3. Five year average annual growth of dividends.

GL4. Five year average annual growth of net income available for common.

GL5. Five year average annual growth of state per capita income.

2. Growth Variables: Short-term (GS)

GS1. Two year average annual growth of total assets.

GS2. Two year average annual growth of operating income.

GS3. Two year average annual growth of dividends.

GS4. Two year average annual growth of net income available for common.

GS5. One year growth of total assets.

GS6. One year growth of operating income.

GS7. One year growth of dividends.

GS8. One year growth of net income available for common.

GS9. One year growth of state per capita income.

3. Payout Variables (PO)

PO1. Cash dividends/net income available for common.

4. Risk Variables (RK)

RK1. R^2 of five year growth of total assets.

RK2. R^2 of five year growth of operating income.

RK3. R^2 of five year growth of dividends.

RK4. R^2 of five year growth of net income available for common.

RK5. Leverage = [capital notes plus preferred stock]/ common.

RK6. Relative size = total assets of bank i/average total assets of sample.

RK7. Market characteristic = log of shares outstanding.

RK8. Market characteristic = log of number of share-holders.

RK9. Capital/Risk Assets = total capital/[total assets minus cash assets minus U. S. securities].

5. Income-Expense Ratios (IE)

IE 1. Loan revenue/operating revenue.

IE 2. Other current operating revenue/operating revenue.

IE 3. Net gain (loss) on securities/operating revenue.

IE 4. Loan revenue/total loans.

IE 5. All interest on securities/total securities.

IE 6. Net income/operating revenue.

IE 7. Net income/[total equity—preferred stock].

IE 8. Salaries and related expense/operating revenue.

IE 9. Interest on deposits and borrowings/operating revenue.

IE10. Net chargeoffs as percent of loans.

6. Asset-Liability Ratios (AL)

AL1. Cash assets/total assets.

AL2. Total taxable securities/total assets.

AL3. State and Political subdivision obligations/total assets.

AL4. Loans/total deposits.

AL5. Total time and savings deposits/total deposits.

AL6. Total borrowings/total liabilities.

---

resent alternative short-term (two and one year) growth rates for total assets, operating income, dividends and net income, respectively. We also hypothesized that the expected growth rate may be a function of the growth in the market served by the bank.[6] As a proxy for market growth we calculated a long-term growth of state per capita income (GL5) as well as a short-term growth rate (GS9). The payout ratio (PO1) is the proportion of net income paid out as cash dividends.

Classification 4 includes variables that can be taken as measures of risk. Items RK1-RK4 are the R^2 of the regression lines for the growth rates

GL1-GL4.[7] Item RK5 is a leverage ratio defined as capital notes and preferred stock divided by common equity. RK6 is a relative size variable calculated as the total assets of the individual bank divided by the average total assets of all banks in the sample. This variable is included since empirical studies by Brigham and Gordon

[6] See for example Robertson [1973].

[7] The R^2 statistic is one measure of the consistency of the compound growth rate over the time period under consideration. The higher is the R^2 value, the more consistently the variable in question increases each year. The lower the R^2, the more unstable is the growth. As suggested by an anonymous referee, an alternative measure of variability could have been the standard error of the regression coefficient of the time variable.

[1968] and Benishay [1961] have found size to be a significant determinant of stock prices in utility and industrial firms. RK7 and RK8 on the other hand are partial proxies for marketability. Since the majority of the bank stocks in the sample are traded over-the-counter, we hypothesized that the risk attached to a security may be a function of the breadth of the market for the firm's stock. Unfortunately, data were not available for the number of shares traded annually as a measure of marketability. Therefore, we developed two proxies for market characteristics: The supply of shares is represented by the shares outstanding (RK7) and the size of the market by the number of shareholders (RK8).[8] In both cases, the log of the value was used to reduce heteroscedasticity. Variable RK9 is a balance sheet characteristic that can be viewed as a risk measure; namely, a capital to risk asset ratio that indicates the extent to which banks allocate funds to higher risk assets.

Classifications 5 and 6 include a variety of profitability, income, expense and balance sheet ratios that are often used to analyze individual banks in terms of sources of revenue, rates of return, expense ratios and asset-liability characteristics. Variables IE1-IE3 are defined as various sources of income as a percent of operating revenue. IE4 and IE5 measure the average rate of return on loans and securities respectively, while IE6 and IE7 measure the rate of return on bank revenue and equity. IE8-IE10 are measures of the relative importance of various expenses such as interest on time and savings deposits, salary and personnel expenses, and chargeoffs.

Items AL1-AL3 are asset composition variables measuring the variation in cash asset holdings and security composition. The overall importance of loans in the portfolio is measured by the loan-deposit ratio AL4. Since data on the types of loans are not consistently available, it is impossible to include variables on the composition of the loan portfolio. AL5 and AL6 represent liability characteristics; namely, the relative importance of time and savings deposits and the relative importance of non-deposit sources of funds. Capital account characteristics are already included in the debt/equity ratio RK5 and capital risk asset ratio RK9.

IV. Empirical Results

As the first step in the process of selecting a final model, the original set of variables was sub-mitted to the stepwise MDA program for each year. The ordering of the variables is based on a process which selects at each step the variable with the highest F-value, given those variables already in the model. Since there is no set rule to determine the optimum number of steps allowed, it is necessary to establish a logical criterion for deciding at which point the iterative process should be stopped. The particular criterion we adopted was to terminate the selection process when the additional variables selected were no longer statistically significant at the 5% level. Given this criterion, the variables selected for each of the six years are shown in Figure 2 along with the number of steps, the number of firms correctly classified at the final step and the overall F-value.

As indicated in Figure 2, the number of steps in which significant variables are added varies between three and six for the six cross-sections. In all cases the overall F-values are significant at the 5% level. If one were solely interested in the ability of the stepwise process to classify banks into high and low groups these results would be impressive because in five of the six years at least 90% of the banks are correctly classified. However, since we are interested in a model consisting of a common set of variables for all years, these initial results are used primarily for screening purposes. The next step is to look for consistent patterns of variables over time.

Selection of Variables for Final Model

An examination of the selected variables reveals several clear patterns. First, traditional bank analysis ratios reflecting asset-liability composition and income-expense characteristics do not enter frequently as significant factors. Rather, variables measuring growth of the firm and its market along with the stability of that growth appear to dominate. Specifically, four variables summarized in Figure 3 tend to enter the discriminant function quite consistently over the six cross-sections. They are: 1) The logarithm of shares outstanding that enters in four of the years, 2) the R^2 of operating income growth that appears in three years, 3) the state income growth variable that enters directly in two years, and indirectly in two additional years through its correlation with the long-term state income growth[9] and 4) the long-term growth

---

[8] In some of the initial tests, the ratio of shareholders to shares outstanding was used as the variable. Although the ratio entered the equation and was significant, the economic rationale for the variable was difficult to justify. Therefore, we decomposed the variable into two parts.

[9] Although both the one year and the five year growth of state income entered twice, we decided to include the one year growth rate for two reasons. First, since a long-term growth rate is already included in the form of net income growth, the inclusion of a short-term rate produces an appealing two growth rate model as suggested by other valuation studies (Malkiel-Cragg [1970]). Second, the use of the five year rate rather than the one year produced evidence of multicollinearity.

Figure 2. Variables Entering Stepwise Multiple Discriminant Analysis 1967-1972

	Variables Entering	
Step	1967	1968
1	Loans/Deposits (AL4)	Log shares (RK7)
2	R^2 asset growth (RK1)	Gain securities/operating revenue (IE3)
3	One year state income growth (GS9)	R^2 operating income (RK2)
4	R^2 net income available growth (RK4)	Chargeoffs/Loans (IE10)
5	R^2 dividend growth (RK3)	
6	Net income/common equity (IE7)	
	1969	**1970**
1	Log shares (RK7)	Log shares (RK7)
2	Five year state income growth (GL5)	Five year state income growth (GL5)
3	Interest income/total securities (IE5)	Interest expense/operating revenue (IE9)
	1971	**1972**
1	Log shares (RK7)	Two year income available growth (GS4)
2	Five year income available growth (GL4)	One year dividend growth (GS7)
3	One year state income growth (GS9)	Two year dividend growth (GS3)
4	Other current operating revenue/oper. rev. (IE2)	Five year income available growth (GS4)
5	R^2 operating income growth (RK2)	R^2 operating income (RK2)

Number of firms correctly classified at final step

Year	1967	1968	1969	1970	1971	1972
Number	38	35	33	36	36	38
Overall F-value	9.10	13.58	13.55	12.88	8.19	13.87

of net income available for common that appears in two years and is correlated in two years with the short-term growth of net income. No other variable appears more than once. Of the 27 total steps allowed in the stepwise process for the six years, the four variables account for 41% of those entered.

Based on this result, the choice of variables for the final model was narrowed considerably. To identify the best final model, four alternatives were then formulated. The first is a model consisting solely of the four variables that enter consistently. Second, in addition to the four basic variables, we add the gain (loss) on securities as a per cent of operating revenue. The reasoning is that the gain variable entered once as a significant factor, was correlated with return on equity that

entered in one year, and was the fourth variable added in the 1969 estimate. Third, in addition to the four core variables we add the ratio of other current operating revenue to operating revenue. Although this variable entered significantly only on one occasion, it was near significance in three other years. Fourth, we combined the basic four variables with the securities gain and other revenue variables as the final alternative.

In order to select the final model, we compare the four alternatives described above on several grounds: 1) The ability to correctly classify banks into the respective groups in each year, 2) overall significance (F-value) of the model and 3) the signs of the discriminant coefficients. With respect to the capability of correctly classifying the banks, the basic four variable model consis-

Figure 3. Variables Appearing Consistently Over the Cross-Sections From the Stepwise Multiple Discriminant Analysis

Variable Name (Number)	1967	1968	1969	1970	1971	1972
Log shares (RK7)	—	Yes	Yes	Yes	Yes	—
R^2 operating income (RK2)	—	Yes	—	—	Yes	Yes
One year growth state income (GS9)	Yes	—	Yes*	Yes*	Yes	—
Five year growth net income (GL4)	Yes*	—	Yes*	—	Yes	Yes

*An asterisk indicates that a variable entered the function that was correlated with the variable in question.

tently classifies a lower proportion (average of 79% for six years) than the other alternatives (an average of 83%). On an overall significance basis the models containing the four variables plus securities gains and the four variables plus other current operating income show comparable F-values that are consistently higher than for the model consisting of the four plus securities gain and other revenue. However, when discriminant functions are calculated for the two remaining alternative models, the sign for the other current operating income variable is consistently negative. The expected relationship for this variable was positive, based on a hypothesis that the variable should reflect the importance of earnings from the diverse

[10]On the other hand, a negative expected relationship may not be illogical if one accepts the view that non-banking subsidiaries cannot be operated profitability.
[11]A related question pertains to the ability of the variables to explain the variation in PE ratios within a regression framework. The results are shown below with + or − indicating the sign of the coefficient and an asterisk indicating significance at the .05 level.

Year	Log Shares	R^2 Operating Income	Growth State Income	Growth Net Income	Gain on Securities	R^2
1967	+	−	+*	+	−*	.315*
1968	+	−*	+	+	−*	.612*
1969	+*	−*	+*	+*	−*	.711*
1970	+*	−	+*	+	−*	.576*
1971	+*	+*	−	+*	−*	.465*
1972	+*	+	+*	+*	−*	.639*

As anticipated, the signs of the coefficients conform closely to those in the discriminant functions and expected relationships occur more frequently. At the same time, the R^2 values are significant and comparable to those obtained in typical valuation studies. Although not obvious from the results shown, it is interesting to note that the proportion of explained variation accounted for by the basic four variables increases steadily in the recent years. This finding is not unexpected given the change in tax laws which occurred in 1969. However, since the gain variable does contribute positively toward correct classification of banks and given the intent of arriving at a consistent set of variables over the six cross-sections, we decided to retain the variable. The apparent decline in importance of securities transactions while the R^2 remains high which are the core of the model.

non-banking activities.[10] Hence, the model selected consists of five variables including the basic four appearing consistently and the securities gains variable.

While the final combination of variables performs satisfactorily in classifying the original sample of banks, adequate testing of the model requires two additional steps.[11] First, the variable included should be subject to rational economic interpretation. Second, validation of the model requires testing on a holdout sample since any classification of the sample banks from which the model is derived is subject to an upward classification bias.

Discussion of Variables

Logarithm of shares outstanding. In the absence of information on share turnover and shares traded annually to represent market activity, we included as a substitute the logarithm of shares outstanding. We hypothesized that as a proxy for market breadth and potential resilience, the variable should be positively related to PE ratios. As indicated in Figure 4, the expected positive sign occurs for each of the six cross-sections.

The R^2 of growth of operating income. Intuitively, one would expect the R^2 to act as a risk variable and be positively associated with PE ratios since the value of this variable increases with the stability of growth. However, the R^2 OI variable entered with a negative sign in four of the six estimates indicating that less stability is associated with higher PE ratios. Such a result is not unreasonable upon further consideration since high growth can be attained only by taking higher risks and by aggressive expansion of bank facilities which may make the growth rate of earn-

Figure 4. Coefficients of the Final Discriminant Function, 1967-72

Year			Variable		
	Log Shares RK7	R^2 Operating Income RK2	State Income Growth GS9	Net Income Growth GL4	Gain (loss) on securities/operating revenue IE3
1967	.008	−.006	2.727	−.382	−0.908
1968	.065	−.141	1.800	.994	−4.364
1969	.050	−.195	1.448	−.121	−3.599
1970	.068	−.102	1.783	.256	−2.196
1971	.035	.079	−1.733	.856	−4.911
1972	.020	.117	1.419	.423	−3.663

ings relatively unstable. Thus, the R^2 variable may be an additional proxy for expected growth.

One year growth of state per capita income. Although a variety of firm growth rates is included in the original set of variables, the growth rate of per capita income in the bank's state enters significantly. Since the variable enters with the expected positive sign in five of the six years, it suggests that higher growth of income is associated with high PE ratios. Ideally, one should measure precisely the growth of the market area of each bank rather than using a proxy such as per capita income. However, this requires accurate knowledge of the market area and there is considerable doubt currently concerning the measurement of appropriate market areas.

As mentioned earlier, previous bank studies have found it difficult to obtain a growth variable explaining variation in bank stock prices. Through a regional dummy variable technique, however, Peltzman [1968] concluded that a dollar of bank capital was worth 20% more in the South and West than in the rest of the country. To test the hypothesis of regional variations in PE ratios an analysis of variance was conducted on the 1967 sample data. The results show no significant differences between regions (as defined by Compustat) and suggest that a more precise market designation is necessary. Consequently, the state income variable was introduced and the results indicate that this breakdown is more plausible. The significance of this variable suggests that the market pays considerable attention to the economic growth of the area in which banks operate and that this growth is expected to be translated into growth of the earning capacity of the individual firm.

Five year growth of net income available. Studies of equity valuation have continually wrestled with the question of measuring expected growth of the firm. While it is clear that growth is an important determinant of PE ratios, it is not obvious how expected growth should be measured given that expectations are not an observable phenomenon. Following the common technique of using historical growth as a proxy, we defined the long-term growth of net income available for common shareholders. As shown in the table, the expected positive relationship occurs for four of the six years.

Gain (loss) on securities/operating revenue. The only traditional bank analysis variable included in the final model is the ratio of securities gains or losses to operating revenue which consistently has a negative sign. The inverse relationship with PE ratios is indicative of the fact that aggressive banks are willing to incur capital losses on securities in order to convert the funds into higher yielding loans. This is quite consistent with a modern approach to the management of bank funds which treats security holdings as a reservoir of funds not for liquidity but for allocation to loans.

Test of Model on Holdout Sample

Overall, our model classifies 83% of the original sample banks correctly. As Morrison [1969] points out, however, this may be an upward baised estimate of the model's classification ability since it is calculated from the same sample that was used to develop the model. Therefore the classification ability was also tested on a holdout sample of 26 banks—13 from the high PE group and 13

Figure 5. Classification Ability of Final Discriminant Function for Holdout Sample

Year	1967	1968	1969	1970	1971	1972
Number of Banks Correctly Classified						
High PE Banks	8	9	6	9	9	8
Low PE Banks	9	11	11	10	9	10
	—	—	—	—	—	—
	17	20	17	19	18	18
Number of Banks in Sample	26	26	26	26	26	26
% Banks Classified Correctly	65.4	76.9	65.4	73.1	69.2	69.2

from the low PE group. The results of this test, presented in Figure 5, show that the model correctly classifies 70% of the banks in the holdout sample. Although it is somewhat less than the original 83% classification rate, the 70% rate is still significantly different at the .005 level from the expected rate of 50% with a chi square test. Thus the classification ability of the model is verified with the holdout sample.

Summary, Conclusions and Implications

The intent of this paper has been to find a limited number of factors capable of discriminating between high and low PE banks. Using an original sample of 40 banks drawn from the Bank Compustat tape, we develop an equation derived from six years of data. The final equation consistently classifies more than 80% of the original sample of banks correctly and also correctly classifies 70% of a holdout sample. Although we could have correctly classified a higher proportion of the original banks by relying completely on the stepwise process, the method used and the final results are more appealing for several reasons. First, the final equation consists of a single set of variables rather than a different combination for each year. Thus, a unique combination of variables is capable of consistently discriminating between high and low groups. Clearly, this is more appealing than suggesting that each year requires a different set of variables as would be implied by a mechanical use of a stepwise procedure. Second, in most cases the signs of the coefficients are

plausible and are not inconsistent with previous valuation studies, although there is some tendency for the magnitudes of values to vary over time.

We do not wish to suggest that the final model presented here is the conclusive answer to the question of the determinants of bank PE ratios. However, we feel that we have avoided the typical pitfalls of previous studies, namely the need to resort to a regional explanation of variations in PE ratios and the acceptance of conclusions that risk and growth are unimportant in bank equity valuation.

What direction should further work in this area take? Given the recent increased availability of bank data from Compustat and the release of report of condition and income-expense information from regulatory agencies, further work in the area of bank equities will be greatly facilitated. From the viewpoint of our efforts, we hope to see work in the general area of valuation models; i.e., empirical testing of valuation models applied to commercial banks. While this has been done for industrials and utilities, efforts on financial institutions have been hindered by the paucity of data. In addition, there are interesting questions related to the impact of mergers, holding companies and other aspects of structure on profitability, growth and hence on price performance. Considerable effort has been devoted to the question of the effects of changing structure on performance measures such as lending behavior, loan rates, etc., but the effects on market price performance have been ignored. Hopefully, the results of this study and the increased accessibility of data will stimulate additional work in the area. □

REFERENCES

Altman, Edward I., "Financial Ratios, Discriminating Analysis, and Prediction of Corporate Bankruptcy," *Journal of Finance* (September 1968), pp. 589-609.

Benishay, Haskel, "Variability in Earnings-Price Ratios of Corporate Equities," *American Economic Review* (March 1961), pp. 81-94.

Brigham, Eugene F. and Myron J. Gordon, "Leverage, Dividend Policy and the Cost of Capital," *Journal of Finance* (March 1968), pp. 85-103.

Dince, Robert R. and James C. Fortson, "The Use of Discriminant Analysis to Predict the Capital Adequacy of Commercial Banks," *Journal of Bank Research* (Spring 1972), pp. 54-62.

Durand, David. *Bank Stock Prices and the Bank Capital Problem* (New York: National Bureau of Economic Research, 1957).

Fredman, Albert J. and James E. Wert, "Bank Stocks Have Entered a New Epoch," *Banking* (January 1970), pp. 49-50, 90.

Haslem, John A. and William A. Longbrake, "A Discriminant Analysis of Commercial Bank Profitability," *"Quarterly Review of Economics and Business* (Autumn 1971), pp. 39-46.

Klemkosky, Robert C. and J. William Petty, "A Multivariate Analysis of Stock Price Variability," *Journal of Business Research* (Summer 1973), pp. 1-10.

Malkiel, Burton G., "The Variation of Public Utility Equities," *Bell Journal of Economics and Management Science* (Spring 1970), pp. 143-60.

Malkiel, Burton G. and John G. Cragg, "Expectations and the Structure of Share Prices," *American Economic Review* (September 1970), pp. 601-17.

Meyer, Paul A. and Howard W. Pifer, "Prediction of Bank Failures," *Journal of Finance* (September 1970), pp. 853-68.

Morrison, Donald G., "On the Interpretation of Discriminant Analysis," *Journal of Marketing Research* (May 1969), 156-63.

Peltzman, Sam, "Bank Stock Prices and the Effects of Regulation of the Banking Structure," *Journal of Business* (October 1968), pp. 413-30.

Pinches, George E. and Kent A. Mingo, "A Multivariate Analysis of Industrial Bond Ratings," *Journal of Finance* (March 1973), pp. 1-18.

Robertson, Norbert, "Banking and Regional Economic Growth," *Bankers Magazine* (Spring 1973), pp. 106-10.

Van Horne, James and Raymond C. Helwig. *The Valuation of Small-Banks Stocks,* Occasional Paper (East Lansing: Bureau of Business and Economic Research, Graduate School of Business Administration, Michigan State University, 1966).

Walter, James E., "A Discriminant Function for Earnings-Price Ratios of Large Industrial Corporations," *Review of Economics and Statistics* (February 1959), pp. 44-52.

Chapter 42

DIVERSIFICATION AND THE CONGENERIC BANK HOLDING COMPANY*

By Peter C. Eisemann

*This article is reprinted, with permission, from *Journal of Bank Research*, Vol. 7, No. 1 (Spring, 1976), pp. 68-77.

A large increase in the number of banking organizations diversifying into nonbank areas took place in the 1960s. The vehicle for this expansion was the one-bank holding company since, unlike multi-bank holding companies, the holding company aspects of one-bank holding companies were unregulated. With the passage of the 1970 Amendments to the Bank Holding Company Act, however, the regulatory distinction between one-bank and multi-bank holding companies was eliminated. The 1970 Amendments brought all bank holding companies (BHC) under equal Federal Reserve Board regulation. In addition, the Board was given more latitude in deciding which nonbank activities should be allowable for BHC expansion.

The general procedure is for the Board to conduct hearings on a proposed nonbank activity and then rule on the permissibility of that activity. If a BHC wishes to enter a permissible activity *de novo,* it only has to notify the Board of its intention; but if the company intends to acquire a going concern in that industry, a formal application is required.

Despite the growing importance of the diversification movement there has been little research on the nonbank aspects of BHCs.[1] The purpose of this study is to shed some light on the diversification potential of congeneric BHCs.[2] More specifically, the study attempts to determine which nonbank activities are efficient for BHC diversification in the Markowitz sense,[3] whether BHCs are indeed diversifying efficiently and finally, the impact that Federal Reserve Board decisions with respect to permissible nonbank activities have had on the diversification potential for BHCs.

Bank Holding Company Diversification

Various possible motives can be hypothesized for the expansion of BHCs into nonbank activities; these include economies of scale, the elimination of functions at market interfaces, the elimination of duplicated activities, an increase in market power, the expansion of product lines, the entrance into new geographical markets, reduced capital costs, increased power and prestige for management, shareholder risk reduction and management risk reduction. It is the last two motives —shareholder and management risk reduction— that are the focal point of this study.[4]

A firm that has as its objective the maximization of shareholder wealth will combine investments whose returns are not perfectly positively correlated in order to reduce total variability of shareholder returns without adversely affecting expected returns. The reduction in risk should have a positive effect on shareholder wealth.

For a congeneric bank holding company this diversification takes the form of the BHC acquiring nonbank subsidiaries.[5] If the returns from these subsidiaries are not perfectly positively correlated there may be an increase in the wealth of the BHCs shareholders.

However, if capital markets are perfect or near perfect this increase in wealth need not be forthcoming.[6] That is because investors could accomplish any diversification needs they had without the assistance of the holding company. They could use "homemade diversification" by purchasing shares in two companies contemplating merger. Thus, investors would gain the portfolio benefits without the merger. If this is the case, the post-merger or post-holding company acquisition value of the securities of a firm would be expected to equal the sum of the pre-merger or pre-acquisition values.

---

[1] There are a few notable exceptions. Alhadeff [1970], Gup [1972] and Lerner [1972] raise many of the relevant issues. Hall [1969] and Chase [1971] examine some of the public policy aspects of the nonbank subsidiaries of BHCs, and Lawrence [1974] focuses on the operating policies of BHCs toward their nonbank subsidiaries.

[2] A congeneric BHC diversifies into activities that are closely related to banking (e.g., sales finance), while a conglomerate BHC diversifies into activities that are not closely related to banking (e.g., steel).

[3] Diversification is efficient in the Markowitz sense if for any given level of risk expected return is as high as possible, and for any given level of expected return the level of risk is as low as possible.

[4] For a discussion of the other motives see Eisemann [1974].

[5] This approach views the BHC as an investment company, investing (by buying or starting de novo) in various bank and nonbank firms.

[6] See Levy and Sarnat [1970] for a proof of this point.

Capital markets are not, however, perfect. Transaction and information costs do exist. In the case of an investor who wanted to hold only a few stocks at one time, there may be some gains from a firm diversifying.[7] By investing in a diversified bank holding company the investor is able to actually invest in a greater number of industries. The investor thus may be willing to pay a higher price for that security. In addition, it is difficult to invest in firms in some industries. In particular, the markets for bank stocks are highly imperfect as are the markets for stocks of most other industries BHCs are entering.[8] By investing in a number of different firms, managers are tied to one firm. To the extent that job security is important, it will pay for managers to diversify internally by acquiring new subsidiaries since this should reduce the variability of shareholder returns for the BHC.[9]

Industry Selection Model

The previous section provided some support for the proposition that both BHC shareholders and managers can gain from efficient diversification. The Markowitz portfolio selection model will be used to determine the efficient BHC structures. As data inputs the Markowitz model requires expected returns and the variance-covariance matrix for all securities under consideration. Instead of viewing the BHC as investing in individual firms though, the BHC will be seen as investing in various industries.[10] The model then determines what industries a BHC should enter rather than which particular firm they should acquire. The required data inputs are industry expected returns and an industry variance-covariance matrix.

The first step is to compute security returns $(r_{j;t})$ for each firm (j) and for each period (t) where

$$r_{j;t} = \frac{P_{j;t} + D_{j;t} + CE_{j;t} - P_{j;t-1}}{P_{j;t-1}}$$

and

$P_{j;t} =$ price of one share of security j at the end of period t

$D_{j;t} =$ cash dividends per share paid during period t

$CE_{j;t} =$ cash equivalent distributions per share paid during period t (e.g. rights)

All values are adjusted for stock splits and stock dividends.

The security returns are then combined for all firms in a particular industry (k) to compute industry returns $(r_{k;t})$:

$$r_{k;t} = \sum_{j=1}^{n} w_{j;t} r_{j;t}$$

where $n =$ the number of firms in the industry

$w_{j;t} =$ weight for firm j in period t

The weights are computed using each firm's relative aggregate market value for that period.[11]

$$w_{j;t} = \frac{P_{j;t} N_{j;t}}{\sum_{j=1}^{n} P_{j;t} N_{j;t}}$$

where $N_{j;t} =$ the number of shares of stock outstanding for firm j at the end of period t

Industry expected returns, variances and covariances are then generated from the industry returns.

Data

Three categories of congeneric industries were chosen for the model. Category one includes some of the industries that are currently permissible for BHCs. The second category includes some of the industries that the Federal Reserve Board has ruled nonallowable. Finally. the third category includes possible industries, those that have been neither rejected nor permitted by the Board. Figure 1 lists the industries used in the model along with the number of firms used to compute the industry returns for each industry.

Monthly data for each firm was collected for the period December 1961 to December 1968. Data selection, collection and validation are explained in more detail in the Appendix.

---

[7] An investor may want to hold only a few stocks and still want to diversify. His reason for only wanting a few stocks may be the reduced transactions costs (e.g., round lots, less time needed to follow stocks).

[8] One excellent study of the imperfections in bank equity markets is Whitaker [1964]. Many firms in industries such as mortgage banking and sales finance are closely held corporations. For some industries there are little or no equities. For example, savings and loans are mostly mutual organizations, and investment banking firms are mostly partnerships.

[9] Managers may well be more interested in earnings diversification than shareholder return diversification. Unfortunately, earnings data was not available so shareholder return diversification will be used as a proxy.

[10] A similar technique was used by Smith and Schreiner [1969] in a study of conglomerate firms.

[11] All computations were also run weighting each firm in an industry equally. However, the results were virtually identical to the results using the relative aggregate market value weights.

Figure 1. Congeneric Industries

Industry	Number of Firms in Industry
A. Permissible Activities	
1. Banking	19
2. Commercial Finance	6
3. Sales Finance	3
4. Small Loan	6
5. Credit Card	2
6. Data Processing	2
7. Leasing	3
8. Mortgage Banking	2
9. Mutual Fund Management	6
B. Nonallowable Activities	
1. Fire and Casualty Insurance	8
2. Investment Banking	2
3. Land Development	6
4. Life Insurance	7
5. Property Management	1
C. Possible Activities	
1. Business Forms	5
2. Detective and Security	1
3. Insurance Agent and Broker	1
4. Mortgage Guaranty Insurance*	1
5. Savings and Loan	6
6. Small Business Investment Company	6
7. Title Insurance	5

* Subsequent to the completion of the empirical work the Federal Reserve Board ruled that mortgage guaranty insurance is a nonallowable activity for the present. Although this activity was found to be closely related to banking the Board felt that the timing was not right for entry. Consequently, mortgage guaranty insurance can still be considered a possible activity.

Figure 2. Mean and Standard Deviation of Industry Monthly Returns

Industry	Mean	Standard Deviation
1. Banking	.00699	.04578
2. Business Forms	.01288	.06559
3. Commercial Finance	.00561	.07389
4. Sales Finance	.01406	.07856
5. Small Loan	.01105	.06448
6. Credit Card	.01948	.10864
7. Data Processing	.02922	.14781
8. Detective	.02734	.11208
9. Fire and Casualty Insurance	.00997	.05734
10. Insurance Agent	.01969	.06463
11. Investment Banking	.01492	.06311
12. Land Development	.02486	.10710
13. Leasing	.01942	.09060
14. Life Insurance	.00248	.67173
15. Mortgage Banking	.00512	.12895
16. Mortgage Guaranty Insurance	.02065	.13286
18. Mutual Fund Management	.01671	.08494
18. Property Management	.02533	.13044
19. Savings and Loan	.00727	.13588
20. Small Business Investment Company	.01832	.09035
21. Title Insurance	.00889	.06248

Figure 3. Efficient Portfolios for Permissible Activities (Industry Proportions in Per Cent)

Portfolio Number	E_p	V_p	1	2	3	4	5	6	7	8	9	10	11	12	13
1	.0292	.1478		NA					100	NA	NA	NA	NA	NA	
2	.0289	.1449							97.55						2.45
3	.0230	.0873						22.51	36.48						41.01
4	.0219	.0815						21.59	28.36						39.31
5	.0213	.0791				4.44		19.6	25.84						37.62
6	.0157	.0565	35.53			13.73		8.3	15.61						26.2
7	.0154	.0555	37.41			14.23		7.7	15.07						25.59
8	.0132	.0485	49.92			17.74		2.45	10.45						19.43
9	.0121	.0456	54.98			19.12	2.22		8.02						15.65
10	.0090	.0413	67.83			18.59	10.82								2.75
11	.0087	.0412	70.32			17.92	11.75								

Notes: Industry numbers correspond to Figure 2
 NA = Industry is not applicable to that category (e.g. business forms is not in the permissible
 group so it could not enter the efficient set of this run)

Figure 4. Efficient Portfolios for Permissible and Possible Activities (Industry Proportions in Per Cent)

Portfolio Number	E_p	V_p	1	2	3	4	5	6	7	8	9	10	11	12	13
1	.0292	.1478							100		NA		NA	NA	
2	.0230	.1025							37.86	62.14					
3	.0245	.0747							21.64	37.73		41.64			
4	.0221	.0625							10.6	18.84		56.94			13.63
5	.0218	.0615				2.01			9.8	17.58		56.94			13.67
6	.0184	.0515	17.87			5.63			6.85	9.88		49.08			10.69
7	.0181	.0506	19.65			5.99			6.56	9.11		48.29			10.39
8	.0147	.0423	35.07	5.57		8.28			3.15	.6		39.83			7.51
9	.0144	.0418	35.89	5.89		8.39	.5		2.9			39.26			7.17
10	.0126	.0389	44.52	6.17		9.69	4.49					32.35			2.79
11	.0118	.0382	50.12	5.31		10.19	6.28					28.11			

14	15	16	17	18	19	20	21
NA	NA		NA	NA	NA	NA	
		10.74					
		12.51					
		.63					

14	15	16	17	18	19	20	21
NA			NA				

Efficient Bank Holding Companies

The expected returns and standard deviations for each industry are presented in Figure 2. One interesting observation from that table is that ignoring covariance effects banking is the minimum risk activity.[12] Initially the industry selection model was run only for those activities that are presently permissible for BHC expansion (see Figure 1). The model was then rerun, but this time the set of possible activities was also included. Finally, the model was run including the nonallowable activities. Figures 3, 4 and 5 present the efficient congeneric BHCs generated by the industry selection model for each of the three runs.[13] These efficient BHCs represent holding companies where an industry is either added or removed from the previous efficient holding company.[14] These holding companies are then plotted in Figure 6 to determine the Markowitz efficient sets. Other holding companies in Figure 6 on the efficient set are simply combinations of the adjoining portfolios listed in Figures 3, 4 and 5.

The following observations can be made from the empirical results. All low risk BHCs contain some banking activity. In fact, the lower the risk level of the BHC the more banking activity the holding company includes. Thus, even when covariance effects are included banking is still the minimum risk activity. One obvious question is the extent to which a BHC that restricts itself to banking suboptimizes? Even if the BHC restricted itself to the permissible activities it could increase its expected return by about 74% (.0069 to .0120) without altering the amount of risk. If the set of possible activities were also included, the opportunity would increase to about 136%; thus by limiting investment to banking, a bank or a BHC substantially reduces expected shareholder returns.

Considering only the permissible activities, the highest risk, efficient holding companies were composed of data processing and, to a much lesser extent, leasing.[15] Middle risk holding companies include data processing, leasing, mutual fund management and banking. Finally, the low risk holding companies include banking, sales

---

[12]Risk is used synonymously with standard deviation.
[13]These portfolios are the corner portfolios.
[14]As before they are efficient in the Markowitz (see footnote 3) sense.
[15]These holding companies, since they exclude banking, are not BHCs.

Figure 5. Efficient Portfolios for Permissible, Possible and Nonallowable Activities (Industry Proportions in Per Cent)

Portfolio Number	E_p	V_p	1	2	3	4	5	6	7	8	9	10	11	12	13
1	.0292	.1478							100						
2	.0282	.1054							48.18	51.82					
3	.0280	.1015							43.42	51.11					
4	.0268	.0858							22.77	39.09				23.59	
5	.0234	.0641							9.63	18.16		44.72		15.88	
6	.0212	.0563							7.69	10.26		45.09	19.25	8.6	
7	.0203	.0538	5.18						7.17	8.52		43.69	19.1	7.75	
8	.0201	.0533	6.1						7.07	8.2		43.43	19.08	7.58	.07
9	.0192	.0508	10.65			1.43			6.45	6.41		41.79	18.8	6.29	.24
10	.0179	.0476	16.75			3.36			5.61	4.01		39.6	18.43	4.56	.47
11	.0161	.0434	22.49			5.98			4.56	.59	3.37	36.29	18.57	1.62	.39
12	.0159	.0428	23.24	.58		6.28			4.35		3.73	35.75	18.57	1.11	.46
13	.0153	.0417	25.19	1.26		6.99			3.73		4.52	34.22	18.3		.38
14	.0148	.0407	28.2	1.68		7.46			2.99		4.76	32.64	17.43		
15	.0128	.0381	40.13	3.58		8.89					4.91	26.4	13.72		
16	.0125	.0379	42.04	3.55		8.98					5.02	25.25	13.27		
17	.0116	.0375	48.83	3.34		9.08	1.77				4.74	21.07	11.17		

Figure 6. Efficient Sets for Permissible, Permissible and Possible, and Permissible, Possible and Nonallowable Activities

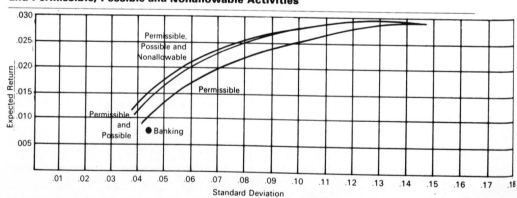

14	15	16	17	18	19	20	21

5.47

14.55

11.62

9.11

8.59

8.48

7.94

7.22

6.13

5.95

5.4

4.84

2.37

1.89

permissible and possible set the domination is not very great and covers mostly the low and middle risk levels. Nonallowable industries that are now in efficient portfolios are property management and land development in the middle risk range; and fire and casualty insurance, investment banking, land development and property management in the low risk holding companies. Excluded industries include the following: commercial finance, credit card, small loans,[16] leasing,[17] life insurance, mortgage banking, mortgage guaranty insurance, mutual fund management, savings and loan, small business investment company and title insurance.

The Record of Holding Companies

One method of examining the diversification record of congeneric bank holding companies would be to take an actual sample of BHCs and compare the performance of those firms to the generated efficient holding companies. However, this approach is not feasible for two reasons. First, current data on the size of BHCs and the size of their nonbank subsidiaries is not publicly available. The second difficulty is that since the nonbank expansion trend only began in the late 1960s, there has not been a sufficient passage of time to allow this type of analysis. It would not be possible, for example, to determine whether the lack of diversification of a bank was attributable to a management decision not to further diversify, or whether there had not been enough time for the BHC to reach its optimal structure.

An alternative, although not as rigorous approach, is to consider those activities BHCs are entering and then compare those activities to the activities that efficient holding companies would enter. Figure 7 summarizes the nonbank expansion of BHCs through September 30, 1973.

From Figure 7 it can be seen that BHCs have been expanding actively into the following efficient industries:[18] Leasing, insurance agent and broker, data processing and banking. While the first two are found in efficient holding companies in the middle-risk range, data processing is found mostly in high-risk efficient holding companies.

However, BHCs are also entering some activities that are not included in any of the efficient holding companies. Two that are being entered

finance and small loans. Perhaps one of the most interesting results is that the commercial finance and mortgage banking industries are excluded from all efficient holding companies.

Adding the possible activities to the permissible activities gives an efficient set that clearly dominates the efficient set for permissible activities only. High risk holding companies include data processing, and detective and security. The middle risk range is dominated by insurance agent and broker, but also includes some sales finance, data processing, detective and security, and leasing. Once again banking dominated the low risk range with business forms, sales finance, small loan, insurance agent and broker, and leasing also included to some extent. The following industries are excluded from all efficient portfolios: Mortgage banking, commercial finance, mortgage guaranty insurance, saving and loan, small business investment company and title insurance.

Although the efficient set for permissible, possible and nonallowable activities dominates the

---

[16] Since small loans was only included in the minimum-return holding company and even then was only 1.77% of the entire holding company, it was considered excluded.

[17] Leasing was also excluded, since its maximum percentage of a holding company was .47.

[18] Of course, these activities are not efficient at all risk levels.

**Figure 7. Expansion of Bank Holding Companies into
Nonbank Activities (January 1, 1971 to September 30, 1973)**

Activity	De Novo Notifications	Acquisition Applications				Total Notifications and Approvals
		Received	Denied	Pending	Approved	
Mortgage banking	216	60	6	16	38	254
Leasing	153	14	3	5	6	159
Investment, financial and economic advisory services	122	5	2	1	2	124
Insurance (broker or agent, underwriting)	255	70	4	32	34	289
Finance company (commercial and consumer)	236	95	3	33	59	295
Data processing	61	10	—	8	2	63
Factoring	25	10	—	1	4	29
Community development	14	1	1	—	—	14
Trust operations	20	3	—	1	2	22
Industrial banking	14	10	1	3	6	20
Management consulting for banks	—	1	—	1	—	—
Savings and loan	—	1	—	1	—	—
Other	5	10	—	5	5	10
	1121	285	20	107	158	1279

Source: Frances E. Wrocklage. "Emphasis in Bank Holding Company Growth Shifts to Related
Activities." *Banking* 66 (January 1974): 29.

quite aggressively are mortgage banking and factoring. While factoring was not included in the model runs as a separate industry, commercial finance, which includes factoring, was a permissible activity and was excluded from all efficient holding companies.

The last industry that was included in Figure 7 that was also included in the model computer runs is the savings and loan industry. Although the table only shows one application, this is deceptive, since savings and loan is not presently a permissible industry; if it is allowed, undoubtedly more applications will follow.

Thus it would appear that BHCs are not doing a very efficient job of diversifying. However, one weakness of Figure 7 is that the performance of individual holding companies is obscured. Although in the aggregate, BHCs may be diversifying inefficiently, it is, of course, possible that some individual holding companies are in fact diversifying efficiently. These possible individual differences disappear when they are aggregated.

Regulation and Efficient Diversification

Of the five nonallowable activities included in this study only one, life insurance, was excluded from all efficient holding companies. However, if Figure 6 is studied it becomes apparent that, although four nonallowable activities are included in the efficient set, they do not add much in the way of increased return for a given amount of risk. The efficient set for permissible, possible and nonallowable activities dominates the set for permissible and possible activities by only a small amount. In other words, the Federal Reserve decisions to this point with respect to the activities that banks may enter have not been very costly to shareholders.

When the potential impact of future Federal Reserve Board decisions is considered, the situation is quite different. The allowable and possible efficient set dominates the allowable set by a substantial amount. Furthermore, by limiting the size of the investment in a permissible activity the holding company could be prevented from reaching its optimal structure. Consequently, the potential impact of future Federal Reserve Board decisions is quite significant.

Summary

This paper has examined the diversification motive for congeneric bank holding companies. An industry selection model adapted from the Markowitz portfolio selection model was used to determine optimal bank holding company structures. It was discovered that bank holding companies that do not efficiently diversify suboptimize significantly. It was further found that actual holding companies do not appear to be diversifying efficiently. Finally, past Federal Reserve Board decisions with respect to allowable nonbank activities have not seriously limited the ability of bank holding companies to efficiently diversify. □

APPENDIX

Firm Selection. Once the list of industries was composed, 4-digit SIC codes were determined for each industry. Firms were then identified using Standard and Poor's *Register of Corporations, Directors and Executives,* Dun and Bradstreet's *Million Dollar Directory* and *Middle Market Directory* various Moody's manuals, trade group listings and telephone books. Firms were then excluded if they were not public corporations, did not have at least 600 shareholders or were not almost exclusively in the business of their industry.

Data Period. The period December 1961 through December 1968 was chosen. Some firms were not used in every period since they were either new after December 1961 or left the industry (through bankruptcy or acquisition) before 1968.

Data. Ending monthly stock price data was taken from the *ISL Daily Stock Price Record, Bank and Quotation Record,* and *National Monthly Stock Summary.* Any questionable prices were checked against at least one other source. In addition, a computer program searched for certain errors. In the case of over-the-counter stocks an average of monthly ending bid and ask prices was used as the ending price. Dividend data was collected using Standard and Poors *Annual Dividend Record.* Rights, stock splits and stock dividends were taken from Prentice-Hall's *Capital Adjustments* and Standard and Poor's *Annual Dividend Record.* The number of shares was found using the appropriate Moody's manual.

REFERENCES

Alhadeff, David A., "The Range of Admissible Activities for Commercial Banks." 1970. (Mimeographed.)

Beals, Ralph E., *Statistics for Economists.* Chicago: Rand McNally and Company, 1972.

Carey, Gerald V., "A Countercyclical Strategy for Bank Holding Companies." *Bankers Monthly,* Vol. 88 (November 15, 1971), pp. 16-17.

Carter H. Golembe and Associates, Inc., *The Nature and Control of One Bank Holding Companies.* Washington, D.C.: Carter H. Golembe and Associates, Inc., 1969.

Chase, Samuel B., Jr. "The Bank Holding Company as a Device for Sheltering Banks from Risk." *Proceedings of a Conference on Bank Structure and Competition.* Chicago: Federal Reserve Bank of Chicago, 1971.

Eisemann, Peter C., "A Test of the Diversification Motive for Congeneric Bank Holding Companies." Ph.D. dissertation, University of Michigan, 1974.

Fama, Eugene F. and Merton H. Miller, *The Theory of Finance.* New York: Holt, Rinehart and Winston, 1972.

Federal Reserve Bulletin, Washington, D.C.: Board of Governors of the Federal Reserve System, Selected Issues.

Fischer, Gerald C., "Market Extension by Bank Holding Companies: History, Economic Implications and Current Issues." *Proceedings of a Conference on Bank Structure and Competition.* Chicago: Federal Reserve Bank of Chicago, 1969.

Greco, Frank J., "Implementation of the Bank Holding Company Act Amendments of 1970: The Scope of Banking Activities." *Michigan Law Review,* Vol. 71 (May 1973) pp. 1170-1211.

Hall, George, "Some Impacts of One Bank Holding Companies." *Proceedings of a Conference on Bank Structure and Competition.* Chicago: Federal Reserve Bank of Chicago, 1969.

Lawrence, Robert J., *Operating Policies of Bank Holding Companies.* Part II: *Nonbanking Subsidiaries.* Staff Economic Study No. 81. Washington, D.C.: Board of Governors of the Federal Reserve System, 1974.

Lerner, Eugene, "Three Financial Problems Facing Bank Holding Companies." *Journal of Money, Credit and Banking,* Vol. 4 (May 1972) pp. 445-455.

Levy, Haim and Marshall Sarnat, "Diversification Analysis and the Uneasy Case for Conglomerate Mergers." *Journal of Finance,* Vol. 25 (September 1970) pp. 795-802.

Lewellen, Wilbur G., "A Pure Financial Rationale for the Conglomerate Merger." *Journal of Finance,* Vol. 26 (May 1971) pp. 521-537.

Mann, Maurice, "The Reality and Promise of Bank Holding Companies." *The Banking Law Journal,* Vol. 90 (March 1973) pp. 181-192.

Markowitz, Harry M., *Portfolio Selection: Efficient Diversification of Investments.* New York: John Wiley and Sons, Inc., 1959.

Melnik, A., and M. A. Pollatschek, "Debt Capacity, Diversification and Conglomerate Mergers." *Journal of Finance,* Vol. 28 (December 1973) pp. 1263-1273.

Mote, Larry R., "The One-Bank Holding Company—History, Issues and Pending Legislation." Federal Reserve Bank of Chicago. *Business Conditions* (July 1970) pp. 2-16.

"One Bank Holding Companies Before the 1970 Amendments," *Federal Reserve Bulletin,* Vol. 58 (December 1972) pp. 999-1008.

Smith, Keith V. and John C. Schreiner, "A Portfolio Analysis of Conglomerate Diversification." *Journal of Finance,* Vol. 24 (June 1969) pp. 413-427.

Whitaker, Gilbert R., *The Market for Bank Stock.* U.S. Congress. Committee on Banking and Currency. Subcommittee on Domestic Finance, 88th Cong., 2nd Sess., 1964.

Chapter 43

COST OF CAPITAL AND DIVIDEND POLICIES IN COMMERCIAL BANKS*

By Shimon D. Magen

And Accompanying Discussion
By Thomas R. Harter

*This article is reprinted, with permission, from *Journal of Financial and Quantitative Analysis,* Vol. 6, No. 2 (March, 1971), pp. 733-746 and 783-784.

I. Introduction

The purpose of this study is to analyze the behavior of the cost of equity capital in the commercial banks by looking at whether there exists an optimal composition of the bank "fund structure"[1] that would maximize bank earnings through the minimization of its cost of funds. The analysis should give an approximate cut-off point for testing such projects as "checking plus," checkless payment systems, etc.

The paper draws on theoretical and empirical work done so far and well known in the literature.[2] The paper also takes a look at whether dividend policies influence banks' cost of capital. Section II gives a sketch of conceptual problems encountered, and Section III covers the investigation, findings, and conclusions.

II. Conceptual Framework

The conceptual framework of the study draws on the present state of the art of the cost of capital theory at the time of writing. The major problems encountered, which influenced heavily the methodology and statistical procedures, were:

---

[1]
Since deposits constitute a considerable percentage of bank resources, and the term *capital structure* has been used in the literature to define the combination of owners equity and long-term debt in industrial and mercantile firms, it is more appropriate to use the term *fund structure* for the banks as a substitute for the term *capital structure*.

[2]
Franco Modigliani and Merton Miller, "The Cost of Capital Corporation Finance and The Theory of Investment," *American Economic Review* (June 1958) pp. 261-297.

David Durand, "The Cost of Capital Corporation Finance" and the "The Theory of Investment: Comment," *American Economic Review* (September 1959) pp. 639-654. David Durand, "The Cost of Debt and Equity Funds for Business," and discussion by Clay J. Anderson and Martin W. Davenport in *Conference on Research in Business Finance* (New York: National Bureau of Economic Research, 1952) p. 254.

Ezra Solomon, *The Theory of Financial Management* (New York: Columbia University Press, 1963).

J. Fred Weston, "A Test of Cost of Capital Propositions," *The Southern Economic Journal* (October 1963) pp. 52-64).

1. *Bank risks*. The distinction between business risk and financial risk
was a major problem. Could there be a distinction between the two risks in a
bank that exercises a very high degree of leverage compared to a nonfinancial
corporation? Does this high leverage introduce a higher degree of uncertainty to
the flow of earnings after the payment of fixed charges?

2. *Dividend policy and growth*. At the early stages of the work, dividend
payout registered a strong correlation to the cost of equity capital, but the
growth rate of bank earnings showed erratic behavior even though growth is
dependent in most cases on the dividend policy.

3. *Bank leverage and debt*. Most of the bank's funds come from the practice
of a very high degree of leverage. For the purpose of analysis, the cost of
equity and bank leverage were defined as:

$$k = \frac{t(rA - ki_1 d_1 - ki_{23} d_{23} - ki_4 d_4)}{A - (d_1 + d_{23} + d_4)}$$

where: k = historical rate of return on bank equity
              capital

        t = 1 - the income tax rate

        r = rate of return on bank assets in %

        A = total bank assets

        ki_1= effective cost of debentures or capital
              notes funds in %

        d_1 = total funds from debenture and/or
              capital notes

        ki_{23} = effective cost of short-term borrowing
              and time deposits

        ki_4 = cost of attracting and administering
              demand deposits in %

        d_4 = total funds from demand deposits.

Combining short-term borrowing with time deposits in d_{23} was necessitated by
the availability of the data. The question of defining debt in the debt capitalization ratios posed somewhat of a problem in the pilot studies performed at the
initiation of this study. Several attempts were made to define the numerator of
this ratio as just debts or debts plus time deposits or just demand deposits.
The findings of these preliminary tests did not justify the exclusion of any debt
capitalization component from the direct leverage measures.

Thus, in the tests to be conducted, we shall use the indirect measures of
leverage i/NOEBIT and i/E-2s used by R. Wippern[3] and the debt capitalization
ratios with the expectations that some might perform better than others.

---

[3] Ronald Wippern, "Financial Structure and the Value of the Firm," *The Journal of Finance* (December 1966), p. 619. For definition of i/NOEBIT and i/E-2s, see pp. 9 and 10.

4. *Other factors*. To shed further light on the determinants of cost of capital, the following additional factors will be tested against the cost of capital: growth of earnings, loan-deposit ratios and variations of the earning flows before and after interest and taxes.

5. *Hypotheses*. The hypotheses on which this paper is based are: The cost of equity capital is a positive function of leverage and a negative function of the dividend payout. The variations in the earning flows should be positively correlated with k and growth negatively correlated with k.

III. Investigation and Findings

Procedure

To test the hypotheses advanced in the previous section it was decided to study the fifty largest commercial banks in the United States as ranked by the size of their assets in 1965. The reason behind the choice of the largest banks was to obtain a sample of observations from banks with a relatively high degree of activity and growth, portraying the state of the banking institutions in the 1950's and 1960's. These banks include banks from the major industrial and financial centers in the country and are spread geographically over the eastern seaboard, midwest, west, and south. They are all members of the Federal Reserve System and the Federal Deposit Insurance Corporation, and thus subject to the same degree of government regulation[4]. Another major consideration in the decision to select the fifty largest banks was the high probability of data availability and the consistency of reporting of such data. Also, these banks offer the whole gamut of banking services and thus are assumed to be subject to the same degree of operating risks. Thirty-six out of the fifty banks are traded over the counter and are quoted in the financial chronicles.

The banks studied are to a certain extent heterogeneous. Though they are all commercial banks, they do differ in size. National Bank of Commerce of Seattle, the fiftieth in the ranking, had over $843-million in assets and the Bank of America, which was first, over $16-billion. The banks differ in the market they serve. Some are strictly·wholesale banks, some are retail, and others combine both characteristics[5]. The banks also differ in the stability of their earnings and the level of these earnings. On the bright side of the data, the banks are homogeneous with respect to their activity-accepting demand and time deposits, providing loans, borrowing for the short and long term, and investing in securities.

A major drawback of the data of this group of banks is the fact that they do not provide a good distribution of observations over a wide range of capital structure. All the banks were levered at between 88 and 94 percent when measured by the debt/capitalization ratio and over a wider range when leverage is measured by the interest-burden ratio. But, then this is the characteristic of the banking industry and the study is performed with this knowledge. It is probable that the inclusion of other banks in the study would have provided a wider range of leverage, but this would not have been typical of large banks.

---

[4]
By "the same degree of government regulation," it is meant the extent of supervision by the F.R. System and other regulatory agencies as to safety and reserves requirements. The paper does not consider the matters of branchings and impact on competitiveness, or the variety of regulations governing states versus national banks.

[5]
The banks were classified into the three categories based on the general knowledge of bankers.

The sample selected is also homogeneous in terms of trend over time. None of the banks had any significant shift in its trend of earnings-per-share over the period studied.

The period covered by the time series analysis to obtain growth and variability measures is 1958 to 1966, a total of nine years covering the later part of the recession of August 1957 to April 1958. In 1959 was the steel strike with its adverse impact on the economy. In the spring of 1960, the recovery was well under way, and economic expansion continued until 1966. The cost of capital tests covered the years 1962 to 1966, since it was decided that these five years provided representative measures for the various tests.

The Variables

Leverage. The leverage variable in banks presented various conceptual and estimation problems. The first decision that had to be made was the general definition of leverage, which was discussed in the preceding section. Next came the problem of measuring leverage by either one of the accepted methods used so far in previous studies. Modigliani and Miller tested their leverage theorem[6] on utilities and oil companies in their original paper with the equation $Y/P = a + b\ L/P$, where Y = net income after taxes, P = market value of common stock, and L = market values of senior securities. Barges, in his critique of the Modigliani and Miller tests, pointed out that the presence of P in the denominators of the dependent and independent variables introduced bias in their statistical procedures[7]. In his own tests, Barges substituted book values for the market values of Modigliani and Miller in the leverage parameters. In his paper a third variation on the same theme is used. The ratio of debt (including deposits) to total capitalization at book value is one of the measures of banks' leverage. Since bank leverage is usually around nine times greater than bank equity capital, it was decided that this measure is more suitable than the conventional debt/equity ratio. In order to recognize that leverage can also be measured in terms of flows rather than stocks, an alternate measure was estimated as the ratio of interest paid to earnings before interest and taxes.

A third measure of leverage which is also used to test the hypothesis is a normalized variation of the interest-burden ratio just mentioned. This measure is estimated as $i/(\bar{E}-2s)$ where i = interest paid by the banks and where $\bar{E}-2s$ = earnings before interest and taxes adjusted by two standard deviations to obtain a trend of earnings free of fluctuations. This measure of leverage performed quite successfully in Wippern's study of nonfinancial corporations.[8] Wippern claims many advantages to this method of estimating leverage. First, it avoids the necessity of choosing between market and book values when using debt/equity or debt/capitalization ratios. Second, it includes an adjustment ($-2s$) for operating risks, thus allowing the performance of the tests across industries belonging to a variety of risk classes. And third, it requires no assumption as to the homogeneity of the firms. Since the sample banks are not completely homogeneous, it was decided to use the model and give it a testing chance on commercial banks.

---

[6] Modigliani and Miller, "The Cost of Capital," p. 261-97.

[7] Alexander Barges, *The Effect of Capital Structure on the Cost of Capital* (Englewood Cliffs, New Jersey: Prentice-Hall, Inc., 1963). p. 22.

[8] R. Wippern, "Financial Structure," p. 619. Wippern included dividends on preferred stock in the numerator of the ratio.

The estimation of leverage in the flow form became a matter of necessity. After leverage was measured by the debt/capitalization ratio, it was discovered that because banks are highly levered, this ratio will result in almost a straight vertical line with all the observations scattered between .88 and .94, which would not have given much latitude in testing the hypothesis. To remedy this problem, it was necessary to recompute all the data and obtain four-digit measures, so that the picture was blown up to larger dimensions. By comparison, the flow measures of leverage in their two forms provided a much wider range of observations. The interest-burden ratio showed a range between .2500 and .8900 with the mean at .6500. The normalized ratio $i/(\bar{E}-2s)$ has a similar range with the mean at .7300.

The last measure of leverage tested is the ratio of debts and time deposits to all debts, deposits, and capital. Since banks pay interest only on debts and time deposits, it was decided to test whether this kind of measurement is a good estimator of leverage. Here again the ratio provided a fairly wide range of observation along the scale. In total, four measures of leverage are used as alternate independent variables in the investigation.

   Cost of Capital. The dependent variable was measured alternately by the yield on bank stocks (NOE/P) and by the Gordon Model. The NOE/P is directly observable from available data, and probably is a good indicator of the market reaction to leverage decisions if such reaction does exist. The NOE/P is also the most widely used rate for pricing stocks and is the reciprocal of the stock market regularly used multiplier P/E.[9] To test the hypothesis, simple linear regressions were performed with the variables measured as follows:

For leverage:

$D/(D+C)$	=	Debentures + short-term debt + time deposits + demand deposits divided by the same + capital for 1962-1966 at book value
$d_{23}/(D+C)$	=	Debentures + short-term debt + time deposits divided by same + capital, at book value
$i/NOEBIT$	=	interest paid per share in 1966 divided by net operating earning before interest and taxes for 1962-66
$i/(\bar{E}-2s)$	=	interest paid per share in 1966 divided by $\bar{E}-2s$ = NOEBIT for 1966 from the trend minus 2 standard deviations.

For the cost of capital:

k	=	NOE/P = Net operating earnings per share for 1962-66 divided by the average of high and low price for the same period
kd	=	D/P (gr_c) where g = the average retention rate for 1962-66 multiplied by the return on capital (r_c) measured as net operating earning divided by the total bank capital at book value.

---

[9] Other possible and equally acceptable measurements would have been the dividend yield on either book or market value. To keep the scope of this study within manageable proportions, it was decided to restrict the measurements of the dependent variable to these two estimators.

The Tests

When the equation was fitted to the data of the sample banks using the alternate definitions of the variables, the results obtained were most surprising.
None of the regression coefficients was statistically significant. All the
standard errors of the coefficients were too large to assure a reliable decision
as to the acceptance or rejection of the hypothesis that the cost of capital
does increase with the increase in leverage as alternately measured here. The
results of the eight combinations of two variables are given in Table 1. The
same relationships were also tested using the logarithms of the variables. The
results did not improve either the regression or correlation coefficients.
Since we found that $i/(\bar{E}-2s)$ and i/NOEBIT produced no better results than the
other measures of leverage and to keep the paper within reasonable limits, these
variables were dropped from the remaining analyses. For the same reason, kd
also had to be dropped.

Cross-sectional analyses, by year. To investigate further the results
obtained above and to eliminate the possible effect of autocorrelation, a cross-
sectional analysis for each year was performed with k as a function of D/D+C
plus the dividend payout ratio defined as:

Po = ratio of dividends paid out in cash to total net
operating earnings averaged for 1962-1966.

The results of the analysis are shown in Table 2.

TABLE 1

SIMPLE REGRESSION STATISTICS: k = f (leverage)

	Variables		a	b	R	F	n	DW
	y	x						
A	k	i/NOEBIT	.0537	.0123 (.0181)	.1059	.4652	43	2.1029
B	k	$i/(\bar{E}-2s)$	.0508	.0130 (.0141)	.1496	.8476	39	2.1531
C	k	d_{23}/(D+C)	.0516	.0285 (.0282)	.1732	1.0211	35	1.7072
D	k	D/(D+C)	-.0210	.0898 (.1580)	.0942	.3226	38	1.9770
F	kd	i/NOEBIT	.0925	-.0186 (.0153)	.1902	1.4633	41	2.1721
G	kd	$i/(\bar{E}-2s)$	.0895	-.0120 (.0134)	.1505	.8111	37	1.9970
H	kd	d_{23}/(D+C)	.0801	-.0003 (.0235)	.0024	.0002	36	2.0739
E	kd	D/(D+C)	-.0718	.1653 (.1320)	.2129	1.5662	35	2.0985

With NOE/P as the dependent variable, the stepwise regression procedure shows that the cost of capital bears no relationship to leverage in any of the five years as indicated by the regression coefficients. In 1965 the coefficient carried the wrong sign.

The dividend payout did not correlate any better. As observed from Table 2, the errors of x_2 coefficient are too large to be meaningful, although three years have the right sign.

Another cross-sectional test was performed substituting $d_{23}/(D+C)$ for $D/(D+C)$. In none of the five years when this test was performed did the dependent variable correlate with leverage in a statistically insignificant manner although all the coefficients, except for 1963, were positive. The payout ratio, Po, did not perform any better. In 1962 and 1966 the coefficients were insignificant but carried positive signs, which is contrary to the hypothesis. Thus, we must conclude that $d_{23}/(D+C)$ is not a good estimator of bank leverage effect on the cost of capital.[23] These results are shown in Table 3.

Introducing other variables. Final regression analyses were performed with additional variables besides the leverage and the payout ratio. The variables introduced were expected to vary with the dependent variable NOE/P and perhaps shed light on its determinants.

It is a widely accepted theory that the growth of a firm's earnings is an important factor influencing the price of stock and the cost of capital. The rationale underlying this phenomenon is that the growth of the firms is a good indicator of future earnings and has per se an informative value to the prospective investor. The expected relationship is that the cost of capital measured by NOE/P should be a negative function of growth. In the analyses the range of the average growth rate was very wide. First National Bank of Oregon had the lowest growth .0307, while United California Bank in Los Angeles grew at .2106. The mean for all the sample banks was .1056.

The asset structure is the other variable introduced in the model and is measured here by the loan-deposit ratio, which is assumed to be a rough estimator of operating risk and would perhaps explain the changes in the cost of capital. The ratio was estimated for the forty-five banks with data. The mean of the ratio was .5912 with a range between .3618 and .7719. The ratio is expected to show a positive correlation with the dependent variable.

Two other variables were also introduced: the variability in net operating earning before interest and taxes (NOEBIT) as another measure of business risk and the variability in net operating earnings (NOE) as a measure of the quality of earning due to bank stockholders.

The four variables were estimated as follows:

Growth	=	average rate of growth in net operating earnings in 1958-66, measured from the trend
L/D	=	average of the ratio of loans to total deposits for 1962-66
CV_1	=	coefficient of variation in net operating earnings measured from the trend, 1958-66
CV_2	=	coefficient of variation in net operating earnings before interest and taxes measured from the trend, 1958-66.

TABLE 2

MULTIPLE REGRESSION STATISTICS: $k = f[D/(D+C), Po]$

Coefficient and Variable	1962	1963	1964	1965
a	-.0427	.0049	.0166	.1099
$x_1 = D/(D+C)$	.0863 (.1666)	.0384 (.1482)	.0500 (.1381)	-.0416 (.1713)
$x_2 = Po$	.0225 (.0247)	.0155 .0281	-.0186 (.0270)	-.0127 (.0200)
R	.1611	.0974	.1437	.1110
F	.2681	.0671	.1313	.0590
n	37	38	38	38

TABLE 3

MULTIPLE REGRESSION STATISTICS: $NOE/P = f[d_{23}/(D+C), Po]$

Coefficient and Variable	1962	1963	1964	1965
a	.0133	.0454	.0600	.0643
$X_1 = d_{23}/(D+C)$	.0204 (.0265)	-.0039 (.0324)	.0192 (.0204)	.0204 (.0285)
$X_2 = $ Payout	.0608 (.0241)	.0086 (.0306)	-.0264 (.0253)	-.0136 (.0201)
R	.4085	.0614	.2622	.1845
F	.5953	.0142	.8832	.4587
n	36	36	36	36

The data for the banks were fitted to the equation:

$$(1) \quad y = a + b_1 x_1 + b_2 x_2 + b_3 x_3 + b_4 x_4 + b_5 x_5 + b_6 x_6$$

where

$$y \;\; = \;\; NOE/P$$

$$x_1 \;\; = \;\; D/(D+C)$$

$$x_2 \;\; = \;\; \text{growth of earnings}$$

$$x_3 \;\; = \;\; \text{payout ratio}$$

$$x_4 \;\; = \;\; \text{loan/deposit ratio}$$

$$x_5 \;\; = \;\; CV_1$$

$$x_6 \;\; = \;\; CV_2$$

The results of the analysis were:

$$y = .1414 - .0327\, x_1 - .0002\, x_2 - .0084\, x_3 - .0865\, x_4 - .0001\, x_5\; .0008\, x_6$$
$$\quad\quad\;\; (.1496) \quad (.0008) \quad (.0243) \quad (.0305) \quad (.0004) \quad (.0006)$$

$$R = .5381 \quad\quad\quad\quad n = 34$$

Only x_3, the payout ratio, remained consistent in sign but not significant. The loan-deposit ratio, x_4, although significantly correlated, carries a negative sign which is contrary to the expected. Leverage remained insignificant. In both tests, x_5 and x_6 representing the variation in net operating earnings and net operating earnings before interest and taxes had zero values. Thus, these variations bear no relationship to the cost of capital. Curvilinear tests did not improve the results.

Interpreting the results. The relationships between the cost of equity and the levels of bank leverage emerge as hazy ones. It seems impossible to find measures that provide consistent relationships of either the hypothesized relationship or definite evidence permitting their rejection.

Whether bank leverage, and whatever determines it, is a relevant factor in the determination of the level of banks' cost of capital over the leverage observed seems to be the problem. We might ask if it is realistic to expect that a single factor--leverage--could be expected to explain the level of the rate of return on a single type of security--bank stocks.

In this age of complex interrelated relationships among a multitude of factors, it just does not seem rational to force the real world into simple equations, especially when dealing with such a unique undertaking as commercial banking. Economic reasoning provides us with the basic variables that should be considered in explaining the cost of all bank funds. Instead of expecting that capital costs be influenced by leverage only, we should expect variables such as the stage of the business cycle in the economy to influence capital costs. Monetary policy and its impact on the money supply and bank credit affect the interest paid and received by the bank, and thus affect banks' earnings.

Beside these macro-factors, there are industry variables such as the competitive structure of the industry. The Modigliani and Miller theorem of independence of k from leverage is based on the perfect market concept which does not apply to our economy and certainly does not fit the industry structure of banking.

The type of service produced by the industry is definitely a factor and a problem in our case. Money is the input as well as the output. Both are regulated as to their cost (interest paid by banks) and their price (interest charged by the banks). This peculiarity, or uniqueness, is probably the major factor responsible for the vague results of our tests.

It seems clear by now that the reason for the lack of any consistent relationship between leverage and the cost of equity must be traced to banks' regulation, which eliminates the financial risk as we normally expect it in the nonfinancial enterprise.

Dividends Payout. In all the tests conducted in this paper the cost of equity-leverage relationship factor emerged as slightly significant and perhaps consistent. The dividend payout ratio was negatively correlated with NOE/P in most cases.

This outcome is not unique to this study. Wippern, in four years' cross-sections, found that the dividend payout was negatively correlated to NOE/P. Benishay in his study of the variability of E/P of corporate equities obtained similar results.[10] The relationship of dividend payment to the cost of capital seems quite clear. In the scale of preference of the stockholders there exists a trade-off between present and future earnings. The period covered, 1962-66, is one characterized by a rising price level. Investors in that period expressed preference to the distribution of bank earnings versus the retention of these earnings. Thus, the higher the proportion paid out of current net operating earnings, the smaller the capitalization rate applied by the stockholders to these earnings in evaluating bank stocks. In the forty-four banks with suitable data, we found that the average payout was .4721 with a range between .3053 and .7116. A second possible reason for the negative relationship is that banks invest in their assets at returns lower than the cost of capital. This would justify the preference of stockholders for banks with the higher payout ratio.

Another explanation of the Po inverse relationship with equity yield was offered by Benishay in the same paper. Benishay claims that the payout ratio represents the extent of the error in the measurement of expected income. Thus, the more observed earnings overestimate expected earnings, the higher will be the observed yield and the lower, the observed payout ratio.

Since the retention rate is equal to 1-Po, the same conclusion may be reached working with the retention rate. Then NOE/P will be positively correlated to $1-P_o$ with the same degree of significance.

Growth and asset structure influence. Finance theory recognizes that the rate of growth of earnings is an important factor in determining cost of capital rates. Durand expected that growth would have had some effect on bank stock prices and made many attempts to measure its impact, but curiously enough failed in his efforts.

In this study, it was expected that given the leverage level, NOE/P would show a negative correlation with the growth rate of earnings. The reasons for the hypothesis are that (1) fixed financing commitments deducted from a growing

---

[10]
    Haskel Benishay, "Variability in Earnings-Price Ratios of Corporate Equities," *American Economic Review* (March 1961). pp. 81-94.

earnings stream constitute less risk to the shareholders and (2) growth increases the earning stream. Thus, a bank whose earnings grow rapidly should be capital- ized at a lower rate of return.

The impact of growth in this study failed to explain any variation in NOE/P. In equation (1), even though x_2, the growth rate, carried the hypothesized sign, its regression coefficient was insignificant. By contrast, studies of non- financial corporations have succeeded in establishing significant negative cor- relation with equity yields.[11] This lack of significance of the growth as a separate explanatory variable possibly lies in the fact that growth, as considered by the market, is inherently expressed in the payout ratio. Another possible explanation is that growth as measured from the earning trend is not a good esti- mator; the growth in deposits or total asset would have been a better alternative.

The loan-deposit ratio as a measure of business risk was expected to show a positive correlation with NOE/P and k . Given a level of leverage, a bank that allocates a higher proportion of its funds to loans should expect higher returns. From equation (1) we see that x_4 is significant but with a negative sign.

Among forty-five banks the mean of the ratio was .5900 with a range of .3600 to .7700.

Stability of the earnings flows. In Section II the question of risk was discussed. It was argued that the variations in net operating earnings before interest and taxes could be used as an indicator of the operating risk and that the additional variations in net operating earnings are indicators of the finan- cial risk. In short, we were trying to use both variations as proxy measures of the quality of the earnings flows.

These two measures of stability did not perform at all in explaining any variations in NOE/P or the level of debt financing in banks. In equation (1), x_5 and x_6 show no tendency to vary with the cost of equity although we did estimate these variations directly from the data and did obtain a wide range in the coefficients of variations estimated.

A possible reason for the lack of adequate performance of these variables is the deficiency of the net operating earnings statistics reported by the banks in those years. Thus the variations around the earnings trend before and after in- terest and taxes may be due to factors other than the banks' revenues, costs and interest-bearing sources of funds.

Banks' data and impact on analysis. Earlier, the heterogeneity of the banks was mentioned. This supports Durand's conclusion made in 1953, that bank stock prices are unsuitable for regression analysis.[12] Regression analysis rests on the common assumption that the independent variables are free of error parameters and that the dependent variable has a random sampling distribution = $a + b_1 X_1 + z$, in which z is a normal deviate with a mean = 0. This assumption leads to fairly reliable estimates of the regression coefficients of X_1. The assumption of error- free, independent variables is not overly ambitious in our case. For instance, the price of stock P in NOE/P is the result of supply and demand forces and is a random variable. The information that leads to such a price can be read without

---

[11]
    R. Wippern, "Financial Structure," p. 621, and Brigham E. and Myron Gordon, "Leverage, Dividend Policy and the Cost of Capital," *Journal of Finance*, (March 1968), pp. 98-99.

[12]
    David Durand, "Bank Stocks and the Analysis of Covariance," *Econometrica*, (January 1955), pp. 30-45.

error from financial reports and is almost free of statistical errors. The same would apply to all deposits, earnings, interest, number of shares oustanding, etc.

At the outset, the data on banks looked deceptively homogeneous. But after looking at closer range, there seem to be certain systematic and individual bank effects that are too strong and that overpower any randomness that might be present in the data. These systematic forces seem to cause either the dependent or independent variables to deviate from the models used in this paper. For example, if the earnings reported by the banks are not really representative of real income, this may bias NOE/P, i/E-2s, i/NOEBIT, G and CV. The systematic omission of loan losses and gains and losses on securities may be responsible for part of this bias, especially when these omissions are not uniform or practiced by all banks.

Bank earnings may be affected systematically by the impact of monetary policy. Regulation Q and the discount rate may not necessarily be representative of the market forces. The absence of these regulations may have allowed these rates to settle at equilibrium levels different from those observed.

The data of banks may also be unsuitable for the intended analysis because of the joint interaction and closeness of movement of banks' cost of funds and rates charged on loans. The regular "buffer" of the production process, which is present in the operation of the nonfinancial enterprise and which separates the costs of inputs from the price of output, is almost absent in the banks.

Of course, one could generalize and state that bank data is unsuitable for regression analysis because of heterogeneity, autocorrelation, and other biases that may infect economic data and render it useless. But heterogeneity and auto-correlation will always be with us, so one must do the best one can.

Conclusions and implications

The findings of this study lead the writer to the following conclusions:

It is not desirable nor does it make economic sense to force all the factors that influence the cost of equity capital into single equation statements. There are too many macro- and micro-factors that exert joint pressures and influences upon these costs.

Leverage in banks apparently does not impart the risk usually associated with leverage in the nonfinancial corporation. Leverage in banks is their stock in trade. The risk associated with it, which is supposed to influence NOE/P, is either nonexistent or completely borne by regulation, insurance, and all the safety procedures applied to banks. In this study and with the methodology used, there is no evidence that the cost of capital is influenced by the degree of leverage in the commercial banks.

If banks were allowed to increase their level of leverage (deposit to capital ratio) in order to improve the return on stockholders' equity and reduce fund costs, the market would not penalize them by raising the capitalization rate applied to earnings. Investors in bank stocks do not expect any premium because of changes in bank leverage. What seems relevant to these stockholders and does affect their rate of capitalization of banks' earnings stream is the dividend payout. Banks that do pay larger percentages of their annual earnings in cash dividends cause their earnings to be capitalized at lower rates than those that retain more. Thus, in the market behavior of bank stocks, dividends seem to count.

This study discovered no conclusive evidence that debt fixed charges cause variations in the net operating earnings beyond those experienced before the deduction of interest and taxes. The findings contradict the theory that the introduction of debt in the capital structure detracts from the quality of earnings.

In commercial banks the operating risk stemming from the composition of assets and the financial risk resulting from added debt are more closely inter-related and subject to management control than in the nonfinancial firms. This hidden link between the risk generated by both sides of the balance sheet is too subtle and difficult to measure by the regular statistical techniques.

Banks have been given a growth image by brokerage houses in the last few years. This image is not justified. The rate of growth estimated either from the trend or as the retention rate multiplied by the return on capital showed no relation to return on equity. Bank stocks should be treated by the market as reliable and stable income securities similar to those of utilities when properly managed.

Whether banks allocate higher or lower proportions of their funds to loans appears to be irrelevant to the stockholders. The market is insensitive as to how banks allocate their funds.

DISCUSSION

Thomas R. Harter: Professor Magen's paper, "Cost of Capital and Dividend Policies in Commercial Banks" is an attempt to measure and explain the effects of financial leverage on the cost of capital for commercial banks. The methodology used is that of linear multiple regression which is inappropriate with regard to his data.

Professor Magen finds no significant relationships between leverage and the cost of capital for commercial banks. This could be expected, because the sample from which the data was obtained included at most forty-three of the fifty largest banks in the country. The sample is not random nor are the elements homo-geneous as Professor Magen suggests. He has defined homogeneity from the point of view that all the banks accept time and demand deposits, provide loans, and invest in securities. The mere activity of providing loans does not make the banks homogeneous, since providing consumer loans is quite different from pro-viding loans to consumer credit companies. Therefore, the methodology used just does not correspond to the data, and the results are likely to be so distorted as to be useless.

The sample Professor Magen uses provides a range of leverage, measured as "debt to total capitalization," from 88 percent to 94 percent. Assuming the methodology to be valid, which is an unlikely assumption, it is quite possible that all of the institutions studied fall within an acceptable leverage range and therefore, the slight variations in the amount of leverage have no effect upon the bank's cost of capital. In other words, all of the banks sampled operate at their optimum capital structures. If the optimum structure ranges from 85 to 95 percent, the sample would show no significant relationship between leverage and the cost of capital.

Professor Magen also finds the relationship between dividend payout (div-idends/net operating income) and the cost of equity (net operating income/price) to be negative but not significant. From this finding he suggests the possibility that banks invest in assets at returns lower than the cost of capital. An alter-native, and probably a more valid conclusion, would be to suggest that the pres-ence of spurious correlation creates the negative effect and, since the coeffi-cients are not significant in most cases, to reserve judgment.

The paper lacks information concerning the collinearity of the independent variables. It is quite likely that the independent variables are not independent. Therefore, the presence of collinearity may be another cause of the insignificant results of the analysis.

As Professor Magen states, "In this age of complex interrelated relationships among a multitude of factors, it just does not seem rational to force the real world into simple equations." I cannot help but wonder why after making the above statement, he forces his analysis into "simple equations." Not only is the analysis forced into "simple equations," but many of the conditions necessary for the use of these equations are violated. However, the problems with the empirical work are to some extent compensated for by the interesting and valuable nonquantitative insights he expresses concerning his topic. It is quite likely that the degree of leverage for a commercial bank is a psychological phenomenon set by depositors. With the advent of deposit insurance the acceptable degree of leverage, of which deposits are the major part, is more a function of the size of the individual deposits than the aggregate deposit size of the bank. Likewise, equity holders are more inclined toward banks with very high levels of financial leverage.

Until the banking community is willing and able to make more detailed information available for analysis, studies in this area should be confined to the simple descriptive type of analysis rather than applying inappropriate quantitative techniques.

INDEX